A HISTORY OF MODERN FRANCE

ALFRED COBBAN

⚜

A HISTORY
OF
MODERN FRANCE

GEORGE BRAZILLER
NEW YORK

BOOK I

⚜

The Old Regime and the Revolution
1715–1799

CONTENTS

INTRODUCTION   9

PART ONE: THE OLD REGIME

1. The Death of the Grand Monarch   13
2. The Regent Fails to Put the Clock Back   21
3. Fleury and National Recovery   31
4. Prosperity and Poverty   40
5. Disorder at Home   53
6. Defeat Abroad   70

PART TWO: THE AGE OF REFORM

1. The Revolution in Ideas   85
2. Revival of Authority   93
3. Prelude to Reform   102
4. The Eve of Revolution   114
5. The Revolt of the Privileged Classes   124
6. Victory of the Third Estate   137

PART THREE: THE AGE OF REVOLUTION

1. The Rising of the Masses   153
2. France under the Constituent Assembly   163
3. Fall of the Constitutional Monarchy   184
4. The Failure of the Brissotins   198
5. The Committee of Public Safety   216
6. Aftermath of Revolution   238
7. Balance-sheet of the Eighteenth Century   254

CHRONOLOGICAL TABLE   261
FURTHER READING   268

MAPS

1 Généralités and Pays d'États   17
2 Gabelles   59
3 Internal Customs   61
4 Parlements and Conseils Souverains   67
5 Revolutionary Paris   161
6 Provinces and Départements   171
7 Eastern Frontier of France during the Revolution   205

INTRODUCTION

THE first object of the introduction is to explain what this history of modern France is not. It is not a strict narrative history, following the course of events year by year. Hence tables of dates have been added to assist the reader. It is not intended to be a textbook giving the facts, all the facts, and nothing but the facts necessary for passing an examination in French history. I have not attempted to spread the history evenly if thinly over the whole period. On the contrary, I have concentrated attention where events are densest and most significant, and passed more rapidly over those periods and aspects which seem of less interest, even if this has meant neglecting much repetitive political manœuvring. Again, the details of foreign relations, in peace and war, are passed over rather slightly. Of course, not all omissions are necessarily deliberate. In some cases they are the result of lack of information. This is particularly so in respect of economic history, for the results of research in this field are still hardly adequate even for a broad picture.

Such gaps constitute one of the major difficulties in compiling the appendixes on Further Reading. These are not intended as anything more ambitious than their title suggests: they represent a rather arbitrary choice and obviously exclude many important works. At least some of my debts are reflected in these lists. There should be added an acknowledgment of what I have learned in supervising the work of those students who have researched on subjects from this period for their doctoral theses in my seminar during recent years. The justification for my treatment of the Girondins can now be found in Michael Sydenham's *The Girondins* (Athlone Press, 1961). An analysis of the membership and motivation of the revolutionary mobs, which has finally eliminated the picture drawn by Taine, is given by George Rudé in *The Crowd in the French Revolution* (Clarendon Press, 1959). The lack of influence of Rousseau's political writings before 1789, and their ambivalence after, is shown by Joan Mac-donald in a study, now being prepared for the press, of their influence during the Constituent Assembly. An analysis of the application of the Civil Constitution of the Clergy in the diocese of Lisieux by Winifred Edington, part of which has been published in French periodicals, revealed, among other things, the acute financial problems it involved. J. P. McLaughlin traced the growth of French annexationist policy from the beginning of the Revolution, and recently J. F. Murley has completed the first detailed account of the circumstances out of which the Revolutionary War between France and Great Britain arose. The counterrevolution has always been a neglected field of study, at least by serious historians. J. A. Johnson, writing a revealing study of the role of Calonne in the counter-revolution, found the origin of its cleavages in the ministerial rivalries of the *ancien régime*; N. F. Richards traced the attitude of the British government in respect of the French monarchy from 1789 to 1802; and the researches of Harvey Mitchell on the counter-revolution, which have partly been published in journals, revealed the actual connection of the comte d'Antraigues with the famous and mysterious Dropmore Bulletins, and also showed how near the Republic came to being overthrown at the time of Fructidor. Turning back to the *ancien régime*, the struggle of the factions for the succession to Fleury, which was only known in general terms, has been subjected to a valuable examination by Evelyn Cruickshanks. G. J. de C. Mead's analysis and survey of the intendants of eighteenth-century France and J. Bosher's account of the efforts to eliminate the internal customs dues will both, I believe, when they are published, add considerably to our knowledge of French administration in the eighteenth century; as, in a different field, will a study by Nora Temple of the government of French towns in the eighteenth century, with special reference to Auxerre and Avalon; and one by Olwen Hufton of the social structure of the town of Bayeux on the eve of the Revolution. Echoes from most of these theses, on the points mentioned, will be found in Volume 1. Another debt which I must express is to Mrs Audrey Munro for coping so efficiently and patiently with my handwriting in this and other books she has typed for me.

I am also indebted to those reviewers and other readers who drew my attention to various small mistakes in the first edition, which have been corrected. The complete resetting of the text for this edition has provided an opportunity to make some more minor improvements; and to introduce one or two passages taking account of research published in the last few years. A set of maps, for the drawing of which I am indebted to Mr E. A. Chambers will, I hope, bring out more clearly than any verbal descriptions can, the administrative complexities of the *ancien régime*.

A. COBBAN

University College, London

PART ONE

THE OLD REGIME

CHAPTER ONE

THE DEATH OF THE GRAND MONARCH

'THE years go by one after the other; time slips past us without our being aware of it; we grow old like ordinary men and we shall end like them': thus Louis XIV in his declining years, conscious of ineluctable mortality. He had seen all his great servants and a whole generation of his subjects pass away. Within a few months, in 1711–12, his son, grandson, and elder great-grandson died, leaving only an ailing baby to bear the hopes of the Bourbon dynasty. 'This time of desolation left so deep a mark,' wrote Voltaire, 'that I have met those who long after, could not speak of it without tears.' The Sun King's day closed not in splendour but amid dark clouds of domestic sorrow, nation-wide discontent, and foreign defeat. When he had first appeared above the horizon, a boy king, riding on an Isabella barb amidst a glittering cavalcade to the ceremony that was to mark the formal ending of his minority, he had seemed to John Evelyn, watching the procession from the window of his friend, the philosopher Hobbes, a young Apollo. 'He went almost the whole way with his hat in hand, saluting the ladies and acclamators, who had filled the windows with their beauty, and the air with *Vive le Roi*. He seemed a prince of a grave yet sweet countenance.' This was in 1651. Sixty-four years later, the body of the old king was laid to rest in the last of his royal garments at Saint-Denis, beside the relics of his ancestors for a thousand years; within a century to be exhumed as indecently as the Jansenist remains he had ordered to be scrabbled up at Port-Royal and scattered to the winds, while petty attorneys and minor officials exercised more arbitrary and terrible powers of life and death than ever the chancellors and ministers of state of the greatest of the Bourbons had wielded, and a jumped-up lieutenant from a wild island, not even in the domains of the Grand Monarch, led the armies of France, under a flag the Bourbons did not know and were never to acknowledge, to conquer and perish in African deserts and Russian steppes.

Louis XIV reigned for seventy-three years and ruled for fifty-five. By 1715 the French monarchy was approaching the end of its long history, but in 1661, when the young king swiftly and ruthlessly hurled Fouquet, all-powerful Superintendent of Finances and heir-expectant to Richelieu and Mazarin, from the pride of place and the magnificence of Vaux-le-Vicomte, newest and loveliest of châteaux, to perpetual prison, it seemed only a beginning. France had been a millennium in the making, now at last she was made. The great nobles, whose ambitions and rivalries had so often ravaged the country and let in the invader, had sunk from the mighty struggles of Burgundian and Armagnac, of Bourbon, Guise, and Montmorency, to the salon politics and mob violence of the Fronde, and from that to the role of mere appurtenances of majesty. After the death of Mazarin and the overthrow of Fouquet the courtiers questioned, anxiously or hopefully, who would be the new favourite and govern France for the king. Their speculations were wasted. Henceforth there was to be no first minister. The king himself was to rule.

Louis never forgot the flight from Paris or the humiliation inflicted on his childhood by the Fronde. Saint-Simon said that he often spoke of those times with bitterness, though the story that he had been neglected by Mazarin and arrived at the throne untrained and unprepared seems to be the reverse of the truth. The lesson Louis drew from the Fronde was that the king must be absolute. To the older principle of divine right, Bodin, a century earlier, in the Religious Wars, had added the more modern idea of sovereignty, and the royal lawyers, under the cardinals, the theory and practice of raison d'état. The idea and the fact of Bourbon absolutism reached their apogee together and found their embodiment in Louis XIV. Never did any prince, said Saint-Simon, possess the art of kingship to such a high degree. No king ever conferred his gifts with better grace, or was more able to make his words, his smile, his very glance, precious to those on whom they were bestowed. He personified majesty, yet nothing seemed to be studied and all was perfectly natural. If the pen of Saint-Simon, more often dipped in vitriol, could say this, we may believe it.

The rigid etiquette that Louis imposed on his court should be judged as the expression not of pettiness of mind but rather of political calculation. The object was to provide the necessary setting for a monarch who was to be the centre of the nation's life with all eyes turned on him. The court was a permanent spectacle for the people: the life of the king passed from birth to death in public. Louis XIV would as soon have neglected his council as the *grand couvert*, at which he dined in the presence of his subjects. Ill and able to do no more than sip a little moisture, he forced himself to the ceremony for the last time on August 24th, 1715. He died on September 1st. A rigorous etiquette was needed if the impression was to be one of majesty and not of confusion. Given this, and a king like Louis XIV to play the principal part, and the court became the scene of a perpetual ballet performed before an audience of twenty million. A more classic background was needed for this than the ramshackle royal quarters in Paris. Although other reasons have been given why Louis left Paris for Versailles — the aversion from his capital induced by the troubles of the Fronde, his love of walking and hunting, the desire to relieve the royal mistresses of the embarrassment of life in a large city — not the least was the need to provide a glorious setting for the court. Versailles was described later by Voltaire as a great caravanserai filled with human discomfort and misery — he himself had been honoured for a time with a little room in the palace just above the privies — but the misery was not on view and the grandeur was.

The court, with its etiquette and ceremony, state dignitaries and royal mistresses, was the ornamental framework of monarchy. It brought the high nobles to Versailles where, away from the sources of their strength in the provinces, instead of civil wars they devoted themselves to palace intrigues and fought for the honour of holding the king's shirt when he rose in the morning, while their ladies quarrelled over the right of sitting on a small stool in the queen's presence. It must not be supposed that the whole nobility of France flocked to Versailles, or it would have needed to be a town larger than Paris. The important fact was that, bereft of the leadership of the greater families, the provincial nobles sank into political insignificance. Versailles was the source of more than honour, it was the fountain of favour; court life was a perpetual struggle for jobs, above all for the sinecures and pensions with which the acquiescence of the *noblesse* in its loss of power was bought. On only one member of the old *noblesse* did Louis XIV ever confer ministerial office: during his reign the royal bureaucracy, which had been so many centuries in the making, took over the government of France. The great feudatories and lesser seigneurs were eliminated from the administrative order and the country was divided up into *généralités* under royal intendants. These were *commissaires départis*, clothed with all the authority of the king, sent out from the royal council and returning to it in due course. Nothing that happened in their *généralités* was too great or too small for their attention. Through their correspondence the whole life of France passed in review like a great and unending panorama before the king's council, sitting in its various divisions day after day.

Acton described Louis XIV as the greatest man born in modern times on the steps of a throne. An unkinder verdict is that he was the greatest postmaster-general: he had a passion for detail — the arms, manœuvres, discipline, uniform of his troops, and his buildings and household establishment above all. He found an ideal instrument for the more serious tasks of government in the person of Colbert. Son of an ennobled merchant family in Reims, official in a financial office, rising under Mazarin to the rank of his chief assistant, Colbert became under Louis XIV, by a cumulation of offices, in effect the dictator of the whole economic life of France. Trading companies and colonies, roads and canals — on the great canal du Midi, from Toulouse to the Mediterranean, 12,000 men were put to work at one time — royal manufactures, the subsidizing of new industries, introduction of foreign entrepreneurs and artisans, creation of an Academy of Sciences, publication of the *Encyclopedia of Arts and Crafts* with illustrations of all known types of machinery: such were some of Colbert's achievements. It should not be forgotten that what, in economic matters, was in 1789 the *ancien régime*, a century earlier had been the New Deal of Louis XIV and Colbert.

This is only one side of the medal. Three-quarters of a century after Louis died, the monarchy, which had reached its height and

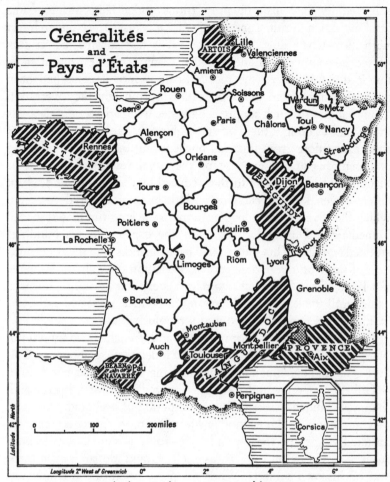

GÉNÉRALITÉS AND PAYS D'ÉTATS

The généralités varied slightly in number during the century. In 1789 there were 33. Except for the pays d'états they were named after the town which was the seat of the intendant. It will be seen how often this is inconveniently placed in one corner of the généralité, far removed from much of the area it administered. When the Constituent Assembly decided that no part of a département should be more than a day's ride away from the *chef-lieu*, it cannot have been uninfluenced by the experience of the *ancien régime*.

The provincial états that survived in the eighteenth century had varying and restricted powers, mostly in matters of finance. One difficulty of writing the administrative history of France is illustrated by the fact that hardly any two of the better-known books in this field agree on what were the actual pays d'états in the eighteenth century.

B

achieved its final majestic proportions under him, was to come crashing down in ruins; and in this case it is just to tax the architect with ill-matched aims. The edifice Louis had constructed far surpassed in complication and size that of any other European state, but it did not exceed the resources of France if these had been adequately mobilized to support it. Unfortunately they were not. Louis had not so much suppressed the declining aristocratic elements in the state as bought them off at a high price, by the perpetuation of their exemptions from financial burdens and the grant of sinecures and pensions at the expense of the royal revenue. The taxable resources of France were further reduced by the creation and sale of a host of venal offices, carrying with them financial privileges, from which the royal treasury lost far more in the long run than it gained immediately. During Louis's reign the expense of his buildings strained and that of his wars ruined royal finances, and the concentration of taxes on the poorer part of the nation drove it to desperate rebellion. In the following two reigns every war brought a financial crisis, until the last one, culminating in political upheaval and coinciding with a famine, turned into a revolution.

French finances were not reformed and French economy did not prosper under Louis XIV, despite the indefatigable labours of Colbert. The trading companies faded into inanition, the state industries — Gobelins tapestry and the like — catered only for a luxury and, therefore, limited market. This was a period of declining prices and of contraction in the economic life of Europe. Great famines devastated France in 1693–4 and 1709–10. The population declined from war, starvation, and disease. The Grand Monarch even made war on his own subjects. When the persecution of the Huguenots reached its climax with the revocation of the Edict of Nantes in 1685, 'le grand Bossuet' called down benedictions on the king's head. 'Proclaim the miracle of our times. Send up to heaven your praises, and say to this new Constantine, this new Theodosius, this new Charlemagne: it is the worthy achievement of your reign. By you heresy no longer exists. God alone could accomplish this marvel.' Saint-Simon, in the pages of his secret diary, expressed a different opinion. 'The revocation of the Edict of Nantes', he wrote, 'without the least pretext or any necessity, depopulated a quarter of the kingdom, ruined its commerce and weakened it in all parts.' It is certain that in spite of efforts to close the frontiers to those flying from persecution, hundreds of thousands of Huguenots, including many of the industrial, commercial, and maritime classes, escaped abroad, while those who remained in France, in the wild country between Gard and Lozère, broke out in the terrible and prolonged revolt of the Camisards. In the cause of religion, Sorel writes, Louis XIV had lost more than he could have gained by the most victorious war, or than could have been demanded by his enemies as the price of the most disastrous peace.

Even in diplomacy and war, which were the essential *métier de roi*, Louis outlived his good fortune. The success of France under the cardinals had been founded on 'la modération dans la force', the classic French foreign policy. Louis XIV, in the words of Sorel, 'le dénatura', because he pushed his ambitions to the point at which they brought about the creation of a hostile coalition powerful enough to defeat even France.

Failure and disaster did not weaken the resolution of the Grand Monarch. Absolutism and bureaucracy kept the country in a frozen grip, apparently immobile. Underneath, new currents were stirring, but they were only to appear on the surface in a new reign. In the midst of defeat and discontent the old king, with his magnificent physique and supreme confidence in divine sanction and the performance of his kingly duty, stood unshaken. In his last years the firmness of the king's character upheld him still, and he was perhaps not undeserving of the title 'great'. Brought to sue for peace from the victorious allies, he rejected the humiliation of himself turning his grandson, Philip V, off the Spanish throne. The heart — or was it the artistic conscience? — of Saint-Simon was melted by the sight of the old king struggling with misfortune. 'Overwhelmed externally by the enemies he had provoked, who rejoiced in his powerlessness, envisaged him as resourceless, and mocked his past glory, he found himself without succour, without ministers, without generals, through having raised and upheld them by favour and whim and by the fatal vainglory of wishing and believing he could create them at will. Anguished at heart by the most personal and poignant losses, with consolation from no one, a prey to his own weakness, reduced to struggle alone against horrors a thousand times more frightful than his most perceptible ills, incessantly reminded of them by those left to him who were dearest and most intimate, who openly and unrestrainedly took advantage of the subjection into which he had fallen, and from which he could not, and did not even wish to relieve himself, though he felt all its burden; incapable moreover, because of an invincible ruling passion and a habit which had become second nature, of casting any reflection on the interest and behaviour of his jailors; in the midst of these domestic bonds, that constancy, that firmness of soul, that appearance of equanimity, that never-changing determination to remain at the helm of state so long as he was able, that hope against all hope, which came from courage and discretion, not from infatuation, that preservation of appearances in everything, of all this, few men could have been capable, and this is what truly entitled him to the description "great", which had been so prematurely conferred on him. It was this which won for him the true admiration of the whole of Europe and that of those of his subjects who witnessed it, and which brought back to him so many hearts alienated by so long and harsh a reign.'

At Denain, in 1712, Villars took advantage of the disruption of the hostile Grand Alliance to end the war with a victory; Torcy conducted the peace negotiations with ability; and France emerged at the Treaties of Utrecht and Rastadt with far less loss than at one time had seemed possible. The last of the agreements was signed in November 1715, but the king of France had died at Versailles on September 1st, at the age of seventy-seven and in the fifty-sixth year of his personal rule.

✤

CHAPTER TWO

THE REGENT FAILS TO PUT THE CLOCK BACK

THE heir to the throne after Louis XIV was a child of five. A regency was inevitable, and — the king of Spain being excluded by the peace treaties — it was also inevitable that the regent should be the prince of the blood nearest to the throne. This was Philip of Orleans, nephew to Louis XIV and the hope of all those whose discontent and rancour had been growing beneath the appearance of conformity imposed by absolute rule. That Orleans was the enemy of all he held dearest Louis XIV well knew, and to political distrust was added personal detestation of him as a rake and unbeliever. Though Orleans had to be regent, the dead king, who aspired to rule France even after his death, had done his best to safeguard his system. He bequeathed effective authority to the royal bastards, begotten of that dazzling, proud, and bad-tempered beauty, the marquise de Montespan, and legitimized in 1714, to the indignation of the old nobility. The duc du Maine, pious and honourable, was appointed by the king's testament guardian of the young Louis XV and commander of the royal guard; he was to be succeeded if he died by his brother Toulouse. Orleans was allowed to be president of a Council of Regency, but the membership of the council was laid down in the will and was not to be susceptible of alteration during the minority. Decisions were to be by majority vote, 'sans que le duc dorleans chef du conseil puisse seul et par son auctorité particulière rien déterminer'. If the vote were equal a fresh vote was to be taken, and only after this, if the council were still equally divided, did the regent have the casting vote. This was to reduce him to a nullity. Louis' testament was an attempt to do what no king could do. It was a flagrant contradiction of his own absolutist principles. On the death of a king his successor was automatically endowed with sovereignty in all plentitude and could be bound neither in law nor in fact by the will of his predecessor. The first act of the regent, in the name of Louis XV, was to emancipate himself from bondage to the dead hand of the great king.

Orleans had behind him the nobles, jealous of the bureaucracy and the royal bastards, the parlements, hoping to regain some of their lost influence, the Jansenists and all who resented the ecclesiastical domination of Mme de Maintenon and the Jesuits. Those who had been discontented by the centralized despotism of Louis XIV looked to him to bring back what were regarded by some sort of historical fantasy as the good old days before the cardinals began the destruction of aristocratic liberties. The parlements were used to quash the will of Louis XIV with due formality, and Saint-Simon has made a dramatic, though hardly historically accurate, story out of it, building up the scene at the parlement from the magnificent entry of the royal bastards, swollen with pride and confidence, to their humiliating deflation and crestfallen departure. It was really a foregone conclusion. The parlements had their right of remonstrance recognized in return for the part they played, though to attribute the trouble they subsequently caused to this episode is to read too much into it. The regent emerged with full powers of royal absolutism but with the intention of using them to bring that absolutism to an end.

Philip of Orleans was a man of culture and natural ability. A good general, he had been kept in the background by Louis XIV's hostility. This was not without cause. Drunken and dissipated, Orleans' reputation was so bad that he was even suspected of poisoning his way to the throne, though without any justification. Living perpetually in the company of loose women and those whom the slang of the regency called 'roués', fit only to be broken on the wheel, he was habituated to debauchery, spiced with outrageous impiety, to the point of being unable to do without it and only able to amuse himself in rowdy orgies. It is said that he was one of those who can take no wine without drunkenness. Perhaps the truth is that he was bored with himself from birth and could only find distraction in wine and women.

Society followed the model set by the regent. The sanctimoniousness and dullness of the later years of Louis XIV were thrown off, like the stiff dresses and sombre hues which Mme de Maintenon had made fashionable. Gay colours, light fabrics and swinging hoops and panniers, copied from the robes of bourgeoises and coquettes, brought lighter modes and manners along with a franker indifference to morals into high society. This was the age of Watteau, by royal appointment 'peintre des fêtes galantes'. There was a general embarkment for Cythera, though the ephemeral moments of love in sun and shade that are seized by Watteau's brush immortalize a generation better characterized by the regent's little suppers. Not, indeed, that it is correct to identify either the good art or the bad morals too closely with the regency. Because political events constitute our basic historical calendar, we tend too easily to assume that other chronological divisions correspond to them. In fact, Watteau's art was already blossoming in the last years of Louis XIV, to open out under the regency and be cut off in full bloom with the painter's death in 1721. Before the seventeenth century had ended, Perrault's *La Belle au bois dormante, Cendrillon, Chaperon rouge* and other stories, published in 1696 and 1697, seemed to announce a spirit of simplicity and lightness. The darker side, too, of a new age, that world of rogues and adventurers in which no man is honest and no woman virtuous, had been reflected, before the Sun King drew his last breath, in the satire of Le Sage. With the *Diable boiteux* of 1707, and *Turcaret* of 1709, says a French writer, 'quelle rancœur d'âme honnête' is revealed. When, with the first part of *Gil Blas*, in 1715, Le Sage showed his hero living on his wits and making fools of the rich and powerful, he was not discovering the new world of the regency, he was merely beginning to feel more at home in a world that was already there before Louis XIV had died. Gil Blas joins hands across the century with Figaro. Meanwhile, out of the personal tragedy of the runaway priest, the abbé Prévost, grew the history of *Manon Lescaut*, sounding a deeper note than the eighteenth century proper could commonly reach. There is more in *Manon* of Racine than of Rousseau. The chevalier des Grieux descends from the high lineage of Phèdre, and could pray like the abbé Prévost, but so unlike the eighteenth century, 'Deliver us from love.'

In politics also the regency must not be dismissed as a mere upstart *opéra bouffe* episode in French history. It represented the culmination of a real attempt to remedy the ills which serious observers detected in French society. The *noblesse de l'épée* had never become reconciled to the position of powerlessness to which the cardinals and Louis XIV had reduced it. As early as 1664 a group of peers commissioned the abbé Le Laboureur to write a history of the peerage for the purpose of putting their claims on a sound historical basis. His work circulated in manuscript, though it was not published until 1740. Fénelon, who had been tutor of the young Duke of Burgundy, the grandson of Louis XIV and heir apparent in 1711–12, denounced royal absolutism. 'I call to my support', he said, 'the memory of past centuries, because it would be blindness to reject the methods that maintained a moderate monarchy for thirteen centuries and to substitute for them others which only facilitate a despotic power, more appropriate to the genius of the Persians, Turks or oriental nations than to our constitution.' These were no isolated sentiments. La Bruyère, in the editions of his *Caractères* published after Louis XIV's invasion of Germany and ravaging of the Palatinate, wrote, 'There is no *patrie* in the despotic state, other things take its place: interest, glory, the service of the prince.' An Oratorian, Michel Levassor, was, it is suggested, the author of the pamphlets entitled *Les Soupirs de la France Esclave, qui aspire après la liberté*. The ideas of Fénelon, who in *Télémaque* taught implicitly the evil of absolutism, were taken up and developed by the Jacobite exile, the chevalier Ramsay.

There was a moment when it seemed as if those who formed the small, secret, aristocratic opposition under Louis XIV had the future at their feet. In 1711 the Duke of Burgundy became dauphin. Fénelon and the Dukes of Beauvillier and Chevreuse, who shared his views, had indoctrinated the new heir and began to draw up plans to abolish despotic monarchy and restore an idealized aristocracy. A year later the Duke of Burgundy died, but Philip of Orleans, with Saint-Simon to urge him on, was himself influenced by the views of what was called 'the faction of the Duke of Burgundy' and as regent he was to attempt to put them into practice. Symbolically, after the death of Louis XIV, the court abandoned Versailles, though the move to Paris was only the continuation of a trend that had begun while he was still on the throne, when the younger nobles, tired of the abode of boredom and constraint that the great king had created, deserted the cramped and crowded discomfort of Versailles for the elegant *hôtels* they built or bought in Paris. The boy king was sent first to Vincennes, but in what was then only a village there was no lodging for his entourage; in 1716 the court was established at the Tuileries, where Louis 'le bien-aimé' grew up, a pretty, spoilt boy, under the admiring eyes of his people. The regent continued to live close by at the Palais Royal.

One of the prime objects of the aristocratic reaction was to reduce the power of the Secretaries of State, described by Saint-Simon as the monsters who had devoured the *noblesse*, the all-powerful enemies of the seigneurs whom they had reduced to dust beneath their feet. Three Secretaries out of four were kept by the regent; but side by side with them he established the so-called Polysynodie, a system of six councils, for war, navy, finance, home, foreign affairs, and religion, composed each of ten members, half official and half noble. This has been treated by some historians as a mere device of the regent to establish a clientele for himself, a piece of lip-service to the new ideas which he never intended seriously. He treated personally with the president of each council, it is said, and neglected to bring many matters of state before the Council of Regency. The fact that Orleans called to the councils his foremost opponents, the bastards, the chief figures of the old court and the former ministers of Louis XIV, makes it difficult to accept this hostile interpretation. No such hypothesis is needed to explain the failure of the Polysynodie. Saint-Simon, himself one of its chief promoters, confessed that the difficulty was the ignorance, frivolity, and lack of application of a *noblesse* that was good for nothing except to get itself killed in war. By 1718 the experiment had failed, the six councils were suppressed, and the regency returned to the old king's system of government through Secretaries of State.

Aristocratic nostalgia for a past that had gone beyond recall was to be dormant for nearly three-quarters of a century more, and when it reawoke was to provoke a catastrophe that those who were aiming in 1715 to overthrow the system of Louis XIV did not dream of, even though another and ultimately fatal ill, which had manifested

itself under Louis XIV, had already reduced the state to a condition
of acute crisis. This was the problem of the royal finances. The
regent thought of declaring the Crown bankrupt and summoning
the States-General, so close does 1715 seem to 1789. The deficit was
indeed greater, proportionally, than that which brought about the
fall of the absolute monarchy under Louis XVI. The last Controller-
General of Louis XIV had proposed to meet the financial difficulty
by the imposition of taxes which would be paid by *noblesse* and
clergy as well as the rest of the nation. The aristocratic reaction was
real enough to prevent this solution from being put into effect. The
interests of the *rentiers* were not yet strong enough, as they had
become by 1789, to prevent the other solution of a partial repudiation
of the royal debts. A Chamber of Justice was set up 'to make the
financiers disgorge'. Composed of magistrates taken from the parlement, it set about its task with a characteristic heavy-handed indifference to justice, condemned petty financiers to the galleys, provoked
suicides, and upset commercial relations to the point at which the
merchants were forced to protest. The wealthier financiers escaped,
the friends of the regent sold immunity to those who could afford
to buy it, and the whole operation produced little gain to the state.
Meanwhile the duc de Noailles, the effective head of the Conseil
des Finances, was able to make limited reforms in financial administration and effect some modest economies.

The regent fully saw the need for more drastic changes and he
believed that he had found the man who could bring them about.
This was the Scot, John Law, son of an Edinburgh goldsmith and
banker, who in the course of an adventurous life had made the
acquaintance of Orleans in the gaming dens of Paris, to which Law
was reputed to resort with a bag of gold coins in each hand. In the
financial capitals of Europe he had learnt that money was only a
means of exchange, that real national wealth depended on population
and supplies, that these depended on trade and that trade depended
on money. The shortage of currency, he truly saw, was one of the
chief handicaps to French economy. The issue by a royal bank of
paper money, guaranteed on the king's credit, could remedy this
deficiency. Credit was the open-sesame to wealth, and therefore
power. How, otherwise, had two tiny states like England and the

Dutch Republic been able to face and defeat the great French monarchy, to raise and support national debts such as France was crushed by, and to extend their trade through all the seas and into all the continents of the world? The regent, nothing if not intelligent and adventurous, saw the force of Law's arguments. The Conseil des Finances was suspicious and the merchants and financiers jealous, but in May 1716 Law obtained authorization from the regent to establish a private bank. Conducted on sound principles, it proved a great success. In August 1717 Law gained a further concession in the form of the trade monopoly with Louisiana, for the exploitation of which he founded the Company of the West. To this was soon after granted the monopoly of trade with the West Indies and Canada. In December 1718 the bank became a royal bank, and in 1719 the company absorbed the old and languishing companies of Senegal, the East Indies, China, and Africa. The financiers, who had not viewed the growth of this banking and trading colossus with equanimity, opposed it as well as they could, the chief centre of financial opposition being the Farmers-General — the financiers who bought from the state for a lump sum the right of collecting the indirect taxes and made what profit they could out of them. Law therefore next proceeded to outbid the Farmers-General and gain for his company the farm of the taxes. Finally, he took over the royal debt, offering its holders shares in the company and asking from the state only a reduced interest of 3 per cent. In 1720 the bank and the company were officially united and Law, who had become naturalized and accepted the Catholic religion, was appointed to the revived office of Controller-General of Finances.

Many reforms were sketched out in the short period of Law's System. Direct and indirect taxes were united under a single system of collection. Following a proposal which had been put forward earlier by Louis XIV's great fortress-builder, Vauban, in his book on the *dîme royale*, a tax to be paid by all classes in the community was planned; it was proposed to suppress a host of unnecessary venal offices; capital was advanced to manufacturers at a moderate rate of interest; debtors were released from prison; a programme of public works was started. But all this was only a beginning, largely on paper in more than one sense. To build up the credit of the com-

pany, on the success of which his system depended, Law had painted
a picture of Louisiana as the new Eldorado, its mountains of gold,
rocks of emerald, mines littered with diamonds, and its inhabitants
simple Hurons ready to exchange all these for the cheapest gewgaws
or manufactures of Europe. To cope with the trade that was expected
from 'le Mississipi', as the company was known, Lorient was
founded in France and New Orleans in America. To provide
colonists, in the absence of volunteers the government took criminals,
vagabonds, foundlings, prostitutes, and shipped them to America by
force; and on the desolate shore where Manon Lescaut died in the
arms of the chevalier des Grieux in romance, many of her sisters
perished in hard fact.

The trade of the company, though not negligible, fell pathetically
below expectation and was quite inadequate to support the inflated
paper currency of the system; but this was the age of speculation,
of the Darien Company and the South Sea Bubble. Noble and base
joined in a frantic struggle for shares in 'le Mississipi' and pushed
their value up to a fantastic figure. Law was besieged by would-be
purchasers: one lady, it was alleged, hired men to shout 'Fire!' to get
him out of his house, and another invaded his bedroom by way of
the chimney. The rue Quincampoix, centre of the stock-jobbing,
had to be closed by the police because of the disorder and bloodshed
that the crowds of speculators from all classes of society caused, but
they only transferred their activities elsewhere. And now the
financiers, helpless in the first days of the system, moved into action.
Public suspicion was aroused that the shares in the company were
not really worth forty times their face value. Great speculators,
princes of the blood like Bourbon and Conti, sold out while the
mania was still at its height. The shrewder copied them. Law
struggled bravely to maintain the stability of the house of cards he
had erected. To keep up the value of his shares he decreed that gold
and silver should no longer be valid currency, but people had begun
to believe that perhaps after all they were safer than paper. In a
desperate attempt to restore the system to solvency Law ordered a
progressive reduction in the value of the shares, but the official
reduction could not keep pace with what soon became a catastrophic
fall. The mob of speculators was now fighting to sell instead of buy.

October 1720 saw the bankruptcy of the system. Law's paper money ceased to be valid currency and in December he fled to London, where, it is said, a special performance at Drury Lane was held in his honour. The play chosen was *The Alchemist*.

Some had made great fortunes out of the system and thousands had been ruined. 'All those', wrote Montesquieu, 'who were rich six months ago are now in the depth of poverty, and those who had not even bread to eat are swollen with riches. Never have the two extremes of society met so closely. The foreigner turned the state inside out as a tailor turns a suit of clothes.' All Law's reforms were lost in the ruin of the system, and the prejudice against a state bank was such that France did not again possess one until Bonaparte was Consul. Interest in maritime and colonial enterprises, on a reduced scale, remained. Lorient and New Orleans survived and slowly grew, to provide visible evidence that 'le Mississipi' had not been entirely a dream. Industry and public works had been given a stimulus, the peasantry had cleared off some of their debts, and the financiers had in many cases increased their fortunes at the cost of the small owners of stock, who were doubtless expendable.

In the economic as in the political structure of France, the attempt under the regency to break away from the regime of Louis XIV and introduce new principles and methods into the running of the state had failed. In foreign policy also a new line had been struck out. Louis XIV in his final years seemed to have learnt the lesson of his defeats and under compulsion to have abandoned the struggle for the hegemony of Europe which had brought him almost to disaster. His last moves have been interpreted as an anticipation of the long eighteenth-century struggle against the natural enemy, England, and a foreshadowing of that Austrian alliance which has been seen by some historians as the master-stroke of French policy, albeit one that miscarried. This is to read too much into what was primarily an attempt to consolidate the one gain that had resulted from twenty-five years of war, the connection with Spain that was the consequence of the presence of a Bourbon on the Spanish throne. It was difficult for the regent to envisage the Spanish alliance in quite the same light. Philip V was, if it were not for the restrictive clauses in the peace treaties, the rightful heir to the French throne. He was, therefore, the rival and enemy of the regent. The ambitions of Philip V and his domineering wife Elizabeth Farnese and minister Alberoni, which led to the organization of a conspiracy against Orleans by the Spanish ambassador, Cellamare, in 1718, forced the regent to look for external support elsewhere. There is a fashion for calling the diplomacy of the eighteenth century secret and attributing it to the personal interests of the ruler, as though the diplomacy of other periods were not secret and were not also influenced by the interests of rulers. The *secret* of the regent was the English alliance, and he had to aid him in putting it into operation his Foreign Minister, the spare, sparkling, intriguing, ambitious abbé, Dubois. The alliance with Great Britain in 1716, which became the Triple Alliance after the accession of the Dutch in 1717, was the work of Dubois and the British minister, Stanhope. By it George I was promised French support against Jacobite claims, and the regent English support against those of Philip of Spain. After a short war Philip V yielded. In 1721 Dubois obtained recognition by Spain of the right of the regent to the French succession, the betrothal of a Spanish Infanta to Louis XV, and — despite his personal life, which was what might have been expected of a regency abbé — a cardinal's hat for himself. The policy of the English alliance was not to last, but at least it was to endure longer than the Polysynodie or Law's System. Despite the failure of his reforming plans, the personal position of the regent was now stronger than ever. All his enemies had been defeated when, in December 1723, he died. Dubois had preceded him by four months. And what might have seemed the beginning of a new chapter proved to be merely an episode in parentheses.

✤

CHAPTER THREE

FLEURY AND NATIONAL RECOVERY

THE duc de Bourbon was ugly, blind in one eye, bandy-legged, and stupid, but as the next prince of the blood he succeeded to Philip of Orleans. The best thing about him was his mistress, Mme de Prie, pretty, intelligent, and ambitious, as was the way of mistresses, daughter of a financier and moving in financial circles, as was also often the way of mistresses in the eighteenth century. Bourbon, for all his limitations, was pleased with the possession of power and conscious that only the life of the young Louis XV stood between the throne and the succession of the son of the regent. To guard against this calamity, or such it seemed to a Condé, the only safeguard appeared to be to marry the king off at once, though he was still only fifteen. As the Spanish Infanta to whom he was officially betrothed was only five, France would have had to wait some time before an heir to the throne could be expected from this marriage. The little Infanta was therefore hurriedly packed off back to Spain, to the fury of the Spanish court. To Bourbon, or his advisers, it seemed a stroke of genius to promote Marie Leczinska, daughter of Stanislaus, ex-king of Poland, to the vacant place in the young Louis XV's affections. True, her father was only a dethroned king, living on a French pension in a modest residence in Germany, while Marie was six years older than Louis XV and no beauty, but the poorer her claims the greater would be her gratitude to her benefactor. Moreover, she was healthy and seemed capable of guaranteeing the succession. Stanislaus had an eye to the main chance, Marie was delighted with her good fortune and the pretty boy to whom she was so unexpectedly offered, and Louis XV all anxiety to be a devoted husband.

The marriage took place in 1725, but the duc de Bourbon did not profit by it for long. He brought about his fall by an unwise attempt to strengthen his position. He tried to make use of the queen to secure the removal from the king's presence of his old tutor, Fleury, Bishop of Fréjus, whose influence seemed dangerously great. This was a fatal error of judgment, for Louis now manifested that capacity for affection and unwillingness to separate himself from those he was used to which was a dominant feature of his character. In June 1726 the young king sent Bourbon to Chantilly and exiled Mme de Prie, with her husband for company, to their château in the country, where she bored herself to death and died, perhaps by suicide, a year later. Without apparent effort Fleury emerged triumphant at the head, under the king, of the machine of state, and the most prosperous and successful period in the history of eighteenth-century France began.

The government of France had been left by Louis XIV half-way between the medieval personal and the modern administrative regimes. It has still in the eighteenth century to be written of mainly in terms of individuals, but there was a governmental machine through which personal rule had to operate. This was, since the regent's attempt at reform had failed, the machine that had been given its final shape by Louis XIV. With few exceptions — the most important being the parlements and the provincial états, of which I shall have to write subsequently — the whole governmental system of France was embodied in the person of the king: he was the state. Divine right was more than a phrase. The king, wrote Bodin at the time of the Religious Wars, is the image of God on earth. When Montesquieu, in his *Lettres persanes*, mocked the memory of Louis XIV, it was clear that the intellectual climate was changing, but the change had not yet touched common opinion, still less affected the assumptions on which the state was based. The court painter Rigaud, who had portrayed Louis XIV in his pride, long after painted Louis XV wearing the same velvet and ermine of majesty, standing in almost the same pose of authority as his great predecessor, so that one almost fails to notice that the subject is a little boy of five years old. Whatever his age or character, the king in person embodied all authority. The law was his and emanated from his simple will. In practice, Fénelon wrote, the king is much more head of the Church than the Pope. The army was a royal army, commanded by the king and fighting under the personal standard of the house of Bourbon. Justice was royal, and whatever the law courts might decide the king could always use his power of *justice retenue* to forestall or override their decision: he could summon any case from the ordinary courts to the Royal Council by *lettre de cachet*. In short, the authority of the king was not that of the titular head of an administrative regime, it was the personal exercise of his individual *bon plaisir*.

Ruling as an individual, the king of France delegated his authority to individuals, and in this way the principle of absolutism passed down through the administrative hierarchy. According to his rank every official was endowed with a fraction of the royal *bon plaisir*. Each, like the king, was in a sense an arbitrary ruler in relation to those subject to his authority, appointed to exercise his discretion, not to act under instruction. This is the meaning of the saying attributed to Louis XV, 'If I were Lieutenant of Police I would ban cabriolets.' Unfortunately he was not Lieutenant of Police, he was merely king, and his only sanction was to dismiss an official who refused to carry out his wishes. Even this power was limited, for most of the royal officials held their offices for payment; their posts were venal and hence assimilated to private property, and could only be taken away from them if compensation equal to their market value were paid. For a royal officer to lose his post was a very rare thing. The result was that the great bureaucratic machine, the product of many centuries culminating in the work of the cardinals and Louis XIV, was to an extraordinary extent in its actual operation independent of the royal will at its lower levels, and at the same time extraordinarily dependent on it at the top.

In theory the king, as well as being supreme judge and lawgiver, head of the armed forces and of the Church, was also the executive in person. He wielded this power through a series of councils. The highest, the Conseil d'état, Conseil d'en haut, or Conseil secret as it was variously called, dealt with the great questions of government and especially with foreign policy. It was presided over by the king and composed of the Ministers of State, who were nominated and dismissed by the king. A second council, the Conseil des Dépêches, was concerned with all internal administration and judicial appeals. Affairs brought before it were reported by Masters of Requests, who, as they had to stand, literally did not have seats in the council and

c

were not members of it. There were, in addition, the Conseil des Finances; a Conseil de Commerce with a fluctuating existence, sometimes separated from and sometimes united to the Conseil des Finances; the Conseil de Conscience, which dealt with the granting of benefices; and finally, the Conseil privé or Conseil des Partis, composed of Councillors of State and Masters of Requests, which exercised the private jurisdiction of the king and was described as 'a tribunal established to judge the judges'. It dealt in particular with conflicts of jurisdiction. The Conseil des Partis was composed, in 1789, of eighty-two Councillors of State and eighty Masters of Requests, who acted as *rapporteurs*; it was the direct ancestor of the modern Conseil d'État. It is sad to have to say, after giving this imposing picture of a conciliar regime, that it was largely a mere façade. The real work of government in the eighteenth century was conducted by other persons and in another way. The heads of the departments of state, who, apart from the Secretary for Foreign Affairs, were not necessarily included in the Conseil d'en haut which in principle decided matters of high policy, were the men who wielded the actual executive power and took the important decisions.

The first of the great officers of state was the Chancellor. President by right of all tribunals, sitting in the parlement above the *premier président*, he embodied under the king all justice. As a sign that while majesty passed away justice was eternal and never died, he alone wore no mourning for the death of a king. The chancellorship was a life office, the last of the great medieval offices of the crown. For this very reason all effective power had been removed from the Chancellor and given to the Keeper of the Seals, who might or might not be the same person. With the power also went the fees. It was said, 'Chancelier sans les sceaux est apothicaire sans sucre', not without justification, for under Louis XV the Seals were worth some 120,000 livres a year.

There were normally four Secretaries of State, for Foreign Affairs, War, the Navy, and the Maison du Roi. The last of these had responsibility for questions of internal security and in particular for Paris, so that he was often called the 'ministre de Paris'. Fifthly, the Controller-General had charge of royal finances, of agriculture, industry, bridges and highways, and in general all matters of internal administration except those in the attribution of the Maison du Roi; and as the complexity of domestic government increased, so his importance grew. The four Secretaries and the Controller-General, each at the head of large and highly developed bureaux, provided the effective government of France, the councils being pushed on one side.

Louis XIV had worked individually with each Secretary, decided with them separately the policies of their offices, and himself provided the unity and co-ordination required if the whole government were to function effectively. If the king could not undertake this task his place could be supplied by *a premier ministre*, such as Richelieu and Mazarin had been. The office was revived in 1722 for Dubois; on his death in 1723 the regent took it for himself and he was succeeded by the duc de Bourbon. Fleury never took the title but he acted as a very powerful *premier ministre*, and while he lived, at least until the last few years, when age began to show its effects even on him, France had a government and a policy, though the Secretaries were increasingly restive under his control. After the death of Fleury, Louis XV decided, or was persuaded, to step into the shoes of his great-grandfather as the effective head of the government, but he had neither the assiduity nor the strength of character to impose his will effectively on the Secretaries. The result was that for the last fifty years of the *ancien régime* France had no *premier ministre*. When one was appointed, in 1787, apart from his personal inadequacy, it was too late to remedy the ills of nearly half a century of weak and divided government. But this is to look ahead. In 1726 Fleury was to take up office with the full authority of the king behind him, though, at the age of seventy-three, it could hardly have been anticipated that he would continue in the same position for another seventeen years.

The modest, smiling abbé, who had become Bishop of Fréjus and was to be cardinal, won the devotion of the young king when he was his tutor and was to retain it to the end of a long life. In the absolute monarchy favour was the first and necessary basis of power, but Fleury was more than a mere royal favourite. In private life a timid, unassertive, friendly though reserved, cautious old ecclesiastic, in office he showed himself to have a will of iron — 'the proudest man in himself and the most implacable that I have ever known', Saint-Simon described him. It was a pride that was put to the service of France. His early poverty had engendered no love of riches in him and his way of life remained simple and unpretentious. While the regent has been condemned for his adventurous policy of innovations, Fleury has been criticized for his conservatism and caution; but they both of them gave France what she needed most, a government.

Fleury brought into the administration hard-working and able ministers. D'Aguesseau, Chancellor for life, was recalled from exile and devoted himself to the continuation of the great work of legal codification begun under Colbert. The former intendant Orry, Controller-General from 1730 to 1746, provided an orthodox, methodical administration. Maurepas built up the navy, while he also functioned as Secretary for the Maison du Roi. D'Angervilliers, Secretary of State for War from 1728 to 1740, was another who had learnt administrative habits as an intendant. From 1727 to 1737 Chauvelin, officially Keeper of the Seals, conducted foreign affairs in collaboration with Fleury, until his efforts to divert French policy on to lines which Fleury did not approve of led to his disgrace and replacement by yet another former intendant, Amelot de Chaillou. France was hardly to know again such a period of stability in governmental personnel.

The third of the great cardinal ministers was not unworthy of the succession to Richelieu and Mazarin. Like his contemporary Walpole, with whom he had more than a little in common, Fleury preferred to let sleeping dogs lie. They both saw the advantage to their countries of a continuation of peace and the opportunity for economic recovery from the wars of Louis XIV, rather than the adventures that the war party in each country was urging and that some subsequent French historians would have preferred Fleury to have undertaken. The European situation when he came into power was uneasy, but Fleury and Walpole were both anxious to preserve peace and rapidly established a personal understanding. The most powerful financier in France, Pâris-Duverney, in a memoir read to the Council, warned that war would be a disaster for French economy. At the beginning of Fleury's term of office Great Britain, under the energetic pressure of Walpole's colleague, Townshend, seemed to be moving in the direction of war with Spain and Austria. The situation of France in the pattern of European powers, and the personal proclivities of Fleury, cast him for the role of honest broker. By continual activity he kept the imminent conflict within the field of diplomacy, and at the price of being charged, at the time and subsequently, with subservience to British policy, he preserved the peace of Europe. The Treaty of Vienna in 1731 closed this episode. None of the fundamental problems of international politics had been solved, no glory had been gained; Fleury had merely preserved peace, which was at the moment the most valuable thing that France could have.

Those who were so anxious to push France into war, preferably with Austria or Great Britain but it did not matter seriously with which, were soon to find a better opportunity. In 1733 Augustus, Elector of Saxony and elective king of Poland, died, leaving as his heir Augustus III of Saxony. The dispossessed Stanislaus of Poland saw in this situation his opportunity; with the backing of a strong French party he proceeded to Warsaw, where a Diet of Polish nobles restored him to the throne. As was usual in Poland, an opposition was immediately formed which chose Augustus III as anti-king. Russia and Austria supported Augustus; and an invading Russian army chased Stanislaus from Warsaw and placed his rival on the Polish throne.

This insult to the father of the French queen and injury to French interests played so completely into the hands of the war party in France that Fleury could do nothing but accept the inevitability of an armed conflict. He let Chauvelin organize a coalition with Spain and Sardinia against Austria; but whereas Chauvelin was also directing his diplomacy against Great Britain, Fleury used his influence with Walpole to secure British neutrality and took care to divert French military action from the Low Countries, where it would have aroused British hostility. While Chauvelin was aspiring after war on the grand scale, Fleury was determined that it should be limited in its scope and profitable in its results. He made no serious attempt to reverse the situation in Poland. A French army occupied Lorraine, but though it crossed the Rhine and captured Phillipsburg, where its commander, the Duke of Berwick, was killed, no attempt was made to penetrate further into Germany. In Italy some territory was conquered in the Milanese by Villars, but he was recalled from an attempt to invade Austria through the Tyrol and died on his way back, the last of the great generals of Louis XIV.

Content with these successes, Fleury began negotiations for peace. At the back of his mind there was the thought that by giving Chauvelin his head and allowing him to push on with an aggressive policy there was a danger that the coalition of Austria, Great Britain, and the Dutch Republic, which had proved fatal to Louis XIV's ambitions, might be recreated. The cardinal was determined to pursue a policy which would not alarm Europe. Secret peace negotiations were therefore begun in 1735, and in 1736, after a short two years' war with no great campaign, France emerged with the virtual acquisition of the duchy of Lorraine. Stanislaus was compensated for the loss of Poland by being made king of Lorraine, where he proved a philosophical and benevolent ruler and turned Nancy into one of the most beautiful minor capitals in Europe, while under his French chancellor the little kingdom was administered practically as a French *généralité*. When Stanislaus died in 1766 it was absorbed uneventfully into France. To reconcile the Emperor to this concession, Francis of Lorraine, destined to marry the Emperor's daughter, was given the succession to Tuscany, and France recognized the Pragmatic Sanction guaranteeing the unity of the Habsburg dominions. Fleury had not only secured a peace which was profitable and a settlement which within its limits was likely to be lasting, he had outmanœuvred his own more reckless colleague and the war party. For his part, Chauvelin had been building up a network of intrigue which, he believed, would intimidate the cardinal. He did not know his man. Rapidly and ruthlessly the ambitious minister was hurled from office into exile. Those who continued to intrigue, or even to correspond with him, paid the price in Fleury's disfavour. Towards Chauvelin the cardinal was henceforth implacable.

Fleury had restored France to the position in Europe which her population and resources justified. In 1739 a French ambassador negotiated a peace between the Holy Roman and the Ottoman Empires which restored Belgrade to the Turks and signified a resurgence of the power of one of France's traditional Eastern allies. At home Fleury's administration was marked by no correspondingly striking achievements. He damped down the fires of conflict over Jansenism and the reviving claims of the parlements, but these, and the connected problem of financial reform, will be best dealt with subsequently, at the point when they effectively take the centre of the stage. The most important feature of Fleury's period of office was undramatic and unmarked. It was the opportunity that a generation of stable government, with no great wars, gave for recovery from the disasters of the reign of Louis XIV and for positive economic advance. For some sections of French society at least, this was the golden age of the *ancien régime*.

❦

CHAPTER FOUR

PROSPERITY AND POVERTY

B Y abstaining from expensive adventures abroad, and providing competent government at home, Fleury established the conditions in which the resources of France could be directed to the task of restoring economic prosperity. Though foreign adventures were subsequently to undermine and finally bring about the collapse of royal finances, until the Revolution they never wholly diverted the country from that pursuit of economic advantage which became a major characteristic of French society in the seventeen thirties. The effect of increasing economic prosperity was to introduce a solvent into its rigid pattern, but we must be careful not to exaggerate the novelty of this factor. The society of the *ancien régime* was never the simple stratification of orders that has so often been described and denounced. Privileged classes and *tiers état* were already, when the eighteenth century began, little more than juridical categories, a formal legal framework which did not correspond to the actual complexity of social life. Acquired riches, which cut across and conflicted with these categories, had become a great force in French society even in the age of the *roi soleil*.

The reign of Louis XIV offered opportunities of wealth and power to the financiers and contractors who raised the loans and furnished the supplies necessary for his wars, fitted out his ships, provided the capital for overseas trade, and began, with government concessions, the exploitation of the colonies. The financier Crozat had, before Law, the monopoly of trade with Louisiana. Samuel Bernard went bankrupt for 30 million livres in 1709 and rebuilt another great fortune on the ruins of the first. The great bankers and financiers inserted themselves intimately into the financial machinery of the state. They fitted out the expeditions to seek overseas supplies, provided the bullion which the French system, lacking adequate credit facilities, required, and farmed the indirect taxes. The constant and indispensable associates of the Controller-General, they were received as honoured guests by Louis XIV and his ministers at Versailles, were viewed with jealousy by the old aristocracy and reviled by the populace as infamous *traitants*. They erected great town houses and châteaux in the country, decorated them with the works of the finest artists of the time, entertained on a princely scale, married their daughters into the aristocracy and bought nobility for their sons. Law's System, with its royal bank and company, was an attempt to take the control of French finances and commerce out of their hands. Its failure, to which they contributed to the best of their ability, brought them back to the position they had won under Louis XIV. The Pâris brothers controlled the liquidation of the system, and the ablest of them, Pâris-Duverney, whose fortune had been built on war-contracts, emerged as one of the powers of eighteenth-century France.

Throughout the century profits came easiest from loans to the king to finance wars and meet deficits, from farming the taxes and from playing the exchanges; commerce interested the financiers less and industry least of all. The highest rank among them was held by the Farmers-General, the group of forty financiers who, every six years, united their resources to buy, through a nominal purchaser, the right of collecting the indirect taxes. For all financiers, however, the career was wide open to their particular talent, especially in the first half of the century. The Pâris brothers were sons of an inn-keeper; the Farmers-General Teissier and La Bouexière began life as valets. More often, however, money bred money. Financiers were apt to find their best jumping-off place in the service of the state, among the army of tax-collectors, receivers, controllers, and treasurers of a host of public services. One small provincial town, say Rennes, with a population of about 20,000, might have nearly twenty of these, all with a foot on the ladder that led to fortune.

There was wealth in eighteenth-century France not only for the financiers. In the eighteenth century, and particularly after 1730, prices began slowly to rise and French economy reacted to the increased stimulation. Another factor was the stabilization of the currency. The relation of the livre and the écu to the gold louis had fluctuated wildly in the past, at the whim of the government. Thus in

February 1724 the louis was worth 24 livres and the écu 6; in December 1725 the louis fell to 14 livres and the écu to 3 livres 10 sous. In 1726 they were fixed at 24 livres and 6 livres respectively, at which figures they remained unchanged from this date until the Revolution.

French overseas trade had suffered from Louis XIV's wars. A quarter of a century of peace at sea enabled it to recover to a point at which the competition of French merchants both alarmed and inspired a bellicose spirit in their English rivals. The French colonies were naturally the basis for this commercial expansion. Canada, with some fifteen ships reaching it a year, and Louisiana with only two or three, were of little economic value, while the French stations in India, so long as their trade was monopolized by the Compagnie des Indes, were generally in financial difficulties. The jewels of the French crown were the little islands of the West Indies. From the Atlantic ports of France four or five hundred ships a year sailed to take part in the trade in slaves from Africa (its morality as yet barely a subject of discussion) and in wine, food supplies, and other goods from France to the Antilles. From the islands the ships returned laden with sugar, rum, and molasses, and a little coffee, cotton, and indigo. All this trade, by the colonial pact called 'l'exclusif', was confined to French ships. The fisheries off Cape Breton Island and the Grand Banks, saved at the Treaty of Utrecht, drew a fleet of little fishing-boats, a fine sight as they put out annually from Saint-Malo to share the dangers of the passage together. They won their profits particularly from the fish they sold to provision the slaves in the Antilles. The Atlantic trade was the most important, but trade with the Levant also experienced a notable revival, stimulated by the success of French diplomacy in the Ottoman Empire.

Colonial trade had increased from some 40 million livres a year in 1716 to 204 in 1756, when the Seven Years War broke out, for what such statistics are worth. By this time France had some 1,800 ships engaged in overseas commerce, which roughly quadrupled between 1715 and 1789. To assist this trade a Bureau de commerce was set up in 1722, and gradually developed a stable and competent administrative personnel, though, especially after 1736, when the Compagnie des Indes lost the monopoly of the trade to the Antilles, the expansion was primarily attributable to the enterprise of individual merchants and shipowners.

The great commercial development was reflected in the growth of the ports. Saint-Malo, held back by the limited draught of the ships that its harbour could take, was confined to the fisheries. The free port of Marseilles flourished on the trade with the Levant. Dunkirk, also a free port, dealt particularly with the Baltic. Le Havre, breaking into the Atlantic trade, was rapidly increasing in prosperity. The port founded at Lorient by Law slowly increased by the trade of the Compagnie des Indes. La Rochelle shared, so far as its harbour permitted, in the Atlantic commerce. Nantes was the town of the wealthy slavers, sending 150 ships a year to the isles. Above all Bordeaux, with the great estuary of the Gironde to shelter its ships, the canal du Midi to link it with Languedoc, and its centuries-old export of wines and brandy to England and northern Europe, exploited the trade to Africa and the Indies. Its commerce and wealth grew steadily till the time of the Revolutionary Wars. Its maritime trade, on one estimate already worth 40 millions in 1724, had increased by 1789 to 250 millions. The merchants of Bordeaux built for themselves great town houses, commissioned the architect Gabriel to plan a fine open *place* fronting the Garonne and flanked by the magnificent Hôtel des Fermes and the Bourse, and housed their Chamber of Commerce in a princely palace. Arthur Young, when he saw the town in 1787, reluctant as he was to admit that anything could be done better in France than in England, had to confess that Liverpool was nothing to Bordeaux.

The most obvious external evidence of the increasing wealth of the eighteenth century was indeed to be seen in the cities. Building enjoyed an unprecedented expansion. Paris grew, on the right and the left banks, into the fashionable new faubourgs of Saint-Honoré and Saint-Germain. In the provincial cities, each a little Paris to its surroundings and separated by a long and tiresome journey from the national capital, governors, intendants, bishops, the aristocracy of sword and robe, financiers and men of affairs, erected their town houses, many of which, surviving as the homes of the wealthy, divided up into bourgeois apartments, or sunk into vertical slums, still constitute a notable feature of the older towns of France. 'Who',

it has been asked, 'has not spent some part of his life in these dwellings with their thick walls and large panelled rooms or more intimate
salons, the marks of age covered by successive layers of paint, with
tall casements opening on the green of garden lawns or on the big
paving-stones of a court, and whose attics huddle together under
red tile or blue slate?'

Rennes, devastated by fire in 1720, was largely rebuilt in the
eighteenth century; in other towns, even without this adventitious
advantage, the work of demolition and rebuilding went on apace.
Who would have guessed, even before the Revolution, that in 1700
Bordeaux had still been a medieval city? While private individuals
built their eternal mansions on earth, elegant, grand, but in their
frequent repetition of the same themes ultimately a little boring,
town planning and the creation of imposing set-pieces on a larger
scale was the work of the royal intendants, who rivalled one another
in the task of beautifying the seats of their authority. After Louis
XIV the threat of invasion or civil war no longer hung over France,
and the ramparts round the cities, which had already often spread
beyond them, having become useless, were converted into public
spaces and promenades, where formal gardens, enclosed with balu-
strades, peopled with statues and shaded by trees, were laid out. At
Nîmes, in the Jardin de la Fontaine, the genius of the eighteenth
century was wedded, with uniquely happy results, to the remains of
the Roman temple and baths. The creation of a *place royale* was
essential to every town that aspired after dignity and standing —
that now called by the name of its own little king, Stanislaus, at
Nancy, with its long, low ranges of buildings and the magnificent
ironwork of its gates and trellises, the loveliest of all. Paris itself
naturally had to have a *place royale*, but since to clear a space in the
heart of the capital would have been intolerably costly, the site
chosen was in the outskirts, on a patch of waste ground between the
gardens of the Tuileries and the wooded Champs-Elysées. Begun in
1757, it took twenty years to complete. The plans were those of
Louis XV's chief architect, A.-J. Gabriel, who, if he introduced no
new motives into architecture, was supreme in his tactful arrangement of the elements he employed, and by his constant striving
after simplicity achieved a restrained elegance. The place Louis

XV, completed in good time to become the place de la Révolution, and now place de la Concorde, proved an admirably convenient site for the austere and functional operations of the guillotine.

Building was perhaps the greatest outlet for the new wealth of France. In addition, the fructifying influence of commercial wealth spread round the great ports, providing distilleries, sugar refineries, shipbuilding yards at Bordeaux, and cotton manufactures in the neighbourhood of Rouen. On the whole, however, the picture presented by French industries in the eighteenth century is very different from that of commerce. Small-scale enterprise, most often that of a single craftsman and his family, or a master with one or two journeymen, predominated. The masters were organized in corporations which, instead of declining as they had done in England, had been given a new lease of life by the legislation of Colbert. This was the high-water mark of the gilds in France, at least in respect of numbers. Poitiers, which had fourteen gilds in the fourteenth century, had forty-two in the eighteenth. Though in some towns, such as Clermont, the state failed to establish, or re-establish them, and in the great ports local hostility kept the system in check, even where the corporation, gild, or *métier juré* did not exist, police control to some extent took their place.

One of the main functions of the corporations was fiscal: they were a means by which, through creating a mass of largely unnecessary offices — either for sale to individuals, whose prime function was to collect fees from the members, or to be bought up by the corporations to prevent them from being purchased by individuals — the state could draw in a little extra revenue. Thus the silk industry of Lyons, which was continually being hindered by the creation, suppression, and re-creation of useless official posts, in 1745 bought up 150 offices of alleged inspectors at a price of 200,000 livres; in 1758 it had to repeat the process at a cost of 133,000 livres. Again, the corporations were obliged to furnish and equip militia men for the army and replace them if they deserted. The silk corporation of Lyons had to provide eighty soldiers in 1742 and another fifty in 1743. The corporative system served also to protect the masters, for the aristocratic character of the gilds was accentuated during the eighteenth century: fees for reception as a master commonly amounted to as much as 2,000 livres and the gilds became largely hereditary. Their aim was in all ways to restrict competition. In 1751 an ordinance was issued prohibiting the circulation of notices in Paris announcing the sale of goods at cheap prices.

To give effect to government control of industry a continual stream of orders poured out, regulating such matters as the quality of raw materials, method of manufacture, and the standard of the finished articles. All these regulations required another horde of officials to enforce them, and the imposition of fees to pay for the process of inspection. They prevented, and were intended to prevent, the development of new methods of manufacture. French industry had in fact been put into a straitjacket by Colbert just at the time when a continual stream of new technical inventions was to call for the greatest flexibility and liberty. Up to the middle of the eighteenth century controls were effectively maintained despite increasing opposition. In the second half of the century the enforcement of the system gradually became laxer, one sign of which was the conclusion of the great struggle over 'toiles peintes' — printed fabrics — by an edict of 1759 which legalized their importation and manufacture. Fashion broke down a ban against which economic theory was powerless.

Industry was held back perhaps even more by shortage of capital than by the regulations of the gilds and state control. Many individual examples of industrial investment could, of course, be given, but such examples should not be allowed to obscure the fact that on the whole comparatively little finance capital flowed in this direction. Large-scale industry, therefore, tended to depend for its capital on the support of the state. The luxury manufactures of the Gobelins and Sèvres were carried on in state factories, as was also the soap manufacture. Other *manufactures royales* were created lavishly and supported by state loans, subsidies, and sometimes monopoly rights. The Jacobite exile, John Holker, who fled from England after being involved in the '45 and set up a textile factory in a suburb of Rouen with the aid of a small team of skilled workers brought over from England, obtained considerable success in his venture. The result was that in 1752 he became a royal manufacturer of velvets and cotton cloths, and in 1755 was appointed Inspector-General of Manufactures.

Here and there, in the eighteenth century, industry developed on a larger scale. At Reims nearly half the textile workers were grouped in factories. There were some ironworks and paper factories. Coal-mining, where it was on any scale, required a concentration of labour, for the control of which a code was drawn up by Orry in 1744. By this, no mining was to be undertaken without the permission of the Controller-General; concessions for mines were granted by the king, proprietors of the surface land being paid compensation; and rules for safeguarding workers in mines were laid down, though as was usual with government regulations they were more often broken than observed. Though many mines were still little better than holes in the ground worked by a handful of miners, under royal encouragement a few fairly large mining establishments were developed. The largest, the mines of Anzin, had 4,000 workers in 1789. Especially in the textile trades, new machines were introduced from England or invented in France; but the fate of the improved methods of silk weaving developed out of earlier experiments by Vaucanson in 1747 is not untypical. The hostility of the silk workers at Lyons prevented their adoption until the idea was taken up by Jacquard at the end of the century and put into practice under Napoleon. For spinning, by 1789 there were perhaps 900 jennies in France: at the same time there were 20,000 in England.

An impressive picture of French industrial advance in the eighteenth century could be drawn by giving a collection of individual examples, and this is sometimes done. In fact, industry was mainly dependent on an army of domestic workers following traditional methods. In the less developed areas, such as Brittany, the peasants continued to weave their own cloths. In Flanders, Picardy, Upper Normandy, and elsewhere, the domestic system of industry prevailed and rural craftsmen worked up the material supplied by merchants, who sometimes also provided the tools of the trade and who collected the finished articles for sale. To avoid gild restrictions there was a tendency for industry to move into suburbs or into the countryside and this movement was encouraged by the government in the second half of the century.

The control of merchants and masters over their workers, and the hierarchical structure of industry, was upheld not only by the system of corporations but also by direct royal edicts. By letters patent of 1749 workers were forbidden under a heavy penalty to leave their masters without written permission or to organize the disposal of their own labour. At Lyons the master weavers had fallen into almost total dependence on the silk merchants. Strikes and violent outbreaks, such as that of 1744 in which the silk workers of Lyons practically took control of the town by violence, were not rare, but they were always repressed, that at Lyons by armed force followed by the torture and execution or sentence to the galleys for life of the leaders. Though some of the masters resented the tutorship of the state over industry, they readily used it to maintain control over their workers and to prevent the introduction of new methods. In the control exercised by the corporations, and the system of state regulation, is to be found one reason why industry in eighteenth-century France, unlike overseas trade and in striking contrast to English industry, remained comparatively stagnant.

Undoubtedly another factor, which also contributed to the industrial backwardness of France compared with England at the same time, was the system of internal tolls, customs, seigneurial dues, *octrois*, and hindrances of all descriptions on domestic trade. Large parts of France were freer to trade with the foreigner than with the main customs area of the *Cinq grosses fermes* which extended over the old provinces of the monarchy. Throughout the century a series of reforming officials devoted themselves to the preparation of plans for the unification of France into a single customs unit, only to be frustrated, time and again, by the opposition of the vested interests of provinces, cities, Farmers-General. The existence of an army of officials to collect the internal customs, and a counter-army of smugglers trying to avoid them, was the chief positive result of this antiquated system. Once again the source of the weakness of eighteenth-century France must be sought in the failure of Louis XIV or his successors to complete the work he had begun. Colbert had initiated the process of customs unification with the creation of the *Cinq grosses fermes*; provincial rights and privileges of all kinds prevented his successors from completing it.

These considerations may help to explain why the great scientific and technical achievements of French genius, although much encouraged by the state, remained to such an extent in the realm of theory and did not produce more positive results in practice. The most successful achievements were in respect of transport. The roads of France, by gradual deterioration of the paved highways of the Romans through neglect or the pilfering of stones, had probably reached their lowest level in the seventeenth century. In 1736 they were put under the Contrôle Général. The great technical Corps of Bridges and Highways, created in 1747, by 1787 consisted of 1 first engineer, 4 inspectors-general, 28 engineers, 60 sub-engineers, 124 inspectors, and an army of inferior grades; its annual budget amounted to 7 million livres for technical services and supervisory personnel alone. The actual work of construction was performed by means of the *corvée*, the forced labour of the population within reach of the main roads, organized and extended to all France by Orry in 1738. Funds were provided by the Treasury or by local and special taxes for those works with which the *corvée* obviously could not cope, and by the end of the century a network of main roads had been created. Radiating out from Paris, and for the needs of the century unnecessarily wide and straight, they were determined by the political predominance of the capital and by military considerations rather than by economic requirements. Arthur Young repeatedly comments on the fineness of the French roads and the lack of traffic on them, even in the neighbourhood of great cities. Transverse connections, linking up the smaller towns and villages and cutting across the great highways, were still inadequate or non-existent. However, to travel from Paris to Lyons by coach, which had taken ten days in the seventeenth century, on the eve of the Revolution only took five. Because of the expense of land transport, goods and even passengers were still conveyed as far as possible by water. Any picture of the Seine at Paris in the eighteenth century will show it lined with long rows of boats discharging supplies from the great hinterland which its tributaries tapped to provision the population.

To draw up a balance sheet of the changes in French economy in the eighteenth century is almost an impossible task, for the picture must seem a contradictory one. Some broad general

D

impressions alone can be given. Overseas trade was developing rapidly
and methods of transport were improving. More efficient industrial
methods were being adopted only slowly and on a very restricted
scale. Meanwhile population was increasing rapidly. The causes of
this growth of population remain mysterious. One can only notice
the absence of great famines, though there was frequently scarcity,
and that no foreign invasions or civil wars ravaged the soil of France.
The plague which swept Marseilles in 1720 was the last of its kind,
though an epidemic is estimated to have carried off 80,000 in Brittany in 1741. Emigration was on a small scale. New crops, such as
maize and potatoes, were slowly coming into use in some areas. But
the expansion of population, beginning, or at least first becoming
marked, in the eighteenth century, is too widespread a phenomenon
to be explicable by any local or restricted causes. The actual figures
are speculative. France had long been the most populated state in
Europe. Its numbers were not surpassed, even by those of Russia,
until after 1789. Under Louis XIV its population had probably been
stationary or perhaps even declining. In 1715 it may have been no
more than 16 or 17 million; by the middle of the century one may
guess at a figure approaching 22, and by the time of the Revolution
it had probably reached 26 million.

Commercial prosperity and the growth of the state machinery
inflated the size of the towns. Paris, in the middle of the century, had
a population of half a million and was steadily increasing, Lyons had
perhaps 160,000, Marseilles and Bordeaux were approaching 100,000.
On the other hand, provincial capitals like Rennes, Dijon, or Grenoble were towns of little more than 20,000. All told, by the end of
the *ancien régime* the urban population of France can hardly have
exceeded two and a half million at most, which left a rural population
of perhaps some 22 to 24 million. It is difficult to avoid the conclusion that France must have been suffering from intense and increasing
rural over-population. This is the other side of the medal, to be set
against the wealth of the mercantile, financial, and official classes, and
of the professional men who to a considerable extent lived on them
and shared in their prosperity.

Only agrarian and industrial revolutions could have saved the
swelling population of France from severe distress as its numbers

pressed increasingly on the means of subsistence, and I have already given reasons why industrial production was rising only slowly. New agricultural methods made practically no headway against the conservatism of the French peasantry, while the limit of profitably cultivable land had possibly already been reached. At any rate, the limiting factor in this respect was not so much land as fertilizers, and these were in short supply because livestock was deficient. The shortage of cattle, horses and sheep in France was partly attributable to the need for each area to be self-sufficient in arable crops, and this in turn was due in part to lack of transport and in part to government policy. The result of the inadequate supply of fertilizing material, as Lavoisier pointed out, was that taking new land — and usually poorer land — into cultivation did little to increase production, for it merely meant that the same quantity of manure was spread over a larger area.

In some parts of France the surplus rural population turned to poorly paid domestic industry, one result of which was to depress wages in the towns. A large floating population worked when it could for the more prosperous farmers, especially at harvest time, and drifted into the towns to provide casual labour at other seasons. The number of vagabonds and beggars, forming themselves some-times into bands which terrorized large areas of the countryside, increased to the point at which they became a social menace. The charitable foundations of the Church had largely disappeared or their resources had been diverted to add to the revenues of more influential if less needy sections of society, though the state gradually began to intervene for the relief of distress in the course of the century. Taine's comparison of the situation of the rural population to that of a man walking through a pond with the water up to his chin — a slight fall in the economic level and he goes under — is not misleading. Only the well-to-do *laboureur*, or the *fermier* who could rent a fair-sized farm, could really live on the product of his land. The majority had to eke out a living by working on the lands of others, engaging in domestic industry, migrating seasonally into the towns, scraping a bare living off the commons and waste, or else starve. That in such conditions the population continued to increase is a mystery which it is for the demographer to explain.

France in the eighteenth century was thus literally a land of prosperity and poverty: but the poverty was concentrated in the inarticulate rural masses, and bad as their conditions were, given the general absence — until 1789 — of rural uprisings or great famines such as had marked the reign of Louis XIV, and the continued increase of population, one is left with the feeling that perhaps, in spite of all, they were better off than they had been in the previous century.

CHAPTER FIVE

DISORDER AT HOME

W HETHER anything that any eighteenth-century government could have done would have remedied the poverty of
the rural masses in France is more than doubtful. But if we
cannot assign the blame for this poverty, we can attribute some
credit for the prosperity of other sections of the community to the
government of Fleury. However, even he could not last for ever.
The disgrace of Chauvelin in 1737 was a warning to those who
opposed the cardinal, but though Louis XV, who clung to old
friends and disliked new faces, refused to be parted from his great
minister, the cardinal's age was not to be ignored. Factions were
growing up at Versailles and among the interested public in Paris,
each with its own candidate for the succession. The fallen minister,
Chauvelin, had his adherents. The cause of the Cardinal de Tencin,
leader of the Ultramontane anti-Jansenists, was energetically
promoted by his intriguing sister, Mme de Tencin, in her salon. A
military faction gathered round the comte de Belle-Isle. The
marshal de Noailles drew support from the ramifications of his
numerous and influential clan at Versailles. The king's mistress, the
duchesse de Châteauroux, and her cousin the duc de Richelieu, hoped
by means of the king's favour to secure a monopoly of patronage.
Finally, the Secretaries of State, strengthened by their long tenure of
office, in spite of their rivalries joined in an effort to save themselves
from subordination to a new *premier ministre*. The king himself, aged
twenty-eight in 1738, might even have been regarded as a candidate
for the succession. Returning, after much hesitation, to the traditions
of his house, he had taken a *maîtresse en titre*, a post occupied in turn
by the three Nesle sisters, Mailly, Vintimille, and Châteauroux, the
last of whom, not without an eye to her own advantage and that of
her friends, encouraged him to take a more active role in the government of his country.

When at last Fleury died, in January 1743, the struggle over the succession reached its climax. Chauvelin, still in exile, had prepared for the long-awaited day by entrusting to an adherent at Versailles a memorandum setting forth his claims to the vacant position and enumerating in no measured language all the faults of the cardinal, which he took it upon himself to correct. Presented with indecent haste to the king immediately after Fleury's death, this memorandum ruined for ever Chauvelin's prospects of returning to office. The duc de Noailles, less ambitious or more subtle, offered Louis for his guidance the instructions which Louis XIV had drawn up for Philip of Anjou when he became king of Spain. 'Do not let yourself be led,' Louis XIV had written, 'be master yourself. Never have a favourite or first minister. Listen to and consult your council, but decide yourself. God, who has made you king, will give you all the necessary wisdom so long as your intentions are good.' Did this echo from the past give the hesitating Louis XV resolution? In any case he announced that he would in future have no first minister but would himself govern.

What this meant in reality was that the faction of the Secretaries of State had won. The business of government would henceforth be done, as it had been under Louis XIV, separately with each Secretary, the king himself providing the necessary co-ordination. Unfortunately this was just what Louis XV was incapable of doing. Intelligent, well-intentioned, conscious of what a king of France and the successor to the roi soleil should be, he was self-distrustful in the extreme, *un grand timide* in whom, said the duc de Croÿ, modesty was pushed to the extreme of a vice. He was incapable of deciding on a policy and supporting it steadily and consistently. Under Fleury, wrote the abbé de Bernis, who was to know the government of France from the inside at a later and less happy stage, 'the king's council had more authority and kept its secrets better, the great corporations of the state were more submissive, the ministers more respected and France more worthy of respect.' Against this we may set the description of the council given by the Cardinal de Tencin after Fleury's death. 'It must be admitted', he writes, 'that the king's council is a council *pour rire*. Only a very small fraction of the business of the state is discussed in it; and after the rapid reading of a memorandum our opinion is asked on the spot, without any time for undisturbed reflection and summing up. Moreover, the lack of interest the king appears to show and the profound silence he maintains is shattering.' D'Argenson, admittedly writing with the bitterness of an ambitious man who had failed in his ambitions, was nevertheless justified when he described the royal council as 'a republic not of citizens assembled to take counsel concerning the well-being of the state, but of heads of factions, each thinking only of his own concerns, one of finance, another of the navy, another of the army, and each achieving his own ends according to his greater or less facility in the art of persuasion'.

Louis XV is hardly to be blamed for not being a Louis XIV. It was his misfortune to have to occupy a representative position for which, either by nature or from the constant and premature publicity which he endured as a child-king, he had acquired a horror. He carried on with aloof dignity the life of a king, surrounded by crowds of courtiers he hardly knew, moving daily through the fixed routine of court ceremonies, stared at from morning to night, the principal boy in a perpetual pantomime; but to concern himself continually with public affairs, to be the statesman who pulled the strings, as well as the puppet who was controlled by them, was beyond his capacity. The intrigues of the court, the appointment or dismissal of officials, his personal and secret system of diplomacy, these could arouse his interest, but public affairs involved so much boring work that they bored him. He had better things to turn his attention to. He sought distraction in hunting and in women, two occupations which if they were always the same were always different, and which filled up the emptiness of his life.

There was never a pause in the holocaust of animals slaughtered, almost daily, for Louis XV was an indefatigable hunter, but the death of the last of the Nesle sisters in 1744 left a gap in the other of his two chief pursuits. It was to be filled by Jeanne-Antoinette Poisson, daughter of a steward to the Pâris brothers, the bankers who after the collapse of Law's System were for a time the most powerful figures in French finances. A financial scandal which made a temporary absence from France desirable for M. Poisson enabled his wife to form a profitable connection with a wealthy Farmer-

General, who in due course married off her daughter to his nephew, Le Normant d'Étioles. The world of high finance in which Jeanne-Antoinette had been brought up was also a world of culture and of what was beginning to be called enlightenment. Young Mme d'Étioles, with her financial connections, intelligence, skill in drawing-room accomplishments, wit, beauty, and a kind of charm which even her enemies had to acknowledge, soon attracted to her house men like Crébillon, the fashionable society novelist; Fontenelle, now getting on for one hundred and a legendary but still lively figure in the world of letters; Montesquieu, not yet the author of *De l'esprit des lois*, but with a reputation for wit based on the *Lettres persanes*; Voltaire, who found her amiable and sincere.

All this was good, but not quite good enough for an ambitious little beauty. There was a higher world than those of finance or letters to conquer. To become accepted in aristocratic society was difficult, the private life of the court was easier to enter if you had something to bring to it, as Madame d'Étioles had, and knew the right person, as she did. A distant relation was body-servant to the dauphin and so in touch with the king, who was on easy terms with his servants. How the first meeting between Louis XV and the new candidate for the vacant place in his affections was arranged is not known, but by September 1745 she was installed at Versailles as recognized mistress, endowed with an estate in the country and the title of marquise de Pompadour. She was to be the king's mistress for five years and his close friend for twenty.

The name of the Pompadour is associated with a world of *objets d'art* — she herself the loveliest if the most ephemeral of them all — in a period when the cult of the lesser arts reached perhaps its height. Paris, in the middle of the century, had five hundred goldsmiths, and a host of skilled craftsmen and shopkeepers were occupied in the production and sale of works of art of all kinds. Mme de Pompadour was one of the most assiduous of their patrons. In one shop, in the rue Saint-Honoré, the account books of which for the ten years 1748–58 have survived, her name appears on an average once a week. When she died it took two notaries, working for a whole year, to draw up the catalogue of her possessions. She is particularly associated with the china manufactory at Sèvres, for it was founded at her instigation to compete with Meissen. Under royal patronage, Gobelins, Aubusson, and Beauvais continued to produce their famous tapestries. Luxury, in ample measure, was tempered by a sense of restraint, an acceptance of limitations, which is evident also in the music that flowed gracefully through such elegant salons. With composers like Rameau and Couperin the music of the century is noble, sober, and classical in operas, or gay but sedate in *bergeries*, *contredanses*, and the accompaniments of *fêtes galantes*. There is little incongruity in adding that this was also the age of the perfection of French cuisine and of the invention of the great wines and cheeses.

To the artistic achievements of the *style Louis XV* the intelligent encouragement of the Pompadour and her brother Marigny, who became Intendant des Bâtiments, contributed much. Exotic influences, particularly in the form of chinoiserie, contributed to the decorative arts of the period, but France escaped the exaggerated styles that prevailed elsewhere in Europe. Perhaps the works of Meissonier represent the only true examples of rococo to be found. Elegance was at its height: one could not ask for more from writing-desks and mirror frames, salt-cellars, fruit bowls, china statuettes. One becomes conscious of the limitations of the period when one approaches the greater arts. Carlo Vanloo, spoilt child of court and capital, produced innumerable undistinguishable society portraits. Nattier painted royal princesses, noble ladies, and wealthy bourgeoises, all with the same gracious smile and vacant countenance, whether they are represented as Diana, Venus, or any other pagan deity or mythological figure. Only Boucher — favourite of Mme de Pompadour — emerges from the crowd of fashionable painters, his pictures, with masterly technique, perpetuating the thoughtless charms of the lascivious little beauties to whose representation in all attitudes he devoted so much of his talent.

In literature it was an age of wit rather than wisdom, of optimism rather than a sense of tragic destiny. Voltaire, it is true, could not persuade himself, at least after the Seven Years War and the earthquake of Lisbon, that all was for the best in the best of possible worlds. The new spirit of pre-romanticism was to come in soon with Rousseau, but that strange Genevan genius did not belong to the

France of mid-century. For the imaginative literature of the age of
Louis XV we must look to lesser figures. 'O to read eternal new
romances of Marivaux and Crébillon,' exclaimed Thomas Gray.
Are the libertine novels of Crébillon still read? Marivaux began to
produce his comedies in 1720. The title of the best known of them,
Le Jeu de l'amour et du hasard, would do for all. Love is no longer
the tyrannical goddess of the classical age, but a mischievous Cupid
who gets his arrows mixed up in a world of lesser nobles and well-to-
do bourgeois, whose too witty valets can pose as gentlemen and
whose too pretty chambermaids be mistaken for their mistresses.
In these comedies we are in a world not of sentiment but of
sensibility. With Marivaux's long novel, the *Vie de Marianne*, there
is added an astringent dose of realism in glimpses of the people, remote
in their lives and thoughts from the elevated sphere in which the
Pompadour glittered and had her being. She has been unduly
identified with an age which she only represented in its transient
beauty. For the political disasters of the period she has unfairly
been held responsible, because she has come to symbolize a generation in which, under a weak king, the irresponsible intrigues of a
frivolous court determined the constant changes of ministers and
policies.

The fundamental weaknesses of the *ancien régime* go deeper than
this, however. The commonest charge against the court, and in
particular against the Pompadour, was extravagance, which, it was
believed, ruined French finances and so brought about the Revolution.
That a lot of money went on palaces, parks, works of art, and even
more on places and pensions for courtiers and their hangers-on, is
undeniable; but in relation to the whole cost of the government of
France the expenditure of the court, excessive as it may have been,
does not play a decisive role. The expense of even a small war was
greater than that of the biggest palace. This does not mean that the
court can be absolved of responsibility for the distress into which
royal finances fell, but the root of the trouble lay rather in the
system of collection of the taxes than in expenditure. Once again
we are forced to seek the source of the evil in the reign of Louis XIV.
The great king endowed France with a modern system of government while retaining a semi-medieval system of financing it. It is

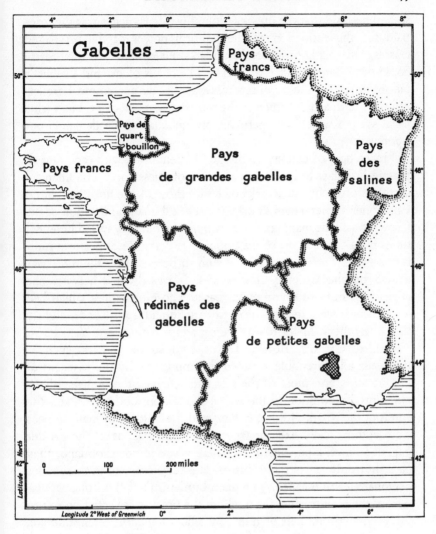

GABELLES

1. pays de grandes gabelles   4. pays de quart bouillon
2. pays de petites gabelles   5. pays rédimés des gabelles
3. pays des salines   6. pays francs

These were the main divisions, but within each of these areas there were many sub-divisions and local variations. The price of salt ranged from 60 livres 7 sous a minot (72 litres) to 1l. 10s. Average prices in each area, though these conceal a wide range of differences, were — 1. 57l.; 2. 33l.; 3. 24l.; 4. 13l.; 5. 9l.; 6. 3l. 15s.

sometimes said that the preservation of fiscal privileges was the price paid for the extinction of the political power of the privileged classes, but this is probably to underestimate what royal authority could have done under Louis XIV. The result of his and Colbert's failure to reform the royal finances was that his successors were left not only with a state which at the moment was bankrupt, but with a fiscal system which was permanently unequal to the demands put upon it.

France had, of course, no budget. Expenditure, with each bureau practically a law to itself, was a matter of guesswork. The financial accounts of each year overlapped with those of the next, so that no Controller-General ever knew what the real financial position of the Crown was. The main tax was the *taille*, the old levy raised in feudal times from the sections of the population that did not perform military service. Each year the total sum to be raised by the *taille* was settled by the Council of Finances. It was divided between the *généralités*, but not on an equal basis. Those provinces which had local Estates were in a position to bargain and got off more lightly than the others. Many towns were exempt from the *taille* — Paris, Versailles, Orleans, Rouen, Lyons, and so on; others, such as Bordeaux and Grenoble, escaped the imposition by the payment of a lump sum, and most of the rest had obtained the transfer of the *taille* into an addition to the *octroi*, the tax on foodstuffs and wine entering the town. Nobles, clergy, and the holders of many offices were automatically exempt where the *taille* was, as in the greater part of France, a personal tax. Where it was imposed on land, they paid, but only on old and out-of-date registers, and in these cases personal wealth escaped. The main burden thus fell on the population of the countryside, from whom the tax was collected, in return for a reduction in their own tax, by fellow *taillables*, often illiterate, incompetent, and arbitrary, with an army of bailiffs and sergeants to enforce payment. The *capitation*, established in 1695 and intended to supplement the *taille* by a tax on wealth admitting of no exceptions, had been whittled down until it was a mere addition to the *taille*. The *dixième*, established in 1710 with a similar object, met with a similar fate.

These direct taxes were supplemented by a vast and complex

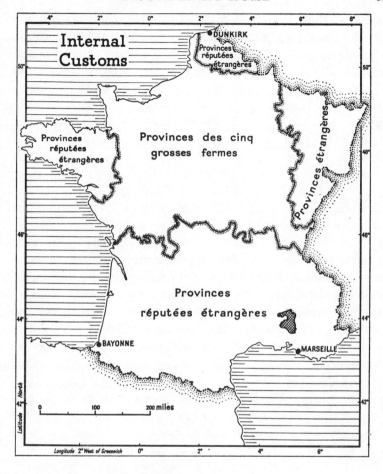

Internal Customs

INTERNAL CUSTOMS

The major divisions of France for internal customs were:
1. Provinces des cinq grosses fermes
2. Provinces réputées étrangères
3. Provinces étrangères

The *cinq grosses fermes* were made into a customs union by Colbert in 1664. The *provinces réputées étrangères* were those excluded from the tariff union of 1664. They retained a congeries of criss-crossing internal customs barriers as well as those on their frontiers. The *provinces étrangères* were those subsequently annexed, which traded freely across the frontiers of France but were separated by customs barriers from the rest of the country. There were three free ports — Dunkirk, Marseille, and Bayonne — but of these only Dunkirk was totally free from external customs of any kind and cut off by a strict customs barrier from the rest of France.

system of indirect taxes. The *gabelle*, the hated salt tax, which between 1715 and 1789 was raised from 23 to 50 million livres, was imposed with such diversity in different parts of France that the price of salt varied from half a sou to twelve or thirteen sous a livre. The inevitable result was a regular industry of salt smuggling, an army of *gabelous* to repress it, and a steady procession of men to the galleys and women and children to prison for offences against the *gabelle*. The great bulk of indirect taxation took the form of the *traites*, customs dues exacted both at the frontier and at innumerable internal customs barriers, the effect of which on French trade and industry I have already mentioned, and the *aides*, excise taxes on such things as drinks, tobacco, iron, precious metals, and leather. Arthur Young, when he saw men and women working barefoot in the country, might have asked how much was added by the *marque de cuir* to the price of shoe-leather in a country where, because of the lack of livestock, it was already in short supply. To describe in a reasonable space the complexities and local variations of this system of indirect taxes would be impossible. They were collected, much more efficiently than the direct taxes, by the great organization of the Farmers-General, but the efficiency, which was reflected in the rapidly mounting price paid for the lease of the taxes, did not increase their popularity.

The Contrôle Général added to its resources by stamp taxes, lotteries, the sale of offices, the *don gratuit* or free gift which the clergy voted to the Crown, not, of course, at an excessively burdensome rate to themselves, and finally by loans to tide over the recurrent crises. The royal treasury could manage to stagger along under this cumbersome system in peacetime, but war inevitably brought a financial crisis. If one is looking for a single reason why France, with its population and resources, should have been defeated by far smaller powers such as Great Britain and Prussia in the eighteenth century, it is to be found in its inability to mobilize the wealth of the country for war. Fleury, by avoiding large-scale war, and Orry, by economical administration, had managed to carry on without grave financial difficulties, though his attempts at economy and his uncourtierlike personality made Orry one of the most hated men in France. It was perhaps not a mere coincidence that the Pâris brothers, to whom his austere financial methods were by no means congenial, succeeded in bringing about his fall in December 1745, just after their protégée, Madame de Pompadour, had risen to favour.

However, if Louis sacrificed Orry to personal enmities and the scheming of the financiers, it was not without giving him a worthy successor. To know how or why anyone was ever chosen for any office, it would be necessary to have a daily, or indeed hourly, bulletin of the intrigues and gossip of the court, but the king was not unconscious of merit when the report of it, or personal impression, could penetrate to him through the network of scandal and backbiting that constituted Versailles. Machault d'Arnouville, the new Controller-General, brought from the intendancy of Valenciennes, was a cold, taciturn, rigid, honest administrator, with a broader horizon than his predecessor had possessed. Called to office with the task of raising the necessary finance for the War of the Austrian Succession, by expedients of all kinds he succeeded in the immediate task. The restoration of peace gave him the opportunity to begin on fundamental reform. In 1749 he introduced the *vingtième*, a tax of one-twentieth on all incomes without exception, for the collection of which he began to organize and train a new administrative personnel.

The struggle over the *vingtième* may be taken as an object lesson in the difficulties of financial reform under the *ancien régime*. The noblesse, naturally, refused to pay, and what sanction could a simple collector of taxes employ against a noble? The parlements and the Provincial Estates had to be compelled to register the edict. The clergy, to whom the idea that they should pay a tax other than their 'free gift' savoured of heresy, took the lead in opposition. They were supported by the *dévot* party at court, with the backing of the queen, the dauphin, and the king's daughters, by the Jesuits, and by the comte d'Argenson, Secretary of State for War and a personal enemy of Machault. The bitterness of the clergy at the prospect of being subjected to compulsory taxation can be appreciated when it is realized that, according to one calculation, on an annual revenue of some 120 million they paid in voluntary taxation some 2 or 3 million. The Pompadour, who had as little love for the clergy as they had for her, put all her influence behind Machault; but the king was susceptible to religious arguments and to pressure from his daughters. The clergy launched a great campaign of prayer to be spared this new affliction, which touched them where they felt it most, and the bishops threatened to abandon their churches. Meanwhile the nobles and *parlementaires* held their fire, more than content to see the battle fought for them by such a powerful ally. Machault could not overcome this opposition. In December 1751 he had to admit defeat. The raising of the *vingtième* on the property of the clergy was suspended and after this the attempt to reform the fiscal system was abandoned.

A weak and divided government was not only incapable of bringing about financial reform, it could not, when the great corporations of the state — the Church and the parlements — were involved, even maintain its own authority and suppress disorder. Curiously, considering that this was the eighteenth century, the prime cause of domestic disturbance was at least nominally religious. There had been in succession three religious struggles in France. The first and bitterest, against the Huguenots, had been effectively ended by Richelieu but reopened by the persecution of Louis XIV. Huguenot despair flared out in the terrible revolt of the Camisards, the last echoes of which reverberate through the eighteenth century. An edict of 1724 forbade heretical religious assemblies, under penalty of sentence to perpetual galleys for men and life imprisonment for women. For Protestant preachers the punishment was death. As late as March 1751 a Protestant religious meeting in the Cevennes was dispersed by the bullets of royal troops. In March 1752 a Protestant preacher was hanged at Montpellier. In 1749 the parlement of Bordeaux ordered forty-six persons to separate for concubinage, that is, for being married by Protestant rites, and declared their children illegitimate and incapable of inheriting their property. In 1752 there was a small Huguenot jacquerie and a new wave of emigration. However, though the case of Calas was yet to come, the persecuting spirit was spending itself and toleration appeared in practice before it was admitted in theory. Even in the first half of the century the treatment of the Protestants depended on the attitude of the local authorities in each *généralité* and varied greatly from time to time; and after 1751 the Church was increasingly on the defensive against a more dangerous enemy.

The second struggle, between Versailles and Rome over the Gallican liberties, had ended in a compromise by 1715. The third, over Jansenism, had apparently ended in 1709 when, under pressure from Louis XIV, the Pope decreed the extinction of Port-Royal, now inhabited, for Jansenism had been rapidly declining in its appeal, only by twenty-two aged nuns. They were dispersed, the property of the convent confiscated, the buildings razed to the ground, and even the bodies in the cemetery dug up to be put in some unknown grave or scattered to the winds. The Jesuits could feel that they had decisively avenged the *Lettres provinciales* of Pascal, but to consolidate their influence over the Church in France it was necessary also to eliminate its deep-rooted Gallicanism. The position of the Archbishop of Paris, Noailles, was the obvious objective to attack, and an opening was provided by the fact that a work published by Quesnel in 1671, which had been recommended by Noailles, was Jansenist in its tendency. Papal condemnation was secured for one hundred and one propositions in Quesnel's book by the famous Bull Unigenitus.

Noailles yielded, but whereas the former controversy had largely been a matter for theologians, this one concerned a popular and widely read work, written in French and not in Latin, and involved the question of the Gallican liberties. For the first time since the Fronde the parlements, so submissive to Louis XIV, refused to register a royal edict, that enforcing acceptance of the Bull. Regarding themselves as the guardians of the rights of the Gallican Church, they took the lead in a struggle that was to continue for fifty years. Though the struggle was still labelled with the name of Jansenism, the so-called Jansenism of the parlements was really a combination of Gallicanism with an attempt to revive their own political power. It enabled them to disguise as an assertion of the independence of the secular power their own claim to authority in matters of ecclesiastical discipline. In the words of the parlement of Paris, they held that: 'The temporal power is independent of all other powers, to it alone belongs the task of coercing the subjects of the king, and the ministers of the Church are accountable to the parlement, under the authority of the monarch, for the exercise of their jurisdictions.' Public opinion, finding little outlet for its religiosity in the official

E

Church, joined in the new Jansenist controversy, especially in the 'thirties, when at the tomb of a Jansenist deacon, Pâris, miracles very inconveniently started to occur. The crowds who gathered to watch the antics into which religious emotion threw the *convulsionnaires* over the tomb became such a menace to public order that, miracles or no miracles, the cemetery was closed by the police.

There followed a struggle over *billets de confession*. The Archbishop of Paris who followed Noailles was Christophe de Beaumont, virtuous, pious, stupid, and a violent partisan of the Jesuits and the Bull Unigenitus. He excommunicated and deprived of the last sacraments those who had not a ticket to show that they had confessed to a priest who accepted the Bull. The parlements retaliated by arresting priests who refused the sacraments to suspected Jansenists. The struggle was now one inside the Church as well as with the parlements, and it was intensified by a new tendency which was developing among the lower clergy. The upper clergy in the eighteenth century were almost exclusively noble, for the Church might well have been described as a system of out-door relief for the aristocracy. A prince de Rohan, Bishop *in partibus* of Campe at the age of twenty-six, could become in succession to his uncle, Bishop of Strasbourg, Grand Almoner of France, Provisor of the Sorbonne, Abbot of the wealthiest abbey in France, and Cardinal. The Cardinal de Polignac, Archbishop of Auch for fifteen years, never once set foot in his diocese. The revenues of many religious houses went to *abbés commendataires*, exercising no religious functions. A large part of the tithes and other revenues of the parish priests was alienated to such nominal abbés or to wealthy upper clergy, save for a meagre *portion congrue* which had to be left for them to live on. The lower clergy therefore provided fruitful soil for the ideas first put forward early in the seventeenth century by Edmond Richer, who had claimed that the government of the Church belonged of right to the whole community of pastors; and the so-called Jansenism of the eighteenth century, which for the parlements was a kind of Gallicanism, for the lower clergy became a kind of Richerism.

To trace the long running fight which went on between the parlements and the Church would be an exhausting and fruitless task. The king, influenced by the *dévot* party, usually took the side of the

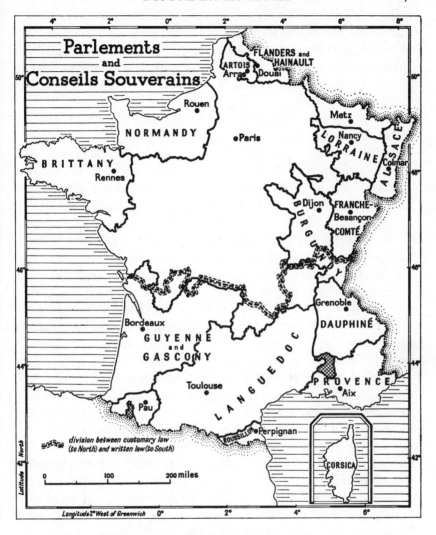

PARLEMENTS AND CONSEILS SOUVERAINS

There were, in 1789, 13 parlements and 4 conseils souverains with similar powers. The vast area from which cases had to be brought to Paris will be noted, and also the small extent of the jurisdiction of some of the lesser courts. If the boundaries of the jurisdictions of the Chambres des Comptes and the Cours des Aides were added, it would be seen that these often failed to coincide with one another or with those of the parlements. In addition to the traditional division of France between the areas of customary and written law, there were a host of varying local laws and feudal customs.

bishops, public opinion that of the parlements; and while in financial matters the parlements were able to prevent reform, in ecclesiastical matters they succeeded in perpetuating discord. The crown found in them its bitterest and most dangerous enemy. It may well be asked how it was that under an absolute monarchy mere law courts could acquire such power.

France had twelve parlements and three sovereign courts, which filled similar functions. The parlement of Paris, its jurisdiction extending over one-third of the country and by far the greatest of these hereditary and venal law courts, dated from the thirteenth century. The other courts, set up when fresh provinces were taken under royal administration, had played an important part in the extension of royal authority. The members of the parlements and of the other courts which shared their powers numbered in the eighteenth century a little over 2,000 in all. Originally recruited from middle-class lawyers, by the eighteenth century membership of the parlements was determined by birth and money, and since the offices were venal they were properties of which their possessors could not arbitrarily be dispossessed. Primarily law courts, the parlements also had extensive police powers over such matters as religion, trade and industry, morals and censorship. Most important of all were their political claims. Registration by the parlements was the normal method of promulgating royal decrees. They could protest against these by *remontrances*, which, intended for the king's eye alone, in the eighteenth century were often published by the parlements for the purpose of stirring up public opinion. If the parlement refused to register a decree, the king could enforce registration by the formal procedure of *lit de justice*. Finally, in the event of continued resistance he could exile individual magistrates or the whole court to some other part of France. The parlements, for their part, could reply by suspending their sessions, thus holding up the course of justice, causing great inconvenience and arousing public opinion in their favour.

Under Louis XIV the parlements knew too well the determination of the great king and feared him too much to provoke his wrath. Louis XIV, it has been said, did not have to crush the parlements; he showed that he did not fear them and that was enough. Under the weaker governments that followed they became the centre of opposition to the royal will. As the last relic of the medieval constitution left at the centre of government, the parlement of Paris, though no more in fact than a small, selfish, proud, and venal oligarchy, regarded itself, and was regarded by public opinion, as the guardian of the constitutional liberties of France. From the revival of its claims under the regency to the moment when it brought the monarchy crashing down in a general destruction of the *ancien régime*, which it shared, it conducted a running war with the Crown. The defence of so-called Jansenism and opposition to financial reform provided the main themes of the agitation. The provincial parlements, in the second half of the century, encouraged by the example of that of Paris, started local wars against the intendants. Thus, while standing in the way of all reforms, the parlements spread a spirit of opposition and revolutionary ideas throughout the country. They undermined respect for the Church and the monarchy prevented the reform of royal finances, and finally, as will be seen, opened the door to revolution. But this is to look far ahead, and meanwhile the weakness and instability of French government after Fleury was to have more immediately harmful consequences in the field of foreign affairs.

❧

CHAPTER SIX

DEFEAT ABROAD

THE disappearance of governmental cohesion in the declining years of Fleury, which led to failure in religious and financial policies, had even more disastrous consequences in the field of foreign policy. The most powerful of the factions which were struggling for the succession to the cardinal in his last years, when he was increasingly unable to hold his own against them, was that which surrounded the ambitious and brilliant comte de Belle-Isle. Grandson of that Fouquet whom Louis XIV had flung from the highest office to perpetual prison in 1661, he had gradually worked his way back into favour. Belle-Isle was a good soldier and distinguished himself in the last battles of Louis XIV. He made a fortune out of Law's System. Charm, ability, tireless energy, ambition, and a mastery of intrigue enabled him to build up a party for himself at court. His chance came when the death of the Emperor Charles VI, leaving a young girl, Maria Theresa, as his successor, threw middle Europe into the melting-pot.

Belle-Isle's aim, or one of his many aims, was to be Marshal of France and Duke, and war was the only short cut to the achievement of this ambition. The young nobles at court, lacking occupation and the opportunity for glory and promotion under the peaceful regime of Fleury, wanted nothing better than war, and Belle-Isle was able to put himself at the head of a powerful faction. The entourage of Louis XV and Mme de Châteauroux encouraged the king to break away from the inglorious caution of his aged minister. The cardinal, though more opposed to foreign adventures than ever, was no longer in a position to treat Belle-Isle as he had treated Chauvelin, and had unwillingly to accept the fact that the ambitious noble was a power at Versailles and let him have his head.

After the death of Charles VI the politics of Europe were centred on the election of a new Holy Roman Emperor. Belle-Isle's grand plan was to secure the choice of a French client, the Elector of Bavaria. To put this plan into operation he was given the key position of ambassador to the Electoral Diet at Frankfurt. There, in feverish communication with the French envoys to all the German courts, with his supporters at Versailles, and with the ambassadors to other courts, he practically made himself the effective Foreign Minister of France. But while Belle-Isle intrigued, Frederick II acted. The Prussian invasion of Silesia in December 1740 precipitated war. Belle-Isle saw the possibility of using Frederick to further his own ends, which was a more excusable mistake at the beginning of the king of Prussia's career than subsequently. He promoted the conclusion of a Franco-Prussian alliance in June 1741, and obtained the command of an army to fight in Germany. Fleury, weakened by age and troubled in mind and body, could not stem the enthusiasm for war. A reconciliation with the Pâris brothers, formerly his enemies, assured Belle-Isle that the necessary supplies would be forthcoming. In August 1741 the French army crossed the Rhine and in alliance with the Bavarians under the Elector, invaded Austrian territory and captured Prague; another French army occupied Westphalia and menaced Hanover; and in January 1742 the Elector of Bavaria was chosen as Holy Roman Emperor. Belle-Isle's policy seemed to have been crowned with rapid and complete success.

It was a precarious triumph, based upon a combination of circumstances which might not prove lasting — the faithfulness of Great Britain under Walpole, the disintegration of the Habsburg Empire, and not least the effective maintenance of control of the French military and diplomatic effort by Belle-Isle himself. The year 1742 was to see all these conditions vanish. Maria Theresa came to terms with the Magyars, reconstituted the Habsburg army, and carried the war into Bavaria. Worse followed. Walpole resigned office, British foreign policy passed into the hands of a minister who favoured intervention against France on the Continent, and by British mediation Frederick II was bought out of the war at the price of Silesia. The Secretaries of State at Versailles, jealous of the predominance of Belle-Isle, intrigued against him, and with the backing of the Secretaries and the queen, Broglie was appointed to command the French army in Bohemia. This change in command was not without its influence on Frederick's desertion, for the king of Prussia admired Belle-Isle and had no faith in de Broglie. Finally, Belle-Isle himself, under the strain of his intense military and diplomatic activities, fell ill, despite which he succeeded, by a brilliant retreat, in extricating the French army from the impossible position into which de Broglie, despite his ability, allowed it to fall at Prague.

But Belle-Isle's halcyon days were over. So recently in all appearance the destined successor of Fleury, the failure of his plans robbed him of all influence. 'If the Marshal of Belle-Isle was not a great man,' wrote a contemporary, 'he was certainly an extraordinary one, but he was soon forgotten.' When Fleury died, in January 1743, there was no question of Belle-Isle as his successor. I have already referred to the victory of the Secretaries of State. Maurepas, d'Argenson, Orry, and Amelot, four able professional administrators, were to hold the government in a sort of commission, with the king himself to direct and co-ordinate their policy. The defects of Louis' character — his uncertainty and self-distrust, his domination by personal motives and interests, lack of assiduity, sudden reversals of opinion — were for the next twenty years to be those of the government of France.

The war — no longer of the Austrian Succession, for Maria Theresa had settled that — dragged on for another five years. Any purpose it had possessed for France at the beginning had been lost by 1742. Lacking any rational objective, the campaigns became a series of diversions — an attack on Sardinia, a projected invasion of England in support of the Young Pretender, a major invasion of the United Provinces. The victories of the most successful of the French generals, Maurice de Saxe, in the last of these campaigns, were ended when he had to be called back to repel an Austrian invasion of Lorraine, where Louis XV, inspired by Mme de Châteauroux — for the Pompadour had not yet come on the scene — to prove himself in the combats of Mars as well as of Venus, had put himself at the head of a French army, only to experience a set-back. Then, at Metz, in August 1744, he fell critically ill. This led to an episode which he did not quickly forget or forgive. The *dévot* party, seizing their opportunity, determined that he should not die in the arms of his mistress, who was driven away, pursued along her route by the hisses of the population, and stoned in her carriage. Louis himself,

believing like everyone else that he was dying, was bullied into making
a public confession of his sins and asking pardon for the scandalous
example he had set his people. The neglected queen and the heir apparent, surrounded by the clergy and the *dévot* party, prepared to
inaugurate a new reign. They were thirty years too soon. Louis
recovered from his illness with astonishing rapidity, *Te Deums*
were sung all over France in a great wave of popular enthusiasm,
and Mme de Châteauroux returned to the royal arms, though briefly,
for she died soon after.

The war continued with better fortune, for Frederick II, alarmed
at the Austrian successes, re-entered the fighting. Meanwhile, the
direction of the foreign policy of France had fallen into new hands,
those of the marquis d'Argenson, a man full of ingenious plans for
the re-establishment of that French hegemony in Europe which
Louis XIV had for a time exercised and which continued to haunt
the imagination of French Foreign Ministers. But even if the plans of
d'Argenson had been more practicable, the opposition of the other
ministers and of the factions at court would have prevented them
from being put into practice consistently. In May 1745 Maurice de
Saxe won the battle of Fontenoy, last glorious victory of the *ancien
régime*, and French troops occupied Flanders. D'Argenson, weaving
a complicated and flimsy web of diplomatic intrigue, failed to take
advantage of the belated military success. Once again, in December
1745, Frederick of Prussia, most treacherous of allies, withdrew from
the war, having consolidated his hold on Silesia. D'Argenson, exposed to violent criticism at Versailles, continued with his tortuous
and unavailing schemes, which were collapsing round him even
before he had properly started to put them into effect; but he was
now no more than nominal Foreign Minister and Louis XV was
taking advice from a variety of diverse and opposed sources. At last,
in January 1747, the king dismissed him.

The chief influence over the conduct of diplomacy and the war
now fell into the hands of Maurice de Saxe, a bastard of the king of
Poland, who had entered the military service of France and who
alone had gained in reputation from this unhappy war. With Maurice
a definite, limited, and attainable objective for French policy at last
emerged: by means of a renewed attack on the United Provinces to

force Great Britain to accept peace. Victory at Laufeldt and the capture of Berg-op-Zoom brought this end within sight. Deprived of British support, Maria Theresa had to reconcile herself to what she thought would be the temporary loss of Silesia, while under the patronage of Maurice a 'Saxon' party at the French court secretly prepared a *rapprochement* between France and Austria. Both Great Britain and Austria were now ready for peace, which after the usual prolonged and intricate negotiations was signed at Aix-la-Chapelle in 1748. Despite the ambitious diplomacy of Belle-Isle and d'Argenson, and the military successes of Maurice de Saxe, France had gained nothing; and this was not strange, for short of European hegemony, which the balance of European forces did not render a practicable end, there was no specific objective to be gained.

True, outside Europe a real conflict of interests between Great Britain and France was developing; but in respect of the struggle for colonies and trade the war settled nothing, and the peace, with a mutual restoration of conquests, represented only an armistice. Moreover, while English concern with the overseas struggle was primary, to France, traditionally aiming at dominance in Europe, it appeared only as a secondary issue, a mere side-show. Therefore, after Aix-la-Chapelle, Louis XV and his ministers, faced with the task of paying for the war and hampered by the opposition of the parlements, forgot the unfinished conflict overseas. Unfortunately for them, whereas their European wars were avoidable and unnecessary, the colonial struggle with England was in the nature of things.

In the New World French missionaries and explorers from the settlements in Canada had been working inland, and by way of the great rivers tracing a route south to Louisiana. A continent was waiting to be opened up, but the royal government was little interested in a colony which cost far more than it brought in. Nor were the French people more interested. Canada attracted few immigrants and its population grew only slowly. The French Canadians slowly increased in numbers from 24,500 in 1710 to 65,000 in 1760. Quebec had 7,000 inhabitants and Montreal 4,000. At the same time the whole of Louisiana, far to the south, was inhabited by 5,000 Europeans. To set against this the English colonies along the seaboard had a population of over one and a half million. On the other side of the world, in the East Indies, France had a network of trading stations, and here the Compagnie des Indes competed with the East India Company not without success, which was increased when, in 1751, Dupleix was appointed Governor-General.

It is easy to comprehend why neither government nor public opinion in France should have cared about Canada or Louisiana, or even the East Indies, when a comparison is made with the resources and profits of the French West Indian islands. Martinique, in the middle of the century, had 17,000 whites and 57,000 slaves, Guadeloupe 9,000 and 33,000, St Domingo, 'the pearl of the Antilles', 20,000 whites and 160,000 slaves. The West Indies accounted for 20 per cent of the total external trade of France in the first half of the eighteenth century. Here was something worth fighting for, but the colonial struggle could not be confined to the West Indies. It continued throughout the world during the years of nominal peace after 1748. French and English colonists clashed in America in the neighbourhood of the Great Lakes. In India, Dupleix entered into the rivalries of the Indian princes and established a protectorate over the Carnatic and a large sphere of influence in the Deccan. The English copied his methods, and in the guise of struggles between local princes a regular war was waged between Dupleix and the representatives of the East India Company from 1750 to 1753. In 1754 the Anglo-French conflict in Canada and India was intensified. The British government decided, although the two countries were nominally at peace, to settle the Canadian struggle by cutting off supplies and reinforcements from France. In June 1755 a French convoy was attacked by Admiral Boscawen off Newfoundland; two French ships were captured, though the rest escaped. On land, military expeditions dispatched under Braddock against the outlying French forts were repulsed with heavy loss.

The French government, in the face of these attacks, could not do less than recall its envoys at London and Hanover. War had still not been declared, but the British navy was ordered to seize all French ships wherever they might be. Over 300 French merchant ships were captured in a few weeks, by what can hardly be described as other than an act of piracy. Versailles sent an ultimatum to London, and by January 1756 the two countries were openly at war.

France had done nothing to provoke this war. Neither court nor country was interested in the icy wastes of Canada, while the Compagnie des Indes, only concerned with trading profits, disavowed Dupleix, who was replaced in 1754 by a governor instructed to liquidate his policy. The trade of the West Indies was another matter. France could hardly sit by passively while French merchant ships were being seized or driven off the seas in time of peace by the British. This war with Great Britain, therefore, could not be avoided. There was, however, another war, starting concurrently, on which a very different verdict must be passed.

Maria Theresa was determined that Silesia should not be permanently lost. To recover it she required an ally on the Continent and that ally could only be France. The brilliant young Austrian diplomat, Kaunitz, sent to Versailles to lay the foundations of an Austro-French alliance, found the French court wedded to pacific ideas. At the same time the British government was negotiating with Austria to secure an alliance which would protect Hanover. Though neither the Austrian nor the British government wished to break their traditional alliance, no agreement for this purpose on mutually acceptable terms could be reached; and since Britain could not rely on Austria to protect Hanover, in January 1756 she concluded the Convention of Westminster with Prussia.

Kaunitz now turned again to France. The difficulty for Austrian policy was that while her prime aim was the recovery of Silesia from Prussia, France was completely unconcerned in this quarrel. It was, therefore, necessary to work on French dynastic ambitions by offering to support a French candidate for the throne of Poland, and even by venturing the suggestion that a son-in-law of Louis XV might be established as ruler of a large part of the Austrian Netherlands. The French royal council was still for the most part committed to the Prussian alliance, and Frederick, by his patronage of enlightened writers, had won for himself propagandists in France who were influential even if they were not conscious of the use that was being made of them. But the influence of writers on foreign policy was limited, and in the state of French government nobody could tell from the ministers nominally in authority what its policy would actually be.

Austrian intrigues might not have succeeded if French foreign policy had not already been confused and confounded. Diplomacy by factions was the natural corollary of government by factions. The *secret* of the regent had been followed by those of Chauvelin, of Belle-Isle, and of the Saxon group. Most important of all, though least suspected at the time, was *le secret du roi*. It was hardly reasonable to suppose that the king would have his own secret diplomacy working in rivalry with and often in opposition to his official agents, yet this was the situation that developed. A habit of private consultation between the king and the prince de Conti on foreign affairs, begun in 1743, developed into a candidature by the latter for the Polish throne, in support of which a system of secret correspondence with French agents to various European courts was built up. In 1752 the comte de Broglie, as ambassador to Poland, became the central figure in this network and he continued as the effective head of it, under the king, after Conti withdrew. The *premier commis* at the ministry of Foreign Affairs, Tercier, was also in the *secret*. Diplomats at foreign courts who were in the organization sent their private reports, as well as copies of the dispatches they had received from the Secretary of State, to the king by way of Tercier and de Broglie. When Tercier was dismissed by Choiseul, in 1759, the last link between the official diplomacy and the king's *secret* was broken, but the latter survived until the king's death fifteen years later. It may well seem extraordinary that Louis should have been willing to toil away, in the privacy of his cabinet, reading the correspondence, personally answering the reports of de Broglie and through him controlling a network of agents in pursuit of one policy, while all the time his Secretaries of State for Foreign Affairs were following contrary policies.

The king's *secret*, aimed at maintaining the alliance with Turkey, Poland, Prussia, and Sweden, separating Austria from Russia, and excluding Russian influence from Poland, was closer to traditional French policy and, it might be argued, more in keeping with French interests than the policy that was officially to be adopted in 1756. Even this, however, was not the work of the Foreign Minister, Rouillé, who was a mediocrity. The Secretaries of State were committed to the Prussian alliance, and Kaunitz, who knew of Louis

XV's taste for secret diplomacy, therefore determined on an indirect approach. The catalyst to bring about the desired reaction in French foreign policy was found in the person of Mme de Pompadour. The titular mistress had ceased to exercise her official functions, in which, as she and the king had both come to realize, she could not share the satisfaction that Louis obtained, at some time in 1751–2. For the next twenty years, until the time of Mme du Barry, the king took his pleasure with an apparently unending series of passing beauties, whose names are largely unrecorded. Their obscure origins aroused the indignation of the court, which felt that the king was ready to confer on mere facile charms an honour that should have been reserved for birth and breeding. Serious hopes were only aroused when it was thought that one of them might usurp the position of the *maîtresse en titre*. For this was not the end of Mme de Pompadour: in a sense it was only the beginning. She ceased to be the mistress to become the closest friend and confidante of the king. Her direct political power has been grossly exaggerated. Her influence, as might have been expected, was in the field of personal relations rather than policies; but in a state whose politics were determined by the factions of a court, personal relations were apt to be the decisive factor. So the Austrians thought when they astutely chose her as the intermediary in their decisive diplomatic manœuvre.

Direct negotiations were engaged between the king and the Austrian ambassador. The council and the ministers were largely excluded from the discussions, the details of which were entrusted to an amiable little friend of Mme de Pompadour, the abbé de Bernis. The revelation of the Westminster agreement between Prussia and Great Britain, which seemed to demonstrate for a third time how treacherous an ally Frederick II was, clinched the issue. In May 1756 France and Austria signed the Treaty of Versailles. Thus was concluded the Austrian alliance, which was to dominate French policy up to 1789. The famous Reversal of Alliances was completed. It represented the abandonment of France's old and decaying allies, Sweden, Poland, Turkey and the German states, in favour of new links with Vienna and St Petersburg. Yet, throughout the long and involved diplomatic manœuvres, which had extended from 1750 to 1756, no positive aim had emerged on the French side. At best the treaty with Austria might have been regarded, though mistakenly, as guaranteeing France against war in Europe while she waged the naval and colonial war with Great Britain. But it should not have required great perspicacity to see that Maria Theresa's object was to secure French support in a war for the recovery of Silesia. Apparently this was not realized at the French court. Frederick II appreciated his danger soon enough, all the more because there were alarming indications also on the Russian side, and rather than allow time for the coalition against him to take the offensive, in August 1756 he fell on Saxony and occupied it; and Louis XV, who had gradually been led on by Austrian diplomacy, found himself committed to a full-scale war in Europe.

The war into which France had been dragged at least began promisingly. Minorca was captured and the British fleet under the unfortunate Admiral Byng repulsed. The French navy, which had been strengthened during the long term of office of Maurepas as Secretary for the Marine, more than held its own on the seas. It was reasonable to suppose that the coalition of France, Austria, Russia, Sweden, Saxony, and other German states would rapidly overcome the resistance of Prussia. What had not been allowed for was the incompetent generalship of the allied armies, the military ability of Frederick, and the coming into office of Pitt in Great Britain. Moreover, for France to join in a system of alliances which enabled Austria to group the German states, with the exception of Prussia and Hanover, both at war with France, under her banner, was a flagrant repudiation of the classic policy of France towards the Empire, which, adumbrated by Henry IV and put into execution by Richelieu and Mazarin, had triumphed in the Treaty of Westphalia.

The French, however, began the continental war with success by invading Hanover. Defeated at Hastenbeck, the Duke of Cumberland signed the Convention of Kloster-Zeven by which he undertook to disband his army. But once again domestic factions prevented France from taking advantage of military victory. The victorious French general, d'Estrées, had made the mistake of quarrelling with Pâris-Duverney, who was in control of supplies, and the powerful financier used his influence with the Pompadour to secure a change in the command. It was, however, her chief rival at court, the duc de Richelieu, professional charmer and favourite of Louis XV, who replaced d'Estrées and proceeded rapidly to fritter away the fruits of victory. In charge of the largest French army, he let it loose on Hanover to pillage the country and fall into a state of complete indiscipline. He disregarded all appeals to join forces with the other French army under the prince de Soubise, which was now closing with Frederick II. The rivalry of court factions thus even determined military policy, for there was no love lost between Louis XV's closest companions, Richelieu and the Pompadour, and Soubise was an old friend of Mme de Pompadour. In November 1757 Frederick took advantage of Richelieu's inaction and routed the French and German troops under Soubise at Rossbach. In December, by the victory of Leuthen over the Austrians, he kept his hold on Silesia. In the early months of 1758, the Convention of Kloster-Zeven having been repudiated, an Anglo-Hanoverian army under Ferdinand of Brunswick drove the French out of Hanover and Westphalia. Richelieu had already been recalled to Versailles, to resume there conquests more appropriate to his talents, but he had done all the damage he could do. A subsequent attempt by French armies to invade Germany was only to lead to the defeat of Minden in 1759.

Overseas, Senegal and Goree fell to the English. Clive's victories in India put Bengal into his hands and enabled him to supplant French influence in the south. In Canada, the strong points of Louisburg, Fort Duquesne, and Fort Frontenac were lost, Wolfe defeated Montcalm at Quebec and the whole colony passed into the hands of the English. In the West Indies, Guadeloupe, Martinique, Grenada, Saint-Vincent, Santa-Lucia were captured by British naval expeditions. At Lagos and Quiberon, the Toulon and the Brest fleets were routed. France itself was exposed to hampering if unsuccessful British raids.

The abbé de Bernis who, according to the memoirs he wrote later, had unwillingly been responsible for launching French policy on this sea of disaster, was already anxious by 1758 to find some haven of peace. He found one, but for himself not for France. He was made a cardinal and sent off to the country. Who was to replace him? The king's council was almost denuded of ability, most of its members aged, and only Belle-Isle rising above mediocrity. The king had even personal grounds for concern. In 1757 a dagger attack had been made on him by the half-mad Damiens, who had taken the anti-royal propaganda of the parlements at its face value. Though Louis was not seriously injured he was alarmed and perhaps even more shocked. Damiens was subjected to the correct legal *question*, and finally tortured to death in a great public ceremony. The opportunity might have been taken to deal with the parlements on a charge of complicity with him. Instead, the two competent, though rival, Secretaries of State, who were most hated by them, were dismissed from office. Thus it was that another d'Argenson, at the Ministry of War since 1743, and Machault, former Controller-General and now Minister for the Marine, fell. Their successors were nonentities. Some means of strengthening the government was urgently required. A protégé of Mme de Pompadour, the comte de Stainville, was therefore called from the embassy at Vienna and made duc de Choiseul and Secretary of State for Foreign Affairs in December 1758.

It was too late to restore the balance of the war: the following year saw the culmination of French defeats. Choiseul had no hope but to extricate France with as little loss as possible. He improved the position by the conclusion, in 1761, of the *pacte de famille* between the Bourbon rulers of France, Spain, the Two Sicilies, and Parma, and in 1762 Spain entered the war on the side of France. With inexhaustible energy Choiseul took over the Secretaryships of War and the Marine, sharing the control of Foreign Affairs with his cousin, Choiseul-Praslin. He was able to conclude peace with Great Britain by the Treaty of Paris in 1763, at a heavy price, but not quite so heavy as the year of disasters, 1759, had seemed to foreshadow. Canada, Senegal, and the West Indian islands of Grenada, St Vincent, Dominica, and Tobago were lost; French possessions in India were confined to a few trading stations; Louisiana was ceded to Spain in compensation for the loss of Florida. As a result of the Seven Years War the first colonial empire of France had been lost and nothing had been gained. The Peace of Paris was the price paid for government by weak and wavering ministerial groups and court factions.

F

PART TWO

THE AGE OF REFORM

⚜

CHAPTER ONE

THE REVOLUTION IN IDEAS

WHILE eighteenth-century France remained politically the France of Louis XIV without the Grand Monarch, socially the nation was changing rapidly and the conflict of social realities with the juristic and formal pattern of society was becoming increasingly acute. Moreover, in ideas this was already a century of revolution, though of a revolution the roots of which lay deep in the past. Even while Reformation and Counter-Reformation were tearing France to pieces in the Religious Wars, Rabelais and Montaigne had initiated a more sceptical attitude to religion, which was continued by the libertine writers of the next century. In the seventeenth century Pascal challenged the moral basis of orthodox thought, and Descartes provided an intellectual alternative to it. While Louis XIV was on the throne there had been little possibility of the open expression of unorthodox ideas, but under the more liberal English and Dutch regimes new ideas were developing rapidly. Newton provided a mathematical system which reduced the physical world to order and demonstrated the reign of law. Locke evolved a theory of human psychology which, through the principle of association, showed how complex ideas could be built up out of the simple data of sensory experience without assuming any innate ideas. His theory of morals marks the emergence of utilitarianism; in politics he justified the English Revolution of 1688 and parliamentary government, and in religion deism.

The infection of new ideas could not be wholly excluded from France during the reign of Louis XIV, even if those who were tempted by dangerous thoughts kept silent or fled abroad. Among the latter the greatest name is that of Pierre Bayle. Because his writings were scattered, unsystematic, often anonymous, his influence is difficult to estimate and may appear less than that of Locke; but in Bayle's writings are to be found all the leading themes of the advanced thinkers of the next century. Locke's ideas had to be translated into the terms of an alien tradition when they crossed the Channel, but in Bayle's writings, though he himself perhaps remained more fundamentally religious, and even Calvinistic, at heart than has been commonly recognized, the climate of opinion was already that which was to become dominant with Voltaire and the Encyclopedists. He fell under the ban of the French state as a Calvinist, even worse, as one who had temporarily accepted Catholicism and then relapsed. The year of the comet, 1680, produced an outburst of superstition, which Bayle, now a refugee teaching at Rotterdam, criticized in his *Pensées diverses sur la comète*, explaining the manifestation on the basis of observed facts as a purely physical phenomenon. He followed this up with a study of the history of the Religious Wars, which set off Catholic and Calvinist accounts against one another and tested both by rational historical criticism.

Bayle was a sceptic, but his scepticism differed from that of Montaigne or La Motte de Vayer, because while he questioned everything he did not end up by disbelieving everything. He accepted what was soundly based on scientific and historical evidence, rationally criticized. The theoretical arguments of Cartesianism and the metaphysics of Leibniz were not for him. To theories he opposed the facts of observation and experience. He was essentially concerned with practical questions. Above all he was a moralist who believed that there was a 'natural idea of equity' in man which was independent of religious revelation. Conscience, he agreed, is the supreme rule of human life, but its judgment on human actions must be in accordance with their results. It was his rejection of the criterion of religious dogma which separated Bayle from his fellow exile, the Huguenot pastor, Jurieu. Bayle's object was to spread the spirit of rational criticism, that of Jurieu to inspire a Calvinist revolt against the Catholic monarchy of Louis XIV. Jurieu's aim was liberty for the true religion, and when he argued for the theory of the sovereignty of the people, it was only the people chosen by God whom he meant. Bayle equally maintained the sovereignty of the political state, but he meant the whole community, held together not by religion but by its common secular interests. No system of government was an absolute good: they all depended on circumstances and should be judged by their results. The whole of this philosophy of life was poured pell-mell into Bayle's *Dictionnaire historique et critique* of 1697, and although he died, at the age of fifty-nine, in 1706, he set the tone and provided the ideas which were to dominate the following century.

Bayle, though he stood above all other critics, did not stand alone. The death of Louis XIV released a dammed-up flood of criticism. Montesquieu's *Lettres persanes*, published when the regency had relaxed the censorship, mocked at the idols, religious and political, of the previous reign. The abbé de Saint-Pierre applied his utilitarian inventiveness, with a range worthy of Bentham himself, to everything from perpetual peace to a patent portable arm-chair. The Jacobite Ramsay followed in the steps of Fénelon with a plea for toleration. Such men, and their kindred spirits, met at the Club de l'Entresol, to which Bolingbroke in exile joined himself, until it was suppressed by Fleury in 1731.

Censorship, of course, was still partially effective in the early years of Louis XV's reign. In 1717 an act of sacrilege was punished by the burning of the culprit, and a charge of speaking with impiety of religion by a sentence to the galleys for life. In 1739 all the printing establishments in forty-three towns were suppressed. Unorthodox ideas, particularly in the field of religion, had to find expression largely in manuscript form. This limited their influence, though the number that have survived of some of these manuscripts is surprising. One investigator found copies of as many as 102 different manuscript treatises expressing unorthodox religious ideas which had been in clandestine circulation in the first half of the eighteenth century. The comte de Boulainvillier, author of the *Vie de Mahomet*, was the centre of one group of heretical thinkers amongst whom such manuscripts circulated; it met at the houses of the marquis d'Argenson and the duc de Noailles, or at the Académie des Inscriptions, until the death of Boulainvillier in 1722. The works of English deists and free-thinkers were translated and circulated in manuscript by such men, but being translations it was also less risky to print these.

By 1730 French writers had passed beyond the moderate deism of most of their English predecessors, though the most notorious of the clandestine writings, the *Testament* of the curé Meslier, was begun as early as 1722-3. Voltaire declared that he knew of over one hundred copies of this extraordinary work, ruthlessly materialist in its views, which treated man as a 'human machine' and not a very successful machine at that. One chapter in Meslier's treatise was entitled, 'The world is not ruled by an intelligent being'. Theology, he declared, made of its God 'a monster of unreason, injustice, malice and atrocity'. Even Voltaire, when he published, much later, extracts from this work, dared not print its violent political and social criticism. In respect of this, indeed, it stands alone, for the general attack was directed almost exclusively against the Church and religious teaching. Published works were much more moderate in tone and are represented by Voltaire's *Lettres philosophiques* of 1734, in which the author popularized Newtonian mathematics, still generally rejected in France in favour of the mathematical theories of Descartes.

Clandestine writings declined after 1740, as the censorship became more lax. The middle of the century marked the turning-point with the publication of a number of major works expressing the new ideas. *Les Mœurs* of Toussaint, in 1748, expounded a secular morality. La Mettrie's *L'homme machine*, in the same year, proclaimed crudely that pleasure is man's only end. Diderot, in a series of philosophical writings of which the most important is the *Lettres sur les Aveugles* of 1749, speculated on the relativity of knowledge and morals. Montesquieu's *De l'esprit des lois*, in 1748, proclaimed the rule of law and inaugurated the comparative study of institutions. Buffon published the first volume of his *Histoire naturelle* in 1749. Condillac, building on Locke, in his *Traité des sensations* of 1754 gave systematic form to a psychological theory which derived all human ideas from experience. By now there was a considerable body of advanced thinkers in France imbued with new and revolutionary ideas on religion, science, history, society, and anxious to spread the enlightenment of which they believed themselves to be the possessors. Diderot conceived the idea of a great Encyclopedia which should be at the same time a compendium of all knowledge and a work of propaganda for the new ideas. Its first volume appeared in 1751.

Orthodox thought was on the defensive, and those who should have been defending it were more concerned with the struggle against the so-called Jansenism of the parlements. The censorship of books was still vigorously carried on by the latter, but with more show than effect. Regularly books were condemned to be burnt by the executioner, and as regularly the publishers produced piles of unwanted remainders to be ceremonially destroyed, and continued to circulate and sell the condemned works as freely as before. Writings which might fall under the ban were published in Switzerland, Holland, and England, or at least alleged to be so on their title-pages and issued without a name of author, attributed to a dead writer, or described as translations.

Fuel was provided for the fire that was now raging against the Catholic Church by episodes of religious persecution which were all the more shocking for being sporadic. Memories of the Camisard revolt, stirred up in a period of economic difficulties and fear of foreign invasion, produced a local panic in Toulouse, of which the bourgeois Huguenot family of Calas, charged with the murder of a son who had been converted to Catholicism, were the victims. The parlement had Calas broken on the wheel and all the property of his family confiscated. The conduct of the trial was so flagrantly unjudicial and incompetent that Voltaire, moved by a combination of genuine indignation at the cruel and irrational verdict of the parlement, pity for the fate of the Calas family, and desire to exploit the judicial murder in the interests of his campaign against the Church, was able to make great play with it and in the end secure the quashing of the verdict by the king's council in Paris. Another case which secured much publicity was that of the young chevalier de La Barre, aged nineteen, who had indulged in some adolescent obscenities which were held to be sacrilege. The *procureur du roi* attempted to save him by means of a *lettre de cachet*, but the local parlement was not willing to let a possible victim evade its clutches in this way. Despite the intercession of the Bishop of Amiens in La Barre's favour, the parlement knew its duty. The rights of religion, which Church and crown had shown themselves regrettably reluctant to enforce in this case, were vindicated by the law. La Barre was sentenced to have his tongue cut out and to be burnt with a copy of Voltaire's *Dictionnaire philosophique*

round his neck. The executioner, more pitiful, only made the semblance of cutting out the tongue and the young man was decapitated
before his body was thrown on the fire.

In spite of the excesses of the parlements it was clear that the
persecuting spirit was dying down in the Church, itself influenced
by the new ideas. This did not temper the force of the cold blast of
scepticism and mockery that Voltaire and the *philosophes* were
directing against Catholicism. The period from 1748 to 1770 may be
said to mark the victory of the new anti-religious ideology. To dismiss this simply as a new kind of unorthodox orthodoxy, as Carl
Becker does, is unfair. The thought of the eighteenth century was
essentially practical. The so-called *philosophes* had no time for metaphysics or dogma, but they were intensely concerned with ethics.
They were essentially empirical in their outlook. They judged the
Church and all other social institutions by their practical results.
Utilitarianism dominated the century and it taught the gospel that
pain was evil and pleasure good. Limited this doctrine may have
been, but in its simple way it appealed to the ordinary educated man
of the age of reason.

In the long run the anti-clerical campaign of Voltaire and the
literary men was to leave the greater mark on the national mind, but
at the time the internecine warfare of the defenders of religion, the
parlements and the Jesuits, was the more dangerous to both Church
and crown. By the middle of the century the parlements had succeeded in reinstating themselves as a power in the land. Their victory
over Machault was followed by an offensive against subsequent Controllers-General, which was copied by the provincial parlements,
waging guerrilla warfare against the intendants. In 1763 the parlement of Paris consolidated its political victory, in alliance with
Choiseul, by securing the appointment as Controller-General of a
parlementaire. The royal administration, in the hour of defeat,
capitulated to the parlements and abandoned its attempts at financial
reform.

The success of the parlements in frustrating financial reform was
followed by the triumphal conclusion of their campaign against the
Jesuits. The Jansenist controversy, even in its limited eighteenth-
century form, was by now dying of inanition: what was left was the

richerism of the lower clergy. But the vendetta of the Gallican *parle-mentaires* against the Jesuits was inexhaustible, and the current of opinion, even if the parlements repudiated and did their best to persecute their unwanted, infidel allies in the literary world, was running against the Society of Jesus.

In this situation the Jesuits were unfortunate enough to have given hostages to fortune. Père Lavalette, Superior of the Mission to the Leeward Isles, had built up at Martinique a great commercial enterprise, which the Seven Years War reduced to bankruptcy. His creditors obtained judgment at Marseilles against the Society, which with great folly appealed to the parlement of Paris. The parlement leapt at its opportunity, condemned the Society to pay all the debts of Lavalette, and then proceeded to set up a commission to examine the Jesuit Statutes. On receipt of the report of this commission, in 1762, the parlement decreed the abolition of the Society of Jesus, as a political body which, on the pretext of combating heresy, had established an alien authority in France and repudiated the sovereignty of the throne. Jesuit doctrines were declared 'perverse, destructive of all principles of religion and even honesty, injurious to Christian morals, pernicious to civil society, seditious, a challenge to the rights of the nation and royal authority, to the safety of the sacred person of the king and to the obedience of subjects, proper to arouse the greatest disturbances in states and to create and support the profoundest corruption in the heart of man.' Louis XV, whose rights were thus vindicated by those who were conducting the bitterest campaign against his government, did what he could to protect the Jesuits and stand between them and the wrath of the parlements; but, emerging discredited from a disastrous war, his government dared not face another domestic conflict. The Society was abolished by royal edict, its property confiscated, and its members dispersed. The *philosophes* may have been spreading irreligious ideas among the educated public: it was the parlements which delivered the greatest blow before 1789 to the Church. One result of the destruction of the Society of Jesus was the cessation of their teaching functions. Oratorians and other orders attempted, as far as possible, to fill the gap that was left in the schools. Many teachers who were either laymen or else in very minor orders had to be introduced — Fouché and Billaud-Varenne both taught in the great school of the Oratory at Juilly. The effect of their teaching on the minds of the coming revolutionary generation can at present only be guessed.

Though exceptions may be found, it is not unfair to say that religion in eighteenth-century France had become largely an external thing, repeating — except when it unconsciously adopted the language and ideas of its opponents — the formulas of the seventeenth century emptied of their feeling; just as religious architecture continued to copy the models of the previous century, exaggerating the theatrical character which even then had given to churches and abbeys something of the feeling of pieces of stage scenery. By the last years of the *ancien régime* the campaign for the secularization of thought appeared to have triumphed, at least in the educated mind. The more positive aspects of the revolution in ideas remain to be mentioned, for this was not merely a negative and destructive movement; but these are so closely bound up with practical developments that they are best discussed along with them as a formative element in the age of reform with which the *ancien régime* was to close.

CHAPTER TWO

REVIVAL OF AUTHORITY

THE Seven Years War left France, potentially still the greatest power in Europe, defeated and humiliated. However, the greatest loss, that of Canada, was of a territory of future and as yet unsuspected potentialities, rather than of an immediately valuable one; and its loss was soon to be avenged by the difficulties which the removal of the French threat produced for the British government in its American colonies. Peace, moreover, provided an opportunity for renewing French strength. Choiseul, if he was not a great minister, was an able and energetic one and took advantage of it. Government by the Secretaries of State and their bureaux was now so firmly established that he could not become an all-powerful *premier ministre*, as Fleury had been without the title, still less a Richelieu or a Mazarin, even if he had been built on that scale. But by accumulating in his own hands and those of his cousin, Choiseul-Praslin, the major offices of Foreign Affairs, Marine, and War, as well as many minor posts, Choiseul was able to provide something more like a united government than France had known since the hey-day of Fleury. That for all his talent and inexhaustible energy Choiseul was not a great minister, was shown at the outset. To ensure himself a peaceful life on the home front he concluded a tacit alliance with the parlements, allowing them to suppress the Jesuits and giving up any prospect of financial reform. This was to abandon from the start the one thing that was essential. Choiseul had willed the end, which was the re-establishment of French power in the world and a war of revenge against England; he did not will the necessary means, which was the restoration of royal authority inside France and the reform of royal finances, without which all other reforms would be in vain.

The bases of Choiseul's foreign policy were the Austrian alliance, which he had inherited, and the Family Compact with Spain, which was his own special creation. Since the Seven Years War had demonstrated how vital naval power was in any war with Great Britain, he vigorously set himself to rebuild the French navy. The fisheries were encouraged, to provide men to man the fleet; an *ordonnance* of 1765 reformed naval administration, giving increased authority to the officers responsible for the navigation of the ships; naval arsenals were multiplied. In 1763 France had some 30 to 40 ships of the line, mostly in bad condition: by 1771 there were 64 well-equipped ships and 50 frigates.

Military changes were introduced at the same time. Choiseul reformed the system by which the captains personally recruited and paid their companies, receiving in return a lump sum: it was naturally to their interests to swell the size of their regiments with dummy entries and to economize on supplies and equipment. Similarly, the colonel was the proprietor of his regiment. Choiseul bought out and retired, despite much noble indignation, many officers, and put recruitment and equipment into the hands of officials of the Ministry of War. He established a school for young nobles preparing to enter the *École militaire*. He converted factories for arms and munitions into royal establishments. The artillery, which had been an independent, self-governing corporation, became a *Corps royal* of six regiments, and the process of equipping it with the new mobile artillery invented by Gribeauval was begun.

The army and the navy Choiseul and his able technical advisers could deal with directly. The colonies, after the Peace of Paris a mere relic of the former French empire, presented greater difficulties; reform in this field meant going against the national tradition and accepting, at least to some extent, the new ideas of free trade put forward by the Physiocrats. This was done all the same. The trading monopoly of the Compagnie des Indes was broken, and imports from the East Indies multiplied two and a half times between the date of the breaking of the monopoly in 1769 and 1776. Efforts at colonization in Madagascar and French Guiana proved expensive failures, but the attenuation of the system of restriction in the French West Indies was reflected in the growth of their population and trade. French strength in the Mediterranean was increased when, in 1768, Choiseul purchased for two million livres from the Republic of Genoa its rebellious possession of Corsica. The opposition of the Corsicans under Paoli, which, although on such a small scale, may perhaps be regarded as opening the history of modern struggles for national independence, was crushed, and Corsica became a French *généralité*. In 1766, on the death of Stanislaus Leczinski, Lorraine was quietly incorporated into France.

Soldier, diplomat, and administrator, ugly and fascinating, calculating and fiery, full of expedients but given to long-range plans, gay and friendly, a frivolous courtier and an incredibly hard-working minister, Choiseul seemed to have everything that was needed to gain high office and make good use of it. Mme de Pompadour was devoted to him. France had had no luck for the twenty years while she was helping Louis XV to keep the boredom of a court and throne at bay: perhaps fortune would change with the brilliant new minister. If it was to do so, the Pompadour was not to know it. She died in 1764 at the age of forty, generally regretted, says the British Ambassador, but not by the people of France. From the balcony of the palace, on a wild, stormy day, Louis XV, wiping the tears from his eyes, watched the funeral cortège leave Versailles. Unequal, despite herself, to his passion, their friendship was unmarred till death separated them. Her political influence has been greatly exaggerated.

The death of the Pompadour had no effect on the position or power of Choiseul. Indirectly at least his fall was to come about, as that of so many other ministers, through the parlements. Choiseul having given way to the parlement of Paris all along the line, it was difficult for it to pick a quarrel with the government. But now the provincial parlements had been aroused to the assertion of their claims, and the struggle against the royal administration was shifting to the provinces. Brittany had been, in 1689, the last of the provinces to receive a permanent royal intendant; it possessed in its Provincial Estates an organ for the expression of the opinion of a tumultuous horde of petty, poverty-stricken, provincial nobles; and its parlement, at Rennes, felt certain of their support in any quarrel it undertook with the king's representatives. The *casus belli* was the construction during the Seven Years War, for purposes of military defence, of a system of roads in the province. These roads could only be made by means of the royal *corvée*, but the Estates of Brittany claimed that to do so was to invade their provincial rights. The parlement supported the Estates and opened a struggle with the intendant, who in this case was collaborating with the military commandant, d'Aiguillon. The representatives of the king carried the war into the enemy camp by depriving the leader of the parlement, the procureur général La Chalotais, of the right of *survivance*, that is of the right of passing his office at death to his son, who as it happened, though this, of course, was no reason for his exclusion from office, was notoriously weak-minded. La Chalotais knew no bounds in the violence of his attacks on d'Aiguillon, who proceeded to have him arrested. The other parlements of France now joined that of Rennes in a chorus of denunciation, and in the assertion of their powers came close to denying the sovereignty of the king. Louis XV repudiated their claims in the *lit de justice* of 1766, in language such as the parlements had not heard for many years. In the face of the tempest, however, d'Aiguillon resigned, though this did not prevent the parlement of Paris from summoning him for trial. Such flagrant defiance of the royal will and open persecution of the king's agents brought even Louis XV to the point of action.

Choiseul's complacency, indeed his secret support for the parlements, now threatened his own position. He seemed at the height of his power when, in 1770, he cemented the alliance with Austria and apparently ensured his future influence by negotiating the marriage of Maria Theresa's daughter, Marie-Antoinette, with the dauphin. This was not to be, from his point of view, as successful a move as he had hoped. Louis XV admired the youthful charm of the new dauphine, but personal difficulties arose when Marie-Antoinette found that the duty of being polite to a royal mistress was too much for a Habsburg princess. She was not entirely to be blamed for this. The new favourite, Mme du Barry, had risen from the poverty of a shop-girl to the rank of royal mistress with the aid of one talent and the most ravishing beauty that the court had seen. Good-natured, easy-going, with charm and charity she won many hearts, including the king's, and became *maîtresse en titre*, an office unoccupied since Mme de Pompadour had died. The du Barry had no political interests, and Choiseul's bitter hostility to her, unless it is accounted for by the story that he had aspired to place his sister in the vacant office of titular mistress, is difficult to explain. Though it did not bring about his fall directly, this quarrel can hardly have strengthened his position with Louis XV.

Despite Choiseul's dominance over foreign affairs and the armed services, his position in the government had not remained unchallenged, for an ambitious and able lawyer, Maupeou, known as an upholder of the king's interests against the parlements, had been given the seals. This was a sign that Louis was not willingly following Choiseul in his subservience to the parlements. Maupeou brought into the ministry the abbé Terray as Controller-General. A curious pair they formed, little, dark, bilious Maupeou, whom his enemies called the Seville orange, and tall, stooping, sombre Terray; alike in their capacity for hard work, ability, ruthlessness, and contempt for popularity.

They had not long to wait before power fell into their hands. Choiseul himself provided the occasion for his downfall. A dispute had broken out between Spain and Great Britain over the Falkland Islands. Choiseul urged the Spaniards not to yield, with promises of support based on the Family Compact. When the question was raised in the royal council, in December 1770, Terray exposed the bankrupt state of royal finances, the result of years of subservience to the will of the parlements. The Choiseuls replied by attributing it, very unreasonably, to Terray's own administration, and a furious debate took place in the king's presence. But Louis had learnt his lesson: he had been pushed into disastrous wars by bellicose ministers in the past. At this moment, war with England over the irrelevant Spanish claims to the Falkland Islands, when the restoration of French strength after the Seven Years War was still incomplete, when royal finances were at their lowest ebb and the parlements were engaged in open hostilities with the king's administration, would have been the height of folly. For once the king asserted himself. Choiseul and his cousin were stripped of all their offices and exiled to their country estates. Parlements, *noblesse*, public opinion were with the fallen minister, whose fate was attributed to the intrigues of the new mistress. In fact the king had saved the country from yet another foreign adventure, which it was in no condition to undertake; and the reforming movement that Choiseul had initiated in the fields that interested him was now to be extended to the domestic field where it was even more needed.

After six months of struggle and intrigue for the succession to Choiseul, d'Aiguillon was brought in as Secretary of State for Foreign Affairs, which was equivalent to throwing down a gage of battle against the parlements. Terray had persuaded Maupeou and the king of what was true enough, that without drastic measures the Treasury could not overcome its difficulties. Such measures could only be carried through by overriding the opposition of the parlements. Maupeou was prepared to undertake this task, and at last Louis XV had been brought to see that either his government or the parlements must rule France.

In a desperate situation Terray began with desperate remedies: repudiation of part of the debt, suspension of payments of interest, and forced loans. These measures dealt with the immediate problem: to put royal finances permanently on a sound basis a general reform was required, which could only be achieved at the price of a bitter struggle with the parlements. Instead of waiting to be attacked, Maupeou took the offensive. By calculated provocations he enticed the parlement of Paris into open rejection of the king's authority. Then, in January 1771, by *lettres de cachet*, he exiled the magistrates, not as was customary to some pleasant country town such as Blois, but to varying and distant destinations, the more violent to remote villages of barren Auvergne in the heart of winter. This act of atrocity, as it was considered, aroused a public outcry, but Maupeou went his way undeterred. He abolished the venal offices of the *parlementaires* without compensation, divided the vast area over which the parlement of Paris had jurisdiction into six parts, and set up new courts, nominated by the king, in which justice was to be free.

It was a veritable *coup d'état*. Provincial Estates, princes of the blood, nobles, the whole world of dependents of the parlements, and the bourgeoisie of Paris, long accustomed to regard the parlements as the defenders of their interests, joined in a furious outcry. Many even of the literary men, who had themselves suffered from the censorship of the parlements, were carried away by the wave of emotion, though Voltaire, with greater understanding of what was at issue, threw himself into the struggle on the side of Maupeou. In spite of it all the new courts were set up and after initial difficulties began to function. The *parlementaires* weakened and accepted concessions which allowed them to return home. Maupeou, having won his initial triumph, proposed to follow it up by a fundamental reform of the whole judicial system of France, reducing the mass of unnecessary jurisdictions, codifying and unifying the laws, reforming the antiquated and barbarous procedure, and creating out of the existing Conseil des Partis a new Court of Appeal and an administrative Conseil d'État. He was not to have the time to put these plans into operation, but it was his secretary, Lebrun, who, as third Consul, was to see them brought into effect in the Consulate of Bonaparte.

With the opposition of the parlements eliminated, Terray was able to proceed with some of the financial reforms which they had so long blocked. Machault's edict of 1749, establishing the assessment and collection of the *vingtième* on a sounder basis, was put into operation. The *pays d'états* remained in a privileged position, but the inequity of the distribution of the taxes was at least reduced. The *capitation* of Paris, the collection of which had fallen into great disorder, was reformed by a new assessment and its product nearly doubled. The new lease of the indirect taxes to the Farmers-General, in 1774, brought in an extra 20 millions.

The weak link in the triumvirate was d'Aiguillon, jealous, petty, and unscrupulous, who perhaps in spite of his conduct of the Ministry of Foreign Affairs was able to keep in office with the aid of court intrigues and even to add to his existing ministry that of War. What may have helped him to keep his job was that he, as well as the du Barry, who was less stupid than was commonly supposed, knew all about the *secret du roi*. Even Choiseul had only suspected its existence. The king's *secret* had become rather disorientated in these last years. The imposition of Stanislaus Poniatowski as king on Poland in 1764 by Catherine had robbed it of the last relics of its original raison d'être. However, de Broglie had provided a new objective in the form of a plan for a war of revenge on Great Britain, and recruited as the representative of the *secret* in London the able young secretary to the French embassy, the chevalier d'Éon. A French agent was sent to report on the defences of the English coast, and a scheme was drawn up by which France, in alliance with Spain and the Northern powers, should be able, when the time came, to throw an invading army across the Channel. These plans were destined to repose in the dossiers of the *ancien régime*, save for an abortive attempt at invasion during the American War, till Napoleon pulled them out; but they provided the occasion for a farcical last episode in the history of the *secret*. D'Éon quarrelled with his ambassador, who was supported by Versailles. He then threatened to reveal the schemes of the *secret* to the British government. Louis, in panic, had an attempt made to kidnap d'Éon, who evaded it and brought a successful lawsuit in the English courts against the ambassador, who had to abandon his post. In 1766 d'Éon agreed to return the documents conveying Louis' instructions, in exchange for a pension of 12,000 livres a year; but he retained other papers with the revelation of which he periodically threatened the French government. However, it was about this time that the chevalier adopted female attire and declared that he was a lady, after which he was taken rather less seriously.

Meanwhile, at Vienna the new French ambassador, the Cardinal de Rohan, discovered that the Austrians had intercepted and deciphered the correspondence of the *secret*, a fact which, through his relation the prince de Soubise, he passed on to the king. The enmity which he experienced from Maria Theresa is doubtless more reasonably explained by the cardinal's inconvenient discovery than by his alleged exploits among her maids of honour. Inherited by Marie-Antoinette, this enmity was at the root of the unhappy and influential diamond necklace affair.

The correspondence of Louis XV in the final years gives one the impression that he himself was beginning to lose the thread of his own secret diplomacy. Although de Broglie more than once begged to be allowed to abandon it, the king was too much a creature of habit to give it up, though it was now practically meaningless. The *secret* ended only with his death when, on the orders of Louis XVI, the papers were deposited with the new Foreign Minister, Vergennes — himself, ironically, a member of the *secret*; so that in him official and secret diplomacy may be said to have come together at last.

Possibly, in these years also, Louis XV may have been paying more attention to home than to foreign affairs, and in this connection d'Aiguillon counted for a good deal less than his colleagues. His irresponsibility was finally demonstrated when he began to negotiate with his old enemies of the parlements against them. But he was a light man and could hardly have swung the balance down against Maupeou and Terray, who had so dramatically and successfully restored royal authority after a generation of weakness. Given a few more years for the country to appreciate the benefits of the new system, there could hardly have been any question of a restoration of the parlements. Freed from their incubus, the reforms which were already in the minds of many, and in the dossiers and *mémoires* of the administration, could be brought out and applied. The tragedy was that the few years that were needed were not given. In 1774 Louis XV was taken ill with smallpox and in fourteen days he was dead. The reforming wave was to continue and to gain in strength, but the forces of resistance that Louis XV had been brought to face and defy only in the last years of his reign were to prove even stronger under his weaker successor, and the contradictions which had been inherent in the social and political system of France since the time of Louis XIV were within fifteen years to bring the monarchy down in ruins.

CHAPTER THREE

⚜

PRELUDE TO REFORM

THE former dauphin, with whom the *dévot* party might have come to power, had died in 1765. The successor was therefore Louis XV's grandson. Louis XVI, king at twenty and full of good intentions, was determined to break with the ways of the corrupt old court and in particular with the tyrannical triumvirate, the protégés of Mme du Barry as he had been taught to see them. All too conscious of his own youth and inexperience, he looked around for an adviser, and was given one by his aunt Mme Adélaïde, in the person of the elderly courtier, Maurepas. A capable and successful minister a quarter of a century earlier, at the age of seventy-three Maurepas found himself called from the wings, where he had long exercised his wit at the expense of the players, back to the centre of the stage, delighted at the freak of fortune which brought him so unexpectedly to the height of influence. If Louis XVI thought he had found his Fleury he was sadly mistaken. Maurepas' only aim was to enjoy his new elevation as long as he could and not to overburden his aged frame with work or his flippant mind with serious thoughts.

The dismissal of Maupeou — last of the great ministers of the Bourbon dynasty — was a foregone conclusion. This was not enough. The *parlementaires*, conscious of their role as the defenders of the constitutional liberties of France, and their supporters who had labelled themselves the 'Patriot' party, rapidly recovered from the disarray and hopelessness into which they had fallen after four years of firm handling by Maupeou. They organized demonstrations in Paris, exploited the legend that Louis XV had speculated in grain to profit from the distress of his people — the so-called 'pacte de famine' — and brought out the mob to invade the courts where the 'parlement Maupeou' sat. It was a tactic that was to be repeated in 1788 and it succeeded in conveying the impression of a great public movement, to which the government yielded by restoring the old parlements. All the achievement of Maupeou was undone. True, the restoration was on conditions, but no one who knew the history of the parlements in the eighteenth century should have expected them to abide by these. In the provinces, as in Paris, the triumph of the combined *noblesse* of the robe and the sword was celebrated as a victory for the people over a despotic monarchy.

But even in this Indian summer of reaction the spirit of reform could not be suppressed. Nothing could be more mistaken than the idea that the eighteenth century was an age of abstract thought. It was, on the contrary, in all the countries where the Enlightenment was a force, and particularly in France and England, one of intense interest in practical reform. To appreciate why this was so we must look a little more closely at some aspects of its intellectual history; for this was the age when science descended, in a sense, from the study to the market-place. Naturally, something was lost in the process, but the strength of the new ways of thought that science brought with it was evident even when they were turned to old uses. The theme of the abbé Pluche's *Spectacle de la Nature* (1732), which went through at least eighteen editions in France, was to prove the existence of God by the evidence of the divine plan in nature. 'Some animals', wrote Pluche, 'are preordained by Providence to live with, and be serviceable to mankind; others to reside in woods and deserts, ... to prove a scourge to all such of the human species as grow profligate and abandoned wretches.' Or again, 'The same hand which made the fishes of the sea, prepared from the beginning the water of which they had need.' Popular science of this sort, admittedly, demonstrated no more than a growth of interest. The barriers against acceptance of new scientific ideas on a higher intellectual level were strong. Even Fontenelle, for all his modernity, clung to Descartes and the *tourbillons* and rejected the Newtonian system. The Jesuits, who, until their expulsion, dominated French education, only accepted Cartesianism about 1730, when it was losing its intellectual validity. Maupertuis, on the other hand, defended Newton's explanation of the movement of comets as early as his *Discours sur la figure des astres* of 1723. Voltaire wrote effective propaganda for Newtonian science, and by 1747 the triumph of the new ideas could be described in the marquis d'Argens' *La philosophie du bon sens* as 'la fureur de l'attraction'.

We must not exaggerate the scientific achievements of eighteenth-century France. The distinguished mathematician d'Alembert, the careful observer of insects Réaumur, among many others, catch our attention; but until we come to Lavoisier it was a period of diffusion, popularization, accumulation, rather than of fundamental discovery. The important new fact was the spread of the empirical attitude. Voltaire, in his *Lettres philosophiques*, and d'Alembert, in the *Discours préliminaire* to the *Encyclopédie*, saw behind Newton the founder of experimental science in Bacon. Abstract, *a priori* thought was almost universally condemned. 'What could be more ridiculous', wrote Condillac in his *Traité des systèmes* (1749), 'than that men awakening from a profound sleep, and finding themselves in the middle of a labyrinth, should lay down general principles for discovering the way out? Yet such is the conduct of the philosopher.' Observe, experiment, collect: this was the method of the eighteenth century and these were activities in which many could join. Salons could be laboratories and literary journals spread scientific news, until even Voltaire thought that the craze for science was going too far. 'I loved physics', he wrote in 1741, 'so long as it did not try to take precedence over poetry; now that it is crushing all the arts, I no longer wish to regard it as anything but a tyrant.'

Empirical science, linked with the sensational psychology and the materialist doctrine, was destined profoundly to influence man's attitude to himself and his institutions. The result was to make environment and education all-powerful over man; the chain of custom, the bondage to the past, was broken at its strongest link. Progress became possible and therefore conceivable. 'We arrive, so to speak', wrote the abbé de Saint-Pierre early in the century, 'at the beginning of the age of gold.' And at the end Condorcet could envisage the human race, 'emancipated from its shackles, released from the power of fate and from that of the enemies of its progress, advancing with a firm and sure step along the path of truth, virtue and happiness'.

The idea of progress provides ample scope for mocking at the shallow optimism of the age of *lumières* from our own peak of

disillusion, but it was not unqualified. 'What is optimism?' asked
Cacambo. 'Alas,' said Candide, 'it is the mania for pretending that all
is well when all is ill.' Voltaire was no stranger to pessimism:

> L'homme, étranger à soi, de l'homme est ignoré.
> Que sais-je? Où suis-je? Où vais-je? et d'où suis-je tiré?
> Atomes tourmentés sur cet amas de boue,
> Que la mort engloutit, et dont le sort se joue.

But his conclusion was not despair, but 'Il faut cultiver notre jardin.'
The whole attitude of mind of the eighteenth century led up to one
thing: practical reform. By the time when Louis XVI mounted the
throne the pressure for reform was such that no government could
ignore it. Maurepas, cynical old courtier as he was, recognized the
need to make a gesture in this direction. While he was casting round
for a reforming Controller-General to give tone to the government,
the name of the intendant of the Limousin, Turgot, was suggested to
him. Maurepas obtained, indeed, rather more of a reformer than he had
bargained for: in Turgot a disciple of the Physiocrats came into office.

The Physiocratic school of thought did so much to influence ideas
in the second half of the eighteenth century that a brief indication of
its major tenets must be given. Quesnay, the founder of the Physiocratic school, was the royal physician. His belief that the land was the
only source of wealth had not a great deal to recommend it from the
theoretical point of view. Its practical conclusions were more important and, indeed, are the real explanation of the success of the
doctrine; for it followed that the land should therefore pay the taxes,
and this meant all the land, which was not to the liking of the great
proprietors, whether noble, clergy, or bourgeois, but would have
been very convenient for the royal Controllers-General. The other
major conclusion was that any restrictions on the circulation of
wealth, and particularly on trade in the products of the soil, was
injurious to national wealth. It followed that all national customs
barriers by which their movement was restricted should be swept
away. If it were asked who was to accomplish these and other
reforms, the answer was the king, for in so far as the first school of
Physiocrats possessed any political doctrine it was roughly that of
enlightened despotism. The most notorious among them was the

eccentric marquis de Mirabeau, the 'friend of man' who loved humanity and hated his own family. Loosely connected with the Physiocrats was Gournay, an inspector of manufactures and Intendant de Commerce, who had a higher conception of the importance of trade and industry and extended the idea of the abolition of restrictions into these fields. He was also less convinced of the potential virtues of the good despot and carried the belief in the advantages of liberty from the economic into the political field.

Turgot was the friend and follower of Gournay. As intendant in the backward *généralité* of Limoges he had attempted to put reforming ideas into practice, to find himself, as his biographer, Dr Douglas Dakin, puts it, 'committed to a perpetual drudgery in administrative bad habits, to a wearisome tidying of endless lumber. He had to collect direct taxation under a system which was archaic, bizarre, wasteful of effort; he had to rectify justice which so frequently miscarried; he must promote the arts of agriculture among an ignorant, surly and beggarly peasantry; he was called to encourage industry and commerce to satisfy a government whose economic wisdom was merely the time-worn prejudice of a medieval town.' His achievements in the Limousin, in these circumstances, if they were on a small scale, were remarkable. Characteristically, of course, it was not his work as intendant but the fact that he had a friend who was also the friend of Maurepas that secured Turgot's appointment to the office of Controller-General.

Whereas Maupeou and Terray had begun by crushing the chief obstacle in the path of reform, Turgot began with the reforms themselves, though on a modest scale. The charge that he tried to force a mass of undigested theories into law *en bloc* is patently untrue. His great mistake, for which perhaps absence from the intrigues of court and council and a certain innocence of the ways of Versailles was responsible, was his concurrence in the recall of the parlements. If he believed that they were likely to pay any attention to the restrictions imposed on them, he was exhibiting a naive optimism. However, the restored parlements remained chastened for a year or so, and during this period Turgot initiated what enlightened opinion expected to be a great reforming ministry. In finance he was able to do no more than take a few minor and hesitating steps. By small economies here and there, despite the opposition of the court, he checked for a time the ever-swelling expense of places and pensions. He introduced reforms into the collection of the *taille* and the relations of the state with the Farmers-General; but if the government was temporarily free from the customary financial difficulties, this is to be attributed to the ruthless policy of Terray rather than the mild reforms of Turgot.

In another matter Turgot reversed the policy of Terray. The price of grain had reached its highest point, before the crisis of 1787–9, in 1770. Terray reacted, as he did to everything, violently, by abolishing the limited freedom of trade in corn which had been introduced during the good harvests of the 'sixties and reviving the traditional policy of state intervention. The parlements and their supporters, though naturally they had no more belief in the liberty of trade than in any other kind of liberty except their own, seized the opportunity to portray Terray as a sinister monopolist, and Louis XV, by means of the mythical 'pacte de famine', as a speculator reaping colossal profits from the deliberate starvation of his people. Popular disturbances broke out but they were soon suppressed. Doubtless the extent to which any government policy could affect the supply and, therefore, the price of corn, was largely imaginary; but in fact there was a steady and substantial decline in corn prices from 1770 to 1774.

The outcry against Terray's policy, factitious as it may have been, predisposed Louis XVI to accept Turgot's proposal for its abandonment. The new scheme was no doctrinaire one: freedom to export grain was still withheld and special precautions to secure the provisioning of Paris were retained. Unfortunately the harvest of 1774 was a poor one. Scarcity ensued, and bread riots and a little *guerre des farines* followed, especially in the countryside round Paris, which was apt to be denuded of foodstuffs because of the demands of the capital. Responsibility for the riots has been attributed to various of Turgot's enemies, but though there is no reason to suppose that they regretted this set-back to his policy, the evidence in favour of the spontaneity of the disturbances is strong. In any case they were suppressed, and the rise in the price of grain, though sharp, was not of long duration.

Other and minor measures of Turgot's reforming administration must be left with a simple mention — the energetic steps he took to deal with a severe outbreak of cattle plague; the replacement of the inefficient old company which had held the monopoly of the manufacture of saltpetre by a *régie*, at the head of which he put the greatest living scientist, Lavoisier, who made the French manufactures of gunpowder the best in Europe and to whose work the later successes of the revolutionary armies were not a little due; the transfer of postal services from a private monopoly into a public service in the department of the Controller-General. More far-reaching plans for the development of education, a measure of local self-government, state provision for the poor, and the reorganization of the army, were also projected.

Both the reforms achieved and those proposed aroused, as all reforms inevitably did, the antagonism of powerful vested interests. Turgot's enemies were soon gathering on all sides. The financiers saw profitable monopolies being taken out of their hands; the Choiseulists, still a strong party at court, their early hopes that Turgot would play their game having been disappointed, turned against him; the *dévot* party and the clergy, well aware of the dangerous intellectual company that Turgot kept and of his commitment to ideas of toleration, had been opposed to him from the beginning — he had tried, unsuccessfully, to secure a modification of the coronation oath by which the king pledged himself to extirpate heretics, and subsequently spoke strongly in the council in favour of measures of toleration for Protestants; the parlements, the natural enemies of any reforming minister, were gradually recovering their confidence and only awaited a favourable moment to unmask their guns. The other ministers turned against Turgot, except for Malesherbes, who had succeeded the corrupt and senile La Vrillière, for fifty years in charge of the Maison du Roi, but who lacked the strength of character, though he had the good intentions, necessary for one who would clean out those Augean stables; Saint-Germain, at the Ministry of War, was himself a reformer but resented Turgot's attempts to revive the influence of the Contrôle Général over the finances of the other ministries; Vergennes, at the Ministry of Foreign Affairs, took little part in domestic disputes; Miromesnil,

Keeper of the Seals, a legal mediocrity, sided increasingly openly with the parlements against Turgot; Maurepas, that fine if somewhat faded flower of the old court, could only conceive of government in terms of intrigue. None of Turgot's colleagues, therefore, could be relied on to support him against his enemies.

Despite the gathering clouds and his own ill health, the Controller-General went ahead with his programme. He submitted his Six Edicts to the king in January 1776. Four of these extended his earlier edicts on free trade in corn to Paris and abolished a host of unnecessary offices which were little more than an excuse for extra impositions on the food trade. The two other edicts were of major importance: the first abolished the *jurandes*, the restrictive gilds which controlled and limited admission to many industries; the other edict suppressed the *corvée* and proposed to raise the funds necessary for the upkeep of roads by a general tax payable by all proprietors of land.

Now the parlement of Paris felt that the time had come to strike: the edicts on *jurandes* and *corvées* were an attack on privilege, and in view of the general intellectual atmosphere any such attack might open a dangerous breach in the wall of privilege which the *parlementaires* were manning with all the greater determination because of their temporary defeat by Maupeou. Despite the opposition of the parlements, and even of his own colleagues, Turgot persuaded the king to register the edicts by *lit de justice*; but Maurepas, who only wanted a quiet life and was now anxious to be rid of his tiresome colleague, succeeded in turning the king against him. In May 1776 Louis dismissed Turgot. As far as was possible, all the work of his ministry was rapidly undone. Even if he had succeeded in his reforms one can hardly suppose that he could have held back the coming aristocratic revolt or saved the *ancien régime*; but it might have died less discreditably had there been more chances of survival for a minister like Turgot.

Any attempt at large-scale reform was clearly doomed to frustration, but the spirit of the age was not to be denied. Through chinks and crannies in the rotted structure of the old regime, reform irresistibly continued to find its way. Two of Turgot's fellow-ministers were in their own fields responsible for important reforms. Saint-

Germain, an old professional soldier who had served the Emperor and the Elector of Bavaria, had fought under Maurice de Saxe and been Minister of War in Denmark, set about reforming the army on Prussian lines. The household troops, expensive, undisciplined, and largely useless, were reduced in numbers, though as their officers, mostly of the higher *noblesse*, had to be bought out at an extravagant price, no more than a beginning could be made in this respect, and even so it aroused the indignation of the court. The militia, a ragged military proletariat of conscripts chosen by lot from the poorest of the population, was useless military material, apart from one company of Royal Grenadiers. Saint-Germain ceased to mobilize them, except for the Grenadiers, and in their stead increased the recruitment of regular troops. He suppressed the École militaire of Paris, which was monopolized by the sons of the higher nobles and wealthy bourgeois, and founded instead twelve provincial military schools, with 600 scholarships for the sons of poor nobles. Among the new officer material thus drawn in there was soon to be a boy called Bonaparte. The administrative system of the Ministry of War was reorganized and a beginning was made in the reduction of venality which prepared the way for its abolition by the Constituent Assembly. Perhaps the most important change of all was the continuation by Gribeauval of the reform of the artillery, commenced under Choiseul but subsequently dropped, thanks to which France entered the Revolutionary War with the most modern artillery in Europe.

All these reforms, as well as improvements in the material conditions of the soldiery, were ignored or opposed by public opinion, which was revolted by the more vigorous discipline that Saint-Germain imposed, and particularly by his rather unhappy introduction of the punishment of beating with the flat of the sword in place of other and not necessarily less severe penalties. Officers and soldiers alike, unused to discipline, showed their resentment. Maurepas was not the man to stand by an unpopular colleague, and Saint-Germain went the way of Turgot and Malesherbes. The *noblesse* continued its struggle against what was now a reforming Ministry of War, and in 1781 secured the issue of a decree requiring the possession of four degrees of nobility for promotion to any rank above that of captain. Of course, no law, under the *ancien régime*, tells us much unless we also know if and how it was put into practice. The result of the reforms of Choiseul and Saint-Germain was that when the noble officers fled in the early years of the Revolution the nucleus of an efficient army remained, which was able to absorb the masses of revolutionary volunteers and conscripts and with them prove itself on the field of battle superior to every other army in Europe.

The winds of reform were by now blowing from every quarter. At the Ministry of Marine, Sartine, yet one more member of the great ministry which inaugurated Louis XVI's reign, built up the navy to a point at which it could challenge British naval supremacy in the War of American Independence, though at a frightful cost to the royal finances. Turgot's memoir to Louis XVI in favour of toleration had achieved no positive results in face of the opposition of the Assembly of Clergy; but on the eve of the Revolution, in 1787, an Edict of Toleration granted the Protestants civil rights, including those of entry into various hitherto prohibited trades and professions, and recognized the legitimacy of Protestant marriages registered with the local authorities, a much resented infringement of the rights of the Church which prepared the way for the secularization of marriage under the Revolution. In 1784 the personal tax which Jews had to pay was abolished. The Church itself was not immune from reform. A Commission des réguliers, established in 1766, forbade the taking of religious vows before twenty-one for men and eighteen for women, and in four years suppressed more than fifteen hundred moribund or practically deserted religious houses. The *portion congrue* which had to be allocated to the parish clergy was raised from 300 livres for curés and 150 livres for vicaires to 500 and 200 respectively in 1768, and to 700 and 350 in 1786. State pawnshops, *monts de piété*, of which there had been only six, were greatly increased in number.

Mainmorte, that last relic of serfdom in France, which was as harmful to agriculture as it was to the unfortunate populations that still lived under it, was suppressed by Necker on the royal domain by an edict of 1779. In 1780 the same minister proposed an improvement in the state of the prisons, though whether much was achieved in this respect is doubtful. The *question préparatoire*, torture inflicted on accused persons for the purpose of obtaining a confession, was abolished in 1780, and the abolition of the *question préalable*, the routine torture of convicted criminals before execution to obtain from them the names of their accomplices, followed in 1788, despite the opposition of the parlements to such interference with the good old ways of doing justice. In 1784, even under a minister with such a reputation as a reactionary as Marie-Antoinette's favourite, Breteuil, there was a general inspection of the cases of all prisoners held under *lettre de cachet*; many were liberated, the use of the letters was henceforth confined to serious offences and the duration of the imprisonment was to be no longer than two or three years. The decision was taken to pull down the Bastille, which now never had more than a mere handful of involuntary guests.

The mud, dirt, and congestion of the streets of Paris were notorious, but the idea that the government had a responsibility for the cleanliness and health of the cities was spreading. A regulation of 1783 laid down thirty feet as the minimum width for roads in future and established a ratio between the width and the height of building permitted along them. Water carriers still thronged the public fountains, but in 1777 a company was formed to supply water from the Seine to houses by means of two pumping engines. Necker, who replaced Turgot in effective control of finances, though as a Protestant he was excluded from the titular office, introduced a number of minor reforms. His successor, Calonne, has no great reputation as a reformer, but he organized a bureau of statistics under Dupont de Nemours, increased grants for road and canal building and harbour improvements, and, as will be seen, produced in the end an extensive plan of financial reform. Vergennes, in 1786, negotiated the free-trade treaty with Great Britain. The initiative for the negotiations came from France and was greeted with profound suspicion by the younger Pitt, who suspected the French even when they appeared to bring gifts. The treaty did, in fact, represent a genuine desire on the part of Vergennes to secure an international *détente*: that this would be a little difficult to reconcile with the intense struggle that French and British agents were at the same time waging for the alliance of the Dutch Republic apparently did not occur to him. The treaty was at least an indication of the extent to which ideas of free trade had penetrated the bureaux.

Behind such reforms we can detect in the background the influence of a growing body of officials and professional men, far from revolutionary in sentiment but becoming increasingly impatient with the barriers that parlements, *noblesse*, and clergy put in the way of every step in the direction of a more efficient state. Such men were only the most influential section of an educated public which had become convinced of the need for drastic changes and which viewed the more barbarous and irrational habits of the *ancien régime* with increasing revulsion. If the reforms would also take political power and social status out of the hands of an effete nobility and bestow them on the competent lesser officials and professional men who already performed most of the actual business of the state, that did not diminish their attraction. At the same time, it would be a mistake to interpret the reforming trend that was now manifesting itself in so many different directions as the simple expression of material interests. It was the flowering of a great humanitarian spirit that had been centuries in the growing. Barbarities and stupidities that were sanctified by the use of ages and embodied in the most cherished traditions of great institutions seemed to be on the point of disappearing like the phantoms of night at dawn.

But much as had been and was being achieved by piecemeal reform, far more remained to be done before the institutions of France could catch up with educated opinion, and meanwhile the forces that looked to the past and aspired to go backward rather than forward were also gathering strength. The dawn of reform was to open the day of revolution, and the revolution, though it was to bring to fruition some of the high hopes of the eighteenth century, was to be fatal to more. The tragedy of the French Revolution lay not in the reaping of a crop of dragon's teeth, but in the frustration of so many noble and apparently practicable aspirations. It was, in the words of Albert Schweitzer, a fall of snow on blossoming trees.

CHAPTER FOUR

THE EVE OF REVOLUTION

I F we ask why reform had to give place to revolution, the explanation, as for the weakness of France under Louis XV, must primarily be given in terms of the personality of the ruler. The condition on which Louis XIV had bequeathed greatness to the French monarchy was that the monarch should be equal to the task imposed on him. It was reasonable, in an age that believed in divine right, to suppose that any personal deficiencies in the actual physical heirs of Saint Louis would be made good by the spiritual nature of their office. Unhappily this spiritual influence had not been conspicuous in the case of Louis XV, and if he had been unequal to his responsibilities Louis XVI was to be even more so. What was to be expected of a rather dull and phlegmatic young man of twenty? Kindly, conscientious, unambitious, devout, he had no vices save a propensity for over-eating. The funeral cortège of Louis XV had been accompanied — or so the story ran — with shouts of 'Voilà le plaisir des dames!': no such cry would ever accompany Louis XVI, alive or dead. Apart from eating, hunting was his chief pleasure and he was a better locksmith — for in true Rousseauist fashion he had learnt a manual craft — than king. He gives the impression of being one of the most uninterested and uninteresting spectators of his own reign. His fate is evidence that good people do not necessarily end happily, especially when they are kings in an age of revolution; but his queen did not end the more happily for being a little less good.

Marie-Antoinette Josèphe Jeanne de Lorraine was the daughter of Francis I and Maria Theresa. At the age of fifteen she took the journey from Vienna to Versailles, a living pledge to the Franco-Austrian alliance. On an island in the Rhine near Strasbourg she quitted the Holy Roman Empire, was symbolically and also literally stripped of her Habsburg apparel, passed over to new French ladies-in-waiting to be robed as a French princess, and stepped on the soil of France the dauphine. As she travelled through the country the enthusiasm and tenderness of the French populace, despite its rags and poverty, moved her to tears, but the little Habsburg princess was not to find Versailles a bed of roses. The party opposed to the Austrian alliance was still very strong and had no love for her. The minister who had made the marriage, Choiseul, had just fallen from power, and though the Austrian court, which had found him too independent, had no regrets at this, Marie-Antoinette always favoured the Choiseulists at Versailles. The old roué who was king of France would have been kind enough to her in his way, but the proud little daughter of Maria Theresa was not prepared to demean herself to the point of recognizing the existence of Mme du Barry; the dauphin, for lack of a minor operation, was no husband to her for the first seven years of their marriage; the king's aunts, *dévot* and dull, regulated the monotonous routine of her life; and Marie-Antoinette was made of too lively a metal to endure all this with patience. The French abbé who had tutored her at the Austrian court reported that she was more intelligent than was generally supposed. 'Unfortunately', he added, 'up to the age of twelve she has not been trained to concentrate in any way. She is rather lazy, extremely frivolous and hard to teach.'

She came to a court whose chief occupation was pleasure, in an age when frivolity had claimed it for its own. Women's attire was becoming more fantasticated, with the queen as the leader of the fashion. The king, said Mme de Campan, disapproved of the excessive luxury in dress but did nothing to check it. The height of elaboration was reached, literally, in the monstrous head-dresses that erected such a heavy burden over such light heads. When the queen passed along the gallery at Versailles, says Soulavie, you could see nothing but a forest of feathers, rising high above the heads and nodding to and fro. Mme de Campan and Soulavie, unreliable on most matters, are perhaps trustworthy on such trifles. Internal decoration, too, was influenced by the same spirit. The nymphs of the opera wanted a less chaste background than the restrained style patronized by Louis XV and Mme de Pompadour and represented by the Petit Trianon, built early in the 'sixties. Arabesques and polychromic ornamentation now spread lavishly.

All this was on the surface, at the beginning of the new reign; but a very different current was emerging from below. Luxury was becoming boring. Marie-Antoinette herself revolted against the tiresome etiquette of the French court. This was the age of Rousseau and pre-romanticism. The classicism of the seventeenth century had dried up and faded under Louis XV. Sensibility reigned, but still with a survival of the restraint of the previous century, until, in the second half of the eighteenth century, human nature took its revenge on the artificiality of fashionable life in floods of lachrymose sentimentality. The *comédie larmoyante*, so much admired and exemplified by Diderot, released natural emotions and portrayed domestic virtues on the stage. 'Back to nature' was to mean more than this when Jean-Jacques Rousseau became its prophet. To identify it with primitivism is a vulgar error. It was a reaction against formality, luxury, elaborate clothes, and etiquette, against the suppression of simple human sentiments and ignorance of innocent pleasures that was the hall-mark of Versailles and the world of fashion. An elegant simplicity was now *à la mode*. The queen could discard her elaborate dresses and hair-styles and have herself painted for the Salon of 1783, her hair unpowdered and unbewigged, in a simple muslin blouse. It was an age of reverie, sentiment, and melancholy, of country fêtes and pastoral pleasures.

Nattier abandoned his mythological portraits to paint his sitters in modern clothing. Chardin devoted his genius to the illumination of humble persons and quiet domestic manners. More popular, and in keeping with the new climate of emotion, were the melting beauties of Vigée Le Brun and the insidious little innocents of Greuze, a finer painter than is commonly recognized. The sorely tried virtue of Rousseau's new Héloïse, close cousin of Pamela, replaced the tougher metal of Marianne and the starkness of Manon. Pictures, Diderot preached in the series of Salons which may almost be regarded as founding art criticism, are only good if they teach moral lessons. Under d'Angiviller as Directeur des Bâtiments 'indecent' works were eliminated from the Salon. Fragonard only achieved official recognition by painting, against his nature, the kind of picture that had now the *cachet* of official approval; after which he returned to the more frivolous masterpieces that reflected his own taste and the spirit of the previous generation. Gluck developed the expression of human emotions in opera.

Beaumarchais brings us to the point at which literature acquires a direct social and political significance. The dramatist was in his own person the symbol of a new age. Pierre-Augustin Caron was the son of a master watchmaker of Paris. His invention of a new escapement, and talent in playing the flute and the harp, opened the doors of the court to him. His charm won for him the office, the fortune, and the widow of a wealthy official, and he became Caron de Beaumarchais. Financial speculations, a *lettre de cachet* and a famous lawsuit, in which he found himself opposed to the 'parlement Maupeou' and took revenge in vitriolic pamphlets, followed. More speculations made him, as a supplier of arms to the American colonies, one of the instigators of French intervention in the American War. He was destined to make and to lose two or three fortunes in his life, to be criticized for dangerous writings under the monarchy and imprisoned as a counter-revolutionary during the Revolution, when he barely escaped the September massacres, to be an agent of Louis XVI and a member of the first commune of Paris. But he survives as the author of *Le Barbier de Séville* and *Le Mariage de Figaro*; and to find in Figaro the spirit of the Revolution is to see in the first breezes of autumn, shaking the petals off the roses one by one, the gales of winter. Figaro, like his creator, belongs to an age when intelligence allied to not too much scruple set out to conquer the world and found only acquired riches and rank in its way. The aim was not to destroy the citadel of vested interest but to occupy it, not to end the *douceurs de la vie* but to enjoy them, in which Beaumarchais was perhaps truer to his generation and class than the serious, puritanical prophets and politicians of revolutionary France. Like practically everyone else he was no revolutionary before 1789, and Figaro ends with a song.

> Or, messieurs, la co-omédie,
> Que l'on juge en cè-et instant;
> Sauf erreur, nous peint la vie
> Du bon peuple qui l'entend.
> Qu'on l'opprime, il peste, il crie;

Il s'agite en cent fa-açons:
Tout fini-it par des chansons. (*bis*)

In this atmosphere Marie-Antoinette withdrew from the stuffy ceremonial of Versailles. With a small group of friends she increasingly spent her time in the freer atmosphere of the little Trianon, that small country-house planned by Louis XV for the Pompadour but never inhabited by her. There, a *jardin anglais*, traversed by a meandering stream, with rustic bridges and an imitation waterfall and leading to a toy hamlet set round the banks of a diminutive lake, provided the setting in which the queen and her friends could dress themselves as stage shepherds and shepherdesses and share the simple pleasures of rural life. Etiquette was thrown to the winds. Marie-Antoinette, fallen from a donkey she had been riding, calls out, 'Hurry up: ask Madame de Noailles [the chief arbiter of court etiquette] what a Queen of France should do when she falls off a donkey.' 'In an age of pleasure and frivolity,' wrote the duc de Lévis, 'intoxicated with supreme power, the queen had no fancy for submitting herself to constraint, and she found court ceremonies tedious. ... She thought it absurd to suppose that the loyalty of the common people could depend upon the number of hours which the royal family spent in a circle of bored and boring courtiers. ... Except for a few favourites, chosen for some whim or because of a successful intrigue, everyone was excluded from the royal presence.' The Princesse de Lamballe, whose devotion to the queen outlasted her loss of favour and who returned to her in the Paris of the Revolution, to be butchered in the September massacres and have her head paraded round the streets on a pike, the Polignacs, greedy and irresponsible, whose favour cost the state half a million livres a year, the handsome young Swede, Count Fersen, who won Marie-Antoinette's heart — these were not the great names of the French court. Maria Theresa, to whom it was all secretly reported by the Austrian ambassador, Mercy, warned her daughter that she did not realize what she was doing. 'I know well enough', she wrote, 'how tedious and futile is a representative position; but believe me, you will have to put up with both tediousness and futility, for otherwise you will suffer from much more serious inconveniences than these petty burdens — you more than most rulers, since you have to rule over so touchy a nation.'

The France that Louis XVI and Marie-Antoinette never saw and that never saw them — for apart from one journey by the king to the new harbour works at Cherbourg they never travelled beyond the group of royal châteaux in the neighbourhood of Paris — was to take its revenge upon them; but the attack was to be launched by the hostile factions at court, which Marie-Antoinette had done so little to conciliate, their enmity intensified by her favour for the Choiseulists. A flood of almost inconceivably scurrilous pamphlets, instigated by her enemies at court, poured out. They attributed to her as lovers practically every eligible male at Versailles, except Fersen: if her children could be bastardized, the king's brother, Provence, might succeed to the throne, and he was not necessarily innocent of complicity in the campaign against the queen. Her reputation was almost ruined when the affair of the diamond necklace came, in 1785, to complete the process.

Napoleon dated the French Revolution from the affair of the necklace. It burst on the public sensationally enough. In August 1785 the Cardinal de Rohan, duke and peer, member of the great Rohan-Soubise clan, one of the three princely houses of France, Bishop of Strasbourg, Provisor of the Sorbonne, Grand Almoner of France, was arrested at Versailles and charged with using the queen's name to procure a fantastically expensive necklace of diamonds from the court jewellers without paying for it. He demanded to be tried by the parlement of Paris. The Minister for the Maison du Roi, Breteuil, who was responsible for the arrest and subsequent prosecution, and, having helped the young Fersen when he first came to court, was also a particular favourite of the queen, exhibited astonishing folly in his conduct of the affair, and above all in allowing the case to be tried before a court composed of the bitterest enemies of the monarchy. It can only be supposed that his personal feud with Rohan, dating from the time when the cardinal had supplanted him as ambassador at Vienna, robbed him of his judgment. The Cardinal de Rohan, moreover, as an enemy of the Austrian alliance, had acquired the ill will of Maria Theresa, who passed her prejudice against him on to her daughter. He himself wanted nothing more than to have his existence recognized at court and to receive the queen's favour. When the comtesse de la Motte, pauperized descendant of a bastard of Henry II, offered herself as an alleged contact with Marie-Antoinette, Rohan was easily taken in. He must have been very gullible: among those he patronized was Cagliostro, Italian adventurer and professional mystifier, who cured his asthma and made him a gold ring out of base metal.

The age of reason was already giving place not only to sentiment but also to superstition. Illuminés and Rosicrucians were spreading from southern Germany into more rational countries, Lavater was founding the new science of physiognomy and Mesmer enthralling society with the mysteries of hypnotism. Mme de la Motte worked her wonders in a more practical way. With the aid of forged letters she persuaded the Cardinal de Rohan that if he would pledge his credit to acquire the diamond necklace for the queen, he would be restored to royal favour. A momentary interview at night, in the gardens of Versailles, with a Paris prostitute dressed up to resemble the queen, completed the cardinal's infatuation. This may have been the fatal episode from the queen's point of view also, for she was anxious that above all there should be no mention of meetings on the terrace. Breteuil, as has been said, was a close friend of Fersen. If anyone knew of the affection between him and the queen it was Breteuil, and a plausible guess may be made that both the minister and Marie-Antoinette suspected Rohan of having ferreted out the queen's secret. This may account for the panic-stricken arrests which followed the revelation by the court jewellers of the transactions relating to the necklace, and the lack of a sense of proportion shown in the handling of the whole affair.

The trial dragged the queen's name through the mire with those of the scum of society. A diamond thief and adventuress, some shady pseudo-gentlemen, an alchemist, a prostitute, a cardinal, and a queen: such were the dramatis personae. The chief deviser of the affair, Jeanne de la Motte, was sentenced to be flogged, branded, and put in the Salpêtrière for life — in fact she escaped after nine months; the cardinal, though found innocent, was banished from the court. The queen was supposed by the public to have sold her favours to him for a necklace of diamonds and then to have jibbed at paying the price. The part that all this played in discrediting her in general opinion and so preparing the ground for the fall of the monarchy is not to be underestimated.

While the weakness of the king and the indiscretions of the queen thus undermined the prestige of the monarchy, public opinion, influenced by the agitation of the parlements, was learning to talk republican language even before it had thought republican thoughts. In more than one way opinion in France was revolutionary before anyone had dreamed of a revolution. An opportunity for the expression in action of such sentiments had been provided when the American colonies revolted against Great Britain. Ideological sympathies joined with traditional Anglophobia to throw French opinion overwhelmingly on the side of the rebels. The Foreign Minister, Vergennes, connived at the sending of arms and supplies to them. French volunteers, including the young marquis de La Fayette, greedy for glory, crossed the Atlantic to fight in the cause of liberty. After the capture, in 1778, of the British army under Burgoyne at Saratoga, Vergennes was able to intervene more openly. The American envoy, Benjamin Franklin, with his unpowdered hair, round hat, brown clothes, and homespun wit, became the idol of Paris society. Vergennes negotiated a treaty of alliance between France and the revolutionary colonies, in which the French king engaged himself, in the event of France entering into the war on the side of the colonies, to claim no conquests in North America or the Bermudas.

As was customary, fighting between France and Great Britain broke out through British aggression on the seas before war was declared. Spain was brought into the struggle on the side of France with the promise of Gibraltar, Minorca, Florida, and British Honduras. The Armed Neutrality proclaimed by Catherine of Russia was joined by most of the other powers of Europe. In 1770 the Dutch Republic entered the war on the side of France and the American colonies. The hour for the revenge of France on the proud island empire which had humiliated her in 1763 had struck.

The last plans of the *secret du roi* now seemed about to be realized. An army of 40,000 was assembled on the Channel coast for the invasion of England, which was to be made possible by a union of the

French and Spanish fleets. As twenty-five years later, when Napoleon was waiting in his camp at Boulogne, the union of the fleets was not effected and the plan came to nothing. However, a body of 6,000 good troops under Rochambeau was conveyed to America to join La Fayette's volunteers, while the bailli de Suffren with a French squadron harassed the British in the East Indian seas. In 1781 a Franco-American army shut up the English general Cornwallis in Yorktown, while the French admiral de Grasse, who had defeated an English fleet under Hood, held the seas outside. Beleaguered by land, and cut off from reinforcements and supplies by sea, Cornwallis capitulated and the colonies were lost.

This was the high-water mark of French success in the war. Soon after, Great Britain recovered naval superiority with Rodney's victory over de Grasse at the battle of Saintes in the West Indies. Gibraltar, besieged by French and Spanish since 1779, was relieved in 1782, though Minorca was recaptured for Spain. It was clear that France could not hope to gain anything by a continuance of the war. A new ministry in Great Britain was prepared to recognize the independence of the colonies. Both French and American governments were now suspicious that the other would seek to conclude a separate peace at the expense of its ally, and after the customary complicated manœuvres peace was finally signed at Versailles in 1783. France regained the small islands of Saint-Pierre and Miquelon off the St Lawrence, Santa Lucia and Tobago in the West Indies, and Senegal and Goree in Africa. It was generally believed that the loss of the American colonies tolled the funeral knell of British greatness, and this was some consolation to France for the meagre results of a war which had entailed so much effort. No one as yet supposed that the price to be paid for American independence was a French revolution.

There were two reasons why this was to be so, the one theoretical and the other material. The second half of the eighteenth century was the period in which democratic ideology rose to influence in western countries. In the American colonies, Great Britain, Geneva, the Austrian Netherlands, Liège, and the Dutch Republic, ideas of democratic government were developing. Except in so far as similar ideas entered, however inappropriately, into the propaganda of the parlements, France had largely been immune from this new current of ideas, for to suppose that the *philosophes* were democrats is an illusion. Alliance with the Americans not merely exposed French society to democratic and republican ideas, but made them fashionable and respectable. Many of the young French nobles who left their wives or mistresses to fight for American independence returned with a new mistress, liberty. 'I was far from being the only one', wrote the young comte de Ségur, 'whose heart palpitated at the sound of the growing awakening of liberty, seeking to shake off the yoke of arbitrary power.'

The influence of the new ideas on French foreign policy was to be demonstrated even in Europe. Louis XVI was to find himself once again the ally of republicans before he became their victim. The Dutch had been led into the American War by their own republicans, the Patriot party. Though the results of the war had been disastrous for the United Provinces, the Patriots continued to control the government and to conduct a violent campaign against the Stadtholder, the Prince of Orange. Since the house of Orange was traditionally connected with England, the Patriots naturally looked to France for support. The association with the anti-Stadtholderian movement in the United Provinces, which was to bring France to the verge of war with Great Britain and Prussia in 1787, was not primarily the work of Vergennes, now in his last years and suffering from ill health, but rather of the chief secretary at the French Foreign Ministry, Rayneval, and the various agents sent by France into the United Provinces. Vergennes died before he could be involved in another war in alliance with republicans, as he had been led into the American War; and though the ministers for the Army and the Marine were prepared to take the plunge, there was one fact which prohibited a new adventure: by 1787, as a result of the American War, the royal treasury was practically bankrupt. The Dutch Patriots had to be left to their fate. But the impending bankruptcy was the second factor, which, though it prohibited another foreign adventure in support of republicanism, was to prepare the way for the coming of revolution in France.

CHAPTER FIVE

THE REVOLT
OF THE PRIVILEGED CLASSES

THE financial crisis was the second major consequence of the American War for France. From 1776 to 1781 the Genevan banker, Necker, who, having made a fortune for himself by shrewd speculation, had come to be regarded as a financial genius, was in charge of French finances. Short, stocky, heavy in appearance and pompous in manner, with an air of self-important benevolence, he seemed to have none of the qualities for success at Versailles. The real architect of his political career was the ambitious Mme Necker, the Suzanne Cuchod of Gibbon's early love, who with the aid of her husband's fortune and her own literary pretensions founded a philosophical salon in Paris. Necker himself played his part by writing an *Éloge de Colbert* and a volume attacking freedom of trade in corn. He thus made himself the spokesman of the opposition to Turgot, and when that minister fell a clever intrigue brought Necker to the notice of Maurepas. A friend of the *philosophes*, but sharing none of the dangerous new ideas of Turgot, enjoying a reputation as a deep thinker and at the same time as a practical man of business with the trust of the financiers and bankers, Necker seemed just the minister needed to restore confidence in royal finances. As he was a foreigner and a Protestant, he was only appointed assistant to the Controller-General, and subsequently Director-General, but he was the effective minister.

In a sense the confidence placed in Necker was justified. He introduced a few minor administrative reforms and made ineffective attempts to limit the extravagance of the queen and her friends. His great expertise, and the one thing he could do really well, was to borrow money. During the American War Necker's reputation, as a minister who could finance a war without new taxation, mounted to the skies. The sum of 530 million livres, which he acknowledged as the extent of his borrowings, was probably a considerable under-statement, and the interest on his loans was between 8 and 10 per cent. The total interest on the royal debt, which had been a modest 93 million in 1774 after the operations of Terray, had risen to over 300 million by 1789, and the responsibility was largely Necker's.

With the aid of skilful and intense propaganda he continued to swim on the crest of a wave of popularity, though in the later stages of the war his position in the government was weakening. To strengthen his hand Necker produced his master-stroke of propa-ganda, by publishing, against all precedent, his *Compte rendu* to the king of the finances of the nation. Preceded by a preamble, in Necker's usual inflated style, which played up to current prejudices and revealed the expansive soul of its author, the *Compte rendu* ex-hibited a happy financial situation, attributable to the wise manage-ment of Necker himself, by whose skill, in spite of war expenditure, the royal accounts had been balanced with a slight surplus on the credit side. For the *ancien régime*, in time of war, this was a miracle. It was also completely untrue, though the nation as a whole, and possibly even Necker himself, were taken in by his specious argu-ments and misleading figures. His enemies delivered a counter-blow by circulating copies of a secret memoir which Necker had pre-sented to the king in 1778, in which he had written of the parlements with considerable contempt. Their ensuing hostility made it im-possible for him to continue to raise new loans, and without these he was lost. Moreover, Maurepas was becoming jealous of the too popular minister.

At this point either Necker's vanity led him to put forward im-possible claims, or knowing that he was at the end of his financial tether, he deliberately set out to provoke his own dismissal. He proclaimed the need for reform and demanded in particular that the expenditure of the Ministries of War and Marine should be brought under the Contrôle Général. This was undoubtedly a much-needed reform, since the financial autonomy of the ministries was an im-portant contributory cause of the permanent deficit. Necker also demanded a seat in the Conseil d'en haut which took the final decisions on foreign policy. Maurepas was now able to go to the king with the threat that all the other ministers would resign if

Necker's claims were granted, and the king and Marie-Antoinette, who both still shared the popular faith in Necker, reluctantly yielded. In five years the Genevan wonder-worker had undone all the work of Terray and imposed on the royal finances a great new burden of debt at excessive rates of interest. What was worse, by his *Compte rendu* he had cut the ground from under the feet of any future Controller-General, for he had demonstrated, to all appearance, that royal finances, even in war-time, balanced and that there was therefore no need for economies or increased taxation. Finally, by linking his resignation with the rejection of proposals for reform he had established his position as a great reformer sacrificed to court intrigues. The Necker propaganda machine was not dismantled and in retirement he remained a power in the land.

The next two Controllers-General were only fleeting figures. The first tried to increase the taxes and to introduce economies. Naturally he fell before the combined wrath of the parlements and the court. The second came into conflict with the Farmers-General and was eliminated in less than a year by a revolt of the financiers. It is tempting to say that with the financiers a new power had appeared in the land, but the memory of the financiers of Louis XIV and of the Pâris brothers should be a corrective to this error. What is true is that the seventeen eighties witnessed one of those periods of speculative mania such as the regency had seen at the beginning of the century. Necker's policy of borrowing had at least made the fortune of a crowd of bankers, some French, a few Dutch or English, and many fellow-Genevans. Rival groups of financiers founded banks and companies, such as those for supplying Paris with water or, appropriately linked with these, for insurance against fire. The Company of the Indies took on a new speculative life. The power of the Press was discovered by those who were playing the market, and the writers they employed to spread false reports to raise or lower the value of shares included more than a few of the later revolutionary journalists, who thus served an apprenticeship to their trade. The king's ministers were brought into the unseemly scramble for profits as allies of this company or that, and what had begun as a struggle between two groups of financiers easily turned into one between two ministries. To safeguard or increase their profits the financiers began to play at politics as well as playing the market, the Swiss and Dutch bankers being in many cases already exiles from their native lands because of their democratic opinions. The American War and the subsequent outburst of speculation made the fortune of the financiers; Necker was their patron saint; his policy of borrowing supplied their life-blood. It was natural, taking all these factors into consideration, that they should have aligned themselves with the new democratic tendencies in France.

The fortunes that individuals were amassing did not help to remedy the increasing financial distress of the state. To cope with this, in 1783 a new and brilliant Controller-General was pushed into office by the favour of the king's younger brother, Artois, and the Polignacs. Calonne, formerly intendant of Lille, had undoubted qualities: incessantly active, fertile in expedients, possessed of personal charm, eloquence, and unlimited self-confidence, he was to fail in all he undertook with a regularity and a cleverness which would have brought success to half a dozen ordinary men who possessed also a modicum of judgment. However, the new Controller-General began by restoring confidence in the stability of royal finances, which had been lacking since the fall of Necker. He reassured the financial world by recognizing the sacredness of the royal debts and paying the interest on them promptly. He rewarded his supporters at court with large gifts and pensions from the funds of the Contrôle Général. He inaugurated an energetic programme of public works, including the great naval harbour at Cherbourg, destined not to be completed until the middle of the nineteenth century. With confidence thus restored, Calonne was able to resume the policy of borrowing, until by August 1786 he also had exhausted the market and could borrow no more.

Calonne was too intelligent to fail to see the need for a fundamental reform of royal finances, and too self-confident to fear to put it into effect when there was no other choice. He therefore now completely changed his tactics and presented the king with a plan for a general land-tax, to which there would be no exceptions, and for the creation of Provincial Assemblies to supervise its collection. Since there was no prospect of persuading the parlements to accept such a proposal, an Assembly of Notables was summoned to deal with them in February 1787. Calonne's belief that he could persuade an assembly of the privileged classes to accept his plans for taxing them is characteristic of that lack of political sense which he invariably exhibited. His chances were not increased by the fact that Necker and his friends had been conducting a virulent campaign against him. Nothing was wrong with the royal finances, they maintained, save the man who was mismanaging them; put Necker back into office and all difficulties would vanish. Inside the ministry, Calonne had a bitter enemy in the queen's favourite, Breteuil, who had managed to secure the support of the successor to Vergennes as Foreign Minister, the mediocre Montmorin. The struggle between Breteuil and Calonne was not decreased in virulence by the fact that they were involved with rival groups of speculators, who were using the ministers to promote their financial interests. Despite support from Artois, the Assembly of Notables rejected Calonne's plans. Exposed to the attacks of the privileged classes on one side and of the partisans of Necker on the other, he was dismissed, disgraced, exiled, and damned as a rogue whose malversations had brought the country to the verge of bankruptcy.

Under pressure from the queen, Louis now appointed to succeed Calonne the Archbishop of Toulouse, Loménie de Brienne; and to increase his authority made him head of the Council of Finances with a Controller-General under him. Soon after, the title of *principal ministre* was revived for Brienne. The Ministers for War and the Marine at once resigned, the former, Ségur, declaring that he was accustomed to do his business direct with the king and not be subject to the authority of any other minister. Once again, after more than forty years, France had a chief minister with the full confidence of the queen, if not of the king. Were the prosperous days of Fleury to be renewed?

As Archbishop of Toulouse, Brienne had presided successfully over the Estates of Languedoc and acquired a reputation as an able administrator. He was an advanced thinker, for a bishop almost too advanced. A distant relation of Mme du Deffand, he had attended her salon and been elected to the Academy with the support of the party of the *philosophes*. He had inspired the movement for the reform of the regular orders, was generous with permits for the use of meat in Lent, forbade burials in churches on sanitary grounds, established free courses for midwives, and bestowed a great library on the city of Toulouse. Evidently he was an enlightened man. He took his religious duties lightly, in spite of which he made great efforts while he was minister to obtain elevation to the rank of cardinal. A friend described him to Mme du Deffand as good-natured, indulgent, gay, easy-going, *insouciant*. He hardly strikes one as possessed of the character needed to push through a great reform, and nothing short of this could now meet the situation. Nor did his team of ministers inspire confidence. At the Contrôle Général under him was an old lawyer, honest but without any financial expertise to supplement Brienne's own deficiencies in this respect. Brienne's incompetent brother was placed in the Ministry of War. At the Ministry of the Marine a former ambassador, La Luzerne, and at Foreign Affairs Montmorin, were already turning their eyes towards Necker, still the popular hero. Breteuil, unwilling to submit to Brienne's predominance, followed Ségur and Castries in resigning and was replaced at the Ministry of the Maison du Roi by a mediocrity. Only the Keeper of the Seals, Lamoignon, had intelligence and firmness of character.

The new principal minister, having played his part among the Notables in opposing his predecessor's plans and bringing about his fall, in office could think of nothing better than to adopt Calonne's proposals practically *en bloc*. Naturally the Notables resumed their opposition, and since obviously nothing more was to be expected from them they were dissolved in May 1787. Brienne now reverted to the normal procedure, of which Calonne had seen the hopelessness, of presenting his edicts for registration by the parlements.

The sovereign courts, as they were called, were by now far more than the constitutional nuisance they had been earlier in the century, and their claims were far-reaching. Earlier they had based their powers on historic rights; as the representatives of the ancient *curia regis* they had claimed to be the guardians of the fundamental law of the kingdom. About the middle of the century they borrowed the idea of 'corps intermédiaires' from Montesquieu and conceived of themselves as the intermediary power between the people and the king. The provincial parlements, from 1755 onwards, asserted their solidarity with the parlement of Paris and kept pace with it in the extravagance of their claims. In the Grand Remonstrances of 1753, which drew the conclusion to the defeat of Machault's financial reforms, the parlement of Paris spoke of 'a kind of contract' between the king and the nation, of which it claimed to be the guardian.

As the century progresses the influence of the contractual school of thought, deriving from Locke, becomes increasingly evident in the literature of the parlements. An anthology of democratic doctrine could be collected from their later Remonstrances. 'It is the essence of a law to be accepted. The right of acceptance is the right of the nation', declared the parlement of Rouen in 1760. Fundamental laws are 'the expression of the general will', it said in 1771. The words 'subjects' and 'people' were being replaced by 'nation' in the language of the parlements. The law, declared the parlement of Toulouse in 1763, depends on 'the free consent of the nation'. By 1788 the parlement of Rennes was proclaiming 'that man is born free, that originally men are equal, these are truths that have no need of proof', and that 'One of the first conditions of society is that particular wills should always yield to the general will.' At the same time, though the parlements claimed to represent the nation, they also called for the revival of the old provincial Estates. 'Give us back', pleaded the parlement of Rouen in 1759, 'our precious liberty; give us back our Estates.' As early as 1763 the Cour des Aides at Paris, through the pen of its president, Malesherbes, had called for a meeting of the States-General.

The Remonstrances and pamphlets in which such ideas were expressed, along with attacks, often in violent and emotional language, on the king's ministers, had wide circulation. Of the Grand Remonstrances of 1753 more than 20,000 copies were sold within a few weeks. One of the constitutional monarchists asked later, 'Who accustomed the people to illegal assemblies and to resistance?' and answered, 'The parlements.' In 1787 their popularity was such that they seemed to be in a position to dictate their will to the king. When Brienne presented his proposals for new taxation they rejected them with contumely and demanded the calling of the States-General. After the edicts had been registered in *lit de justice*, the parlements declared the registration null and void. Amid mounting popular excitement they were exiled to Troyes in August 1787. Brienne, still attempting conciliation, sent agents after them to try to win over individuals by bribes and promises, and even offered the dismissal of Lamoignon, who was known to favour stronger measures. On the promise of the withdrawal of the edicts, the parlement returned to Paris in November and consented to register further royal loans on condition that the States-General was summoned. But the ministry and even the more moderate members of the parlement were becoming alarmed at the popular clamour that the agitation had aroused, and it was agreed that the States-General should only meet after several years' delay. However, the proposed loan proved too large and the delay too long for the parlements, and the agreement was almost at once broken.

From its return in November 1787, to May 1788, the parlement harassed the ministry with protests and remonstrances, and the provincial parlements joined in the hunt. The weakness of government at the centre was reflected in the *généralités* by the intendants who, apart from the fact that, being nobles themselves as well as royal officials, their loyalties were divided, dared not take strong measures, which were only too likely to be disavowed at Versailles, against the local parlements. To add to the financial distress of the Crown, the collection of taxes was beginning to break down. Even the loyalty of the army, under its noble officers, was in doubt. The Keeper of the Seals, Lamoignon, the only man with any strength of character in the ministry, now forced Brienne's hand. At last a minister of Louis XVI had been brought to realize that there was only one way out of the impasse, and that the way of Maupeou. Two of the wildest of the *parlementaires* were arrested, and on May 8th, 1788 the parlements were suspended, forty-seven new courts being created to take their place. A plenary court, nominated by the king, was entrusted with the duty of registering royal edicts. At the same time a number of legal reforms which the parlements had hitherto blocked were passed into law. The parlements had now the choice between submission and open resistance. Conscious of the strong forces that supported them, they chose the latter. What were these forces?

In the first place, they had the backing of the Church. The

Assembly of the Clergy, invited to vote a *don gratuit*, drew up Remonstrances in its turn, protested against the suspension of the parlements, and insisted on the immunity of clerical property from taxation. Then the dukes and peers of France associated themselves, by a collective letter, with the protests of the parlements. The duc d'Orléans, representative of the next line in succession to the throne after the Bourbons, had put himself forward as a spokesman for the parlements in November 1787 and been exiled to a château in the country for his pains, but an agitation was continued in Paris by a little mercenary Orleanist faction which saw the possibility of greatness descending, even on such scabrous shoulders, if the difficulties of Louis XVI became insuperable.

The *noblesse*, in former times the enemies of the magistrature, now made common cause with it in defence of their financial privileges, which they needed all the more because of the debts which their gaming, their extravagant mode of life, and the passion for building had piled on them. Indebtedness had almost acquired a prestige value: he who owes two millions, it was said, is obviously twice as great a noble as he who only owes one. They too had learnt to nourish aspirations for provincial self-government. Following on largely abortive attempts by Necker and Calonne, in 1787 Loménie de Brienne had established a system of Provincial Assemblies; but these were intended to facilitate royal administration, not to put authority into the hands of the *noblesse*, who were demanding not these limited assemblies but full-blown Provincial Estates. The *parlementaires* were long practised in the art of stirring up popular disturbances through the lesser world of *avocats*, clerks, and ushers who depended on them for their livelihood. Seconded by the *noblesse*, they organized riots in the provincial capitals, at Bordeaux, Dijon, Pau, Toulouse; in two provinces, Brittany and Dauphiné, the disturbances went beyond mere rioting. At Rennes the intendant and the commandant were attacked in the streets and besieged in the latter's town house. The poverty-stricken nobles with whom Brittany swarmed organized seditious assemblies and prepared for battle against the royal troops. At Grenoble the parlement remonstrated against the royal edicts. Exiled by royal order, it refused to obey, and, supported by the *noblesse* of Dauphiné and the people of

Grenoble, organized a revolt which sacked the house of the commandant and took control of the city by force. Representatives of the *noblesse* and of the towns illegally convoked the Estates of Dauphiné for the first time since 1628.

Before this nation-wide revolution of the privileged classes the king capitulated; for it was a confession of defeat when, on August 8th, the States-General were summoned to meet on May 1st, 1789. The situation was desperate and Brienne patently unequal to it. He resigned, to be followed shortly by Lamoignon, and on August 25th the king called Necker back to office. The exposure of the falsity of the *Compte rendu*, and the intrigues of Necker and his partisans against subsequent ministers, had destroyed the king's trust in the Genevan banker; but the nation looked to him as a saviour. He was, indeed, indispensable. The treasury was empty and payments had been suspended, while the privileged classes were in open revolt. Necker's reappointment solved, if only momentarily, both difficulties. His earlier record reassured the privileged classes — had he not proved that it was possible to meet the needs of the state without fresh taxation? — and the confidence that the financial classes had in him enabled the government to raise a loan. He knew his power and insisted on the rank of Director-General of Finances and Minister of State: the other ministers were nonentities. 'At last', commented Mirabeau, 'M. Necker is king of France.' If he was, he knew as little what to do with his power as the real king. He had no policy but to wait for the States-General somehow miraculously to cure the ills of the nation. Meanwhile, the order for the recall of the parlements was issued and a second Assembly of Notables was summoned to give advice on the manner of convocation of the States-General. For long enough the privileged classes had sown the wind: they were now about to reap the whirlwind.

On September 23rd, 1788, the parlement made its triumphal re-entry into Paris, amid the plaudits of the crowd, the ringing of bells, and firing of cannon. On September 25th it registered the declaration convoking the States-General, with the instruction that they should be composed in the manner observed the last time they had met. This was in 1614, but legal memories were long. It was a fatal move. There was an outburst of indignation. The falsity of the propaganda of the parlements was at last revealed. By 'the nation' they had all along meant themselves, but there was another nation, outside the ranks of the privileged classes, which would not be content with a National Assembly in which its representatives were restricted to one-third of the membership, and were always in a minority of one to two when the three Orders voted. The Third Estate, suddenly and dramatically, appeared on the scene. The eighteenth century had seen a great increase in its numbers and wealth. The royal bureaucracy, with its host of minor juridico-administrative officers, the professional civil servants of the great ministries, the crowds of lawyers, the doctors, surgeons, chemists, engineers, lower army officers, artists, writers, bankers, merchants and their clerks — all these formed a social nexus which provided the men who did most of the work of government as well as of the professions, but who were kept out of the highest offices by lack of *noblesse* or at least of the entry to the court, and humiliated socially by the thought that they belonged to a lower caste. For a generation they had supported the demands of the parlements for the recognition of the rights of the people, because they took the people to be themselves. Towards the manual workers of the towns and the tillers of the soil in the countryside, of course, their attitude was very much that of the privileged Orders towards themselves: the masses did not exist for them except as supporters of their natural leaders of the educated middle classes.

The declaration of the parlement of Paris on September 25th produced a rapid intensification of the debate which was being conducted in a vigorous pamphlet literature, and a change in its tone. It has been calculated that for the next six weeks new pamphlets appeared at the rate of twenty-five a week, and the main target was the privileged Orders. Memorials and petitions poured out demanding double representation for the Third Estate and voting by head instead of by Order. Though sudden changes are admitted in practical affairs, there is a tendency to regard movements in ideas as only taking place slowly, by the process of a gradual evolution. This is not necessarily so. In a period of intense political excitement the development of new political attitudes may be catastrophic in its suddenness. Such a period was that from 1788 to 1794. The few weeks after September 25th, 1788, witnessed the most revolutionary change of all. The Third Estate, which had been faithfully seconding the struggle of the privileged classes against royal despotism, suddenly discovered that its supposed allies were its enemies. The cause of the nation, which had hitherto been the war-cry of the parlements, was taken over by the Third Estate, and the advocates of its claims annexed the title of Patriots. Whether there was any organized control of their activities has been much debated. The alleged Masonic plot can be left where it belongs in the realm of legend. The Orleanist conspiracy has a little more substance. The duc d'Orléans certainly had his hireling faction, centred on the Palais Royal. He was quite prepared to be a Patriot king if Louis XVI could be eliminated, and would shrink from no means, however despicable, of achieving his ambition. But at most the Orleanist faction exercised a localized and minor influence. There was also the famous and mysterious Society of Thirty, which included leading members of the liberal *noblesse* such as La Fayette, Condorcet, La Rochefoucauld-Liancourt, and the Bishop of Autun, better known as Talleyrand, and was attended also by the abbé Sieyes, who had made a name for himself by writing the most popular of all pamphlets against privileges, 'Qu'est-ce que le Tiers État?', and by Mirabeau. It met at the house of Adrien Duport, a young *parlementaire* who had thrown in his lot with the Patriots of the Third Estate. Many of its members had formerly advocated the cause of the American Revolution. There are no grounds, however, for attributing a decisive influence to the Society of Thirty: it was a symptom, not a cause, of a nationwide movement.

The first objective of this movement was double representation of the Third Estate. When, on December 27th, 1788, the royal council met to decide this question, Necker, faithful to his policy of never doing anything that might harm his popularity, proposed the doubling of the Third Estate. The Keeper of the Seals, who alone opposed the proposal, wrote that Necker's argument was that the royal authority had everything to fear from the two higher Orders and everything to gain by allying itself with the people. This was, indeed, the way in which the declaration in favour of doubling the representation of the Third Estate was interpreted in the country:

the king, it was believed, had thrown in his lot with the people. He became overnight a popular idol. Assemblies of nobles in the provinces issued protests, in Brittany *noblesse* and Patriots came into armed conflict; but Necker and the council, with the acquiescence of the king, had by a stroke of the pen defeated the revolution of the privileged classes. A new and great weight had been thrown into the balance: at the very moment when the parlements and the *noblesse* thought themselves victorious, a new revolution, which was directed against them, had already begun.

CHAPTER SIX

VICTORY OF THE THIRD ESTATE

I T is natural to feel a disinclination to attribute great events to petty causes. The changes in French society and the revolution in ideas were perhaps bound to find their reflection in political and institutional developments sooner or later; but this is not equivalent to saying that the French Revolution was inevitable. What form the impending social and political changes were to take, and when they were to come about, and how, were matters to be decided by circumstance. The Revolution was not a Niagara in the stream of national life, its incidence and situation determined by the presence of a single great fault in the social strata: it was rather the result of the confluence of a host of contributory currents, small and great, flowing together to swell suddenly into a mighty flood. Changes in the structure of French society and government might have been imposed from above, or they might have been the result of a gradual evolution. In so much as it happened, a revolution was doubtless inevitable and this was necessarily the revolution that actually occurred. But to understand the way in which it came about, the end of the *ancien régime* must be studied almost on a day-to-day time-scale and in relation to the lesser as well as the greater forces: and since all these influenced the course of the Revolution, they also played their part in determining the society that should emerge from it.

The most realistic contemporary analysis of the factors which made the Revolution possible was that of Robespierre.

In states constituted as are nearly all the countries of Europe, there are three powers: the monarchy, the aristocracy and the people, and the people is powerless. Under such circumstances a revolution can break out only as the result of a gradual process. It begins with the nobles, the clergy, the wealthy, whom the people supports when its interests coincide with theirs in resistance to the dominant power, that of the monarchy. Thus it was that in France the judiciary, the nobles, the clergy, the rich, gave the original impulse to the revolution. The people appeared on the scene only later. Those who gave the first impulse have long since repented, or at least wished to stop the revolution when they saw that the people might recover its sovereignty. But it was they who started it. Without their resistance, and their mistaken calculations, the nation would still be under the yoke of despotism.

The calling of the States-General was undoubtedly the critical step, for it meant the abdication of absolute monarchy. It was made necessary, as has been shown, by the financial difficulties, which were in essence the result of the resistance of the privileged classes throughout the century to the attempts of the king's ministers to introduce financial reforms. Without the parlements to act as the point of crystallization it is doubtful whether the *noblesse* and clergy could have made their resistance effective: the restoration of the parlements in 1774 was therefore the fatal moment for the monarchy. A far stronger king than Louis XVI would have been needed to crush the opposition of the privileged classes, which steadily grew during the next fifteen years, now spreading underground like a heath fire, now bursting into flames on the surface. Only when royal authority had been weakened, and the king humiliated and forced to refer the problem of governing France to an elected assembly, did the Third Estate enter into the struggle in its own right, put forward its own claims, and in so doing transform what had been an aristocratic Fronde into a revolution of a new kind, such as Europe had not witnessed before.

The parlements, *noblesse*, and upper clergy had certainly not desired or expected their revolt to be taken over and diverted to its own ends by the Third Estate. In its turn, the Third Estate also was to find that it had started something that it could not easily stop. As the forces of revolution swept onward in a destructive torrent, overwhelming faction after faction which, while it was riding on the crest of the wave, imagined it was leading and controlling the onward rush, it seemed to those who were being swallowed up by the advancing tide that some hidden hand must be at work; and so in a sense there was, but it was not the secret societies or the plots and conspiracies of legendary history. The hidden force at work, which provided a continual supply of inflammable material to feed the fire of revolution, was one which the eighteenth century, with its belief in the power of government and its predominantly political out-look, did not recognize, though it was plain enough to see. It was simply the supply and the price of food, which meant primarily bread, or grain of which bread could be made, for bread was truly the staff of life: it constituted the major element in the cost of living of every poor family, that is, of between three-quarters and four-fifths of the population of France. When other foods were unobtain-able there was scarcity, only when bread was lacking was there famine.

Here is the hidden factor which explains why parlements, nobles, and Third Estate were in turn able to promote and profit by the revolutionary movement. If a chart of popular disturbances during the eighteenth century is drawn up, it will be found that they coincide fairly closely with periods of high bread prices. It seems probable that, while the condition of the people improved consider-ably in the first few decades after 1715, subsequently there was a drastic deterioration. I have suggested above that the main cause of this was the pressure of a growing population on an economy which, if developing rapidly in some sectors, in the essential productivity of agriculture and industry was progressing only slowly. The reign of Louis XVI was marked by a general economic regression, but French economy being so largely an agrarian one, the ultimate catastrophe occurred when, after a period of economic deterioration, there came the disastrous harvest of 1788. The worst time after a bad harvest was always the summer following, when the produce of the previous year's harvest was exhausted and the new harvest had not yet been brought in. The point of maximum distress was thus timed, as though by an unkind fate, to coincide with the open-ing sessions of the States-General.

Disturbances were spreading all over France in the spring of 1789. They were too widespread and disorganized to be regarded as other than a spontaneous expression of popular distress. From intendant after intendant, during April and May, were flooding in reports of bread and grain riots. These were particularly liable to break out when stocks of grain were being moved about the country, and of course the greater the shortage the more grain was liable to appear in transport, as towns and provinces tried to protect themselves from starvation by buying it wherever a supply could be found. Since the cheapest form of carriage for a bulk article, and indeed the main form of transport in the eighteenth century for anything, was by water, much grain was seen travelling down the rivers and canals or round the coasts. From this arose a popular belief that it was being exported to create an artificial shortage and so increase the profits of monopolists. Who were the villains of the piece was not quite clear, but it was evidently a plot to starve the people for the advantage of speculators. The owners of seigneurial rights, who were still taking their share of the diminished harvest and selling it at greatly enhanced prices, naturally did not gain in popularity. Finally, as well as attacks on convoys of grain, and an intensification of hostility to the seigneurial regime, there arose a nation-wide demand for the fixing of maximum prices, involving violent demonstrations against the local authorities, who were responsible for price control. The lower strata of the rural population, which had little or no land, provided recruits for bands of half-beggars half-brigands who terrorized the countryside. The reliance of many in the country on domestic industry, which normally helped them to make ends meet, now merely aggravated the distress, for bad harvests involved a general slackening of economic activity and so a great decline in the demand for industrial goods. Starving country workers fled to the towns to swell the ranks of the urban unemployed. From 1787 to 1789 there is evidence that unemployment in French industry rose to a general level of 50 per cent.

That the economic crisis was intense cannot be doubted, though it must not be exaggerated: we do not read of people starving to death. In 1789 there was a distressed but not a dying population. The great famine of 1709–10 seems in fact to have been the last in which there was a large death-rate directly from starvation. Was the change due to improved facilities for the transport of food, or — as is more likely — to the development of governmental efforts to provide food for the people in time of shortage? The correspondence of the intendants bears witness to the frantic efforts they were making to provision the distressed populations of their *généralités* and to the humanitarian spirit that had grown up in the course of the eighteenth century. The dangerous factor was the coincidence of food shortage with a period of intense political agitation: the distress of the masses made them malleable material for successive opposition groups. The bands of mountaineers who invaded Pau in June 1788 in support of the nobles and the parlement had been told that the king intended to impose new and yet heavier taxes on them. The legend of the 'pacte de famine', which the parlements and *noblesse* had employed against Louis XV and Maupeou, was renewed against Louis XVI. Popular agitation was intensified and kept at fever heat by the continuation of economic difficulties at a time when all France was being summoned to elect its representatives to the States-General.

The opinions that found expression in political form were, of course, not those of the most distressed sections of the population. The opposition of the privileged Orders to the doubling of the representation of the Third Estate released the latter from its alliance with the privileged classes and enabled it to put forward its own programme; the drawing up of *cahiers* in the countryside opened the door to the expression of the grievances of the peasantry; but in neither town nor country did the masses of the population have much opportunity for the statement of their views, even if they had been coherent and articulate enough for expression. The *cahiers* of the towns put forward the claims of the well-to-do middle classes, and the parish *cahiers* those of the *laboureurs*, the better-off farmers. Summarizing the *cahiers* very briefly and inadequately, we may say that the bourgeois in the towns demanded equality of status with the privileged classes, and the peasants in the country freedom from seigneurial dues, relaxation of royal taxation, both direct and indirect, the re-diverting of the tithe to its proper purposes, and the ending of what was seen as a general exploitation of the country by the town. There is much more in the *cahiers* than this, but only a lengthy discussion could do justice to the many problems involved in their interpretation. However limited their scope, discounting local peculiarities, such as protests from Lorraine against the bad breath of sheep being allowed to infect the pastures, against the growing of potatoes, which was said to spread diseases in the arable land, against *cabarets* which led the poor into dissipation, or against the introduction of textile machinery which robbed them of work, and some of the more abstract clauses, a programme could have been compiled from the *cahiers* of the Third Estate which would have made a practicable and effective scheme of royal reform. The monarchy might conceivably have been saved if some such programme had been put forward in the first place by the government. Necker, pressed to take the initiative, gave as the excuse for his inaction the resistance that such a programme would provoke from the nobles and the clergy. He was, after all, only a clever banker, and statesmanship could not be expected of him; but to suppose that an initiative was psychologically possible for the king and his ministers would be to forget both the persons concerned and the repeated humiliations inflicted on royal authority by the privileged Orders in the course of the previous fifty years. In any case, an inert king, with a weak ministry, was not capable of striking out an independent line in opposition to the court, for which the interests of the privileged Orders were paramount.

The drawing up of the *cahiers* and the choice of representatives thus went on with no control or guidance from above. The elections were an appeal to a France which the court never knew, the France of quiet market towns and small provincial capitals, of secluded manor-houses, modest vicarages, humble farms. Versailles, which had for so long been the voice of France, found that in the decisive hour France could speak for itself and choose its own representatives. Naturally, the elections being held in the provinces, it was men from the provinces who were chosen to be sent to represent them at Versailles. Paris was to reassert its supremacy in due course, but in 1789, for a short moment, the provinces had their hour. To the Second Estate, few of the court nobility were elected but many of the provincial *noblesse*, with rare exceptions bringing with them no contribution to the counsels of the state but their intransigent determination to defend their ancestral rights and their declining fortunes, so closely bound up with their privileges. For the First Estate, the lower clergy, aided by the system of election to their Order, sent to Versailles some 200 parish priests out of 300 representatives: for the first time the ideas of Richerism on the government of the Church seemed within reach of achieving practical expression. The Third Estate, also, elected almost exclusively local men. These were, to the extent of over 40 per cent, the holders of minor offices in the juridico-administrative system of local justice and government. Lawyers, most of whom would have aspired to a similar office when they had acquired or inherited sufficient capital to purchase one, constituted one-fourth of the Assembly, and other professional men another 5 per cent; the world of commerce, finance, and industry was only represented by some 13 per cent of the deputies. Despite the overwhelmingly rural nature of the electorate, at most only 7–9 per cent of those chosen were agriculturists.

On May 4th, 1789, the States-General met at Versailles and went in procession to hear Mass at the church of Saint-Louis. The next day they held their opening session. The order of proceedings, and even the garb of the participants, had been laid down by the court master of ceremonies with due regard to precedents. As these dated at latest from 1614, it is not to be wondered at if the Third Estate was somewhat restive at regulations which instructed them to be attired in their customary suits of solemn black, to keep their hats off when the nobles and clergy followed the king in donning theirs, to be received by the king in a different manner and room from those prescribed for the first two Orders, and to enter the Assembly by a side door after the clergy and nobles had walked in by the front. Besides this, the royal officials in charge of the proceedings, accustomed to dealing with the intimate etiquette of the court, were overwhelmed when they had to organize a mob of over a thousand provincials. At the opening session of the States-General there was considerable confusion, long delays, and when the voice of authority spoke, in the person of the Keeper of the Seals, it was largely inaudible. Necker, and, after his voice also gave way, a substitute, then droned on for more than three hours in a speech full of complicated financial explanations. He called on the privileged Orders to give up their exemptions from taxation, but made explicit the royal capitulation to the aristocratic revolution by leaving it to the three Orders to decide separately on which subjects they would be prepared to deliberate and vote in common.

The Third Estate, which had flocked to Versailles full of enthusiasm, expecting and prepared to follow a strong royal lead, was profoundly disillusioned. On what it rightly regarded as the crucial issue the king had come down on the side of the privileged Orders. Only a union of the Orders would give the Third Estate — the nation as it regarded itself and as Sieyes and other pamphleteers had taught it to believe — a majority and the possibility of passing the reforms it desired. This, then, became the first object of the Third Estate, and the tactic it adopted to secure its end was one of passive resistance; it refused to take any other step until its demands in this respect had been satisfied. At the same time it appealed to the king in the name of the 'natural alliance of Throne and People against the various aristocracies'. On June 17th, tired of waiting, it arrogated to itself the title of National Assembly, thus implicitly asserting its possession separately of all the powers of the States-General, almost implying that it was, as Sieyes had claimed, everything, and the other two Orders nothing. Moreover, the Third Estate had the advantage, on this question of the union of Orders, of being united, whereas the First and Second Estates were divided. Many of the lesser clergy sympathized far more with their brethren of the Third Estate than with their own aristocratic superiors, and a group of democratic curés was working hard to secure the adhesion of the clergy to the Third Estate. A small group of liberal nobles also was sympathetic, though the great majority of the *noblesse* had no intention of capitulating to the demand for union.

When it became patent that only the king could break the impasse it was decided to hold a joint session, though the royal council was too divided to have any settled idea as to what it proposed to do at this. On June 20th the large hall which the Third Estate used was closed to facilitate the alterations in accommodation necessary for the royal session. Through a misunderstanding the members had not been informed, and when they found a detachment of troops occupying the building it seemed to them that their Assembly was being dissolved by force. Gathered in an indignant mob in pouring rain outside the closed doors, they followed their president, Bailly, the eminent astronomer who had taken liberty for his pole-star, to a neighbouring indoor tennis-court, the nearest large building that offered shelter. There, with only one open dissentient, they took the oath never to separate, and to meet wherever circumstances dictated, until the constitution of the kingdom and public regeneration had been established and consolidated. Two days later, their hall still being closed, they assembled in the church of Saint-Louis and were now joined by 149 members of the clergy.

The royal session was due to be held on June 23rd. Necker had at last resolved to do what should have been done at the outset and to present the States-General with a royal plan of reform. The strength of the opposition to this proposal in the royal council perhaps justified his belief that it would have stood no chance of acceptance earlier, but circumstances were even now hardly more favourable. The elder son of Louis XVI and Marie-Antoinette had died early in June. History does not pay much attention to private grief, but the consequences of this loss were far-reaching. The court went into retirement at Marly. There the king was surrounded and indoctrinated by courtiers, headed by his younger brother, Artois. The parlement of Paris, now belatedly converted to the cause of royal authority which it had done so much to undermine, sent secretly to the king to call for the dispersion of the Third Estate by force. The result was that at the royal council which drew up the final instructions for the royal session, although the form of Necker's proposals was retained, their substance was drastically altered. At the eleventh hour the aristocratic revolution reasserted itself. The declaration drawn up for the king to read embodied its maximum concessions and minimum demands. It was an aristocratic and not a royal programme.

Necker absented himself on June 23rd, when the three Orders assembled for the royal session amidst a considerable show of armed force, the Third Estate characteristically being kept waiting in the rain while the privileged Orders were being seated. The declaration of the king's intention that was read to the Assembly provided the ground plan for the conversion of France into a constitutional monarchy and suggestions for a whole range of important reforms; but the vital fact was that it promised the royal sanction for the

K

abolition of fiscal privileges only when the privileged Orders had agreed to this, and therefore presumably only on their own terms. The king was made to declare that the distinction of the three Orders should be preserved in its entirety and that the decisions of the Third Estate on June 17th were null and void. He ended by ordering the Assembly to disperse and resume meetings in their separate chambers on the morrow.

If there were not so many fatal occasions in the Revolution one would be tempted to say that it was in the royal session that the monarchy sacrificed the possibility of alliance with the nation and bound its fate to that of the privileged Orders. In essence the royal session was the counter-revolution, and it had already come too late. On June 25th a group of liberal nobles followed the majority of the clergy in joining the Third Estate. Now there were some 130 clergy and 241 nobles sitting separately, and 170 clergy and 50 nobles who had joined the Third Estate. What caused the king to reverse his policy drastically and to issue instructions, on June 27th, for the privileged Orders to join the Third Estate, has never been made clear. Perhaps the rumour, which prevailed at the time, of 40,000 armed brigands who were said to be preparing to march on Versailles, is the nearest we shall ever get to an explanation. It receives support from the fact that orders were at the same time secretly issued calling up 20,000 troops from the provinces. The Janus deity of fear, with its other face of terror, was already unveiled: it was to preside over the destinies of the Revolution from beginning to end. Unwillingly, in obedience to the king's instructions, the recalcitrant nobles and clergy entered the Assembly, in a deathly silence, on June 30th. The Third Estate had won its first battle. That night Versailles was illuminated. Crowds paraded in front of the palace shouting '*Vive le Roi!*' '*Vive Monsieur Necker!*' The king and queen appeared with their children on the balcony, but it was observed that the queen was in tears.

The court, however, had merely postponed the struggle. As troops steadily poured into the neighbourhood of Paris and Versailles, under the command of the Marshal de Broglie, it felt strong enough to show its hand. On July 11th Necker and his supporters in the council were dismissed and Necker himself was ordered to leave the country. The queen's favourite, Breteuil, was brought back to lead a government which would put an end, it was hoped once and for all, to this nonsense of the Third Estate. The constitutional struggle was about to turn into a civil war.

It would be tempting to declare that the court now took the initiative in an appeal to force, as the privileged classes already had in the disturbances of 1787 and 1788; but we could only say this by averting our gaze from what had been happening all over France in the course of 1789. The aristocratic Fronde had weakened or destroyed royal authority everywhere, and the power to keep a distressed populace under control no longer existed. In town and country disturbances were endemic. Paris itself was becoming ungovernable. In April the rumour, an untrue one, that a wallpaper manufacturer named Réveillon had advocated a reduction in wages, started a riot which burnt down and pillaged his house, and was only repressed with much bloodshed. What was very odd was that Réveillon was well known for his good treatment of his own workers, none of whom took part in the affair. In July mobs attacked and burnt the customs posts surrounding Paris, which were a natural object of hatred to a starving population; but there is a curious report that two posts belonging to the Duke of Orleans were spared. Both at the time and subsequently such popular movements have been attributed to the machinations of enemies of the regime, particularly to the agitation of Orleanist agents. In the absence of proof all one can say is that on the one hand Orleans and his agents were certainly fishing in troubled waters, and on the other that the misery of the populace was quite sufficient to explain outbursts of violence without hypothesizing the operations of any hidden hand behind the scenes. The alleged, and probably exaggerated, Orleanist plot was provided with some semblance of plausibility by the fact that the gardens of the Palais Royal, which had been commercialized and turned into a popular pleasure resort, with shops, cafés, and entertainments, had become a centre for democratic agitators. Some were doubtless in the pay of Orleans, but his resources were limited and certainly not equal to starting the widespread agitation that developed.

There was ample reason in the second week of July for the Third Estate to feel itself threatened. The dismissal of Necker, still the idol of the people, and the concentration of troops, largely foreign, near Paris, were evidence of an impending military coup. Orators at the Palais Royal called the people to arms. Mobs formed daily, in an increasingly feverish political atmosphere, ready to defend liberty and their lives against the threatened military dictatorship. But where could they obtain arms, for weapons were expensive and few private individuals outside the ranks of the *noblesse* possessed them? The rioting crowds turned to the municipal authorities, who in face of the general disorder were helpless. Besieged in the Hôtel de Ville by a threatening mob, the Provost of Merchants, de Flesselles, could do nothing but try to divert them elsewhere, for example to the Invalides, which on the morning of July 14th was raided by a large mob seeking for arms.

Crowds were now surging everywhere about Paris, gathering round all public buildings, and not least before the Bastille, the frowning fortress whose guns were menacingly directed on the poor quarter of the faubourg Saint-Antoine which surrounded it. Rumour and pamphleteers had for years been disseminating a picture of its dungeons packed with wretched state prisoners. It was the obvious stronghold from which the royal troops would sally forth to commence their slaughter of the Parisians. It was in fact garrisoned by eighty Invalides and thirty Swiss. The mob before it sent a deputation to the Governor, de Launay, who promised not to fire unless attacked. The outer courts, which had been left unguarded, were filled by an agitated crowd. Across an unguarded drawbridge they penetrated to the inner court, and although they were still quite incapable of invading the fortress itself, the defenders in panic fired on them, with considerable slaughter, arousing among the besiegers a spirit of fury that could not easily be appeased. At this point a new factor came into play. A detachment of rebellious Gardes Françaises marched to the Bastille with five cannon they had taken from the Invalides. Under fire they got their guns into position and trained them on the main gate. The incompetent de Launay now lost his head metaphorically, in advance of losing it literally, and surrendered, with a promise of safe conduct for himself and his troops. As the garrison emerged some were seized by the infuriated crowds and slaughtered, and the rest hustled off to the comparative safety of prison. De Launay himself was struck down, and his head, cut off with a butcher's knife, paraded round Paris on a pike. The Provost of Merchants, for his efforts to prevent the arming of the populace, was seized by another mob at the Hôtel de Ville and suffered a similar fate. The prisoners who poured out of the dungeons of the Bastille consisted of four forgers, two lunatics, and a dissipated young noble. The people set about demolishing the fortress, but the task was taken over by professional housebreakers, who made a considerable profit out of the affair. The episode was a striking one, but the actual events have been greatly exaggerated by the romantic historians of the nineteenth century. Only some 800 individuals were able to justify their claim to the title of 'Conquerors of the Bastille', and these were a mere handful of the agitated crowds who were ranging Paris. The significance of the fall of the Bastille lies in its symbolic value. The important fact was that the king had lost control of Paris and even with the troops called to Versailles had no prospect of regaining it.

In the face of the Parisian revolution, what would be the reaction of the new ministry? Fear had set the populace of the city in motion and now fear dictated the varying responses of the court. The revolt of the Gardes Françaises seemed to spell doom: even the foreign regiments were of doubtful loyalty. Breteuil counselled a withdrawal of the court to Compiègne and the restoration of order by military force; Artois and Condé supported him; but Louis XVI was not the man for strong decisions. Did he even yet appreciate the seriousness of the situation? On the day of the capture of the Bastille he returned late from the hunt and wrote in his diary, 'July 14th, nothing'. Suspicious of the ambitions of his brothers, and even more of those of Orleans, he hesitated, but sent to the Marshal de Broglie to ask if he could guarantee an escort to Metz. De Broglie was discouraging: he was not sure of his troops, he said. What subsequent policy, he asked, did the king propose to follow when he had reached Metz? To this there was no answer. Since he feared to leave, Louis had no choice but to submit. He dismissed Breteuil, recalled Necker, and on July 17th went with fifty deputies to the Hôtel de Ville of Paris to receive from the hands of Bailly the national cockade of red and blue, the colours of the city, with white for the house of Bourbon in between, symbol that Paris had reconquered its king.

Artois, generally regarded as the inspirer of the attempted military coup, Condé, the Polignacs, Breteuil, and their adherents, could no longer safely stay in France, denounced by pamphleteers and mob orators as enemies of the people. They fled across the frontier and the emigration had begun. In the next two months some 20,000 passports were delivered. The privileged classes had proved themselves, at the first test, incapable even of defending themselves. The falsity of their position was revealed when it appeared that the authority of the crown, which they had done so much to undermine, was the only bulwark for their own privileges. In the first two weeks of July the Third Estate, which they had ignored or treated as a dependent ally, had taken over the Revolution from them. It now had the burden of maintaining the state thrust upon it, along with the twin problems of reshaping French society and government after a pattern closer to its own interests and ideals. The door was wide open to reform: but the identity of the figure that was advancing through the door seemed somehow different, its shape and size uncertain and vaguely menacing.

PART THREE

THE DECADE OF REVOLUTION

CHAPTER ONE

THE RISING OF THE MASSES

THE revolt of Paris, in which culminated the nation-wide disturbances of 1789, and the general collapse of royal administration, confronted the members of the Third Estate with the problem of taking steps to protect property and restore some semblance of law and order to France. In their turn, like the privileged classes before them, they were to find that they had started something they could not stop, and that a movement which they had envisaged as one of moderate constitutional and social reform was to become a revolution of a very different nature and scope. Their response to the new challenge was dictated by circumstances. All through the Revolution we find that theory plays little part in determining policies, though it has played much in their subsequent interpretation. The actions of the revolutionaries were most often prescribed by the need to find practical solutions to immediate problems, using the resources at hand, not by preconceived theories.

The Parisian populace, which by its rising had frustrated the plans of the court and saved the Third Estate, was not moved solely by altruistic political emotion; it had its own grievance in the high price and shortage of bread. A week after the fall of the Bastille, Bertier de Sauvigny, intendant of Paris, and his father-in-law, Foulon, who were responsible for food supplies, were seized by a mob besieging the Hôtel de Ville and massacred. Their heads — it was an *ancien régime* custom — were stuck on the end of pikes. A man in the uniform of a dragoon, followed by a large crowd, pushed his way into the meeting of the municipal body with a chunk of bleeding flesh, saying, 'Here is the heart of Bertier.' When it was proposed to bring in the decapitated head also, messengers were sent out to inform the populace that the council was engaged on important business and preferred not to have the head of its former intendant on the agenda. The electors, who had been chosen in the first place as secondary electors for Paris to the States-General but had never dissolved, now constituted themselves the municipal authority, appointed Bailly, the eminent scientist, as mayor in place of the murdered Provost of Merchants, and took over such government as the city was capable of.

Events in Paris reflected those that had been taking place up and down the length and breadth of France. In some towns an understanding was reached between the old municipal authorities and the new revolutionary ones. Elsewhere revolutionary committees simply took control by main force. Before the changes were given legal sanction by the law on municipalities of December 14th, the municipal revolution was a *fait accompli* practically everywhere in France. The new authorities, however, required a means of restoring some degree of law and order. It was to their hand in the equally spontaneous growth of a citizen guard, which had been springing up everywhere for the dual purpose of protecting property from indiscriminate pillage and defending the Third Estate from suspected or real aristocratic plots. This also was given official recognition: it became the National Guard, and on the morrow of the fall of the Bastille the hero of the American expedition, La Fayette, was appointed to its command in Paris, which made him, as the royal army disintegrated, potentially the most powerful man in France.

Municipal authorities and National Guard represented the determination of the well-to-do Third Estate to take over the responsibility for government, local as well as national, that had fallen from the hands of the royal officials. In calling to its aid the people of Paris the Third Estate had let loose more dangerous forces than it realized, but it did not feel any strong remorse for the assassination of Bertier and Foulon. Was this blood, then, so pure, Barnave asked in the National Assembly, making himself, as so many others were to be, the apologist of terrorism before he became its victim. In the countryside, however, a different revolution had been taking place, and one which the Third Estate viewed in a very different light. If 1788 saw the last Fronde, 1789 saw the last jacquerie.

It must be frankly admitted that the history of eighteenth-century France as I have given it up to this point has been, apart from a few sentences, the history of one-tenth of the French people. Glacier-like, the rural masses of most nations before the nineteenth century remain anonymous and concealed, even from contemporaries, beneath the surface. That France was suffering from the effects of rural over-population I have already suggested, and equally that, short of a great increase in production, for which the conditions did not exist, there was no remedy for the consequent distress. The result was an increasingly bitter struggle for the diminishing slice of cake — or rather of bread — that remained to go round. Land hunger was its most obvious manifestation. By 1789 peasant proprietors owned perhaps one-third of the land of France, though, in ignorance of what proportion of the arable this included, and knowing something of the great variations from district to district, we must realize that such a statement tells us less than it seems to. Arthur Young, who continually complains that wherever there is the property of great nobles it is bound to be forest or waste, might have reflected that possibly this may have been because so much of the more cultivable land had already passed out of their possession. Round the towns the wealthy bourgeoisie and *noblesse de robe* had invested heavily in land, on which they put farmers, or *métayers* on a stock and land lease. The more prosperous peasants were also building up their properties with some success.

Short of confiscating the lands of the Church, and although this suggestion had been made earlier it was not a practical one before 1789, the only land that might still be thrown into the market was the common land of the village communities. A royal edict of 1767 established a procedure for the enclosure of these which was to the advantage of the possessors of seigneurial rights and the larger proprietors. There were, however, also complaints in the *cahiers* that enclosures gave patches of land to the poorer villagers and so made them less amenable as hired labour. The better-off peasant proprietors, the *laboureurs*, thought that they lost more than they gained by enclosure of the commons and therefore opposed it, with considerable success, for they exercised the strongest influence in the rural communities. The bitterest struggle in rural France during the last years of the *ancien régime* was between the peasant proprietors and the possessors of seigneurial rights.

The seigneur might be a noble or a bourgeois, he might even be a prosperous peasant, for seigneurial rights were no more than, to quote a legal treatise of the time, 'a bizarre form of property'. Such rights were the *banalités*, the compulsion to use the lord's mill, bakehouse, or winepress, the *cens* or quit-rents, a kind of perpetual ground rent, *péages* or tolls on road or river, the right of keeping pigeons or rabbits to feed on the peasants' crops. Innumerable local dues, in kind or money, were added to such more general ones. The seigneur himself in his court, through some petty local attorney appointed to act as his judge, adjudicated on disputes over his own rights. Appeals were to the parlements, which, as the magistrates were themselves large purchasers of seigneurial rights, had no doubts on which side the scales of justice should be tilted. Indeed, without the juridical backing of the parlements the whole system of seigneurial rights might have collapsed, for the royal officials had no interest in the maintenance of a system which removed income from those who were taxable into the hands of those who could not be taxed. In the course of the eighteenth century, perhaps partly owing to the purchase of seigneurial rights as a form of investment, they came to be exacted with increasing severity. A class of professional *feudistes* took over the task of drawing up and revising the *terriers* in which the dues were recorded, resurrecting long-forgotten claims from old manorial rolls. A skilful *feudiste*, working on a commission basis, could secure a greatly increased return to the seigneur, and — since the latter possessed all the documents — without much danger of the claims being disproved, though legal cases over them were endless.

Seigneurial dues were an anachronistic relic, a survival of feudal lordship which the peasant proprietors resented all the more because they were now the real owners of the land on which the dues were imposed; but the spirit of the push for increased seigneurial dues that was the main feature of the so-called 'feudal reaction' that preceded the Revolution was much more commercial than feudal. *Mainmorte*, retaining some of the features of personal servitude, and the *capitaineries*, or hunting rights in forest areas, were more truly feudal, but they were restricted in their incidence to certain areas. They were regarded as incompatible with the ideals of a century of enlightenment, and moreover non-nobles normally did not possess them, so they were generally condemned. On the other hand the Third Estate in the towns had little quarrel with the seigneurial dues. Their *cahiers* said little on the subject until they were faced with the demands of the peasants. Demands for the abolition of seigneurial dues were subsequently inserted in the more general *cahiers* of the Third Estate, though usually with a provision for compensation.

The deputies of the Third Estate evidently did not contemplate dealing in a hurry with a grievance which did not affect them personally. Moreover, seigneurial dues were a form of property. To denounce 'feudalism' in the abstract was all very well: to attack a widely owned property right was another matter. In fact the Third Estate did not launch the attack: the decision was taken out of its hands. Just as the parlements and *noblesse* found that they had started a movement among the bourgeois which went far beyond their own aims, so the bourgeois were to repeat the experience with the peasants. The bread riots of the spring and early summer of 1789 prepared the way for a general breakdown of social discipline in the countryside. Here and there, throughout France, abbeys and manor-houses were attacked, game was trapped illegally, the peasants ceased to pay their dues. The breakdown of royal authority in the towns intensified rural unrest. Belief in an aristocratic plot — and there were in fact little local aristocratic plots, apart from what was going on at Versailles — spread like wildfire. In the third week of July there were risings in the Norman *bocage*, in Franche-Comté, the Mâconnais, and Alsace.

Towards the end of July these sporadic risings were caught up in a different and more extensive movement which has come to be known as the Great Fear — a panic terror of brigands who were supposed to be descending on the peaceful villages of France. Over large areas the Great Fear raged like a forest fire. The legendary brigands were never clearly identified. In the north-east, where there had been the troubles of the Fronde, they were called the Mazarines, and in the centre 'la bande anglaise' — shades perhaps of the Black Prince and the White Company still surviving in the age-old peasant memory. The association of an aristocratic plot with the menace of rumoured brigands set a pattern that was to be repeated more than once in the Revolution. At the time of the September massacres it was the criminals of the Paris prisons who were expected to be let loose by the aristocrats on the wives and children of Patriots. Given the picture of the Revolution as a rising of the riff-raff of the towns and the landless proletariat of the country, such fears are meaningless. When it is realized that the revolutionary masses were not these, but rather the master craftsmen, shopkeepers and the like in the towns, and the peasant proprietors in the country, they become easily explicable.

The prosperous professional men and officials of the Third Estate, who had seized control of the Revolution from the privileged classes, had no intention of letting it slip from their hands, but the game they were playing, even if unconsciously, was a dangerous one. After the affair of the Bastille they regained control of Paris with the aid of the new municipal authorities and the National Guard. The countryside presented a more difficult problem. The peasants rarely attacked individuals, their objective was usually to burn the manorial rolls, overthrow enclosures and restore common lands, kill game, and 'have fires out of the Grand Duke's wood'. Regular troops and National Guards were sent out from the towns to repress such disturbances and protect property rights. Where effective action was possible the rioters were seized and, after trial before summary courts, hanged. In most areas, however, the authorities were powerless before the resistance of the peasantry. Unless something was done rapidly to remedy the situation, it was evident that it would soon be completely out of control. But from what quarter could a lead be given?

There was one more or less organized political body at Versailles. A group of deputies from Brittany had formed the plan of meeting daily in a café for the purpose of concerting their policy. They were joined by deputies from other provinces and by some who were not deputies. The Breton Club — only after it had followed the Assembly to Paris and hired a hall from the Jacobin convent in the rue Saint-Honoré was it to be known as the Jacobin Club — became a rallying point for the Patriots, as those who aimed to complete the victory of the Third Estate called themselves. It was probably in private discussions at the Breton Club that the conclusion was reached that only by swift and drastic concessions could peace be restored to the countryside, and that the only hope of passing the necessary laws was to take the National Assembly by surprise and rush them through in a night session. The duc d'Aiguillon, peer, commandant of the King's Light Horse, a great landowner and one of the liberal nobles who had led the secession to the Third Estate, was chosen to put the manœuvre into effect on the night of the fourth of August; but, perhaps because he had learnt of the scheme and saw a personal advantage in anticipating d'Aiguillon, the initiative was seized from him by another liberal noble, the vicomte de Noailles, nicknamed for his lack of lands 'Jean sans-terre' and therefore perhaps all the more ready to give away the property of others. D'Aiguillon followed him, and then a fury of renunciation swept the Assembly. The privileges of nobles, tithe-holders, provincial Estates, cities, corporations, were hurled on the bonfire. At two o'clock in the morning, exhausted but triumphant after its orgy of self-sacrifice, the Assembly decreed a solemn *Te Deum* and adjourned.

Second thoughts brought a measure of repentance. The next week was spent in tidying up and whittling down the concessions of the night of the fourth of August. The Assembly had gone much farther than had perhaps originally been intended. An attempt was made, in drawing up the definitive legislation, to rescue what could be saved from the holocaust by inventing a distinction between those rights which were 'feudal' in origin, that is, derived from personal servitude, and those which were of the nature of property, derived from a contractual relationship. The former were to be abolished without compensation and the latter to be made redeemable. The distinction was a difficult one to draw in law and impossible in practice. The peasants simply disregarded their former obligations and stopped paying their dues, and no Assembly in Paris had any means of forcing them to do otherwise. When, finally, in July 1793, the Convention decreed the suppression of all remaining 'feudal rights' without compensation, this was merely the recognition of a *fait accompli*. The peasant proprietors won their victory in 1789. So far as they were concerned the Revolution was over: their role for the rest of its history was a purely passive one, except where, as in Brittany and the Vendée, they turned into active opponents.

For the National Assembly the unrest of the towns and the peasantry was a diversion from its proper task, which was to give France a new Constitution. Royal co-operation in this task was still less than half-hearted, and aristocratic opposition vigorous and vocal. The king, it was feared, had not drawn the necessary lesson from the fourteenth of July and the Patriots came to think that only another dose of the same medicine would make him fully amenable to their wishes. In Paris, popular agitators and journalists were keeping the people in a fever of political excitement with denunciations of aristocratic plots. Neither the respectable leaders of the Patriot party in the Assembly, nor the less respectable agitators in the streets, could have taken effective action, however, if it had not been for the continuing and even increasing economic distress of the populace. The incident which set fire to this inflammable material was so petty as to give ground for the suspicion that it was merely the occasion and not its cause.

On October 1st a dinner was held at Versailles for the officers of the Flanders Regiment newly arrived there. When the king and queen appeared to acknowledge their loyal acclamations, Blondel's song 'O Richard, O mon roi, l'univers t'abandonne', from Grétry's opera, was sung amid enthusiastic demonstrations. Nothing happened for four days, which is odd if this episode is to be regarded as the provocation which led to the October Days, but indeed the whole story of what did happen is an odd one. On October 5th women gathered before the Hôtel de Ville demanding bread: this was quite normal. Getting no satisfaction the cry was raised — by whom? — that they should make their way to Versailles to appeal to the king. Several thousands set out, gathering numbers as they went. It was a gloomy, wet, October day, hardly the best one for a spontaneous demonstration. Now, however, the tocsin was being rung through Paris, district assemblies were meeting, National Guards and others were gathering, especially before the Hôtel de Ville, where La Fayette, on horseback, was trying unavailingly to control the situation. The watchword still seemed to be to march on Versailles. At four o'clock in the afternoon the Municipal Council authorized

La Fayette to move off with the National Guard, and now there appeared for the first time a definite objective: the king was to be brought back to Paris. With a mixed body of National Guards and others, La Fayette set out. At Versailles Louis XVI, who as usual had been out hunting, returned in the afternoon, interviewed a deputation of the women who by now were congregated before the palace, and promised them a supply of bread for Paris. That evening

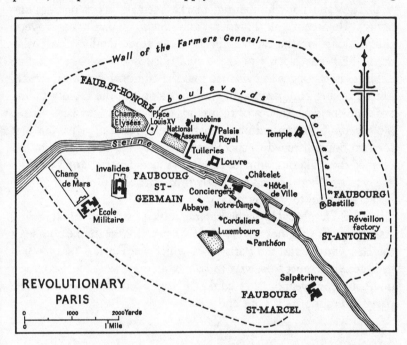

the main body of the Parisians arrived, settled down for the night as best they could or ranged about the streets of Versailles and the courts of the palace. At early dawn on the next day a few hundred of the demonstrators found a way into the palace, slaughtered some of the royal bodyguard whom they encountered and penetrated nearly to the queen's apartments before they were repulsed.

Morning saw serried masses in the courtyard before the palace, now with one cry, 'To Paris!' Was resistance to an armed mob of some 20,000 possible? It seems not to have been contemplated. The

L

idea of flight had again been urged on the king and queen, only to be rejected by them, perhaps for fear of leaving the throne vacant for Orleans, whose inspiration was suspected behind the march on Versailles. The only course left was to yield as graciously as possible in the circumstances. In the afternoon of October 6th the triumphal procession set out on the muddy march back to Paris: National Guards armed and royal bodyguard disarmed, wagons laden with corn and flour lumbering, market men and women straggling along, Regiment of Flanders and Swiss Guard, La Fayette riding alongside the carriage bearing the royal family, also beside them the heads of two of the Royal Guards on pikes, a hundred deputies in carriages as evidence that the National Assembly would keep the king company, and, trudging along in the rapidly failing twilight, the dark shapes of thousands of nameless Parisians. At ten o'clock on a gloomy autumnal night the royal family, having first for two hours listened to speeches before the Hôtel de Ville, at last reached the Tuileries, whence Louis XIV had departed for Versailles 118 years earlier, and camped down in hurriedly cleared rooms as best they could for the night.

In the October Days the capital took possession of king and Assembly. For the next five years Paris was to dictate the course of the Revolution, and the Paris mob, which the Patriots of 1789 had used for their purposes, was to prove, as they were to discover in due course, a weapon that could be employed by more than one party and to more than one end.

CHAPTER TWO

FRANCE UNDER THE
CONSTITUENT ASSEMBLY

IT is easy in retrospect to see the fatality of the situation that had been created by October 1789 and the price at which the Third Estate had bought its victory. At the time few appreciated the full implications of what had been done and none knew if the victory was final. For that reason the triangular conflict of monarchy, aristocratic reaction, and democratic revolution continued. The king, having lost the initiative from the beginning, was doomed henceforth passively to follow circumstances, always their victim and never their master. The opposition to the Revolution was to come not from the monarchy but from the aristocratic revolution, the leaders of which had taken flight and were already preparing to instigate a counter-revolution from abroad, having given up hope of successful resistance within France. Their belief was that it would be easy to reconquer their privileges by an invasion with the aid of foreign powers: what this might imply for Louis XVI and Marie-Antoinette did not much concern them. They followed from the beginning, therefore, a wrecking policy: the worse the excesses into which the Revolution fell, they thought, the sooner it would be over.

The Third Estate itself could not believe in the completeness of its victory. The Patriots continued to attack the Crown, though they had no practical alternative to royal government to propose. In spite of their suspicions, they could not rid themselves of the idea that government was the function of the king and his ministers. On the other hand, distrusting the court and the queen profoundly, they could not trust Louis XVI's ministers to govern. Obviously the result was to make all government impossible, but this practical consequence was only gradually to be revealed. Meanwhile the National Assembly, though it continually interfered with the administration through its committees, assumed that its task was not to rule but to draw up a constitution. It was literally a Constituent Assembly. Since this was the eighteenth century, the first step inevitably was to lay down general principles in the form of a Declaration of Rights, which was accepted by the Assembly on August 26th, 1789.

A whole book could be written — indeed books have been written — on the Declaration of Rights. Little need be said here about the confused debate over its origins. American precedents are obvious but not fundamental, for even without these the same intellectual influences which produced the American Declaration would have operated in France. What were these influences? Not the little-read and less-understood *Social Contract* of Rousseau, nor the writings of the *philosophes*, so little concerned with political theory. If a source in eighteenth-century France is looked for, it will be found in the Remonstrances of the parlements, and behind these in the ideas of the Natural Law school of thought, which provided the basic content of current political thinking. The Declaration begins with the assertion that men are free and equal in rights. This was not intended to eliminate social distinctions, but their justification henceforth was to be utility. The object was to abolish distinctions based on privilege, and break the monopoly still retained by the privileged Orders of the higher posts under the government, which was already a social anachronism. All careers are henceforth to be open to talent equally, but this is where equality stops. The right of property is recognized as natural, inalienable, sacred, and inviolable. Freedom from arbitrary arrest and imprisonment, freedom of opinion 'even religious', freedom from taxation without consent, are recognized as political rights. Law is the expression of the general will, by which is meant the will of a representative assembly, for the idea of the general will was common in eighteenth-century political thought and is not to be interpreted in the subtle philosophical sense given to the term by Rousseau.

The Declaration of Rights was the death-warrant of the system of privilege, and so of the *ancien régime*. In this respect it inaugurated a new age. Yet in the history of ideas it belonged rather to the past than to the future. The age of individual rights was not beginning but ending. The Declaration was the conclusion, not the commencement, of a great intellectual development, and is far from summing up the revolution in political ideas that the democratic movement of the later eighteenth century brought about. A shorter and often unnoticed decree of the Constituent Assembly, passed after the forcible removal of the king to Paris, tells us more. This decree changed the royal title from 'Louis, by the grace of God, King of France and Navarre' to 'Louis, by the grace of God and the constitutional law of the state, King of the French' — *roi des Français*. It was a recognition that divine-right monarchy belonged to the past. It was more than this: it meant that the state had ceased to be simply a territory, or collection of territories, under a single authority; it had become a people, a nation, and as the Declaration of Rights said, 'The source of all sovereignty resides essentially in the nation.'

To understand fully the significance of this change in political ideas we must look back to the treatise which expressed in the clearest language the political ideals of the Third Estate on the eve of the elections to the States-General. Sieyes' famous 'Qu'est-ce que le Tiers État?' was primarily an attack on the privileged Orders and an assertion that the Third Estate was the nation; but Sieyes did not stop at this, he went on to tell the nation what its powers were.

> The Nation exists before all things and is the origin of all. Its will is always legal, it is the law itself … Nations on earth must be conceived as individuals outside the social bond, or as is said, in the state of nature. The exercise of their will is free and independent of all civil forms. Existing only in the natural order, their will, to have its full effect, only needs to possess the *natural* characteristics of a will. In whatever manner a nation wills, it suffices that it does will; all forms are valid and its will is always the supreme law.

In the ideas of Sieyes, and in the practice of the Revolution, a national sovereignty far more extensive in both theory and fact than the monarchical sovereignty of the *ancien régime* was let loose on the world. This national sovereignty was not, like the sovereignty of the people in Rousseau, confined to the drawing up of general laws by an assembly of the whole people, such as was conceivable only of a little state hardly as big as the smallest Swiss canton. For Sieyes, as for the French Revolution, the full power of the absolute and unlimited sovereignty of the people was attributed to a representative assembly, which, it was assumed, being the embodiment of the people, was not susceptible of any limitations, nor of needing any, for the people could not be supposed to be capable of exercising tyranny over itself. At the very moment, therefore, when restrictions on the exercise of political power were being laid down with an eye to the authorities of the past, a new political authority was set up which was by its very nature emancipated from all such restrictions.

The contradiction was crystallized in the opposition between the two leading political ideas of the revolutionaries. The idea of the separation of powers, incorrectly attributed to Montesquieu, who had argued for a balance and not a rigid separation, was employed to exclude executive influence from the legislature; on the other hand, the principle of popular sovereignty justified the legislative assembly in any invasion of the sphere of the executive. Although the full effects of the emancipation of sovereignty from all restraints were not to be seen for another century and a half, the revolutionary and Napoleonic quarter of a century in France provided some indication of what they would be. At the same time it must not be supposed that the Constituent Assembly was conscious that it was inaugurating anything other than a liberal and individualist regime.

Two years of discussion in committee and of debates in the Assembly were required before the Constitution was completed. Much of this discussion was too detailed and technical to arouse public interest, but one of the issues which provoked a major controversy arose at an early stage. The first constitutional committee of the Assembly proposed, towards the end of August 1789, that the king should be given an absolute veto on legislation. The Patriot orators and journalists started a popular agitation against the proposal. As one revolutionary journal put it, presumably not in irony, the speed with which the populace became instructed on this 'truly delicate and profound question' was incredible. Who could have guessed, in the summer of 1789, how little it would matter whether the king had an absolute or a suspensive veto, or no veto at all? The episode is of significance, coming between the fall of the

Bastille and the October Days, as an indication of the interplay between the Patriot party in the Assembly and the Parisian agitators.

The threat of a popular rising was a form of blackmail that the more advanced section of the Assembly continually used against its opponents. But mobs require leaders, and to provide this intermediate leadership an underworld of political agitators and journalists grew up which was capable of being used, when the revolutionaries themselves split, by one faction against another, and in the end of becoming a power in itself. This is to look ahead. The Constituent Assembly, even if it was ready to make use of popular unrest to put pressure on the king, had no intention of sharing its political authority with the lower social strata, as it made clear in the debates on the franchise. It was, of course, difficult to talk grandly about the sovereignty of the people in theory and at the same time refuse political rights to a large section of the sovereign people — difficult but not impossible. Sieyes provided the necessary formula in the shape of the distinction between active and passive citizens. All adult males were citizens, but only those who paid a direct tax equivalent to the value of three days' labour in the year were active citizens with the right of voting. A much higher qualification was required for membership of the electoral assemblies: the qualification for sitting in the Legislative Assembly was to be the payment of a tax of a *marc d'argent*, about 52 livres. In this way it was hoped that the principle of democratic sovereignty might have the sting taken out of it and effective power remain in the hands of the propertied classes. This was the issue which produced the most violent division in the ranks of the Third Estate. A few members of the Assembly, including particularly the deputy from Arras, Robespierre, and a large body of agitators and journalists in Paris, denounced these proposals as creating, in the words of one of them, Marat, an 'aristocracy of wealth'. In the end, before the Constitution was finally passed into law in 1791, the qualification of the silver mark was dropped, though the other property qualifications remained.

The year 1790, following on an improved harvest in 1789, was, apart from some mutinies and a good deal of scattered unrest, a comparatively peaceful year. The optimism and idealism of the early phase of the Revolution still set the prevailing tone, and the rosy light with which France was suffused seemed the promise of dawn rather than the darker hues of sunset. The Revolution, perhaps for most of the nation, was something won, not something yet to be fought for, and as such it was celebrated, in the summer of 1790, all over the country. Out of many possible illustrations may be chosen the civic fête of June 20th, held by a society formed at Paris for the purpose of commemorating the tennis-court oath. Arranged in a procession the participants march from Paris to Versailles, in their midst four victors of the Bastille bearing a tablet of bronze with the tennis-court oath inscribed thereon, and four other victors carrying stones from the demolished fortress. At Versailles the municipality welcomes them and a guard of honour from the Flanders Regiment presents arms. The procession proceeds to the tennis-court, where all present renew the oath 'dans un saisissement religieux'. After speeches, in the course of which one orator tells them that their children will flock to that sacred spot as the Muslims to Mecca, four aged men seal the tablet in the walls. With mutual embracings the municipality, the National Guard of Versailles, and the Flanders Regiment escort them to the gates of the town. On the return journey a halt is made in the bois de Boulogne, where a repast for 300, 'worthy of our ancestors', is served by young patriotic nymphs on tables decorated with the busts of the friends of humanity, Rousseau, Mably, Benjamin Franklin. For grace the first two articles of the Declaration of Rights are read. A toast is proposed by Danton to the liberty and happiness of the whole world; Robespierre, Barnave and other prominent revolutionaries follow with equally appropriate toasts, and women dressed as shepherdesses crown the deputies present with oak leaves. Now the four victors of the Bastille bring on a model of it, which they place on a table. National Guards surround it and destroy it with their swords, one hopes carefully, for in the midst is found, O joy, O ravishment of the spectators, a baby dressed in white, symbol of oppressed innocence and new-born liberty; also a red Phrygian cap, which amid applause is placed on the baby's head, and several copies of the Declaration of Rights and extracts from the works of Raynal and Rousseau, which are scattered among the spectators. With this final gesture the celebration is ended. It seems all very fresh and innocent and even naive, but unless we can recapture some of the spirit in which such fêtes were held and trees of liberty were planted, and judge them without undue cynicism or wisdom after the event, we shall fail to understand an essential element in the revolutionary victory. This spirit was what Wordsworth recalled when he looked back to the days when he was a companion of the young republicans of Blois.

> Bliss was it in that dawn to be alive,
> But to be young was very Heaven! O times,
> In which the meagre, stale, forbidding ways
> Of custom, law and statute, took at once
> The attraction of a country in romance!
> When Reason seemed the most to assert her rights
> When most intent on making of herself
> A prime enchantress to assist the work,
> Which then was going forward in her name!
> Not favoured spots alone, but the whole earth,
> The beauty wore of promise — that which sets
> (As at some moments might not be unfelt
> Among the bowers of Paradise itself)
> The budding rose above the rose full blown.

In this idyllic landscape, or cloud-cuckoo land of political ideals, the ardent revolutionaries dwelt, while the Constituent Assembly laboriously debated the constitutional proposals, and the king's government continued its decline into ever-increasing impotence. Urgent problems demanded attention. Something had to be done to restore local government. Since there could be no question of abolishing the communal councils which had sprung up spontaneously all over France, they remained the basic element in the new system of local government. In place of the thirty or so *généralités* France was divided into eighty-three departments. The essential object of this change was to destroy the provincial spirit, so bound up with the traditions of the *ancien régime* and the system of privilege. At the same time the electoral principle, with a property qualification, was substituted for the monarchical principle of nomination. Before 1789 local government had been controlled almost exclusively by officials appointed from above; after 1789 it was entirely in the hands of committees elected from below. In the long run, with its system of municipalities or communes, and departments, the Constituent Assembly had laid sound foundations, as a century and a half of subsequent history was to show; but immediately its legislation was vitiated by two glaring gaps. The new local authorities were given considerable powers, but no provision was made for financing their activities. Naturally, within a year they were bankrupt. Further, no administrative machinery was created to connect the local and central government. If it is added that a natural conflict of interests rapidly developed between the departmental directories, representing the wealthier classes, and the communes, in which a poorer though still propertied section of the population was represented, it is evident why the disintegration of central government was to be accompanied, and indeed partly caused, by a parallel collapse of local government.

Apart from the reorganization of local government, the most urgent problem before the Constituent Assembly was finance. In the spring and summer of 1789 the collection of the taxes, both direct and indirect, had broken down. Fiscal equality was achieved at a bound in a situation in which nobody paid any taxes at all. At the same time the National Assembly demonstrated its financial orthodoxy by ordering the resumption of payments of interest on the royal debt. The financial burden was also immensely increased by the achievement of a reform which the Controllers-General of the past had never dared to introduce. All venal offices were abolished. This was undoubtedly the removal of one of the greatest abuses of the *ancien régime*, and, more remarkable, it was the work of an Assembly composed, so far as concerned the Third Estate, of venal officers in the proportion of some 43 per cent. The explanation of what might otherwise seem an act of extraordinary self-abnegation on their part is that before 1789 at least some of the offices had already been declining in value, and that it was not abolition without compensation.

The solution to the fundamental financial problem was a simple one. It had been commonly held that the property of the Church was in some way different from other property. As early as August

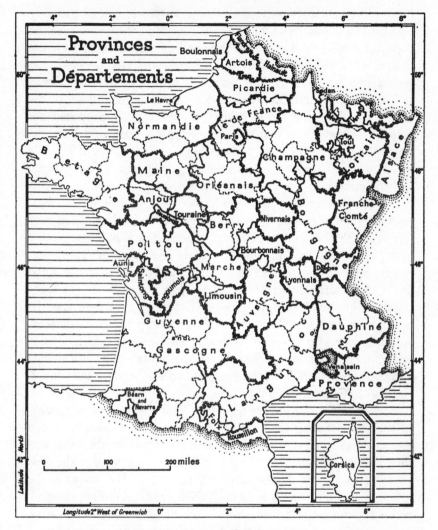

PROVINCES AND DÉPARTEMENTS

The provinces of France varied in size from the huge area of Guyenne and Gascony to the petty Boulonnais or Aunis. Some of them, for example Brittany, Normandy, Alsace, Dauphiné, retained a strong provincial feeling. Others had been from the beginning artificial agglomerations of territory. By the eighteenth century they had lost practically all their administrative significance. Only in a few cases did the généralités correspond to them. Yet provincial tradition must have counted for something in 1789, for the map shows how often the new departmental frontiers did in fact follow provincial boundaries.

1789 left-wing deputies were asserting that ecclesiastical property belonged to the nation. Occasional outbursts of anti-clerical feeling appeared during the summer of 1789 and the upper clergy were the objects of attack along with the *noblesse*. On October 10th the secular-minded and ambitious Bishop of Autun, better remembered as Talleyrand, whose life, declares a biographical dictionary of the time, 'would be the secret history of our epoch', proposed the nationalization of ecclesiastical property, on condition that the state took over the financial responsibilities of the Church. The sale of Church lands, he declared, would bring in two milliards of livres, and the upkeep of the clergy would cost only 100 million a year. It seemed, if one may put it so, a heaven-sent solution to an otherwise insoluble problem. That so much valuable land had been kept out of the market in the dead hand of the Church had long been a grievance to the land-hungry bourgeois and peasants. The lower clergy, who were promised an annual salary of not less than 1,200 livres for a curé, apparently stood to gain materially by the proposals. With very little opposition, on December 19th, the sale of the first 400 million livres' worth of Church properties was decreed. Among those who negotiated for their purchase was Marie-Antoinette. That it was to be the first step in the secularization of the state and the commencement of a still unfinished war between the Church and the Revolution hardly anyone guessed.

Backed by the proceeds of the sale of Church lands, paper money, in the form of assignats, was issued. It was to be bought in and destroyed as money returned to the Treasury from the sales, and thus the fear of inflation, which had haunted France since the time of John Law, was dissipated. With the aid of the assignats the interests on the *rentes* could be paid, the bottomless budget plugged, and a breathing-space ensured in which the Assembly could bring into operation a new and reformed fiscal system. In fact, instead of stabilizing the situation, as it supposed, the Assembly had primed the pump of continued revolution. Inflation was to be the root cause which perpetuated economic distress and so provided the raw material for future upheavals; but this consequence must not be pre-dated. There had been, before 1789, a shortage of currency in France, and therefore a certain amount of slack existed to be taken up before the rope began to tighten. The assignats, which were at a slight discount of 5 per cent when they were issued, had only fallen from 95 to 91 per cent of their face value by January 1791 and to 87 per cent in July. It is after this date that the catastrophic fall begins. The Constituent Assembly, by confiscating the lands of the Church, had given itself two years in which to complete its work.

While the nationalizing of Church lands aroused little opposition, the imposition of the Civil Constitution on the Church, by a law of July 1790, was to have a very different reception. In the new organization, bishops and curés were, on the best democratic principles, to be elected by those on the roll of active citizens. The religious orders were dissolved, except provisionally for those engaged in teaching and charitable work. In these laws for the first time we come to a development which was determined mainly by ideological considerations rather than by pressure of circumstances. The anti-clericalism of Voltaire and the *philosophes* had bitten so deeply into the minds of those who represented the Third Estate at Paris that the extent of the opposition which their reorganization of the Church was to provoke was hidden from them. Unknowingly, they had added religious schism to the other causes of political and social unrest. Open opposition was slow to develop, however. The clergy themselves, to begin with, were at a loss to know what to do. The king, after some months' delay, ratified the Civil Constitution. The oath of loyalty to the Constitution, which was imposed on all clergy, was taken only by seven bishops out of 160; but of the lower clergy possibly about one-third took the oath. In the local variations the religious map of nineteenth-century France was already sketched out, with four main centres of opposition to the Civil Constitution, in the north-east (Nord and Pas-de-Calais), Brittany and its environs, part of the mountainous region of the centre (Lozère and Haute-Loire), and an area in the east (Bas-Rhin and Moselle). Divided and hesitant, the Church waited for a lead from the Pope, who, anxious not to do anything that would imperil the Papal possessions of Avignon and the Venaissin, postponed a decision as long as he could. Only in March 1791 did the Vatican take the plunge, declare the Civil Constitution destructive of the Catholic religion, and denounce the 'monstrous right' of liberty of thought and writing.

Soon after, when the Vatican suspended all priests who did not withdraw their acceptance, a movement of retraction began among the clergy who had taken the oath. The Constitutional Church, in spite of a great shortage of qualified clergy, was to survive for a decade. The war that had been started between Church and state was to continue to the twentieth century.

To catalogue the laws, most of them of a more permanent nature than the ecclesiastical legislation, in which the Constituent Assembly continued the great age of reform inaugurated before 1789, would be a long task. Their keynote was liberty. All offices were opened to Protestants in 1789; there was opposition from Alsace and Lorraine to the granting of rights of citizenship to Jews but this was finally voted three days before the Constituent Assembly dissolved. The attempt, when the States-General met, to prevent the publication of reports of its meetings was frustrated by Mirabeau, who adopted the device of turning his journal into the form of a periodical report to his constituents. Until the revolution of August 10th, 1792, the Press enjoyed the most absolute liberty. The theatre was equally freed from control and became, like the Press, a medium of political propaganda.

The proposal to abolish slavery in the colonies, put forward by the Société des amis des Noirs, met with opposition from the strong vested interest of the plantation owners, many of whom were resident in France, and from the merchants engaged in the Atlantic trade. The Declaration of Rights was a little difficult to reconcile with slavery, but the Constituent Assembly gallantly swallowed its principles, which, however, having penetrated to the Antilles, were to provoke a devastating revolt there. The principle of liberty also ran into difficulties in its application to the traditional authority of the father of the family. This was henceforth restricted to children under the age of twenty-one and the powers of imprisonment it carried with it were limited, though not abolished. The secularization of marriage was a logical corollary of the anti-clerical ideology, but the Constituent Assembly only reached the point of proclaiming the principle that marriage was a civil contract. Civil marriages and secular registrations of births and deaths were to be established by law in 1792, when a system of civil divorce was also introduced.

The laws of inheritance, which varied from province to province, presented too controversial a problem for the Constituent Assembly to solve. The principle of equality of inheritance between children was generalized in 1790, but specific prohibitions against willing property unequally were only introduced in 1793.

That the criminal laws and the law courts, both civil and criminal, needed drastic reform was generally agreed by enlightened opinion before the Revolution. On the future of the parlements, which clung to the use of torture and the good old ways, there were no two opinions in the Third Estate; they were first put on permanent vacation and then abolished, a new system of courts being set up in their place. 'Imaginary crimes' — heresy, lèse-majesté, and magical practices — were no longer recognized. Mutilations and all forms of torture were removed from the list of punishments, leaving only deportation, imprisonment, and death. The aristocratic privilege of decapitation was extended to the whole nation, with the aid of a new invention, incorrectly attributed to Dr Guillotin. What all this meant in the way of humanitarian progress cannot easily be over-estimated.

Along with liberty and equality the National Assembly proclaimed the sanctity of property, though this did not include 'feudal' privileges or the lands of the Church. What it meant was the free exploitation of recognized property rights; it therefore implied the extinction of the system of state control of trade and industry. The corporations were suppressed; but when the workers of Paris assumed that liberty meant the liberty to strike, the Assembly replied with the law Le Chapelier, prohibiting associations of workers. Even the left-wing in the Assembly did not oppose this law. In the country a major issue was that of enclosures. In spite of rural hostility, which had been manifested before 1789 and was expressed in the parish *cahiers*, the Assembly went as far as it dared, in the face of this opposition, in authorizing and encouraging them. Finally, all internal restrictions on the free passage of goods were abolished, the long-elaborated plans for a single tariff at last emerging from the bureaux of the Contrôle Général and being put into effect by the officials who had struggled unavailingly for their acceptance before 1789. On the other hand the protective system of tariffs on goods coming into France was strictly preserved, for the free-trade treaty of Vergennes with England had aroused a torrent of opposition and the economic crisis was attributed, however incorrectly, to it. Similarly, the monopoly of colonial trade was maintained. Altogether, the National Assembly cannot be charged with slavish adherence to theoretical principles of liberty in its economic legislation.

While the foundations were thus being laid for the future, the present had been forgotten and France was fast sliding into a state of anarchy. The collapse of the civil administration was serious, but even worse was the spread of indiscipline among the armed forces of the crown. Revolutionary committees of soldiers and sailors were formed, which came into conflict with their officers. The most notorious among many outbreaks was that in August 1790 at Nancy, where the regiment of Châteauvieux, after the cruel punishment of the *couvroies*, a kind of running the gauntlet, had been inflicted on two insubordinate soldiers, mutinied and with the aid of the mob took control of the town. The marquis de Bouillé, in command of the army of the East, stormed Nancy with heavy loss on both sides; several of the mutineers were sentenced to death and some forty-one to the galleys. Though the National Assembly voted thanks to Bouillé, political agitators were able to make good use of the episode for propaganda purposes.

Revolutionary clubs played a leading part in such disturbances, and indeed in a state in which the old authorities had collapsed and the new ones had hardly begun to function it was inevitable that such revolutionary groups should become the real centres of power. The establishment at Versailles of the Breton Club, later to become the Jacobins, has already been mentioned. The deputies who belonged to the club constituted an influential left-wing pressure group in the Assembly. By such forms of social assistance as the distribution of vouchers for cheap bread, and by giving pecuniary or legal help to poorer patriots in distress, they acquired a popular clientele, though not until October 1791, when additional galleries were constructed and their sessions thrown open to the public, could they be said to have fallen under the influence of the mob instead of influencing it. The prestige of the club was so great that it was able to survive extensive secessions. It far surpassed in influence the other political clubs, such as the right-wing Club des Valois and the left-wing club of the Cordeliers, which was led by extra-parliamentary agitators like Danton, Camille Desmoulins, Anacharsis Clootz, friend of humanity, and the poetically self-named Fabre d'Églantine.

All over France similar political clubs were formed by local revolutionaries. Establishing a system of correspondence with the Paris Jacobins, many of them came to adopt its name and look to it for leadership. By 1793 there were probably between five and eight thousand such clubs, with a nominal membership of perhaps half a million, though the active membership may have been much smaller. The Jacobin Clubs gradually came to usurp the powers of local government, and later, under the Committee of Public Safety, became in effect auxiliary administrative bodies as well as centres of propaganda and electoral influence. The role of the clubs in revolutionary France is yet one more example of the victory of practical considerations over theory, for in theory any kind of party organization was regarded as factious and held in disrepute. The very idea of concerted action among the deputies in the Assembly was looked on with suspicion. The justification for the part played by the clubs was given by a speaker at the Jacobin Club of Paris in April 1793: 'Patriots do not form a party,' he declared, 'that designation can only be applied to the intriguers of the Convention.' It was through the Jacobin Clubs that the more advanced revolutionaries were gradually able to impose their rule on France. The pattern remained to the end what it had been in the beginning: the exploitation of popular discontent and the stirring up of mob passions, whether against aristocrats or priests, or simply political opponents.

The Jacobins, of course, were not the mere 'vauriens' of royalist legend. At the commencement the high subscription of 36 livres, with 12 livres entrance fee, as well as the level of the debates, were sufficient safeguard against this. Although the membership of the Jacobin Clubs was broadened later, it has been shown that even under the Terror they remained largely middle-class in composition: the tax assessments of the Jacobins were well above the average. They were opposed both to the rich and to the propertyless. They came from the cities and small towns: though there were clubs in villages they seem to have exhibited little activity, and the rural masses, after the summer of 1789, were either passive or hostile to the Revolution. What held the Jacobins together was less class interest than a common ideology, which became increasingly narrow with the development of ritual, tests of orthodoxy, purges, and public confessions. Being only a small minority in the whole nation they came to think of themselves as a chosen body, an elite, 'the very small number', Camille Desmoulins put it in 1791, 'of those to whom only the witness of their conscience is necessary, the small number of men of character, incorruptible citizens.'

If we want to understand the revolutionaries we must remember above all that they had been nurtured on a classical education. Robespierre, asked what constitution he wanted, replied 'That of Lycurgus.' Plutarch, Livy, Tacitus were their teachers; Brutus the consul, Brutus the tyrannicide, and Cincinnatus their models. They wore Phrygian caps, built triumphal arches, and erected statues — usually of not very durable plaster — to all the classical virtues, crowned their heroes with laurel wreaths, converted the appropriately classical church of Sainte-Geneviève into a Pantheon to hold the mortal relics of their prophets and martyrs, and if they had to die, did it when they could in the old Roman fashion. They were to have senates and councils of ancients, bearers of the fasces, consuls, and in due course an emperor. But even their classicism, as I have already implied, was not an invention of the Revolution. In the plastic arts its triumph was already manifest before 1789. Hubert Robert's landscapes, with ruined temples and fallen columns, earlier in the century testified to the interest in the antique. The French Academy at Rome was the centre from which a more rigorous classicism spread and the crucial moment was when the most brilliant of the rising young artists in France, David, went there with the Prix de Rome in 1774. The new style won its decisive victory with David's 'Oath of the Horatii', exhibited in the Salon of 1785. When the Revolution came it merely set the seal on his artistic triumph. While Vigée Le Brun emigrated, and Fragonard for a time took refuge in Provence from the new hard climate, David became the unchallenged leader of revolutionary art. He put his already great reputation and his artistic genius to the service of the Revolution. The Jacobin Club, of which he had become a member, commissioned him, on the first anniversary of the tennis-court oath, to immortalize it in paint. His drawing for this, exhibited in 1791 and widely reproduced, is, of course, an imaginative reconstruction, influenced by subsequent political events, and not a contemporary record. It was destined never to be finished, for the artist entered the Convention, and politics, or political art, made increasing demands on him until Thermidor. He was to be, for a time, practically the artistic dictator of France. Contrary to an old story, he used his influence, as a member of the Commission of Monuments, to save the artistic treasures of France and he protected Fragonard. If his huge canvases won him his contemporary fame and made him the official artist of Jacobinism, however, it is by his magnificent portraits that he survives as one of the greater painters of France. In modern times, at least, official art is generally bad art. David's contribution to the propagation of Jacobin ideology must be spoken of in its place.

All this is to anticipate. Between 1789 and 1791 such consistency as the Jacobin Clubs were later to give the Revolution was lacking. Agitators and journalists were stirring up trouble and the Constituent Assembly was unable to control the rising tide of anarchy. To condemn the Assembly, in the language of Burke, as a collection of country curates and petty provincial attorneys is absurd. Though a majority of the members were, naturally, local notabilities who as individuals have left no mark on history, there has perhaps never been an assembly in French history which contained so much talent. What its members lacked was what in the nature of things they could not have acquired — political experience. If in this respect one man stands out in contrast to almost all the other members of the Constituent Assembly, it was not because he was wiser or better than the rest, but because he, almost alone, recognized as if by a native instinct the necessary conditions of a parliamentary regime.

Mirabeau, younger son of the physiocratic marquis, won notoriety before the Revolution for his amorous adventures. He published works of varying degrees of scurrility and obscenity and attempted to break into public life by way of the back-stairs of diplomacy and shady finance. The Revolution provided the opportunity for him to turn to a better use the energy and ability which had gone to waste under the *ancien régime*. Even before his election to the States-General Mirabeau had written to the Foreign Secretary warning him of the need for the ministry to adopt a plan of action in order to remain in command of the situation and avoid the dangers of aristocratic plots and democratic excesses. No notice was taken of his advice, and the government was to fall a victim to both in turn. Elected a member of the Third Estate, Mirabeau, with his stentorian voice, massive build, lion-like mane, and domineering countenance, its natural ugliness accentuated by the ravages of smallpox, at once became a leading figure. For the Assembly itself, filled with worthy and high-minded characters amongst whom he was as out of place as Gulliver among the Lilliputians, he had the utmost contempt. But he concealed this. I have never known any man who, when he wished, could be more seductive than him, wrote the young Genevan Dumont, one of the group of experts who prepared Mirabeau's speeches and whose backroom services enabled him to speak, as no other member of the Assembly could, with authority on any and every subject. Mirabeau at the outset made himself the voice of the Third Estate against the privileged Orders, to which he belonged by birth, but it was for the purpose of strengthening, not destroying, monarchical authority. 'I am the only one in that patriotic horde', he said on one occasion, defending in private the need for royal authority, 'who can speak thus without performing a volte-face. I have never adopted their romance, nor their metaphysics, nor their useless crimes.' Necker he despised as only a strong, ruthless man can despise a weak-minded sentimentalist. While maintaining his reputation as a staunch revolutionary by violent-sounding, though often moderate in content, speeches, he established secret relations with the court. Marie-Antoinette was willing to pay him, but not to trust him. 'We will never be so wretched, I believe,' she wrote, 'as to be reduced to the painful extremity of having recourse to Mirabeau.' The king and queen never understood the reason of his demand for a ministry responsible to the Assembly, a principle, he rightly declared, 'more important even, if possible, to the king than to his people'. With the man who should have been his natural ally, La Fayette, head of the National Guard and a popular idol, mutual dislike made it impossible for him to work. Even apart from such personal difficulties, Mirabeau's plan of action could hardly have achieved success. His position was essentially false, fated as he was to arouse the distrust of the court by demagogic speeches in the Assembly, and of the revolutionaries by his attempts to preserve the authority of the crown. In January 1791 he still wielded enough influence to be elected President of the Assembly. In April he died, worn out by toil and excesses, at the age of forty-two. 'O people,' wrote Marat, 'render thanks to the gods, your most formidable enemy has fallen.' To Mirabeau himself was attributed the dying phrase, 'I carry in my heart the funeral knell of the monarchy.'

Only after Mirabeau's death, and two years too late, did Louis XVI and Marie-Antoinette put into effect the advice that he had consistently given them to fly from Paris and set up the royal standard, with all who would support it, in a provincial capital. Mirabeau's advice had been to go to Rouen, in conservative and phlegmatic Normandy, flanked by the Catholic and royalist forces of Brittany and the Vendée. The king and queen, when at last they saw no hope but in flight, chose the destination they had contemplated in 1789, Metz, where Bouillé, after the suppression of the mutiny at Nancy, still maintained some kind of discipline among his troops, and from whence the frontier could easily be gained. The devoted Fersen made the arrangements for the escape. At half-past ten at night, on June 20th, 1791, by an unguarded door, the king and queen, with the king's sister, Mme Élisabeth, the two royal children and their governess, left the Tuileries in a waiting carriage. At the gate of Saint-Martin they changed into a heavy berline prepared for the journey and at a slow pace took the road. Meaux, Châlons, Sainte-Menehould were passed, and the little town of Varennes — fatal name — was reached between eleven and twelve o'clock on the night of June 21st. More than once in their slow progress the royal family had been recognized but allowed to pass unchallenged. At Varennes they met with a stauncher patriot and were stopped. The squadrons sent by Bouillé to safeguard his sovereigns, ranging in what seems a rather confused fashion about the countryside, missed them, and were unable to rescue them from the bands of peasants gathered at Varennes. The tragic journey back to Paris, far longer and more pitiful than that of October 1789 from Versailles, was accompanied by the shouts and threats of hostile crowds, only prevented from inflicting personal injury on the royal family by the presence of an escort of National Guards and the arrival of Barnave and two other deputies.

The king and queen re-entered the Tuileries on June 25th as prisoners, yet prisoners whom the Assembly would not or could not do without; for it was on the point of completing its task and presenting for the royal signature a monarchical constitution. Voices outside the Assembly, in the journals and on the streets, were now openly calling for a republic, but the members of the Constituent Assembly were not prepared for such a revolutionary step: even Robespierre believed that a monarchy was necessary. Therefore they had to pretend that the king had never fled: he had been kidnapped.

The popular agitation was not to be so easily diverted. A great demonstration was organized in the huge open space of the Champ-de-Mars, where a petition calling for the king's abdication was drawn up. After a preliminary meeting on July 16th, 1791, the meeting on the following day was inaugurated by the lynching of two men found hiding under the steps leading up to the platform. Serious proceedings began with the signing of the petition. Meanwhile Bailly, mayor of Paris, and the Municipal Council, along with La Fayette, had decided that precautions must be taken. Martial law was proclaimed for the first time, the red flag hoisted, and a detachment of National Guards sent to the Champ-de-Mars. There a shot rang out, from which side is not known. General firing broke out, some fifty of the crowd as well as two National Guards were killed, and the demonstrators were dispersed. The use of force against a popular movement was followed by measures against its instigators. Leaders of the popular clubs were arrested or went into hiding and the more extreme journals were suppressed. A secession to the Feuillants threatened to extinguish even the Jacobin Club. In the face of this unexpectedly strong action the agitation collapsed. For the first time it seemed that authority was capable of asserting itself.

In the summer of 1791 the Constitution was, considering its slow progress during the previous two years, fairly rapidly completed. A last-minute move to strengthen the monarchical element in it might

have succeeded if it had not been for irresponsible opposition from
the right. As it was, Barnave, who had entered into a secret correspondence with the queen after conversations on the road back from
Varennes, wrote to her, 'The constitution is a very monarchical
one.' The king formally appended his signature on September 14th,
and on September 30th the Constituent Assembly was dissolved.
Before this it had taken one decisive and fatal resolution, in voting
the self-denying ordinance by which its members disqualified themselves from membership of the new Legislative Assembly. The
motives of Robespierre, who proposed this decree and thus at a
single stroke eliminated all the moderates who at last were showing
signs of realizing the need for government in France, are obvious;
but he could not have secured its acceptance without the support of
the right, whose hatred for the constitutionalists led them to deal
this last blow to their enemies even if it was to prove fatal to themselves and to the king. As the moderate marquis de Ferrières
wrote, 'The Great Aristocrats and the Wild Men combined to pass
the decree.' By it, all those who had learnt painfully something of the
conditions of parliamentary government were to be eliminated
temporarily from the scene. New men, in a new Assembly, were to
take over the task of consolidating the gains of the Revolution and
restoring a stable government to France.

CHAPTER THREE

✠

FALL OF THE CONSTITUTIONAL
MONARCHY

'THE Constitution', wrote Mirabeau's disciple Dumont, 'was a veritable monster: there was too much republic for a monarchy, and too much monarchy for a republic. The king was an hors-d'œuvre.' Such a judgment was obviously written after the Constitution had failed. The Legislative Assembly that met for the first time on October 1st, 1791 had no such forebodings of disaster; despite the flight to Varennes it intended to make the constitutional monarchy work. Although some 136 of its members joined the left-wing Jacobin or Cordeliers clubs, many more, about a third of the total number of deputies, put their names down at the more moderate Feuillants, formed as a break-away from the Jacobins. The leadership of left-wing opinion in the new Assembly was taken by the small but active group who were called, from the name of their most prominent member, the Brissotins. Brissot, son of a restaurant proprietor of Chartres, came from a lower social stratum than even the most advanced of the members of the Constituent Assembly. He had left school at fifteen to become a lawyer's clerk and subsequently graduated in the underworld of literature; he wrote propaganda for financial speculators trying to rig the markets, possibly joined the London factory which was publishing pamphlets against Marie-Antoinette for the purpose of having them bought up and suppressed by the police, and associated with the more advanced and idealistic leaders of the Third Estate. In 1786 he entered the service of the Duke of Orleans, to which so many political adventurers gravitated. After the meeting of the States-General he founded the *Patriote française*, which became one of the chief journals of the extremer revolutionaries. He played a part in the organization of the Champ-de-Mars demonstration of July 1791 and was elected in September 1791 for Paris. The charges of dishonesty which the royalists in the earlier part of his career, and the Jacobins subsequently, directed against him, have little more justification than the fact that he was a poverty-stricken adventurer always short of funds. He died poor, which is a good if not a decisive defence. He was sincere in his way, yet a born intriguer, full of plans, facile, optimistic, ambitious, and above all a light man. His febrile activity gathered a brilliant group round him in the Legislative Assembly, including Vergniaud — one of the greatest orators of the Assembly, who as a leading light of the bar at Bordeaux was elected by the department of the Gironde — and other members of the same deputation.

Those who were labelled Brissotins were not a party — they were too few — but at most a faction, held together by ties of personal friendship, a common rather sentimental idealism and a vague republicanism. They took the lead in pressing for decrees against the émigrés and the refractory priests who had not taken, or had withdrawn, the oath to the Civil Constitution. In doing so they were necessarily provoking an open conflict with the king, for Louis XVI, so weak where his own interests were concerned, was sincerely religious and at the same time could not easily sanction positive measures against the émigrés, including so many of his own friends and relations. What the Brissotins wanted, apart from power, it is not easy to say. In their attempt to achieve this, however, they were to prove more unscrupulous, if less ruthless, than their enemies of the Mountain were to be later. They had one trump card: war, they rightly thought, would play into the hands of the left wing and enable it to rally popular passions behind it. Brissot and his friends therefore set to work to bring war about.

On the other hand, the outbreak of war between revolutionary France and Europe can only be presented as the result exclusively of a Brissotin intrigue by taking the immediate occasion for the cause. Brissot had the war card in his hand, but if he had not, there can be little doubt that someone else would have played it instead. To treat the outbreak of war as the mere result of a faction struggle is to forget the history of the previous half-century, during which France had known in foreign affairs nothing but defeat. In 1787, when British and Prussian intervention forced the government to abandon the Franco-Dutch alliance in humiliating conditions, Arthur Young had found everywhere an outcry for war with England. When the States-General met, the desire for national unity was the earliest form taken by the patriotic spirit. The first measure to this end could be regarded as a mere formality: Corsica, already a French *généralité*, was declared part of the French Empire. It was not until September 1791 that Avignon and the Venaissin, after a bloody struggle between revolutionaries and the adherents of the papal authorities, were annexed. In the independent enclaves of the German princes on the left bank of the Rhine the laws against feudal dues were applied and protests rejected 'in the name of the sacred and inalienable rights of nations'.

It must not be supposed that the Constituent Assembly was bellicose in sentiment. On the contrary, it was imbued with the profoundly pacific ideals of the great writers of the eighteenth century. War, the revolutionaries believed, was a wicked habit of despots: a nation could not be aggressive. When, in 1790, the Anglo-Spanish conflict over Nootka Sound seemed about to develop into open war and Spain called for French support under the terms of the Family Compact, the Assembly insisted that the right of declaring war belonged to the nation and not to the king, and added the famous declaration renouncing all wars of conquest and pledging the French nation never to employ its forces against the liberty of any people. Such sentiments represent fairly the idealistic pacifism of the opening stages of the Revolution, but in this, as in so many other respects, circumstances were to be more influential than ideas.

Old Europe resounded with denunciations of the Revolution, which found their most fulminating expression in Burke's *Reflections on the Revolution in France* in November 1790. Round the frontiers of France gathered little congregations of émigrés, the king's younger brother, Artois, with Calonne to direct his tactics, at their head, stirring up counter-revolutionary movements in France and urging the powers to launch an attack for the purpose of restoring the *ancien régime*. The French Patriots could hardly have been expected to know that the powers had no intention of doing anything of the kind. In Great Britain the government of the younger Pitt was wedded to peace and quite content to see France, as Windham put it as late as 1792, 'in a situation which, more than at any other period, freed us from apprehension, on her account'. Austria and Prussia, chiefly concerned with the dangers arising from Russian policy and looking to the possibility of further spoils in Poland, were also not regretful to see French military power eliminated, or so they thought, from the map of Europe; while Catherine of Russia was only urging them to strike at France for the purpose of ensuring a free hand for herself to pursue further annexations in Eastern Europe. The appeals of the émigrés to the courts of Europe were therefore met everywhere with expressions of sympathy combined with a determination to do nothing to put it into practice.

The counter-revolution was not even united. Marie-Antoinette, with Breteuil to represent her and the king abroad, was profoundly, and not without reason, suspicious of Artois and his party; but at the same time was sending secret letters to her brother, the Emperor Leopold, denouncing the Constitution and the Assembly and calling for armed intervention. 'We have no longer any resource', she wrote, 'but in the foreign powers: at all costs they must come to our aid.' The famous manifesto of Pilnitz, on August 27th, 1791, showed how little they intended to respond to her appeal. Leopold and the king of Prussia satisfied their elastic consciences and their convenience at the same time. They proclaimed the common interest of all the sovereigns of Europe in the fate of the king of France, and declared themselves ready with the co-operation of these sovereigns to restore the king to a situation in which he would be free to strengthen the foundations of monarchical government. This was a formidable threat in appearance: in substance it amounted to nothing, for the signatories well knew that the other powers were not willing to join them. Marie-Antoinette's disappointment was bitter: 'The Emperor has betrayed us,' she wrote. The revolutionaries did not see it in this light and anticipated at any moment a descent of foreign armies, spearheaded by the corps of émigrés and supported by an aristocratic rising inside France. It was not far from this fear to the idea of a preventive war to anticipate the attack.

The apparent threat from without met and intensified a growing bellicose trend within France. Austria was the hereditary enemy and the Austrian alliance had long been denounced by court factions as the source of all evil. Moreover the Revolution was already an international revolution, not merely because of the universal applicability of its ideas but in actual fact. The democratic movement of the second half of the eighteenth century, as I have said, had not been peculiar to France. America, England, Ireland, Geneva, the United Provinces, Liège, and the Austrian Netherlands witnessed similar movements, though only in America had the revolution achieved success. Democratic refugees from abroad flocked to France, some of the more distinguished to offer their advice and cooperation to the leaders of the French Revolution, even to be elected to the Legislative Assembly, others to join the underworld of agitators and journalists in Paris. They exercised a continuous pressure for French intervention in their homelands, which they represented as only waiting the signal to rise, overthrow their feudal and despotic rulers, and cast in their lot with France. The Brissotins formed the point of crystallization for all the tendencies leading France in the direction of war, and Brissot launched the campaign in a speech of October 20th, 1791, which denounced the émigrés and called for their expulsion from the territories around France. 'In the event of a refusal', he told the Assembly, 'you have no choice, you must yourselves attack the powers which dare to threaten you. The picture of liberty, like the head of Medusa, will terrify the armies of our enemies.' In November another member of the Brissotin faction, Isnard of the Var, invented the formula 'a war of peoples against kings'.

The agitation for war was now reinforced unexpectedly from within the government, and by the Minister for War who had been put into office by the influence of the moderates. This was the comte de Narbonne, commonly regarded as an illegitimate son of Louis XV, current lover of Mme de Staël and later to be an aide-de-camp of Napoleon. A noble and officer, Narbonne had thrown in his lot with the Revolution, but his aim, except that they both saw in a war the opportunity for political power, was precisely the opposite of that of Brissot. Narbonne shared the views of that section of the right which regarded a successful war on a limited scale as a means of restoring the power of the crown. Their calculations were not unsuspected among the revolutionaries, but few of the latter dared to criticize the war fever, and only one opposed it with consistency and force. This was Robespierre, who, at first favourable to the idea of a declaration of war, had rapidly seen the possibility that it might play into the hands of the king. In a series of great speeches at the Jacobin Club, early in 1792, he attempted, practically single-handed, to stem the tide of war. Crush our internal enemies first, he said, and then march against foreign ones; in an even more striking phrase, 'No one loves armed missionaries.' Europe, he declared, with true insight, wants peace; the émigrés are powerless; the immediate threat to the Revolution is entirely within France.

The duel at the Jacobin Club between Robespierre and Brissot over the question of war was to weigh heavily on the future of the Revolution, for it was at the root of their subsequent discord. At the moment the forces on the side of Brissot and the war party were overwhelming, and Robespierre was left for the time being defeated and practically isolated. The Brissotins, with the almost unanimous support of the Assembly, forced the ministry to resign in March 1792. Narbonne did not reap any reward from his advocacy of war, for he had lost office shortly before this in consequence of a quarrel within the ministry; but the leading figure in the new government was an even more determined advocate of war. Dumouriez was a professional soldier who, although not a noble, had risen to the rank of maréchal de camp before the Revolution, when he had also played a minor diplomatic role in the service of the anti-Austrian faction. After the outbreak of the Revolution he built up a reputation for himself as a patriot and established contacts with Brissot and the deputation from the Gironde. At the same time he maintained an indirect connection with the king and was sending him secret memoirs through an intermediary. Intelligent, active, intriguing, and ambitious, Dumouriez saw fame and fortune in a successful war directed by himself. The Brissotins could feel that in him, unlike Narbonne, they had an ally who would play the same game as themselves. Along with Dumouriez, a group of ministers loosely connected with the Brissotins came into office, the king's advisers having now decided that the best way to disarm the opposition was to give it the responsibility of government. This was not necessarily a mistaken idea and it might have succeeded had the new ministers possessed more of the raw material of statesmanship. After Dumouriez, the most important ministers were Roland, a worthy civil servant and husband of Mme Roland, and the Genevan financier Clavière, of whom Mirabeau, whom he had provided with a financial policy and most of the speeches with which to defend it, said that he had the intelligence of a man and the emotions of a child.

With Dumouriez the ideas of the anti-Austrian party at the French court, so long frustrated, were at last carried into effect. His plan was to isolate Austria by ensuring the neutrality of the other powers, for which purpose the young marquis de Chauvelin, with Talleyrand to advise him, was sent to the court of St James, and the comte de Custine, who had fought with distinction in the American War, to Berlin. The Emperor was summoned to reduce his armaments, which were said to be threatening France. When this demand was rejected, Dumouriez persuaded his colleagues to propose a declaration of war. Louis XVI and Marie-Antoinette, seeing their salvation in the chance of French defeat, accepted the proposal, and on April 20th, 1792 the king presented it to the Legislative Assembly. The only member who dared to speak against it was shouted down. In a transport of acclamation from Assembly and galleries the declaration of war was carried with only seven opposing votes.

Nothing was ready for the war on which France had so lightheartedly launched. The Legislative Assembly had not even made the preparations for which Narbonne had asked while he was minister. The army was in a deplorable condition. Out of some 9,000 officers about 6,000 had abandoned their commands. Whole regiments had disintegrated. Arms and all other provisions of war were lacking. Battalions of volunteers, the famous 'blues', so-called from the colour of their uniforms as contrasted with the white coats of the old royal army, had been raised by the Constituent Assembly, but though full of enthusiasm they fell short of what had been hoped for in numbers. With this inadequate and ill-supplied army it was proposed to wage war on Europe; but the Brissotin faction was counting on a general rising of the neighbouring populations in their favour and Dumouriez shared this expectation. Since, to enable such risings to take place, the presence of French armies was necessary, a general offensive was planned. La Fayette, in command of the French forces, starting from Metz was to move to Givet, that salient of French territory pointing like a spearhead at Liège, where, as in the Austrian Netherlands, there had already taken place a democratic revolution which the Austrians had repressed by force. From Liège, Brussels would be within short marching distance. It all sounded simple in Paris, so simple that the date for the offensive was advanced at the last minute. La Fayette was given a mere six days to move his army to Givet, an adequate time if logistics were entirely ignored.

The first encounter with the enemy proved how mistaken were these facile calculations. A small body of 3,000 men, which crossed the frontier in the direction of Tournai, was halted by a few cannon shot and the order was given to withdraw. Panic seized the French and they fled in disorder back to Lille, where they massacred their general and some Austrian prisoners they had taken. Similar episodes occurred elsewhere and the offensive had to be abandoned almost as soon as it had begun. France lay open to the enemy and was only saved by the scholarly and traditional generalship of the aged Duke of Brunswick, who was not prepared to advance until all conceivable preparations had been made and all precautions taken.

The hopes of Brissot and his friends had proved false at the outset. Instead of reaping the fruits of an easy victory they found themselves saddled with the responsibility for military disaster. Nor was this their only concern. Economic difficulties, endemic throughout the Revolution, were becoming more acute, partly indeed as a result of the strain imposed on France by the war. The assignat fell to 47 per cent of its face value in March 1792. Although the harvest of 1791 had been fair the food crisis reappeared, for the peasants were unwilling to sell their produce for a rapidly depreciating paper currency. Grain riots once again became widespread. In consequence of a negro revolt in St Domingo, in August 1791, the supply of sugar was cut off from France. In January 1792 shops with stocks of sugar were sacked in Paris and the populace helped itself to other foodstuffs as well. The Assembly, tied to progressive economic as well as political ideas, did not contemplate abandoning the principle of internal free trade and made no attempt to remedy the shortage of grain. For the Brissotins there were two possible courses of action: to join with the moderates in repressing disorder, or to throw in their lot with the more advanced revolutionaries. The dilemma was to haunt them until it finally brought them to the guillotine, for they could make up their minds to follow neither course of action consistently. For the time being they fell back on their well-tried tactic of denouncing the treachery of the court and aristocratic plots. That there were such plots and that the court was hoping for defeat is true, but they were not the cause either of the actual defeat or of the economic distress. This did not deter Brissot, who had confessed earlier, 'We have need of some great treachery.' The secret manœuvres of Marie-Antoinette and the court were not so secret but that suspicions of them had been aroused. Backed by these, the theme of an 'Austrian committee', planning an invasion of France to restore absolute monarchy, was put into circulation and successfully exploited.

For once Paris was not the chief centre of disturbance. The outbreak of war had stimulated counter-revolutionary movements all over France and particularly in the south, against which the revolutionaries reacted with vigour. The Jacobins of Marseilles, having won their victory in the great port, sent out flying columns to Aix, where they disarmed a regiment of Swiss, to Arles where they forced the royal troops to evacuate the town, and, under the leadership of the famous Jourdan Coupe-Tête, to suppress the counter-revolutionary movement at Avignon. The same kind of spontaneous revolutionary action was taken elsewhere, not without an occasional massacre, and the Brissotins conceived the idea of calling on the militant revolutionaries of the provinces to swing the balance in their favour at Paris. Contingents of National Guards were summoned to the capital to defend the Revolution. In this way, with that genius for political miscalculation which seemed natural to them, the Brissotins called into existence the very force that was to prove fatal to themselves.

The war having proved thus far such an unhappy speculation, they could find no better way of diverting public indignation from their own failure than to continue to stir up popular feeling against the monarchy. Their ally, Roland, the ineffective Minister of the

Interior, on July 10th addressed a letter, drawn up in fact by Mme Roland, to the king, indicting him for his veto on the decrees penalizing refractory priests and creating the camp of provincial National Guards at Paris. The letter was written in terms of a severe and priggish reprimand. 'I know', wrote Mme Roland, 'that the austere language of truth is rarely welcomed near the throne.' It conveyed a barely veiled threat of revolutionary measures. Even Louis XVI could not swallow this from his own government. He dismissed Roland and his two chief supporters in the ministry and replaced them with obscure Feuillants.

All that the Brissotins and Roland had succeeded in doing was to pour oil on the flames of popular unrest, already growing dangerously fierce. The leadership and organization of the revolution of 1792 are rather better known than those of the similar movement in 1789, but much still remains obscure. Marat, in the *Ami du peuple*, was waging a campaign of general denunciation, in which he did not spare Brissot, who, he wrote, 'apprenticed to chicanery, became a would-be wit, a scandal-sheet writer, an apprentice-philosopher, a fraudulent speculator, a crook, a prince's valet, a government clerk, police spy, publicist, municipal inquisitor, legislative senator, faithless representative of the people, abettor of the ministerial faction and finally henchman of the despot.' Hébert, in the *Père Duchesne*, poured out similar denunciations, larded with obscenity in a would-be popular tone, and other revolutionary sheets joined in the outcry. With the raw material of distress among the people to work on, a rising was prepared in clubs and secret committees by agitators drawn from varied ranks of society. Such were Santerre, the brewer of the faubourg Saint-Antoine, and the butcher Legendre, both well-to-do tradesmen; the marquis de Saint-Huruge, a de-classed noble adventurer; Alexandre, a former *agent de change*, now commander of a company of National Guard gunners; Rossignol, a jeweller's workman; and Fournier, son of a respectable bourgeois family, who was called 'the American' because he had been in America at the time of the American Revolution. The considerable number of foreign agitators on the fringe of politics included Lazowski, a Pole and former prosperous Inspector of Manufactures whose post had been suppressed early in the Revolution, and Rotundo, an Italian

N

teacher of languages and a crook. Whether more substantial political figures can be detected in the shade behind these agitators of the streets, or whether it was purely a group of such men who prepared the manifestations of June 20th, remains uncertain. On that day, in the face of rather feeble opposition from the municipal authorities, an armed procession was formed which demanded admission to the Assembly. For an hour National Guards, women, citizens with *bonnets rouges* and pikes, singing the revolutionary song, 'Ça ira', one with a calf's heart on the end of a stick and the inscription 'Aristocrat's heart', filed through the hall. The mob then moved to the Tuileries, penetrated into the palace and even reached the royal apartments. For two hours they flowed round the king shouting and demonstrating, sticking a red cap on his head and giving him a glass of wine to drink with them. He put up with it all with great courage. His demeanour, and perhaps an element of good temper in the crowd, prevented any bloodshed. As evening fell the demonstrators melted away. Whatever had been intended by the demonstration, it had failed.

Despite this warning, Brissot and his friends continued to play with fire. Their object was to use the threat of mob violence to intimidate the king into restoring Roland and the other Brissotin ministers to office. On July 3rd Vergniaud delivered a speech which was a general indictment of Louis XVI, in whose name, he said, foreign armies were descending on France. Yet shortly after, Vergniaud himself was one of the authors of a secret letter to the king, calling on him to restore the Patriot ministers to office and promising to save him if he did so.

The general unrest was not diminished by the issue, on July 25th, of a manifesto by the Duke of Brunswick threatening Paris with military execution and total subversion if there were the least violence offered to the royal family. On July 8th the National Guards summoned from the provinces, the famous *fédérés*, began to arrive in Paris. Though 25,000 had been called for, only 4,500 came, and some of these were subsequently diverted to a camp at Soissons; but what they lacked in numbers they made up in revolutionary ardour. The Brissotins soon discovered their miscalculation, for the *fédérés* were seized on and indoctrinated by the more advanced revolutionaries of Paris. Even more ominous was the fact that Robespierre, who had regained his influence in the Jacobin Club and whose reputation was higher than before, since events had justified his opposition to the Brissotins earlier in the year, now abandoned his defence of the Constitution and advocacy of legal methods.

The situation in Paris was all the more alarming because of the equivocal attitude of the municipal authorities. As was the case elsewhere, a cleavage had developed between the conservative Departmental Council and the more revolutionary Commune. Bailly resigned his office as mayor of Paris in November 1791, and in a contest between La Fayette and Pétion, a lawyer from Chartres who had made a name for himself in the Constituent Assembly as an advocate of the popular cause, the latter was elected. It is noteworthy that only 10,300 voted in the election, and that the court, to vent its spite on La Fayette, supported his more radical opponent. Pétion's partisans called him 'Aristides', and Mme Roland said that he was incapable of the slightest evil action. He was to render the insurrectionaries an essential service by sanctioning the distribution from the arsenal of up to 50,000 arms, lacking which the popular rising could hardly have succeeded. Full of good intentions, his strongest passion vanity, he was a weak man, a fitting fellow-traveller of the Brissotins and, like them, quite unequal to the task of controlling the popular movement they both played their part in provoking. Lower in the ranks of the municipal hierarchy was a more formidable figure, the Deputy Procureur Danton. The Commune included advanced revolutionaries among its members, and by opening its galleries to the public in March 1792 it was exposed, like the Assembly and the Jacobin Club, to the direct pressure of popular passions. Below the Commune there were the Sections, the meetings of the local constituency divisions of Paris, which on July 25th were declared permanent. Meeting at any hour, and if necessary without break, they provided forty-eight centres from which the leaders of insurrection could conduct their campaign.

The Brissotins were still not clear whether they were for or against the revolt that was evidently brewing in Paris, and perhaps did not even know whether it was for or against them. By a decree of the Legislative Assembly, pikes were distributed to all citizens and the ranks of the National Guard were opened to members lacking the tax-paying qualification for active citizenship. In a speech to the Jacobin Club on July 29th Robespierre, who had slowly been aligning himself with the revolutionary movement and establishing contact behind the scenes with its leaders, gave it a more specific programme than it had hitherto possessed. He called for a complete renewal of political personnel by the election of a National Convention based on universal suffrage. The agitation thus now had the support of one of the unquestioned leading figures in revolutionary politics and the Brissotins had been by-passed by the movement they had started, to the advantage of Brissot's most bitter personal enemy. Robespierre was well on the way to revenge for his defeat in the debates at the beginning of the year. There are signs in their journals that the Brissotins were now trying to hold back the revolt they had done so much to provoke, but it was too late.

Political excitement continued to increase until, on the night of August 9th, the Section of the faubourg Saint-Antoine, where lived the master craftsmen, who, followed by their journeymen, had won a reputation as the stalwarts of revolutionary action, summoned three representatives from each Section to the Hôtel de Ville. There they set up a revolutionary Commune side by side with the legal one. The night was a hot one, doors were open, many of the populace in the streets, crowds gathering here and there, and excitement mounting. Towards eight o'clock in the morning a column left the faubourg Saint-Antoine under the command of Santerre. Among the *fédérés*, the Bretons and Marseillais had already begun to march on the Tuileries. The king, who had decided to review the National Guard on duty before the palace, was greeted with cries of 'Vive la Nation' and hostile demonstrations. Finally, seeing the peril of their situation, the royal family fled for protection to the Legislative Assembly. The Marseillais and Bretons, who had now reached the Tuileries, penetrated into its forecourt and fraternization with the Swiss commenced. Suddenly firing broke out from the windows, at whose order and whether by the Swiss or the gentlemen of the king's guard is not clear. Some seven Marseillais were killed and the firing became general on both sides. Now arrived the column from the faubourg Saint-Antoine, bringing cannon with which they drove the defenders to take cover within the palace. The king sent orders to the Swiss to cease fire and retire to their barracks, after which their resistance disintegrated and the fighting turned into a massacre. Altogether the attackers lost 373, while some 800 nobles and Swiss were killed in the fighting or massacred subsequently. If, as Karl Marx says, each historical event is enacted twice, the first time as tragedy and the second time as farce, the tenth of August followed the pattern of the attack on the Bastille with extraordinary fidelity, but it was far from being a farce. It was a new revolution in its own right; but just as the fall of the Bastille had to wait until the October Days for its logical conclusion to be drawn, so the tenth of August remained for a time an unfinished revolution.

The Legislative Assembly had now lost the initiative. It could only register the results of the struggle at the Tuileries. It suspended Louis XVI from his functions, but it was as much the victim of the new revolution as he was. The Brissotins tried to save what they could from the wreck of their policy. The monarchical constitution clearly being dead, they summoned a National Convention, to be elected by universal suffrage, for the purpose of framing a new constitution. Roland and his friends returned to office in a provisional Executive Council, but they had to offer a pledge to the victorious insurrection in the form of the appointment of Danton to the Ministry of Justice. He, as well as Marat and Robespierre, had kept in the background during the fighting of the tenth of August, but they were the real victors, though months of political struggle were to follow before their victory was consolidated.

CHAPTER FOUR

✦

THE FAILURE OF THE BRISSOTINS

THE revolution of the tenth of August succeeded in destroying the authority of the Legislative Assembly and overthrowing the monarchical constitution, but it solved none of the problems which had brought about their collapse. Indeed, by intensifying internal cleavages it made the military situation of France more desperate. The revolutionaries were saved in the event less by their own efforts than by the slowness of Brunswick's preparations and the weakness of the forces which Austria and Prussia, counting on a general disintegration of the French army and a counter-revolution inside France, had committed to the campaign. The invasion was in effect a side-show for them: their real concern was with Russia and developments in Poland. Brunswick commanded an army of 42,000 Prussians, 29,000 Austrians, and 6,000 Hessians, a force which in normal circumstances would have been regarded as inadequate for a serious invasion of France. After months of delay, at last, on July 19th, he crossed the French frontier by the traditional route of invasion, penetrated between the two French armies of Sedan and Metz, and marched on the fortress of Longwy. Badly supplied, the Prussians pillaged the countryside and met with a hostility that should hardly have been unexpected. Slowly moving forward, dragging with them an immense baggage train, they reached Longwy on August 20th. Under a comparatively slight bombardment the inhabitants cried out for capitulation and the garrison was allowed to march out on condition of not serving during the remainder of the war. After staying six days at Longwy the Prussians moved on. Verdun was the next objective: it yielded, after an even slighter bombardment, on September 2nd. The invasion seemed to be turning into a military promenade.

In Paris, the Legislative Assembly was dying daily as more and more deputies drifted back to their homes in the provinces. Political

excitement had not ended with the attack on the Tuileries. The
general opinion of the revolutionaries, and perhaps of most of the
population of Paris, was that the tenth of August had saved France
from an aristocratic plot, timed to coincide with the invasion.
Orators and journals demanded the punishment of the guilty, and
the Assembly yielded to the popular demand by arresting large
numbers of suspects, including many refractory priests. Riots,
sporadic murders, and attacks on property were daily occurrences.
The panic produced by the apparently inexorable advance of Brunswick was increased when La Fayette, having vainly tried to lead his
army back to suppress the revolution in Paris, fled to the Austrians.
With the fall of Longwy the road to the capital seemed open. The
Legislative Assembly took no adequate measures to meet the danger,
apart from deciding to raise an additional 30,000 men from the
National Guard in Paris and the neighbouring departments for the
defence of the country. By September 20th, 20,000 had been sent
off to the frontier.

The situation of France and the general climate of opinion provided growing weather for a renewed popular panic, which has
obvious similarities with the Great Fear of 1789 and the more artificially contrived *complot des prisons* later. Rumour had it that, when the
Prussians were within reach of Paris, a 'fifth column' of aristocrats
and priests would break out of the prisons to strike at peaceful
citizens and murder the women and children of those who had
marched to the frontiers to defend the *patrie*, at the same time
letting loose the cut-throats and criminals of the jails to join in the
massacre of patriots and the pillage of their property. When the
news of the attack on Verdun reached Paris on Sunday, September
2nd, the Commune issued a panic-stricken proclamation: 'To arms!
The enemy is at the gates!' The tocsin was sounded and the drums
of the National Guard called the citizens to the Sections. Whether
the subsequent events were planned in advance, and if so by whom,
will probably never be known. At two o'clock in the afternoon a
convoy of suspects, being moved from the Mairie, insulted by
shouts and wounded by blows on their way as was now normal,
reached the Abbaye prison, where a small mob, becoming more
menacing, demanded an immediate trial, lacking which it attacked

the prisoners and massacred seventeen out of twenty-two. At about four o'clock another band broke into the prison of the Carmes, where there were more than two hundred priests. After some initial murders, a kind of mock tribunal was set up, which called the priests before it one by one and after a few questions turned them out to be assassinated with the simple weapons that were to hand and their bodies thrown into a well. Similar scenes took place at other prisons. At the Salpêtrière women who were branded as criminals were picked out for trial and thirty-five of them were hacked down. It may not be true that female victims were raped, or that obscene mutilations were performed on the body of the princesse de Lamballe, but the *massacreurs* were well plied with wine and there was a good deal of drunken sadism mixed with their patriotic ardour. The massacres continued sporadically from September 2nd up to September 7th. As late as September 10th a party of fifty-three prisoners, sent from Orleans to be tried at Paris, was set on at Versailles by a mob, to which the escort joined themselves, and slaughtered. Although the events at Paris were the most dramatic and have attracted most attention, similar episodes occurred in the provinces on a smaller scale, which suggests that though the actual *massacreurs* were few in number they were only giving bolder and bloodier expression to a state of mind shared by many.

Of some 2,600 prisoners in Paris, it is estimated that between 1,100 and 1,400 were massacred. Among the victims were 225 priests, about 80 Swiss or members of the king's bodyguard, and between 49 and 87 other political prisoners. The remainder, between 67 and 72 per cent of the total, were ordinary common-law criminals. Throughout the period when the massacres were taking place the authorities remained in a state of almost complete passivity, at most making some weak efforts to limit the number of victims. The general public was either equally terrified of interfering with the butchery or else shared the sentiments that inspired it. Only the fear of a general outbreak of anarchy led the authorities belatedly to pluck up their courage. On September 6th the Commune of Paris issued a proclamation calling for a cessation of the massacres. The Brissotins, who had remained helpless spectators while the bloody harvest they had sown was being reaped, now began to repudiate their responsibility and represent the massacres as a manœuvre to eliminate themselves. In this they were not entirely without justification, for on either September 1st or 2nd Robespierre had denounced them to the Commune as accomplices of Brunswick. They could also regard the massacres as an attempt to influence the elections to the Convention which were proceeding concurrently.

Though the atmosphere of September 1792 was not that best calculated for the free expression of the will of the people, the Convention is commonly taken as the embodiment of revolutionary democracy. The accuracy of this interpretation depends, of course, on what one means by democracy. There were few voters. Many were excluded by law or force; fear or indifference kept others away from the electoral assemblies; the rural population had largely ceased, if indeed it had ever begun, to play an active part in politics. Altogether perhaps one-tenth of the primary electors went to the polls, and of those they chose to represent them at the secondary elections a quarter abstained. The Convention thus represented an effective vote of some 7.5 per cent of the whole electorate, and the votes even of these were not always freely cast. At Paris the Electoral Assembly transferred itself, on the proposal of Robespierre, who was himself the first to be elected, to the hall of the Jacobin Club, where the votes were given orally, in the presence of a tumultuous public. Marat, more closely identified than any other leading personage with the September massacres, was also elected. Brissot did not obtain a single vote in Paris. Elsewhere it was very different. In the provinces the Brissotins were all re-elected, along with a mass of provincial deputies who had no particular affiliations. If the revolution of the tenth of August had been intended to remove them from the political scene, it had failed. Brissot and his friends were to be given a second chance, and in much more favourable conditions, for when the Convention met the wave of terror was receding and the events of September 2nd were to provide the justification for a counter-attack on Robespierre, Marat, and their supporters.

The general lightening of the political atmosphere was due to more than a sentimental reaction against the deeds of the terrorists. As the panic aroused by the Prussian advance had created the terrorist outburst, so a dramatic change in the situation on the frontiers was to eliminate, at least temporarily, the chief grounds for panic and with them the Terror. After the flight of La Fayette, the command of the armies on the north-east frontier had been given to Dumouriez. Still clinging to his plan for an invasion of the Austrian Netherlands, he began to take up his position on the Belgian frontier; but in face of Brunswick's advance he had to abandon this. He moved south and concentrated the French forces, calling up Kellerman to join him, in the hills behind the Argonne, taking the risk of practically denuding the northern frontier for this purpose. On September 7th Brunswick reached the Argonne, and following his customary policy of manœuvring the enemy out of position, began to move round Dumouriez, expecting him to retreat, as on orthodox principles he should have done. Kellerman and the other French generals were all convinced of the necessity for withdrawal, but Dumouriez now had his hour of greatness. He drew his forces closer together on the semicircle of hills surrounding the little village of Valmy and there awaited the attack of Brunswick's army, which had moved in an arc round the French position and stood between it and Paris.

On the foggy morning of September 20th Brunswick's forces came unexpectedly under fire from Kellerman's guns. The value of Gribeauval's reform of the artillery and of Lavoisier's powder was now to be proved. Moreover, apart from two battalions of volunteers, the French consisted entirely of regiments of the line of the old army, with many men and officers who had fought in the American War, whereas the Prussian army, which had not fought a serious campaign since the time of Frederick the Great, had never been under fire. After a few local panics, the French troops held firm before the counter-cannonade of the Prussians. Firing went on till nightfall and neither army budged. Brunswick was now in a difficult position. While the Prussians cut the French army off from Paris, it stood between them and the supply base at Verdun, on which they depended for their foodstuffs. The weather throughout the campaign had been frightful, torrential storms made Brunswick's circuitous communications even more difficult, and dysentery was ravaging his troops. Though only a few hundred men had fallen on either side, he really had little choice but to withdraw. As he did so, Dumouriez might have launched an attack with considerable chance of destroying the Prussian army; but for him Austria was always the enemy and he still had his eyes fixed on Belgium. Brunswick was therefore allowed to retreat to the frontier unmolested while Dumouriez moved his armies to the north, to resume his plan for an attack on the Austrian Netherlands.

In Paris the victor of Valmy was the hero of the hour. Roland had not forgiven the general, who had been responsible for his dismissal earlier in the year, but Dumouriez had the support of Danton, now the strong man of the government. One of the most controversial figures in the history of the Revolution, Danton, son of a solicitor of Arcis in Champagne, was a mass of contradictions. Of good education and culture, able to purchase for 78,000 livres, mostly of borrowed money it is true, the office of an *avocat* to the king's council, in 1789 Danton set himself up as a mob orator and agitator at the left-wing Cordeliers Club. He obtained, in 1791, a post under the Commune of Paris. His role in the various revolutionary *journées*, and especially the revolution of the tenth of August, was suspected, probably rightly, but he always remained sufficiently in the background to escape direct responsibility. During these years, while he was building up a reputation as a tribune of the people, Danton was living extravagantly and in spite of this managing to accumulate a considerable fortune. The evidence for his venality — he certainly obtained money from the court and possibly from other sources — is overwhelming, but what services, if any, those who paid him received in return, remains unexplained. Venality did not prevent him from acquiring the stature of a colossus among the petty intriguers and street-corner orators of the factions. He was, indeed, literally a huge man, whose inexhaustible energy and force of personality recalled the figure of Mirabeau. A great orator, Danton was one of the few revolutionaries who practically never wrote his speeches, which is the reason why, when we have so many complete speeches of his contemporaries, all that survives to remind us of the torrent of oratory that could overwhelm his opponents is a collection of fragments. The contradictions running right through Danton's character rob him of true greatness. He could stir up popular passions and organize revolutionary *journées*, yet, with too much magnanimity and too little hatred in him ever to be really a man of blood, he would endeavour to save the victims of the passions he had himself aroused. He attracted a group of corrupt adventurers round him, but it is almost impossible to doubt the sincerity of his patriotic invocations. He probably took bribes to betray the Revolution and his country, yet there is no evidence that he betrayed them. Easy-going, fond of his pleasures, lazy, the crisis of France in the autumn of 1792 stirred him to tireless activity. When Dumouriez came to Paris before the new offensive, Danton rallied the revolutionaries behind him, supported his efforts to discipline the volunteers, and obtained from Santerre, now commander of the National Guard at Paris, a part of his artillery for the campaign.

The invasion of the Netherlands is not to be interpreted as the mere result of the personal ambition of Dumouriez, nor as simply the renewal of the traditional anti-Austrian sentiments of the *ancien régime*. Equally, it was not just an expression of revolutionary ardour: there were more material interests at stake. With the aid of Belgian resources the French could hope to restore financial stability and obtain supplies for their armies. It must not be thought that the wars of loot began only with Napoleon, though it would equally be wrong to suggest that the revolutionaries thought only of the economic benefits that would come to them from liberating neighbouring territories. Patriotism reaches its height when it can combine ideal ends with material benefits. On the crest of a wave of revolutionary patriotism, therefore, in the autumn of 1792, the French armies flooded over the frontiers to north-east and south-west. Savoy and Nice were occupied in September. In October, Custine took Spires, Worms, Mainz, crossed the Rhine in pursuit of the Austrians, and occupied Frankfurt. In November, Dumouriez, with 40,000 men, routed the Austrians at Jemappes and entered Brussels in triumph, to the sound of bells ringing and through streets lined by Austrian deserters, for the most part Belgians incorporated in the Austrian army.

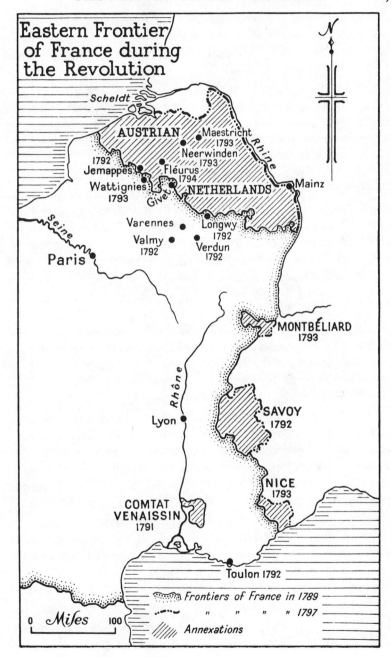

Eastern Frontier of France during the Revolution

Scheldt

AUSTRIAN

Maestricht
1793

Neerwinden
1793

1792
Jemappes

Fléurus
1794

Wattignies
1793

Givet

NETHERLANDS

Rhine

Mainz

Varennes

Longwy
1792

Valmy
1792

Verdun
1792

Paris

Seine

MONTBÉLIARD
1793

Rhône

SAVOY
1792

Lyon

NICE
1793

COMTAT
VENAISSIN
1791

Toulon 1792

0   Miles   100

Frontiers of France in 1789

"   "   "   " 1797

Annexations

The Convention, carried away by these successes, proceeded to lay down the principles of revolutionary war in two decrees which had wide European repercussions. On November 19th it offered help to all peoples who wished to recover their liberty; and on December 15th decreed the abolition of feudal dues, tithes, and all corporations in occupied territories, and the establishment in them of popularly elected governments. Less idealistic aims appeared in other clauses of the same decree. All the property of the ruler and his agents or supporters, the treasury and other public offices and corporations, lay or religious, in occupied territory was to be taken under French protection; French national commissaires were to be appointed for the purpose of co-operating with the locally elected administrations on measures of common defence, of procuring clothing and supplies for the French armies, and meeting the expenses of the occupying forces. These decrees, and the speeches which accompanied them, were an open defiance to the powers of Europe, and the first acts of the Convention were no more calculated to reassure them.

The Convention began its task by abolishing the monarchy. To symbolize the opening of a new era it henceforth dated its decrees from the year One of the Republic. With this, united action ended and open conflict began between the two small factions which the Convention had inherited from the Legislative Assembly. On one side were the Brissotins and Rolandists, to whom a number of new members joined themselves; on the other, the Jacobin deputation from Paris, which became known, from the seats it took high up at the back of the Assembly, as the Mountain. The mass of the deputies formed the Plain, or Marais, and were uncommitted to either faction, but their main allegiance at first naturally went to those like Brissot and the deputation from the Gironde whose names they knew, rather than to the Paris extremists whose reputation in most cases hardly extended beyond the capital.

Brissot and his friends had returned from their electoral campaign in the provinces conscious of victory and burning to avenge their defeat of August, as they rightly saw it, on those whom they regarded as the real leaders of that revolution, Robespierre, Marat, and

Danton. Personalities, not policies, still dominated their tactics and determined their alliances and enmities. Danton, who after the election had given up his ministry in order to be able to take his place in the Convention, leaving Roland as the chief minister in so far as there was one, made approaches to them but was repulsed. 'I cannot associate the idea of a good man with that face', said Mme Roland. However, the new deputies from the provinces did not yet appreciate the bitterness of the feuds that had developed in Paris. Attempts to persuade the Convention to put Robespierre and Marat on trial failed to win the support of the Plain. The Mountain transformed its position from one of defence to offence by a more subtle tactic. The Brissotin faction was faced with the nemesis of its earlier attacks on the monarchy in the form of a demand for the trial of the king. The discovery, at the Tuileries, of the secret *armoire de fer*, containing the royal correspondence with Austria, was the death-warrant of Louis XVI. After the revelation of the papers it contained his trial could not be avoided. Robespierre saw clearly the dilemma in which the Brissotins were placed and pressed the issue remorselessly. If they opposed the trial, or voted for the innocence of the king, they could be denounced as royalists and traitors, as well as in effect tacitly repudiating and confessing the dishonesty of their earlier denunciations of Louis; if they voted for the king's death they sacrificed moderate support and were left isolated. Vergniaud and Brissot attempted to evade the fatal vote by pleading for a referendum, but Robespierre, who had often advocated a direct vote by the people when it suited his purpose, would have none of it now; the proposal was rejected. There was not a shadow of doubt in anyone's mind that Louis had been guilty of treachery, as indeed he had from the point of view of revolutionary France. In the decisive vote, 28 were absent, 321 voted for penalties other than death, 13 for death but with a respite, 26 for death but with a debate on postponement of execution, and 361 for death without qualification, an absolute majority of one. The king's trial had reduced the Brissotins and Rolandists to chaos, and proved how little they formed an organized party with a settled policy, for their votes were to be found scattered on all sides. In a subsequent debate on the proposal for a respite, which was rejected by 380 to 310, the opposition to sparing the king's life was led by Mme Roland's young paladin from the south, Barbaroux.

The fate of Louis XVI, it might be said, had been settled on the day when he signed the decree for war with Austria; by it he became the king of a nation that had reduced him to the status of a constitutional rubber stamp, the leader of a crusade against those whose only declared motive was to protect him from his own subjects and restore his power. King at the same time of the Revolution and of the counter-revolution, whatever he did or did not do, the essential falsity of his position spelt doom. On January 21st, 1793, Louis XVI was carried through roads lined with the National Guard and a silent populace to the Place de la Révolution, formerly Place Louis XV, and there guillotined. For the regicides there could now be no turning back.

At the moment there seemed little occasion for second thoughts. The offensive that had been launched by the victories of Dumouriez and Custine was carrying all before it and the Convention was intoxicated with success. It proclaimed the annexation of Savoy in November 1792. The Scheldt, closed except to the Dutch since the Treaty of Münster in 1648, was declared open to all shipping. In January 1793 Danton proclaimed the doctrine of natural frontiers, often, but incorrectly, attributed to Louis XIV, and thereby staked a claim to the Rhine frontier. These actions were bound to lead to an extension of the war, but the Convention did not wait for its enemies to take the initiative. The former calculation on English neutrality was now forgotten: the time had come for the Seven Years War to be avenged, as well as the more recent humiliation of 1787. Anglophobia in France was hardly less strong than hatred of the Austrians. For the purpose of maintaining English neutrality, as I have said, early in 1792 the young marquis de Chauvelin had been sent over to the court of St James as French ambassador. His first dispatches, probably dictated by Talleyrand and his Swiss adviser, du Roveray, were moderate and raised no hopes of an imminent revolution in England; but when Chauvelin was deprived of these experienced advisers and came to realize that such views only aroused suspicions at Paris of his loyalty to the Revolution, he changed his tune and produced more acceptable reports. The French Foreign Office was not relying on mere official information, however. It had sent over a small army of secret agents to spy on the English and on one another, whose reports drew a picture of a nation waiting only the call from France to burst the bonds of tyranny. The British government itself was disturbed by the association of French agents with the English Jacobins. It was not these activities, however, but the deposition of Louis XVI, in whose name Chauvelin's credentials ran, that led to the withdrawal of official recognition from the ambassador, though unofficial contact was maintained with one or two of the more respectable of the French agents. It was inevitable, when the news of the execution of Louis XVI was received, that Chauvelin and the French official mission should be ordered to quit England. The breach of diplomatic relations with France did not necessarily mean war, even though the decrees of November 19th and December 15th, and the opening of the Scheldt, were regarded as sufficiently provocative to justify military and naval preparations.

On the French side there was also hesitation. The Brissotins, the Executive Council, with its weak but not stupid foreign minister, the former journalist Lebrun, and even some of the Mountain, including Robespierre, hesitated before the final step and saw the dangers, external and internal, that a general war with all Europe would bring on the new Republic. Such doubts, however, were reserved for their secret thoughts and expressed in public, if at all, only with great caution; for the revolutionary leaders were now at the mercy of the patriotic ardour which they had been whipping up for the past three years. Public opinion, including that of the great majority of members of the Convention, had no reservations or private doubts. When the comte de Kersaint, Breton noble and naval officer, and as such sharing the traditional Anglophobia of the French navy, delivered a resounding call for war with England on January 1st, 1793, he spoke for the Convention. Brissot, who had lived in England, was Anglophile in his private sentiments, but here once again we see how little the Brissotins formed a coherent party, for Kersaint had been one of their most ardent supporters in the attack on the Mountain. Similarly, while Brissot and some of his friends were trying to postpone war with the Dutch, Dumouriez

o

was pressing for the invasion of the United Provinces. In the presence of general enthusiasm for war the revolutionary leaders found it easier to win popular applause by denouncing pacific tendencies as treachery to the Revolution than to attempt to moderate the bellicose ardour of their followers. Nor should the influence of the foreign revolutionary refugees, whose only hope of gaining power in their own countries lay in French assistance, be underestimated. On February 1st, 1793, Brissot himself introduced the decree of the Convention declaring war against Great Britain and Holland. It was voted unanimously. In March hostilities were declared against Spain, and the French Republic was soon at war with all Europe except Switzerland and Scandinavia.

France had still no effective government to conduct the war. A Committee of General Defence, including three representatives from each of the committees of the Convention, had been set up on the proposal of Brissot, but it had no executive powers and remained ineffective. The army, from which the volunteers had been flowing back home after Jemappes, was in no condition to conduct a major campaign. The Convention decreed the raising of 300,000 men, but met with much opposition in its attempts to put the measure into effect. In these circumstances, the frustration of the hopes that had been raised by Jemappes rapidly followed the extension of the war. Early in March the French army besieging Maestricht was driven back in disorder, and Dumouriez, perhaps foreseeing further defeats, addressed a letter to the Convention attributing the reverse to the policy of the ministers and the tactless and tyrannical conduct of the French commissaires in Belgium. On March 18th the Austrian general, Coburg, defeated him at Neerwinden and he was compelled to evacuate Brussels. The scheme for a quick victory over Austria was in ruins.

The French general was left with the second and more secret part of his plan to attempt: this was to march his army on Paris and restore the Constitution of 1791 with the young Louis XVII as king. After a secret meeting with the Austrian general Mack, in which they reached an understanding, he was allowed to withdraw the French armies to the frontier unmolested. Representatives of the Convention, where suspicions of Dumouriez's intentions were growing, were sent to summon him to the bar of the house. They were arrested on his orders and handed over to the Austrians; but his efforts to persuade the army to march on Paris failed, and on April 5th he too passed over, with most of his general staff, like La Fayette before him, to the Austrians.

Meanwhile, farther south, Custine had been driven back and forced to give up the left bank of the Rhine. Within France the first of the provincial revolts against the Revolution broke out when, in March, the Vendée rose in arms against the attempt to enforce conscription for the army. The accumulation of disasters renewed the panic mentality that had been responsible for the events of August and September 1792, and as on former occasions, popular unrest was fed by economic distress. The expense of the war intensified the torrent of inflation — at the moment when war was declared on Great Britain and Holland 800 million of new assignats had to be voted by the Convention to meet its initial cost — and inflation meant a new food crisis. Leaders were now beginning to appear in the streets of Paris who differed from earlier popular agitators in that their primary demand was for the remedying of the economic distresses of the populace, and for economic and not political measures to bring this about. One of the most prominent of these was Jacques Roux, accused in 1790 of instigating a peasant rising, who had been elected as one of the constitutional clergy in Paris and had acquired influence through his violent speeches at the Cordeliers Club. Another of the *enragés*, as they were called, was a prosperous postal official named Varlet, who became a successful mob orator, though he failed to obtain a hearing from the Convention or the Jacobins. How far these were men of violent temperament, anti-parliamentary by nature, who were prepared to exploit the sufferings of the people to build up a following for themselves and climb into power by way of rioting in the streets, and how far they genuinely believed in the economic views which they put forward and which differentiated them from the rest of the revolutionaries, whether advanced or moderate, it is difficult to say. To the members of the Convention, the *enragés*, because they advocated a revival of the economic controls of the *ancien régime*, seemed crypto-counter-revolutionaries; but whereas the Brissotins and the ministers offered nothing but open hostility to them, the Jacobin Mountain, with greater political realism, was prepared to use them against its political opponents so long as it seemed possible to do so.

In February 1793 food riots, led by Jacques Roux, failed to achieve anything. Another popular movement, in March, in which the *enragés* probably had secret support from the Mountain, was checked only after the destruction of the Brissotin printing-presses. The treachery of Dumouriez, combined with military defeat, led to a revival of fears of foreign invasion and counter-revolution, and gave an increased impetus to unrest; but the Convention, which remained preoccupied with the faction fight between Brissotins and the Mountain, could only agree on increasing the severity of the repressive legislation against counter-revolutionaries. The punitive laws against refractory priests and émigrés were intensified; a Revolutionary Tribunal was set up to judge traitors; representatives on mission were sent out to strengthen the Revolution in the provinces; a decree condemned to summary execution all rebels taken in the act. The numbers who were to perish by this last law are uncalculated and probably incalculable, but they were to exceed by far the victims of the Revolutionary Tribunal. On March 21st watch committees were set up in every commune: they were to become one of the principal instruments of the Terror. On April 6th, at the proposal of the Brissotin Isnard, a Committee of Public Safety was formed, entrusted with the duty of supervising the Executive Council and elected for a month at a time. The most important new feature was that it was given 100,000 livres for the payment of its agents and another 100,000 for secret expenses.

Most of the machinery of the revolutionary government and the Terror was thus created in the spring of 1793, and it was the work of a Convention in which the Brissotins still retained considerable influence. This was evidently suffering, however, from the inadequacy of their efforts to cope with the national crisis. A change was needed not in machinery but in personnel. In the election of the first Committee of Public Safety the Convention marked its dislike of the faction fight that Brissotins and the Robespierrist Mountain continued to wage, by the choice of middle-men, like Danton and Barère, uncommitted to either faction. Danton was to devote the next two months to an attempt to mediate between the hostile factions, relying on the votes of the Plain. The Mountain, for its part, wanted no mediation and was prepared to repeat its tactics of the previous year, though the situation was now not so simple as it had been then. In August 1792 the aim had been to secure the dissolution of the Legislative Assembly; now they wanted to purge the Convention of their chief enemies, without destroying it, and with it themselves, altogether. Whether the Mountain, behind the scenes, organized a new popular movement at the end of May 1793, or whether it was the work of the lesser men of the Commune of Paris and the Sections, unwittingly playing the game of the Mountain, again cannot be said. Whatever its inspiration, on May 28th an insurrectionary committee drawn from the Sections was set up at the Archbishop's Palace. As in August 1792, a revolutionary Commune was constituted and Hanriot, a former customs official and a swaggering braggadocio, usurped command of the National Guard.

On June 2nd a huge mob, including many National Guard with their cannon, concentrated round the Tuileries where the Convention sat and demanded the arrest of the factious members. This meant specifically the leading Brissotins, the two ministers associated with them, Lebrun and Clavière, and the members of a Commission of Twelve which had been formed to repress the Commune. However spontaneous the action of the mob may have been, it is hardly likely that this list of chief enemies of the Mountain could have been drawn up without inspiration from above. Among those attacked, only the Breton lawyer, Lanjuinais, a constitutional monarchist, with the Mountain shouting him down and crying for the deputation from the mob to be admitted, dared to denounce the illegal authority which had surrounded the Convention with armed men and cannon and was offering it a petition which he boldly described as 'dragged through the mud of the streets of Paris'. When the butcher Legendre called to him, 'Come down or I'll fell you', it is said that Lanjuinais replied, 'First of all decree that I am an ox.' On the other hand, a number of the Brissotins weakly offered to resign their legislative functions. Only the young Marseillais, Barbaroux, the Antinoüs of Mme Roland, joined Lanjuinais in defying the armed hordes outside and their advocates within the Chamber. While the debate proceeded in the Convention, Hanriot and his forces ranged remorseless without and cut off all avenues of escape. It was finally Couthon, the devoted follower of Robespierre, which is not without significance, who demanded to be carried, for he was partly paralysed, to the tribune and there proposed that the Convention accept the demands of Hanriot and his forces, and decree the arrests they were demanding. There was no roll-call, but Hérault de Séchelles, who had taken over the presidential chair, declared the decree carried.

In the following days many deputies signed protests, which were later to be used to justify more arrests and to build up the legend of a great and menacing Girondin Party; but the more timid, in considerable numbers, left Paris, and the Jacobins of the Mountain, with the mob behind them, secured control of the Convention. Their situation was potentially dangerous; they had to prevent the popular movement which had given them control of the rump Convention from getting out of hand and overthrowing it. The solution was a simple one: they voted the demonstrators a payment of 40 sous a day in compensation for their lost days of labour, and in return secured the dissolution of the insurrectional committee. To prove their impeccable principles, the Mountain presented the Convention with a democratic Constitution, drawn up by a committee of Jacobins, which was rapidly passed into law and as rapidly consigned to a cedar chest, to be kept moth-proof, inviolable, and inoperative until the end of the war.

As a result of the uprising of June, the political situation had been drastically changed. One side in the faction fight having been decisively defeated, there was no scope left for mediators in the Convention. Some of the middle-men, like Barère, rapidly aligned themselves with the victorious Mountain. Danton and his group, who had dominated the Committee of Public Safety for its first three months, now lost their places on it. When the Committee was re-elected in July it included Hérault de Séchelles, Jeanbon Saint-André, Saint-Just, Couthon, and Prieur of the Marne, from the Mountain, along with Barère and Robert Lindet, from the Plain, who had joined them. Robespierre entered the Committee in July, in August Carnot and Prieur of the Côte d'Or, and

in September Billaud-Varenne and Collot d'Herbois. Apart
from Hérault, who was rapidly eliminated, this completed the
great Committee of Public Safety, which was to hold power
for the most critical year of the Revolution, from July 1793 to
July 1794.

CHAPTER FIVE

THE COMMITTEE OF PUBLIC SAFETY

WITH the new Committee of Public Safety, revolutionary France for the first time had an effective executive government and an Assembly from which the opposition had been eliminated. For the next twelve months the Convention was to be the faithful echo of the powerful Committee and the ministers its mere agents, poor creatures, the American ambassador described them, hardly daring to blow their own noses without permission. Such a concentration of power was unprecedented, but it would have been of little avail if it had not been in the hands of a group of men who were equal to the opportunity they had created. The great Committee of Public Safety embodied the results of a ruthless struggle for survival of the fittest in the internecine warfare of revolutionary politics. The result was a government of perhaps the ablest and most determined men who have ever held power in France. The desperate situation of the country forced unity on them. Though there was to some extent a division of labour, the attempt of historians to discriminate among the members of the Committee between the 'politicians' who conducted the Terror and the 'administrators' who reorganized the army and the government and saved France has not survived the test of more detailed research: the glory and the terror were bound up together and the members of the Committee stand out too clearly as individuals in the round to be reduced to pasteboard silhouettes or identified by any conventional labels. The only way of dealing with them is to take them one by one.

We can dismiss rapidly Hérault de Séchelles, a strikingly handsome young noble of the robe who, with distinguished ancestry, wealth and ambition, had thrown in his lot with the Patriot party. The role he played on the occasion of the revolution of June 2nd made him temporarily a leading figure in the Convention. He presided over the fête at the Champ-de-Mars to celebrate the acceptance of the Constitution of 1793, and cut a fine figure as he presented the chalice of lustral water that poured from the breasts of the Statue of Liberty on the altar to the deputies as they filed up one by one. Insouciant, gay, with aristocratic connections and a mistress whose husband served in the army of the king of Sardinia, he was out of place among the hard, uncompromising men of the Mountain; he naturally lost his position on the Committee and in due course his head.

The remaining members were made of very different metal. Billaud-Varenne and Collot d'Herbois stand apart from the others. These were the real men of blood. Collot had been a not very successful actor and dramatist, whose histrionic talent served him well with a popular audience. He was the one member of the Committee who was a mob orator and may have owed his position to the Committee's need to keep in touch with the subaltern agitators of the streets on whom their power in the last resort depended. Billaud-Varenne, though commonly linked with Collot as a mere terrorist, was an abler and more interesting figure than is usually recognized. Son of a lawyer of La Rochelle, he became a teacher in one of the schools of the Oratory, where a colleague was Fouché, and like him entered revolutionary politics. He built up connections with the Commune and the Sections of Paris and supported in the Convention the movement of June 2nd. By no means a mere vulgar agitator, he had produced books and pamphlets which indicate serious thought on the problems of government and was perhaps to be responsible for the great law of Frimaire reorganizing local government in November 1793.

The two Prieurs are the members of the Committee whose personalities emerge least from the pages of history. Prieur of the Marne, a lawyer from Châlons-sur-Marne, spent much of his year of office on mission to the armies and the departments. The other Prieur, of the Côte d'Or, an engineer officer when the Revolution broke out, was a friend of Carnot and played a useful part in the organization of the supply of munitions of war. Lazare Carnot had before the Revolution been a captain in the engineer corps. His failure to prove noble descent, despite persevering efforts, robbed him of both marriage with the girl he loved and further advancement in the army. He was to be the organizer of victory. Almost equally important for the salvation of the Republic, though history has neglected him, was Robert Lindet, with special responsibility for food supplies. Forty years later, in Balzac's *Les employés*, the old concierge at the ministry compares the modern 'paper-scratchers' with the hard-working officials he knew when he was young. But that, he adds, was under Robert Lindet. Jeanbon Saint-André, a Protestant from Montauban who after a career in the merchant navy became a pastor, was to spend much of his year in the Committee of Public Safety organizing the navy at Brest. Barère de Vieuzac owned a small fief and held legal office at Tarbes in the Pyrenees. Prosperous, eloquent, with ingratiating manners and literary tastes, he combined social and professional success. Elected to the Constituent Assembly in 1789, he reported its debates in the *Point du Jour*, moved steadily to the left with the current of revolutionary opinion, gained influence in the Convention as a facile orator and was to be the regular reporter to it of the views of the Committee of Public Safety. Ornamenting its measures of proscription with flowers of rhetoric, he became 'the Anacreon of the guillotine'. Couthon, the little, lame lawyer from Auvergne, gentle and idealistic, was devoted to Robespierre, whom he was to follow to the bitter end. On mission at Lyons, he moderated the violence of his colleagues; but, not a man of blood himself, he could make bloodthirsty speeches, and his reputation has lived by what he said rather than what he did. The other close associate of Robespierre was a very different figure, Saint-Just, a terrifying young man, only twenty-one when the Revolution broke out. 'His arrogance surpasses all bounds', protested Carnot, and Camille Desmoulins, 'He carries his head like the Holy Sacrament.' The political essays and draft constitution he wrote during the Revolution are the ground plan of a Spartan republic. On mission to the armies he showed that he was a man of action. Pity and moderation were not in his vocabulary.

With such ruthless and able men as his colleagues, to treat the Committee of Public Safety as the dictatorship of Robespierre is patently absurd. Yet there is a sense in which the little lawyer from Arras was the one man who was essential. Precise and even elegant in dress, prim in manner, living decently and dying poor, an eminently respectable figure but capable of winning love as well as admiration, the part he played in the Revolution has been reduced to nonsense and himself to a meaningless horror by the systematic blackening of his reputation after Thermidor. Robespierre's rise to a position of pre-eminence among revolutionary politicians has been made inexplicable by the biased reporting which concealed his effectiveness as a speaker in the Constituent Assembly. Though he spoke always as if he were the voice of the people, he was no mere demagogue: he held out almost single-handed against the war fever in the spring of 1792 and later was to face and defeat *enragés* and Hébertists. 'I have seen him', wrote a fellow-member of the Constituent Assembly, 'resist the entire assembly and demand, as a man aware of his own dignity, that the President should call it to order.' His 'sea-green' incorruptibility may not be an attractive virtue, but it was not too common a quality and not confined to mere freedom from pecuniary temptations. Robespierre, it was truly observed, was a dangerous man because he believed everything he said. He was compared to the leader of a sect. He sought out the faithless like an inquisitor. He was a political Calvinist to whom principles were everything and men nothing. It would be too much to expect that as well as being virtuous he should also be likeable; yet no man in the history of the Revolution had more devoted friends and followers. He can be admired or hated, excused or condemned, he should not be belittled. When David, in 1832, went to see the aged Barère, on his bed of sickness, to speak to him of a plan for portraying the great men of the Revolution, the old revolutionary sat up and with a commanding gesture declared, 'Do not forget Robespierre! He was a man of pure integrity, a true republican.'

The Committee of Public Safety had an apparently desperate task before it. Not only was France at war with most of Europe, but Paris was at war with most of France, and for this widespread civil war it is only fair to say that the Committee was itself in large measure responsible. The Mountain, in its conflict with the Brissotins, and above all in the methods it had used to destroy them, had sowed the seeds of civil strife and was now to reap the harvest. Yet if we ask what the struggle with its opponents had been about, it is hard to give a satisfactory answer. The leaders of the Mountain are difficult to distinguish in their social and political ideas from the

Brissotins. Both factions believed in the sacred rights of property and the principle of economic freedom; both had abandoned their earlier support of constitutional monarchy, the Brissotins possibly with more alacrity than their opponents; both recognized the sovereignty of the people and neither regarded the people as including a propertyless proletariat; in their attitude to the religious question the Brissotins tended to exhibit more extreme anti-clerical sentiments than the Mountain; both, in speeches and in their journals, had invoked popular violence; the Brissotins had taken the initiative in attempting to proscribe their enemies in the Convention. The difference between the two factions is to be looked for chiefly in their attitude to the problem of the turbulent populace of Paris and the agitators who could exploit its fears and passions. Two things were guaranteed to arouse these: military defeat, and the economic pressure of high prices and shortage of supplies. In the spring and summer of 1792, and again in the spring of 1793, the Brissotins found themselves responsible for disaster to the armies. In economic matters they were too wedded to the principles of free trade to be able to take any steps to alleviate popular distress. The Mountain was free from governmental responsibility for the former and was prepared to compromise with its principles in dealing with the latter. A further source of strength to the Mountain were the contacts it had established with the leaders of the Paris mob. The Jacobins did not hesitate to call in the Sections and Commune of Paris to redress the balance in the Convention; but by accepting, even on grounds of expediency, the demands of the revolutionary Commune and aligning themselves with the mob, they were purchasing the support of Paris at the price of a break with the more conservative provinces. The Brissotins, by the operation of the same causes, found themselves looking for support to the provinces against Paris. They were therefore again put in a position to be outmanœuvred by the Mountain and represented as federalists aiming to destroy the unity of France, and as allies of the royalists who had been attempting to raise provincial revolts since the beginning of the Revolution.

The most dangerous and long-lived of these revolts was that in the west. Measures against the Church aroused resentment in

Catholic Brittany, but what ultimately provoked the outbreak of large-scale civil war in the Vendée was the attempt to apply conscription in the spring of 1793. By June the Vendéan rebels were masters of a wide area in the west and besieging Nantes. In Normandy there was a minor rising which was easily repressed. At Marseilles and Bordeaux the representatives on mission were expelled by force. At Lyons, where the silk industry was stagnating, the National Guard revolted, threw the mayor of the city into prison with many of his supporters, and massacred some 200 of the local Jacobins. Some of the deputies proscribed on and after the rising of June 2nd, who had fled from Paris, joined these uprisings; but most of them either went into hiding or were captured and perished miserably. They had neither provoked nor were they able to profit by the outbreak of civil war.

Externally the situation continued to deteriorate. On the north-eastern frontier foreign invasion again threatened with the fall of Valenciennes. The port of Toulon revolted and was handed over by the royalists to the English. The factions in Paris were brought vividly to a sense of their peril when Charlotte Corday stabbed Marat to death on July 13th, 1793. His body with its wound was exhibited to the public next day; and the same night, after a procession by the light of torches, with muffled drums and firing of cannon, was interred in the garden of the Cordeliers. No more fatal event than Marat's murder could have occurred for the moderates or for any who could be suspected of moderatism. The imprisonment of all suspects was decreed and the revolutionary committees in the communes of France became in effect the masters of life and death. Representatives sent out on mission from the Convention, to enforce a *levée en masse* of all unmarried men between eighteen and twenty-five, repressed opposition, sometimes with moderation, sometimes, as Carrier at Nantes, with massacre and bloodthirsty sadism. In Paris the Revolutionary Tribunal, which had operated slowly hitherto, speeded up its production under the impulsion of the Public Prosecutor, that devoted public servant Fouquier-Tinville. The guillotine cut a swathe through the ranks of counter-revolutionaries and revolutionaries alike. Marie-Antoinette, after a trial in which all the indecent slanders of her enemies of the old court were dragged up to discredit her, was executed in October, a tragic figure, sketched on her last journey, all her beauty gone, by the bitter pen of David. Brissot, Vergniaud, and twenty-nine of those arrested with them, their mouths silenced at their trial by a decree of the Convention, died, sacrificial victims on the altar of the republic they had striven to achieve. Roland, Condorcet, Clavière, Pétion evaded execution by suicide. The Duke of Orleans, unworthy Philippe-Égalité, mounted the steps of the guillotine instead of the throne and died with more dignity than he had lived. Mme du Barry perished shrieking her head off, and Élisabeth, sister to the dead king, with religious devotion. Military leaders who had been defeated were guillotined to encourage the others. In Lavoisier was executed the former Farmer-General; it was a pity that France's greatest scientist had to die at the same time. 'Les dieux ont soif,' cried Camille Desmoulins, and they cared little whose blood was poured out for their libation.

The victory of the Mountain and its allies of the left brought to power also those who were not satisfied with the compromise represented by the Civil Constitution of the Clergy, and enabled the anti-clericals to launch a violent campaign of dechristianization. A new republican calendar dated the year One from September 22nd, 1792, and introduced a ten-day week, which had the advantage of eliminating Sundays and substituting a rest-day every ten days for one every seven. Extremists took matters into their own hands, holding anti-religious processions in the streets and attacking churches and priests. In Notre-Dame the festival of liberty, personified by an actress suitably garbed and elevated on an artificial mountain in the choir, was celebrated. Among the continual deputations of patriots, intoxicated not only with revolutionary ardour, which helped to pass the time of the Convention, may be singled out for distinguished mention a procession of one of the Paris Sections. National Guards with their drums were followed by a group of women dressed in white to symbolize what is not said, and a double file of men clad in cassocks, chasubles, and copes, carrying with them the spoils of Saint-Germain-des-Prés, including all the utensils of superstitious practices, and escorting a black drapery beneath which was supposed to be the dead body of fanaticism. After the robed men had executed dances to the sound of the 'Ça ira' and other revolutionary tunes, the demonstrators took their seats on the now unpopulated right side of the Convention, while their orator delivered a speech which was received with transports of universal joy. Three days after this, on November 23rd, 1793, the Commune closed all the churches in Paris. What the Committee of Public Safety thought of these proceedings is not revealed; but while some members, like Collot, shared the sentiments of the dechristianizers, most of them saw political dangers in thus alienating the great mass of the French people, which had not been greatly concerned at the confiscation of church property or even the establishment of the Constitutional Church, but would be likely to react more positively to an open war on religion. Robespierre, who preferred to have things done decently and even the Terror conducted with some appearance of law and order, was too good a Rousseauist in his religious ideas not to see behind dechristianization the sinister shade of atheism.

However, the left-wing extremists now had the bit between their teeth and seemed on the point of bolting with the Revolution. The economic situation was playing into their hands. Since the beginning of the revolutionary war the assignat had been falling rapidly and by July 1793 had lost 77 per cent of its face value. The economic distress of the populace of Paris, which had been exploited by successive political factions for five years, presented a challenge and a threat to the Committee of Public Safety; all the more because, perhaps somewhat disillusioned at the failure of a series of political revolutions to bring about any improvement, the people were now listening to agitators who demanded economic measures such as the punishment of monopolists and profiteers and the fixing of maximum prices. In the description of the spokesmen of this agitation, men like Jacques Roux and Varlet, as the *enragés*, the wild men of the Revolution, is reflected the horror with which the respectable middle-class citizens of the Convention, however extreme they were in their political views, regarded the prospect of any interference with the economic order. But the Mountain, having overthrown their opponents with the aid of the populace of Paris, had now to pay the price or be overthrown by an alliance of dechristianizers and *enragés* in their turn. Unlike Brissot and Roland, they were political realists and accepted the necessity of doing something to alleviate economic distress. They put French economy on a war basis, inaugurated a policy of requisitioning, and imposed a maximum on the prices of essential goods. Their measures improved the situation temporarily. By the end of 1793 the assignat had risen to 50 per cent of its face value.

The *enragés* were few in number, their propaganda was ideological and lacking in demagogic appeal, and their proto-socialist ideas ill-adapted to win the support of the small masters who formed the backbone of the revolutionary mobs. The Committee of Public Safety, having stolen the practical points in their programme, clapped them into prison as counter-revolutionaries. A very different threat was presented by the movement of the sans-culottes, all the more dangerous because it was so inchoate and incoherent. What the sans-culottes wanted is almost as difficult to say as what they were. Their name indicates that they did not wear knee-breeches, which is about as useless a class distinction as could be found. They constituted the militants of the Sections of Paris, the professional revolutionaries who spent their time at the Section meetings, orating and denouncing in an alcoholic haze. Their leaders, men like Hébert and Chaumette, were themselves professional revolutionaries on a higher level, interested mainly in power for themselves and the guillotine for their enemies. If they stood for anything it was for anti-clericalism, but only for this, one suspects, because the clergy were easily-identifiable victims against whom to whip up popular passions. They maintained their control of the Sections by packing them with a clientele paid for attendance, or in the less sans-culottist districts with supporters from outside, and by strong-arm methods. Hébert's *Père Duchesne* flourished with the aid of a large government subsidy for its free distribution in the provinces and the army. It is now unreadable. If murder had to be advocated, at least it might have been done with the literary qualities of a Marat. All the *foutus* and *bougres* of Hébert are as stale and artificial as their author. It is difficult to find anyone else in the whole history of the Revolution as completely contemptible as the leaders of the sans-culottes. Perhaps in the end even their followers thought so, for when the time came for their elimination hardly a voice was raised in their defence. The threat of sans-culottist anarchy was removed in two stages. Towards the end of 1793 the Committee of Public Safety re-established the control of the central over local government.

For the first time since 1789 France had a real government. Along with determination at the centre was needed the machinery for regaining control of the provinces. This was provided by the law of the fourteenth of Frimaire, year Two (December 4th, 1793), of which the chief author may have been Billaud-Varenne. All subordinate authorities and officials were put under the authority of the Committee of Public Safety, except for the police, which remained in principle the responsibility of the Committee of General Security. National agents, placed in control of the districts, were to report every ten days to the two supreme Committees. The movement that had commenced with a spontaneous outburst of communal liberties had thus ended, only four years later, with the creation of a far more ruthlessly centralized system of administration than even the *ancien régime* had known.

With a strong impulse now coming from Paris, the military fortunes of the Revolution, both within France and on the frontiers, improved. In October, Lyons fell to the republican army. Its defenders fled or were massacred and the total destruction of the city was decreed. Toulon, bombarded by the artillery of the young Corsican, Bonaparte, surrendered in December. The Vendéans, after a series of victories, failed to capture Granville in the Cherbourg peninsula and establish contact with the British fleet. Their armies, divided and lacking coherent leadership, became dispersed and were defeated, though the massacres and counter-massacres which marked this bloody and cruel civil war prohibited any lasting pacification for another seven years.

Despite the anarchic conditions in France, conscription had given the Committee of Public Safety an army of some 650,000 by July 1793. However badly equipped and clothed they were, this was a formidable body of men, inspired by revolutionary ardour, and far surpassing in numbers any armies that could be brought against it. In October the allies under Coburg were defeated at Wattignies by Jourdan; in Alsace, Hoche crossed the Vosges and drove back the

P

enemy; Savoy was freed by Kellermann; the Spaniards were driven across the Pyrenees.

These victories strengthened the hand of the Committee of Public Safety in Paris. As well as the dangerous movement of the *enragés* and the dechristianizers, who had found a would-be leader in the demagogue Hébert, journalist of the professionally obscene *Père Duchesne*, opposition was reappearing from another quarter in the early months of 1794. The austere economic policies of the Committee of Public Safety were not to the liking of the crowd of political adventurers, government contractors, and financiers who had found patriotism a profitable speculation. The game of playing the markets and speculating for a rise or fall in the shares of companies, which had created mutually profitable alliances between the world of finance and that of government in the years before the Revolution, had not ceased with the triumph of virtue. Indeed, the fall of the assignat and the need for vast contracts to supply the revolutionary armies provided opportunities for speculation to reach unprecedented new heights. Foreign financiers, Belgian, Dutch, Swiss, Austrian, congregated in Paris, and found an ample supply of politicians, even in the pure atmosphere of the Mountain, who were open to the lure of wealth and women. It is difficult to believe that the speculators had any political principles, but some of them were associated with the Hébertists and dechristianizers on the left, and others with a new tendency which was appearing to the right of the Committee of Public Safety, demanding a relaxation of the Terror.

Danton, more capable of wild bursts of energy than of persistent political action, had ceased to play a leading role in revolutionary politics after he left the first Committee of Public Safety. For months he had withdrawn with a new young wife to his home at Arcis-sur-Aube. If he were not entangled with corrupt financiers himself, he certainly had many friends who were, and when they came under attack in November 1793 from the Hébertists and their financial allies, he returned to Paris to their aid. To save those who were already in prison, though not necessarily to the exclusion of more disinterested motives, Danton put himself behind a campaign for the relaxation of the Terror. With the approval of Robespierre, the

Dantonist Camille Desmoulins, one of the most brilliant if one of the least reliable of revolutionary journalists, launched, in the *Vieux Cordelier*, a devastating attack on the system of spies and informers which in the name of patriotism was turning France into a police state. The machinery of denunciation, arrests, and executions was indeed getting out of control: it was being used by all kinds of subaltern agents and petty agitators for their own private ends. The *Vieux Cordelier* and the campaign for clemency found so unexpectedly wide a public welcome that Robespierre became alarmed and withdrew his support. Collot d'Herbois and Billaud-Varenne reacted violently, and the forces they could rally in Paris were still too powerful to be repudiated. Robespierre therefore drew back from his tentative alliance with Danton and temporized.

Meanwhile, on the other flank, the Hébertists were still a potential threat to the regime. In March 1794 Robespierre decided to finish with them. At the same time, to carry the whole Committee with him, he had to abandon his half-hearted protection of the Dantonists. On March 24th, Hébert and his chief lieutenants were sent to the scaffold. The 'Revolutionary Army', a little private army of a few thousand sans-culottist heroes of the home front, which had been used for requisitioning food from the surrounding countryside, suppressing opposition by force, and as a side-line closing the churches and dechristianizing, was dissolved in Paris; its numerous provincial copies had already disappeared. Danton and his friends followed their enemies to the guillotine on April 5th. The complicity of both factions with alien financiers was used to represent their execution as the suppression of a 'foreign conspiracy'; the fact that many who perished had already been under arrest for months enabled the police to present it also as another 'prison plot'. In eliminating by a bold stroke to right and left both Dantonists and Hébertists, the Committee of Public Safety had won the most brilliant victory in the history of the Revolution, but it had also destroyed many of the men whose command of the mob had brought it to power.

Henceforth the Committee was to rule in an increasing void, though its efforts to create a favourable public opinion must not be underestimated. Apart from the official or semi-official press, the greatest and perhaps the most successful propaganda effort took the form of the grandiose processional pageants that were organized by David. To celebrate the anniversary of the revolution of the tenth of August and the promulgation of the Constitution, the Convention voted the sum of 1,200,000 livres for the fête of August 10th, 1793. Delegates of the primary assemblies from all over France, members of the Convention, of the clubs, and a miscellaneous collection of the sovereign people, gathered at the Place de la Bastille, and after speeches, songs, and salvoes, formed in procession, with chariots and floats symbolizing the republican virtues, moving down the boulevards, with halts at triumphal arches or colossal plaster figures, till they reached the altar of the *patrie* in the Champ-de-Mars. Huge crowds watched or participated in the celebrations, which lasted from seven in the morning to eleven at night. Another famous occasion was the Fête of the Supreme Being, at which Robespierre set fire, with a torch handed to him by David, to a huge cardboard figure of Atheism, which went up in flames, exposing to view a rather smoky statue of Wisdom, after which the whole Convention, and delegates from the Sections, ascended an artificial mountain where appropriate ceremonies were performed.

Similar fêtes, though on a smaller and simpler scale, were held in the provinces, where the communes were dominated by small groups of ardent revolutionaries organized in Jacobin clubs and receiving guidance from Paris. The membership of the clubs was perhaps half a million at their height; but active membership was much smaller, and there were constant complaints of non-attendance at meetings. They fell under the influence of small cliques of militants, which obtained control of local affairs. Thus in Metz 61 Jacobins out of 148 held government office, and at Toulouse 103 out of 731. They exploited their offices and used popular violence to establish petty local tyrannies. Though the majority of the Jacobins were men of the middle classes, who stood for the smaller property owners against both the rich and the propertyless, the bond that united them was not class but faith. The Jacobin clubs had many of the characteristics of a political church, with rituals, tests of orthodoxy, public confessions, and purges. Their members thought of themselves as a body of the elect, marked out by the possession of virtue, or patriotism: they were the elite of the Revolution. Yet as they became increasingly mere cogs in the revolutionary machine, and from the point of view of efficiency rather incompetent ones, their ardour cooled and their spontaneity disappeared. This was what Saint-Just meant when he complained, 'La Révolution est glacée.'

Success, in fact, brought to the fore the basic contradictions in revolutionary ideology, for a clear demonstration of which we must examine the political evolution of the man who was the mind and the conscience of Jacobinism. Robespierre's strength, and ultimately perhaps his weakness, lay in his greater awareness of the significance of ideas in a period when ideas, if — as I have tried to show — they seldom determined practical decisions, played a large part in the formulation of political and social policies. To put it at the lowest, they provided the symbols over which and in the name of which the struggle was waged, and it was no Homeric battle over the dead body of a hero, for the ideas themselves were living forces which developed and even changed sides as the Revolution progressed. Robespierre himself was the true child of a century which had been so strongly concerned with ethical questions. The basic problem for him was the application of moral principles in government; and with the optimism of the pre-revolutionary world he believed it was not a difficult one. As Montesquieu said, immorality was the basis of despotism and virtue of the republic. To find the morality suppressed in the corrupt society of the *ancien régime*, it was only necessary to release the natural virtue of the people. Political virtue was thus equated with the sovereignty of the people. To restore their sovereignty to the people was to inaugurate the reign of virtue. With the victory of the Mountain it seemed that this had been achieved and all opposition should then have come to an end, for there could not be two separate and different expressions of a single, sovereign will. Since, on the contrary, opposition continued and even grew, Robespierre was faced with the need for an agonized reappraisal of his position. The explanation was soon obvious to him. We have built the temple of liberty, he said, with hands corrupted by the chains of despotism. Intriguers were still at work, perverting the naturally good will of the people. Practical considerations were added to theoretical ones. France was torn into fragments by internal strife. We need, he wrote, 'une volunté une'. On what could it be based? At first, it seemed, on the people of Paris, 'the citadel of liberty'. But even here there was corruption. Intriguers were at work in the Convention, in the Sections, in the clubs other than the Jacobins. Robespierre was driven to believe that while the people in normal times rule by virtue, in times of revolution to virtue must be added terror. His programme was not merely one of repression, however. Opinion, he knew, was the basis of political power — had it not been the instrument of his own rise? — and it was not enough to repress hostile opinion on the platform, in the Press, at the theatre: something must be put in its place. Hence good writings, speeches, pamphlets, journals, were to be encouraged and distributed widely. A national system of education, something which he had formerly opposed as dangerous to individual freedom, must be set up. Great pageants were to be organized for the purpose of propaganda. The ground plan of a totalitarian state, it seems, was being laid down, so far were Robespierre and the Jacobins being driven — by force of circumstances and the logic of their theory — from their earlier liberal views.

Yet to read their policies in unduly modern terms would be a mistake. Even at the height of the Terror Robespierre remained, so far as he could, a defender of religious toleration. When a letter was received from the president of a commune asking what measures should be taken against women detected wearing crosses, he referred it to the *bureau de police* with the comment that the writer must either be a fool or a rogue. A circular of the Committee of Public Safety ordered the local authorities not to persecute Anabaptists, and to allow those conscripted for the army to serve as pioneers or in the transport or else to purchase exemption. Such signs of moderation did not endear Robespierre to the extremists. The ultimate crisis, in theory as well as in fact, was to come for Robespierrist democracy when even the purged Convention, which he had called more than once the 'boulevard (i.e. the bulwark) of liberty', was to turn against him. The circle of virtue was narrowing. There are two peoples in France, he declared in May 1794: 'One is the mass of citizens, pure, hungry for justice and loving liberty. It is this virtuous people which pours out its blood to establish liberty, which overcomes foreign enemies and shakes the thrones of tyrants. The other is that collection of factious intriguers, appearing everywhere, turning everything to abuse, seizing the tribune and often public office, who use the education which their advantages under the *ancien régime* gave them to deceive public opinion.' 'I see the world', he cried despairingly in his last speech of all, 'peopled with dupes and knaves.' The will of the people, which expressed their sovereignty, had by now long ceased for him to be the actual will of an actual majority; it had become an ideal will incarnated in 'the few generous men who love virtue for its own sake'.

Having said all this, it must be added — and it is equally true — that practical circumstances dictated to theory. The rule of the Committee of Public Safety was essentially a war dictatorship. Under it, for the first time in modern history, appeared the phenomenon of a nation in arms. By 1794 France had over 850,000 men in its armies. Soldiers of the old regiments of the line, volunteers, and conscripts were gradually fused into a single fighting force. Authority and discipline were restored. The ability of the generals was tested by the pitiless crucible of war and failure was a death sentence. It was under the Committee of Public Safety that the generals who were to lead the armies of France in victory across Europe were discovered and tested — Jourdan, Hoche, Pichegru, Masséna, Moreau, Davout, Lefebvre, Sérurier, Augereau, Brune, Bonaparte — eight future marshals of Napoleon among them. Youth had its chance along with ability: the average age of the generals was thirty-three, of the Committee itself thirty-seven. Commissaires sent out from Paris kept the armies and their generals faithful to the Revolution; and as confidence increased it became possible for a general to risk at least a minor reverse without having to contemplate the guillotine. The new artillery and the tactics evolved by military theorists in the last years of the *ancien régime* served the revolutionary armies well. National factories for the manufacture of arms were extended.

Behind the scenes in France there had been those, in particular Danton, who saw in the repulsion of the enemy from the soil of France the possibility of opening peace negotiations and ending at the same time the war and the Terror. The revolutionary ardour of the Committee was not to be held back thus. 'Who dares to speak of peace?' cried Barère, and answered, 'The aristocrats, the moderates, the rich, the conspirators, the pretended patriots.' Carnot deployed the French armies for a fresh advance on the Austrian Netherlands, and after months of complicated manœuvres Jourdan defeated Coburg at Fleurus on June 26th, advanced to Liège and Antwerp. Belgium fell again under French occupation.

At sea, the efforts of Jeanbon Saint-André to restore efficiency to the French navy after the loss of so many capable officers and the breakdown of discipline, were, through no fault of his own, less successful. The revolutionary effort at sea has been, until recently, underestimated. It was not unambitious. The pre-revolutionary plans of de Castries for the construction of ships were implemented and expanded. The naval war against Great Britain called for a treble armament — flotillas of small boats to guard the coastal trade, a fleet of ships of the line capable of engaging the British navy, and an invasion fleet to put into effect long-cherished plans for invasion. A remarkable effort of construction was in fact achieved, though it was to be frustrated, largely by the internal revolts. The royalist seizure and the British occupation of Toulon robbed France of one fleet. Even more serious were the effects of the revolt of the Vendée, which kept supplies of material and men away from the great naval bases of the Atlantic coast in a vital period. Jeanbon Saint-André had also to deal with the efforts of local revolutionary committees to undermine discipline in the ports and the fleet. In spite of all difficulties, one main object of the French navy, which was to break the British blockade and enable convoys of food ships from America to reach France, achieved some measure of success. The greatest of the convoys, protected by the Brest fleet, at the price of heavy losses, in three long days' fighting culminating on June 1st, 1794, against a British fleet under the command of Howe, was enabled to reach port safely.

Whether the arrival of the Brest convoy had any substantial effect on the food situation in France cannot be said. But from the point of view of the Committee of Public Safety nothing could have been more fatal than military or naval success. A regime which had been founded on defeat was not stabilized by victory. Moreover, the economic problem remained intense despite all the efforts of the Committee, and it was easier to offer a distressed population scapegoats to be immolated on the guillotine than a solution to its economic problems. The defeat of foreign enemies and the crushing of organized opposition inside France was therefore followed not by a diminution but by an intensification of the Terror. An analysis of the number of official executions shows that its incidence varied greatly in different parts of France and that it reached its height in the departments where civil war raged. To give even an approximation to the number of those who were killed in one way or another in the course of the Terror is impossible, but one estimate of the number of suspects put under arrest arrives at the figure of 300,000. Every suspect had friends and relations whose sympathies were bound up with his fate. The more there were arrested, the larger grew the silent hosts of fear and hatred surrounding the great Committee. As the Terror became more and more a mindless, reasonless machine, it fell increasingly and indiscriminately on all sections of the community. Of those who were guillotined after trial, 85 per cent belonged to the Third Estate, some 6.5 per cent to the clergy, and 8.5 per cent to the *noblesse*. The Committee of Public Safety, at the time and since, has, it is true, been saddled with the blame for police measures many of which are attributable to the one other Committee, that of General Security, which had survived and retained its autonomy. The latter regarded police as its special province and, composed of purer terrorists and perhaps mere terrorists, was responsible for a large proportion of the rank and file arrests and executions, though the great political trials, conducted by the two Committees jointly, have left a deeper mark on the pages of history.

An unsuccessful attempt to assassinate Collot d'Herbois, and a merely suspected one on the life of Robespierre, produced sufficient terror in the breasts of the ruling faction to evoke the law of the twenty-second of Prairial (June 10th), introduced by Couthon, with Robespierre presiding over the Convention. This deprived the proceedings of the Revolutionary Tribunal of the last semblance of judicial trial and allowed no verdict but acquittal or death. The largest and most miscellaneous batches of prisoners were now dispatched to the Tribunal *en route* for the guillotine. From March 1793 to June 10th, 1794, 1,251 persons had been executed at Paris; from June 10th to July 27th, there were 1,376 victims. The members of the Convention, even those not threatened hitherto, began to fear for their own necks, and the whole country, including the small ruling faction and its adherents, stifled in a miasma of suspicion and fear.

So long as the Committee of Public Safety remained united its authority could not be shaken. The Press, public opinion, and all the organs of administration were under relentless control. But the successes of the armies, completed in the victory of Fleurus, by relaxing fear of the foreign enemy, undermined the unity of the Committee. The law of Prairial aroused alarm in the Convention of the use that might be made of it by the Robespierrists. In the Committee of Public Safety violent disagreements arose between Carnot and Saint-Just over the conduct of the war, in which Robespierre supported Saint-Just, and Carnot had the backing of his fellow-technicians, Robert Lindet and Prieur of the Côte d'Or. The Committee of General Security found its authority challenged by a new police committee composed of Robespierre, Couthon, and Saint-Just. Robespierre personally provoked the resentment of the strong anti-religious element in the Committee of General Security, as well as exposing himself to barely veiled ridicule, by founding his new religion of the Supreme Being and celebrating it in a great public festival. Although the Convention followed him, in his new sky-blue coat, in procession to the Champ-de-Mars, it was with its tongue in its cheek. However classical the education and ideas of the revolutionaries, a *pontifex maximus* did not enter into their pattern of a republic. While he had antagonized Carnot and the men of the Plain, who had followed the Mountain and taken their share of responsibility for the Terror when it seemed the only way of establishing a government strong enough to save France, Robespierre had also aroused the fears of those who were terrorists by nature and perhaps for the pure love of terrorism. Deputies who had been in charge of the repression in the provinces, men like Carrier, Fréron, Fouché, Tallien, had been called back from their bloody work by the influence of Robespierre and knew that he would not spare them when the time came for him to act. They were joined in scarcely veiled opposition by the Committee of General Security and by Collot and Billaud, who had never been Robespierrists. Barère — one of nature's middle-men — struggled to the last to effect a reconciliation in the Committee of Public Safety, but it had become divided into factions which hated and distrusted each other too deeply for them to be able to continue to work together. The conflict could only be settled by the elimination of one side or the other.

Robespierre still had many cards in his hand. He had defeated those who had dared to oppose him in the Convention so often that it did not occur to him that his mastery of the majority could be shaken. The Commune of Paris was packed with his devoted followers, and its armed force, under Hanriot, would be loyal to him. He felt supremely confident and only bided his time to strike. For a month after the passing of the law of Prairial he waited, isolating himself from all but his closest adherents and manifesting his displeasure by abstaining from attending the meetings of the Convention and the Committee of Public Safety. On the eighth of Thermidor (July 26th), the lowering storm broke. Robespierre came to the Convention and denounced his enemies in terms which were menacing enough to carry a threat of death to all his opponents and vague enough to include practically anyone. He demanded, in effect, a blank cheque on the guillotine to fill in as he pleased. The speech was a masterly one, but for once oratory was not enough. The next day the conspirators, desperate men who knew that it was Robespierre's life or theirs, took the offensive. The moment Saint-Just and Robespierre tried to speak, their voices were drowned with cries of 'Down with the tyrant'. A Mirabeau or a Danton would have made himself heard; the Robespierrists included no orator of that calibre, and in any case Collot d'Herbois, in the chair, gave them no chance. Tallien struck the first blow. In turn, Billaud-Varenne, Barère, Vadier, Fréron, took up the attack. In a tumult the Convention voted the arrest of Robespierre and the small group that devotedly gathered round him, before they could rally support in the streets or their allies in the Commune could come to their aid.

The man who should have saved the situation, Hanriot, probably drunk as usual, got himself arrested, was then released, but failed to make any use of the forces he commanded. The Commune sounded the tocsin and gathered a mob of some 3,000, but perhaps because the imposition of a maximum on wages had discontented the people of Paris, perhaps because arrests and executions had robbed them of the leaders of the street-fighters who had carried the Mountain into power, it remained inactive. The Convention outlawed Robespierre with all who supported him, and recruited a force of some 6,000 men from the moderate Sections, under the command of Barras, a member of the Convention, *ci-devant* count and infantry officer, who thus laid the foundations of his political fortune. The situation still seemed in the balance. The arrested Robespierrists, who had been freed in one way or another, joined with the members of the Commune at the Hôtel de Ville; but the troops of the Commune who should have defended them had dispersed and they found themselves surrounded by hostile forces. Paris, which had followed Robespierre for so long, and on the support of which he relied unquestioningly, had deserted him. All was lost, only death remained. He was shot through the jaw, almost certainly in an attempt to commit suicide. On the tenth of Thermidor, Robespierre, his brother Augustin, Saint-Just, Couthon, Hanriot, and seventeen others were hurried to the guillotine. 'He had on the sky-blue coat he had got made for the Feast of the *Être Suprême* — O Reader, can thy hard heart hold out against that?' wrote Carlyle. The next day the Robespierrist Commune was exterminated: seventy-one heads fell in the biggest single holocaust of the Revolution. The Thermidoreans had won their victory, and in making an end to Robespierre and his faction had ended far more than they knew. They had ended the Revolution.

They had saved their own heads. Two days earlier and they might have saved also, unknowingly, the one great poet of their generation in France. On the seventh of Thermidor André Chénier, in whose lyrics a purer classical genius shone than that age of pseudo-classicism knew, died, at thirty-two, on the guillotine as an enemy of the people. His elegy, 'La Jeune Captive', written in prison, is in every anthology. One might think that, in 'Néère', he had foretold it and his fate.

> Mais telle qu'à sa mort, pour la dernière fois,
> Un beau cygne soupire, et de sa douce voix,
> De sa voix qui bientôt lui doit être ravie,
> Chante, avant de partir, ses adieux à la vie ...

CHAPTER SIX

AFTERMATH OF REVOLUTION

THE regime that succeeded to Robespierre and the great Committee of Public Safety had been brought to birth by a *coup d'état*, it was to live by *coups d'état* and to die by a *coup d'état*. The Thermidoreans were united only in their fear of Robespierre. There is little to admire in them: no motive higher than self-preservation inspired their desperate attack, no ideals justified their executions, no laurels crowned their victory. Men like Carnot, Robert Lindet, Prieur of the Côte d'Or were the best of them, practical and limited men driven to ruthless action by fear of the dangerous courses into which the Robespierrists were once more leading the Revolution. Other Thermidoreans were men like Cambon, one of the few who had entered revolutionary politics from the world of commerce and who had appropriately obtained control of revolutionary finances; Vadier and his supporters of the Committee of General Security, hoping, with the Robespierrists eliminated, to seize control of the machinery of terror and use it to establish their own rule; Fouché, Billaud-Varenne, Collot d'Herbois, fearing the turning of their own weapon against themselves; Tallien, a petty official before the Revolution, sent as terrorist commissaire to Bordeaux, to have his heart melted by the beautiful Thérèse Cabarrus and to rescue her from the impending guillotine; Barras, who was to emerge as the strong man of the Directory; Fréron, son of the old literary opponent of Voltaire, god-child of King Stanislaus of Lorraine, Cordelier, journalist of the *Orateur du peuple* in which he had rivalled Marat in denunciation and appeals to violence, colleague of Barras in a bloody proconsulate at Toulon and Marseilles, cruel and corrupt Conventionnel. Such were the first leaders of the Thermidorean reaction.

Thermidor was a counter-revolution but it was not effected at a single blow. The raw material of revolution, the turbulent and

distressed populace of Paris, remained, but its political power had
been undermined and for this the great Committee of Public Safety
was perhaps itself responsible. In consolidating its authority the
Committee had unwittingly destroyed the foundations on which that
authority rested. The great Terror had swept up in its indiscriminate
slaughter so many of the agitators of the street-corners and clubs;
there had been, in the long succession of *journées*, such a wastage of
leaders of revolt, that the mob never again became a coherent force.
Henceforth it was an army without officers, anarchic, irrelevant.
The politicians of the Convention, who had used and then cast aside
the men of the streets, could not supply their places. The general staff
of terrorist warfare had guillotined its own non-commissioned officers and its army had disintegrated. After Thermidor, Fréron
stepped in and turned the chief weapon of the Jacobins against
themselves. With a little group of adherents, and with invocations to
the shade of Marat, he gathered round him former Dantonists,
enragés, and many others, fresh from the prisons of the Convention, with bitter memories to avenge, and directed them against
those who were denounced as *la queue de Robespierre*. With such
men he united, in an unnatural and temporary alliance, the *jeunesse
dorée*, not very gilded perhaps, of minor officials, lawyers, bankers'
clerks, and the like, young aspirants to as yet unachieved social
position. Among the Thermidorean mobs were doubtless also
many of those who had formerly constituted the street army of the
Mountain and the Commune, men ready to rally to any cry, so
long as it gave them an opportunity to range through the streets,
hunting, beating, tearing to pieces whoever was designated as the
quarry, and seeking any opportunity of looting that offered.

These former Cordeliers and ex-Hébertists, with far more experience in the actual control of the streets than the Robespierrist
Jacobins ever had, organized street bands which abandoned the
uniform of the carmagnole, the peasant blouse and loose trousers.
The Muscadins of the Thermidorean reaction affected a very different
style, dressing in coats with square shoulders, tight breeches,
wearing blond wigs, carrying weighted cudgels, and chanting
'le Réveil du peuple'. Based especially on the Palais Royal, whence
had issued agitators in a very different cause only five years earlier,

they chased known Jacobins through the streets and attacked their headquarters in the rue Saint-Honoré, providing an excuse for the new rulers of France to close the club. A counter-terror appeared spontaneously in the provinces. In the Lyonnais, where the deeds of the Jacobins had not been forgotten, a self-styled Company of Jesus assassinated former terrorists and their women and threw the bodies in the Rhône. In a new prison massacre — but this time the prisoners were the Jacobins — there were ninety-nine victims. Convoys of arrested terrorists were waylaid and the prisoners put to death. The massacres spread to all the surrounding departments. At Nîmes, Marseilles, Aix, Orange, and elsewhere in the south a White Terror raged, conducted by bands calling themselves the Companies of the Sun.

From the prisons of the Jacobin Terror the suspects poured out, saved by Thermidor from the guillotine and with their sequestrated property restored to them. The enemies of the Mountain re-emerged from concealment or prison to take their seats again in the Convention, where a strong right wing of some 150 members reappeared and temporarily found an unexpected leader in the reformed terrorist Tallien. The complexion of the two governing Committees changed as each monthly election brought in new figures. On September 1st, Barère, Billaud-Varenne, and Collot d'Herbois left the Committee of Public Safety. The Revolutionary Tribunal, reorganized after Thermidor, inherited, as its first great post-Thermidorean trial, the case of the Nantais, dispatched in January 1794, when Carrier was on mission at Nantes, to the prisons of Paris. Originally numbering 132, deaths during the months in prison had reduced their numbers to ninety-four. Their trial turned into a continuous indictment of Carrier, who himself appeared as a witness for the defence. He alleged that while at Nantes he had been concerned exclusively with the organization of food supplies and even professed himself unconnected with the arrests. This did not save him. The Nantais were acquitted amid scenes of enthusiasm. The next day Carrier was denounced at the Convention as a 'cannibal', and he and his associates were sent to the Revolutionary Tribunal. A host of witnesses, freed from fear, appeared to testify against him. He at least ended bravely. After a hopeless attempt to deny the overwhelming evidence, he admitted his deeds, exculpated those who were tried with him as mere agents executing his orders, and was condemned to the guillotine. After Robespierre, he became the symbol of the Terror and there was little need to blacken his reputation as Robespierre's had been blackened.

The reversal of the terrorist machine and the repudiation of Jacobin policies was not completed at one blow. Early hesitations were shown by the passing of a decree translating Marat to the Pantheon. The whole Convention escorted the honoured remains of the Friend of the People to the temple of the great men of the Republic in September 1794: they were expelled again, with less ceremony, in February 1795. The Public Prosecutor, Fouquier-Tinville, arrested soon after the ninth of Thermidor on the denunciation of his old enemy Fréron, was not brought to trial till the following March. He defended himself on the ground that he had merely carried out the orders of the Committee of Public Safety as a faithful civil servant should, but in spite of this he and fourteen jurors of the Revolutionary Tribunal passed beneath the knife to which they had condemned so many others.

While the reaction was progressing, however, the causes of popular unrest had not been brought to an end. A distressed populace still existed to be called into action. On April 1st, 1795, the twelfth of Germinal, it broke out in rioting. That there were still politically motivated leaders is shown by the cry of the crowd which invaded the Convention: bread and the Constitution of 1793, but they were obscure and ineffective men. The day of Germinal was little more than a large-scale riot, suppressed without difficulty when the National Guard from the western Sections of Paris was brought up. Its supporters in the Convention dared not declare themselves and the riot merely provided the new majority with an excuse for turning against the three most prominent terrorists left in their midst, Collot d'Herbois, Billaud-Varenne, and Barère. Their deportation to Guiana and the arrest of some twenty other deputies was decreed. Collot rapidly died there of yellow fever; Billaud-Varenne settled down as a farmer in the tropics with a devoted negro girl named Virginie and spent the rest of his life in an obscure and Rousseauist pastoral idyll; Barère, for the first time in his life, it was said, failing to sail with the wind, remained in France and lived to beg for jobs from Bonaparte, to be exiled during the Restoration, and to die a poor pensioner of Louis-Philippe.

The discontents which had provoked the riot of Germinal were not diminished by its failure, and protests and minor demonstrations against food prices were of daily occurrence. If the Convention did nothing to improve the economic situation, it took more effective precautions of another kind. The law prohibiting the army from penetrating within a certain distance of Paris was suspended and troops were brought to the outskirts; officers of suspected Jacobin tendencies were purged, including a young Corsican, Bonaparte; the National Guard was reorganized, excluding the poorer citizens. Precautions were certainly needed, for agitation was spreading among the people of Paris, little revolutionary cells were forming, manifestoes were being distributed calling on the people to rise. On the morning of the first of Prairial (May 20th, 1795) the tocsin was sounded in the faubourg Saint-Antoine and in the neighbouring Sections; crowds of women gathered, mobs were formed, arms seized, and the traditional march on the Convention began. As in Germinal, however, there seems to have been no central body to organize and control the demonstration and no co-ordination with a party in the Convention to exploit it. Bread and the Constitution of 1793 was still the cry. The entry to the Convention, which, contrary to tradition, tried to defend itself, at the price of the life of one member whose head was more traditionally put on a pike, was forced. Despite the howling presence of the mob, Boissy d'Anglas, in the presidential chair, boldly refused to suspend the session. Only after some hours of disorder did the few members who sympathized with the demonstrators venture to put into the form of a motion their demands. Meanwhile the National Guard, now composed of opponents and no longer of allies of the revolutionary movement, had been called out, had seized strategic points in the city and marched to the protection of the Convention. Towards midnight they drove out the mob at the point of the bayonet. The next day the insurgent Sections reassembled and again surrounded the Convention, but a pitched battle with its defenders was somehow avoided. On the third day detachments of the army entered

Paris, disarmed the faubourg Saint-Antoine, and the crisis of the Thermidorean regime was over. It only remained for the Convention to arrest and condemn, by a summary military court, the six deputies who had supported the insurgents. On the steps of the Tribunal, hurried from condemnation to execution, they stabbed themselves; three died on the spot and the others were borne bleeding to the guillotine, one, who had died en route, already a corpse when he was thrust beneath the knife. The remaining members of the great terrorist Committees were arrested, only Carnot being saved by a cry, 'He was the organizer of victory'. In the Sections there was a general denunciation and disarmament of former Jacobins and sans-culottes. The companies of gunners attached to the National Guard were dissolved, which was to rob insurrection of one of its chief weapons.

While the personnel of the Terror was thus being disbanded and dispersed, its governmental machinery had been rapidly dismantled. The changes that were made, and the precautions that the Convention took to safeguard its authority, are not only important in themselves, they also reveal clearly the administrative arrangements that had made the great Terror and the dictatorship of the Committee of Public Safety possible. The first step was to change the Committee of Public Safety from being in effect a self-perpetuating oligarchy and the master of the Convention into its servant. It was henceforth to be renewable by one-fourth every month, and retiring members could not be immediately re-elected. Its functions were reduced to the control of foreign affairs and war, and there was a general distribution of governmental authority among the Committees of the Convention. In the provinces the revolutionary committees of the communes, which had been among the chief agencies of the Terror, were suppressed and a new army of representatives on mission was sent out from the Convention to assist in orientating local government to the new line. In Paris, which had been the stronghold of the Committee of Public Safety, despite the temporary dislocation of the revolutionary forces, both at the top and at intermediate levels, there was still a fear that they might reassert themselves unless they were deprived of the means of doing so. A series of administrative measures was enacted, therefore, which

effectively destroyed this possibility. The headquarters staff of the
National Guard, put under the direct control of the Committees of
the Convention, was to be changed every ten days. The Sections
were to meet only once in every decade and the payment of 40 sous
for attendance was suppressed. The revolutionary committees were
reduced from forty-eight, one for each Section, to twelve, one for
each *arrondissement*, and were renewable every three months. The
dreaded Commune, which had been first the creator and then the
instrument of the terrorist dictatorship, disappeared altogether with
the suppression of the administrative unity of Paris. It was replaced
by two commissions of officials, one for police, responsible to the
Committee of General Security, which also had the right of calling
in the armed forces, and the other for taxation. Paris had ceased to
rule France, it had ceased even to rule itself.

The Thermidoreans thus demolished the structure by which the
Mountain had dominated France. In the Convention all that remained of that once fearful height was a tottering and diminishing
crête. The work of destruction had been almost too successful, for it
was carried on, far beyond the intentions and expectations of the
Thermidoreans, by strong winds of public opinion which were
sweeping France and bringing with them hopes of a royalist
restoration. The problem for the historian now is not why the
monarchy fell but why it was not revived, and this is an easier
question to answer. The brothers of Louis XVI, identified with
foreign invasion and émigré hopes of revenge, had excluded themselves by their words and deeds. The little son of Louis XVI and
Marie-Antoinette, the prisoner of the Temple, would have provided
the ideal solution. A mere child but the legitimate king of France, his
presence on the throne would reconcile the nation to its government and in his name, under a revived Constitution of 1791, the new
rulers of France could exercise power without fear of a counter-
revolution and therefore without terror. Boissy d'Anglas, whose role
during the days of Prairial had marked him out as the key man of
the new order, was cautiously preparing the way for a return to constitutional monarchy, when, on June 8th, 1795, the little boy, on
whose life so many hopes for France rested, and who stood, had
the ambitious young Corsican who was now expiating in disgrace

his former association with the Mountain but known it, between him and an empire, died of tuberculosis, exacerbated or caused by his shocking ill-usage in prison. 'The death of the young king, Louis XVII', wrote the moderate royalist Mallet du Pan, 'is at this moment the most fatal of events. It has consternated and discouraged the constitutional monarchists, and ensured the triumph of the republicans and the success of the new farrago of nonsense which they are going to decree under the name of a constitution.'

Worst of all, the death of the little Louis XVII meant that the comte de Provence was now Louis XVIII. He celebrated his accession by issuing a manifesto from Verona proclaiming merciless punishment of the regicides and the restoration in its entirety of the *ancien régime*, with the parlements restored to their old powers, the higher Orders back in their privileged position, and Catholicism again the exclusive religion of the state. This was an open warning that the counter-revolution was prepared to make no concessions to the new France. It was also evidence that the émigrés were as out of touch with reality as ever. A restoration on these terms was only conceivable if the revolutionary regime could be overthrown by force, and the improbability of this was to be demonstrated once again in 1795. In February Charette, the most prominent of the leaders of the Vendéan rebels, signed a pacification at La Jaunaye with the republican authorities, and by May the whole of the west had temporarily laid down its arms. When, in June, the long-awaited expedition of the émigrés, with belated British support, at last sailed to the promontory of Quiberon in southern Brittany, it was too late. Defeated by Hoche, those of the luckless royalists who could not escape in the British fleet were captured and butchered.

The Thermidoreans, after a year of hesitation and uncertainty, had now no choice but to attempt to consolidate the Republic by providing it with a new Constitution. Sieyes reappeared once again to offer a plan, which was, as usual, patently unworkable. The chief author of the Constitution of the year Three was the leader of the moderates, Boissy d'Anglas. It was based on a dual fear of democracy and dictatorship. Universal suffrage was abolished and elections were to be indirect. A restricted franchise gave political power to the propertied classes. 'We should be governed', declared Boissy d'Anglas, 'by the best, and the best are those best educated and most interested in upholding the laws. With very few exceptions you will only find such men among those who, possessing property, are attached to the country containing it and the laws which protect it.' To prevent any concentration of power such as had fallen into the hands of the Committee of Public Safety, the executive and legislative powers were separated and the latter was put into commission by being entrusted to a Directory of five. Finally, to prevent the electorate from supposing that it could do as it pleased, priests and former émigrés were disfranchised, along with all those under arrest or accusation, that is all former leading Jacobins, and a decree was passed compelling the electors to choose two-thirds of the members of the new legislative body from among the surviving members of the Convention. This Constitution was submitted to a plebiscite in which it obtained just over a million votes. There was only a pitiable 200,000 for the decree of two-thirds. As thirty-three of the Paris Sections rejected the decree almost unanimously, only the votes of the remaining fifteen Sections were counted.

The obvious determination of the rump Convention to perpetuate its power provoked unrest in Paris, culminating in a rising on the thirteenth of Vendémiaire (October 5th, 1795). Barras, who had been successful against the Jacobins in Thermidor, was again entrusted with the defence of the Convention, this time against moderates and royalists. He called to his aid the victor of Toulon, the young general Bonaparte, temporarily unemployed because of his associations with the Mountain. Troops to the number of some 6,000 were brought up to protect the Convention, threatened by about 25,000 men from the Sections; but Bonaparte had also cannon and did not hesitate to use them. Before musket and cannon fire the Sections fled, leaving behind them two or three hundred killed and wounded: Parisian revolts, whether of the right or left, were evidently out of date. Vendémiaire delivered a sharp check to the royalist revival. It did more, it brought the army into politics: but the consequences of that were not yet to be appreciated.

With the Directory a new age in the history of France begins. A class of new men, with newly acquired wealth and office, was emerging as the ruling element in the state. They were, naturally, not the cultured upper bourgeoisie of the *ancien régime* — the Farmers-General, higher judicial officers and administrators, and the like — but the purchasers of national property, war contractors, speculators, profiteers, and politicians. Declassed nobles mingled with jumped-up plebeians to form a society of nouveaux riches in which the vices of the court met and fused with those of the courtyard. Salons reappeared, gathered round the elegant mistresses of revolutionary politicians and generals — the lovely Mme Récamier, Joséphine de Beauharnais, Mme Tallien, formerly Thérèse Cabarrus and yet to become Princesse de Chimay, but best known to history as 'Notre Dame de Thermidor'. The brilliant daughter of Necker, Mme de Staël, less decorative but with a mind nourished on the conversation of the great intelligences and wits of the last years of the *ancien régime* in the salon of her mother, provided a centre for intellectual society.

The end of the Terror, with its popular and puritan austerities, was also marked by a revolution in dress. The exaggerated fashions of *incroyables* and *merveilleuses* were the visible sign of the birth of a new society, with men in badly-cut coats, padded shoulders, high collars, immense cravats and admiral's hats, and its women half-naked in pseudo-classical robes, gathered up in the high-breasted directoire style and falling in long diaphanous folds to the Grecian sandals. An affected 'de-boned' speech, leaving out the consonants, was adopted by the *jeunesse dorée*.

Wealth was now quite fashionable again, for a wild inflation followed the abandonment of the economic controls of the Committee of Public Safety. In August 1795 the daily expenditure of the government amounted to 80 to 90 million and the receipts to between 6 and 8 million. The assignat of 100 francs fell to 15 sous. Markets were deserted, vagabondage and brigandage endemic, and misery widespread. The deputies protected themselves by calculating their salaries in myriagrammes of cheese. The armies could only live by pillage. The towns were saved from wholesale starvation by free distribution of food, requisitioned from the peasantry, who were not thereby the more reconciled to the new regime.

In these conditions it was natural that the ideas of the *enragés* should reappear in the form of the primitive kind of communism advocated by the petty official Babeuf and his small band of followers who called themselves the Equals. His attempted conspiracy, in May 1796, attracted a few hundred former terrorists, including well-to-do professional men, and was financed by former Jacobins who were sworn enemies of the Directory. Government spies were in the movement from the beginning and it was crushed with little effort.

The real menace to the Directory came from the other side. Royalists within France were plucking up their courage and emerging from hiding or passivity; many were trickling back into France across the frontiers. The British government, through its envoy in Switzerland, William Wickham, was pouring in secret agents and supplying them lavishly with money. When the partial elections of April 1797 came round, only eleven former deputies to the Convention were returned out of 216. The majority of the new members were constitutional monarchists. Despite the debacle of Vendémiaire, if the royalists had been united and competently led, and the émigrés capable of offering a modicum of concessions, France was theirs. This was to ask too much. The elements in France which were potentially favourable were alienated by the programme of the émigrés. The peasants were little enough interested in republican politics, but they did not contemplate with equanimity the loss of the confiscated noble and church lands and the revival of seigneurial dues. The new governing class which had acquired wealth and jobs during the Revolution had no desire to sacrifice them. The constitutional monarchists found all their efforts to come to terms with the pure royalists rebuffed. In the army, more or less isolated from the changing opinions of the country, the republican sentiments of earlier years still survived.

Yet, with a majority in the legislative bodies, and with Carnot and Barthélemy sympathetic in the Directory itself, it seemed inevitable that the monarchists should assume control of France by constitutional means. Their success in taking over the reins would have meant peace, for in 1797 negotiations had been opened with the British at Lille, and throughout the summer had been dragging on. Peace and war hung in the balance, turning on which party gained control at Paris. The decisive factor was to be not the politicians but the generals, who had a professional interest in war. The two republican Directors, Reubell and La Revellière-Lépeaux, were joined, after much hesitation, by Barras. In September 1797 the three decided to take action against their colleagues and the royalist majority in the chambers, fully aware that if they did not do so their cause was lost. There was no question now of arousing a popular movement to save the republic. As in Vendémiaire the army was the decisive factor, and a mere constitutional provision that excluded armed forces from the neighbourhood of Paris was a feeble barrier against it. Bonaparte, on campaign in Italy, sent his rough lieutenant Augereau to maintain the stability of the republic at home while he pursued its conquests abroad.

On the morning of the eighteenth of Fructidor (September 4th, 1797) Paris woke up to find itself under military occupation. Barthélemy was arrested and Carnot fled. The legislative bodies were purged, the elections of forty-nine departments quashed, all opposition journals suppressed, and seventeen of the more prominent enemies of the triumvirate despatched to the 'dry guillotine', French Guiana, where eight of them rapidly died. A few hundred priests were also sent to Guiana, and a similar number of other opponents of the regime were tried by military courts and shot. For a short period it was a new Terror — one inspired not by republican ardour but by political calculation. The republic had been saved and even the appearance of liberty lost. With the aid of the army the politicians of the Directory still held precariously to their power and kept the centre of the stage, but the tramp of marching men increasingly drowned their voices, and from the wings the figure of Bonaparte cast a deepening shadow.

The decisive step, it might have been thought, had been taken earlier, when the Revolution had bound up its fortunes with war. France committed itself to ultimate military government, it may be said, when for the third time, in 1795, after Prussia, Holland, and Spain had accepted French terms and Belgium had been incorporated in France, it continued an aggressive war against Austria, aimed chiefly at the conquest of northern Italy. The motives for the Italian campaign were very mixed ones, but not least financial. Exaggerated conceptions of the wealth of Lombardy and Tuscany, of Genoa and Venice, tempted the invader as in centuries past. The riches of Italy lay waiting to be liberated by the ragged but battle-tested armies of revolutionary France.

Bonaparte, who had won the confidence of the Directory when he saved it in Vendémiaire, was given command of the army of Italy. He put the ideas of the *ancien-régime* strategist, Guibert, into practice, with a genius for improvisation all his own. Sardinia was beaten to the ground in the spring of 1796 and granted peace at the price of Nice and Savoy and the dismantling of the defences of the Alpine passes. Heavy convoys of bullion and works of art arrived in Paris as the first-fruits of the conquest of Italy. Serious opposition to the French armies was to be expected when they came into contact with the Austrians, who were defeated at Arcola in November 1796 and Rivoli in January 1797. Peace preliminaries were signed at Leoben in April, and in October the Treaty of Campo-Formio brought peace with profit. The Emperor recognized the French annexation of the former Austrian Netherlands and the left bank of the Rhine, and the creation of a new Cisalpine Republic out of the conquests in northern Italy. In return the French, who had occupied the territory of the Venetian Republic, handed it over to Austria, having first looted it of everything of value they could find, including the great bronze horses of St Mark. The peace treaty, like the campaign, was the personal achievement of Bonaparte, who, having intervened decisively in the domestic politics of France when he sent Augereau to implement the *coup d'état* of Fructidor, was now also determining the foreign policy of the republic.

Only Great Britain remained to be dealt with, peace negotiations, which had been conducted in a leisurely manner at Lille, having been abruptly broken off. The British naval victories of St Vincent over the Spaniards and Camperdown over the Dutch, in 1797, made the prospect of a successful invasion of England an unpromising one. Bonaparte advised the Directory against it, but showed little enthusiasm for the idea of concluding peace, which Great Britain might now be expected to accept on terms favourable to France. In this situation there emerged the plan of an expedition to Egypt. In May 1798 Bonaparte sailed from Toulon with 400 ships, 40,000 troops, and a considerable body of scientists, scholars, and officials, for it was intended to turn Egypt into a French colony, as well as using it as a base for the destruction of English commerce and a stepping-stone to the creation of a French empire in the East. After the French fleet, having successfully escorted the expedition to its destination, had been caught by Nelson at anchor in Aboukir Bay and destroyed, the French army was cut off. Few of the soldiers who were marching across scorching sands, trying to apply the policy of living off the country in a land where even the inhabitants found it difficult enough to live, were ever to see France again. The mirage of the wealth of the East faded in the deserted ruins of Alexandria and the wretched huts of Cairo. Egyptian opposition was easily crushed, but the international repercussions of the invasion were unfavourable to France. It brought Turkey into the alliance with Russia and Great Britain, and Russia, her interests in the East threatened, for the first time took an effective part in the European war. The Second Coalition of 1799, uniting Britain, Russia, and Turkey, was then joined by Austria. Defeated in Italy and on the Rhine, with an army shut up in Egypt, France was threatened again with invasion.

The Directory, which had welcomed the Egyptian expedition as a means of removing an ambitious and dangerous general from the scene, found that it had brought a new continental war upon itself and one which it lacked the energy or ability to cope with successfully. The political situation in France was now changing once more. Reubell, the Director most associated with the war policy, but also the ablest of them, retired. He was replaced by Sieyes, that 'mole of the Revolution' as Robespierre called him, who had for long been intriguing in search of an opportunity to show once again, and perhaps this time with success, his genius as a maker of constitutions. He secured the removal of the other Directors, except Barras, whose energy seemed to have evaporated and who presented no danger, and replaced them with nonentities. This was clearly only a preliminary measure, but preliminary to what? Since Thermidor, France had been living under a regime of improvisations. A government lacking real support in the country had been reduced to a see-saw policy of playing off royalists against republicans, conservatives against Jacobins — these two distinctions are not the same. To draw up a fair verdict on a period which has never received the detailed study that has been devoted to the earlier years of the Revolution is impossible. The work of the Directory has perhaps been underrated and the achievements of the Consulate which followed correspondingly overrated. Considerable efforts were made to restore budgetary equilibrium and stability to the currency, with very limited success. Good harvests in 1796 and 1798 improved the supply of food. Industrial production remained lower than it had been in 1789, and to the loss of ocean commerce resulting from the maritime war with Great Britain was added the closing of the markets in the Levant after the invasion of Egypt.

In 1799 economic difficulties and the defeat of the armies brought about a last tentative resurgence of the Jacobin spirit. The Directory, by its measures to conscript men, requisition supplies, and raise forced loans, had to a certain extent provoked this revival. After the expulsion of the royalists by the *coup d'état* of Fructidor in 1797, the Council of the Five Hundred acquired a republican majority which in the crisis of 1799 showed itself still capable of by now largely meaningless Jacobin gestures, using language like 'la Patrie en danger' and calling for a new Committee of Public Safety. On the other side, royalist revolts broke out in the south-west and in Brittany. These were easily put down, while Paris made no move in response to the agitation of the neo-Jacobins. Troops were now permanently stationed in the capital to repress any attempt at a popular rising, but of this there was no sign. The political passions of the so-recent past had little life remaining in them. All that France wanted was a chance of tranquillity, peace at home and abroad, and the latter at least seemed within reach. A successful campaign by Masséna in Switzerland pushed back the Russian army and removed the threat of foreign invasion. Bonaparte, who had returned hurriedly from Egypt with his principal lieutenants to save the country, when he landed at Fréjus on October 9th, found that France had unfortunately already been saved. The invincible conqueror, who had just, or so it was thought, founded a new empire in the East, was not received with any the less enthusiasm.

The immediate crisis being over, the apparent need for urgent measures had vanished, but Sieyes was not ready to abandon his schemes so easily. In the course of ten years he had fetched half a circuit about the world of politics and reached his political antipodes. Whereas in 1789 he had stood for the unlimited sovereignty of the legislature, his aim now was to expand and consolidate the authority of the executive. This meant a further *coup d'état* at the expense of the legislative bodies, which could only be effective by calling on the co-operation of a popular general, who could be none other than Bonaparte. Did Sieyes believe that, having served his purpose, a general, especially a Bonaparte, would then retire quietly into the background? It is possible: he was vain enough to believe anything. Bonaparte, to whom all the factions now looked anxiously, though he had nothing but contempt for Sieyes, saw the advantage of a temporary alliance with him. Talleyrand acted as the intermediary between them. Fouché, uninvited, gave his support. To depict Bonaparte as advancing, vice and crime on either hand, to the over-throw of the republic would be poetic licence, but not inexcusable. The number of those actually implicated in the conspiracy of 1799 was small, but in a sense the whole nation was Bonaparte's accomplice, for propaganda in the journals had worked up a fear of terrorist plots, behind which the real conspiracy lay concealed.

An alleged terrorist conspiracy provided an excuse to move the legislative councils to Saint-Cloud outside Paris. This transfer was carried through on November 9th, 1799. The next day, the eighteenth of Brumaire, when the Council of the Five Hundred met, there were violent speeches against Bonaparte, despite the efforts of his brother, Lucien, who was in the chair. Bonaparte, who entered to harangue the Five Hundred, lost his head and denounced them wildly. They replied with cries for a vote of outlawry. He fled outside and called on the guards to support him. While the soldiers hesitated, Lucien emerged and saved the situation by a dramatic appeal to them to rescue their general from the daggers of assassins. This lie did the trick. The Five Hundred were driven out by the troops and France's first essay in parliamentary government had come to an end.

CHAPTER SEVEN

BALANCE-SHEET OF
THE EIGHTEENTH CENTURY

THE age that began with the death of a king ended with the virtual death of a republic. Such beginnings and such endings draw arbitrary lines across the pages of history. They are artificial interruptions in the grand unfolding theme of national life. Yet if history is, in the words of Carlyle, the essence of innumerable biographies, there are — among those whose lives, added together, make up the grand total — the millions who count in the statistical averages and generalizations, and the few who, because of their positions or personalities, cast a measurable individual weight into the balance. That Louis XIV and Napoleon Bonaparte fall into the latter category cannot be doubted. The disappearance from the scene of the former, and the rise to power of the latter, were events momentous enough to write finis to one age and incipit to another.

Between the grand monarch and the emperor there is, in France, no figure of comparable political magnitude, none of those men who can define an age and stamp the mark of their personalities on it. The French eighteenth century is not a period of great, dominating political figures. Yet if no one man counted overmuch, more men — and women — counted for something than possibly at any other time. The great mass forces of the modern world had not yet been born, while the individual — at the end of the century sometimes even the obscure individual — had at last emerged from the anonymity of the Middle Ages. If it was not a century of greatness, for the student of *l'homme sensuel moyen* there is no more fruitful field. The eighteenth century was also something more: it was, and above all in France, the nursery of the modern world. Ideas and social forces, the seeds of which were doubtless sown much earlier, can be seen now pushing above the surface, not in the neatly arranged rows of the careful gardener but in the haphazard tangle of nature. Yet they *can* be seen and distinguished: the field is no longer a seed-bed but it is not yet a jungle, and a pattern is discernible. The simple interpretations imposed on eighteenth-century France by historians writing under the influence of later social and political ideologies may have to be abandoned, but the history that is beginning to emerge from more detailed studies, if it is more complex, is still coherent, it is not a chaos of unrelated facts.

The basic pattern of the age was inherited from the immediate past. French society and government bore the impress of the personality of Louis XIV throughout the century which witnessed his decline and death. If Louis XV and Louis XVI failed and were to be hissed off the stage, it was in part because they were mere understudies, and not very good ones at that, trying to fill the role of the greatest actor of majesty that France had known. Only Napoleon, and he only for a short period, could successfully play the part that had been created by the grand monarch. Failing a great king, a great minister, supported by the king, could have given France the government that she needed; but the intrigues of a court were not breeding ground for greatness, and after Fleury the whole system of government was calculated to prevent the king from finding the minister France needed; or if he found him, from giving him the necessary authority. This does not mean that the ministers of the eighteenth century deserve all the condemnation that has been lavished on them by historians who only admire success. There were among them many able and honest men who could provide efficient administration: what they could not provide was a united government and a consistent policy. And when eventually, for lack of a policy, the absolute monarchy collapsed, the revolutionary regime which followed seemed to be attempting to push the weakness of the *ancien régime* to its logical conclusion by turning anarchy into a form of government. In a sense, therefore, the dominant factor throughout was a negative one: the void left at the centre of the machine of state by the death of Louis XIV.

It was for the very reason of lack of central control that French society was able to develop so rapidly and freely and at the same time in such contradictory directions. First, when the king had become the prisoner of a court, instead of the court being the mere decorative background for the king, the way was open for aristocracy to re-emerge from the political insignificance into which it had been thrust in the shadow of the bureaucratic colossus erected by Louis XIV, to recapture the highest offices of state, and in the end perish in a bid to gain control of the state itself. That many of the old nobility of Louis XV and Louis XVI were the sons or grandsons of those who had been, a generation or two earlier, the new nobles of Louisquatorzian officialdom is of little import. They intermarried with the old *noblesse*, their new names were lost in old titles, and they inherited more of the spirit of the Fronde than of the upstart administrators of Louis XIV. The *noblesse de l'épée* drew closer to that *noblesse de robe* which in its parlements had for centuries past upheld the authority of the crown against a turbulent *noblesse* of the sword, but now itself aspired to usurp the authority of which it had formerly been the docile guardian. The parlements renewed on a more permanent basis the alliance with the aristocracy that they had momentarily consummated during the Fronde. The Church, reduced to subservience to the crown by the Concordat of Francis I and kept in obedience by the Gallican liberties, its wealth and its higher offices put in the hands of the king to be given as rewards or taken away as punishments for the loyalty or disloyalty of the great houses of France, in the eighteenth century looked rather to its allies and relations of the aristocracy than to the crown. The higher Church posts had either by long use become practically hereditary in great families, or else were distributed, as the prize of court intrigues, not to maintain the authority of the crown, but to bolster up ministerial or aristocratic factions. Thus by 1788 the *noblesse* of the sword, robe, and church, which throughout the century had waged parallel campaigns against royal authority, had come so close together that they could unite in a single aristocratic revolt.

Yet their combined forces, dominant at Versailles, and with their centres of power in every cathedral, abbey, parlement, great château, or petty manor-house scattered through provincial capitals and countryside, though they were able to reduce the royal administration to impotence, were themselves to reveal only their weakness when they were challenged by another force which they had never associated, which indeed had never associated itself, with a claim to power. Looking backwards, the theme of eighteenth-century history in France is the rise of the Third Estate, but how many could have guessed this before 1789? Do we yet fully know what it means, for who were the Third Estate? We can give them another name and call them, if we will, the bourgeoisie, but this helps us no more, for what was the bourgeoisie? All that was not *noblesse* or people, we may reply. It may be suggested that the Third Estate consisted largely of officials, professional men, rentiers, and non-noble landowners; but for any more detailed or reliable estimate we shall have to wait until the social history of the period has been written.

However it was constituted, the problem remains why the Third Estate came to have the power to overthrow the combined aristocracies of France. In the course of narrating the history of this great overthrow, the explanation has perhaps emerged incidentally, for clearly it was not the bourgeoisie, whoever they may have been, who rioted in the market places, sacked the manor-houses and burnt the manorial rolls, dragged cannon to the Bastille, marched to Versailles, or mutinied in the army and fleet. The men who did these things, and constituted the rank and file of the peasant revolts and the great revolutionary *journées*, were peasants, craftsmen, artisans, small shopkeepers, soldiers. It was by making use of their discontents that the Third Estate was able to overcome the resistance of the privileged Orders and divert the Revolution to its own ends. Once this fact is realized a restatement of the problem becomes possible. The grievances of the people in town and country need not be recapitulated, nor the breakdown of social discipline which at least in part followed from the aristocratic revolt. The real problem is how a class of officials, lawyers, financiers, rentiers, landowners, was able to acquire the leadership of a popular movement constituted mainly of peasants and craftsmen. What did such leaders and followers have in common? To ask the question is to go a long way towards answering it. What they had in common was evidently not economic interests, though each group had its own interest which, to the best of its ability and in so far as it understood that interest, it pursued. What they had in common was an enemy,

R

primarily the *noblesse*, but along with it the superior clergy, *noblesse* of the robe, higher officials, and some sections of the wealthy such as the Farmers-General: in other words all those who might be described as belonging to the privileged classes.

Privilege was the enemy, equality the aim, though it must be remembered that the equality desired by the Third Estate was an equality not of property but of status. This was the inspiring motive of a social grouping which possessed talents, education, and at least moderate wealth, and yet was denied the position and status to which it thought these things entitled it. The peasants also found their primary objective in the assault on privilege and played their part in the events of 1789 under this banner. The better-off peasantry having achieved their principal aims, and the remainder lacking the cohesion or consciousness for more than sporadic unrest, they dropped out of political life. The Revolution was henceforth mainly an urban phenomenon, kept alive in the towns, and above all in Paris, by the unrest of a populace which suffered increasingly from the pressure of high prices and shortage of supplies. The under-mining of authority, the breakdown of police control, and the disintegration of the army led to a situation in which even a com-paratively small popular demonstration could intimidate the Assembly. The political factions of the left naturally took advantage of the weapon they found to their hand and used it to overthrow their opponents; but the alliance of the Mountain with the masses was fortuitous and effected only a temporary diversion of the main stream of the revolution of the Third Estate. The populace gained little from it, except possibly during the period when the war economy of the Committee of Public Safety for a time halted inflation, and then only at the price of the Terror.

When the new revolutionary army was sufficiently profession-alized and disciplined to be used in the streets of Paris, the political role of the people was at an end. But as the politicians of the Third Estate, having made use of the populace, had found themselves at the mercy of their own instrument, so the oligarchy which emerged after Thermidor and leant on the army found its policies determined by the generals, until one rose above all the others and became the autocrat of France. Then, and only then, did the logic of Bourbon absolutism finally triumph over the liberal ideals of the Constituent Assembly, and divine-right monarchy find, with Bonaparte, its historical sequel in the sovereignty of force.

Yet, though the later regimes of the revolutionary decade were to leave their mark on France, it was under the Constituent Assembly that the real harvest of the eighteenth century had been gathered in. Its work was lasting because it was built on foundations which had been solidly laid and because it was the culmination of a social revolution which, underneath the formal, juridical structure of society, had been quietly proceeding for centuries. We can call it the triumph of the bourgeoisie if by this term we mean the venal officers, lawyers, professional men, proprietors, with a few financiers and merchants, who invested their money, for the most part, in land or *rentes*, after venal offices were no longer available. The Revolution gave them the opportunity to obtain some of the lands and more of the offices of the privileged classes and to complete the process of rising to become the ruling class in France. They were not, by and large, a commercial or industrial class; their wealth was only to a minor degree derived from trade or industry, and it did not go back to fertilize the economic life of the nation. In their way of life they were the heirs of the obsolescent *noblesse*, and if they were bourgeois their aim was to be 'bourgeois vivant noblement'. The pattern of life which they copied and gradually made their own was that of the eighteenth century, the graces of which they were to perpetuate, to the best of their ability, into a modern world. Their eyes remained turned to the past in which their ideal had been set.

The victors had no wish to go beyond the social and political victory they had won, nor had they any intention of sharing their gains with the petty shopkeepers, craftsmen and journeymen, and all the *menu peuple* of the towns who had fought their battle for them. Equally, in the countryside, the better-off peasant proprietors were satisfied with what they had gained, indifferent to the grievances of the share-cropping *métayers*, and hostile to the barely conscious demands of the landless labourers. Out of the Revolution, therefore, there emerged a new and even stronger system of vested interests than had preceded it. Perhaps human capacity for change is limited: at any rate, the Revolution seemed to have effected changes so great that for a time they inhibited further progress. It did not inaugurate but brought to an end a great age of social transformation. The paradox of French history is that a revolutionary settlement was to provide the basis for a profoundly conservative pattern of society.

Yet it would be a narrow view to portray the Revolution as concerned only with material interests: the eighteenth century was an age of intellectual and moral as well as social development. Humanitarian and utilitarian reforms that had existed only on paper, or at best had received only scattered and partial expression before 1789, were given fuller effect in the legislation of the revolutionary assemblies. In one field, admittedly, the eighteenth century had sown dragon's teeth: clericalism and anti-clericalism were to bedevil French politics into the twentieth century. The phenomenon of anti-clericalism is, however, far from being understood: to attribute its outburst among the revolutionary masses merely to the influence of the *philosophes* is unsatisfactory, but if its tap-roots went — as they well may have done — deep into the obscure recesses of the popular mind, from what sources they drew nourishment, and driven by what inner urge it pushed its way to the surface, remain unsolved and perhaps insoluble problems. We can only add this to the sum total of all that the Enlightenment bequeathed to the Revolution and so to modern France, of which, intellectually and morally, as well as socially, the pattern had been already set when, on the eighteenth of Brumaire, Bonaparte made himself First Consul. Undeniably, the Enlightenment set up ideals that the revolutionaries could aspire towards more often than they could achieve, yet what they did achieve would give the French eighteenth century greatness if nothing else did.

CHRONOLOGICAL TABLE

⚜

1643	Accession of LOUIS XIV
1648–53	The Fronde
1651	Formal ending of minority of Louis XIV
1661	Beginning of Louis XIV's personal rule
1685	Revocation of Edict of Nantes
1697	Bayle's *Dictionnaire*
1701	War of Spanish Succession begins
1713–15	Peace of Utrecht
1713	Bull Unigenitus
1715	Death of Louis XIV. Accession of LOUIS XV
1715–23	Regency of Philip of Orleans
1716	Establishment of Bank by Law
1717	Creation of Mississipi Company
	Triple Alliance of France, England and Holland
	Watteau paints 'L'Embarquement pour Cythère'
1718	Quadruple Alliance of France, England, Holland, Austria
	Conspiracy of Cellamare
	Abandonment of Polysynodie
1718–19	Law acquires the General Farm of the taxes
1720	Collapse of Law's System
1721	Montesquieu's *Lettres persanes*
1722	Dubois becomes *premier ministre*
1723	Deaths of Dubois and Orleans
	Bourbon as *premier ministre*
1724–31	Club de l'Entresol
1725	Marriage of Louis XV and Marie Leczinska
1726	Disgrace of Bourbon
	Fleury becomes chief minister (without the name)
	Stabilization of livre
1731	Treaty of Vienna
	Marivaux's *La Vie de Marianne* (completed 1748)
	Prévost's *Manon Lescaut*
	Convulsionnaires of Saint-Médard
1733	Outbreak of the War of the Polish Succession
1734	Voltaire's *Lettres anglaises*

1735   Fleury signs peace preliminaries with Austria
1737   Disgrace of Chauvelin
1738   Treaty of Vienna: Duchy of Lorraine attributed to Stanislaus
        and on his death to France
1739   Outbreak of war between England and Spain
1740   Death of Emperor Charles VI
        Rise of Belle-Isle
1741   Franco-Prussian alliance. France enters the War of the
        Austrian Succession
1742   Loss of influence by Belle-Isle
1743   Death of Fleury
1744   Illness of Louis XV at Metz
        Strike of silk workers at Lyons
1745   Mme de Pompadour becomes titular mistress of Louis XV
        Fontenoy: victory of Marshal de Saxe
        Dismissal of Orry
1748   Treaty of Aix-la-Chapelle ends the War of the Austrian
        Succession
        Montesquieu's *De l'esprit des lois*
1749   Buffon's *Histoire naturelle* (completed 1788)
        Machault's tax of the *vingtième*
1751   First volume of the *Encyclopédie*
        Failure of Machault's attempt at financial reform
1754   Recall of Dupleix from India
        Condillac's *Traité des sensations*
1755   British attacks on French ships
1756   Agreement of Westminster between Prussia and Great
        Britain
        France and Austria conclude Treaty of Versailles
        Outbreak of Seven Years War
1757   Defeat of Soubise by Frederick II at Rossbach
        Attack on Louis XV by Damiens
1758   French armies evacuate Hanover
        Voltaire's *Candide*
        Helvétius's *De l'esprit*
        Choiseul appointed Secretary for Foreign Affairs
1759   Minden: French defeat
        Loss of Quebec, Guadeloupe, Martinique, etc.
        French naval defeats of Lagos and Quiberon
1760   Rousseau's *Nouvelle Héloïse*

1761	Family Compact between France and Spain
1762	Execution of Calas
	Rousseau's *Contrat social* and *Émile*
1763	Peace of Paris
1764	Death of Mme de Pompadour
	Dissolution of Society of Jesus in France
1765	Execution of La Barre
1766	Lorraine incorporated in France
1768	French purchase of Corsica from Genoa
1770	Marriage of the dauphin and Marie-Antoinette
	Fall of Choiseul
1770–4	Ministry of Maupeou and Terray
1771	Exile of parlements
1774	Death of Louis XV. Accession of LOUIS XVI
	Fall of Maupeou and Terray
	Maurepas acquires chief influence in government
	Recall of parlements
1774–6	Turgot as Controller-General
1776	Turgot's six edicts
	Fall of Turgot
1777–81	Necker in charge of finances
1778	France enters War of American Independence
1781	Necker's *Compte rendu*
	Dismissal of Necker
	Capitulation of Yorktown
1782	Defeat of de Grasse at naval battle of Saintes
1783	Treaty of Versailles ends War of American Independence
	Calonne becomes Controller-General
1784	Beaumarchais' *Mariage de Figaro*
1785	Affair of the diamond necklace
1786	Vergennes' commercial treaty with Great Britain
1787	Death of Vergennes
	February: Meeting of the Notables
	Fall of Calonne
	May: Appointment of Loménie de Brienne as *principal ministre*
	Dissolution of Notables
	Edict of toleration of Protestants
	August: Exile of parlement of Paris
	September: Anglo-Prussian intervention in Dutch Republic
	Recall of parlement

1788   May: Suspension of parlement and creation of Plenary Court
           by Lamoignon
        June: Revolt at Grenoble
           Resignation of Brienne and Lamoignon
        August: Convocation of States-General
           Return of Necker to office
        September: Recall of parlements
        December: Royal council approves decree doubling Third Estate

1789   January: Revolt at Rennes
        February: Sieyes' 'Qu'est-ce que le Tiers État?'
           Bread and grain riots in spring and early summer
        April: Réveillon riots at Paris
        May: Meeting of STATES GENERAL
        June 17th: Third Estate adopts title of National Assembly
        June 20th: Tennis-court oath
        June 23rd: Royal Session
        June 27th: King orders first two Orders to join third
        July 14th: Fall of the Bastille
           Recall of Necker
        July-August: Grande Peur
        August 4th–11th: Decrees abolishing feudal rights and privi-
           leges
        October 5th–6th: October Days
        October 21st: Decree on martial law
        November, December: Secularization of Church lands and issue
           of assignats decreed
        December: Law on local government

1790   July: Civil Constitution of the clergy
        August: Mutiny at Nancy
        September: Resignation of Necker
        November: Burke's *Reflections on the Revolution in France*

1791   April: Death of Mirabeau
           Papal Bull condemns oath of Civil Constitution
        June 21st: Flight to Varennes
        July 17th: Meeting at Champ-de-Mars dispersed by National
           Guard
           Formation of Feuillants Club
        August 27th: Declaration of Pilnitz
           Negro revolt in St Domingo

1791   September: Annexation of Avignon and Venaissin
                   Constitution of 1791 voted
                   Dissolution of Constituent Assembly
        October: Meeting of LEGISLATIVE ASSEMBLY
        November: Pétion elected mayor of Paris
1792   March: Formation of Brissotin ministry
        April 20th: France declares war on Austria
        June 12th: Letter of Roland to Louis XVI
        June 13th: Dismissal of Roland, Servan, and Clavière
        June 20th: Popular demonstrations in Paris
        July 11th: 'La Patrie en danger'
                   Manifesto of Duke of Brunswick
        July 25th: The Sections declared permanent
        August 10th: Attack on Tuileries
        August 19th: Flight of La Fayette
        August 20th: Fall of Longwy
        September 2nd: Fall of Verdun
        September 2nd–6th: September massacres
        September 20th: Valmy: retreat of Brunswick
        September 21st: Meeting of CONVENTION
        September 22nd: Abolition of monarchy
        September: French occupation of Savoy and Nice
        October: Custine crosses the Rhine
        November: French victory at Jemappes, occupation of Belgium
                   Annexation of Savoy
        November 19th: Decree of Convention offering help to all
                        peoples wishing to recover their liberty
        December 15th: Decree on treatment of occupied territories
        December: Trial of Louis XVI
1793   January 21st: Execution of Louis XVI
        February 1st: French declaration of war on Great Britain
        February, March: Food riots led by Jacques Roux and Varlet
        March: French declaration of war on Spain
                Revolt of the Vendée
                Revolutionary Tribunal set up
                Dumouriez defeated, evacuates Netherlands
        April: Treason of Dumouriez
                Establishment of Committee of Public Safety
        May: First law of the maximum
                Revolt of Lyons

1793   May 31st: Rising in Paris
June 2nd: Arrest of Brissotins
June 24th: Constitution of 1793 voted
July 13th: Assassination of Marat
       Robespierre enters Committee of Public Safety
       Suppression of remaining seigneurial rights without
         compensation
August: Toulon delivered to English
     Levée en masse declared
September: Law against suspects
       General maximum established
October: Lyons revolt repressed
       Execution of Marie-Antoinette
       Execution of Girondins
       Dechristianization campaign
December: Toulon retaken by revolutionaries
December 4th: Law on local government of 14 Frimaire
       Defeat of Vendéans

1794   March 24th: Execution of Hébertists
April 5th: Execution of Dantonists
June 1st: Naval battle off Brest
June 8th: Fête of the Supreme Being
June 10th: Law of 22 Prairial reorganizing Revolutionary
       Tribunal
June 26th: French victory at Fleurus: reconquest of Belgium
July 27th–28th: 9 Thermidor — Fall of Robespierre
September 1st: Billaud, Barère, and Collot leave Committee
       of Public Safety
November: Jacobin Club closed
December: Trial and execution of Carrier
       Abolition of maximum

1795   February: Pacification of La Jaunaye
April 1st: Day of 12 Germinal
April: Deportation of Billaud, Collot, Barère decreed
     Peace of Basle between France and Prussia
May: Peace with Holland
May 20th: Day of 1 Prairial
June: Death of Louis XVII
July: Quiberon: defeat of émigrés
     Peace between Spain and France

1795   August: Constitution of Year III voted
            Law of the two-thirds
        October 5th: Revolt of 13 Vendémiaire
                    Dissolution of Convention
        November: Rule of DIRECTORY begins
1796   May: Conspiracy of Babeuf
            French victory at Lodi
        November: French victory at Arcola
1797   January: French victory at Rivoli
        April: Preliminaries of Leoben
                Partial elections return constitutional monarchists
        May: Bonaparte occupies Venice
        September 4th: *Coup d'état* of 18 Fructidor
        October: Treaty of Campo-Formio
1798   May: Departure of French expedition to Egypt
        July: French victory at Battle of the Pyramids
        August: Aboukir Bay: Nelson destroys French fleet
1799   March: War of the Second Coalition
        May: Sieyes enters Directory
        June 18th: Day of 30 Prairial
                La Revellière and Merlin expelled from Directory
        March–July: Austrian and Russian successes
        August: French defeat at Novi
        September–October: Russian army defeated in Switzerland
        October: Return of Bonaparte to France
        November 9th–10th: *Coup d'état* of 18 Brumaire

FURTHER READING

To provide a full bibliography, or even a list of all the books, articles, and some unpublished material used in writing this history is not practicable. Ample bibliographies, up to the date of their publication, may be found in Lavisse, *Histoire de France*, vol. 8, pt ii: H. Carré, *Louis XV, 1715–1774* (1911), vol. 9, pt i; Carré, Sagnac and Lavisse, *Louis XVI, 1774–1789* (1912); Lavisse, *Histoire de France contemporaine*, vol. i: P. Sagnac, *La Révolution (1789–1792)* (1920); vol. ii: G. Pariset, *La Révolution (1792–1800)* (1920); Halphen et Sagnac (ed.), *Peuples et civilisations*, vol. 11: P. Muret, *La Prépondérance anglaise (1715–1763)* (1937), vol. 12: P. Sagnac, *La Fin de l'ancien régime et la révolution américaine (1763–1789)* (1941), vol. 13: G. Lefebvre, *La Révolution française* (1951, trans. 1962); *Clio: Introduction aux études historiques*: E. Préclin et V.-L. Tapié, *Le XVIIIe siècle* (2 vols., 1952); *Clio:* L. Villat, *La Révolution et l'Empire*, vol. 1, *Les Assemblées révolutionnaires, 1789–1799* (1936); *Thémis: Histoire des Institutions*, by J. Ellul, vol 2 (1956). A useful bibliography of the eighteenth century, including works on France, is *A Select List of Works on Europe and Europe Overseas 1715–1815*, edited by J. S. Bromley and A. Goodwin (1956). The list of books which follows should be regarded as no more than a guide to further reading.

Among general histories, the Lavisse volumes and the *Peuples et Civilisations* series, both already cited, are of value. The Larousse *Histoire de France* (1954), edited by Marcel Reinhard (vol. ii: R. Mousnier, *La France de Louis XV*, and M. Reinhard, *La Crise révolutionnaire*), is a very readable, sound summary, magnificently illustrated. Ph. Sagnac's *La Formation de la Société française moderne* (2 vols., 1946), which surveys French social development from 1661 to 1789, provides an introduction to many important aspects of the period, but is too general in treatment, often because the fundamental research has still not been done, to provide a satisfactory synthesis.

The Ancien Régime

Original sources for the French *ancien régime* offer an embarrassing richness. The memoirs, of which there are hundreds in print, have to be treated with caution. Apart from their inherent faults as historical sources, many are later fabrications not even written by the authors to whom they are attributed. Thus the famous *Souvenirs* of Mme de Créqui, which passed through over a dozen editions, represent a bookseller's venture of the eighteen thirties, Mme de Créqui, who knew the Versailles of Louis XIV and met the Emperor Napoleon at the Tuileries, being an admirable figure on whom to hang an anecdotal history of the whole century. The history of eighteenth-century France is still littered with the debris of such apocryphal or unreliable memoirs. Among those that are genuine must be named, first and foremost, the memoirs of Saint-Simon. In addition to the monumental and essential edition in 41 volumes by Boislisle (1879–1928), there are various volumes of selections, some in translation. D'Argenson's *Journal* (9 vols., 1859–67, also available in translation, 1909) represents the views of a disappointed minister, the *Journal* of Barbier (ed. in 4 vols. 1847–56 and in 8 vols. 1885) those of a gossiping lawyer, on the reign of Louis XV. Between them they have done a good deal to distort its history. The most reliable history of the court of Louis XV is the *Mémoires du duc de Luynes sur la cour de Louis XV (1735–1758)* (17 vols., 1860–5). Another interesting view of high society is presented in the *Mémoires du comte Dufort de Cheverney* (ed. R. de Crèvecœur, 2 vols., 1909). The story of the *secret du roi* has been completed by the publication of the *Correspondance secrète du comte de Broglie avec Louis XV (1756–1784)* (ed. by D. Ozanam and M. Antoine, 2 vols., 1956–). The literary world is reflected in the *Correspondance littéraire, philosophique et critique de Grimm, Diderot, etc.* (16 vols, ed. M. Tourneux, 1877–82). The people and daily life of Paris appear in L. S. Mercier's *Tableau de Paris* (many editions), with an abridgement in English, *The Waiting City: Paris, 1782–88* (trans. G. H. Simpson, 1933). An interesting account of a peasant household is Rétif de la Bretonne's *La Vie de mon Père* (ed. M. Boisson, 1924), for the author, though he achieved fame by the description of less simple manners, was himself the son of a peasant. The parish *cahiers* of 1789 throw much light on conditions in the countryside, though it must be remembered that these, like Rétif de la Bretonne, generally reflect the views of the better-off class of peasant farmers called *laboureurs*. An interesting selection of the observations of foreign visitors is given in C. Maxwell's *The English Traveller in France, 1698–1815* (1932). Among the sources quoted in this collection is the naive and fascinating *Diary of a Scotch Gardener at the French Court at the End of the Eighteenth Century*, by T. Blaikie (ed. F. Birrell, 1931).

The classic study of the *ancien régime* in relation to the Revolution is de Tocqueville's *L'Ancien Régime et la Révolution* (many reprints and also in translation). Taine's *L'Ancien Régime* is a brilliant piece of writing, but lacks the depth and intellectual honesty that has enabled de Tocqueville's book to retain its value. F. Funck-Brentano's *L'ancien régime* (1926, translated as *The Old Regime in France*, 1929) is an amusing, lively, anecdotal apology for France before the Revolution. P. Gaxotte's *Le Siècle de Louis XV* (revised ed., 1933, translated as *Louis the Fifteenth and his times*, 1934), which aims at rehabilitating the memory of Louis XV, may serve as a corrective to the many equally superficial works which have denigrated him. The *Dictionnaire des institutions de la France aux XVIIᵉ et XVIIIᵉ siècles* (1923) by M. Marion is an invaluable work of reference.

For many aspects or periods the historian will have to turn to books written in the nineteenth century, which he will neglect at his peril. I propose here, generally, to confine myself to more recent and more easily available works. Apart from the valuable notes and appendixes to Boislisle's edition of Saint-Simon, the most complete account of the Regency is Dom Leclercq's *Histoire de la Régence* (3 vols., 1921). An introductory book is H. M. Hyde, *John Law* (1948). There is no satisfactory biography of Fleury, but on his foreign policy we have two sound studies, P. Vaucher's *Robert Walpole et la politique de Fleury, 1731–1742* (1925), and A. M. Wilson, *French Foreign Policy during the Administration of Cardinal Fleury* (1936). Among P. de Nolhac's many pleasant if slight works on the French court and eighteenth-century art, the most useful for the historian is *Louis XV et Madame de Pompadour* (1928). Nancy Mitford's *Madame de Pompadour* (1954) is eminently readable and sound. J. G. Flammermont's *Le Chancelier Maupeou et les parlements* (2nd ed., 1885) is scholarly and detailed but, writing at a time when the propaganda of the parlements was still taken at its face value, the author failed to appreciate the achievement of Maupeou and Terray, which still awaits its historian. The best book on Turgot, which also throws much light on the problems of local and central government, is D. Dakin, *Turgot and the Ancien Régime in France* (1939). On the affair of the diamond necklace there are, of course, innumerable books; the best, though it inevitably leaves some problems unsolved, is still Funck-Brentano's *L'Affaire du collier* (5th ed., rev., 1903, also in translation). An account of French foreign policy in the Dutch crisis of 1784–7 is given by A. Cobban in *Ambassadors and Secret Agents: the Diplomacy of the First Earl of Malmesbury at The Hague* (1954), which also throws light on the defects of French diplomacy in the eighteenth century.

The more recent work on the *ancien régime* has tended to deal with special subjects rather than periods or episodes. There is no study of the system of government as a whole. The machinery of central government, rather than the way in which it worked, is described in P. Viollet, *Le Roi et ses ministres pendant les derniers siècles de la monarchie* (1912). A summary of the machinery for collecting indirect taxes is provided by G. J. Matthews in *Royal General Farms in eighteenth-century France* (1958). Funck-Brentano corrects some mistaken ideas in *Les Lettres de cachet* (1926). H. Carré's *La Fin des parlements, 1788–1790* (1912) provides a short general description of the parlements as well as narrating the history of their final phase. F. Ford in *Robe and Sword* (1953) concentrates his attention mainly on the social composition of the *noblesse de robe* and its connections with the *noblesse de l'épée*; and R. Forster's *The Nobility of Toulouse in the Eighteenth Century* (1960) shows that at least in one area there was a shrewd, hard-working, commercially-minded provincial *noblesse*. Flammermont's *Remontrances du parlement de Paris au XVIIIᵉ siècle* (3 vols., 1888–98) is an essential source. A useful survey of the political ideas of the parlements is made by R. Bickart in *Les Parlements et la notion de souveraineté nationale au XVIIIᵉ siècle* (1932). The only general study of the intendants is P. N. Ardascheff, *Les Intendants de province sous Louis XVI* (trans. from Russian, 1909) which, however, needs much correction. Among many local studies the most recent, as well as the most important, is H. Fréville, *L'Intendance de Bretagne, 1689–1790* (3 vols., 1953). On French finances we have the first volume of M. Marion's *Histoire financière de la France depuis 1715* (6 vols., 1914–31), to which should be added the same author's *Machault d'Arnouville* (1892).

General outlines of international relations are given by G. Zeller in *Les Temps modernes, ii. De Louis XIV à 1789 (Histoire des Relations internationales*, ed. P. Renouvin, vol. iii, 1955), and P. Rain, *La Diplomatie française d'Henri IV à Vergennes* (1945). Useful general surveys of French colonial history are H. Blet, *Histoire de la colonisation française* (2 vols., 1946), and H. J. Priestley, *France Overseas through the Old Régime* (1939). The history of French Canada is treated by G. M. Wrong, *The Rise and Fall of New France* (1928). On Dupleix there is A. Martineau, *Dupleix, sa vie et son œuvre* (1931), and H. H. Dodwell, *Dupleix and Clive* (1920).

For the study of economic developments the general survey by H. Sée, *Histoire économique de la France* (vol. i, ed. R. Schnerb, 1948), is a useful introduction. An excellent outline of the social structure of France before the Revolution is given by Sée in his *La France économique et sociale au XVIIIᵉ siècle* (1925, trans. as *Economic and social conditions in France during the eighteenth century*, 1927). H. Carré in *La Noblesse de*

France et l'opinion publique au XVIIIe siècle (1920) describes the various divisions of the *noblesse*. The older books of A. Babeau, *La ville sous l'ancien régime* (2nd ed., 1884), *Le Village sous l'ancien régime* (5th ed., 1915), etc., provide much interesting, if scrappy, information which it is difficult to obtain easily elsewhere. On the army the most useful work is L. Mention, *L'Armée d'ancien régime* (1900). The effect of the shortage of suitable timber on French naval power is shown in P. W. Bamford's *Forests and French Sea Power, 1660–1789* (1956).

On the conditions of the peasantry important works, though they cover a broader period, are H. Sée's *Les Classes rurales en Bretagne du XVIe siècle à la révolution* (1906) and Marc Bloch's *Les Caractères originaux de l'histoire rurale française* (new ed., 1952), with a second volume of supplementary material published in 1956 by M. Dauvergne. G. Lefebvre's monumental *Les Paysans du Nord pendant la Révolution* (1924) contributes much to the understanding of the conditions of the peasantry before as well as during the Revolution. An interesting examination of the attempts to introduce more advanced methods of agriculture into France is A. J. Borde, *The Influence of England on the French Agronomes, 1750–1789* (1952).

Turning to industry, A. Rémond's study of the Jacobite exile who became a leading French industrialist, *John Holker, 1719–1786* (1944), M. Rouff, *Les Mines de charbon en France au XVIIIe siècle, 1744–1791* (1922), and G. Martin, *Nantes au XVIIIe siècle, l'ère des négriers, 1714–1774* (1931), may be mentioned among other specialized studies of such topics. An important contribution to the economic history of the period is C. E. Labrousse, *Esquisse du mouvement des prix et des revenus en France au XVIIIe siècle* (1934), which prepared the way for his fundamental analysis of economic conditions, *La Crise de l'économie française à la fin de l'Ancien Régime et au début de la Révolution* (1944). On the economic thought of the physiocratic school we have G. Weulersse, *Le Mouvement physiocratique en France de 1756 à 1778* (2 vols., 1910) and *La Physiocratie sous les ministères de Turgot et de Necker, 1774–1781* (1950).

Behind the economic developments were technical advances, of which a remarkably full and reliable outline is given by R. Mousnier in the *Histoire générale des civilisations: Le XVIIIe siècle*, by R. Mousnier and E. Labrousse (1953). On the same subject is S. T. McCloy, *French Inventions of the 18th Century* (1952). The life and multifarious activities of the greatest French scientist of the century, Lavoisier, who also made many contributions to technical advance, are described in D. McKie's *Antoine Lavoisier* (1952), and among important works on the history of science

P. Brunet's *L'Introduction des théories de Newton en France au XVIIIe siècle* (1931) is notable.

In the field of religion, the Jansenists have been treated by A. Gazier, *Histoire générale du mouvement janséniste depuis ses origines jusqu'à nos jours* (2 vols., 1922), which is favourable to them, and E. Préclin, *Les Jansénistes du XVIIIe siècle et la Constitution civile du clergé* (1928). The Protestants of France, whose existence is often forgotten, are dealt with by J. Dedieu in his *Histoire politique des protestants français, vol. ii: 1715–1794* (1925). The influence of the new climate of opinion on the Roman Catholic Church is shown in R. R. Palmer, *Catholics and Unbelievers in eighteenth-century France* (1939). A revealing study of the most famous act of persecution of pre-revolutionary France is David D. Bien's *The Calas Affair* (1958).

A general survey of eighteenth-century French thought is Kingsley Martin, *French Liberal Thought in the Eighteenth Century* (2nd ed., 1954). *The Philosophy of the Enlightenment* (trans. 1951), by E. Cassirer, is subtle, but to my mind misleading. Carl Becker's *The Heavenly City of the French Philosophers* (1932) is a brilliant essay but also carries one line of interpretation of a many-sided movement too far. It is severely, but in my opinion justly, criticized in a series of studies edited by R. O. Rockwood, *Carl Becker's Heavenly City Revisited* (1958). A recent interpretation of the Enlightenment, which differs fundamentally from that of Becker, is A. Cobban's *In Search of Humanity: the Role of the Enlightenment in Modern History* (1960). The essential introduction to the thought of the eighteenth century is the masterly work of Paul Hazard, *La Crise de la conscience européenne, 1680–1715* (3 vols., 1934), which has been translated. Probably the best book on the Encyclopedists is R. Hubert's *Les Sciences sociales dans l'Encyclopédie* (1923). A useful selection is *L'Encyclopédie of Diderot and d'Alembert: Selected Articles* (1954) by J. Lough. A. M. Wilson's *Diderot: the Testing Years* (1957) is the first volume of what is likely to be the authoritative life of the famous Encyclopedist, who is in some ways the most stimulating and provocative thinker of eighteenth-century France. The older books on French opinion in the eighteenth century by Aubertin, Roustan, and Rocquain have largely been superseded and are not reliable guides. A general survey is D. Mornet, *La Pensée française au dix-huitième siècle* (1926), and a much more detailed study is provided by the same author in his *Origines intellectuelles de la révolution française* (1933). An interesting study of the spread of the new ideas is I. O. Wade's *The Clandestine Organisation and Diffusion of Philosophic Ideas in France from 1700 to 1750* (1938).

S

The history of French literature in the eighteenth century is hardly distinguishable from that of French thought. Perhaps for this reason a satisfactory general history of literature as such is hard to come by. F. C. Green's *Minuet* (1935) is an attractive *rapprochement* of some English and French themes. There is no space for a list of books on individual writers. E. Carcassonne, *Montesquieu et le problème de la Constitution française au XVIIIe siècle* (1927) is a thorough discussion of the influence of Montesquieu, especially on the parlements. The basic work on Voltaire is still G. le B. Desnoiresterres' *Voltaire et la société au XVIIIe siècle* (2nd ed., 8 vols., 1871–6), to which may be added A. Bellessort's brilliant *Essai sur Voltaire* (14th ed., 1933). The most important study of Rousseau's political thought in relation to its origins is R. Derathé's *J.-J. Rousseau et la science politique de son temps* (1950). Similar in its basic interpretation of Rousseau is A. Cobban's *Rousseau and the Modern State* (1934).

On architecture there is R. Blomfield, *History of French Architecture, 1661–1774* (2 vols., 1921), and L. Hautecœur, *Histoire de l'Architecture classique en France* (vols. 3 and 4, 1943–5); on painting, L. Gillet, *La Peinture de Poussin à David* (2nd ed., 1935), and R. Schneider, *L'Art français: XVIIIe siècle* (1926). A detailed compendium of the spread of French artistic influence through Europe is provided in L. Réau's *L'Europe française au siècle des lumières* (1938).

The Revolution

It would doubtless be an exaggeration to say that the amount of original material in print on the revolutionary decade in France is equal to that available for the whole of the rest of modern history put together, but to any historian of the revolutionary period it must seem no more than a pardonable exaggeration. A few of the better known original sources alone can be mentioned here. The many volumes of *cahiers* which have been edited are essential for the study of social conditions in France on the eve of the Revolution. Arthur Young's *Travels in France in 1787, 1788 and 1789*, available in many editions, the best being that of the French translation by H. Sée (3 vols., 1930), is invaluable, though the views of Arthur Young need a good deal of correction. The flood of memoirs continues in the revolutionary period. Among the more important are E. Dumont's *Souvenirs sur Mirabeau* (ed. J. Bénétruy, 1950), the *Correspondance inédite, 1789, 1790, 1791* of the marquis de Ferrières (ed. H. Carré, 1932) and the *Mémoires de Madame Roland* (ed. C. Perroud, 2 vols., 1905).

An extensive sample of revolutionary journalism is provided in G.

Walter's *La Révolution française vue par ses journaux* (1948). There are also extracts from the journals in L. G. Wickham Legg's *Select Documents illustrative of the history of the French Revolution. The Constituent Assembly* (2 vols., 1905). There is a modern edition of Camille Desmoulins' famous *Le Vieux Cordelier* (ed. H. Calvet, 1936). *L'Ancien Moniteur* (30 vols., 1850–4) is a reprint of the journal which, by the skill of its editors in following the official line as faction after faction rose to power or fell, survived throughout the period and can be regarded as reflecting the governmental view at each stage. It should be noted that up to February 3rd, 1790, this reprint is a later compilation. *The Principal Speeches of the Statesmen and Orators of the French Revolution, 1789–1795*, edited by H. Morse Stephens (2 vols., 1892), has unfortunately long been out of print and is difficult to obtain. An interesting collection of contemporary verdicts on Robespierre is made by L. Jacob in *Robespierre vu par ses contemporains* (1928). The most convenient selections of laws and decrees are J. M. Thompson's *French Revolution Documents 1789–94* (1933, reprinted) and *L'Œuvre législative de la Révolution* by L. Cahen and R. Guyot (1913).

A definitive edition of the writings, speeches, and correspondence of Robespierre is in progress and there are editions of the writings, letters, and speeches of many other prominent revolutionaries. The famous pamphlet of Sieyes, 'Qu'est-ce que le Tiers État?' has had no reprint since 1888, which is regrettable, for it is essential to the understanding of the political ideas of the revolutionaries.

The study of the historiography of the Revolution has become a subject in itself, but cannot be dealt with here. The histories of Mignet (1824) and Thiers (1823–7) still have something to tell the student of the Revolution. Carlyle's *French Revolution* (1837) is in a class by itself. Michelet's history (1847–53 and many subsequent editions) is closer to Carlyle than to modern scholarship. Louis Blanc's twelve-volume history (1848–62) brought in new themes inspired by his socialistic ideas. De Tocqueville's masterpiece has been cited above. Taine's history (1882–7) is a brilliant polemic. Aulard's *Histoire politique de la révolution française* (1789–1804) (1901, translated in 4 vols., 1910) is the first general history based on the results of modern scholarship, but, as its title suggests, is mainly political in approach. Jaurès' *Histoire socialiste*, vols. 1–4 (1901–4), is valuable, not only because it inaugurated the study of the Revolution as a struggle of social classes, but also for its interpretation of some of the major episodes. This line of research was continued by A. Mathiez, whose *La Révolution française* (3 vols., 1925–7, translated in 1928), which ends in

Thermidor 1794, is still one of the best general histories of France in these years. A masterly history of the whole revolutionary age is Georges Lefebvre's *La Révolution française* (3rd ed., 1951, now trans.). The best account by an English historian is J. M. Thompson, *The French Revolution* (1943), and a valuable short introduction, embodying the results of modern research and concentrating particularly on the opening stages of the Revolution, is that by A. Goodwin, *The French Revolution, 1789–1794* (1953). There is much important material in the shorter studies of Aulard, Mathiez, and Lefebvre. The histories by Madelin and Gaxotte are readable but of little serious value.

Turning to more detailed monographs on the history of the Revolution, the finest account of the outbreak of the Revolution is G. Lefebvre's *Quatre-vingt-neuf* (1939), translated as *The Coming of the French Revolution* (1947). The most thoroughly worked out, though not convincing, exposition of the conspiracy thesis of the origins of the Revolution is A. Cochin's *Les Sociétés de pensée et la Révolution en Bretagne, 1788–1789* (2 vols., 1926). Relevant to the aristocratic revolution are Carré's *La Fin des Parlements*, cited above, P. Renouvin, *Les Assemblées provinciales de 1787* (1921), and J. Egret, *La Révolution des notables: Mounier et les monarchiens* (1950). *La Grande Peur de 1789* by Lefebvre (1932) is a model of historical detection. The legend that the members of the Jacobin clubs were drawn from the lowest strata of the population was dissipated by C. C. Brinton's *The Jacobins* (1930). D. Greer in *The Incidence of the Terror during the French Revolution* (1935) and *The Incidence of the Emigration during the French Revolution* (1951) analysed the social composition of the victims of the Terror and of the émigrés. A stimulating if perverse Trotskyite interpretation of the social struggles of the Revolution, in which Robespierre appears as the supreme counter-revolutionary, is D. Guérin, *La Lutte des classes sous la première république* (3rd ed., 2 vols., 1946). The Revolution of August 10th, 1792, is described in Mathiez, *Le Dix Août* (1931). P. Caron's *Les Massacres de septembre* (1935) is a work of minute and detailed research. Taine's picture of the revolutionary mob is successfully criticized by G. Rudé in *The Crowd in the French Revolution* (1959). A major reinterpretation of revolutionary politics, which demolishes the legend of a great Girondin party, is M. J. Sydenham's *The Girondins* (1961). The episode of *Les Sans-culottes parisiens en l'an II* (1958) is described in massive detail by A. Soboul; and R. Cobb deals, in many articles and a forthcoming book, with the little, local *armées révolutionnaires*. The only comprehensive study of the composition and achievements of the great Committee of Public

Safety is R. R. Palmer's *Twelve who Ruled* (1941). On the Thermidorians we have Mathiez, *La Réaction thermidorienne* (1929), and Lefebvre, *Les Thermidoriens* (1937); and for the Directory *Le Directoire* (ed. J. Godechot, 1934) by Mathiez, and *Le Directoire* (1946) by Lefebvre. A. Vandal's *L'Avènement de Bonaparte* (2 vols., 1907–8) is brilliantly written; it may overpaint the scene and exaggerate the defects of the directorial regime, but until more work has been done on this phase of revolutionary history no judgment of the faults and merits of the Directory can be much more than a guess.

The best short survey of the constitutional history of the Revolution is the introduction to *Les Constitutions et les principales lois politiques de la France* by Duguit and Monnier (many editions). In later editions the introduction remains unchanged so far as concerns the revolutionary period. A valuable survey of revolutionary institutions is the *Histoire des institutions de la France sous la Révolution et l'Empire* (1951) by J. Godechot, to whom we also owe *Les Commissaires aux armées sous le Directoire* (1937).

The standard work on international relations is A. Sorel, *L'Europe et la Révolution française* (8 vols., 1885–1904), though Sorel's work is susceptible of many major corrections and additions. A shorter account is P. Rain's *La Diplomatie française de Mirabeau à Bonaparte* (1950). A. Fugier's *La Révolution française et l'Empire napoléonien* (1954) is rather slight on the revolutionary period. A significant reinterpretation of the outbreak of the revolutionary war is made by G. Michon in *Robespierre et la guerre, 1791–2* (1937). R. Guyot's *Le Directoire et la paix de l'Europe* (1911) is a major contribution to diplomatic history. Closely linked with foreign relations is the story of the Vendée, on which the literature is vast but partisan. E. Gabory, *L'Angleterre et la Vendée* (2 vols., 1930–1), has the virtue of using the extensive English as well as French sources. The effect of the Vendée on French naval power is revealed by N. Hampson in *La Marine de l'an II* (1959), which gives more credit than is customary to the Committee of Public Safety for its efforts to build up the French fleets, though showing also the reasons for its comparative lack of success.

A useful introduction to the economic policy of the revolutionaries, with extensive bibliographical references, is provided by the first chapters of S. H. Clough, *France: a History of National Economics, 1789–1939* (1939). The importance of bankers and financiers in revolutionary politics emerges in J. Bouchary, *Les Manieurs d'argent à Paris à la fin du XVIIIᵉ siècle* (3 vols., 1939–43). On the finances of the government we have

Marion's *Histoire financière de la France*, cited above, and S. G. Harris, *The Assignats* (1930). The significance of the struggle initiated by the *enragés* was revealed by Mathiez in *La Vie chère et le mouvement social sous la Terreur* (1929). Lefebvre's *Paysans du Nord*, cited above, and his *Questions agraires au temps de la Terreur* (1932) throw much light on the problems of the countryside. Interesting technical material on agriculture is to be found in O. Festy, *L'Agriculture pendant la Révolution française* (1947).

The relations of the revolutionaries with the Papacy and the question of Avignon are described in A. Mathiez, *Rome et la Constituante* (1910). Recent Catholic historians of the religious policy of the revolutionaries are A. Latreille in *L'Église catholique et la Révolution* (1946–50), rather hostile to the Revolution, and J. Leflon in *La Crise révolutionnaire, 1789–1848* (1949), remarkably free from bias.

Among a host of biographies only a few can be selected for mention. J. M. Thompson's *Leaders of the French Revolution* (1929) contains a series of short but penetrating sketches. G. C. van Deusen, *Sieyès: his life and his nationalism* (1932) is concerned mainly with Sieyès's ideas. The standard work on the Mirabeau family is L. and C. de Loménie, *Les Mirabeau* (5 vols., 1878–90). Other biographies are O. J. R. Welch, *Mirabeau* (1951), L. Barthou, *Danton* (1932), L. R. Gottschalk, *Marat* (1927), L. Madelin, *Fouché* (2 vols., 1900). The best and most detailed life of Robespierre is by J. M. Thompson (2 vols., 1939). M. Reinhard has written the authoritative life of Carnot (1950–2).

On literature and art may be mentioned P. Trahard, *La Sensibilité révolutionnaire, 1791–1794* (1936), D. L. Dowd, *Pageant-Master of the Republic: Jacques-Louis David and the French Revolution* (1948), and L. Hautecœur, *L'Art sous la Révolution et l'Empire* (1953).

BOOK II

❧

*From the First Empire to the
Second Republic
1799–1871*

CONTENTS

INTRODUCTION   9

PART ONE: THE FIRST EMPIRE

1. France in 1799   13
2. From Consulate to Empire   16
3. Napoleonic Foundations of the Nineteenth Century   22
4. The Napoleonic Empire: Rise   41
5. The Napoleonic Empire: Fall   57

PART TWO: THE CONSTITUTIONAL MONARCHY

1. The Restoration   73
2. Clericalism and Anti-Clericalism   83
3. The Foundation of the July Monarchy   94
4. Louis-Philippe   106
5. An Age of Idealism   114

PART THREE: THE SECOND REPUBLIC AND THE SECOND EMPIRE

1. 1848: from the February Days to the June Days   133
2. The Triumph of Louis Napoleon   146
3. A Bourgeois Empire   157
4. L'Empire c'est la Paix   170
5. Towards the Liberal Empire   182
6. The Price of Dictatorship   196
7. Plus ça change   211

CHRONOLOGICAL TABLE   222
FURTHER READING   230

MAPS

❦

1 The French Empire and its satellite states, 1812   52

2 The eastern frontier of France, 1814–71   74

3 The conquest of Algeria, 1830–48   111

Paris in the nineteenth century   194

INTRODUCTION

THE second book of this history of modern France—originally the second volume—covered the whole period from 1799 to the Second World War. This meant that the treatment of twentieth-century history in particular had to be much abridged. This fact has been criticized, and in answer to these criticisms I have now divided the former second volume into two parts. To the original second volume of the history, which now ends in 1871, I have added a short concluding section. The new third book is largely rewritten and carries the story of France from 1871 to the present day.

I have taken this opportunity to correct a number of slips and must express my gratitude to all who have pointed them out to me.

A. C.

PART ONE

❧

THE FIRST EMPIRE

CHAPTER ONE

FRANCE IN 1799

THE pattern of French society, and even its physical setting, received so strong an imprint in the eighteenth century that the mark of that age still remains in many aspects of national life the dominant characteristic of France. In its provincial capitals, the solid eighteenth-century quarters, well-planned enclaves, or graceful urban extensions in a semi-rural setting still recall the memory of a more elegant age. In Paris, when the older buildings were swept away under the Second Empire and even the street plan modernized out of recognition, the eighteenth century survived in the great town-houses scattered from the Chaussée d'Antin through the faubourg Saint-Honoré to the Seine, and by way of the place de la Concorde across the river to the faubourg Saint-Germain. Under Louis XV, Paris, pushing outwards, had swallowed up the limits traced by Charles V in the fourteenth century and their western extension of 1631 under Louis XIII. The hated wall of the Farmers General, built in 1785 as a customs barrier with imposing monumental gates, took in a vast new area, stretching round the western and northern heights of Passy, Chaillot, Belleville, and Ménilmontant, including — south of the river — the faubourgs Saint-Victor, Saint-Marceau, Saint-Jacques, and Saint-Germain, and curving back round the Champ-de-Mars. At the end of the eighteenth century much of this new territory was not yet built up; within the barrier, beyond the Bastille and the Temple in the east, were fields and scattered houses with their gardens. In the west the Champs-Élysées were woodland crossed by roads and wandering paths, and the Champ-de-Mars a huge open space. Paris proper still huddled together within the boulevards that marked the site of its former fortifications, a solid agglomeration of high, closely-packed, terraced houses separated by winding, narrow streets and alleys, noisy with street cries, busy with passers-by, crowded and dangerous with carriages and wagons of all kinds, strewn with rubbish and filth lying about in heaps or carried along in the torrents of water pouring after a storm down the wide gutters, across which pedestrians could pass dry-shod only by little plank bridges. After a decade of revolution the house-fronts were dilapidated, their plaster falling, paint-work peeling, and shreds of posters flapping in the wind. At night, when there was no moon, an occasional *lanterne*, jutting out from the wall, shed a feeble and after 1789 a rather sinister light in these dark canyons. For all the fine architecture of the classical age, and the palatial *hôtels* of the wealthy, urban amenities were rare. Voltaire, in 1749, had called for such improvements as fountains to supply pure drinking water, roads adequate for the traffic of a great capital, and worthy public buildings, especially theatres. The narrow and squalid streets of Paris, he declared, should be widened, and fine buildings which were concealed from sight by a huddle of houses freed from their squalid surroundings. It was a century later before his hopes for Paris began to be realized, and then to the artistic taste of the Second Empire instead of that of the age of Louis Quinze.

Paris, at the end of the eighteenth century, was still in some respects an homogeneous city. Though there were faubourgs like Saint-Antoine and Saint-Marceau, inhabited mainly by small masters and their journeymen, and new wealthy quarters like the faubourg Saint-Germain, in much of older Paris the homes of the well-to-do, of the middling people and of the poor existed under the same roof. It might almost be said that class stratification was vertical, the rich and the poor entering by the same door, the former to mount by a short and broad staircase to the impressive apartments of the first floor, the latter to climb high up by ever narrowing stairs till they reached the attics in the mansard roof.

From Paris and the provincial capitals already radiated out the network of great roads that so impressed Arthur Young, as did the lack of traffic on them. The new industrial regions of France have witnessed many changes since the eighteenth century, but the great ports were already considerable cities. They still glory in their eighteenth-century quarters, while to many smaller towns and villages, scattered up and down the length and breadth of the country, alteration has come only slowly and imperceptibly. It was from the provinces that was drawn, then as now, much of the busy, scurrying population of the ant-heap of Paris, and many a Parisian, his fortune made or lost and his active life over, withdrew to pass his declining years in the quiet town or village of his childhood, along with the men who had been boys when he was a boy, who had not stirred from their native soil and who were the millions of France. Perhaps 600,000 lived in Paris at the end of the eighteenth century. The total urban population of France must have been well under two millions. Probably some 95 per cent of France's 26 millions lived in isolated farms, hamlets, villages, and small country towns. Mountain and forest still covered, as they do today, large tracts of country, though under pressure of rural over-population farming had pushed into marginal land on moor and hill-top that has since been abandoned. Agriculture, little influenced by the new methods developed in eighteenth-century England, followed its routine of the Middle Ages. Industry was still largely domestic.

In all these fundamental respects it matters little whether we are writing of 1789 or 1799. The Revolution did not materially add to or subtract from the basic resources of France, though it altered the use that was, or could be, made of them. What France had that still endowed her, at the end of the eighteenth century, with a potentially greater strength than any other country, was the largest population in Europe under a single government, apart from Russia, and even that had only just caught up with France. The application of the steam engine to industry was hardly yet a factor in national strength; and this apart, France had a technical skill and equipment second to none. The Revolution had freed her from the trammels of the *ancien régime*. Paris, which for some five years had tried to rule France, had been disciplined with the aid of the armies drawn from the un-political rural millions. All was ready for a great general to con-centrate the newly released forces into a centralized despotism and direct them into a bid for world empire.

CHAPTER TWO

FROM CONSULATE TO EMPIRE

ENTURIES do not usually end so punctually as the French
eighteenth century did with the year 1799; though in another
sense, as I have suggested, the France of the *ancien régime*
still survives. For both its sudden conclusion and its persistence the
chief responsibility must be attributed to Bonaparte. With his sense
of realism, executive capacity, and ruthless strength of will, he wrote
finis to the doubts and feuds of the revolutionaries, and imposed,
out of the materials to hand, a new-fashioned framework on France,
which was to last in its essentials to the present day. For the very
reason that it was an artificial superstructure, which bore the weight
of the state without ever being consciously shaped to the society on
which it was arbitrarily imposed, it prevented the natural growth
of institutions which might otherwise have taken place. This is, of
course, wisdom after the event. When Bonaparte was brought to the
chief office in the republic, though there was a general feeling that a
new period had opened, the politicians who had effected the *coup
d'état* did not appreciate what they had done, any more than those
who had overthrown Robespierre five years earlier.

On the morrow of brumaire, Bonaparte himself had only taken
the first step, though a long one, on the path to Empire. He had yet
to show that he was more than a successful general and to consolidate
by the arts of politics what he had staked out a claim to by those of
war. The original proposals for the new constitution came from that
self-appointed Solon of the Revolution, Sieyes. Given a third
opportunity to demonstrate his genius at making constitutional
bricks without straw, he framed a system of legislative bodies
ingeniously devised to remove all effective political power from the
sovereign people without attributing it to anyone else. In the best
revolutionary tradition he was proposing to set up an imposing
machine of government without providing any motive power to

work it. The central position in the whole complicated system was to be occupied by a Conservative Senate, and if we ask how this was to be created we come to the heart of the matter: it was to be nominated, in effect, by Sieyes. The executive power, on the other hand, was to be entrusted to a Grand Elector with powers so carefully cabined and confined that he could do nothing by himself: this role was reserved for Bonaparte. We can hardly be surprised that for the third time Sieyes' plans proved abortive. His proposal for drawing the teeth of democratic sovereignty by attributing the right of voting to electors nominated from above—'authority must come from above and confidence from below', to quote his new-style formula for democracy—suited Bonaparte well enough, as did the various devices for preventing the legislative chambers from exercising any real power. But Bonaparte was determined that he himself, as First Consul, should have effective and undivided executive authority. Even the other two Consuls were to be little more than rubber stamps. The result of his revision of the constitutional proposals was that whereas the age of divine-right monarchy had ended in 1789, the age of dictatorship began in 1799. Sieyes, who had written the birth-certificate of the Revolution, also signed its death-warrant. He accepted, soon after, a large estate from Bonaparte, and confined himself henceforth to drawing-room politics. In a popular vote on the constitution, which was in effect a plebiscite for or against General Bonaparte, the people performed what was to become its customary role in dictatorships in exemplary fashion: 3,011,007 voted for and 1,562 against.

The politicians of Paris did not immediately acknowledge the finality of brumaire. No sooner was Bonaparte installed in power than they began to intrigue against him. For his part, the First Consul set about consolidating his position by winning over, through the personal charm which he had at his command, as well as by material favours, men of all parties, revolutionary or royalist, so long as they were willing to forget their principles in his service. All the arts of popularity and propaganda were put to work. The propertied classes, old and new, saw in Bonaparte a saviour of society. A mixture of clemency and force pacified the rebellious departments of the west. The outlines of a new administrative structure for

France were drawn up and—more important—put into effective operation. A peace offensive—and peace the French people now ardently longed for, gone the warlike passions of the early 'nineties— was launched by personal letters from the First Consul to George III and the Emperor; but peace, he was careful to tell the French people, could only come after victory. This was also necessary if he was to be able to put an end to the political intrigues of Paris and consolidate his personal authority.

The military situation was unpromising. When the year 1800 began the remnants of the defeated French army of Italy were still hanging on in Genoa in imminent danger of starvation, and their final collapse would open the door into France. Therefore, leaving Moreau in charge of an offensive on the Rhine, Bonaparte hastily gathered an army at Dijon and descended on Italy by way of the Great St Bernard. The campaign which followed was confused and unplanned. Important documents which might have revealed too much about it were destroyed by Bonaparte subsequently, and his own dispatches are a tissue of lies, so that it is difficult to know exactly what happened. The decisive clash of the French and Austrians at Marengo on June 14th, 1800, took Bonaparte by surprise, with his army scattered. He was saved by the return, in the nick of time, of the division he had sent off under Desai. It was a soldiers' battle, won by the staunchness of the Guard and the dash of Desai, who was killed in the fighting. Bonaparte, in a dispatch from the battlefield, provided for him a romanticized death: a dead man could be no rival. By the battle of Marengo Lombardy was regained and France relieved from the threat of an Austrian invasion. Meanwhile Moreau had advanced through Bavaria, occupied Munich, and in December, after routing the Austrians at Hohenlinden, was within fifty miles of Vienna.

Bonaparte had not waited for the completion of the German campaign to return to Paris, where, he knew, his enemies, Carnot prominent among them, were counting on defeat or at least a stale-mate in Italy to enable them to overthrow the Consulate. Instead, hot on the heels of the news of Marengo, Bonaparte came spurring across France to pluck the fruits of victory. The Guards, who had served him so well, were brought back hurriedly to enter Paris with their general on the morning of the Quatorze Juillet, so that their entry could coincide with the celebration of the fête of the Bastille. The faubourg Saint-Antoine, where Robespierre had once been the idol, turned out its sans-culottes in their thousands to hail the triumph and welcome the victor.

Peace with victory was now within reach. The Holy Roman Emperor, threatened by French armies advancing from southern Germany on Austria itself and from northern Italy on Venetia, acknowledged defeat. By the Treaty of Lunéville, in February 1801, French possessions on the left bank of the Rhine, from Switzerland to the sea, and the French satellite states — the Cisalpine and Ligurian Republics in northern Italy, the Helvetic Republic in Switzerland, and the Batavian Republic of the Dutch — were recognized. The hereditary princes of the Empire who lost territory on the left bank of the Rhine were to be compensated within Germany, and France, as a party to the treaty, was to participate in the process of territorial redistribution. This was to open the door to large-scale French intervention in the Holy Roman Empire.

Now only England remained in the way of complete pacification. To ensure her isolation Bonaparte negotiated an agreement with Russia, and conciliated Spain by the grant of the duchy of Tuscany to the Bourbon Duke of Parma. Under Russian leadership the Armed Neutrality was formed to oppose British attacks on neutral shipping, but the assassination of Paul I of Russia, and the bombardment of Copenhagen, dislocated it. In Egypt the isolated French army had been forced to capitulate by a British expeditionary force. These, however, were peripheral events. Faced with the bankruptcy of their European policy, Pitt and Grenville resigned and a new British government was ready to conclude peace with France. The negotiations were long and difficult, but slowly and reluctantly Great Britain gave up a large part of her conquests: it is true they had mainly been at the expense of former allies and not of France. In March 1802 the Treaty of Amiens was signed; Bonaparte had achieved peace for France and could proceed to collect the fruits of victory.

The change from Consulate to Empire was to be effected with the aid of victories abroad and plots at home. Marengo was followed on

December 24th, 1800, by an attempt to blow up Bonaparte on his way to the opera. The attempted assassination was the work of a group of royalists under the Vendean leader, Georges Cadoudal, but the First Consul seized the opportunity to eliminate the unreconciled Jacobins, whom he regarded as his more dangerous opponents. Many of them were sent to rot to death in Guiana or the Seychelles.

The signature of the Treaty of Amiens enabled Bonaparte to secure the passing, by a majority of three and a half millions to eight thousand, of a new plebiscite making him Consul for life. The next step followed fairly soon after. Cadoudal, who had taken refuge in England after the failure of his plot in 1800, organized a new attempt on Bonaparte's life in 1803, possibly with the connivance of Windham among the British ministers. Moreau, whose victory at Hohenlinden had been deliberately played down by Bonaparte to enhance his own glory, and Pichegru, returning secretly from England where he had taken refuge since his failure to overthrow the Directory, were also implicated. The conspiracy was discovered before it could be put into effect. Cadoudal and his group of desperate men were arrested and executed; Pichegru was imprisoned in the Temple and found strangled one morning. According to the official theory he had committed suicide, as enemies of dictators are apt to do. Moreau, against whom the evidence was weaker, and whose victories were too recent for him to be disposed of so easily, was allowed to go into exile.

Bonaparte now decided that the royalists must be taught a lesson, as the Jacobins had been. The young duc d'Enghien, the last of the Condés, was seized on territory neighbouring France, brought back over the frontier and shot as an émigré in foreign service. There was nothing to link him with the plot of Cadoudal: it was an exemplary murder. As a Corsican perhaps Bonaparte regarded it as a legitimate exercise of the right of vendetta, his own life having undoubtedly been threatened by royalist plots. The much-publicized Cadoudal conspiracy also provided an appropriate atmosphere for the final transmutation of the First Consul into the emperor. The Senate, duly prompted, passed the necessary legislative measures and the subsequent plebiscite, now de rigueur, gave popular sanction by

3,572,329 votes against 2,579 to the establishment of an hereditary Empire. This was perhaps less of a shock to republican sentiment than one might think, because, as early as 1789, the term empire had been in use to describe the French state, as a means of avoiding the word monarchy without falling into that of republic. The religious sanction was the one thing lacking, Napoleon felt, to make him a real emperor. It could be provided. Pius VII was prepared for what to a less holy-minded man might have seemed a humiliation, if it could be regarded as a further step to win France back to the fold, and agreed to perform the ceremony of crowning Napoleon in Notre-Dame. There were many difficulties to be smoothed out but— except that the Pope, or according to the version at the time of the divorce, Josephine herself, insisted that Napoleon should go through a religious ceremony of marriage with her, which he did in strict privacy—in most matters the emperor had his own way. Anointed by the Pope, Napoleon himself placed the crown on his own head. The day was December 2nd, 1804.

❧

CHAPTER THREE

NAPOLEONIC FOUNDATIONS OF THE NINETEENTH CENTURY

WHEN he became First Consul Napoleon Bonaparte was only thirty years old, but already marked as a man of destiny. The impecunious son of what passed for a gentle family in Corsica, after the French conquest he went with government assistance to the school at Brienne and then to the École Militaire, whence he emerged as sub-lieutenant of artillery. The Revolution was the time, the army was the career, for an ambitious young man. Short, but thin and muscular, he had good looks, though little notice should be taken of portraits in which he is already the Byronic hero of the coming romantic movement. He had tremendous energy and a powerful and disciplined memory. He could work continuously for long periods, with only snatches of sleep. In order not to disturb his habits, says his police official, Réal, he had taken care not to form any. He had a thirst for glory, fed partly on the writings of the pre-romantics but more on the history of the great conquerors of the ancient world, Caesar and Alexander, for this was also the period of the classical revival. Although he read Rousseau and was not uninfluenced by the ideals of the Enlightenment, his contribution to the legal code which bears his name showed a natural preference for the more conservative and less enlightened ideas of the *ancien régime*. Politically his bent was towards despotism untrammelled by divine right. His experience of the Revolution had left him with a deep contempt, not unmixed with fear, for the people. For politicians he had the dictator's natural aversion. He was not without humane instincts, and was capable of kindness in private life, to say nothing of the charm which he could turn on at will; but such qualities vanished when they stood in the way of his success. Even early in his career, before overweening egoism had quite mastered him, when military considerations demanded it he was entirely ruthless. There is no evidence that bloodshed mattered a scrap to him, or that he ever thought, as a Marlborough or a Wellington did, of economizing in the lives of his soldiers. The mass attack on which he relied depended on not counting the cost in dead and wounded. A French colonel describes him riding, as was his custom, over the field of Borodino after the battle, rubbing his hands and radiant with satisfaction as he counted five dead Russians to every one French corpse. I suppose, the colonel adds sardonically, he took the bodies of his German allies for Russians. Such nobility as might have been given, even to the career of a military despot, by the service of some end, although a mistaken one, was lacking. Apart from his own personal glory, the only other ambition he had at heart was to found a dynasty. When, in his last campaign, he might have saved much for France by abandoning his dream of empire, he was incapable of such moderation, or even realism. After all this, to say that he was an adventurer is an anti-climax; but it is not irrelevant or unimportant. Coming from islanders whose social institutions were the *banditti* and the *vendetta*, he carried the same standards into a country where the Revolution had already shown how uncertain were the conquests of the Enlightenment. For fifteen years France and Europe were to be at the mercy of a gambler to whom fate and his own genius gave for a time all the aces. He always cheated at cards and his carriage had diamonds concealed in its lining in case of hurried flight.

The short intermission from continual war that the Treaty of Amiens inaugurated gave Bonaparte the opportunity to establish the bases of a new government. As soon as he became First Consul he began the task of reconstruction. The simulacrum of representative institutions was preserved as a sop to revolutionary tradition, with an advisory Senate, a Legislative Body which could vote but not speak, and a Tribunate which could speak but not vote. Since the last, powerless as it was, did not invariably say just what the emperor wanted, it was reduced in membership to fifty, divided into sections, and finally, in 1807, abolished. The Legislative Body, chosen by the Senate and composed mostly of obscure former revolutionaries, was then ungagged but remained a passive register of the emperor's will. The Senate, including many of the great names of the period, at first sight looks a more substantial body, with real legislative powers; but for all their distinction, its members were a mere collection of nominees, serving only to give dignity to their master's decisions.

If we turn from the legislative to the executive, even the façade of limitation on the will of the emperor disappears. The reorganization of the ministries had mostly been effected during the Revolution. Foreign Affairs, War, and Marine, to which was attached Colonies now that France had lost them all, remained as before 1789. The Keeper of the Seals became the Minister for Justice. The most important changes were the result of amalgamating, and then sub-dividing on more logical grounds, the Contrôle Général and Maison du Roi, out of which emerged the Ministry of Finances and the Ministry of the Interior. Finally, like all dictators, Bonaparte required a Minister of Police. A State Secretariat was also set up, through which the First Consul controlled and co-ordinated the policies of his ministers.

Over the Police the ex-terrorist Fouché, later, when titles were handed round, to become the duc d'Otranto, reigned, with the assistance of a choice collection of scoundrels gathered from the police of the *ancien régime* and the underworld of the Revolution. At Foreign Affairs Talleyrand was indispensable. Berthier at the War Office was an invaluable chief of staff. Lucien Bonaparte, the first Minister of the Interior, though efficient showed signs of independence which could not be tolerated, least of all in a brother, and was soon dismissed. Finances were entrusted to Gaudin, formerly a high official of the Contrôle Général. There was, of course, no first minister, and the ministers never constituted a cabinet. The Emperor consulted them individually, took their advice or gave them their orders as it pleased him, like an *ancien régime* monarch. Louis XIV had at last found a successor and France was again ruled by the *bon plaisir* of an autocrat, but one enfranchised from the bonds of aristocratic and provincial privilege and control-ling a new-fashioned and far more efficient administrative machine.

At the centre of the new administrative structure was the Council of State. Napoleon, for all his seizure of arbitrary power, was no mere vulgar dictator imposing unconsidered decisions on a servile nation. An expert himself in the matter of war, he knew the value of experts. He was also, at least when he first came to power, conscious of his own limitations and of his need for a body of specialists who, without possessing political power, could provide him with the advice he needed in all fields of government. The Council of State was intended, in the first place, as the means of his own political education. It was also to draw up laws and administrative regulations and expound them to the legislative bodies: it was in fact the real legislative organ. The Councillors of State took the place of the masters of requests and councillors of the *ancien régime*, from whom the intendants and higher officials had been recruited. They formed a permanent corps whence Napoleon could draw *missi dominici* for the varied tasks of imperial government. The sections into which the Council was divided supervised the various fields of government and provided him with a means of checking and controlling the actions of his ministers. The importance he attributed to the Council was well shown in his advice to the former *parlementaire* and constitutional monarchist, Roederer, one of Bonaparte's associates in the *coup d'état* of brumaire, not to accept a nomination to the Senate but rather to enter the Council of State. 'In that', the First Consul said, 'there are great things to be done; from that I will draw my ambassadors and ministers.' The advice, as was inevitable with Bonaparte, was not disinterested. He was counting on the Council of State, more than on any other of his administrative bodies, to draw into his service able men from all fields and from all points on the political scale, except the most intransigent republicans and royalists. Former magistrates and high officials of the *ancien régime* sat side by side with men who had made their mark in the struggles of the Revolution, generals of the revolutionary armies with civilian technicians and scientists.

What was to be ultimately the greatest achievement of the Council of State, the creation of a system of administrative law, was as yet a minor activity; but as well as its major role in the central government it exercised an unlimited supervision over local administration and all public establishments, and gradually filled in the details of the administrative and financial system sketched out under the Consulate. From its creation in 1800 to 1813, 58,435 separate cases were brought up for examination in the general assembly of the Council; the number dealt with annually rose from 911 in 1800 to 6,285 in 1811. While the Council of State formed the ideal instrument for an absolute regime, its work was far too valuable for any subsequent government to dispense with its services. Though under Napoleon it was no more than an instrument without any independence, the Council of State developed in due course a tradition and an *esprit de corps* of its own and became the unshakeable corner-stone of the French bureaucracy. In the absence of an effective parliamentary system it provided, along with the administrative substructure, the ferro-concrete framework of government, which was to enable French society to survive and emerge comparatively unchanged from so many political upheavals. At the same time, and for this very reason, it also stood in the way of the creation of effective parliamentary institutions. Through the Council of State and his other administrative institutions, the shadow of Napoleon continued to darken the following century. He had given France, when she needed it after the stresses of the Revolution, a steel corset on which she was to become dependent and from which she was to emancipate herself only slowly and painfully and never completely.

The system of centralized bureaucracy called for the creation of machinery of local administration which could carry the will of the government at Paris into the most remote communes. Administrative centralization, as de Tocqueville pointed out, was not an invention of Napoleon. The modern prefect can trace his ancestry back to the intendants of Louis XIV and Richelieu, and even to the *sénéchaux* and *baillis* of the Middle Ages; but the element of continuity, though important, must not be exaggerated. The *ancien régime* still retained too many medieval relics for the writ of the central government to run unchallenged and unimpeded through the provinces. The great achievement of the Revolution, for good or ill, had been to make a *tabula rasa*, administratively speaking, of France. The system of democratic councils with which the Constituent Assembly endowed, as by a stroke of the pen, its new administrative divisions, could not survive the strains of the Revolution. Already under the Committee of Public Safety a big step had been taken in the direction of the restoration of central control. Under the Directory the local authorities became increasingly weak and corrupt, though the more exaggerated accounts of Directorial decay are perhaps the work of Bonapartist propaganda. However, an official report of 1799 declared, 'The pillage of public funds, attacks directed on public officials, the inertia of a great number of them, the assassination of republicans—such is unfortunately the picture which several departments present.' The picture had at least some truth in it and was perhaps more generally true than was admitted.

Bonaparte and his advisers, in 1800, had no doubt what was wrong: it was the attempt, still surviving in theory, to govern the departments and communes by a system of elected councils. In the basic law on local government of the year VIII the elective principle was eliminated from the appointment of all local officials. Local councils still survived in name, it is true, but their functions were reduced to microscopic proportions. As Chaptal, wealthy proprietor and scientist, ennobled before 1789, and the successor to Lucien Bonaparte at the Ministry of the Interior, put it, 'These popular councils are placed, so to speak, to one side of the line of executive action: they do not hamper in any way the rapid progress of the administration.' In fact adequate precautions were taken to ensure that they should not do so. They were not allowed to meet for a longer period than fifteen days in the year; their chief function was to give their approval to the distribution of taxation between the various *arrondissements*, towns, and villages of the department. All administrative authority in the department was placed in the hands of a prefect, appointed from Paris, with sub-prefects under him. The latter were generally local men and often former revolutionaries, but a job was a job. They had no independent authority. The first list of prefects included many Jacobins who had rallied to Bonaparte, as well as former *ancien régime* officials. The prefects, unlike the sub-prefects, were never local men. There has been much discussion whether they were mere passive agents of the central government. They probably possessed less independence than the former intendants; but since, even now, instructions took eight days to reach Toulouse from Paris, and the newly invented system of telegraphs was only used for important communications, mostly military, detailed control of the prefects' actions was obviously difficult. Lucien Bonaparte in a circular of the year VIII said, 'General ideas must come from the centre. I note with regret that some of you, with praiseworthy intentions doubtless, concern yourselves with the interpretation of the laws ... It is not this that the government expects of its administration.' That the prefects were the officers of a central government and subject to the same kind of obedience as was expected of officers of the army was made quite clear by putting them into uniform. It was a dignified one—blue coat, white waistcoat and breeches, silver thread on collar, cuffs, and pockets, a *chapeau français* ornamented with silver, red scarf with silver fringes, and a sword—but one wonders what an intendant would have said if he had been expected to wear a uniform.

The first task of the prefects was that of economic restoration. In a note of 1800 Bonaparte wrote, 'The 36,000 communes in France represent 36,000 orphans, heirs of the old feudal rights, which have been abandoned or pillaged for ten years by the municipal guardians of the Convention and the Directory.' Now the communes were to be taught that they had a master and a more efficient one than the medley of *ancien régime* authorities. This is not to say that the prefects could afford to ride rough-shod over all local feeling. Under the Empire the local notabilities re-emerged as the dominant interest and the prefects and sub-prefects found it wise to remain on friendly terms with them, for their mutual advantage. Of the general ability of the prefects and the valuable work they did in restoring administrative good habits to the departments there can be no question. Taine once expressed the regret of not having had the experience of serving for a year as secretary to one of Napoleon's prefects.

The prefects had other tasks besides that of promoting the economic well-being of their departments. They had to collect favourable votes for the plebiscites: the success with which they performed this duty foretold their future political role. Gradually, as the war pressed increasingly heavily on French life, its requirements came to dominate the activities of the prefects. They drew up lists of conscripts, authorized exemptions, sought out deserters, confiscated horses for the army, looked after troops in passage, and guarded prisoners of war. As early as 1801 a prefect is found complaining that the enforcement of conscription occupies one-third of the employees of his prefecture and that these are barely sufficient. Continually increasing military demands bore so heavily on the departments that by 1814 their financial resources had been exhausted.

In the later years of the Empire the personnel of the administration underwent considerable changes. Especially from 1809 onwards, Napoleon, with the weakness of a new man for real gentlemen, tended to appoint former nobles to office. A host of émigrés flocked back to take up good jobs, to introduce more easy-going methods into the prefectures, and leave the real work to their secretaries-general. From 1810 all prefects were given the title of count or baron and ordered to assume coats of arms. Many were now secret royalists, ready to accept the emperor's pay while he was in power, but prepared to desert him with cynical haste in 1814. During the Hundred Days the prefects exhibited what would be a comic, if it were not equally a cowardly and treacherous anxiety to be on the winning side. Official adulation of the emperor was carried to extreme lengths. A prefect of the Pas-de-Calais, formerly officer of the Royal Normandy regiment, apostrophized his department, when it was about to receive a visit from the Emperor, thus: 'You are about to see him, that Napoleon, proclaimed so justly the greatest of men in the greatest of nations ... Dieu créa Bonaparte et se reposa.' As soon as Napoleon lost power the same official addressed his devotions with equal fervour to the duc de Berry, only to renew his loyal protestations to the emperor when he returned from Elba. Among those with a genius for guessing which way the cat was going to jump and getting there in advance, the prize must be held by M. de Jessaint, prefect of the Marne uninterruptedly from 1800 to 1838. The fact is that the prefectoral system was an immensely powerful instrument in the hands of the central government, but its power was entirely derivative. While the regime was strong at the centre the prefects could guarantee to control the rest of the country; but a *coup d'état* in Paris could shatter the whole fabric, for no element capable of standing by itself existed in the provinces. The prefectural system, for all its merits, combined the vices of excessive rigidity and excessive instability. It was to be in no small measure responsible for the alternation of revolution and reaction that marked the history of nineteenth-century France.

Besides creating a unified administrative machinery, Napoleon laid down the legislative basis on which it was to operate. The idea of reducing the varied laws of France to a uniform, written code was inherited by the Revolution from the *ancien régime*. The work had been begun by the *Ordonnances* drawn up under Colbert and d'Aguesseau. The revolutionary Assemblies set up committees to complete the work of codification, but they were never able to catch up with the mass of their own legislation. In 1800 Bonaparte appointed a committee of distinguished lawyers to draw up a civil code, and gave them five months to do it in. After their draft code had been discussed in the Council of State, the First Consul himself being present at about half of the meetings though of course he had not the legal knowledge to make a serious contribution to them, it was submitted to the legislative bodies, where criticism was so hostile that it did not obtain final acceptance until 1804. The criticism to which the Code was subjected, though it infuriated Napoleon, was largely sound. His role was not to frame the Code but to see that the lawyers came to a conclusion, good or bad, without further delay. For some of the worst features he was personally responsible. Such were the deterioration in the legal status of women, who were allowed no control over the family property and could not acquire, sell, or give property without their husband's consent; the re-introduction of confiscation as a legal penalty; and the use of the fiction of civil death. The First Consul's influence was also responsible for the tightening up of the laws of marriage and divorce and the restoration of paternal authority in the family. The great gains of the Revolution, however, were maintained: equality before the law, the principle of religious toleration, the abolition of privileges and seigneurial burdens. Property rights were strictly maintained and there was particular emphasis on the interests of the small owner. Property was to be inherited equally by all legitimate children at death, except for a certain disposable proportion: to this provision has been speculatively attributed the limitation of families in nineteenth-century France. Perhaps the most important feature of the Civil Code was that all its 2,281 articles could be contained in a single fairly small volume. It was to be the most effective agency for the propagation of the basic principles of the French Revolution that was, or perhaps that could have been, devised. It was carried by the French armies through Europe and thence spread across the world. There followed in France a Code of Civil Procedure, cumbersome and mostly copied from *ancien régime* rules, a Commercial Code, and a severe and arbitrary Criminal Code, which was all the same a model of enlightenment compared with the barbarous laws that still prevailed in Great Britain.

The Revolution had in nothing failed so completely as in its finances. The first step towards their rehabilitation was taken by Gaudin, head of a division in the Contrôle Général before the Revolution and after the eighteenth of brumaire Minister of Finances, when he removed the assessment and collection of direct taxation from the control of local authorities and formed a central organization charged with the task. France, however, has never been able to draw the major part of its revenue from the wealthy, and the new rich were no more willing to pay for the privilege of being governed than had been the old privileged orders. All indirect taxes had been abolished by the Constituent Assembly, though the Directory reintroduced them on playing cards and tobacco. Napoleon revived the tax on salt, brought back the hated *droits* on wine and cider, and created a *régie* for their collection. The Directory had also reestablished local *octrois*; these were greatly extended under the Empire and the central government took an increasing proportion of them.

In 1800 was founded another of the great and permanent creations of the Consulate, the Bank of France. Though with semi-public functions, this was a private bank, its shareholders represented by a general assembly of the 200 most important, who elected the fifteen regents and three censors. The Bank, like the other Napoleonic institutions, was to remain a power in France throughout the regimes which followed.

In 1802 the French budget was balanced, but this was only a temporary success. The existence of private and military funds under the direct control of the emperor prevented the imperial budgets from ever being more than paper exercises, with little relation to the facts. No institutional reforms could put the country on a sound financial basis in time of continual war; and there was never sufficient confidence in the permanence of the regime for the government to draw, as Great Britain did to such a great extent, on loans. Moreover, Napoleon had a profound suspicion of them. He had to fall back, just like the *ancien régime*, on expedients, and live from hand to mouth. And like the Revolution he exploited the conquered countries, to such an extent that it might almost be said that war was a financial necessity for France.

Yet another of the loose ends left by the Revolution for Napoleon to cut and tie up in his own fashion was the problem of a religious settlement, and this also was largely, if not essentially, an administrative question. Whether religious differences still remained, in 1799, a source of danger to France, or whether the increasingly tolerant *modus vivendi* reached by the Directory could have survived, is a much disputed point on which agreement is unlikely to be reached; but it can be agreed that religious persecution during the Revolution had not merely failed to destroy the hold of the Roman Catholic religion on the people, it had strengthened religious feeling and played some part in promoting a religious revival. The more moderate policies of the Directory were perhaps more dangerous to the Church than active dechristianization. The secularization of education — a circular of the year VIII ordered teachers in the central schools to avoid 'everything that pertained to the doctrines and rites of all religions and sects whatever they may be' — may be regarded as initiating a struggle that was to continue to the present day.

The Catholic Church had certainly something to gain in this respect from the renewal of state support. There were also powerful inducements to the state to abandon its policy of religious neutrality and secularization. The complete pacification of the Vendée and Normandy would undoubtedly be greatly facilitated if the support of the clergy could be gained. This would also powerfully aid in the assimilation of the Belgic provinces and other newly acquired territory where the Catholic religion was strong. Bonaparte himself was aware of the sentimental appeal of a vague kind of Rousseauist religiosity, though one can hardly envisage him as a disciple of the Savoyard vicar. Religion, like every other ideal, was to him a means to an end, his own power. Sayings attributed to him represent truly his essential attitude — 'Religion is a kind of inoculation which by satisfying our love of marvels guarantees us against charlatans and sorcerers'; 'Society cannot exist without inequality of wealth, and inequality of wealth cannot exist without religion.' Walking in the park at Malmaison he is alleged to have said, listening to the bells, 'What an impression that must make on the simple and credulous ... How can your philosophers and ideologues answer that? The people must have a religion and that religion must be in the hands of the government.'

The Vatican, for its part, despite its denunciations of the Revolution, was prepared to make considerable concessions to regain official recognition in France. The new Pope Pius VII, elected in 1800, a simple and holy monk with little knowledge of the world, was not violently hostile to the Revolution, and papal agents had been sent secretly to Paris as early as September 1800. The victory over Austria and the Peace of Lunéville in February 1801 made it desirable to come to terms with a France which now controlled all northern Italy. Secretly instituted negotiations were concluded in July 1801. To minimize the inevitable resistance of the strong anti-clerical elements in the legislative bodies, Bonaparte waited until the Peace of Amiens had been concluded before he announced the Concordat, in April 1802. Characteristically, having secured an agreement, he proceeded to distort it in his own interest by means of the issue of Organic Articles. Even so, many of the former revolutionaries exhibited open hostility to the Concordat and Fouché issued a mocking circular. By the Concordat the Vatican agreed to the institution of a new episcopate which should contain a proportion of bishops from the Constitutional Church, recognized the alienation of Church lands as permanent, and accepted the payment of clerical salaries by the state. Catholicism was described as 'the religion of the great majority of citizens', and its practice was to be free and public so long as it conformed to such police regulations as were required by public order. By the supplementary Organic Articles Bonaparte tried to turn the Concordat into the instrument of a new and stronger Gallicanism. No papal bull was to be published, nor any papal representative to function in France, without the permission of the government. The bishops were placed under the close control of the prefects and the lesser clergy lost the

c

considerable independence of episcopal authority they had formerly enjoyed. Subsequent concessions to religious opinion included the suppression of the official ten-day cult, already practically dead, the restoration of Sunday as the day of rest for officials, and of the Gregorian calendar; children were to be given only saints' names or those of the great figures of antiquity; the payment of salaries was extended to all clergy and the actual salaries were increased; religious orders reappeared in France, with official sanction for women's orders and for male missionary orders, while others, such as the Jesuits, were tolerated by official connivance; primary, though not higher, education was restored to the control of the clergy.

Despite all these concessions the Vatican was not quite happy about the bargain it had concluded. The Pope protested against the Organic Articles and only consecrated the bishops Bonaparte had chosen from the Constitutional Church after two years' delay. On the face of it the Concordat was a great victory for Bonaparte and a master-stroke of policy. The emperor was able henceforth to use the clergy as an instrument of government. They celebrated his victories with *Te Deums*, published his imperial proclamations from their pulpits, delivered patriotic sermons, stimulated conscription, and promoted loyal sentiments. An Imperial Catechism was issued for the purpose of 'binding by religious sanctions the conscience of the people to the august person of the Emperor'. A national fête was created for the day of the Assumption which was also Napoleon's birthday and turned out conveniently to be the saint's day of a newly discovered St Napoleon. Yet with all this he failed to obtain any permanent religious sanction for his rule. In the last years of the Empire the barely concealed royalist sentiments of most of the clergy undermined the loyalty of the people and prepared the way for his fall.

The religious revival, of which the first great manifesto was Chateaubriand's *Génie du Christianisme* in 1802, would have come about without Napoleon. The Concordat, by pushing Gallican principles farther than ever before, and this in the interests of no divine-right sovereign, did much to discredit Gallicanism and strengthen the ultramontane tendency in the French Church. It also reduced the lower clergy to a position of total dependence on their bishops, and made the bishops themselves much more dependent on the Papacy than formerly. The act by which the Pope, in agreement with Napoleon, deposed the whole episcopate of France, including many lawfully appointed and consecrated bishops, marked a great step forward in the assertion of papal authority. The thirty-seven *ancien régime* bishops who were excluded from their sees by the Concordat kept the allegiance of a small group of the faithful who founded what was called *la petite Église*. The injury to vested interests and nice consciences, and the elevation of a dozen somewhat grisly constitutional bishops, was a cheap price to pay for such a great extension of papal authority. The ultimate result was immensely to strengthen the influence of the Vatican in France. Napoleon had won for himself an unreliable and temporary ally, and he had bequeathed to his successors a Church which would henceforth never willingly be the junior partner of the state. The intermittent struggle between Church and state which bedevilled French politics for the following century and a half was as much the inheritance of the Napoleonic Concordat as of revolutionary anti-clericalism.

That hierarchical conception of society which made it easy for Napoleon to come to terms with the Roman Church, so long as he imagined that he had safeguarded his own position at the apex of the pyramid, was applied also, though less appropriately, to the organization of the Protestant churches. Their pastors became salaried officials and like the curés took an oath of loyalty. Their synods and consistories were chosen from the wealthier adherents of the faith and controlled by the secular authorities. Louis XIV had failed to extirpate French Protestantism, Napoleon succeeded in domesticating it.

While Napoleon restored official recognition to the Roman Catholic Church, he had no intention of returning the control of education they had possessed under the *ancien régime* to the ecclesiastical authorities. But he needed a system of education to provide administrators and technical experts for the service of the state. The Revolution had destroyed the old system of education but created nothing to put in its place apart from a limited number of central schools, which were neither sufficiently traditional in their curriculum, nor sufficiently authoritarian in their discipline, for Bonaparte's taste. They would produce, he thought, liberals and ideologists, for neither of which was there room in the Napoleonic state. Bonaparte himself expounded the basic principles of his theory of education: 'So long as children are not taught that they must be republican or monarchist, catholic or irreligious, etc. ... the State will not be a nation, it will rest on insecure or vague foundations ... In a properly organized state there is always a body destined to regulate the principles of morality and politics.' Defending the law of 1802 on education, presented to the Legislative Body, ironically enough, by Fourcroy, a leading chemist, another of Bonaparte's necessary experts, Roederer, declared that Latin must be restored to its primacy and quasi-monopoly in the educational system. There followed an almost complete return to the syllabus and methods of the *ancien régime*, which lasted with little change until the reforms of 1865. The central schools were replaced by lycées, boarding-schools with a semi-military uniform and discipline and military training from the age of twelve.

In these the new elite of France was to be formed with the aid of some 6,000 national *bourses*, of which rather more than a third were reserved for the sons of officials and officers. They led on to the specialized schools of law, medicine, and pharmacy, the *école militaire spéciale* and the famous *école normale*, founded in 1808 to prepare for service in schools and universities 300 young men chosen by competitive examination. These were to provide the technical experts needed by the Empire. On a lower level, secondary schools, established by municipalities or individuals, gave the education needed for commercial or minor administrative posts. At the bottom, the primary schools were left to the initiative of the communes and the teaching orders, and were now too few to bestow even a modicum of literacy upon more than a small fraction of the population. The educational system was placed, by a law of 1808, under the control of a single imperial university. The whole structure formed a rigid hierarchy, under a Grand Master nominated by and responsible to the emperor. An imposing bureaucratic apparatus centred in Paris was charged with regulating the educational life of France down to the smallest detail. If, today, the Rector of a university cannot appoint his secretary, dismiss a cleaner, or modify an academic course without reference to Paris, it is in obedience to the dead hand of Napoleon.

In the lycées religion was kept, by Napoleon's prescription, to the 'necessary minimum'. Primary education, on the other hand, he was content to leave in the hands of the Church. Under the influence of its Grand Master, Fontanes, the University was increasingly subjected to clerical influence. The schools run by priests prospered at the expense of the state lycées. Even before his fall the instrument created by Napoleon to dragoon the mind of France was escaping from his control, and the conflict between secular and clerical education, which was to be one of the dominant themes in the history of the following century, was emerging.

Where the task was simply one of repression, the success of the Napoleonic system was less qualified. The press became a mere instrument of imperial propaganda, and papers which were not sufficiently docile soon disappeared. A censorship controlled the publication of books. Theatres were put under the Ministry of Police and reduced in Paris to eight. Even in the midst of a desperate war, at Moscow in October 1812, Napoleon could concern himself with drawing up the regulations for the Comédie-Française, a gesture illustrating less his interest in the promotion of the drama than his determination to ensure that every medium for the expression of opinion remained under strict control.

The First Empire was hardly the milieu from which literature was likely to emerge, and very little did. The mock-heroics of *Ossian*, translated in 1801, suited the emperor's literary taste. The romantic melancholy of Chateaubriand's *Atala* and *René*, Mme de Staël's assertion, in *Delphine* and *Corinne*, of woman's right to happiness, but also of the unhappiness that is the fate of superior persons, Joseph de Maistre's theocratic ideals, had no appeal to him. Of these authors only Chateaubriand stayed under Napoleon's rule. Most of the writing of the Empire falls into the category of journalism or propaganda rather than literature.

In painting also the Empire has little to its credit. Fragonard, when he died in 1809, had long been an anachronism. David was capable of magnificent portraits, but he was prepared to serve

Napoleon as faithfully as he had served the Jacobins and wasted his talents on huge, neo-classical, historical set pieces. In such a painting as his 'Sabine women interrupting the battle between Romans and Sabines', every figure, down to the smallest child, is posed in a rhetorical attitude, consciously playing a part on the stage of history, just like David's own contemporaries of the Revolution and Empire. The whole scene is as moving as the waxworks of Mme Tussaud which also date from the same period. A more poetical spirit is infused by Prud'hon into his classical compositions: the Empress Josephine reclines in reverie and classical *déshabillé* on mossy rocks amid a romantic landscape. But most of the painting of the period is frank propaganda. David rearranges the Coronation of Napoleon to order, as he had already done the Tennis-court Oath. Napoleon's charger rears up as his master with an heroic gesture points the way across the Alps to a stage army in the background. The baron Gros paints huge battle scenes to the glorification of the emperor and his Marshals. He was perhaps the most successful of the official painters of the Empire until he committed suicide.

Napoleon himself was represented *ad nauseam*, the hero leading the charge across the bridge at Lodi, presenting the eagles to his legions, riding his chariot in a Roman triumph or apotheosized as a classical deity, sparing the conquered on the battlefield or subjecting the proud, visiting the victims of plague, rousing by his very presence the spirit of devotion in the wounded and dying. It is quite clear that the French painters of the period and Goya—of course, a painter on a different scale of magnitude—were not illustrating the same war. But it would be a mistake to judge the political success of Napoleon's artists by their artistic merits. Their influence in the formation of the Napoleonic legend and in creating and perpetuating a romantic attitude to war is not to be under-estimated. More important for the history of art is the group of young men—Ingres, Vernet, Géricault—which was appearing in the last years of the Empire.

The decorative taste of the Empire was luxurious and heavy, adding Egyptian and Etruscan motives to the influence of the now triumphant classical revival. The provincial cities were not important enough to receive much imperial attention, and there the eighteenth century largely survived, but considerable steps were taken towards the spoiling of Paris. Napoleon required a grandiose setting for the capital of his Empire, and of course a classical one. Triumphal arches—such as the Étoile and the Carrousel—were de rigueur. For public buildings the correct thing was temples; so we have the temple of finance—the Bourse with its sixty-four Corinthian columns; the temple of religion—the Madeleine; the temple of the laws—the palais Bourbon, all heavy pastiches and all equally unsuited to the purposes for which they were intended. The proportions of the place Vendôme were ruined by sticking in its middle, in place of the destroyed royal statue, a monstrous column, in imitation of that of Trajan. To enable the Napoleonic monuments to be seen, the process of driving long straight roads through Paris, which was to be carried much further under the Second Empire, was begun. Unlike the lath and plaster erections of the Revolution, the buildings of the Empire were made to last—unfortunately, for they embody too well the emperor's chief aesthetic rule: 'Ce qui est grand est toujours beau.'

Literature and art could not be expected to flourish in the hard climate of the Empire. Speculation about society was even less likely to be encouraged. In 1803 Napoleon suppressed the Academy of Moral and Political Sciences. On the other hand the natural and mathematical sciences have usually seemed able to accommodate themselves quite happily to absolutism. Apart from the guillotining of Lavoisier as a Farmer General, the Revolution and Empire did nothing to check scientific progress. The older generation of mathematicians and physicists such as Lagrange, Laplace, whose name is identified with the theory of nebulae, Monge, mathematician and accomplice of Bonaparte, and the botanist Lamarck, overlapped with younger men—Cuvier, who brought geology and palaeontology to the aid of zoological studies, Ampère, the founder of electromagnetism, and the astronomer Arago. In psychology, Destutt de Tracy and Cabanis continued the materialist theories of Condillac.

All this—art or science—is incidental or irrelevant to the history of the Empire. Napoleon's peculiar and lasting achievement was the work of the Consulate—that administrative reorganization which, in perspective, can be seen as bequeathing not only to France but to much of the rest of the world, the most powerful instrument of bureaucratic control that the Western world had known since the Roman Empire. It was not a framework for the kind of society that the idealistic liberals of 1789 had imagined themselves to be inaugurating, nor should we treat the Napoleonic system, as it often has been treated, as the mere logical sequel to the *ancien régime* and the Revolution, and Napoleon simply as the heir of Louis XIV and the Committee of Public Safety. This is to underestimate the scope of his achievement. The Grand Monarch did not leave an imprint on French institutions that can be compared with the heritage of the emperor. His immediate successors might repudiate his work, they could not undo it, and the Napoleonic state was long to outlive its author and the ends to which he had directed it.

✤

CHAPTER FOUR

THE NAPOLEONIC EMPIRE: RISE

THE Consulate was more important in the history of France, though not of Europe, than the Empire. What remains is a ten-years' wonder, the history of conquests as dazzling as they were ephemeral, of armies marching and counter-marching from Lisbon to Moscow, and peace a brief breathing-space between wars. If we ask, as the Greeks would have done, what was the end of the Napoleonic state, the answer must be war. In war it had begun, war remained its raison d'être, and by war it was to end.

The Treaty of Amiens could not in the nature of things be more than an armistice, but it provided an opportunity for extra-European policies to be developed by Bonaparte. With France's position in Europe consolidated, he looked to the restoration of her overseas empire. Louisiana and the colony of St Domingo had been gained from Spain; and the colonies which had been conquered by Great Britain during the Revolutionary War were restored to France, which thus had in 1802 a larger colonial domain than in 1789. The position was less favourable than it might seem, but to understand the reason for this we must briefly look back over developments in the West Indies since 1789.

The Revolution had at first seemed a golden opportunity for the wealthy planters of the French Antilles, the Grands Blancs, in the name of self-government (the usual demand of those who want to oppress others) to relieve themselves of the control of the authorities in Paris. At the same time, to prevent the liberal ideas of the Constituent Assembly from being applied to the colonies, a number of big colonial proprietors had formed in Paris, in June 1789, a club to defend their interests, called from its meeting-place the club Massiac. On the other side, the Société des Amis des Noirs rallied anti-slavery opinion. The liberal tendency was the stronger in the Assembly, and it was joined to a belief in centralized control. The principle that the colonies are an integral part of France was first enunciated by the Revolution in a decree of March 1790; it was repeated in August 1792 and again in the constitution of the year III. The extension of civic rights was much slower and more reluctant. In May 1791 coloured men who were sons of a free father and mother were given the vote. This was only some 5 per cent of the whole black or mulatto population, but both white and black now began to take up arms. In an attempt to restore peace the Legislative Assembly gave political rights to all free men, and sent over to St Domingo, in September 1792, commissaires and 6,000 troops to enforce its policy. The planters resisted and their leaders signed a treaty temporarily delivering the islands to the British, in return for military and naval assistance. The commissaires, in desperation, proclaimed the enfranchisement of all blacks who would join them. Meanwhile, in July 1793, the Convention had abolished the slave trade, and in February 1794 was to vote the abolition of slavery. In the confused triangular struggle of English, French, and coloured that followed, the chief victor was the yellow fever. But by 1798 the great negro general Toussaint-Louverture was undisputed ruler of St Domingo; while in Guadeloupe a revolutionary commissaire with the aid of the negroes had driven out a British force of occupation.

The legislation of the Revolution had, in spite of everything, made important reforms, but the French colonists, supported by Bonaparte, had no intention of accepting them. The constitution of the year VIII laid it down that the colonies should be ruled by special laws; in 1802 they were placed under executive regulations and exempted from legislative control. The department of the colonies in the Ministry of the Marine, staffed with *ancien régime* officials from whom Bonaparte took his advice, willingly abandoned all the reforms of the Revolution. The French trading monopoly was restored in the West Indies. Slavery was re-established where it had been abolished, negroes were excluded from France, and mixed marriages prohibited. It is reasonable to suppose that the influence of the creole Josephine reinforced Bonaparte's native illiberalism in his dealings with the colonies. In the lesser islands small military expeditions from France restored French authority without difficulty. St Domingo, where Toussaint-Louverture had established an autonomous authority with himself as governor though recognizing French suzerainty, presented a more difficult problem. To solve it Bonaparte despatched an army of 30,000 under General Leclerc, with instructions to gain the confidence of the negroes and arrest their leader. Toussaint was seized and sent to France, where he died within a year in prison, to be remembered in one of Wordsworth's greatest sonnets. The removal of the one negro leader with authority and statesmanship intensified the ferocity of the servile war against France. Those of the French who were not killed by the negroes were exterminated by disease, and the pearl of the Antilles passed for ever out of French possession.

Louisiana was lost in a different way. Officially annexed in March 1803, it was sold to the United States in December. The remaining scattered colonies fell to English naval expeditions in the course of the following years. The loss of the first French Empire, begun in 1763, had been completed by Bonaparte. He was too much a man of the *ancien régime* to be really interested in colonies save as pawns in the military struggle, and his imagination turned more easily to the East than to the West. There, the army he had left behind in Egypt, defeated by a British expeditionary force in 1801, had capitulated; but Napoleon's eyes still saw the Mediterranean as the route to India, where French agents were hard at work. His troops remained at Leghorn and Ancona on the west and east coasts of Italy; treaties were concluded with Tripoli and Tunis; Algiers, after the pillage of a French ship, was threatened with attack; French diplomacy was active at Constantinople; and a French agent, Sébastiani, was sent on a mission to Syria and Egypt. All this, while perfectly within French rights, was not likely to reassure her recent enemies.

Military movements on the Continent were also a source of alarm to Great Britain. French control over the satellites was strengthened. In Italy, Piedmont was divided into six departments and its army amalgamated with the French; the Ligurian Republic became a French military division; and Bonaparte appointed himself president of the Cisalpine Republic. In the north, French troops continued to occupy the Dutch ports. By an Act of Mediation the Swiss cantons were reorganized and French control was established over the

Alpine passes. Italians, Swiss, and Dutch were all called on to furnish contingents of conscripts for the French army.

None of these measures, except the retention of troops in Holland, was an infringement of the Treaty of Amiens. The new *casus belli* was to arise in the Mediterranean, where Great Britain had undertaken by the Treaty of Amiens to restore Malta to the Knights of St John, but on second thoughts, despite her treaty obligation, could not bring herself to abandon such a valuable strategic position. British intransigence was encouraged by secret negotiations with Russia, also alarmed at the evidence of Bonaparte's interest in the Near East. On January 30th, 1803, the *Moniteur* published Sébastiani's report on his tour there, in which he seemed to be putting forward, in language referring to the British in terms of contempt, proposals for a French reconquest of Egypt.

Why did Bonaparte, although he toned down the report slightly, publish such a provocative document at a moment when—though we need not attribute any noble dreams of permanent peace to him —he was not yet ready for a renewal of war? The answer seems to lie in the natural incapacity of a dictator for understanding the politics of a parliamentary country. The vulgar and immoderate personal attacks of the British press, which he attributed to the inspiration of the British government, drove him to fury; and the language of the parliamentary opposition led him to believe that the country was too divided by political conflicts to react strongly to his provocations. British opinion, on its side, had now overwhelmingly decided that Bonaparte was merely using the peace as an armistice during which to prepare for further aggression. The British government was determined to obtain further securities. Bonaparte, who had given hostages to fortune overseas and had not yet rebuilt French naval strength, was also suspicious of the reliability of his Russian alliance. He therefore temporized and even offered concessions. A British ultimatum on April 23rd insisted on the continued occupation of Malta for ten years, the cession of the neighbouring island of Lampedusa to Great Britain, the evacuation of Holland by French forces, and the recognition of the Italian satellites only on condition of compensation for Sardinia and Switzerland. This was in effect a repudiation of the terms of Amiens. Bonaparte

offered more concessions but the British government would be
satisfied only by the integral acceptance of its ultimatum. Failing
this, negotiations were broken off and the war renewed in May 1803,
after fourteen months of uneasy peace.

The Treaty of Amiens had not contained the conditions of a
lasting peace. Bonaparte was not prepared permanently to accept a
situation in which Great Britain outweighed France in naval power
and in overseas empire; Great Britain, for her part, did not regard
French military hegemony in Europe as compatible with her own
security. War was inevitable in these circumstances: the problem
was how it could be waged, how the land and the sea power could
measure their strength against one another. The British could seize
French shipping and mop up the French colonies again one by one;
but they could only intervene in Europe by means of alliances.
Bonaparte's problem on the other hand was to find some means of
bringing his far greater military power to bear directly against
England. His solution was the Boulogne camp and invasion across
the Channel.

All through the wars of the eighteenth century plans for the
invasion of England had accumulated in the dossiers of the French
ministries. Bonaparte put these into practice on an unprecedented
scale. No attempt was made to conceal his preparations. The
Bayeux tapestry was brought to Paris for exhibition as a reminder
of a previous successful invasion of England from France. By the
summer of 1804 there were six to seven hundred invasion barges
and a Grand Army of over 100,000 men gathered on the coast at
Boulogne. A year later they were still there. The French admiral
Villeneuve's manœuvre to entice the British fleet to the West Indies
had failed to produce that temporary French control of the Channel
which was necessary for the invasion. The battle at Trafalgar, into
which Villeneuve was driven by Bonaparte's reproaches, brought
about the destruction of the French and Spanish fleets and guaranteed
British control of the seas for the rest of the war. But even before
the battle Napoleon had—he believed temporarily—abandoned his
invasion plan and struck camp at Boulogne.

Russia, which had decided on war with France, and Austria,
under pressure from Russia and alarmed at the growth of French

power in Italy and Germany, joined Great Britain to form the Third Coalition in July 1805. By the end of August the Grand Army was marching across southern Germany in seven columns. By agents and informers Napoleon already knew exactly the dispositions of the Austrians. He fell on the incompetent Austrian general, Mack, at Ulm and routed him. The Russian allies, with another Austrian army, barred the French advance at Austerlitz where, on December 2nd, in turn they were overwhelmed. Twice defeated, Austria concluded a humiliating peace at Pressburg.

Prussia, alarmed at the continual growth of French power in Germany, which it had so far done much, passively and even actively, to promote, now belatedly took to arms — the most highly polished, as well as the most antiquated, in Europe — to be humiliatingly crushed at Jena in November 1806. Russia, which alone remained of the European allies, was defeated in the bloodiest and most hard-fought battles Napoleon had so far been engaged in, at Eylau and Friedland, in 1807.

The sequel was the meeting of Napoleon and Alexander on the raft at Tilsit, on June 25th, 1807, when Napoleon dictated the terms of peace. Prussia was reduced to a mere torso. Russia had to make major concessions in the Near East, abandoning the Ionian Islands to Napoleon, evacuating the Turkish provinces of Moldavia and Wallachia on the Danube, accepting the Continental System, and, if Great Britain did not agree to Russian mediation, concluding an alliance with France. Napoleon was master of Europe west of the Russian border. The frontiers of France were extended to the Rhine in the north-east and to take in Piedmont, Parma, Genoa, and Tuscany in Italy. They were bordered by a glacis of satellite states — the former Batavian Republic, now the Kingdom of Holland, under his brother Louis; the Confederation of the Rhine, with Bavaria, Württemburg, Baden, and other states, and the electorate of Saxony promoted to be a kingdom; the Kingdom of Westphalia, formed out of the territories of the deposed rulers of Brunswick and Hesse-Cassel, with the subsequent addition of part of Hanover, placed under Napoleon's younger brother, Jerome; Prussian Poland, formed into the Grand Duchy of Warsaw, under the King of Saxony; the Helvetic Republic; the Kingdom of Italy, based on

Lombardy-Venetia and stretching down the coast of the peninsula through the eastern part of the Papal States to Ancona, with the privilege of having Napoleon himself as its king, crowned in 1805 with the iron crown of Lombardy at Milan, his step-son, Eugène Beauharnais, being Viceroy. The western half of the Papal States, surrounded by French power, still had a precarious and short-lived independence; but to the south the Kingdom of Naples—not of the Two Sicilies, for sea-power and a British force under General Stuart which won the small but significant battle of Maida in 1806, kept the French armies on the landward side of the Straits of Messina—was given in 1806 to Joseph Bonaparte, who was succeeded, when he was transferred to the throne of Spain, by Murat, not so much in his capacity of cavalry general as in that of husband of Caroline Bonaparte. Napoleon had done well by his clan. This was not to be the farthest limit of his empire, but already Russia and Austria were the only continental powers not dominated by him.

How was it that France, which under Louis XIV had known no such success, which since Fleury had had no luck in its foreign policy and known hardly anything but defeat, within fifteen years had acquired the hegemony of Europe? The military genius of Napoleon is part of the answer; the improved weapons, which he inherited from the reforms of the later years of the *ancien régime*, another part. But neither leadership nor material would have won victories without the men, the armies which had grown out of the ragged battalions of the Republic. What the Revolution had bequeathed to Napoleon was a large body of veterans, by now all really professional soldiers, many of them trained in the army of the line before 1789 and all blooded in the battles of the Republic. Young men of adventurous spirit, ability, and ambition from all ranks of society, seeking the quickest path to advancement, furnished the officers. The wars of the Revolution provided a supply, though a wasting one, of able generals. The masses that were required to be poured into and amalgamated with these cadres to fill out the armies of the Empire were provided by conscription. Although there were many exemptions and evasions, between 1800 and 1812 Napoleon raised well over a million men from France; a week at the depot to equip them and give them a rudimentary notion of military discipline, and they could be sent to the front, to be fused with trained men and learn the art of war on the field of battle. The brutal punishments which were regarded as necessary to discipline in British and other armies had been abolished by the revolutionaries. *Esprit de corps*, honours, and the spirit with which Napoleon inspired his soldiers from top to bottom, were a better substitute.

To picture a French army, using French resources, as conquering Europe would, however, not be correct. From the beginning of the Revolutionary War the French armies had lived off the country, and as their wars were always, until 1813, fought on foreign soil, the main burden did not fall on France. The numbers of men raised from France, though large by *ancien régime* standards, were not excessive. Up to 1812 the annual average works out at some 85,000, and this from a France which was steadily expanding its frontiers. As well as Piedmontese, Belgians, Dutch, and inhabitants of some German states, which were subjected to the laws of conscription when they were annexed, levies were raised from the satellite states. The army that invaded Russia in 1812 had contingents from every nation of Europe: of its 700,000 men only a third were French.

It was in moving the huge bodies of men he commanded across the map of Europe and concentrating them on the chosen field of battle that Napoleon showed his greatest military genius. The battle engaged, solid columns were flung at the enemy, a method that was costly in lives but the most efficient way of using masses of half-trained or untrained conscripts; it was successful until it met the concentrated fire of the English regiments of the line.

The most important factor of all in the Napoleonic conquests was the result of a technical change. The art of war seems to progress through alternate periods in which the defence and the offensive predominate. At the end of the eighteenth century the mobility of armies was greatly increased; the French were the first to exploit this and Napoleon was the first great master of the new techniques. Improved road surfaces, light field-guns, organization of armies in divisions, moving along different roads and therefore able to live off the country and dispense with cumbersome baggage-trains, the concentration of artillery fire and infantry attack—these methods, learnt from the military theorists of the *ancien régime*, especially

Guibert, author of the *Essai général de tactique* of 1772, were put into practice by Napoleon, with such effect that by 1807 all Europe, except Russia, was at his feet.

After Tilsit it might have been thought that Napoleon would rest on his laurels, content with his unchallenged military supremacy. The capacity for accepting a limit to his ambition was against his nature, but we need not resort simply to an explanation in terms of personal character; the perpetuation of war was in the nature of his regime, but in a more subtle way. England remained unconquered and after Trafalgar could apparently only be conquered by a restoration of French sea-power to the level at which it could challenge and defeat the might of the British navy. With the resources of France and all the satellite states to draw on, one might have thought that the creation of a new navy would not have been beyond Napoleon's power. If he chose another way of attack it was not, perhaps, because he recognized the restoration of French naval strength as impossible, but because he believed implicitly that this other way, while ensuring the collapse of British power equally, and perhaps more expeditiously and certainly, possessed also other and inherent attractions which made it desirable in itself. The Continental System was a device for bringing Great Britain to her knees, but it was also, quite apart from this, a method of increasing and consolidating the wealth and therefore the greatness of France. Moreover the Continental System was not invented out of nothing by Napoleon: it was a development of the policies of the Republic and the *ancien régime*.

The use of economic weapons in the struggle for power was not new. The revolutionaries had used them in their war against Great Britain. The hated commercial treaty of 1786 was annulled immediately after the declaration of war in 1793. All British goods were excluded from France; all shipping entering French ports had to be French or that of the country from which the goods came. 'Let us decree', cried Barère, 'a solemn navigation act and the isle of shopkeepers will be ruined.' As early as 1795 there was a proposal to use the alliance with Dutch naval power to exclude British trade from the Continent. Napoleon did not have to invent the Continental System; as in so many other fields, he found an idea already in existence and merely applied it with his own method and whole-heartedness. It was generally believed that British power rested on her naval strength and her subsidies—the guineas of Pitt; and both these on the profits she derived from trade. To destroy that trade by cutting off its markets would ruin her finances and rob her of her power as effectively as if every port in the British Isles were sealed: thus could the sea power be blockaded from the land.

This, however, is only one side of the Continental System. There was also the thought that what England lost France could gain, taking the place of her rival as the great industrial nation of Europe, and drawing in by her exports the wealth that would be barred to England. The Treaty of Amiens gave Napoleon the respite he needed to begin his policy of Bonapartist Colbertism by injecting a stimulus into French industry. His efforts were vigorous and at first not unsuccessful. Schools were set up for technical training, prizes offered for inventions, industrial fairs organized, Jacquard's machine for silk weaving was brought into use. Great French chemists, Lavoisier, Fourcroy, Berthollet, discovered new methods of dyeing, bleaching, and tanning. Industrialists and technicians visited the factories of Great Britain, and British machines and workers were imported into France, where they were put into operation with the aid of government credits and patronage. The French industrialist, Richard Lenoir, by 1810 had six cotton spinning mills with 3,600 workers in Normandy. Ternaux, a wool manufacturer of Sedan, employed 24,000 workers. Between 1788 and 1812 the number of looms increased from some 7,000 to 17,000 and the workers from 76,000 to 131,000. Such details, however, must not be allowed to give the impression of rapid industrial progress. The Revolution and the Empire may have provided a stimulus in some directions, but it is doubtful whether the pace had in fact increased. By 1815 French industry, it is estimated, was at the level of mechanization reached in Great Britain by 1780. Domestic labour was still the norm. Little workshops, with a master man and a few *compagnons*, working from one to five looms, still overwhelmingly predominated even in the textile industry. The small scale of industry is revealed by a few figures: 452 mines with 43,395 workers, 41 iron-works with 1,202, 1,219 forges with 7,120, 98 sugar refineries with 585. At Marseilles the soap industry had 73 workshops and 1,000 workers. The industrial revolution in France, of which there were notable signs before 1789, was progressing very slowly. The energy of the nation had been diverted first to civil strife and then to conquest.

The authoritarian and hierarchical spirit of the emperor, as well as the victory in the Revolution of the men of property, was reflected in the labour laws of the Empire. In 1803 was introduced the *livret*, a kind of passport and police visa, which every worker had to possess and in which were recorded all his changes of employment, reasons for leaving each job, and wages. It was kept by the employer and without it a worker could not be employed and would be regarded as a vagabond. Strikes were vigorously prohibited under severe penalties. The *compagnonnages* only survived clandestinely. Working conditions were miserable, though there seems to have been a modest rise in real wages up to 1810 and a fall after this.

Napoleon, like his predecessors, was chiefly interested in power, and in prosperity only as a means to power. His commercial policy was therefore at the service of his political ends. His conquests gave him ample opportunity to exclude British trade from the Continent, beginning with the occupation of Hanover in May 1803, which enabled him to close the mouths of the Elbe and the Weser. These measures, along with the prohibition of, or heavy duties on, colonial produce, increased the cost and diminished the supplies of raw material for French industry. This policy was intensified and systematized by the Berlin Decrees of 1806. By the Milan Decrees of December 1807 any ship which had called at a British port, paid a duty to Britain, or even been examined at sea by the British, was made a lawful prize. The result was in effect to exclude neutral shipping, on which Europe now depended for its supplies from overseas, from ports under French control. The British Orders in Council, blockading all French ports, were imposed more effectively by a fleet which swept the seas, and by raiding privateers. French privateers, the most successful of whom was the famous Surcouf, took a heavy toll of British shipping, at a rate of nearly 450 losses a year; but a high percentage of British exports (from 25 to 42 per cent) and re-exports (71 to 83 per cent) continued to go to the Continent. In the attempt to prevent this, Napoleon organized an army of customs officials round the coasts of Europe. The extent to which the Continental System

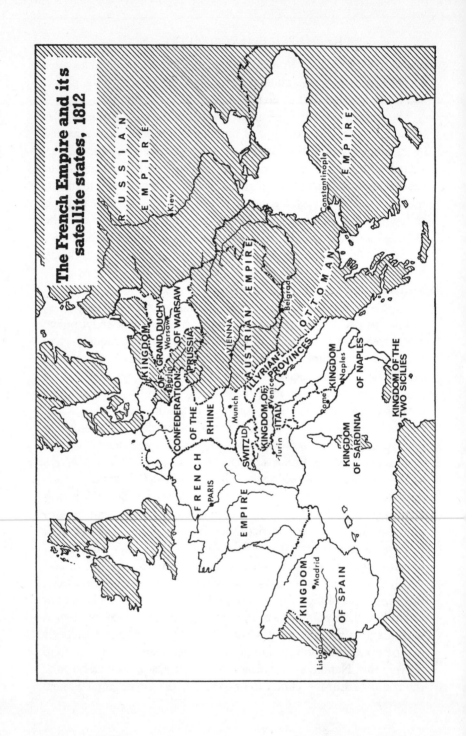

The French Empire and its satellite states, 1812

dictated the aggressions of the Empire, such as the invasion of the Iberian peninsula, has perhaps been exaggerated; but annexations were at least influenced by the needs of the System. Napoleon's aim was, in his own words, to close every port from the Sound to the Hellespont to British shipping.

To portray the Continental System, as it has been portrayed, as an attempt to create a great pan-European economic union, is to attribute to Napoleon a degree of enlightenment in the pursuance of his ends which dictators do not usually possess. If it had been this the System might conceivably have aroused less resentment in the rest of Europe. On the contrary, it was, as I have already said, a device not only for defeating England, but also for ensuring French economic supremacy. The economies of the other nations were subordinated and geared to that of France. His object, Napoleon declared in 1810, was to encourage the export of French goods and the import of foreign bullion. Thus, new frontiers in Italy, with high customs barriers between them, were devised to enable French industrial products to capture the Italian market. The Grand Duchy of Berg, centred on the Ruhr valley, already a growing industrial area, was cut off from its markets in the Netherlands and the Baltic by high tariffs. The export of Italian textiles to southern Germany was prohibited. Raw silk from Piedmont was directed to Lyons and away from the silk workers of Lombardy by means of tariff adjustments. French manufactures could be exported freely into Holland, but Dutch goods had to pay customs dues to enter France.

As has already been indicated, these efforts to turn France into the great industrial nation of Europe failed. The loss of colonial raw materials was incompatible with their success, though desperate efforts were made to improvise substitutes. The growing of woad was promoted in the south-west of France, where its production had flourished in the Middle Ages, to replace colonial indigo; chicory provided a substitute for coffee and beet for the sugar cane. Attempts were made to introduce the growing of cotton in southern Italy, but the cotton industry languished for lack of raw materials. The substitutes had at the time only mediocre success.

The decisive factor in Napoleon's attempt to create a French industrial empire was that he was not merely setting land power against sea power, but land communications against sea communications, at a time when transport by water was immeasurably cheaper than transport by land. If the rivers of Europe had flowed in a different direction the prospects might have been brighter, but the great strategic roads that were driven across France and stretched out to the French Empire could not materially diminish the cost of land transport. Despite all Napoleon's efforts, French foreign trade under the Empire never regained the level it had reached in 1789. In Bordeaux, wrote the American consul in 1808, grass was growing in the streets and at the great quays a mere handful of vessels with cargo swung in the tide.

When the economic crisis of 1811–13 burst on Europe, though the contemporary crisis in Great Britain would suggest more general causes, Europe naturally attributed it to the Napoleonic system. In France itself, at Mulhouse 40,000 workers out of 60,000 were unemployed, and 20–25,000 at Lyons. Napoleon, who had learnt during the Revolution to fear starving urban mobs, modified and opened loopholes in his economic legislation, and this was the effective end of the real enforcement of the Continental System, though it had already broken down largely in practice. Round the coastline of Napoleonic Europe, from Gothenburg in Sweden, Heligoland, Gibraltar, the Balearics, Malta, after their capture in 1809 the Ionian Isles, a flood of contraband goods seeped into Europe. Smuggling became one of the most remunerative and by no means the least numerous of professions. It was conducted sometimes by official subterfuge, sometimes by force of arms. Administrators and generals, and the customs officials themselves, made a regular trade of corruption. Against universal smuggling the Napoleonic machine of repression that had been created was powerless. When confiscated goods were ordered to be burnt, valueless rubbish was destroyed in their place. Smuggling became so much an organized trade that smuggled goods were even insured against seizure. The rate at Strasbourg on illicit goods destined for France was 30 per cent. Napoleon himself connived at the infringement of his own laws. He wrote to his brother Louis to fix the point where English smugglers were to land to purchase Dutch gin: what was essential, he believed, was that they should be made to pay in bullion and not in goods. But at Hamburg, English clothing and shoes were being bought for the French army.

It was only after the economic crisis of the latter years of the Empire that Napoleon had recourse to the organized breach of the Continental System by the method of licences. Since Great Britain was doing the same, an interchange of goods developed between the two countries at war. French ships were allowed to trade with England under a neutral flag; unfortunately, once outside Napoleon's clutches they generally stayed outside, to swell the merchant marine in British service. The licences were, of course, expensive, and there were heavy duties on the imported goods, so that fiscal motives were not absent from Napoleon's mind. Finally, the opposition that his economic policies had always aroused in the rest of Europe spread to France. The commercial and industrial classes began to detach themselves openly from a regime the burden of which went on increasing and the benefits diminishing.

Empire and military glory were in the end as incompatible with economic progress as the political chaos of the Revolution had been. And the Emperor himself, if he had started as the heir of the Revolution, was turning in his social policy into something more like the restorer of a pseudo *ancien régime*. The creation of the Legion of Honour in 1802, against the advice of many of his supporters, was an early sign of his anti-egalitarian tendencies. Once he was Emperor he needed a court, the nucleus of which was provided by the six Grand Dignitaries of the Empire — Grand Elector Joseph Bonaparte, Grand Constable Louis, Arch-chancellor of State Eugène de Beauharnais, Grand Admiral Murat, Arch-chancellor Cambacérès, and Arch-treasurer Lebrun — four relations plus the former second and third consuls. For the ceremonies of the new court a series of Grand Officers of the Crown, drawn from the *ancien régime*, provided the correct tone. Mme Campan was there to explain to the Ladies of Honour and the Empress how Marie-Antoinette used to do things. A whole gamut of titles, from duke to chevalier, was recreated and made hereditary on the granting of an appropriate entail. Sons of ministers, councillors of state and the like, and the nephews of archbishops, became counts. Prefects were barons or counts. Altogether Napoleon created over 3,000 nobles. Of course, a real noble was even better. Those among the *ancien régime* nobility who rallied to the imperial banner were singled out for favour. They came increasingly to dominate the court and the administration as the Empire reached its zenith.

⚜

CHAPTER FIVE

THE NAPOLEONIC EMPIRE: FALL

IN 1807, after Tilsit, there was a reorganization of the ministries, in which Talleyrand lost the Ministry of Foreign Affairs, though he was made a Grand Dignitary. He had already decided that Napoleon's ambition would bring him to ultimate ruin, and having served him well and gained a huge fortune by the acceptance of bribes, he was now secretly negotiating with Napoleon's enemies. He had never believed in the wisdom of the humiliation of Austria. In the course of 1808 Talleyrand and Fouché, when Napoleon was absent in Spain, began to make plans for the choice of a successor, who was apparently to be Murat. Napoleon did not remain in ignorance of this. When he returned he dismissed Talleyrand with a torrent of abuse; but the ex-bishop, ex-revolutionary, ex-Minister of Foreign Affairs, ex-Grand Chamberlain, continued to haunt the court like a vulture of ill omen biding his time. Fouché, former terrorist and regicide, Minister of Police since 1799, and a particular friend of Josephine, had been useful to Napoleon as a link with the revolutionaries, but subsequently established a position also as a kind of patron to many royalists. During the Revolution, while a leader of the anti-religious party, he had protected priests, especially members of his old order of the Oratory. His contempt for the Concordat was unconcealed, not for lack of a clerical capacity for dissimulation but from a natural independence of mind. He was the least servile of all Napoleon's servants and the humanest minister of police a dictator ever had. But when, in 1810, Napoleon discovered that Fouché had been engaging for the past year in secret negotiations with England, his dismissal was inevitable. Though Talleyrand and Fouché waited to be dismissed—and it is a sign of their confidence that they feared no more—it is evident that they had deserted Napoleon by their own choice and were preparing for a future in which they foresaw his inevitable defeat. It was an ominous sign. Their successors, often former royalists, were men of inferior calibre and untried loyalty. Whereas at first Napoleon had gathered round him a collection of the ablest men in France, his later appointments were increasingly influenced by favouritism and court intrigue. He now wanted flunkeys, says Chaptal bitterly, not advisers.

Intolerance of criticism was only one sign of the degeneration that was beginning to come over the emperor, both physically and mentally. His decline may be said to have begun even before the Empire had reached its height. His aggressions were increasingly irrational. Thus the Pope had not realized the nature of the relationship which Napoleon assumed to have been created by the Concordat. 'So far as the Pope is concerned', he wrote, 'I am Charlemagne'; if the Pope did not behave he would be reduced to the status of bishop of Rome. For military purposes, French troops had already occupied the Adriatic coastline of the Papal States and the port of Ancona. In 1809 the Papal States were annexed to the French Empire and the Pope was arrested and carried off to captivity. His subsequent refusal to collaborate with Napoleon, though inconvenient, especially because it prevented the filling of vacant sees in France, had surprisingly little practical result.

The French intervention in Spain was to have more momentous consequences. Under Godoy, Prince of the Peace, an adventurer who had made the queen his mistress, Spain had become a French satellite. To extend French control over the whole peninsula, a joint Franco-Spanish army invaded Portugal in 1807. Napoleon, however, was not satisfied with the aid he was getting from Spain. Under direct French rule, he believed, this backward and priest-ridden nation could be modernized and so contribute far more to the strength of the French Empire. The sordid intrigues which followed in the Spanish court need not delay us. In May 1808 the king and queen and the heir Ferdinand were summoned to Bayonne and by threats made to sign away their rights over Spain. Godoy was imprisoned, regretted only by the infatuated queen and a few other mistresses. Joseph Bonaparte, brought from the throne of Naples, was put on that of Madrid.

Even before Joseph entered his new capital, where he was able to stay on this occasion only for eleven days, a spontaneous insurrection all over Spain had imperilled some 150,000 French troops dispersed over the whole peninsula. In July one force had to capitulate at Baylen and in August another, beaten at Vimiero by a hurriedly dispatched British expeditionary force under Wellesley, signed the Convention of Cintra and was shipped back to France. Joseph and the remaining French troops withdrew behind the Ebro. All this was unprecedented. If allowed to succeed it might set a fatal example. The veteran corps of Victor, Mortier, and Ney were called from Germany and a great French army was assembled under Napoleon on the Ebro. The Spaniards were routed and driven back. A small British force under Moore retreated to Corunna and was evacuated by sea. Joseph was reinstated in Madrid. However, the diversion effected by Moore's army had drawn back the French forces from their triumphal sweep through the peninsula. After this Napoleon returned to Paris and never came to Spain again. During the remainder of the wars of the Empire, Wellington from his base in Portugal, and the Spanish guerrillas, were to tie down a large French army permanently. In Napoleon's winter campaign of 1808 he had over 300,000 men in Spain; in the spring offensive of 1810 the number rose to 370,000; in the crisis of the Empire in 1812 there were 290,000 and in 1813 still 224,000. The wastage by battle and disease was heavy all through. If it was a side-show it was a very expensive one: henceforth Napoleon was to have to fight on two fronts.

The French reverses in Spain may have played some part in the resurgence of Austria, which had remained unreconciled to the humiliation of Austerlitz and had since been reorganizing her military forces. A hard-fought campaign from April to July 1809 ended in another Austrian defeat, at Wagram; but Napoleon's position was still not secure. The Tyrol had revolted, Venetia had been captured by the Austrians, Prussia and Russia were hesitating on the brink of war, far away to the west Soult had been driven out of Portugal, and a British expedition had landed in Walcheren. Even Wagram, though an Austrian defeat, was not a rout, and was only worth an armistice. But when it became clear that Russian aid was not coming, and that Vienna itself was exposed to attack, the Austrian emperor gave up the struggle and bought peace with more

territorial concessions—a large part of Galicia to the Duchy of
Warsaw, Salzburg and the Tyrol to Bavaria, the Illyrian provinces,
in accordance with the requirements of the Continental System, to
direct French rule.

Victory still followed the imperial eagles but one thing was
lacking to Napoleon's ambitions. The intrigues of Talleyrand and
Fouché had made the insecurity of his position clear. His clan evidently depended entirely on himself: there was no hope in it for the
establishment of a Bonapartist dynasty. Josephine would now
never give him a child, but he knew through a mistress, in 1807,
that he was capable of getting one. For some time schemes for a
divorce and re-marriage had been mooted, and after a few unsuccessful approaches to the old dynasties, the Habsburgs, unlucky in
battle, remembered their tradition—*Bella gerant alii; tu, felix
Austria, nube*. They had an available princess, Marie-Louise, ready
for the sacrifice, and as the young Austrian minister Metternich
wrote, the Austrian Emperor 'will shrink from nothing that may
contribute to the welfare and peace of the state'. He would however
have shrunk from a civil marriage, which in any case would not have
been adequate for Napoleon's purpose. Josephine therefore had to
be got rid of, not by a divorce, but by a declaration of the nullity
of her marriage. This involved proving the invalidity of the religious
ceremony which she and Napoleon had gone through on the eve of
the coronation in 1804. Though performed by a cardinal—Napoleon's uncle, Fesch—this marriage had been clandestine, it was
argued, and without adequate witnesses. To complete the conviction
of the religious court that tried the case, it was established that
Napoleon had acted under compulsion from Josephine. The religious requirements of the Church were thus met, and it was disappointing—seeing that everything was in order—that thirteen
cardinals out of twenty-seven should have stayed away from the
marriage ceremony with Marie-Louise in 1810. Napoleon in revenge
assigned to them compulsory residences and forbade them to wear
their robes of office. Hence they became known as the black cardinals. In 1811 was born the little boy who was proclaimed King of
Rome but never to inherit an Empire in which the cracks were
already visible.

Now that Austria had been once more defeated, and by the dynastic alliance had apparently accepted defeat, Russia remained the only continental power that was not subordinate to France. The nominal ties of Tilsit could not prevent the growth of mutual suspicion and conflict of interests. Alexander and Napoleon suspected each other —and rightly—of preparing an attack when the opportunity came. They had more concrete grievances. Napoleon strengthened his position in the Baltic by the annexation of Oldenburg in December 1810, although Alexander's sister was married to the heir to the Duchy, and despite the guarantees of Tilsit. He began to move his troops eastwards, garrisoning Danzig, turning the Grand Duchy of Warsaw into a great military base and gathering huge magazines of supplies there. Meanwhile Russia, like the rest of Europe, was suffering from the economic crisis. To cope with the consequent discontent Alexander imposed heavy duties on French imports and opened his ports to neutral shipping. In effect he was withdrawing Russia from the Continental System, and although British trade with Russia was insignificant, this may have influenced Napoleon. More alarming was the fact that in May 1812 Russia concluded peace with the Turks. This was perhaps the decisive event, for Napoleon knew that it freed Alexander's hands in a way that nothing else could have done. Alexander had also concluded an agreement with Bernadotte of Sweden, received promises from Austria that her support for Napoleon would be only formal, and was negotiating secretly with Great Britain. Of all this Napoleon was not unaware. A defensive reaction would have been against the nature of the man and his system. War it had to be.

On June 24th, 1812, the Grand Army began to cross the Niemen. Napoleon had gathered in the Grand Duchy of Warsaw 675,000 men and 1,350 cannon. Poles, Prussians, Austrians, Dutch, Swiss, Italians, all the nations of Europe had sent their conscripts tramping across Europe. Russia was to be overwhelmed by sheer weight of numbers. Instead it was Napoleon's own military machine that, in the long barren distances of Russia, was to collapse under its own weight. As the Russian armies avoided battle and withdrew, Napoleon moved forward, his armies struggling on through the heat of summer. At last, in front of Moscow, the Russians stood and

Napoleon could fight the battle for which he had been longing. But it was not the *coup de grâce* he needed to deliver. At Borodino some 30,000 of his troops were killed, and though the Russians lost more they retreated in order. The occupation of an empty Moscow, the burning of the city, the retreat after five weeks' waiting for peace emissaries who never came, with an army already reduced to about 100,000, with officers and men, baggage-trains, horses, carriages loaded down with the spoils of Russia's conquered and looted capital, across a region that it had already desolated, in the rain and mud of autumn, turning to the snows of winter—all this is a many-times-told tale of greed and cruelty, heroism and despair. After the tragic crossing of the Beresina on November 27th, famine and frost and the pursuing Russians completed the annihilation of the army of the Empire. It was not beaten in battle; under the stress of a long, starving retreat, the great cosmopolitan military machine collapsed and disintegrated, leaving behind it a legend in history. Some 1,000 of the Guards, out of the great host that had set out, held together when Ney recrossed the Niemen on December 14th.

Napoleon had already, on December 6th, deserted an army that no longer existed and was hastening back to Paris, where the essentially ephemeral nature of his regime had just been demonstrated by the Malet conspiracy. In this extraordinary episode a republican general, Malet, and a royalist priest, Lafon, both in custody as political prisoners, came near to overthrowing the Empire in its capital by the simple device of forging a document announcing the death of Napoleon and the constitution of a provisional government under the banished general Moreau. In his name Malet assumed command of Paris, and arrested the Minister of Police, the War Minister, and the Prefect of Police—all in the space of a single morning. Only when the commander of the Paris garrison challenged the news, and the little band of conspirators failed to keep up the pretence of Napoleon's death successfully, were they resisted. Then, of course, they were easily seized and after a rapid trial executed. It was a gallant adventure and deserved a better sequel. It was also clear evidence that the whole government of Napoleon rested on the cohesion of the military and administrative machine he had created and that this in turn depended exclusively on his person.

Back in Paris, Napoleon set the administration to the task of raising conscripts from France, for the first time really ruthlessly. Europe was now rising everywhere against his domination, but there were still Napoleonic armies and garrisons far and wide. Indecisive battles against Russians and Prussians, at Lützen and Bautzen, in May 1813, were followed by an armistice. If Napoleon had been capable of concessions, he might now have kept the Austrians out of the war and disintegrated the alliance; but such moderation had long since ceased to be possible for him and the struggle was resumed. He had some half a million men in the field, the allies rather more. Moreau was advising them and Bernadotte bringing an army down from Sweden. A French victory at Dresden in August was followed, in October, by the battle of the nations at Leipzig. After this, with its soldiers dead in battle or by disease, deserters or prisoners, or uselessly shut up in fortresses scattered about Germany, the army of 1813 followed that of 1812 into the void. Only a fragment retired across the Rhine.

More conscripts were called up from France: there were no foreign allies or dependents left to exploit. Still, in December 1813, Napoleon refused to negotiate in time for a recognition of the 'natural frontiers' of France. By now the armies of the coalition were in Switzerland and on the Rhine, and Wellington had crossed the Pyrenees. In January 1814 Murat deserted Napoleon and Italy was lost. In France itself his regime was patently breaking down. It had entered the winter of its discontent. Under the frozen surface of dictatorship resentment brooded. Conscription had reached the point at which it was meeting open resistance even from the inert peasantry. They were touched more closely when Napoleon's armies, fighting for the first time on French soil, supplied themselves by the normal method of requisitioning which had carried them all over Europe. The *droits réunis*, the hated taxes on alcoholic drinks, tobacco, and salt, were a long-standing grievance of the peasantry. Industry had lost its markets with the collapse of the Empire and unemployment was widespread in the towns. Commerce was languishing and the finances in disorder. The clergy, who had never quite forgotten their loyalty to the Bourbons, were a centre of opposition everywhere. All those who had acquired wealth and jobs saw the need to insure against the future. An underground royalist movement, a kind of royalist and catholic freemasonry, which had been created in 1810, was reviving the memory of the Bourbons in a country that had begun to forget them. But though the royalists were active and beginning to emerge above ground, the nation as a whole remained passive.

When the allies invaded France, it accepted the foreign invaders as passively as it had borne the rule of Napoleon. Épinal surrendered to fifty cossacks, Reims to a platoon, Chaumont to a single horseman. The one demand of the country was peace. The Senate, called together by Napoleon in December 1813, performed its last act of homage towards the man to whom so many of its members owed fame and fortune. But the Legislative Body, that collection of insignificant yes-men, voted by 223 to 51 an address of unprecedented independence: 'Our ills are at their height. The *patrie* is threatened at all points of the frontier; we are suffering from a destitution unexampled in the whole history of the state. Commerce is destroyed, industry dying ... What are the causes of these unutterable miseries? A vexatious administration, excessive taxes, the deplorable methods adopted for their collection, and the even crueller excesses practised for the recruitment of the armies ... A barbarous and endless war swallows up periodically the youth torn from education, agriculture, commerce, and the arts.' This was strong language, and the Legislative Body ended with an appeal for abandoning the ambitious schemes which had been for twenty years 'so fatal to all the peoples of Europe'. No wonder that Napoleon banished the authors of the address, forbade its publication, and prorogued the Legislative Body.

If he had been willing to buy peace by renouncing the Empire he might still have got it and remained the ruler of France. In February and March 1814 negotiations with the allies at Châtillon proved that he could not bring himself to do this. Instead, with a small army of some 60,000 men, largely untrained conscripts, he manœuvred brilliantly between the invading armies in the east of France and inflicted reverses on them. The requisitions and brutalities of the invaders aroused patriotic feeling in the occupied areas, but this did not spread to the rest of France. The allies, realizing the scarcity of Napoleon's troops, ceased to play his game, by-passed his forces, and advanced on Paris. On March 29th, in accordance with orders from Napoleon, Marie-Louise and the King of Rome left the capital. All the higher officers of state were commanded to leave with them but many found means of remaining. On March 31st Paris capitulated and the troops garrisoning it moved to Fontaine-bleau, where Napoleon established his headquarters. The same day the allied forces entered through the porte Saint-Denis, marched across Paris amidst curious crowds and bivouacked in the Champs-Élysées.

A provisional government, of which Talleyrand was the leading member, was set up. The Senate and the Legislative Body voted the deposition of Napoleon. But who was to take his place? Talleyrand, who had established close relations with the Tsar, had largely won him over to a restoration of the Bourbons. The Paris press, now under royalist control, agitated for a restoration. But the allies were still hesitant. Europe had been conditioned to fear the French nation and was still alarmed at what it might do if an unpopular regime were forced on it. At this stage what was happening in the south-west was perhaps decisive. The army of Wellington, having crossed the Pyrenees, was advancing towards Toulouse in pursuit of Soult. A small British force, detached from the main army, was sent off to occupy Bordeaux. The imperial authorities fled across the Gironde, and on March 22nd the British advance-guard, to which a squadron of young royalists had attached themselves, entered the city, to be welcomed by the Mayor of Bordeaux, a member of the royalist secret society of the Chevaliers de la Foi, with a white cockade and the cry of 'Vive le Roi'. In the afternoon arrived the duc d'Angou-lême, greeted with wild demonstrations of joy. The influence of this spontaneous French rejection of Napoleon and proclamation of the Bourbons, on both the allies and the French leaders in Paris, was considerable. Napoleon himself, faced with the refusal of the mar-shals to engage in another battle, had abdicated in favour of the King of Rome and sent plenipotentiaries to Alexander. It was already too late to save even this from the wreck. Marshal Marmont, despite a short-lived mutiny among his troops, marched them to the enemy lines and surrendered. On April 6th Napoleon abdicated

E

unconditionally. Four days later, so slow did news travel, the last battle of the allied invasion was to be fought, a bloody assault in which Wellington overcame Soult's entrenchments before Toulouse.

On April 12th the comte d'Artois, as lieutenant-general for his brother, Louis XVIII, entered Paris in triumph. Through decorated streets and applauding crowds, he went to Notre Dame where the *Te Deum* was sung. Louis XVIII himself landed at Boulogne on April 24th and, received everywhere with enthusiasm, moved slowly to Saint-Omer where he met a delegation from the Senate and issued a royal proclamation. 'Louis, by the grace of God, King of France and Navarre', recalled by the love of his people to the throne of his fathers, promised France representative government in a Senate and Chamber of Deputies, taxation only with consent, public and individual liberty, freedom of the press, freedom of religion, responsible government, judicial independence, a career open to talent, and — not least — that no one should be punished for opinions or votes during the fallen regime, the recognition of the national debt, of pensions, grades, and military honours, of titles of both the old and new nobility, and of the sales of national property. It was a compromise between divine right and the Revolution, rather to the advantage of the latter. On May 3rd Louis XVIII and the royal family made their ceremonial entry into the capital.

Napoleon, largely by the mediation of Alexander, was meanwhile journeying to a smaller kingdom in Elba. While he travelled through country that had experienced the allied occupation his reception was favourable, but as he moved south, according to the Prussian commissioner who accompanied him, it became increasingly hostile. He got through Lyons at night. At Orange there were shouts of 'Vive Louis XVIII', and at Avignon 'À bas le tyran'; he saw himself hanged in effigy and after this disguised himself in an old blue coat, put up a white cockade, and preceded his carriage in the guise of a courier. Later he dressed himself as an Austrian officer. He embarked from Fréjus, where he had landed fifteen years earlier on his way home from Egypt, leaving then also a defeated army behind, but with the triumphs of brumaire and the Empire before him. Fearing assassination he refused to embark on the French ship provided for him and sailed to Elba in a British frigate. He left a France which, it has been estimated, had lost in his wars 860,000 men between the ages of 23 and 44, half of them under 28.

The Restoration did not begin well. Talleyrand confined himself to foreign affairs. The old system of government by a conseil d'en haut, with no chief minister, no unity, and therefore no policy, was revived. The two most important ministers were baron Louis for Finance, and Dupont, remembered only for his defeat at Baylen and perhaps unmerited disgrace, at the Ministry of War. By an austere financial policy Louis put the budget into better shape, but at the price of maintaining the unpopular *droits réunis* and of economies which cut down pensions and salaries. Dupont's policy demoralized the army. He retired many officers and put many more on half-pay, brought into it, over the heads of Napoleonic veterans, a host of émigrés who had never seen a battlefield or commanded a man, recreated the Household Guard—the Light Horse, Grey and Black Musketeers, the Cent Suisses, and the rest, crammed with dissatisfied royalists, expensive, intriguing, and useless—6,000 men, all with the rank and pay of officers, costing twenty million francs a year. 'The indignation and exasperation of the army', wrote Philippe de Ségur, himself a noble of the *ancien régime* but one who had acquired other ideas and other loyalties in the Imperial Army, and a veteran of the Moscow campaign, 'had become so violent that at the Tuileries, among the officers of the Old Guard on half-pay, spectators like myself of the reviews which were held, I had difficulty in preventing an outburst.' The flag also was already a burning issue. 'They imposed on us', wrote de Ségur, 'the flag under which they had fought us.' At the same time, the old court ceremonies and the king's household were recreated as though nothing had happened since 1789.

Napoleon at Elba was not uninformed of the dissatisfaction in France, and at the end of ten months was sufficiently dissatisfied himself with ruling a tiny island in place of half Europe to be ready to set out on his last and most reckless venture. On March 1st, 1815, he landed with 1,050 troops, once again at Fréjus, and avoiding this time royalist Provence, took the mountain road from Cannes to Grenoble. Opposition melted away wherever he appeared. By itself the march from Fréjus to Paris is sufficient evidence of his magnetic personality. It is clear, however, that what he could appeal to now was primarily the loyalty of the old soldiers to a great leader, and their habit of obedience. The survival of revolutionary sentiments, and the possibility of their re-awakening, was shown at Lyons, where enthusiastic crowds added to cries of 'Vive l'Empereur' those of 'À bas les prêtres', 'À bas les nobles', 'Mort aux royalistes'.

The news of Napoleon's landing reached Paris on March 5th. Before anything could be done, on the next day he was at Grenoble, and in the capital complacency was rapidly being succeeded by frantic and futile orders and counter-orders, and something approaching panic. The defection of Ney, in command of the royal troops in Franche-Comté, was decisive. At midnight on March 19th, Louis XVIII, accompanied by a few horsemen only, took the road for Lille. Finding the garrison there hostile, he crossed the frontier to Ghent.

Napoleon was once again master of France, but what use would he make of his revived authority? He announced that he had given up the Grand Empire, but was alarmingly ambiguous as to the scope he envisaged for the French Empire to which he now promised to limit himself. No promises could have disarmed the enmity of the other Great Powers. They declared Napoleon outside the pale of civilized society and had 7–800,000 men under arms to back up their ban.

To give the new regime a more liberal cloak, Napoleon issued, with the advice of Benjamin Constant, an *Acte additionel*, proposing a constitution not so very dissimilar from that adumbrated in Louis XVIII's *Charte*. Either believing in Napoleon's professions of liberalism, or thinking him a lesser evil than the Bourbons, Carnot emerged from retirement to become Minister of the Interior. But even if Napoleon had been sincere, and there is little reason to suppose that he was, he could not give France what its people still wanted more than anything else—peace, or its ruling classes what they wanted—stability, and security for their property and jobs. The chief reason for his successful return, after the loyalty of the old army, was the passivity, the political inertia of the nation. Of course, protestations of loyalty flowed in from the same officials who a year earlier had hastened to offer their allegiance to Louis XVIII and were to repeat the performance once the emperor had been defeated. The weakness of the royalists was shown by their inability to offer serious resistance, except in the Vendée, where a rising pinned down 30,000 men whom Napoleon could well have used in Belgium.

The thought of an appeal to the masses, if it ever entered Napoleon's head, was rejected. There is no evidence, of course, that the masses would have risen, or what they could have done if they had. Instead, the governmental machine was put into operation in the orthodox way to raise a new conscript army. 600,000 men were called up, but when Napoleon invaded Belgium he could only assemble an army of 125,000, though these included many veterans, gathered back in France from the scattered remnants of his former armies. He marched off, leaving treachery behind him in the person of Fouché, once again Minister of Police, working with the liberals, protecting royalists, in secret correspondence with Metternich and Talleyrand at Vienna and Artois at Ghent, and revealing half of what he was doing to Napoleon, with a foot in every camp. He calculated on Napoleon's survival for some three months, in the course of which the duc d'Otranto reckoned to make himself—as for a short while he was to be—indispensable to all parties.

In Belgium, the only forces ready to oppose Napoleon were 120,000 Prussians under Blucher, and a mixed force of Belgians, Dutch, Hanoverians, and English under Wellington. The Prussians were driven back at Ligny and Wellington's forces, held by Ney at Quatre Bras, retreated on the hill of Mont-Saint-Jean near the village of Waterloo. There, on June 18th, Napoleon flung his massed columns at them with little attempt at manœuvre, in increasingly desperate attacks as the threat of the Prussian army, coming up on his flank, became greater. In the later stages of the battle only a retreat could have saved the French army, but Napoleon knew that farther off were the Austrians and Russians, and that if he did not win his first battle his chance was gone for ever. The retreat therefore became a rout and his last army vanished.

> Comme s'envole au vent une paille enflammée
> S'évanouit ce bruit qui fut la grande armée.

Back in Paris, on June 21st, Napoleon still talked of fighting on, draining the country of men, but there were none now to follow his frantic egoism. He signed his second abdication. If he had not done so the Chambers would have done it for him.

The liberals in Paris, being rid of the emperor, did not want to replace him with a king, least of all a Bourbon. The man of the moment, however, was Fouché, who had turned to the royalists. He secured the withdrawal of the French army covering Paris and by a series of masterly manœuvres was able to present to Louis XVIII, returning as rapidly from the frontier as he had fled there, a peaceful and unopposed restoration, and himself as his Minister of Police.

Meanwhile, Napoleon was *en route*, by way of Rochefort, though he did not suspect this as yet, to St Helena. From the *Bellerophon*, on which he had taken refuge, he wrote to the Prince Regent in a last fine gesture, 'I come, like Themistocles, to seat myself at the hearth of the British people.' The hearth of the British people was a very cold one but we need not waste too much sympathy on Napoleon. The last fling of his ambition had to be paid for, like the earlier ones, by France; not only in the loss of life and the expense of war, but in a severer treaty of peace. France was reduced to the frontiers of 1789, with the additional loss of one or two small areas for strategic reasons, the most important being the Saar, its future economic importance not yet suspected. An indemnity of 700 million francs was extorted. The works of art looted from Europe were to be returned. The fortresses of the north and the east were to be occupied by 150,000 allied troops for a period of from three to five years. The price of the Hundred Days in the terms of a treaty can easily be stated: its price in terms of the subsequent history of France remains undefinable.

PART TWO

THE CONSTITUTIONAL MONARCHY

✤

CHAPTER ONE

THE RESTORATION

THE Second Restoration was to take place under very different auspices from those that had presided over the First. Fouché prepared the way for it in Paris. Talleyrand, hurrying back from Vienna, met the king at Saint Denis — where the kings of France had been buried for centuries, until the revolutionaries dug them up — and presented Fouché (vice leaning on the arm of crime, Chateaubriand said) to Louis XVIII, who accepted the regicide as his Minister of Police. It was a very different homecoming from the first. Even if Wellington and the king's advisers, who urged on him the necessity of accepting Fouché and Talleyrand as his ministers, were mistaken in believing that this was the only way to a peaceful second restoration, the fact that they believed it, and that the king yielded to their opinion, is in itself significant of the latent weakness and even contradiction in his position; for despite his ministers Louis XVIII did not intend to return the second time, any more than he had come back the first, as the king of a crowned revolution. When, on the news of the abdication of Napoleon in 1814, a courtier announced to him, 'Sire, you are King of France,' he had replied, 'Have I ever ceased to be?' His sense of indefeasible, hereditary, divine right, which supported him in the years of exile, had become second nature. It gave him a dignity which his physical appearance might otherwise have prohibited. Immensely fat and walking only with difficulty, he occupied the throne like an old idol, self-sufficient in divinely sanctioned egoism. If he compromised with new conditions it was without faith and with very little hope.

Louis XVIII's English exile had not taught him the virtues of parliamentary government. At bottom he shared the views of his younger brother, who once declared that he would sooner earn his living as a wood-cutter than be King of England. This did not mean that the restored Bourbons intended, even if they had had the power,

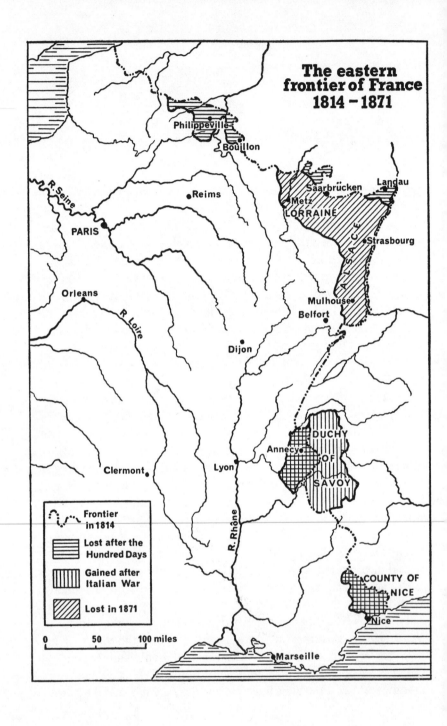

The eastern frontier of France 1814–1871

R. Seine

Philippeville

Bouillon

Reims

Landau

Saarbrücken

Metz

LORRAINE

PARIS

Strasbourg

A L S A C E

Orleans

R. Loire

Mulhouse

Belfort

Dijon

Clermont

Lyon

DUCHY

Annecy

OF

SAVOY

R. Rhône

Frontier in 1814

Lost after the Hundred Days

Gained after Italian War

Lost in 1871

COUNTY OF NICE

Nice

0   50   100 miles

Marseille

to bring back the absolute monarchy. The question is often discussed as though there were no other choice, at least in ideology, than that between the absolutism of a Louis XIV and the principles of the Revolution. This is to forget that it was not the ministers of Louis XVI but the émigrés who returned in 1814, and that the kings of the Restoration had formerly been, when they were Provence and Artois, the leaders of the Counter-revolution. Their programme had been that of the aristocratic revolt, of the Assembly of Notables and the Royal Session of 1789. These were the political ideas that Louis XVIII and his advisers embodied in the Charter of 1814.

The concessions it offered should not be underestimated. The recognition of the principles of liberty and equality, with which it commenced, perhaps meant less, but not in practice so much less, than it had in 1789. More important was the assurance that a curtain of forgetfulness was to be dropped over opinions and votes expressed before the Restoration: this was necessary if the political, administrative, military, and religious personnel which had served the Empire was to continue to serve the restored monarchy. The Civil Code and all existing laws which were not contrary to the *Charte* were maintained in force: this was to retain the administrative and social structure given to France by Napoleon, and here the fundamental contradictions of the Restoration begin. To superimpose the pseudo-Gothic of an aristocratic reaction on the pseudo-classical pillars of the Napoleonic system was to create a piece of wedding-cake architecture, essentially ephemeral.

A second problem was that of land owership. It was met by a recognition of the inviolable right of all existing property, including specifically all the lands of the Church and the émigrés which had been confiscated by the Revolution and had passed to new possessors. Legal recognition of the changes in land ownership was doubtless inevitable, but could those who had been despoiled reconcile themselves to the fact that even if the king was enjoying his own again, they were not?

Thirdly, religious toleration was proclaimed. This was an achievement of the eighteenth-century Enlightenment, consolidated by the Revolution; but Roman Catholicism, a declining, emasculated force in the eighteenth century, was now moving towards a new militancy on the crest of a wave of religious revival. The immediate question was whether it would continue passively to tolerate its enemies. A more fundamental issue was whether the anti-clerical spirit, now deeply rooted among the educated classes, would ever be prepared to accept willingly the recognition in the *Charte* of the Catholic, apostolic, and Roman religion as the official religion of France, and the close alliance between Church and state that was the natural corollary. A minor problem, but one which was to give the Restoration much trouble, was slurred over in the clause which recognized both the liberty of the press and the right of the government to repress its abuse.

When we turn to purely political issues, contradictions are equally apparent in the *Charte*, though here there was more scope for a compromise to be worked out in practice. The aim was to establish a constitutional but not a parliamentary monarchy. The king embodied the executive power and had the initiative in legislation; but a parliament composed of two chambers was to discuss and vote the laws and the taxes, and the Chamber of Deputies had the right of impeaching the king's ministers before the upper chamber. These provisions were illogical but reasonable. They were to prove quite workable and to give France a valuable apprenticeship in parliamentary government. The issue that had divided the *noblesse* in 1789, the creation of a house of peers, was settled without any dispute, and here perhaps the examples of Great Britain and of the institutions of the Empire were not without influence. An assembly of the highest dignitaries, lay, ecclesiastical, and military, of both the old regime and the Empire, nominated by the king, formed a decorative, impressive, and workable upper chamber.

The fundamental problems of the Restoration were, however, essentially extra-political in the narrower meaning of politics. Louis XVIII recognized clearly what they were when he wrote to his brother, in 1817, that he did not intend to be the king of a divided people. 'All the efforts of my government', he said, 'are directed to the effort to fuse the two peoples, who exist only too much in fact, into a single one.'

Unhappily the Hundred Days had broken the spell of general reconciliation which seemed for a moment to be operating in 1814.

A White Terror raged in the south before the central government was able to regain control. La Bourdonnaye, in the Chamber at Paris, demanded chains, executioners, tortures. 'Defenders of humanity', he cried, 'learn how to shed a few drops of blood to spare a torrent of it.' Doubtless to the disappointment of such real enthusiasts, the legal proceedings resulted only in a few thousand imprisonments. Fouché connived at the escape of many of those who had compromised themselves during the Hundred Days. Ney, bravest of the brave, whose execution was undoubtedly a political blunder, was given every opportunity of escaping before his trial, even though his desertion to Napoleon had been flagrant.

The first step out of the provisional for the Second Restoration was the election of a Chamber of Deputies. The government of Talleyrand and Fouché appointed the prefects and the presidents of the electoral colleges, and perhaps assumed that having chosen the makers of elections, the election was as good as made. But, not for the last time in the nineteenth century, it was shown that there were limits to what the administration could achieve by electoral management. Local notabilities dominated an election which took place in two stages, the primary electors having the task of choosing the actual electoral colleges. Out of a total electorate of 72,000, those who voted numbered 48,000. The result, which has never received a fully satisfactory explanation, was an overwhelmingly reactionary and royalist assembly, the famous Chambre introuvable. In the face of this striking repudiation by the electorate even the cleverness of Talleyrand and Fouché could do nothing and they faded from the scene. In their place Louis XVIII called on the duc de Richelieu, whose disinterested loyalty was well known, who had proved his capacity as an administrator in the service of Russia, where he had been governor of the newly conquered territory on the Black Sea, and who because of his long absence was uninvolved in any of the factions of the Emigration. Wellington said of him that his word was equal to a treaty. His colleagues, however, were weak, and the Chambre introuvable ungovernable. Louis XVIII has been praised for breaking with the reactionary elements which dominated it and at the same time blamed for rejecting, at the outset of his reign, the principle of parliamentary government; but the former was probably inevitable and the latter he had never accepted. The Chamber was dissolved in September 1816 and in the new elections the government of Richelieu obtained a working majority. Under him, by one of those remarkable financial recoveries which are a feature of French history, the indemnity imposed after the Hundred Days was paid off and the occupying armies withdrew in November 1818. Richelieu resigned in December 1818 but he had brought France back into the comity of nations.

The resignation of Richelieu, much more than the dissolution of 1816, was the proof that the regime was still a monarchical and not a parliamentary one, and that a minister could not hold office without the favour of the king. Louis XVIII was not ill disposed to the minister, but behind the scenes he was taking the advice of a personal favourite. This was Decazes, son of a notary of the Gironde. Decazes had become Prefect of Police for Paris after the Hundred Days, as such obtained access to the king, and completely won his devotion. 'Come to receive the tenderest embraces of thy friend, thy father, thy Louis', the king would write to him. Decazes has perhaps been unduly written down because of the way in which his political fortune was built up. If he had not an elevated character and was no great statesman, he was successful in reconciling the role of royal favourite with moderate concessions to the left. In the new government, of which he was virtual though not nominal head, he combined the offices of Police and the Interior. Where Richelieu's administration had rested on the centre but looked for support towards the right, Decazes, equally with a centre government, relied on the support of the left.

The difficulty for any such government was that the one strongly organized and coherent party in Parliament belonged to the right. This was the party of the Ultras or pure royalists. It looked towards the king's brother, Artois, and represented the purest ideas of the Counter-revolution. Its strength in the country came from the support of the secret society of the Chevaliers de la Foi. Its leader in the Chamber of Deputies was the able parliamentarian, Villèle, and in the Chamber of Peers it had Polignac, Montmorency, and Chateaubriand to speak for it. The paradox was that the pure royalists from the beginning found themselves in opposition to the king; the less pure royalists who supported him formed the political centre, with a right wing represented by Richelieu and a left wing by Decazes. The left proper, only gradually returning to the political arena after the fiasco of the Hundred Days, took cover under the title of Independents.

With the revival of political life had come also that of political thought. The chief theorist of the left was Benjamin Constant, who saw the safeguard of the liberal principles to which he was devoted in a parliamentary monarchy after the English fashion, and whose political thinking, possibly for that reason, has lacked in France the recognition it deserves. The centre-left found its theorists in the doctrinaires Royer-Collard, Barante, Guizot, de Broglie, Charles de Rémusat, who saw political life as a careful balancing of interests, and recognized no authority but that of law, or impartial reason, which however they tended to identify in practice with the interests of the socially dominant classes. The Ultras obtained doctrinal support from the writings of the theocrats, Joseph de Maistre, de Bonald, and Lamennais, for whom politics was the handmaid of religion and kings were the servants of the Pope, in whom was embodied the divine will on earth.

Political realities were far below this realm of high theory. They have to be discussed in terms of the membership of parliaments and cabinets, of party manœuvres, franchise adjustments, and electoral wangling. The *pays légal*, those who had the vote, was restricted to some 90,000 electors in a nation of well over twenty-six millions, the qualification being the payment of 300 francs in direct taxation. Since by far the greater proportion of the wealth of France was in the form of land, and it was in land that those who had made money chiefly tended to invest it, this was primarily a landowners' franchise. To be eligible to stand as a candidate it was necessary in addition to be subject to a tax of 1,000 francs and to be over forty years of age. The number of possible candidates in the whole of France was some 15,000 of the wealthiest men. Nothing very revolutionary, it might be thought, could emerge from such an electorate. An analysis of the last Chamber of Deputies of the Restoration gives 38·5 per cent higher officials, 14·8 per cent engaged in trade, finance, or industry, 5·2 per cent belonging to the liberal professions, and

41·5 per cent large landowners, apart from such members of the previous categories as were also landowners, as probably most were.

The large proportion of the deputies who had played a part in public life under the Revolution and the Empire is an indication that the Restoration assemblies were not likely to be wholly swayed by Ultra views; nor was there much chance for the left in the elections. But to obtain a reliable body of supporters the government had to resort to methods of electoral management such as had been used experimentally under the Directory and were to become classic in nineteenth-century France. Reducing the taxes of known opponents for the purpose of robbing them of the franchise was a common device. To prevent appeals against exclusions, the lists of electors might be posted up only at the last moment, at night, not in alphabetical order, and at a height which made them unreadable without a ladder. The prefects who managed the elections for the government saw to it that all government servants voted for the right candidate. Electoral meetings were prohibited. The electoral colleges were presided over by officials, and although the ballot was in theory secret, supporters of the government took care not to conceal their votes.

Once in the Chamber, the functions of the deputies were limited. The choice of ministers rested in the hands of the king, and the cabinet system was as yet only imperfectly evolved. Under Talleyrand, Richelieu, and Decazes there was an effective President of the Council, who co-ordinated the policy of the ministers. Villèle, on the other hand, when he became head of the government, adopted the practice of working alone with the king, and Charles X aspired to be himself the real leader of the ministers. The identification of the last of the Bourbons with the policy of his government was so close that it was impossible to prevent the fall of the government from bringing with it the abdication of the monarch.

In spite of the narrowness of the franchise and the control exercised by the government over elections, the multiplicity of parties stood in the way of stable administration during the Restoration. Decazes tried to conciliate the opposition, but when he went to the country in 1819 the result was merely an electoral victory for the left, in which even the former constitutional bishop and regicide,

Grégoire, was returned, it is true with the aid of ultra-royalist votes. This was a blow to Decazes, but the fatal event for him was the assassination, in February 1820, of the duc de Berry, as he was leaving the Opéra. It was an isolated crime but it gave an opening to all the enemies of the minister, and enabled them to force Louis XVIII reluctantly to abandon his favourite and recall Richelieu to office. To bring under control the reviving political activity, laws permitting the arrest of suspected persons, extending the censorship of the press, and conferring a double vote on the wealthier members of the electorate were passed. In September 1820 the birth of the posthumous son of the duc de Berry guaranteed the continuance of the Bourbon line.

The left now began to flirt with revolutionary movements. Representatives of small secret societies met under the chairmanship of La Fayette to discuss insurrectionary plans; but Richelieu, who was as well informed of these plans as the left-wing leaders themselves, took steps to make them aware of this fact and the embryo revolution was still-born. The international secret society of the Carbonari, which had perhaps as many as 40,000 members in France, was stirred into activity by the revolutions in Spain and Naples, but achieved nothing beyond a few petty local disturbances. The best known was the attempt of the four sergeants of La Rochelle to subvert their regiment. Denounced, they were arrested, tried, and executed. The left, however ineffectively, was thus abandoning the policy of compromise; the right was preparing to take over power; and the centre, on which Richelieu based his government, was fast disappearing.

France under the Restoration was not yet a parliamentary monarchy, and when the second Richelieu ministry fell, in 1822, it was again not because of a change in the balance of power in the Chamber but because the king had acquired a new favourite. Some years earlier a young woman named Zoë, Countess of Cayla, had sought the royal protection in a lawsuit against an 'unworthy spouse'. Beautiful, witty, and aged twenty-seven, Mme du Cayla won her suit and the royal affections at the same time. Given the age and infirmity of the king she could hardly become a royal mistress in the full sense of the term; but every Wednesday she visited the

Tuileries for a private game of chess with the king, during which the doors of the royal apartment were guarded; and every day she wrote the king a letter, in composing which she was assisted by Villèle. Not surprisingly, Villèle, who had entered the government in 1820, in September 1822 became President of the Council.

Villèle, a minor noble from Toulouse, short, ugly, intriguing, and ambitious, was the leader of the ultra-royalist party in the Chamber of Deputies, so that even without Mme du Cayla he would have been the appropriate minister for the royalist reaction. He was inexhaustible in his capacity for work, a master of detail, and unwilling to share his authority with anyone. Louis XVIII, now completely preoccupied with his health and Mme du Cayla, left the control of affairs almost entirely to his brother and successor, Artois, along with Villèle, whose great achievement was in the field of finance. Between 1822 and 1827 he put public finances in France on foundations which kept them sound and stable until the crisis of the twentieth century. The task of establishing a budgetary system and strict control of governmental expenditure, which had proved beyond the powers of the Controllers General of the *ancien régime*, but to which the Finance Ministers of Napoleon had made an important contribution, was now completed. This was perhaps the most important service of the Restoration to France. It was the return to peaceful international relations which made financial stability possible, of course. It is no accident that while the eighteenth and twentieth centuries, which were centuries of large-scale wars for France, were marked by instability in the national finances; the nineteenth century, with no really great and prolonged war between 1815 and 1914, was one of balanced budgets.

Peace after 1815 also brought with it a marked improvement in trade. According to one set of statistics French foreign trade more than doubled between 1814 and 1825. It is true that according to another set it remained stationary, but the former seems on the face of it the more likely. Altogether the Restoration gave France efficient and honest government, and, so long as Louis XVIII lived, moderation and a reasonable degree of stability, which endured long enough to prove that there was no inherent reason why it should have broken down.

CHAPTER TWO

CLERICALISM AND ANTI-CLERICALISM

T HE failure of the Restoration was not primarily in the field of
government, where it was weak, but in that of religion, where
it was strong. Although the succession of Charles X may
have precipitated the crisis, its beginnings can already be seen under
Louis XVIII. Europe, in the early years of the nineteenth century,
witnessed a widespread religious revival. This strongly affected the
French Church, in which there was now a zealous episcopate and a
lower clergy gradually growing in number and unexceptionable in
devoutness. Religious houses for women increased from 1,829 in
1815 to 2,875 in 1830. Orders for men were tolerated, though only
in the case of three missionary orders were they authorized by law,
but these also were increasing in number. The Jesuit-inspired Congregation engaged in energetic religious propaganda throughout
France. An attempt was even made to annul the Napoleonic Concordat and return to the relations between Church and state that had
prevailed under the *ancien régime*; but the terms of the Concordat —
and this is perhaps the ultimate judgment on it — were too favourable
for the Papacy to abandon and the negotiation for its revision proved
abortive.

The Gallicanism of the Restoration was an anachronism, as became quite evident after 1830, when there was no longer a king
with the sanctity of hereditary divine right on the throne. With
Bonald, de Maistre, Lamennais, force of argument and literary
talent were both on the side of the Ultramontanes. The religious
revival naturally worked to the benefit of Rome. Gallicanism
now stood for the authority of the French bishops, authoritarian
and often aristocratic, with all the enhanced power conferred on
them by the Concordat over the lower clergy, who could be transferred from parish to parish, or deprived of their office, at the
bishop's arbitrary will. No wonder that a habit of looking, or even

appealing, to Rome grew up among the clergy: they had no one else to appeal to.

Napoleon had attempted to use the Concordat to reduce the Church to the role of an instrument of the state: under the Restoration there seemed a danger that the state might be made the instrument of the Church. In the interests of religion the episcopate did not hesitate to call on the support of the administration. With the Ultras in power this tendency was intensified. The Panthéon, purged of the infidel remains of Voltaire and Rousseau, was given over to religious uses. Secondary education was placed, in 1821, under the supervision of the bishops. A high ecclesiastic, Mgr Frayssinous, was appointed Grand Master of the University. In 1824 the appointment of all teachers in primary schools was given to the episcopate. In 1822 two new press offences were created — criticism of the divine right of kings and outrage on religion. A law against sacrilege made the profanation of sacred vessels punishable with imprisonment for life, and in the case of profanation of the consecrated host with death, though in fact the law was never applied.

When Charles X, who succeeded to the throne in 1824, was crowned in the cathedral at Reims, it was with all the apparatus of the religious revival. The assembled multitude cried 'Vivat Rex in aeternum'; but it was noted when the king returned after the ceremony to Paris that his reception in the capital was distinctly lukewarm. Eternity was to last for five years.

While the depth and seriousness of the religious revival in France must not be underestimated, its limitations also should not be forgotten. Rationalism and anti-clericalism had driven too deeply into French soil to be easily uprooted. The intellectual life which had flourished under the *ancien régime* had been blighted but not killed by the frosts of the Revolution and the Empire. Now, in a milder, if still somewhat austere climate, it reburgeoned as in a new spring. Science continued its progress, uninfluenced by, and uninfluencing, the changing political scene. Lamarck, who had studied under Buffon, links the zoology of the encyclopedists with the evolutionary theories of the nineteenth century. Cuvier practically created palaeontology, and Ampère has been called the Newton of electricity.

The son of the great Carnot, Sadi Carnot, founded thermo-dynamics and Fresnel produced the wave theory of light.

History experienced a remarkable revival, amounting almost to a rebirth, under the Restoration. The famous École des Chartes was founded and the publication of the great collections of memoirs relating to the history of France was begun. Barante's *History of the Dukes of Burgundy* (1824–6) was as successful as a novel, and Augustin Thierry wrote a notable history of the Norman conquest of England (1825). Guizot's *Essais sur l'histoire de France* (1823) was followed by the six volumes of his lectures on modern history at the Sorbonne in 1828–30. As opposition became bolder, historians turned to more recent times with the histories of the French Revolution by Thiers in 1823–7 and Mignet in 1824.

Above all this was a period of rebirth in literature. The new romantic spirit which crossed the Channel with Walter Scott and the Rhine with Mme de Staël's *De l'Allemagne* (1810) was in the beginning religious, monarchical, hierarchic, its eyes turned backwards to the Middle Ages. Lamartine, Victor Hugo, Mérimée, Alfred de Vigny, Stendhal, Chateaubriand raised the flag of romanticism. The paintings of Géricault and Delacroix might have been conceived as illustrations of their writings. The new trend appeared in music with Weber, Rossini, Berlioz.

Literature was not at first hostile to the Restoration, which represented emancipation from the strait-jacket of the Empire and an age of poetry after prose. Louis XVIII, a patron of poetry, impressed by the merit of a young beginner in the art who had determined to do what few dared to attempt—make literature a career—gave him a pension of 1,000 francs, and so eased the first steps of Victor Hugo, whose writings were to be a changing illustration of his age. He was the son of a general of Napoleon, who had somehow picked up the title of count in the service of Joseph in Spain. After 1815 General Hugo, like so many others, transferred himself to the service of Louis XVIII, and by discovering a noble family of Lorraine with the same name, which had conveniently died out, annexed a more distinguished ancestry for himself. Victor Hugo was not only a poet but a vicomte; and in both capacities Catholic and royalist, writing poems on the death of the duc de Berry, the funeral of

Louis XVIII, the war in Spain, attending the *Sacre* of Charles X at Reims.

But despite its initial affiliations the new wine of romanticism was too heady to be confined in the old bottles of Restoration politics or Vatican religion. Literature has during the last two centuries traditionally migrated to the opposition in France. In the years that preceded the revolution of 1830 romanticism deserted Catholicism and monarchism and formed an alliance with liberalism, carrying into the camp of its new partner some of that passionate vigour and anti-rationalist spirit which it had perhaps in part acquired from its former ally. Victor Hugo's *Préface de Cromwell*, a more notable piece of writing than the unplayable drama it introduced, is an invocation to liberty; and in 1830, in the preface to *Hernani*, Hugo denounced the Ultras of all brands.

The clerical reaction continued without the support of many of its former adherents in the literary world. Charles X, who presided over a regime which was now throwing off the hesitations and compromises which had marked the reign of Louis XVIII, had forgotten little; in intellectual goods his mind was so sparsely furnished that there was little for him to forget. At sixty-seven still youthful in manner and child-like in mind, he was determined to be king. However, he continued to support Villèle, whose government had added foreign victory to its financial successes.

The civil war, which had begun in Spain in 1820, could not leave the sister Bourbon monarchy in France unconcerned. Villèle, who was anxious to avoid military intervention, managed to drive the extremer Montmorency out of the ministry on this issue; but his place was taken by Chateaubriand who adopted the same policy. Despite Villèle's reluctance, in 1823 a French army was despatched to restore the Bourbon King of Spain, an ill-omened venture which unexpectedly achieved rapid and complete success. The invasion was little more than a military promenade. By lavish expenditure the financier Ouvrard, in charge of supplies, bought both provisions and an almost unopposed passage through Spain. French intervention re-established the king on his throne without difficulty. Comparisons were drawn, naturally, between this speedy success and the disasters that had encompassed Napoleon's armies in Spain. Villèle was not the better disposed to Chateaubriand because his policy had proved successful, and when the Foreign Minister refused to support a governmental finance measure took the opportunity to secure his dismissal. This was a great mistake, for Chateaubriand flung himself into opposition with vigour, taking the influential *Journal des débats* with him. The Spanish war, thus, though successful, crystallized an incipient split in the ranks of the right, and promoted the growth of a royalist counter-opposition. This is in part attributable to the narrowness and inflexibility of Villèle; but it is difficult not to believe also that the royalists were so unaccustomed to the compromises necessary in government, and the nobility so deeply imbued with the Frondeur spirit, that opposition came naturally to them.

They had a material reason for dissatisfaction. Disappointed under Louis XVIII, with Charles X the émigrés expected at last to receive the fruit of their sacrifices in the form of the undoing of the revolutionary land settlement. Villèle gave them the laws on sacrilege, the press, and education, but they wanted something of greater substance. The solution Villèle found was to create 30 million francs in annual new *rentes*, representing the interest at 3 per cent on a capital nominally of a thousand million francs, at which the value of the confiscated property was calculated, in fact of about 630 millions. The former émigrés, or their heirs, now numbered some 70,000 and the indemnity to be divided between them came to an average of some 1,377 francs a year each. It did not satisfy their wishes, while it exacerbated the feelings of the great majority of persons of property who felt that in one way or another they were paying for it.

The propertied men who were aggrieved by the indemnity to the former émigrés included also those who were most suspicious of the clerical influences at work in the new reign. The outburst of anti-clerical propaganda which occurred in 1825 has been attributed to the subtle tactics of the liberal opposition, hoping to achieve by this means the electoral success which it had not been able to gain by more legitimate methods. All the measures in favour of the Church and religion were attributed to the influence of the Jesuit Congregation; the existence of the secret Chevaliers de la Foi was unknown to the general public. In fact, while the extent of the clerical reaction was exaggerated, the strength of anti-clerical feeling in France had also been underestimated. If the liberals were able to use the fear of clericalism to achieve political results that could not have been achieved by more direct methods in a country that was not very interested in politics, this is in itself proof of the strength of anti-clerical sentiment. It was the major current in a rising tide of hostility against Charles X and his government. What two and a half years of Ultra rule had done was shown in March 1827, when the king, reviewing the National Guard of Paris composed largely of the well-to-do middle class, was greeted with cries of 'Down with the Jesuits!', 'Down with the ministers!', 'Vive la liberté de la presse!' It was hardly possible to impose any sanction in reply except to dissolve the National Guard.

Meanwhile the extreme Ultras had been becoming increasingly discontented with what they regarded as the excessive moderation of Villèle. A naval intervention in the Greek struggle for independence, which resulted in the successful engagement of Navarino in 1827, had little repercussion in France. If Villèle was to remain in office, he would have to try to secure a change in the composition of the Chamber of Deputies; but after elections held in November 1827 the government found itself with some 160 to 180 supporters in the new house, against an approximately equal liberal opposition, and with a group of 60 to 80 extremists forming a royalist counter-opposition on its right flank. Villèle had now no choice but to resign. The king appointed a ministry of technical experts, without any President of the Council, though the new Minister of the Interior, Martignac, was its spokesman in the Chambers and is often referred to as its head. This government offered some minor concessions to the left, especially in matters of education; but it was clear that it would not be more than a stop-gap. Charles X was determined not to compromise with the liberal opposition, and if the Villèlists and the royalist counter-opposition could be brought to work together a majority of the right seemed still possible.

The fall of the last Bourbon king of France was so little determined by the nature of things, that in spite of the acute struggle over clericalism it took almost inconceivable imbecility on the part of Charles X and his minister to bring it about. For the new king also had his favourite. This was Polignac, his 'dear Jules'. In secret correspondence with Polignac by the back-stairs of the palace, a new ministry was arranged. Jules de Polignac, a prisoner of Napoleon from 1802 to 1814, was an *exalté* with no grasp of political realities. To him was added La Bourdonnaye, who had been identified with the White Terror of 1815, as Minister of the Interior, and Bourmont, who had deserted Napoleon on the eve of Waterloo, as Minister of War. At the Ministry of Justice was Courvoisier, a recent convert from infidelity to Catholicism, whose chief political guide was the Apocalypse. The government thus oddly constituted took office in August 1829. For six months it proceeded to do nothing, while the opposition prepared itself for resistance. Under the patronage of La Fayette, the society *Aide-toi le ciel t'aidera* organized electoral committees. The students of Paris formed a republican society called *Jeune France*. Inspired by Talleyrand and organized and financed by the banker Lafitte, the Orleanists made their preparations and founded a new paper, the *National*, edited by the liberal historians, Thiers and Mignet.

While the forces of the left were gaining coherence, the ministry was becoming increasingly incoherent. Except for Polignac it was completely renewed, with ministers whose names are not worth recording. The Chamber was dissolved and elections were held in June and July 1830. The customary methods of administrative pressure were employed, and the king issued a personal appeal to the electors to support the official candidates. All was in vain: the opposition won 274 seats against 143 for the government, and 11 of doubtful allegiance. The Polignac ministry had been decisely rejected by the *pays légal*. Everything would now depend on whether the king was prepared to accept the verdict of the electorate and appoint a President of the Council who could work with the new Chamber.

Charles X and Polignac had no such intention. Divine right could not make compromises. Moreover they wore fresh laurels of victory, won in the colonial field, on their brows. After Napoleon the French overseas empire was an attenuated one. In 1815 France possessed five trading stations in India, the isle Bourbon (formerly La Réunion), Saint-Louis and Gorée in Senegal, the small West Indian islands of Guadeloupe and Martinique, Guiana in South America, and the rocky islets of Saint-Pierre and Miquelon off Newfoundland, chiefly valuable because of the fishing rights that went with them. It was not much. The Restoration picked up the scanty and broken threads of French colonial policy, resuming rather the traditions of power politics of the *ancien régime* than the more liberal if muddled policies of the Revolution; there was nothing to inherit from Napoleon. Expansion began in Senegal and a foothold was won in Madagascar; but the major achievement of the restored Bourbons was the result of the Polignac ministry's need for prestige: the expeditions to Spain and Greece were followed, in 1830, by one against Algiers. Efficiently organized and well led by Bourmont, anxious to retrieve his reputation, in three weeks it achieved complete success; the foundation stone of the French North African Empire had been laid under the last and least considered of the legitimate sovereigns.

News of the victory at Algiers reached Paris on July 9th. Charles X and Polignac, encouraged by this success abroad, proceeded to take the steps necessary to reverse their electoral defeat at home. On July 10th Polignac produced the first draft of proposals which, after discussion in the King's Council, were issued on July 25th as the Four Ordinances. These prohibited the publication of any journal or pamphlet of less than twenty-five pages without official authorization; dissolved the Chamber which had just been elected; restricted the effective use of the franchise to the wealthiest 25 per cent of the existing electors; and convoked the electoral colleges to choose a new Chamber.

The first step in opposition was taken by the journalists, led by Thiers and the *National*. They issued a manifesto calling on France to resist. Shops and workshops in Paris were closed on July 26th: the king, as though to model himself on Louis XVI, spent the day hunting. Polignac, who in his blind infatuation did not for a moment expect the opposition to pick up the gage of battle which he did not even realize that he had thrown down, had taken no military precautions. Indeed the best troops, to the number of 40,000, were in Algiers. On July 27th, when it began to dawn even on Polignac that the situation was not quite normal, Marmont was put in charge of the garrison of Paris. On July 28th rioting began in the streets. A number of deputies met and sent a deputation to Polignac which he refused to see. By July 29th, Marmont having found it necessary to concentrate his troops, Paris was in the hands of the rioters, who had lost some 1,800 killed against 200 among the soldiers in the course of the fighting. The deputies now decided to accept the leadership of the revolution to prevent it from falling into the hands of extremists, and the Orleanist Lafitte joined other deputies in a self-elected municipal council, the next day to promote itself to the rank of provisional government. Three days of street fighting—*les trois glorieuses*—had been sufficient to overthrow the restored monarchy.

On July 30th Charles X at last recognized that something had happened and that concessions were necessary; but already on the walls of Paris was the placard, drawn up by Thiers and Mignet, calling on the people to place the Duke of Orleans on the throne. The self-chosen provisional government invited him to become lieutenant-general of the kingdom. Orleans, who had been hesitating at a safe distance from Paris, accepted and on August 1st appointed provisional ministers. Meanwhile Charles X, threatened by the populace of Versailles, had taken flight to Rambouillet. There he himself appointed Orleans lieutenant-general and abdicated in favour of his own grandson, *l'enfant du miracle*. Orleans himself still had some legitimist scruples, and if he had accepted this solution it might have been better for France and better perhaps in the long run for himself. The monarchical principle would have been preserved, the fatal cleavage between legitimists and Orleanists averted, and a parliamentary government set up in the name of the legitimate line. But the Orleanists had waited and intrigued too long for this moment to give up the prize at last within their grasp. Orleans convoked the Chambers and announced the abdication of Charles X, without any reference to his grandson. The fallen king slowly made his way with the royal family to Cherbourg, where he dismissed his bodyguard and took ship for England.

The Restoration had failed: this does not prove that it was from the beginning inexorably doomed to failure. On the contrary, the Revolution of 1830 seems at first impression rather the result of a series of accidents, and above all of the obstinacy of Charles X, who went from blunder to blunder as though driven by a blind fate, or as though the little sense there had ever been in that addled pate had entirely vanished with age. He was such a nonentity as to be hardly worth a revolution, and indeed, looking behind the passing events of 1830, one can see that it was not really directed against him; it was against the anachronistic reappearance of a *noblesse* which believed that the eighteenth century had never ended and a clergy which, since the eighteenth century was, so far as the Church was concerned, a rather unfortunate episode, looked back to the century of the Compagnie du Saint Sacrement, Bossuet, and the Revocation of the Edict of Nantes. On the other hand, an important section of the educated classes in France, even if they thought that religion might be good for the masses, did not intend that priests should rule, or that their own sons should be educated by them. They turned against a regime in which the influence of the Church seemed to be increasingly dominant.

They also found that the Restoration was robbing them of one of the chief perquisites resulting from the Revolution. The new aristocracy of office created by the Revolution and Napoleon found its ranks swollen after 1815 by an unwelcome accession of strength from *ancien régime* families, who joined in the competition for even the humblest official appointments, and who, because of their ancestry and loyalty to the crown, had what seemed an unfair advantage in the game. The unemployed educated proletariat, searching for a career and especially concentrated in the student population of Paris, which has been wrongly seen as a factor in 1789, was perhaps a reality by 1830. At a higher social level the bankers and businessmen of the Chaussée d'Antin looked with jealousy on the aristocratic exclusiveness of the faubourg Saint-Germain. The monarchy, which might have bridged the gulf between ancient names and new fortunes, in the person of Charles X allowed its policies to be dictated and its councils to be monopolized by clergy and *noblesse*. At the same time, inconsistently, it attributed the franchise exclusively to men of wealth. It is true that this was mainly wealth in the form of land, but the extent to which land had passed into the possession of new men was perhaps not realized. Only this can explain the fact that the Restoration lost the support of even such a restricted electorate.

One thing more was needed to make a revolution possible: a mob to riot in the streets of Paris. Economic conditions supplied the material to fill this gap. The population of France had increased by nearly two and a half million between 1815 and 1830, without any marked increase in agricultural or industrial productivity in these years. After a short economic recession in 1817, a new and severer crisis began in 1826 and was to last until 1832. In 1828, out of 224,000 workers in the department of the Nord 163,000 were receiving some form of charitable assistance. That misery alone does not make revolutions is suggested by the significant fact that the populace provided insurrectionary mobs only in Paris, where the political agitation was concentrated.

Having won Paris with the aid of the mob, the journalists and politicians speedily brought the disturbances under control. The *noblesse* as a whole had perhaps not put up much of a fight in the first Revolution, outside Brittany and the Vendée. In 1830 they offered no resistance at all. In 1789 and the subsequent years at least they fled abroad to start a counter-revolution; in 1830 they merely gave up their jobs and took refuge in that abstention from public life which has been called *l'émigration intérieure*, which robbed France of the services of a host of families whose position and traditions called on them to contribute to the ruling elite, but who had learnt under the bureaucracy of an absolute monarchy to disassociate rights from duties and who had ceased to be a governing class while remaining an aristocracy.

CHAPTER THREE

THE FOUNDATION OF THE JULY MONARCHY

I N 1830 a political movement which had begun as an attempt to force Charles X to dismiss an unpopular minister turned into a revolution. The republican leaders, who now re-entered the political arena with the Paris mob behind them, were determined that the monarchy should disappear with the monarch. They had a ready-made candidate for president of the republic they believed they were about to establish in the person of the Commander of the National Guard, La Fayette, that distinguished relic of 1789, who was far too ingenuous and well-intentioned, and convinced of other people's good intentions, ever to succeed in politics. If a republic had been possible in 1830 he would have made an admirable president, but to the politicians, financiers, and men of property who had led the campaign against clericalism, the émigrés, Polignac, and Charles X, the Republic was still a name of terror. La Fayette was to be, in 1830 as in 1789, a mere cathartic agent, who precipitated events without really sharing in them.

The only practical alternative to a republic seems to us so obvious that there is a temptation to believe that the revolution must have been encompassed for the purpose of bringing it about. For the third time the shadow of an Orleanist conspiracy appears on the stage of history, and undoubtedly the Orleanist alternative to the Bourbons had been envisaged by some during the Restoration. There is no evidence, however, of the existence of any real conspiracy. The change in the dynasty was not a consciously calculated result of the 1830 Revolution: it was a pragmatic response to largely fortuitous circumstances.

The incoherence of the July Revolution was demonstrated in its first government. La Fayette and the *conventionnel* Dupont de l'Eure represented the Revolution, Sébastiani and Gérard, Napoleonic generals, the Empire; Guizot and baron Louis had served Louis XVIII, the banker Lafitte and the journalist Thiers were active in the Orleanist interest, Casimer-Périer and the duc de Broglie had been less committed opponents of the Bourbons.

There is little significance in this *olla podrida* of a government. More important in the long run than those who were included was the fact of those who were excluded, or excluded themselves. Each of the successive revolutions in modern France has eliminated a section of the political personnel. In the 1830 Chamber of Deputies, 52 members refused to take the oath to the new king and 68 others lost their seats. There was a holocaust in the administration—20 of the 38 members of the Conseil d'État, 76 prefects, 196 sub-prefects, 393 mayors or deputies, were dismissed. Of 75 generals, 65 were removed from the active list. Practically the whole diplomatic corps was changed.

This was not enough for the more violent revolutionaries, who were determined on revenge for the bloodshed of the streets and called for blood in return. The government would have been very glad to forget all about revenge, but under pressure from public opinion it had to bring the last ministers of Charles X to trial before the peers. While the National Guard, or at least its more advanced members, surrounded the Chamber and threatened lynch law, the accused ministers were got away by a trick to Vincennes. In their absence they were sentenced to life imprisonment and released a few years later.

To the new king and the more conservative among his supporters, the great danger seemed indeed to be the National Guard and its commander La Fayette. Aged as he was, he remained the symbol of revolution, but not for long. When his proposals, including a generous extension of the suffrage and a ministry of the left, were rejected, he resigned. The National Guard was reorganized by a law of March 1831 which confined effective membership to those who paid direct taxation; and although its officers were elected, its administration and finance were put under the control of government officials. It was to be the bulwark of the regime—or so they thought.

The hopes of a great international revolution, which have always accompanied domestic revolution in France, were also to be frustrated.

The July Revolution had sparked off a Belgian revolt against the Dutch. But if the left saw this as the opportunity to reverse the decisions of 1815 and renew the conquests of the First Republic, Louis-Philippe knew that the other powers would never tolerate a French annexation of Belgium. He believed that Great Britain might be persuaded to accept an independent Belgium, and appointed Talleyrand ambassador in London to implement this policy. He accepted the perpetual neutrality of the new state—envisaged as a safeguard against France—to win British support, and he resisted manfully the temptation presented by the offer of the new throne of Belgium to his son, the duc de Nemours. The success of his policy was demonstrated when, in August 1831, the Dutch king, rejecting the decisions of an international conference, launched his army against Belgium. Louis-Philippe was able, with British approval, to dispatch an expeditionary force which preserved Belgian independence.

The conservative nature of the July Revolution was marked from the start and embodied in the terms of the new constitutional Charter. It could hardly have been otherwise when the Chamber which drew up the Charter of 1830 was the last elected, on the narrow Restoration franchise, under Charles X, minus the ultraroyalists. There was inevitably a breach with the divine-right monarchy, and if the constitutional changes were more marked in symbols than in positive institutional arrangements, those who made them knew that men are governed by symbols. The new king would have been Philip VII or Louis XIX if he had succeeded legitimately to the throne; instead he became king as Louis-Philippe. In recognition of the fact that he was one of the new national sovereigns of the nineteenth century he took the designation—already given to Louis XVI in 1789—of *roi des Français* instead of *roi de France*. And that he was the heir of the Revolution and not of the Bourbons was shown by the return to the tricolore, in place of the white flag and the fleur-de-lys, the personal emblems of the dispossessed dynasty. Louis-Philippe had fought under the flag of the Revolution at Jemappes. According to a story, when he first appeared in revolutionary Paris and was greeted with cries of 'À bas les Bourbons!', Thiers and Mignet rapidly produced a placard announcing, 'Ce n'est pas un Bourbon, c'est un Valois'. This was nonsense: his ancestry was nothing to the point. His raison d'être was to stand between France and a republic.

Yet the principle of popular sovereignty was tacitly admitted. The Charter was not a concession granted (*octroyé*) by the king, as in 1814, but a declaration of the rights of the nation. Apart from this, the changes made in it were significant, but hardly revolutionary. Catholicism was no longer to be 'the religion of the state', but the religion 'professed by the majority'. The power of suspending or dispensing with laws was specifically taken away from the king, who also had to share the initiative in legislation with parliament. Censorship was to be abolished for ever: which meant that journalists in future were, with certain qualifications, to be allowed to publish before they were damned.

The sessions of the upper chamber were to be public, though when the Charter was drawn up views on its future composition were too contradictory to allow more to be said than that the question of the peerage would be re-examined later. The interests of the king in this matter coincided with left-wing opinion, and a law of December 1831 suppressed the hereditary peerage and made the upper chamber in effect a house of royal nominees. This was a more important decision than might be thought: aristocratic France was doubtless already dead of the kind of pernicious anaemia which had been sapping it for centuries, but this was the last nail in its coffin. The 'Corinthian capitals of polished society' had been finally knocked away, and their removal left the bare structure of power exposed in all its rather unlovely nakedness. Perhaps those, like Guizot and Broglie, who opposed the measure, were not wrong in fearing its social and political implications. The government of France could now be seen to be a combination of bureaucracy and plutocracy. The legitimist gentry and aristocracy withdrew into their manor-houses, or the salons and inner courts of the faubourg Saint-Germain, and abandoned public service of all kinds, though they returned to the army later in the century. Political power was shared by the king and the Chamber of Deputies. What this meant in practice can be seen from an examination of the electoral laws. The age of eligibility as a deputy was lowered from forty to thirty, and the *cens*, or electoral qualification, to the payment of 200 francs annually in direct taxation. In this respect it seemed that a revolution had been made to raise the total electorate of France to a number estimated in 1846 as 241,000, some 2·8 per cent of the male population over the age of twenty-one. Moreover, since even the great Revolution had never ventured to introduce such a frightful socialistic measure as an income tax in France, direct taxation fell mainly on real estate. There-fore about 90 per cent of the tiny electorate of Orleanist France, it has been calculated, obtained their qualification from taxes on prop-erty, the remaining 10 per cent representing commerce, industry, and the professions. The so-called 'bourgeois monarchy' was in fact an oligarchy of landowners. In the absence of a more detailed analysis of Orleanist society, we must not read too much into this statement; but at least it suggests that the landed wealth of the coun-try was no longer mainly in the hands of old legitimist families, but partly in those of a class of new men, who had doubtless made their wealth in many ways in the course of the *ancien régime* and the Revolution. Their figures, like that of père Grandet, dominate the novels of Balzac. Their new wealth had largely been invested in land, and they were now a well-established propertied class, with a suffi-ciently strong sense of its own interests to use the revolution of 1830 to oust the Legitimist-clericalist regime of the restored Bourbons, and at the same time prevent the republicans from acceding to power.

The narrow oligarchical pattern extended from central to local institutions. The Municipal Law of 1831 established elected councils, but on such a narrow basis that a town of 5,000 inhabitants might have only 300 electors, one of 15,000 could have 700; and towns of 100,000 might reach the figure of 3,000 electors. Even these petty municipal oligarchies were kept under strict government control. The *maires* continued to be chosen by the central government for the larger towns, and by the prefect for the rest.

It was not to be expected that France would at once settle down peacefully after the disorders of 1830. The economic depression continued into 1832, and while in Paris political interests called the tune, in Lyons, always more influenced by economic considerations, industrial disturbances continued. Although the silk weavers of Lyons had not suffered from unemployment, the prices paid by the merchants for their handwork had been greatly reduced and the tariff to which they were accustomed was abandoned. In October 1831 a mass demonstration won the restoration of a minimum tariff of payments, but it was soon repudiated by the merchants. In November, at a review of the National Guard of Lyons, ill-feeling developed between the wealthier members with an elaborate uniform and the artisans in their ordinary clothes. The next day a crowd of several hundred weavers started to go round the town proclaiming, and enforcing, a strike. They were fired on and eight were killed. This was the normal pattern for a revolutionary outbreak in nineteenth-century France. It set fire to Lyons. The weavers rose as a man, barricaded the streets, descended from their quarter on the hillside of the Croix-Rousse. They were joined by companies of the National Guard and in pitched battle with the royal troops captured Lyons. Having won their victory, they policed the city, set guards on the Monnaie and the Recette Générale, and repressed all looting, for these were Lyonnais, sober and serious workers, master craftsmen, men of order. But of course not quite of the prevailing order, as the government realized. A large body of troops was despatched to Lyons, its National Guard was dissolved, the prefect—who had been too reasonable—was dismissed, and the tariff of prices revoked. The workers of Lyons were crushed, but not for good.

In Paris, at the same time, the effervescence assumed a different form. As always, political and ideological motivation was more evident than economic in the capital. There it had not been forgotten that the threat which had stimulated the July Revolution had been clericalism, and the struggle of clericalism and anti-clericalism took a little while after 1830 to settle down. At the outset a group of ardent Catholics had been stirred up by the July Revolution to envisage the possibility of a reconciliation of religion with liberty and to found a journal to advocate this. The leaders—it is not certain if there were any followers—were Lamennais, by now a republican, Lacordaire, a liberal, and Montalembert, a romantic medievalist. Their paper, *L'Avenir*, founded in October 1830, was abandoned in November 1831. While it lasted it had advocated, among other proposals, the abolition of censorship, freedom of education, universal suffrage, and the separation of Church and state. In 1832 the

Encyclical *Mirari vos* pronounced the wickedness of all these ideas and the editors submitted to the verdict of the Pope.

Anti-clericalism was less easily brought under control, and it is not certain that all those in positions of power wanted it to be controlled. Whatever its deeper roots, anti-clericalism naturally appears above ground wherever the aspiration of priests to political power and the exercise of control over the life of society brings them into conflict with secular interests. The Church in France had overbid its hand in the 'twenties, so naturally it lost some tricks in the 'thirties.

Anti-clerical sentiments formed the excuse for a violent outbreak on February 14th, 1831, when a Mass for the duc de Berry, assassinated ten years earlier, was held at the Church of Saint-Germain-l'Auxerrois, with white flags and fleurs-de-lys, a congregation of devout legitimists, and rows of aristocratic carriages with armorials waiting outside. It is difficult to believe that a crowd of rioters also found themselves there by accident, or that they unintentionally allowed the legitimists to depart without more than an ugly scene, before beginning the real attack. A detachment of the National Guard which now arrived escorted the priests away through the mob, which was left to pull down and destroy images, crucifixes, and all the destructible furnishings of the church. Some of the rioters then made their way to the archbishop's palace, next to Notre Dame, where a fine thirteenth-century building and a great library offered the prospect of even more enjoyable destruction. Books are always a temptation: they burn so well. The task was broken off when night fell, but was resumed the next day till the whole building had been demolished. In true revolutionary tradition mock religious rites were performed in the ruins. Similar scenes were witnessed in other towns, the authorities remaining neutral. Then, as rapidly as it had flared up, the agitation died down. The episode is a curious one. It is difficult to believe in the spontaneity of the outburst, but who organized it, and how did it spread through France? How far was there a deep-rooted and extensive anti-clericalism among the urban population, and how far was it artificially incited, the work of a mere handful stirred up by bourgeois anti-clericals? If we knew more about the provincial movements it might be possible at least to attempt to answer these questions.

Even the legitimists contributed to the prevailing disorder after 1830, with one feeble attempt to reverse the decision of July. The duchesse de Berry, mother of the legitimist heir, the young comte de Chambord, was the heroine of this romantic adventure. She travelled in disguise across France from Marseilles, finding, like Bonnie Prince Charlie in similar circumstances, much profession of loyalty but little willingness to take up arms, until she reached the old centre of royalist resistance, the Vendée. There, a small rising was easily crushed. The duchess escaped and went into hiding but was captured later in the year. It then gradually became impossible for her to hide the fact that she was pregnant. Obviously this could not be a second *enfant du miracle*, and she had in the end to confess to the awful truth, that she was re-married to a minor Italian count. This ended the political significance of the romantic duchess. As a royalist supporter said, a mistake might have been forgiven the duchesse de Berry, a marriage excluded her from the royal family. This pathetic episode was the sum total of the counter-revolution after 1830: things had certainly changed since 1789.

The last outbreak of violence linked with the July Revolution came in 1832, when the funeral of General Lamarque, a former Napoleonic general and a popular member of the Chamber of Deputies, was used by republicans and Bonapartists—to whom legitimists joined themselves—as the excuse for an attempted insurrection in Paris. The army and the National Guard, both now well under government control, suppressed it at the cost of some 800 killed and wounded. After this it was clear that the revolutionary movement was over; indeed this miserable affair looks forward to the street affrays of the Third Republic rather than back to the great *journées* of 1789 and 1792.

The new regime might not have survived its growing pains if it had had to rely on its first government. Its leading figure, in so far as there was one, was the banker Lafitte, but his conduct of affairs was so notoriously incompetent that he had to resign. Since France could not yet afford the weak government that Louis-Philippe really preferred, power fell into the hands of the most forceful of the existing ministers. This was Casimir-Périer, who declared that his policy was to combine order with liberty; but there is no doubt that the emphasis was on the former. France, he said, must be governed. In the elections of July 1831, Casimir-Périer made it clear that his government had no intention of being neutral. The prefects were instructed to use all their influence to secure the return of suitable candidates, though everyone was so new and untried that they found it difficult to know who was suitable. However, the great majority in the new chamber was conservative and prepared to accept a strong hand so long as there seemed any danger of reaction or further revolution.

Of the two bankers who had been patrons, and perhaps financiers, of the liberal movement under Charles X, Lafitte inclined to the left, whereas Périer, who regarded 1830 as not a change of system but only of person, was a leader of the 'resistance' to any liberal concessions. Naturally, whereas Lafitte has left the reputation of a weak minister, Périer was able to justify his reputation as a strong man. The new President of the Council also found his task of pacifying France facilitated by the ending of the economic slump. Louis-Philippe, however, whose position was now becoming securer, was not altogether happy with a strong minister who kept him out of cabinet discussions, and it was perhaps rather a relief to him when the cholera epidemic, failing to observe the strict class discrimination of the Périer regime, carried off his Prime Minister in May 1832.

Although the struggle to put curbs on the revolution had now in effect been won, the republican secret societies were still agitating and there was a good deal of repressed popular discontent. The government determined to take the offensive. The popular associations were attacked by direct prohibitions, by extending penalties from the organizers to all members, and by transferring trials arising out of breaches of the laws against political associations to courts without juries. The debate on these proposals suggested that the prime motive behind the new law was the fear of political revolution. The insecurity of the regime was still such that all opposition seemed dangerous. Resistance, declared Guizot, is turned by the opposition leaders into revolution. Thiers described the opposition as an illegal government, prepared to use the associations to overthrow the legal government. And in fact the Society of the Rights of Man was planning an armed rising, and a secret committee was formed to organize it. But in the event the government itself was responsible for provoking the armed outbreak.

Lyons was once again the scene of the major disturbances. In February 1834 the silk merchants again reduced their rate of payment to the weavers. A ten-day strike failed and the silk weavers returned to work. The city was peaceful when the government arrested six leaders of the strike, and anticipating the opposition that this action was bound to arouse, sent 10,000 troops to occupy the strategic positions and chief buildings of Lyons. Sporadic rioting broke out, and as so often, the authorities only offered a weak resistance until the insurrection had thoroughly developed. This is often attributed to callous calculation; it seems more likely to have been due to a natural slowness to react, and perhaps to mere stupidity. The rising, having been allowed to develop, was then ruthlessly crushed. A merciless struggle went on for four days. The royal troops gradually forced their way back into the town, while the forts on the outskirts bombarded the rebel-held quarters.

At the news of the revolt of Lyons troubles also broke out in many other towns, but only in Paris was there an attempt at actual insurrection. There, in the quarter of the Marais, some desperate republicans and their followers erected barricades. But Paris had a large garrison, and a National Guard which feared social revolution and the revolt of the workers more than anything else. They descended on the tiny nucleus of revolution, crushed it without difficulty, and proceeded to engage in a little private massacre in the rue Transnonain. Daumier made one of his most pathetically effective cartoons of it. The government might defend the actions of its supporters on the plea that it was just that those who had appealed to force should perish by force. Another view might be that what had happened in Paris was an attempt to exploit the genuine economic grievances of the workers by a small faction of political republicans. And yet a third view is that the republicans had played into the hands of the authorities, who were not sorry to have the chance of damning the workers of Lyons as revolutionary republicans for their attempt to defend their standard of living, and the republicans of Paris as social revolutionaries because of their connections with the workers' movement.

After the failure of this pathetic attempt at a revolution, out of 3,000 prisoners rather over 100 were selected for trial—a moderate measure of repression compared with the sequel to social struggles later in the century, when class hatred had become much more intense. And after the danger, or supposed danger, was over, public sympathies began to veer on to the side of the accused, whose trial was thoroughly mismanaged. Twenty-eight of them escaped from prison; and apart from a number of sentences to deportation or imprisonment, most of the prisoners were only condemned to periods of police supervision. On the whole, in spite of the massacre of the rue Transnonain, the republicans had discredited themselves by the events of 1834 and the government had behaved with comparative moderation.

An attempted assassination of Louis-Philippe in July 1835, by a bomb explosion which killed several National Guards, other persons round the king, and spectators, strengthened the hand of the government further, for the assassin, a Corsican named Fieschi, had been assisted by two members of the Society for the Rights of Man. Steps were taken after this to check the incitements to violence in the republican press. The Charter of 1830 had abolished censorship, but this did not mean that the government was powerless in its relations with journalists. Political journals had still to deposit a substantial sum as caution money. Conviction on such charges as offering an affront to the king or holding the government up to contempt might bring a fine of 1,000 francs, accompanied by a term of imprisonment for the editor. On the other hand, though juries were chosen only from the wealthy class which possessed the right of franchise, they had a regrettable tendency to acquit journalists charged with press offences. Louis-Philippe and his government continued to be showered with insults, and portrayed in venomous caricature by Daumier, Grandville, and other less brilliant but equally bitter cartoonists.

Casimir-Périer, from whom Louis-Philippe had been relieved by the hand of fate, was succeeded by a 'doctrinaire' ministry, including the able conservative peer Broglie, Thiers, and Guizot, with a 'non-political' general, Marshal Soult, as nominal head. This was still much too strong a government for a king who wanted to hold the reins himself. A palace intrigue eliminated Broglie in April 1834, but after nearly a year of confusion he returned in March 1835, making the condition, like Casimir-Périer, that the cabinet should not meet in the presence of the king. But Broglie's authoritarian style was as little to the liking of the Parliament as of the king, and in February 1836 he lost his majority again. Louis-Philippe had now to split Thiers and Guizot, which he did by inviting Thiers to form a ministry. It lasted only six months; the king broke with Thiers over foreign policy, and then called on Molé, a peer who had served Bonaparte and the Bourbons in turn, and was equally willing to serve the house of Orleans. He was an official and a capable one, not a statesman; but it was an official that Louis-Philippe wanted, for, as he put it in rather unkingly language, 'c'est moi qui mène le fiacre.' The series of events that began in July 1830 may be said to have been completed now, with all political or social opposition to the new monarchy driven underground, and Louis-Philippe himself the real head of his own government.

CHAPTER FOUR

LOUIS-PHILIPPE

THE one and only Orleanist king came to the throne at the age of fifty-seven. He was already sixteen in 1789 and had been educated in the sentimental philanthropy of the *ancien régime* by Mme de Genlis. His presence in the armies of the Revolution provided Orleanist propagandists with the material for a military reputation, which somehow never stuck. An émigré in 1793, as the son of Philippe Égalité and an officer of the revolutionary army, he could hardly seek refuge among the allies. Wanderings in neutral countries, such as Switzerland, Scandinavia, the United States, and disagreements with Great Britain, occupied the next twenty years, leaving him a man of neither Revolution nor Counter-revolution, a suitable king for a regime of the *juste milieu*; leaving him also with a love of wealth and power which were concealed beneath habits of bourgeois modesty. What he lacked was style. Louis-Philippe had neither the decadent grace of the eighteenth century nor the romantic panache of the nineteenth. He was gossiping, fussy, undignified, and with his pear-shaped face a gift to caricaturists. Above all, he was already ageing when he came to the throne. The skill and determination he showed in 1830–1 too soon turned into smug complacency and self-satisfied intrigue.

Yet Louis-Philippe had a good deal over which he might well feel self-satisfied. He had a model queen in Marie-Amélie of the Sicilian Bourbons, and five sons—Joinville, Orleans, Nemours, Aumale, Montpensier—handsome, distinguished, able in their different fields, and damned for ever by the wit who called them a family of brilliant second lieutenants. Within ten years he had established himself so firmly on the throne that his dynasty seemed secure. Legitimism had ceased to be a political force; republicanism was discredited among all proper-minded people and reduced to an underground intrigue; and that Bonapartism was not to be taken seriously had been shown when it could not even make a bid for power in 1830, as well as by the Strasbourg fiasco of Louis Napoleon in 1836, of which more later.

Hopes of a Napoleonic restoration apparently ended with the death of the young duc de Reichstadt, son and heir of the emperor, *l'Aiglon* of romantic legend, in 1832. So innocuous did the Bonapartist legend seem, that the regime even tried to exploit it. Thiers filled in the gaps in his political activity with the composition of his *History of the Consulate and the Empire*. In 1833 Napoleon I was put back on the Vendôme column, though in civil attire. And in 1840 Joinville was sent to fetch the emperor's remains from St Helena for reburial in the Invalides. The second fiasco of Louis Napoleon, this time in the form of a day excursion to Boulogne in 1840, showed once more that Bonapartism was not a force in France. Orleanist politics could pursue their placid if erratic course undisturbed by any fear of rapids ahead.

The absence of any effective nucleus of opposition was perhaps one reason for the weakness of Louis-Philippe's governments. The other was his own aversion from ministers with policies of their own. Molé was obviously no more than a stop-gap. With all the great figures in parliament ranged against him, his tenure of office was uncertain. In 1839 he appealed to the electorate, and in spite of all that official pressure could do, lost some thirty seats. The king had to look for a successor. He was in the dilemma of George III: weak ministers could not control parliament, and strong ministers pursued their own policies. Soult reappeared transiently, then Thiers, but once again foreign policy was the apple of discord. Since 1832 Louis-Philippe had been the effective manager of French foreign policy. He prided himself on his knowledge of Europe and his success in coping with its problems, not without some justification. He had kept the peace, brought about a *rapprochement* between France and the other great powers, played his part in solving the Belgian problem satisfactorily, and maintained French prestige.

Unfortunately he had given one hostage to fortune by encouraging Mehemet Ali's revolt against the authority of the Sultan. French opinion, tending to divide the world between friends of France and others, enthusiastically supported the Pasha of Egypt.

But the success of Mehemet Ali, when war with Turkey broke out again in 1839, alarmed the other great powers, which in July 1840 issued an ultimatum calling on him to cease hostilities or face military intervention. French opinion was indignant. Thiers was all for war in defence of the French protégé, though it would be without an ally and against the four other great powers. France had a good deal at stake. With officers, teachers, businessmen, and loans, she was the dominating influence in the Egypt of Mehemet Ali, and stood to gain or lose a major position in the Near East according as Mehemet Ali succeeded or failed. Thiers was the minister for a foreign policy that recalled the ambitions of Napoleon. On the other hand, the British government saw French influence in the Ottoman Empire as a menace to vital British interests. To British representations Thiers replied that France would never tolerate the use of force by the other European powers against Mehemet Ali. This has been regarded as a policy of bluff, though it was one that might have led to war. But when British and Turkish troops intervened in Syria, and the local population turned against the occupying Egyptian forces, Thiers realized that he had over-estimated the strength of Mehemet Ali and accepted the situation. Having done so, he still wanted to save his face by making the threatening and now meaningless gesture of inserting a bellicose statement in the speech from the throne in October. This was too much for Louis-Philippe, who had been watching with increasing alarm Thiers' policy of going to the brink of war before he withdrew. He now exercised his influence in the Chamber to overthrow Thiers.

The game of general post that the king had been playing with his governments since 1832 was resumed with the appointment of Guizot as Minister of Foreign Affairs and Soult as nominal President of the Council. Contrary to all expectation, however, the new ministry was to last, with minor changes, to the final catastrophe. Guizot was perhaps the most intelligent and high-minded minister ever to preside over the ruin of a political system. A Protestant, with all the austerity of a French Huguenot, he accepted the politics of wealth and influence; a distinguished historian with profound critical powers, who envisaged behind changing circumstances the movement of great historical forces and the evolution and conflict of classes, he behaved as if he thought his own regime could somehow escape from historical fatality; a doctrinaire who had asserted mildly liberal principles under the Restoration, he never moved beyond the narrowest interpretation of them when he was in power.

Disdain for all opposition, and a certain noble serenity, insulated him from the effects of the attacks that were continually made on him, but he gave the impression of rather more deviousness than seems compatible with his elevated character. He was undoubtedly a man of remarkable intellectual calibre, but one must not exaggerate the political skill that was shown by his long tenure of power; Guizot was free from the weakness which had undermined previous ministers — the intrigues of the king — for Louis-Philippe had found a minister who was indispensable to him. As for the support of parliament and the country, that was guaranteed by the electoral system. Each constituency had its college, many as small as 150 voters, and easily managed by the administration. The whole conduct of the elections was in the hands of the prefects, sub-prefects, and *maires*, one of whose chief functions was to secure the return of the official candidate. They practised every form of chicanery that was possible before the Second Empire turned the system of official candidatures into a fine art, though perhaps only fully in the election of 1846. Not that it mattered much: the propertied class was satisfied so long as its own wealth and social position were safeguarded. It was entirely content with a profoundly conservative regime that proposed no changes at home, and only such adventures abroad as were likely to involve no new taxes.

True, a new French Empire was founded under the constitutional monarchy, but this was the result more of the force of inertia than of considered policy. The Orleanist monarchy saw no profit or prestige in colonies, and if the forward movement begun under the Bourbon Restoration did not cease, this was due rather to the officials than to the ministers. After the first step had been taken with the attack on Algiers more determination was needed to stop the slow forward movement than to continue it. From the three initial conquests of Algiers, Oran, and Bône, French occupation was gradually extended until, in 1839, the Arab chief Abd-el-Kader abandoned his treaty and took to arms in the endeavour to check its progress.

Bugeaud, promoted corporal on the battlefield of Austerlitz, who had already had much experience of fighting in Algiers, was put in charge by Guizot. He dealt with the threat of scattered Arab warfare by lightening the equipment of his troops and organizing them in mobile columns. He had under his command Cavaignac, Changarnier, Lamoricière, and the king's son Aumale, a group of able subordinates, but it took an army of some 88,000 men and several years campaigning before Abd-el-Kader was finally defeated and captured in 1847. The war was bloody and barbarous on both sides. The Algerians massacred their prisoners; the French destroyed crops, orchards, villages, and asphyxiated 600 men, women, and children, who had taken refuge in a cave. Behind the fighting, colonization was slowly but steadily proceeding. By 1847 Algeria had 109,000 Europeans, about half of them French, and the new French empire with its promises and problems was solidly founded. It was the achievement of the constitutional monarchy, even though Louis-Philippe had taken no particular interest in it himself.

Foreign policy was what Louis-Philippe regarded as his special expertise, for he knew Europe well, though he knew it as an exile. Yet he had no luck in international affairs after the initial and well-deserved success over Belgium. The trouble was that, while he was wisely determined not to get involved in war, he hoped to collect some useful trophies at a cheaper price. As the failure of the gamble on Mehemet Ali showed, this was not possible. Louis-Philippe always felt something of an outsider among the sovereigns of Europe. If Victor Hugo's account of a conversation of 1844 is to be believed, the king confessed to a belief that both France and its ruler were hated by the kings of Europe, and he himself even more than France. 'I tell you frankly, they hate me because I am an Orleans, and they hate me for myself.'

This was perhaps the reason for the *rapprochement* with Great Britain, though to call it an entente is to stretch the meaning of the term. Superficially friendly relations were patched up after the failure of Mehemet Ali and the dismissal of Thiers. Queen Victoria paid a state visit to Louis-Philippe in 1843, when she seems to have been mostly impressed with the muddle and lack of dignity of the French Court. The French king repaid the visit the following year.

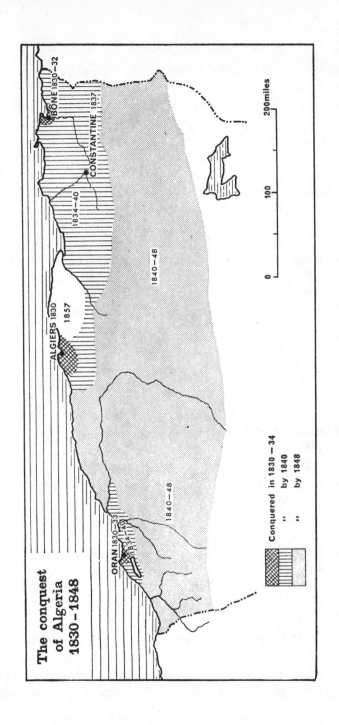

The conquest
of Algeria
1830–1848

BÔNE 1830–32

CONSTANTINE 1837

CONSTANTINE

1834–40

1840–48

ALGIERS 1830

1857

1840–48

ORAN 1830–33

1834–40

1840–48

0   100   200miles

Conquered in 1830 – 34
     "   "   by 1840
     "   "   by 1848

Essentially the so-called Franco-British entente was no more than an expression of the personal liking and mutual trust of the French and English ministers, Guizot and Aberdeen. It was not even proof against a trivial dispute in a Pacific island, which arose out of the rivalry of French and English missionaries in Tahiti, and the not altogether incomprehensible habit of the local ruler of accepting the protectorate of whichever power had last sent a gun-boat there. An ambitious English missionary named Pritchard, who believed that the flag followed the Bible, attempted to interfere with this amicable arrangement and got himself expelled by the French in 1844. This produced much British indignation, for these were the days of *civis Britannus sum*. Under pressure from the Foreign Office, the French government expressed its regret, which aroused corresponding French wrath. In 1847, the French protectorate was recognized, which restored the situation as it had been before the Pritchard affair, but rumblings of discontent continued. As for the shadowy entente, that vanished when Palmerston returned to the Foreign Office in 1846.

Anglo-French rivalry had been particularly evident in the affairs of Spain, where marriage with the young queen Isabella was a political triumph which either the house of Coburg or that of Orleans might aspire to. Since either could have been happy with her, it was decided, in September 1843, that by a mutual renunciation, neither should enjoy the prize. But Guizot, who was being out-manœuvred by Palmerston, had to take counter-measures. He arranged a double marriage of the duc de Montpensier, son of Louis-Philippe, with the sister of Isabella, while the queen of Spain herself was to marry her cousin. Thus it was assumed that in due course there would be an Orleanist heir to the Spanish throne. However, there must have been a miscalculation somewhere, for Isabella had a son almost at once and the whole rather sordid intrigue came to nothing.

The lack of a glorious foreign policy, along with a supposed revival of Bonapartist sentiment, have been accounted main factors in the failure of the Orleanist monarchy. It will be more convenient to discuss the part played, or not played, by the 'Napoleonic legend', and the attempts of Louis Napoleon Bonaparte, at Strasbourg in

1836 and Boulogne in 1840, to exploit it, at a later stage. As for the lack of a glorious foreign policy, the belief that this was a cause of the revolution in 1848 may go back to a phrase of Lamartine, in 1839, which has had only too much success, — 'La France est une nation qui s'ennuie'; but there is no reason to suppose that the poet was complaining of the absence of military glory. Like so many young literary men a royalist under the Restoration, Lamartine had become a liberal by 1830, and under the Orleanist monarchy was converted to the principle of universal suffrage, in reaction against the narrow and selfish plutocracy that ruled France. There was a cleavage growing up in France, not so much between the two nations of Disraeli's *Sybil*, for unlike Great Britain, France had not yet come anywhere near that stage of industrial development, but between the mind and heart and ideals of France and its political and social structure. Genius was bored, as it normally is, with the rule of vested interests. Louis-Philippe had nothing to offer to a romantic generation.

✣

CHAPTER FIVE

AN AGE OF IDEALISM

THE politics and economics of the July Monarchy were perhaps no more sordid than such things usually are: if they seemed so it was because this was a generation of unexampled idealism, of romantic and not always rational hopes or despairs, and of a widely diffused religiosity which was now spilling over the bounds of the Catholic revival, producing a crop of new cults in England and America, and in France becoming closely linked with schemes for social regeneration.

In the history of art and literature there is no dividing line at 1830. Theocracy, of course, became a memory then; the romantic writers who had been royalists, like Hugo and Lamartine, now moved over to liberalism; and the humanitarian themes of the Enlightenment were resumed, though with a more emotional tone infused into them by the revival of religious feeling, the new sense of history, and the cult of the people. Politically, romanticism may be said to have migrated to the opposition in 1820, though a simple formula like this can hardly do justice to such a complex movement, with such diverse sources.

The strongest influence over the nascent romantic movement had been that of Rousseau, who set the tradition of romantic melancholy, self-inquiry, reverie, which was continued by Bernardin de Saint-Pierre and Chateaubriand. Lamartine, in the *Méditations* of 1820, brought the Rousseauist spirit of soul-searching, sorrow for lost love, search for religious consolation, into poetry. There was something deeper and more classic in the pessimism of Alfred de Vigny; and the lyrical spirit was to be carried on in the sentimental, easy, and attractive poems of Alfred de Musset, in the prose of Théophile Gautier, who inspired the ballet *Giselle* (1841), which remains the perfect expression of a certain romantic feeling, and in the charm of the rustic Berrichon romances of George Sand.

But this muted note was not the characteristic or the dominant one in French romanticism. More exotic influences were also at work. Normally, in the history of art and literature, inspiration has come from France and spread to the rest of Europe; but the French spirit has been too self-contained and insular, and the French too unwilling to read foreign languages, for much to be accepted back in return. The Emigration and the Empire temporarily changed this situation. Mme de Staël's *De l'Allemagne* in 1810 introduced France to *Sturm und Drang*. Shakespeare was adapted for the French stage in the late 'twenties by Alfred de Vigny. Gérard de Nerval translated *Faust* in 1828. One cannot pretend that the romantic drama which flowered in France under these influences was quite up to the level of Shakespeare or Goethe. It was closer to, and more directly influenced by, the historical novels of Sir Walter Scott, which had a great vogue in France under the Restoration, and inspired in 1826 the austere *Cinq-Mars* of de Vigny, in 1829 the *Chronique de Charles IX* of Mérimée, and, going back to the Middle Ages, that astonishing, ridiculous, and wonderful source-book of romantic clichés, *Notre-Dame de Paris* by Victor Hugo, in 1831.

The historical movement was also evident in painting. Delacroix painted scenes from recent and ancient history—the 'Massacres of Scio' (1824) or the 'Death of Sardanapalus' (1829)—with brilliant colour and drama. Géricault, as in his most famous painting, the 'Raft of the Medusa' (1819), drew scenes of violent action and death. With Daumier romantic art became the expression of the social conscience and abandoned the Middle Ages.

Romantic medievalism had its most disastrous effects in architecture. The destruction of famous medieval buildings, including Cluny, mother house of the Benedictine Order and greatest abbey of medieval France, aroused the indignation of both romantic and religious medievalists. Led by Montalembert and Victor Hugo, a press campaign produced a Commission on National Monuments, with Prosper Mérimée as its secretary. The chief living authority on medieval architecture, Viollet-le-Duc, was put in charge of the work of preservation. Alas, the most complete neglect would have been more salutary. A new Vandal invasion could not have done worse, for that would merely have pulled down whereas Viollet-le-Duc also rebuilt. Moreover he did not work alone but had his emulators. Abadie raged through the west, restoring: at Angoulême he dealt with the deficiencies of the cathedral by taking down everything that was not text-book thirteenth-century style—this was most of the cathedral—and rebuilding it as he thought it ought to have been built if the medieval architects had read the right text-books.

In literature and art the more ridiculous aspects of romantic medievalism, which was never married very happily to French traditions, can easily be overstressed. In contemporary life it was linked with an awakening of the social conscience. For all its enlightenment and humanitarianism, the eighteenth century never really faced the problem of poverty; perhaps it believed, with the Church, that the poor we shall always have with us. Particularly after the July Revolution, however, the humanitarian tradition of the Enlightenment combined with a new, and largely Rousseauist, religious influence, to make the amelioration of the condition of the poor the central object of social thought. 'Religion', wrote Saint-Simon in his *Nouveau Christianisme*, 'should direct society towards the great end of the most rapid amelioration possible of the lot of the poorest class.' The goodness of the people became a romantic doctrine, and the people were now no longer the idealized peasantry and honest craftsmen of the Rousseauist illusion, still surviving in the rustic idylls of George Sand, but the ragged and starving populace of Paris. They appeared in medieval guise in Hugo's *Notre-Dame*, and in a more contemporary costume in Eugène Sue's serial, *Les Mystères de Paris*. The fellowship of poet and pauper was exemplified by de Vigny, himself from a family of lesser nobility ruined by the Revolution, in his play *Chatterton* (1835), in which also can be detected the first shots in the war that was now beginning between the artist or man of letters and bourgeois society.

Though there was much idealistic republicanism, the battle was against a social order based almost exclusively upon distinctions of wealth, rather than against the monarchy as such. True, Louis-Philippe was for many the symbol of this social order, but the prosaic nature of the Orleanist monarchy has been exaggerated. The sons of Louis-Philippe were, in their various ways, a surprisingly intelligent and cultured group of men. The heir to the throne, the duc d'Orléans, had genuine literary interests; his duchess, the adorable Hélène, was an admirer and patron of Victor Hugo. It was through her influence that Hugo became one of the exceptional men of literary genius in France to be admitted to the Académie Française before he was moribund, if at all, and it was through the duchess that he became a peer of France. He never forgot his debt to the house of Orleans or wrote ill of Louis-Philippe.

The cartoonists were less sparing of the king. The editor of *Charivari* fought a running battle with the censorship, and if a great cartoonist like Daumier experienced short prison sentences, it did not prevent him from creating a gallery of sub-human figures out of the Orleanist officials, judges, lawyers, and financiers. The character who symbolized the whole regime was taken from an inferior play about an amoral adventurer named Robert Macaire, who was built up by the great actor of the period, Frédéric Lemaître, into a monster of cynical rascality, and portrayed by Daumier as an out-at-elbows ruffian. He became the type of a society on the make, with no conscience, no pity, no standards of conduct. On a higher literary level we have the long series of novels that make up Balzac's *Comédie humaine*, which exhibits a society dominated by money, a world of men of property like the Forsytes without their principles. Oddly enough, Balzac himself, with his grandiose ideas, frantic struggle for fortune, financial adventures, bankruptcies, passionate love affairs, and craving for luxury, was a man of his age almost to exaggeration, and like so many of his own characters, and for the same reason, he was a believer in authority and the social function of religion.

The wealth of the rich might have seemed less blatant if it had not been for the equally unconcealed misery of the masses, particularly in Paris. The population of France grew from some 29 millions in 1815 to nearly 36 millions in 1851, and since the countryside already supported as many as it could under existing conditions, the bulk of the increase took refuge in the towns, particularly Paris. There was as yet no industrial development in France equal to providing them with work. Paris in 1848 had nearly 65,000 industrial undertakings, of which only 7,000 employed more than ten workers. It is probable that the standard of living of the urban populace had deteriorated drastically since the eighteenth century.

The government, dominated by laissez-faire ideas, as well as by class interests, made no attempt to improve conditions.

In the third and fourth decades of the century many writers, a class in which the social conscience seems to have been more lively than in others, were acutely aware of the conjunction of extreme wealth with dire poverty. They were passing over from humanitarian sympathy to aggressive criticism of the social order and positive proposals for a new and better one. Thus Lamennais, under the Restoration a leading Catholic apologist and offered a cardinal's hat which he wisely declined, found after 1830 that there was no room for his liberal ideas inside the Church. His *Paroles d'un croyant* marked the breach with Rome and he then moved on from religious heterodoxy to political liberalism. The people was the new Messiah, and Lamennais wrote passionately of its sufferings in *Le Livre du peuple* of 1841: 'They have said you were a flock and that they were your shepherds; you, the beasts; they, the men. Theirs, therefore, your fleece, your milk, your flesh. Pasture under their crook and multiply, to warm their limbs, quench their thirst, and satisfy their hunger.'

Lamennais himself did not offer any remedy for social injustice other than liberal democracy, though he was one of the founders of Catholic social reform. But this was a period of intense and original social speculation, in which socialist ideals first burgeoned. The greatest name to be mentioned in this connection is that of the comte de Saint-Simon, of *ancien régime* nobility, who had fought in the war of American Independence and became an ardent revolutionary in 1789. His enthusiasm was not lessened when he made a fortune by speculating in nationalized property. An extravagant way of life under the Directory ruined him and he turned to plans for social regeneration. Among his collaborators were the young historian Augustin Thierry and the founder of positive philosophy, Auguste Comte. These fell away, but when Saint-Simon died in 1825, he left behind him a small band of disciples, including Hippolyte Carnot, future minister of the Second Republic, Michel Chevalier, the economist and later adviser of Napoleon III, and the Péreire brothers, the financiers of the Second Empire. The leadership of the group, which was rapidly developing into a Saint-Simonian church, was taken over by the 'père' Enfantin, who turned it into one of the many nineteenth-century religions of love, and whose practical exercises in that direction brought him into conflict with the law. The real importance of the ideas of Saint-Simon was only to appear under the Second Empire.

Another social theorist whose writings pre-date 1830 was Fourier, in whom, as in the whole movement of which he is not the least eccentric representative, the influence of Rousseau is marked. The evils of civilization and the inability of government to remedy them are traced to property; the emphasis has now shifted from politics to economics. The social compact is seen as guaranteeing the rich the enjoyment of their wealth and impunity for their crimes. Fourier's solution was based—and this again indicated a new century—on new psychological principles, in which the passions were more important than the reason. He saw human nature as based on the *papillonne* or principle of variety, and to cater for this each man should take many jobs, not merely in his life but in each day. Fourier's new society was to be organized in Phalanges—self-contained communities which were to produce, on a principle of co-property, all that they consumed. The practical significance of these ideas was slight. Fourier, like nearly all the socialist or Utopian writers of the period, was not as mad as he sounds, but he was planning for a pre-industrial world.

Among others, Buchez, the co-editor of the forty-volume *Histoire parlementaire de la révolution française*, combined Christianity and co-operation in the name of science. Pierre Leroux, a former Saint-Simonian, developed the idea of a religion of humanity. Cabet, who was influenced by Owenite ideas from England as well as by a Rousseauist faith in the goodness of human nature, described a Utopian community in his *Voyage en Icarie*, and subsequently tried to realize it in America. Louis Blanc, a journalist, produced the idea with the most immediate appeal. His *Organisation du travail*, in 1839, was a simple but effective assertion of the 'right to work', and proposed to put it into practice by state intervention on the labour market. The most influential of all these socialist writers in the long run, as well as the most striking personality, was the working printer Proudhon, who became the *bête-noire* of the bourgeois by his work

Qu'est-ce que la propriété? (1840), in which he gave the answer to his own question — 'C'est le vol.' But his great influence on the French labour and socialist movements came later in the century.

The social thought of the period is a remarkable mixture of sense and nonsense, of a realistic appreciation of social evils combined with the proposal of sometimes fantastically Utopian solutions. The element of escapism that is to be detected in this literature is also to be seen in the novels of adventure that proliferated at the time, exploiting the new medium of newspaper serials. Alexandre Dumas ransacked history for picturesque periods; Eugène Sue found mysteries in Paris; Mérimée and Balzac combined romantic themes with realistic detail. Béranger played a part, by his popular lyrics, in turning the propaganda of the First Empire into a Napoleonic legend.

Yet even in the hey-day of the Romantic movement there were signs that it would not last. Stendhal's *Le Rouge et le Noir* and *La Chartreuse de Parme* are packed with romantic detail, but the spirit of their author was closer to that of the eighteenth century. Gautier's *Mademoiselle de Maupin* belongs to the same perverse genre as *Les Liaisons dangereuses*. In 1838 a young actress, Rachel, played Racine in a way that swept the trivialities of romantic drama off the boards. And already, while the romantic wave seemed to be engulfing everything, signs of a new attitude were appearing. Théophile Gautier, whom Lanson has described as the pivot of French literature in the nineteenth century, proclaimed the new gospel of 'art for art's sake' as early as a preface of 1832. Gérard de Nerval looked back to the *illuminés* of the eighteenth century and forward to the symbolists. That literature was not unaffected by the current preoccupation with the social problem can be seen in the novels of Hugo, Balzac, Sue, George Sand; and the first attempt at a scientific treatment of it brought the beginning of sociological thought, particularly in the work of Auguste Comte. He began as a teacher of mathematics and a disciple of Saint-Simon, but soon broke away and devoted the remainder of his life to developing the school of Positivism, which by an equal misconception of the nature of science and of religion, offered a new secular religion of science to those who had lost their traditional faith but could not manage without an

inspired teacher and at least one form of certainty. More distinguished thinkers, like Renan and Taine, experienced strongly the
influence of Comte's positivism, which has continued to exercise a
spell over the French mind.

However wild or *a priori* much of the social thinking of the first
half of the nineteenth century in France was, at least men were
speculating about the problems of society. But between this thought
and the policies of government there was an almost impassable gulf.
The men who ruled France were not economically minded, and their
electorate, as has been said, was largely one of landed proprietors.
Hence the ruling elite was not likely to be interested in industrial
development; and the comparative backwardness of French social
conditions and economic development, for which the social structure of the *ancien régime* and the diversions of the Revolution and the
Empire were in part responsible, continued under the so-called
bourgeois monarchy.

A glance at some figures will easily substantiate this statement.
The horse power at the service of French industry in 1832 was under
1,000; by 1848 it had multiplied by nearly seven times, but in Great
Britain six times as much machine power had already been employed
in the 'twenties. In 1790 French production of coal was about one-
twentieth of that of Great Britain. Its production increased by about
three times under the July Monarchy, but it was still not sufficient
to satisfy even the modest needs of France. The amount of iron
ore mined more than doubled; but behind a high protective tariff
the price of iron was far higher than in Great Britain and production
far lower. Modern methods were only gradually introduced in
smelting. The last charcoal furnace in France ceased production in
the course of the First World War.

More progress was made in transport but adequate capital for its
development was lacking. There was a historical reason for this.
The provision of highways and bridges in France had always been
the prerogative of the public service of the Ponts et Chaussées, and
it was traditional for the state to finance them. Under the July
Monarchy the nation demanded improved means of transport and
the government was in fact prepared to go a long way towards
meeting this demand. It could only do so, however, by government

expenditure; and as fast as the announcement of a programme of public works aroused support, the finance necessary to pay for them aroused opposition. Moreover, since the wealthy class which formed the narrow electorate also included those who contracted for the works, suspicions of corruption, which were often too well founded, were naturally aroused. Some progress, of course, was made. A law of 1836 on the construction and upkeep of local roads was of considerable benefit to the rural population; and the length of canals in use doubled under the July Monarchy.

Railways were developed very slowly and with a good deal of discouragement from above. When a line was projected from Paris to Saint-Germain, Thiers declared it might be worth constructing as an amusement for the Parisians; and the scientist Arago warned against the menace to human health involved in travelling by rail. Private capital was unwilling to risk itself in the construction of railways; while the Charter blocked the spending of public money on them. In 1842 a compromise was reached by which the state should buy the land, and plan and lay out the lines, while private capital supplied the actual rails and rolling-stock. There followed, from 1844 to 1846, the first French railway mania. It was of short duration and was followed by a collapse of railway shares and a financial crisis. Too many of the new lines, indeed, had been constructed to serve the interests of local politicians rather than economic demand. In 1848 many of the little local lines were bankrupt, and France had 1,921 kilometres of railways, compared with 3,424 in Prussia and 6,349 in Great Britain.

The first half of the nineteenth century in Great Britain has been described as the period of the race between population and industrialization. In France, while population was increasing only slowly, the level of production was rising even more slowly. Inevitably the standard of living fell and the material for a social revolution piled up, at least in the large towns. A bad harvest or a slump in business would produce a critical situation. Economic factors do not make revolutions by themselves, however, and to understand how the Orleanist regime met its fate we must turn back to politics.

For all the apparent strength of the Guizot administration, it was attacked with increasing vehemence from both left and right—this should not have surprised a regime which claimed to represent the *juste milieu*. The attack from the right took the form of a challenge to its educational policy. The quarrel was bound to become acute with the progress of both religious and state systems of schools. The achievement of the Restoration in education has seldom been adequately appreciated. A decree of 1816 laid it down that there should be a school in every commune and that education should be free for the children of parents who could not afford to pay. This represented an ideal rather than a fact, but by 1820 out of 44,000 communes there were schools in 24,000, a great advance on the previous situation.

The last government of Charles X issued an abortive law reorganizing the teaching service. Guizot, in 1833, repeated the effort in a law which has been called the first charter of primary education in France. Each commune, or group of neighbouring communes, was to have a primary school, and each department, or group of departments, a training college for elementary school-teachers, the *école normale primaire*. Between 1830 and 1848 the number of *écoles normales* grew from 12 to 47. Secondary schools were obligatory in the chief towns of each department, and in all towns with more than 6,000 inhabitants. These schools were either conducted by lay *instituteurs*, teachers who had to have a certificate from a training college, or by brothers of a religious order who were exempted from the requirement. This privilege of the religious schools of course ensured that the state schools would gradually come to be educationally superior. At the same time, by putting the teachers under rigid local and central control, the law of Guizot ensured that they could only escape from the control of the Church by falling under that of the state.

The importance of the role of the teachers in inculcating law and order and a proper respect for the powers that be was recognized from the beginning, recognized that is in principle, but not in material recompense. Guizot's circular to the teachers in 1833 was engagingly frank on this point. 'A profound sentiment of the importance of his work must sustain and animate the teacher,' he wrote; 'the austere pleasure of having served mankind and contributed to the public weal must be the worthy payment which his conscience alone gives him. It is his glory to use himself up in sacrifices and to expect his reward only from God.' This was true to the facts, if tactless; but a class of underpaid teachers, with at least more instruction than the petty local tyrants of Church and state who rendered them fully conscious of their social and financial inferiority, was not in fact likely to provide a cement of society.

Of course, the more schools there were, the more intense became the competition between Church and state for the control of them. The July Monarchy had started off, as we have seen, to the accompaniment of a violent anti-clerical reaction against the clericalism of the Restoration. The affiliations of the Church, moreover, were naturally with the divine-right monarchy and therefore with the legitimists. By 1841, when the new Archbishop of Paris, Mgr Affre, paid an official visit to the king, relations between Church and state seemed much ameliorated; but a strong faction in the Church, led by the clerical journalist Louis Veuillot and the *Univers*, persistently agitated against what was called the 'University monopoly' of education. The parties of the left retaliated by reviving the Jesuit bogey. In 1843 Michelet and Edgar Quinet published jointly the courses they had given at the Collège de France under the title *Des jésuites*; but the clerical campaign, organized by the Catholic writer Montalembert, was the more effective.

The government offered a new law on education in 1844, making various concessions. Quinet's lectures were suppressed. Guizot brought himself to declare, in 1846, that children belonged to the family before the state, and that the state did not claim the exclusive right of education: religion also had its rights. Unfortunately clerical ambitions had grown with the success of the clerical propaganda, and it turned out that the new educational law proposed by the government, because it provided definitions where there had previously been laxity, threatened to make the situation of clerical education worse instead of better. Moreover the anti-Jesuit campaign had unexpected success. Montalembert and the party of 'liberty of education' were dissatisfied. Legitimism, which was also practically invariably ardently Catholic, remained unreconciled to the rule of

Louis-Philippe. Religious opinion was in no state of mind to support the regime in an emergency, if one occurred.

On the other side, the left, so badly defeated in the early 'thirties, had been continuing its apparently hopeless opposition in the press and at the polls. The *National*, edited by Armand Marrast, denounced the corruption of the political system unceasingly, though it only called for moderate and peaceful reforms. Those for whom it was too moderate, inspired by the eloquent young lawyer, Ledru-Rollin, the rising hope of the more advanced reformers, founded, in 1843, the *Réforme*, as an organ of more democratic opinion. The radicals were now rallying their forces for the first time since the disaster of 1834, and in the demand for universal suffrage they had found a principle on which to unite.

Though Ledru-Rollin, surprisingly, given such a narrow franchise, secured election to the Chamber of Deputies, the parliamentary opposition as a whole had really more quarrel with the personnel than with the system of government. In 1845 Odilon Barrot and Thiers, tired of seeing another minister instead of themselves in office for the unexampled space of nearly five years, joined forces on a programme of electoral and parliamentary reform. It seemed the only way to shift Guizot, and it gave them the opportunity to join in the cry, always popular in France, of corruption.

In 1846 Guizot appealed confidently to a satisfied electorate, which hardly needed the nips and nudgings of the prefects to be gathered safely into the fold. The governmental machine could congratulate itself on a notable triumph when, after the elections, the address from the throne was accepted by a vote of 248 to 84. The majority was indeed almost too large for its own good. There were too many 'progressive conservatives', like de Tocqueville, in its ranks—enough in fact to elect an opposition candidate as vice-president of the chamber. The awkward subject of parliamentary reform and the extension of the franchise reappeared, though the government produced the—to it—decisive argument that if the country—that is the existing privileged class of electors—had wanted the franchise to be extended, it would have shown this in the election. Guizot revealed behind the demand for the extension of the franchise the terrifying shadow of universal suffrage, and made the classic pronouncement, 'Il n'y aura pas de jour pour le suffrage universel.'

The cry of corruption was still the most effective weapon that the opposition had, and though there is no reason to suppose that the Guizot regime was any more corrupt than those which preceded or followed it, circumstances enabled this cry to be exploited effectively at what was to be a critical time. A criminal trial in 1847 brought out in evidence the correspondence of a former Minister of War, which revealed large payments, for the purpose of securing industrial concessions, to the then Minister of Public Works, Teste, now President of the Appeal Court and a peer of France. Teste was prosecuted and attempted suicide. Both of the former ministers were condemned to civic degradation and three years in prison.

This was followed by the affair of the duc de Praslin, who battered his wife to death for love of an English governess. Brought to trial before the peers, he succeeded in committing suicide with arsenic. Together these cases were taken as a revelation of the manner of life of the governing class, which itself had its confidence sapped by such apparent justification for the continual denunciations of corruption to which it was subjected.

Meanwhile the parliamentary opposition, seeing how hopeless the situation was in the Chamber, determined to carry the campaign to the country. In July 1847 it organized the first of a series of political banquets, at which leading orators denounced the government, made much play with corruption, and called for parliamentary reform. Thiers, who abstained from the banquets, was himself conducting an unrestrained campaign of speeches in the Chamber against the foreign policy of Guizot. The minister and the king, confident in their parliamentary majority and forgetting how little it really represented in the country, did not weaken before the verbal attacks from all sides. In January 1848 they prohibited further banquets, and the opposition, now becoming a little alarmed at its own boldness, but unwilling to lose face by yielding too obviously, made a private arrangement with the authorities. Its supporters were to assemble for the banquet, but to accept a police order to disperse peaceably, and the case would then be tried in the courts. This was very reasonable for it was really only a squabble between different factions in the small governing class. Banqueteers do not come from the ranks of the disinherited, and the opposition only wished to exert sufficient pressure to put themselves and their friends in, and Guizot and his friends out.

But while the parliamentary leaders were preparing to retreat, their followers were pressing forward. The two journals, the *National* and the *Réforme*, were the centres of a more determined agitation. They called on the people of Paris to take up the struggle that the deputies had abandoned. This was to introduce a factor into the situation which on all sides had been curiously ignored. It is a striking comment on the class structure of France that the governing class, engaged in its political rivalries, does not appear to have thought that the condition of the people was anything that needed to be taken into consideration.

A bad harvest in 1846 and potato blight had affected most of Western Europe. An industrial crisis also brought widespread unemployment. The slump had perhaps touched bottom in 1847 and the curve of economic activity was beginning to rise again, but those who were suffering from it, with little attempt at relief from public or private charity, could hardly be expected to appreciate this fact. Again, as in 1787–9, and to a lesser extent in 1830, a political agitation coincided with an economic crisis, and those who had started the agitation, found that it led them much farther than they ever intended or expected. As in 1830, the basic fact was the refusal of the king to be parted from his minister until it was too late, and in his fall the minister dragged the king down with him.

In place of the abandoned banquet of February 22nd, 1848, there was a popular procession of protest through the streets. The government felt the need for a counter-demonstration, and though the king had not reviewed the National Guard since 1840, it was summoned to his defence. Unwillingly it assembled on the morrow at the *mairies* of the different *arrondissements*, but as its members made their way to their appointed places they called out, 'Vive la Réforme!' presented a petition at the Palais Bourbon, where the Chamber of Deputies sat, sang the Marseillaise, prevented the troops of the line from controlling the crowds, and shouted 'À bas Guizot!' Unwillingly Louis-Philippe, after a fatal delay, through the veils of

aged self-satisfaction and obstinacy appreciated that something unusual was happening, and asked for the resignation of his minister.

Now it was seen that there had in fact been some point in his
clinging to office, for the whole system disintegrated when the man
who had been the key-stone of the arch fell. Indignation among those
who had staked their whole political future on the survival of the
regime, was followed by a *sauve-qui-peut*. The politicians began to
look for an alternative, and in the streets the crowds were getting
out of hand. The king appointed Molé to succeed Guizot, and
Bugeaud, who had mastered Paris in 1831 and 1834, to the command of the army. The dismissal of Guizot took some of the edge
off the crowds ranging up and down the boulevards, and it still
seemed that the situation might be saved. But then, late on the
evening of February 23rd, occurred the incident which turned a riot
into a revolution. Victor Hugo gives a vivid description of the
episode. He writes:

> The crowds which I had seen start cheerfully singing down
> the boulevards, at first went on their way peacefully and with-
> out resistance. The regiment, the artillery, the cuirassiers
> opened their ranks everywhere for their passage. But on the
> boulevard des Capucines a body of troops, both infantry and
> cavalry, was massed on the two pavements and across the road,
> guarding the Ministry of Foreign Affairs and its unpopular
> minister, M. Guizot. Before this impassable obstacle, the head
> of the popular column tried to stop and turn aside; but the
> irresistible pressure of the huge crowd weighed on the front
> ranks. At this moment a shot rang out, from which side is not
> known. Panic followed and then a volley. Eighty dead or
> wounded remained on the spot. A universal cry of horror and
> fury arose: Vengeance! The bodies of the victims were loaded
> on a cart lit with torches. The cortège moved back amidst curses
> at a funeral pace. And in a few hours Paris was covered with
> barricades.

On February 24th the king replaced Molé with Thiers, ordered
Bugeaud to withdraw his troops, and spent the day in political
negotiations. Paris was now in the hands of the mob, which had

captured the Hôtel de Ville and advanced on the Tuileries. After the disaster of the previous day there seems to have been no serious thought of an appeal to the army, though it was still loyal and had its links with the dynasty. The sons of Louis-Philippe were closely associated with the army. The duc d'Aumale had fought in Algeria, where he was now governor-general; the duc d'Orléans was popular in military circles because of the interest he had always taken in the army. Nevertheless, outside Paris, and once the riots had triumphed there, not a shot was fired in defence of the dynasty.

On the afternoon of February 24th, collapsing in senile despair, Louis-Philippe abdicated in favour of his grandson, the little comte de Paris. It was the end of a regime that had been so lacking in principle that it could only be known by the name of the month of its founding, as the July Monarchy.

I

❧

PART THREE

THE SECOND REPUBLIC AND
THE SECOND EMPIRE

CHAPTER ONE

1848: FROM THE FEBRUARY DAYS
TO THE JUNE DAYS

1848 IN France was a revolution by accident. If the revolution had not happened then, it may be said, as of other revolutions, that it would have happened at some other time, whenever the 'conjuncture' — the term in current French historical jargon that has replaced the 'psychological moment' — was appropriate. But of course, if it had occurred later or earlier it would have occurred in different circumstances and would have been a different revolution. The revolution was not the fore-ordained result of the emergence of new social forces that could not be contained in the old institutions, for none of adequate importance had yet arisen; it was rather the accidental though highly probable result of the inherent weakness of government in France. Since 1789 no regime had possessed the conditions necessary for stability. A series of political upheavals had fragmented conservative forces, the unity of which was the prerequisite of political stability, by introducing ideological cleavages which cut across economic ties and destroyed the cohesion of the forces of property and order. Simplifying the situation, we may say that in 1848 the propertied classes were split between the old *noblesse*, legitimists, and clericals, for whom an Orleanist king was worse than no king at all; those men of property and officials who liked to think themselves liberal, who were inclined towards anticlericalism and reasonably satisfied with Louis-Philippe; and a rising class of educated and professional men, of varied economic standing, with republican sympathies. As for the mass of rural small proprietors, because of the memory of 1789 the peasants were still labelled in the public mind as potential revolutionaries: the events of June 1848 were to show how mistaken was this opinion, but in February there was no way in which their weight could be cast into the scales against change.

Indeed, hardly any element in French society outside Paris could materially influence events in the crisis of February. This was a second inheritance from the Revolution and Napoleon: authority had been concentrated so thoroughly in the ministries at Paris that whoever held Paris held France. And Paris, of course, was the most difficult part of France to hold. Under the Orleanist monarchy it was a witch's cauldron fermenting with dangerous ideological ingredients.

The collapse of divine right left a void, which the revolutionaries of 1789 attempted unsuccessfully to fill. Their principles were too self-contradictory, and too difficult to reconcile with hard political and social facts, to provide the ideological basis for a new society. The new ruling classes that emerged from Revolution and Empire had used democratic and egalitarian ideas to justify their attack on the older privileged classes, but with no intention of allowing the same principles to be turned against themselves. France, throughout the nineteenth century, was an oligarchy of wealth, especially landed wealth, and office; but unlike the British governing classes in the same period, the French elite was insecure, not only because its internal divisions went much deeper, but also because it did not believe in itself. It had no reason to: it had neither inherited an old tradition of government nor had it evolved any Burkean or Benthamite philosophy to provide a moral basis for its new powers and privileges. Too often its self-justification took the form of a cynical assertion of material interests. At the same time it lacked the crude virtues of a get-rich-quick society. Sunk in a stubborn and unimaginative defence of its vested interests, it lacked the enterprise necessary even for its own economic progress. With only a little harshness, we might say that the French ruling class, heir of the great Revolution, was devoid of social conscience, devoted— inevitably—to its own property rights, and indifferent—not quite so inevitably—to the conditions of life, or death, of the populace beneath it. Because the ruling classes were weak they feared to make concessions in advance, but were quick to appeal to force when a threat had materialized. The Orleanist monarchy has been unfairly blamed for its failure to alleviate the misery caused by the economic crisis of the 'forties: this is to be attributed to the forces of society rather than to the fault of the government.

There was no reason to fear any threat to the social order from conditions in the countryside or in the provincial towns, apart from Lyons. Paris was another matter. The population of the capital was both growing and changing in character. The centralization of the life of France in Paris played its part in promoting the drift of population there, even from comparatively distant provinces and before the railway era. Beginning as a seasonal immigration, it turned into a permanent transfer. Under the Orleanist monarchy the population of Paris, within what were to be the increased limits of 1860, grew from roughly 860,000 to 1,250,000. There had been little industrial development to give work to these extra arms, and little increased agricultural production to provide food for the mouths. There is no coincidence in the fact that two countries which escaped serious trouble in 1848 were the only two in which industrialization had made substantial progress — Great Britain (but not Ireland) and Belgium. In France the population, already before 1789 rather more than the country could support without a declining standard of living, had continued to grow, though at a slower rate, with no substantial industrialization to assist in its absorption.

How a political quarrel between the Ins and the Outs unintentionally set fire to this inflammable social situation has already been indicated. Perhaps it would not have done so if there had not already been 1789 to provide such a model. So de Tocqueville thought. In the presence of the revolutionary mob which invaded the Assembly, he could not persuade himself, he said, that there was a real danger of bloodshed, despite the muskets and bayonets and sabres. 'Nos Français,' he wrote, 'surtout à Paris, mêlent volontiers les souvenirs de la littérature et du théâtre à leurs manifestations les plus sérieuses.' It seemed to him, he added, that they were playing at the French Revolution rather than continuing it. The revolution of 1848, Marx said, could find nothing better to do than to parody that of 1789–95. Nevertheless the fighting in February was real enough to destroy a monarchy; the days of June 1848 were to see a bitterer social war than ever the first Revolution knew; and an empire was to emerge from the republic in four years instead of fourteen.

Once the regime of Louis-Philippe and Guizot had collapsed in Paris, its hollowness was shown by the rapidity with which its adherents joined in a general *sauve-qui-peut* and proclaimed their allegiance, along with legitimists, republicans, clericals, anti-clericals, liberals, socialists, and all, to the revolutionary government. In its opening days this was a revolution of fraternity and universal love. The hero of Flaubert's *L'Éducation sentimentale*, after the February Days revisiting the fair friend whom he had left on his previous visit in a somewhat disgruntled frame of mind, found that the revolution had restored harmony.

> Now that all was peaceful and there was no cause for fear, she kissed him and declared herself for the Republic—as Monseigneur the Archbishop of Paris had already done, and as, with a marvellous alacrity, the Magistrature, the Council of State, the Institute, the Marshals of France, Changarnier, M. de Falloux, all the Bonapartists, all the legitimists, and a considerable number of Orleanists, were to do.

The government to which France entrusted its fate, of course provisionally, on the morrow of the February Revolution, was as accidental a product as the revolution itself. The Chamber of Deputies, which was an Orleanist chamber, was watching with hearts full of sentiment the lovely Duchess of Orleans, mother of Louis-Philippe's grandson in favour of whom he had abdicated, and listening to emotional appeals on their behalf—'The crown of July', declared Odilon Barrot, 'rests on the head of a child and a woman'—when the *blouses* and the National Guards burst into the hall with shouts of 'À bas la Chambre', 'Plus de députés'. The courage of the members and the hopes of the dynasty vanished together: only a republican government would pacify the mob. Out of the tumult the names of seven leading republican figures—Lamartine, Ledru-Rollin, Marrast, Arago, Crémieux, Marie, Garnier-Pagès—emerged. At the Hôtel de Ville a left-wing demonstration had put forward the socialists Flocon and Louis Blanc, and a solitary, symbolic (of nothing in particular) worker, Albert. These names were added, and thus did France receive its new government.

The first act of the Provisional Government was to proclaim the right of universal suffrage, swelling the electorate overnight from a quarter of a million to nine millions, and laying the foundations for the subsequent Bonapartist dictatorship. Next, it abolished slavery on all French territory, thus freeing about half a million slaves, a belated reform, introduced without any preparation or precautions, which brought immediate economic disaster to the slave colonies.

A more pressing problem was that of unemployment in France, and principally Paris. The general European slump had reached bottom in 1847 and conditions were slowly improving; but in France the uncertainty produced in the business world by the revolution prohibited any recovery and in 1848 the economic crisis was intensified. Shops were closed, craftsmen without work, men dismissed from the few factories; credit was lacking, private charity quite inadequate, and government assistance totally absent. To the starving horde of unemployed, or to those who were vocal amongst them, one idea had filtered down. How the economic position had changed in the past half century is shown by the shape of this idea. They no longer, as between 1789 and 1794, called for a maximum on prices; the demand now was for work, embodied in Louis Blanc's formula, *le droit au travail*. It is evidence that the labouring masses in the towns now thought of themselves primarily as producers rather than as consumers.

In a revolutionary situation something had to be done to satisfy their demands or those of their spokesmen. It was not too difficult to find an innocuous solution. Louis Blanc and Albert, political innocents compared with the politicians, were put at the head of a Parliament of Industry which met at the Luxembourg and was allowed to talk its way through the crisis. Louis Blanc's plan for National Workshops, which involved the state in providing credits for industry, was rejected. To the Minister of Public Works, Marie, and many others, it seemed a revolutionary proposal, alien to the spirit of brotherhood that had prevailed in February. If the name National Workshops was adopted, it was only as a sop to the followers of Louis Blanc; in fact all the Workshops, or Ateliers, ever amounted to was a system of registering the Paris unemployed for the payment of a wretched dole. By June 1848 some 120,000 were in receipt of this pittance and the lists had been closed to exclude perhaps 50,000 more. To give the impression that something was being done, a young engineer named Thomas was entrusted with the task of organizing the so-called Workshops. In spite of opposition, he managed to set about 12,000 men to work levelling a small hill on the site of what was later the boulevard Montparnasse. The prevailing attitude of mind among the wealthy classes, though intensely protectionist in relation to foreign trade, was sternly non-interventionist in respect of internal economic activity. When the government of Louis-Philippe had proposed to meet the economic crisis of 1847 by a programme of public works, a legislative body of proprietors naturally rejected the proposal. The Provisional Government, in so far as it ever even contemplated the same programme, met with the same resistance.

Orthodox economics also insisted, and more successfully than in 1789, that the National Debt was sacred. To maintain public credit, interest continued to be paid scrupulously on state loans, the budgetary gap being filled by imposing an extra tax of 45 centimes, which fell mainly on the peasantry. This was the most misconceived of all the Provisional Government's measures. Whereas the National Assembly of 1789 had, intentionally or unintentionally, lightened the burdens of the peasantry, the revolution of 1848 actually increased them. Here is at least one factor which helps to explain the changed attitude of the peasants to revolution.

The mutual fear and suspicion of the middle classes and the populace in Paris, which had been violently intensified, though not created, by the economic crisis, came into the open very early in the revolution. On March 16th the better-off members of the National Guard, distinguished by their uniform and fur caps, staged a rather futile demonstration which is known as the manifestation of the *bonnets a poil*. There followed on the next day an imposing and far larger counter-demonstration by masses of Paris workers. The situation was tense but Ledru-Rollin, known as the most sympathetic to the people among the middle-class republican leaders, acquired considerable, though not lasting, prestige by pacifying the demonstrators. Though the great body of conservative republicans did not trust him and detested his ideas of moderate social reform, it was evident that he could not be dispensed with while the danger from below existed; so he had to be tolerated.

In the key position of Minister of the Interior, Ledru-Rollin had the responsibility for organizing the election of a Constituent Assembly. Universal suffrage represented a leap in the dark, and the more they thought about the implications of this sudden and unprepared granting of their democratic demands, the darker the outlook seemed to the democratic factions; for the great mass of the new electors were illiterate peasants, likely to follow the lead of their clergy, local landowners, and notables. The only hope the left-wing politicians could see lay in a postponement of the elections, to give them time to indoctrinate the peasants and teach them who their real friends were. Hence a series of petitions flowed in from the clubs of Paris in favour of postponing the elections, which was also one of the demands of the demonstrators of March 17th. In more general terms it may be said that the democrats of 1848 were faced with the constant dilemma of democracy: can the sovereign people, if it so wishes, be allowed to abdicate, has it the right to repudiate democracy? Suppose it chooses to follow a conservative, or even a reactionary policy, instead of a progressive and reforming one, is this permissible? The members of the great Committee of Public Safety had been faced with the same question and their answer was the Terror. Ledru-Rollin and the republicans of 1848 did not contemplate this solution. They would doubtless have been less despised by historians if they had been more bloody-minded. Unfortunately they were idealists who believed in their own principles.

Within the limits which seemed legitimate to him, Ledru-Rollin did what he could towards the winning of the elections. The essential first step was the replacement of the Orleanist administrative machine. All the prefects, and all but twelve of the sub-prefects, were dismissed, and revolutionary commissaires appointed in their place. By mid-April tried republicans were at the head of practically every department. The Provisional Government instructed them not to imitate the usurping governments of the past in corrupting the electors. Ledru-Rollin, rather more frankly, addressed them with the rhetorical question 'What are your powers?' and replied, 'They are unlimited ... The elections are your great task.' By this he meant that the duty of the commissaires was to enlighten the electors and purge the administration of non-republican officials who might exercise a dangerous influence.

The discredited and disorganized Orleanist machine could not resist Ledru-Rollin. On the other hand the clerical party, with an anti-Orleanist record behind it, was not afraid to engage in open political agitation under the leadership of Montalembert's central Committee for Electoral Liberty. It was supported energetically by most of the bishops. Few leaders of the Church were as far-seeing as the bishop of Viviers, later Cardinal Guibert, who wrote:

> I am convinced that we are doing an imprudent thing, and that the few votes in favour of religious liberty we may be able to send to the Chamber are not worth the sacrifice of the fine position we have won by our isolation from political power since 1830.

Faced with the clerical threat, the Minister of Education, Hippolyte Carnot, called on the village school-teachers to counteract the clergy by spreading the republican faith. This was the beginning of the ideological struggle between the *curé* and the *instituteur*, but the struggle was as yet a very uneven one. The Church was still far stronger than the state in the rural communes, and the republicans were not unaware of this fact. Possibly they fixed on Easter Sunday for the elections in the hope of keeping the faithful away from the elections. If so, it was a gross miscalculation. Mass was celebrated at an early hour in the morning, and the villagers marched to vote with the priest at the head of the procession, sometimes in harmony, sometimes in undignified rivalry, with a republican *maire*.

Apart from propaganda, a game at which the local notabilities and priest could usually defeat Ledru-Rollin's commissaires, the elections were notably free. The failure of the more advanced republicans supported by Ledru-Rollin is evidence of that: Ministers of the Interior did not normally lose elections in nineteenth-century France. There was a poll of 84 per cent and the vote of the peasantry ensured that the Constituent Assembly should be in a majority conservative and traditionalist in its complexion. Four-fifths of the deputies were men of the district which elected them; four-fifths were also over forty; nearly 700 out of nearly 900 were men of substance paying a tax of over 500 francs a year. Half the deputies were monarchists, divided into some 300 Orleanists and 150 legitimists.

About 350 were committed to support the clerical campaign for freedom of education. There was a mere sprinkling of red republicans, and still fewer socialists. The conservative nature of the Assembly was demonstrated by the voting on two proposals. Only 82 members supported a motion recognizing the right to work; and only 110 out of 900 were in favour of that most revolutionary of all measures, a graduated income tax. Of course, even a vote of one in eight for such a measure would have been inconceivable in the great French Revolution. Ledru-Rollin's attempt to secure an advanced republican Assembly had thus decisively failed. His influence in the government naturally declined, and he would probably have been pushed out of it by the new Assembly if it had not been for the support of Lamartine, who thereby sacrificed much of his own prestige.

It was an Assembly interested in political, but opposed to all economic change. From the beginning it exhibited the besetting sin of the Second Republic, an obsession with political dogma. This appeared in the Assembly's insistence on turning the Provisional Government into an Executive Commission, appointed by the Assembly, which had the duty of deliberating on policy, while a separate body of ministers had the duty of carrying it out. This division was introduced for the purpose of maintaining the sacred principle of the separation of powers.

The left-wing leaders of Paris, frustrated by the elections, carried on an increasingly bitter agitation in the press and the popular clubs. Their violent speeches, invocations to social revolution, songs like

> Chapeau bas devant ma casquette,
> À genoux devant l'ouvrier,

did not lessen the alarm of the middle and upper classes. Since one thing that all France definitely wanted was not to be involved in a revolutionary war, with characteristic ineptitude the club leaders decided to use a petition for assistance to the Polish revolution as the excuse for an attempt to overthrow the National Assembly by a mob demonstration after the established model. This attempted 'push' on May 15th, under the revolutionary leaders, Barbès and Blanqui, who hated one another even more than they hated their opponents, was easily put down by the regular troops and the National Guard. Its only result was that practically all the left-wing agitators disappeared from the political scene, either in flight abroad or into prison. Hence they cannot be held responsible for the great popular rising of June.

The revolt of the June Days is one of the most mysterious episodes of its kind. It is not easy to find another popular movement, especially of such magnitude, in which not a single leader, even of the second or third rank, can be identified. The psychological preparation for the June Days is not difficult to see, and it can be granted that there was plenty of inflammable material in Paris. The hope of salvation, with which the unemployed and starving masses had poured out of their garrets and cellars in February, had given place to disillusionment when under a republic economic conditions became worse instead of better. Class hatred in Paris reached perhaps its highest point, before the Commune, in 1848. De Tocqueville, returning to the capital after the elections, found the aspect of Paris terrible and sinister.

> I saw society split in two: those who possessed nothing united in a common greed; those who possessed something in a common fear. No bonds, no sympathies existed between these two great classes, everywhere was the idea of an inevitable and approaching struggle.

It is a classic fact of revolutions in a predominantly agrarian economy that the late spring or early summer is the point of greatest danger, when the previous year's harvest is exhausted and the new one has not yet come in. Semi-starvation was the lot of the masses of unemployed in Paris. The dole handed out by the so-called National Workshops was only a slight alleviation of their misery, and even so, many of the unemployed were excluded from it and the National Assembly was determined to get rid of it as rapidly as possible. For the chairman of the Labour Committee of the Assembly, the comte de Falloux—a devoted son of the Church and proud aristocrat, whose grandfather, a cattle-merchant, had been ennobled by Louis XVIII in 1823—the National Workshops were 'a permanent and organized strike', 'an active centre of dangerous agitation'. To the suggestion that if they were dissolved there might be resistance he replied, 'Have you not the National Guard? ... Take what measures you choose, we guarantee they will not meet with serious resistance; and if we do encounter it, let us not be afraid to use force, force without the shedding of blood but that moral force which belongs to the law.'

As a result partly of de Falloux's pressure, on June 22nd it was decreed that all unmarried workers in the National Workshops should join the army, and the remainder go to the provinces, under penalty of losing their payments. This seems to have been the spark which set off the rising in Paris, though how or why is far from clear. It is alleged that those who were enrolled in the National Workshops did not in fact participate in the June Days to any great extent, but there is no doubt that it was, as it seemed to contemporaries like de Tocqueville, a workers' movement, a revolt of the helots, a servile war. The numbers involved in the actual fighting must not be exaggerated; they were probably not more than 20,000, one in ten or less of the workers of Paris. Their first step was to erect barricades, which cut off the poorer quarters of Paris. These were necessary because with the black powder then used it was difficult to fire from other than a standing position. Held by desperate men, with flanking fire from windows, in the narrow, winding streets of old Paris, the barricades could only be taken when cannon had been set up against them, which was a slow and dangerous process. Then, when a barricade had been rendered untenable, its defenders could move back, breaking through the party walls of the houses, to another line of defence prepared in advance.

The unresisted opening stages of the revolt were possible because of the absence of troops, which was due not to calculation but to the difficulty of provisioning them in Paris and to the lack of barracks; but once the regular troops were brought into action the result was a foregone conclusion. The general entrusted with putting down the revolt, Cavaignac, a staunch republican but also intensely conservative, moved in infantry and artillery steadily for the kill. The army was reinforced by detachments of National Guard, volunteers from the provinces, where the hatred of Paris had reached fever pitch. Even at the time of the election of the Constituent Assembly de Tocqueville had been struck with the spirit of fraternity which sprang up between all owners of property, rich or poor, in his rural department of the Manche, and the universal hatred and terror which they experienced at the thought of the 'anarchists' of Paris.

In six days of bitter street fighting the rebel quarters were conquered street by street. How many of the insurgents were killed in the struggle or shot out of hand when captured cannot be estimated. The prisoners, thousands of whom were to be sent as forced immigrants to Algeria, were piled into improvised dungeons such as Flaubert describes:

Nine hundred men were there, crowded together in filth, pell-mell, black with powder and clotted blood, shivering in fever and shouting in frenzy. Those who died were left to lie with the others. Now and then, at the sudden noise of a gun, they thought they were all on the point of being shot, and then flung themselves against the walls, afterwards falling back into their former places. They were so stupefied with suffering that they seemed to be living in a nightmare, a funeral hallucination. The lamp hanging from the arch looked like a patch of blood; and little green and yellow flames flew about, produced by the effluvium of the vaults. Because of a fear of epidemics a commission of inquiry had been appointed. On the first steps its president flung himself back, appalled by the odour of excrement and corpses. When the prisoners approached a ventilator, the National Guards on sentry duty stuck their bayonets, haphazard, into the crowd, to prevent them from loosening the bars.

The National Guards were in general pitiless. Those who had not been in the fighting wanted to distinguish themselves now, but all was really the reaction of fear. They were avenging themselves at once for the journals, the clubs, the mobs, the doctrines, for everything that had provoked them beyond measure in the last three months; and despite their victory, equality (as if for the punishment of its defenders and mockery of its enemies) was triumphantly revealed—an equality of brute beasts on the same level of blood-stained depravity; for the fanaticism of vested interests was on a level with the madness of the needy, the aristocracy exhibited the fury of the basest mob, and the cotton night-cap was no less hideous than the *bonnet rouge*. The public mind became disordered as after a great natural catastrophe, and men of intelligence were idiots for the rest of their lives.

Victor Hugo said that in the June Days civilization defended itself with the methods of barbarism. They were a turning-point in many respects. The army, like the peasants of which its ranks were so largely composed, passed from one side of the barricades to the other in June 1848. The Grande Peur of 1789, Valmy and Jemappes, the four sergeants of La Rochelle, and a host of other memories identified the peasant with social disorder and the army with revolution. Almost at a blow the myth—for it had become a myth by 1848—was ended: the peasant became the embodiment of social conservatism and the army the bulwark of order.

CHAPTER TWO

THE TRIUMPH OF LOUIS NAPOLEON

A FTER the June Days the army held power in France and the Assembly survived under its protection. 'This poor Assembly', wrote Victor Hugo, 'is a true soldier's girl, in love with a trooper.' The trooper was Cavaignac, whose principles excluded military dictatorship. He took the place of the discredited Executive Commission and appointed a moderate republican ministry to hold office while the Assembly completed its constitutional proposals. It did this by November. The constitution it made was much more influenced by theory than any of the preceding constitutions since 1789. The change in social ideals in the course of sixty years can be seen in its preamble, which—significantly enough—took the place of the former Declaration of Rights. The individualism of 1789, with its emphasis on rights, now had to share its claims with a recognition of duties and a new emphasis on fraternity. This may not have meant much in the France of the June Days, but even lip-service was a sign of a changing climate of opinion. Politically there had been rather less change in republican ideals. There was still the old attempt to reconcile the principles of separation of powers and sovereignty of the people. All power comes from the people, but this power must be divided: the conclusion was the election of a single chamber and a unique head of the government, both by universal suffrage and both directly responsible to the people, the one entrusted with total legislative authority and the other with all executive power.

The crucial decision as it turned out later, and indeed as it appeared at the time, was the embodiment of the executive power in the person of a president elected directly by the whole nation. The election of the president by direct universal suffrage was supported by the right and the moderates, and opposed by Ledru-Rollin and the red republicans. The fear of the tyranny of a Convention still haunted moderate opinion: de Tocqueville warned against the danger of turning the president into a mere agent of the Legislative Body. Grévy, the author of a famous amendment, admitted the danger, but saw a more dangerous precedent in the career of Napoleon I. 'Are you sure,' he asked the Assembly, 'that there will never be found an ambitious man, anxious to perpetuate his power, and if he is a man who has been able to make himself popular, if he is a victorious general, surrounded with the prestige of that military glory which the French cannot resist, if he is the offspring of one of the families which have reigned over France, and if he has never expressly renounced what he calls his rights [there could hardly have been a more obvious reference to Louis Napoleon], if commerce is languishing, if the people are in misery ... will you guarantee that this ambitious man will not succeed in overthrowing the republic?' The answer was given by Lamartine: If you want to do so, he said, confuse the legislative and executive powers, add the judicial and call your system by its true title—the Terror. He admitted that there were names which attracted the crowd as a mirage draws the flocks to it; but concluded, in a phrase from which his reputation has never recovered, 'Il faut laisser quelque chose à la Providence.' The Grévy amendment was defeated by 643 to 158 votes and the Second Republic had committed a delayed suicide.

The presidential election followed in December 1848. Among the candidates Cavaignac was the standard-bearer of the conservative republic and Ledru-Rollin of the red republicans; Raspail and a sprinkling of other candidates represented the left-wing; and there was a name of destiny—Louis Napoleon Bonaparte.

It is time to say something of Bonapartism as a political movement in France, now that at last it was on the point of becoming one. It may seem paradoxical, yet it is probably true, that the Napoleonic legend, while essential to the existence of the Second Empire, played only a secondary part in its creation. About the origin of the legend there need be little dispute; it was the deliberate creation of Napoleon I, by his official propaganda while he was Emperor, and in the imaginative picture he tried to draw while he was in exile of himself and his aims. To the legend of the pacifier who suppressed the internecine strife that had been tearing France apart, the protector of religion who had brought persecution to an end, the saviour who rescued society from the Jacobins and the Terror, the administrator who gave France efficient government and restored its financial and economic prosperity, the great general and military hero who had made Europe into a French Empire, was added an even more mendacious picture of the great champion of liberal ideals, of freedom for the oppressed nationalities of Europe, and of peace. In 1815 the facts were a little too close for all this to have very much effect, and by 1830 the Napoleonic legend was no more than a romantic survival of no political significance. It seemed so little dangerous that the Orleanist regime did not hesitate to exploit Bonapartist sentiment for the purpose of acquiring a little badly needed popularity.

The two adventures of Louis Bonaparte, at Strasbourg in 1836 and Boulogne in 1840, confirmed the belief that Bonapartism, if it was not a spent fire, was one that was too damp ever to burst into flames again. The Emperor's nephew, it is true, had shown rather more skill with the pen than with the sword. He had produced, in 1832, a volume of *Rêveries politiques*—possibly not the best title to advertise its author as a man of action. More effective for the creation of a public image of the pretender—even if only an *image d'Épinal* like the popular cut-outs of Napoleon and his soldiers—were an artillery manual and a booklet on the extinction of pauperism. Louis Napoleon Bonaparte's most important production was *Des idées napoléoniennes* in 1839. This should have been taken more seriously than it was. As with later dictators, if it had been possible to believe that Louis Napoleon meant what he said, the subsequent history of France would have come as less of a surprise to contemporaries.

After the Boulogne adventure, Louis Bonaparte's light was extinguished for the next six years by not very rigorous imprisonment in the fortress at Ham, where he was provided with the modest amenities of life including a mistress, and from which he walked out disguised as a builder's labourer in 1846. In February 1848, therefore, he was again a potential saviour at the disposal of France, only hardly anyone as yet seemed to think of him in that capacity. He made a fleeting appearance in Paris soon after the revolution but found the political climate uncongenial and returned to London, where by enrolling as a special constable against the Chartists he did something to bury the memory of the carbonarist and conspirator and build up a picture of himself as the defender of law and order. So slight was the Bonapartist sentiment in France on the morrow of the revolution, that a Bonapartist paper could only survive from February 25th to March 3rd, and the tiny group of devotees of Louis Napoleon could make no impression on public opinion.

By June there was evidently a change in this respect. Possibly the apparently imminent collapse of the social order had already started the swing to a potential saviour of society. Supplementary elections then returned Louis Napoleon for Paris and four other departments, with practically no organization or propaganda to support his candidature. This should have been an omen, but a miscalculated letter that he sent from London to the President of the Assembly aroused feeling in the Assembly against him. Wisely he appreciated that the time was not yet ripe and resigned. Further elections, in September, saw him returned in five constituencies and at the head of the Paris list. Despite this, the republicans of the Assembly for the most part remained unimpressed by the Bonapartist danger. When he rose in the Assembly, the insignificant appearance of the bearer of such a great name, and a halting speech in a German accent, convinced them that they were right. But though it would still be an exaggeration to speak of a Bonapartist party, supporters were gathering and conducting a more active propaganda, by journals and by the production of prints, medals, brooches, and knick-knacks of various kinds with Napoleonic inscriptions or associations.

As the presidential election came nearer the obscure Bonapartists who had been backing what had seemed for so long a forlorn hope found themselves joined by more prominent figures. Ambitious Orleanist politicians like Thiers and Odilon Barrot, disappointed in their expectation of office by the revolution they had done so much to provoke, hoped to use Louis Napoleon to return to power. Barrot called him 'our excellent young man', and Thiers, who advised him to shave his moustache, said he was 'a cretin whom we will manage'. De Tocqueville, with a mixture of shrewdness and misjudgment, described him as 'an enigmatic, sombre, insignificant numskull'. Whatever their views of him personally, many former Orleanists, unfettered by attachment to political principles but with a keen eye on the main chance, prepared to jump on the Bonapartist band-wagon. More idealistic motives inspired Victor Hugo, who also kept a sentimental attachment to the memory of the Emperor his father had served. From the time of the *Ode à la colonne* his poems had done as much as any writings, except those of Béranger, to keep the Napoleonic memory alive. In 1848 he saw himself as the prophet and adviser of a liberal Bonaparte; and Louis Napoleon was not indifferent to the prestige that the support of France's greatest poet could give. After the election the poet was a guest at the first dinner given by the new president at the Elysée. The offer of the Madrid embassy tempted Hugo, with his memories of imperial Spain, but it was not what he had hoped for. In youth he had declared, 'Je veux être Chateaubriand ou rien,' and Chateaubriand had been Foreign Minister. Though disappointed, he continued to support the president until December 2nd added political to personal disillusionment.

The beautiful Miss Howard, with whom Louis Bonaparte had lived since 1846, came over in the autumn of 1848 to add her fortune to the others that were being invested in his future, and after the election to be for a time official mistress in the prince president's little court. Spiritual support was added to secular. The clerical party, headed by Montalembert and Falloux, was legitimist in principle but prepared to do a deal with Louis Bonaparte in the interest of clerical control of education. Because Louis Napoleon had the support of the great banker Fould, it has been supposed that the financiers and also the industrialists were among his backers; but in fact they were more firmly Orleanist than the politicians, and suspicious of both the ideas and the associates of Louis Bonaparte. On the other hand his connection with the Saint-Simonians brought him the support of that sect and its adherents, such as the Péreire brothers. While the republicans remained aloof, some socialists saw hope in Bonapartism.

The two great journals of the February Revolution opposed the Bonapartist candidature, the *Réforme* supporting Ledru-Rollin and the *National* Cavaignac. Louis Bonaparte had on his side Girardin's *Presse,* because of its editor's enmity to Cavaignac, the *Constitutionnel* under the influence of Thiers, Victor Hugo's *Événement,* and a number of provincial journals. But though the Bonapartists spent as much as they could on propaganda in the press, they only had the support of a minority of papers.

It is possible to believe that even if he had had none of this support Louis Bonaparte might still have been elected President. The populace in the large towns had no reason to vote for the victor of the June Days and the repressive and reactionary regime with which he was identified. The peasants of the countryside, who formed the great mass of the voters, were under the influence of a panic fear of red terror and confiscation of property spread by the men of order; they needed a saviour of society and who could fill that role better than a Napoleon. 'The idea of authority is attached to that name', wrote Barante, 'and it is authority that they want.' The idealism behind Ledru-Rollin, the social conservatism and official influence behind Cavaignac, were powerless against this wave of emotion. Ledru-Rollin secured 370,119 votes, Cavaignac 1,448,107, and Louis Napoleon 5,434,226; on the extreme left Raspail had a pitiable 36,920. Lamartine's star had long since set: in all France he could only gather 17,910 votes.

The first act of the new president was to take the oath of loyalty to the Republic and swear to defend the constitution. If he had any mental reservations he kept them to himself; he was always good at keeping his own counsel. He appointed a conservative Orleanist ministry under Odilon Barrot, which reflected the political complexion of the Assembly, left the government to them, and devoted his time to tours through France. This enabled him to exhibit his real brilliance as a propagandist, and at the same time to leave the onus of repressing the forces of the left on the Assembly. The red republicans had reacted to their defeat by drawing closer together in a nation-wide organization under the name of the Solidarité Républicaine, with central and local committees and a staunch Jacobin, Delescluze, as its secretary. The task of repression was begun with the outlawing of this society in January 1849.

The Constituent Assembly had no real justification for its continued

existence now that the constitution had been made and put into
effect, but it hung on as long as it could, in a moribund condition.
Finally it had to dissolve and in May 1849 elections were held
for a Legislative Assembly. The conservative forces of all kinds,
sometimes called the 'party of order' though they were too divided
to constitute a real party, organized themselves for the election
through a committee in the rue de Poitiers. It included legitimists,
Orleanists, Bonapartists, Catholics, and even moderate republicans.
The prefects, who had replaced Ledru-Rollin's commissaires, now
returned to their customary role and played a large part in the
elections. Of course, the supporters of order obtained a large
majority of 500 out of 750 members. The conservative republicans
of the *National*-Cavaignac school were reduced to a small group of
70; the men of February—Lamartine, Dupont de l'Eure, Garnier-
Pagès, Marie, Marrast, Carnot, and others—were rejected by the
country. What was unexpected and alarming to the forces of order
was the comparative success of the red republicans, with 180 seats.
Ledru-Rollin came second on the Paris list. The explanation, of
course, lay in abstentions from voting, especially of many of the
peasantry. The total vote in the country had sunk to 40 per cent of
those entitled to vote, and of these one-third had voted for the reds.
Evidently the left was still far from defeated. But what the conservative forces could not achieve in the elections, the left-wing
politicians in Paris managed to do in a single day. Undeterred by the
lessons of 1848 they staged a futile attempt at revolution on June
13th, 1849. Whereas in 1848 the cry had been Poland, now it was
Rome. There was at least this justification for the demonstration:
that a French force under Oudinot was about to overthrow the
Roman Republic and reinstate the authority of Pius IX, which it did
shortly after. The attempted insurrection in Paris and a number of
provincial towns obtained no popular support. Ledru-Rollin and
most of the left-wing deputies fled abroad, others were imprisoned;
and the government and the Assembly had a fair excuse for passing
more severe repressive legislation.

As well as an energetic suppression of the reds by police measures,
the conservatives now began to feel that a more positive inculcation
of the principles of social order was needed. The 'panic of property'

which followed the June Days had weakened the anti-clericalism of many of the propertied classes and of their leaders such as Thiers. The merit of clerical education as a means of instilling the principles of social discipline and the sacredness of property into the minds of the lower orders was now more adequately appreciated. It found expression in an educational law proposed by Falloux in June 1849 and finally voted in March 1850. Meanwhile, in January 1850, had been voted the so-called 'little law' on education. This attributed the appointment and dismissal of primary teachers to the prefects, a right which they kept until 1944. The *loi Falloux* itself gave members of religious orders the right of opening schools without requiring any further qualification, and introduced councils with strong clerical elements to control the University.

On a general policy of weakening the left, the president and the Assembly were able to co-operate. But Louis Napoleon soon showed the Barrots and the Thiers that he was not the puppet president they thought they had elected. In October 1849, though it still had a majority in the Assembly, he dismissed the Odilon Barrot ministry and issued a message justifying his action to the country. 'To strengthen the Republic menaced on all sides by anarchy,' he began, turning against themselves the chief weapon of the parliamentary factions, 'to maintain externally the name of France at the height of her renown, men are needed animated by a patriotic devotion, proof against everything, who understand the need for an undivided and strong rule and for a clearly formulated policy, who will not compromise authority by irresolution, and who will be as deeply conscious of my responsibility as of their own.' For his new ministry, therefore, he chose new men from outside parliament; and to show that it was to be a presidential and not a parliamentary government, he appointed no president of the council. He himself was to be its head.

President and Assembly, however, were still capable of receiving a shock from the country. In March 1850 by-elections were held to replace the 30 deputies condemned after the events of June 13th, 1849. In the face of intense repression the democratic republicans rallied their forces once again. Despite all the efforts of the administration the left won 20 seats out of the 30, and in Paris the three left-wing candidates were returned with large majorities. In a sub-sequent election to fill a vacancy at Paris, the novelist Eugène Sue, now a name of terror to the respectable classes who had read his newspaper serials with avidity, was returned.

The panic of the Assembly revived: in spite of all the measures of repression, universal suffrage was still, it appeared, dangerous. In May 1850, therefore, a law was introduced to deprive of the franchise all who had suffered any condemnation by the courts—given the repressive legislation this would eliminate most of the militants of the left—and all who had not three years' residential qualification in the same canton. The effect was to exclude about three million out of nine and a half million voters. Supported by Thiers with an un-measured denunciation of the 'vile multitude', the law was passed in May 1850 by a majority of 433 to 241. It gave the president the opportunity to present himself once more as the defender of the rights of the people, and his demand for the abrogation of the law, in November 1850, was only rejected by 355 to 348.

Louis Napoleon had by now attracted to himself the support of a substantial group in the Assembly. By his propaganda tours, and the fact that his star was obviously still rising, he obtained an increasing backing in the country. He particularly worked on the army, and in January 1851 felt strong enough to dismiss the republican general Changarnier, who commanded the forces, both regular and National Guard, in Paris. Despite its earlier suspicions, the world of business, fearing a renewal of disorder when the president's mandate came to an end in 1852, and dissatisfied at the rather slow recovery from the slump, was now beginning to see its best hope in the continuance of Louis Napoleon at the head of the state.

Unfortunately this was not possible, or so it seemed. The con-stitution did not permit the re-election of the president. To over-come this obstacle the administration organized a campaign of petitions for its revision. So energetic and so successful were the prefects, that nearly all the Conseils Généraux in France supported the plea for revision. The Assembly yielded to this pressure by appointing a commission to examine the question, which concluded against the proposal. A vote in July 1851 was by 446 to 278 in favour of revision, but this was not the constitutionally necessary two-thirds majority. There was a renewed flood of petitions, but now Louis Napoleon and his little group of intimates had decided to settle the matter in an extra-parliamentary way.

The support of the army was ensured by bringing over from Algeria Saint-Arnaud and other colonial generals, with no civilian prejudices in favour of republics or parliamentary methods. The Bonapartist inner circle was now fairly complete. Louis Napoleon's half-brother Morny, a gambler of genius, was the chief organizer of the *coup d'état*. De Maupas, a *préfet à poigne*, was brought from Toulouse to become Prefect of Police. Persigny, who had shared Louis Bonaparte's defeats before 1848, rightly joined in his coming triumph. After several postponements the coup was finally fixed for December 2nd, the anniversary of Austerlitz.

On the night of December 1st–2nd the conspirators moved into action. Troops under an Algerian general occupied the Imprimerie Nationale, the Palais Bourbon, newspaper offices, printing works, and the main strategic points in Paris. In the *mairies* of the *arrondissements* the drums were broken, the bell-towers of the churches were guarded. The Parisians woke in the morning to find placards announcing the dissolution of the Assembly, the restoration of universal suffrage, new elections, and a state of siege in Paris and the neighbouring departments. In an *appel au peuple* the president accused the Assembly of conspiracy—a nice touch—and fomenting disorder. A proclamation to the army declared, 'Soldiers! it is your mission to save the country.' Sixteen members of the Assembly and some 80 other known opponents were seized by troops in their homes. Some 300 deputies, excluded from their chamber, met in the *mairie* of the *X*^e *arrondissement* to protest, and were duly arrested in their turn.

On the morning of December 2nd the saviour of society, accompanied by his generals, rode out from the Élysée. In a city occupied by 50,000 troops there was little danger, but also, to his disappointment, little enthusiasm. There were even some slight hostile demonstrations, but the day passed with no sign of resistance. On December 3rd, however, Victor Hugo and a few republicans formed a committee to organize opposition. A barricade was erected in the faubourg Saint-Antoine and on it a deputy, Dr Baudin, was killed.

His name was not forgotten. The danger was slight for the masses were on the side of the dictator. When Flaubert's hero asked a worker if they were not going to fight, he received the answer, 'We're not fools enough to get ourselves killed for the bourgeois! Let them settle it themselves!' They did in their way. On December 4th more barricades appeared, manned by a few hundred republicans who had not forgotten 1848. The generals were determined to have done with this nonsense: 30,000 troops, with artillery, musket, and bayonet, were let loose against the resistance, which was crushed in a few hours. Only a few hundred were killed, either in the fighting or shot when taken prisoner. The most dramatic episode occurred on the boulevard Poissonière, where the soldiers, in a state of natural excitement, fired several volleys into a large crowd of passive onlookers. It was not a very glorious beginning for the Second Empire.

✦

CHAPTER THREE

A BOURGEOIS EMPIRE

IT was difficult to make a *coup d'état* without breaking some heads as well as an oath, and so Louis Napoleon had found, doubtless to his regret for he was a humane man. If he could have obtained the power and glory by honourable and peaceful methods he would certainly have preferred them. In addition he had to begin with repression, not so much because the feeble resistance in Paris and a few minor movements in the provinces needed repressing, as because unless there were some repression there would hardly have seemed any reason for a *coup d'état*. Altogether 26,884 arrests were effected throughout France. Of those arrested, 9,000 were transported to Algeria and 239 to Cayenne, 1,500 expelled from France, and 3,000 given forced residence away from their homes. Soon after, a commission of revision freed 3,500 of those sentenced, and by 1859, when an amnesty was offered to all the remainder except Ledru-Rollin, the number still penalized was only 1,800. The Second Empire might have been astonished at its own moderation and one would have expected it easily to live down the slight splashes of blood that accompanied its birth-pangs. Somehow it did not, and even the Emperor never quite put them out of his mind.

One of the first steps of Louis Napoleon was to confiscate the extensive property which Louis-Philippe, with almost excessive paternal affection, had collected for his large family as well as for himself. It was used to make grants to societies for mutual aid, for constructing workers' dwellings, and so on; but it looked a little too much like bribery with stolen property, even for a number of Louis' supporters. His enemies called it 'le premier vol de l'aigle'.

Such comments showed a bad spirit. It was desirable that the country should envisage recent events in the proper light; so by a decree of February 17th, 1852, largely the work of Rouher, the press was brought under a more severe control than it had known since the First Empire. No journal dealing with political or social questions was to be issued without the permission of the government; the caution money was heavily increased; the list of press offences was enlarged and penalties strengthened; those accused of press offences were to be tried without a jury; after three warnings to Paris journals by the Minister of the Interior, or to provincial ones by a prefect, a journal could be suspended by administrative action and in the last resort suppressed.

The general clauses of a new constitution did not need long discussion, for Louis Napoleon regarded himself as invested with constituent authority by the plebiscite that had confirmed his seizure of power. The president was to have, as before, the nomination of all officials, from top to bottom, as well as of the Senate, the Conseil d'État, the High Court of Justice, and the ministers. There was to be a Legislative Body, elected by universal suffrage in single-member constituencies, in which the prefects and sub-prefects, experts at electoral management, the majority of whom had passed over from the service of Louis-Philippe to that of Louis Napoleon, could make certain—by all the traditional devices—that only the official candidate had much chance of succeeding. The result of the elections that were held in March 1852 was a foregone conclusion. Four legitimists, one independent, and three republicans (who refused to sit) were elected; the remaining 253 members were official candidates, chosen by the administration to uphold the Bonapartist cause in the constituencies. The labourers were not considered unworthy of their hire: in the same month the salaries of the prefects were doubled. 'The dictatorship with which the people has entrusted me ceases today', declared Louis Napoleon in an official pronouncement on March 30th. It was only to cease, in the humiliation of Sedan, eighteen years later.

The possibility of failure seemed far removed at the outset. The new regime was lucky in the stars under which it was born, for the lean years in European economy were at an end and the new government was able to take advantage of a rising tide of economic activity. Shares rose rapidly in value on the Paris market. The Bank of France reduced its interest rate to 3 per cent. A triumphal tour of a regenerated France in the autumn of 1852 by Louis Napoleon was followed by the proclamation of the Empire and a plebiscite in which 7,800,000 voted yes and 250,000 no.

Even allowing for two million abstentions this was a decisive endorsement of France's new ruler. Yet what kind of man he was very few knew. Aged forty-four in 1852, he was still almost completely an unknown quantity to the country that had entrusted its destinies to him. The son of Josephine's daughter Hortense Beauharnais, and Napoleon's brother Louis, the un-Napoleonic appearance of Napoleon III, as he chose to be known, and the adventures of Hortense subsequent to his birth, had led to doubt being cast on his paternity, though almost certainly without justification. He was brought up by his mother, after she and Louis had separated, among the flotsam and jetsam of the Empire in exile. It was the drifting, raffish life, in Germany, Italy, England, Switzerland, of a cosmopolitan adventurer. Queen Victoria, when she met the new Emperor, remarked that unlike Louis-Philippe, who was 'thoroughly French', Louis Napoleon was 'as *unlike* a Frenchman as possible', and much more German than French in character. She was a shrewd judge and meant it as praise.

The first political action of the young Louis Napoleon was in Italian, not French, politics. He joined an abortive Carbonari rising in 1831 and had to fly the pursuing Austrians in disguise. Possibly the tutorship of Philippe le Bas, son of the Robespierrist, had aroused his youthful idealism. His first political declaration — the *Rêveries politiques* of 1832 — proposed the regeneration of France by a peculiar combination of Napoleon II and the Republic. Only after the death of the duc de Reichstadt was it possible for Louis Napoleon to put forward the Bonapartist claim on his own behalf.

It is difficult to know at what stage he began to feel he was a man of destiny. Queen Victoria, when she met Napoleon III in 1855, was impressed by his genuine belief that all he had done and did was only in fulfilment of his destiny. But if a superstitious belief in his fate deceived him, it need not deceive us or lead us to underestimate his real abilities. Chance had not dealt Louis Napoleon many cards apart from his name. He was no orator and wisely chose to listen rather than speak, unlike Louis-Philippe, whose garrulity was a legend. The charm which he could exercise over other men, and even more over women, owed little to advantages of appearance. Greville describes him as 'a short thickish vulgar-looking man'. Practically all the Bonapartes, of course, were rather vulgar. In addition, Louis Napoleon had no taste in literature or art. It would be an interesting question whether the official art of the Second Empire was, or was not, more boring, pretentious, and vapid than that of the First. That there was no originality in Louis Napoleon does not perhaps matter, for originality is not normally conducive to political success. On the other hand, like the first Napoleon he had a great capacity for picking up other men's ideas; his mind was immensely receptive. It can hardly be denied that between his election in 1848 and the *coup d'état* in 1851 he played his cards with great shrewdness and beat the politicians at their own game. He had more natural generosity and humanity—when his ambitions did not get in the way—than most dictators; and his sympathy for the lot of the French working-man went beyond the mere requirements of the cult of popularity. If we say that in the last resort he had no moral scruples, this is to refer to his single-minded devotion to the quest of power, in which he gave those who observed him the impression, if not of the frantic possession of a Hitler, at least of a quieter, but equally unswerving kind of somnambulism. Louis Napoleon's taciturnity gave the illusion of depths that were not there. It is difficult to dislike him; but equally difficult to respect him.

Napoleon III never became more than an adventurer, even when he was on a throne; and for all his triumphs he never seems to have enjoyed them. Perhaps he was already prematurely old when success came. Perhaps he had trained himself to sacrifice everything else, including happiness, to success in his chosen objectives. Only in some such way can his marriage be explained. Evidently the new emperor would have to marry if he was to perpetuate his dynasty. Negotiations for one or two minor royalties had proved abortive when, unfortunately, Louis Napoleon's roving eye was caught by a Spanish beauty in transit through Paris. She was of noble birth, twenty-six years old, and a notorious virgin. It was a challenge and he attempted his usual gambit of seduction, which totally failed. Even fairly mature Spanish grandees were not easily seduced, especially if there was the prospect of something better. In January 1853 it materialized in the form of marriage. 'She has played her game with him so well,' wrote the British ambassador, 'that he can get her in no other way but marriage.' But though she was beautiful, an admirable model for a fashionable painter like Winterhalter, with all the dignity that Napoleon III himself sometimes lacked, and in the end exhibited courage and greater force of character than the Emperor, Eugénie was a bad choice in almost every other respect. She was not very intelligent, but very religious, or at least clerical in a Spanish way. Her influence, and that of her friends, over the policy of the Second Empire was almost invariably unfortunate. There were personal difficulties too. Her mother, it turned out, did not live up to her daughter's standards: she collected debts and lovers. Eugénie, on the other hand, proved to be one of nature's virgins, incapable of responding to the emperor's sensuality, and he periodically resorted to Miss Howard, now created comtesse de Beauregard, and subsequently to many others. After the birth of the Prince Imperial in 1856, which nearly cost the empress her life, marital relations ceased.

However, the succession was secured, so far as the life of one heir could do so, and the element of loyalty to a dynasty, though a very new one, could begin to play a role in politics. Bonapartism was more than mere attachment to a name. An opponent might say that it was a synthetic substitute for real political principles, a combination of inconsistent and irreconcilable objectives, of value only as propaganda. But among the supporters of Napoleon III there was one group, with which he himself had considerable sympathy, which —so far as its ideas went—could supply the Second Empire with a policy and some sort of working philosophy behind it. These were the Saint-Simonians, now more or less recovered from the père Enfantin's aberrations. Saint-Simon as the John the Baptist of Positivism may be left where he belongs, in the classes on moral philosophy of the écoles normales. 'It seems', writes one normalien, 'that his best title to fame is in having transmitted from Condorcet to Comte the idea of a positive policy founded on social science.' A better claim may be found in the implications of his well-known parable. Suppose, Saint-Simon says, France were to lose suddenly its fifty leading scientists of all kinds, artists, architects, engineers, doctors, bankers, merchants, ironmasters, industrialists in every

L

branch, masons, carpenters, and workers in every craft—it would immediately sink in the scale of civilization and become inferior to all those countries of which it is now the equal. On the other hand, suppose it kept all its leading men of science, arts and crafts, commerce and industry, but lost the whole royal family, all the ministers and counsellors of state, the prefects, judges, archbishops, bishops, and all other ecclesiastical dignitaries, and in addition the ten thousand wealthiest landed proprietors living solely on the income from their property—the loss would undoubtedly grieve the French, being a humane people, but it would not materially affect their prosperity or their position in the world. In other words, Saint-Simon was asserting the primacy of the productive classes in society, of economic over political ends. It was also a protest against the dominance of the conservative propertied classes which was established by the Revolution.

Saint-Simon died in 1825, but his disciples continued and systematized his ideas of economic progress. The problem before France, as they saw it, was stated by Michel Chevalier in *Des intérêts matériels en France* in 1838. The new ruling class, he says, has won political power only in alliance with the people. If it is not to be overthrown in its turn it will have to meet the material demands of the people. This can be done only by means of the development of credit, communications, and education. The events of 1848 went a long way towards justifying this analysis, but they also showed that the position of the propertied classes was stronger than he supposed and that they had no intention of adopting Chevalier's remedy, or any other, except that of crude repression. They viewed the Saint-Simonian idea of the expenditure of large sums by the state to counter economic depression with horror. The Saint-Simonians themselves were not unaware of the strength of the opposition to their ideas and looked to strong government as the only means of economic and social reform. It was natural, therefore, that they should have welcomed the coming to power of Louis Napoleon, who himself had been attracted by the novelty and promise of Saint-Simonian ideas. They provided him with an economic programme, and with some of the personnel to put it into practice. The expansion of credit, railways, industry, trade, even the rebuilding of Paris, for which there had been a Saint-Simonian plan in 1832 — in fact, practically all the major economic developments, and therefore nearly all the real and lasting achievements of the Second Empire — derive from the inspiration of Saint-Simon and his followers. Though on a smaller scale and in a more restricted field, Saint-Simon might almost be called the Bentham of nineteenth-century France.

The key to economic progress in France lay in the growth of credit, as the Saint-Simonians correctly saw. It is sometimes assumed that the Second Empire was promoted, in their own interest, by the financiers. The truth is rather, on the contrary, that the financiers were promoted by the Second Empire. The affiliations of most high finance were with the old order of Orleanism or with the conservative republic. The only names that stand out on the side of Louis Napoleon are those of the Péreire brothers and Achille Fould. Existing banks and orthodox financiers catered mainly for the wealthy and conservative *rentiers*, interested principally in government loans. For the growth of industry new banks were needed. The Comptoir d'Escompte, founded in 1848 and developed with the encouragement of the emperor, was primarily a commercial bank. Later it developed considerable colonial and Far Eastern interests. The Crédit Foncier, founded in 1852, was given a monopoly of mortgage finance, and its moderate terms facilitated the extensive rebuilding of the towns of France during the Second Empire. The Crédit Agricole dealt in farm mortgages and other agricultural finance; it ran into difficulties later, but this was after 1870. Private banks were also developed, the most famous being the Crédit Mobilier of the Péreire brothers, Saint-Simonians, who plunged heavily in French and foreign railways, a French steamship line, and government loans. Later, in 1863, the Crédit Lyonnais was set up; conducted with the traditional caution of the Lyonnais businessmen, it has flourished to the present day.

A wave of economic expansion followed the establishment of the Empire. It was concentrated particularly on the development of railways. After a slow beginning, the companies were rationalized by being reduced to six, and the pace of construction was so accelerated that by 1859 France had nearly three times as great a length of line as in 1851. By 1870 France had almost as extensive a network of lines in operation as Germany or Great Britain. Railway development stimulated, of course, the production of coal and iron. The consumption of coal was trebled, and the use of horse power in industry quintupled, between 1851 and 1870. The average price of steel was practically halved. The greatest of the iron-works, at Le Creusot, was bought by the Schneider brothers in 1836 when its annual production was 5,000 tons; in 1847 it was 18,000, and the increased pace of growth under the Second Empire is shown by the rise from 35,000 tons in 1855 to 133,000 in 1867. In the same period the foreign commerce of France practically trebled.

Meanwhile the growth of the French population had slackened, so that the increased wealth of the country was not swallowed up by the excess of mouths. Moreover the shift from the country to the town continued. The proportion of urban population grew from 24 per cent to 31 per cent, and this probably represented a rise in the average standard of life in the countryside, for it was the landless labourers and the poorest element there which declined most. The growth of railways, which played their part in facilitating the movement from the country, also broke down some of the traditional rural isolation.

The share of the state in providing the actual finance for this general economic development should not be exaggerated. Up to 1860 the public works programme was financed mainly by private investment. Budgetary expenses for this purpose were indeed smaller than they had been under Louis-Philippe; whence those developments in which for one reason or another the private investor was not interested — roads, canals, ports — languished. The same was true of agriculture. The peasants, whose votes had established the Second Empire, were those who profited least from it. They were suspicious of all new methods; the legal structure of France protected the small proprietor in his jealous independence of any interference, and the sub-division of the land prohibited any general or co-ordinated schemes of improvement.

The programme of public works which Louis Napoleon inaugurated was in his mind a continuation of the policy of the First Empire. He himself wrote of Napoleon I, 'The public works, which the Emperor put into operation on such a large scale, were not only

one of the principle causes of domestic prosperity, they even promoted great social progress.' While these motives were certainly
present to the mind of Napoleon III, the propaganda value of public
works was also not absent, particularly if they could be effected in
full view of the public. The improvement of Paris, in continuation
of the work of Napoleon I, was therefore among the first projects
to be taken in hand after the *coup d'état.*

The need to render Paris, like all the other great urban agglomerations of Europe, habitable was patent enough; but it would be a
mistake to attribute the improvements solely to the pressure of hard
facts. Reforms, in Paris as in London, did not come about by the
automatic pressure of circumstances; they were the conscious
achievement of the disciples of a Saint-Simon or a Bentham, and in
France the result of deliberate policy. It was not confined to the
capital: at Lyons, the prefect Vaïsse effected an almost equally
dramatic transformation.

The first attempt of Napoleon III, after the *coup d'état,* to promote
a policy of public works was frustrated by the conservative financial
ideas of the officials in charge, but in 1853 one of the most energetic
of the prefects was brought to Paris. This was the Alsatian Protestant,
Haussmann, who had hitched his administrative wagon to the rising
star of Louis Napoleon as early as the presidential election of 1848.
As a godson of Prince Eugène, Haussmann had almost an hereditary
claim to be regarded as a Bonapartist. Forceful and cunning,
ambitious, unprincipled, formidable in bulk and character, he was the
ideal agent for the Second Empire in a grade a little lower than the
highest. He was to be Prefect of the Seine from 1853 to 1870. Such
a man did not shrink from unorthodox, but up to a point justified,
financial methods. The theory behind them was simply that the new
values created by the reconstruction of the older sectors of Paris
would themselves pay for the work that had to be undertaken.

The scope of Haussmann's demolition and reconstruction is
amazing. He gave Paris eighty-five miles of new streets with wide
carriage-ways and pavements shaded with trees. Private enterprise
lined them with houses and shops, to a height and with a façade
prescribed by the authorities, and in a style that represented Haussmann's idea of architectural beauty, for the Prefect of the Seine had

the born philistine's conviction of his own impeccable artistic taste. Viollet-le-Duc, apart from the injury he did to Notre-Dame, was kept out of the rebuilding of Paris by Haussmann, who was neither romantic nor medieval. His passion, like that of Napoleon I, was for vistas. The place de l'Étoile looks very fine from the air: it is a pity that it is not normally seen from that angle. Napoleon III, indeed, reproached Haussmann that in his love of straight lines he neglected the needs of traffic. The new railway stations, for example, were left without adequate approaches.

The best things in the re-planning of Paris were due to the influence of Napoleon III. His memories of London inspired the creation of many squares and other open places. The Bois de Boulogne, which had been a rather dull royal forest, cut across by long straight avenues for the hunters, was given by the emperor to the city. At the instigation of Morny a race-course was created at Longchamps; it rapidly became a fashionable social resort, the profits on which largely paid for the transformation of the un-interesting *bois* into a landscaped park. A similar treatment was accorded to the Bois de Vincennes on the east of Paris. Napoleon III was also responsible for the construction of the Halles, the great central market, as a functional structure of metal and glass.

Apart from the long straight roads he drove through Paris, and the vistas they afforded, Haussmann's greatest achievement was in the drainage of the city. The sewers of Paris before him are luridly described by Victor Hugo in *Les Misérables*. By the end of the Second Empire the visit, especially of the great sewer which Hauss-mann liked to call his Cloaca Maxima, was a tourist attraction. A further virtue of the sewers was that they had been built without tearing anything else down, for much of old Paris and many fine and historic buildings were sacrificed to make it a Second Empire city. A sentimental regret for what was lost, and even an aesthetic distaste for what replaced it, would neither, perhaps, be justified if a fine modern city with improved living conditions had been built. But the tradition of urbanism, the Florence of the Medici, the Paris of Louis XV, the Nancy of king Stanislaus, had now come down to the boulevard Malesherbes and the place de l'Opéra. Behind the state-prescribed façades of Haussmann's streets the builders could put up what they liked, and often new and more imposing slums replaced the older and more picturesque ones. Running water was only supplied at the option of the owner of a building, who often decided that it was an unnecessary luxury, since it involved the payment of a water rate. The function of the grand new sewers must not be mistaken: they were to remove the rain-water from the streets and prevent flooding. Sanitary, or rather insanitary, refuse still had to be carted away by an army of men at night in the traditional fashion, or sunk in cess pits, or deposited illegally in streets and gardens. Another, equally unpleasant, aspect of the city was the large area taken up by decaying bodies. Haussmann is not to be blamed for this; his plans for a great municipal cemetery outside Paris were successfully resisted by those who were determined that when they could do no more mischief there alive, they should leave their dead bodies to pollute the air and drinking water of the city.

The attention that was paid to Paris was not given to its surroundings. The wall of the Farmers General (on the line of the present outer ring of boulevards), with its sixty gates, was now no longer the effective limit of occupation. A shift of population was taking place to the large area between this wall and the fortifications of the Orleanist monarchy. Railway works and factories attracted a suburban population; and many of those who continued to work in Paris were drawn outwards by the cheapness of living in what was becoming a huge, poverty-stricken, higgledy-piggledy encampment of shacks. However, in the great enterprise of Haussmann good and bad were mixed up together, and his achievement suited his day and generation. Contemporaries who began by opposing and went on to mock his efforts, came to admire the results.

The crown of them all was to be the new Paris Opéra, built by Charles Garnier, inspired by the eighteenth-century Bordeaux Opéra, and calculated for the gratification of a society even richer and more luxurious than the eighteenth-century mercantile aristocracy of Bordeaux, as well as for a less chaste artistic taste than that of the age of Louis XV. Within and without it was loaded with decoration in all the styles known to history. A separate carriageway led into a private entrance to the imperial box, for Napoleon remembered the attempt by Orsini and the murder of the duc de Berry. A huge entrance hall and elaborate stairs, for the arrival and reception of foreign or French notabilities; a foyer for the circulation of the fashionable throng; an auditorium surrounded by boxes to preserve the privacy of wealth and rank or facilitate amorous intrigue; a stage as deep as the auditorium, on which the most grandiose spectacles could be presented — such was the Paris Opéra, a worthy setting for the luxury and splendour of Second Empire society, where Napoleon III and his empress might shine amidst the wealthiest *nouveaux riches* and the most beautiful courtesans of Paris. This was a dream picture: in 1871 the Opéra was still unfinished. It was completed, with the constitutional laws of the Third Republic, in 1875.

The Second Empire was the real bourgeois monarchy, an age of plutocrats without the culture or taste of an eighteenth-century Farmer General, of fashionable priests without the religious feeling of a Lamennais or a Lacordaire, of well-disciplined academics without the intellectual distinction of the Orleanist scholars, of glittering *demi-mondaines* whose possession was one of the chief forms of ostentatious expenditure and signs of worldly success. The fashionable painters and writers were even more insignificant than is usual in modern times. Apart from Daumier's cartoons, Millet's paintings exhibiting the dignity of labour, and Courbet's bourgeois-shocking realism, the only painters of real distinction were the rebels of the Salon des Refusés in 1863 who, rejected by official art, founded the great Impressionist school of the Third Republic. The most lasting artistic creations that belong properly to the Second Empire are the comedies of Labiche and the operettas of Offenbach. What was on a higher level represented either a survival of the romanticism of the early century, or a direct or implied protest against the new society and its standards. Victor Hugo, fulminating in exile from the Channel Isles, launched *Les Châtiments* against 'Napoléon le Petit'. The cult of realism that is associated with the Third Republic developed in fact under the Second Empire, which recognized its enmity when the publications of *Madame Bovary* and *Les Fleurs du Mal* were prosecuted in 1857.

If we want to see the spirit of the Second Empire at its best and most triumphant, we must look at the Exhibition of 1855, organized in imitation of the Great Exhibition of 1851 in London, but representing none the less a genuine aspiration after economic progress and pride in the beginnings of achievement.

CHAPTER FOUR

L'EMPIRE C'EST LA PAIX

A N age of materialism and money-making was opening, selfish and—especially after the June Days—hag-ridden with class hatred, but all classes were striving, with varying success, for the same thing—a higher standard of living. The desire for adventures, either domestic or foreign, if it ever existed, was over. Nationalist historians have represented a nineteenth-century France constantly harking back to the military glories of the First Empire. Nothing could be more misleading. There were many grievances against the July Monarchy, but its lack of bellicose ardour was not one of the causes of the 1848 Revolution. If the left-wing republicans and socialists aroused the opposition of the nation under the Second Republic, it was not least because of the fear that they might involve France in war with Europe. Louis Napoleon had judged the desires of the country rightly when he proclaimed, 'l'Empire, c'est la Paix.'

They had not changed by 1853, when the Russian occupation of Moldavia and Wallachia led to a Russo-Turkish War. France was involved because she claimed to be the protector of Roman Catholic interests in the Near East, and a quarrel over the custody of the Holy Places had been the occasion, if not the cause, of the Russo-Turkish war. The French emperor was indignant at the Russian aggression and at what seemed to him a humiliation for France; but though clerical support might have been expected, the country as a whole entered the Crimean War not only without enthusiasm, but with patent reluctance. However, confused as were the events leading up to the outbreak of war in March 1854, the responsibility of Napoleon III for them was comparatively slight. Nor can he be held personally responsible for the incompetence with which the war was conducted, particularly by his British ally.

The news of the fall of Sebastopol in September 1855, after much disappointment and disillusionment, was greeted in France with an outburst of rejoicing. It was assumed to mean peace, and if it had not meant peace, opposition to the continuance of the war would have been widespread. The Peace Congress was held at Paris in the spring of 1856. It was a triumph for Napoleon III, though what France gained by the war it is difficult to say.

If the Crimean War was the result of accident, the same can hardly be said of the next war that the Second Empire was involved in. The legend of Napoleon I as the liberator of Italy, the early association of Louis Napoleon with the Italian Carbonari, and his genuine nationalist ideals, given his obstinate, fatalistic habit of clinging to the ends he had once set himself, made it certain that the emperor would endeavour to do something for Italy. Cavour was fully aware of this and played on Napoleon III in all the ways he knew. The insane attempt by the Italian revolutionary, Orsini, to assassinate Napoleon III and Eugénie as they arrived at the Opéra, which killed eight people and injured many more, was just the thing to appeal to the over-clever mind of an ex-conspirator as an opportunity to turn it to precisely the opposite ends from those that any reasonable calculation could have anticipated. Orsini, of course, had to be executed, but first he had to play the role, which his appearance and the emperor cast him for, of the romantic patriot. Through his would-be assassin, Louis Napoleon was able to proclaim indirectly his allegiance to the ideal of Italian liberation.

The next step was the secret conference with Cavour, in July 1858, at Plombières, where, in the absence of his ministers, the emperor reached a verbal agreement envisaging war against Austria. The Italian war, which was now planned, shows even more clearly than any of the other wars of the Second Empire, that they are not to be attributed to pressure from below, or to the French desire for glory, so beloved of historians, or to a supposed need to cement the emperor's authority. They were the necessary result of his foreign policy, which he kept largely in his own hands, partly through belief in his star, and partly because he never fully trusted any of his ministers. This was why, says Émile Ollivier, 'he adopted the custom of dealing directly with the ambassadors on important occasions, to the exclusion of his ministers.' The meeting at Plombières was followed by a year of declarations which seemed to make war inevitable, yet which, under the pressure of French and European opinion, stopped short of actually provoking it. There is a possibility, indeed, that Napoleon was playing an insidious game of bluff, which would be characteristic of him, and hoping in the end to achieve something without war. His last-minute agreement to a European congress to discuss the future of Italy, though he pretended to those who wanted war that it was not intended seriously, casts some doubt on the sincerity of his bellicose gestures. The cunning of Cavour and the folly of the Austrians robbed him of the choice and in April 1859 war began.

Despite these equivocations, the Italian War was esssentially the emperor's own. The ministers were opposed to it; the clergy and those who followed their lead, the peasantry and most of the better-off classes, were against it. Only the enemies of the emperor, the republicans and their clientele in the towns, viewed it with favour. The emperor had seemed to be working for war by all the methods he could, with little regard for scruple, or even for French interests, as if he were infatuated. It was the even greater folly of the Vienna government and the Austrian ultimatum that gave him the chance to bring France into the war on a temporary wave of anti-Austrian sentiment. Whatever the feelings of the peasants who furnished the mass of the troops, their departure for the war brought cheering crowds into the streets of the cities; and when the Emperor himself, leaving Paris from the Gare de Lyon, had to pass through the workers' quarter of Saint-Antoine, there were scenes of great enthusiasm.

Perhaps as a Bonaparte, Napoleon III was expected to be, and may —though this is more doubtful—have expected himself to be, a military genius. Really, considering his total lack of military experience, the fact that he did not get his armies into a complete mess, indeed into rather less of a muddle than professional generals had done in the Crimean War, or than the Austrian generals did with the troops opposed to him, is very much to his credit. The Austrians, who had advanced into Piedmontese territory, were defeated first at Magenta, which saved Milan, and then at Solferino, after which the French and Piedmontese were on the point of invading Venetia.

It is unlikely that this luck would have lasted, and there were other considerations which called for serious reflection. Things were not turning out quite as Napoleon III had expected. Revolutions in the smaller Italian states were throwing them into the arms of Piedmont. The revolt of the papal province of Romagna increased the opposition of the French clericals to the war. Prussia was mobilizing on the Rhine. The Austrian forces were now in a stronger position, resting on the famous fortresses of the Quadrilateral. Solferino had brought enough glory and bloodshed for both the emperor and his people. As after the fall of Sebastopol, only now even more so, there was a general cry for peace. All this might easily have been anticipated, but it apparently took Louis Napoleon by surprise. He reacted quickly by opening negotiations with Francis Joseph, and less than three weeks after the battle an armistice was concluded at Villafranca.

By its terms, Lombardy was to be ceded to France, for her to transfer to the Kingdom of Sardinia; but Austria was to keep Venetia, and in the Italian states which had revolted their former rulers were to be restored. Since he had failed to unite all Northern Italy to Piedmont, Napoleon could not claim the cession of Savoy and Nice to France, which had been part of the agreement with Cavour. The fact that the other Italian states were united to the Kingdom of Sardinia in the course of 1860, and that France could consequently annex Savoy and Nice, was a purely adventitious gain, but it meant that at the last minute the emperor's luck had held. Though some clerical and right-wing support was alienated, and the Foreign Minister, Walewski, whose sympathies were with the papal cause, had to resign, republican and left-wing opinion—which presented a much more serious opposition—became more favourable to the Empire. The real miscalculation of the Italian war lay in its effect on the European situation, but this was only gradually to be revealed.

Napoleon III was much more interested in asserting the role of France among the Great Powers than in developing imperial ambitions outside Europe. In the colonial, as in every other field, it is difficult to trace a consistent policy through the aberrations of the Second Empire. The emperor began with a prejudice against Algeria, which he called 'un boulet attaché aux pieds de la France'. His romanticism, or his national ideas, or perhaps even his idealism, brought about a drastic reversal of policy in 1863, when, in a public letter to the Governor General, he condemned the confiscation of native land for the colonists. 'Today', he declared, 'we must convince the Arabs that we have not come into Algeria to oppress and despoil them, but to bring them the advantages of civilization ... Algeria is not a colony properly speaking, but an *Arab kingdom* ... I am just as much the emperor of the Arabs as of the French.' One result of this new orientation of French policy was a drastic diminution in colonization, and attempts to introduce large-scale capitalist enterprise which failed. The government of Algeria continued to be in military hands until 1870, when a parliamentary inquiry condemned the system and the government restored the authority of the prefects.

Senegal, considered of secondary importance, had the good fortune to be governed from 1854 to 1865, with a brief gap, by one of the wisest colonial administrators France has had. This was Faidherbe, an engineer captain in 1854, who established a system of indirect rule and extended French authority inland. When he retired, he had wrested large populations from the overlordship of the Moors and sketched out the plan of an extensive and prosperous colony. He established the pattern of pacification, organization, and assimilation which was to be continued with remarkable success for many years. In 1857 the port of Dakar was founded. Attempts to develop the native agriculture of Senegal were markedly successful. A cadre of able colonial administrators was built up. Altogether, in Africa under the Second Empire we can see the beginning of the modern problems of colonial government, and tentative answers, emerging sometimes through the influence of the emperor, and sometimes in spite of him.

In the Far East French missionaries and merchants led the way, to be followed by small expeditionary forces. An Anglo-French punitive force in 1860 occupied Peking, burnt the Summer Palace, and looted everything it could lay its hands on, to show the superiority of European civilization. A French force annexed Cochin-China in 1862 and a French protectorate was established over Cambodia.

Nearer home, Turkish massacres of Christians in Syria led to a French expedition there in 1860, which afforded the occasion for international recognition of France's traditional interests in the Levant. Finally, it was in 1859 that Ferdinand de Lesseps began the construction of the Suez Canal, in spite of English opposition. The most ambitious of the overseas projects of Napoleon III was to be in Mexico, but this must be dealt with later, at the moment when the reckoning was sent in.

This colonial expansion was carried on without any suggestion of rivalry or conflict with Great Britain. This is all the more remarkable because French opinion, throughout the Second Empire, was even more than normally Anglophobe. At the Congress of Paris it was remarked that an uninformed observer might have thought the Russians the allies and the British the recent enemy. Yet Napoleon III was determined not to make the mistake of his uncle and allow himself to be drawn into hostilities with Great Britain. This determination, in the light of his European ambitions, was undoubtedly wise, and perhaps all the more so because it ran counter to the dominant trend of French opinion, while in England anti-French feeling was so strong that coastal fortifications were constructed and corps of volunteers enlisted for defence against France.

After the Italian war, the emperor began seriously to reflect that perhaps after all the Empire ought to mean peace. Fear of further wars was beginning to weaken confidence inside France. He had by now thoroughly stirred up Europe and shattered the status quo. This may have been one reason for the negotiation of the Cobden free trade treaty with Great Britain. It was intended as a gesture of reassurance. In a letter published in January 1860, Napoleon announced that peace would be used to develop national wealth and improve the conditions of the agricultural population and the workers. At the same time he had a genuine belief in the benefits to be derived from the adoption of free trade principles. Chevalier had persuaded him to accept the plan for a commercial treaty with England before Cobden met the emperor. It had not been a difficult task, for Napoleon III had a genuine interest in the well-being of the populace of France, and believed that a reduction in the traditionally high French tariff wall would promote it.

He kept his plans secret from those ministers who were not likely to agree with them. Walewski, who was out of sympathy both with the Italian and the commercial policy, was removed from the Foreign Ministry in December 1859. In January 1860 Napoleon published a letter to his Minister of State, Fould, in which he announced measures for the improvement of French agriculture and industry with the aid of government loans, in preparation for the commercial treaty. Because the Legislative Body, weak as it was, would not abandon protective duties quietly, the emperor resorted to a reduction by executive action. Cobden and Chevalier negotiated the Anglo-French free trade treaty, which was signed in January 1860. The French industrialists, fanatical protectionists, reacted with combined panic and fury. Petitions were got up; manufacturers descended on Paris to protest — those from Rouen even chartered a special train — but all to no avail. By the terms of the treaty France agreed to bring absolute prohibitions of import to an end, and to reduce her tariff to a maximum of 30 per cent within two years and 25 per cent in five years. Great Britain practically abolished all customs dues on imports from France, except for those on wines and spirits. In actual fact the French government went further than it had promised in reducing customs rates.

Commercial treaties followed with other states. In matters of trade the Second Empire was the only liberal regime France has ever known. It did not seem to harm French prosperity. The small ironworks, still dependent on wood, the iron mines of the north, rapidly being worked out, were hurried to their end by foreign competition, but British competition brought down the price of iron and so stimulated the growth of railways and the introduction of machinery.

On the other hand, the hopes of a period of international peace to be promoted by the adoption of a free trade policy were hardly fulfilled. In the 'sixties the Second Empire was entering on a period of misfortunes and mistakes. Though he had his long-term objectives, the actual policy of the emperor had always developed as a series of lucky improvisations. Now his luck was changing, or perhaps we might say that the unpaid debts resulting from earlier gambles were coming in for payment. He was less equal to them than formerly, because a disease of the kidneys and bladder was increasingly weakening him and sapping his capacity for decision.

In the 'fifties Louis Napoleon had built up the prestige and influence of France in European councils with considerable success. What this meant was that France was returning to the position among the Great Powers that her population, wealth, and military potential justified. It is also fair to say that for a number of different reasons the competition inside Europe was not formidable at this time, while the emperor sedulously avoided any serious dispute with Great Britain. But in the 'sixties the situation began to change, partly as a result of Napoleon III's own actions. His semi-romantic, early-nineteenth-century ideas of foreign policy were no longer appropriate in the harsher climate of blood and iron that was sweeping over Europe; and also it must be admitted that, in the age of Cavour and Bismarck, Louis Napoleon was out of his class.

There was another, and perhaps more fundamental, cause of the failure of French foreign policy in the 'sixties. France could now only maintain her prestige and keep up her relative position among the Great Powers of Europe by preparing for, and facing the possibility of, eventual war. But by 1860 the French nation had fought in ten years two more wars than it wanted. The emperor himself had his fill of war and moreover was well-informed of the strongly pacific trend of public opinion. This was perhaps the decisive factor, which needs to be emphasized. Napoleon III never forgot that he had been brought to power by the masses of the people. His authority had not been created by, nor did it depend on, the army. There was no great party machine, as in modern fascist and communist dictatorships, to hold the people down. His was a personal and plebiscitary dictatorship, and what the people had given the people might take away. The emperor was therefore almost pathologically conscious of his dependence on public opinion, and lacking the machinery — apart from a press of which the known subservience was the measure of its lack of influence — or the modern techniques for manufacturing opinion, he had often, indeed too often for the well-being of the country, to follow it. The problem was to discover what the public, in so far as a public existed, was thinking. Here the Second Empire had to fall back on the method of earlier regimes, by relying on a

M

continuous flow of reports on the state of opinion from its own administrative agents.

Dependence for information on those who have a vested interest in representing the situation in the most favourable light, for naturally they do not wish to cast discredit on their own services or their efforts to influence opinion, can prove very dangerous, and leave a government—as it left Louis-Philippe and Guizot—in sublime ignorance of their own isolation from the country. The stronger the government, the greater the danger of this. The governments of the Second Empire were weak, though the regime was not equally weak. The prefects and other officials would doubtless generally have been anxious to provide the answers that their superiors wanted if they had known what these were, but often they did not; and particularly in his later years the emperor was genuinely trying to discover what public opinion demanded, in order to satisfy it. Sometimes, it is true, he initiated policies under the impression that they would win popular favour, and then found it difficult to liquidate them when this proved a miscalculation. But he was no longer prepared, as he had been when he assumed responsibility for the Italian War and the Treaty of Commerce, to swim against the tide.

When Poland revolted against Russian rule in 1863 the Emperor followed opinion faithfully in first alienating Alexander II and sacrificing what was almost a Russian alliance by protesting against the suppression of the Poles, and then exhibiting his weakness by doing nothing to follow up the protest, beyond proposing a congress. Great Britain, suspecting French ambition to recreate a Polish client state in Eastern Europe, refused to support this proposal. The next year, when Prussia and Austria seized the duchies of Schleswig and Holstein, it was Great Britain that proposed the congress, and Napoleon III, in a futile hope of extracting compensation from Prussia on the Rhine, who refused his support. Neither France, nor Great Britain, of course, was prepared to fire a shot in support of the smaller nations of Europe; in these circumstances their notes and diplomatic manœuvres could not be anything but useless gestures.

In 1866 came the Austro-Prussian War, in preparation for which Bismarck had played Napoleon III like a cynical animal trainer with a greedy but rather stupid beast, enticing him into the desired position with the proffer of a choice morsel—of not clearly specified territory on the Rhine—but all the time intending to snatch it away at the last moment. Louis Napoleon, of course, was not foolish enough to count on Bismarck's gratitude for the reward of his neutrality. He believed that Austria was the stronger of the two Germanic powers, and with his old pro-Italian and anti-Austrian obsession, gladly saw Italy join in on the side of Prussia to redress the balance and wrench Venetia from the Austrian Empire. His miscalculation was basically due to the fact that the Austrian Empire was still for him what it had been for Napoleon I, the real enemy in Europe. Prussia, on the other hand, was seen as the weak state defeated at Jena and a natural ally of France. French opinion also, as Bismarck had assured himself through his informants in France in advance of the war, was determined that France should keep out of it. Louis Napoleon even contemplated an alliance with Prussia and Italy against Austria; and when Thiers in a brilliant speech warned France against a policy that was setting up a united Germany and Italy as dangerous rivals to France, Napoleon went out of his way to repudiate this view and proclaim his belief in the primary interest of France in smashing the Vienna settlement of 1815. After the rapid Prussian victory, the Foreign Minister, Drouyn de Lhuys, and the empress were for immediate war, and this was the moment when France might have resorted to war with the best chance. Unfortunately, although French sentiments were now anti-Prussian, the habit of sitting on the side-lines and cheering or booing without intervening in a dangerous game had gone on too long to be changed overnight. France was still profoundly pacific and Napoleon had done nothing to prepare French opinion for the necessity of resisting Prussian aggression. At the critical moment he was ill, and his strongest minister, Rouher, was opposed to armed intervention. All the emperor could fall back on was the notorious 'policy of *pourboires*' —territorial compensation to be extracted by weakness from strength —the left bank of the Rhine, Belgium, Luxembourg. What Great Britain, the German states, and the states involved in the proposed bargain, when it became known—and Bismarck saw to it that it did —thought of these proposals need not be said.

Meanwhile the French garrison, kept in Rome under pressure from the French Catholics but withdrawn in December 1866, had been brought back in October 1867. A small French force assisted the papal troops in repelling Garibaldi at Mentana. This completed the antagonization of Italy. Between 1863 and 1867 Louis Napoleon succeeded in alienating practically every state of any importance in Europe.

Outside Europe earlier colonial successes had led up to a much more ambitious scheme to undo what Napoleon III might well consider the mistake that Napoleon I had made in selling Louisiana. As always, a series of accidents seemed to mark the path of Napoleon III to the end which, when he had attained it, could be seen to have been in his mind all the time. A moderately reforming and anti-clerical government in Mexico under President Juarez having repudiated the foreign loans incurred by its predecessor, in 1862 a debt-collecting Anglo-Franco-Spanish expedition was sent to Mexico. When the other two contingents withdrew, a French force remained at Vera Cruz to experience a defeat at the hands of Juarez' men. This, of course, had to be avenged for the sake of French honour and imperial dignity. Reinforcements were therefore sent out, which captured Mexico City and organized an Assembly of Notables. This offered the throne of Mexico to a Habsburg prince, Maximilian, put forward by Napoleon III. The Civil War meanwhile prevented the United States from opposing the breach of the Monroe Doctrine.

A mixture of motives inspired this attempt to establish a client state of France in the Americas. To the expected extension of national power and prestige was added the hope of economic gain — perhaps a persistence of the legend of the wealth of the Indies. Morny had a more personal hope of gain in the form of a commission of 30 per cent on the repayments to a great Swiss creditor of Mexico. There was strong Catholic support for a plan which promised to overthrow the anti-clerical Juarez government; at Rome the French campaign was proclaimed a crusade. The French expedition proved a much bigger military commitment than had been expected; in the mid-'sixties nearly 40,000 of the best French troops were tied up on the wrong side of the Atlantic, when the balance of Europe was being changed. The situation was not improved by the fact that the French general, Bazaine, quarrelled with the other leaders of the imperial forces, married a young Mexican girl, and may have had ambitions of setting up as a ruler on his own. Guerrilla warfare dragged on with a continued drain of men and money—the adventure rapidly becoming intensely unpopular in France—until the end of the American Civil War announced the end of the French intervention in Mexico. In 1867 the French troops were withdrawn, while Maximilian remained to be shot by the Mexicans, and his empress went mad. It was a tragic end to a squalid and foolish adventure. Worse was to follow, but before tracing the foreign policy of Napoleon III through to the final catastrophe, it is necessary to say something of the concurrent decline of his authority at home.

⚜

CHAPTER FIVE

TOWARDS THE LIBERAL EMPIRE

LITTLE has been said so far of the politics of the Second Empire. But the impression should not be given that apart from its foreign and colonial adventures, the only thing that really counted in its history was economics. The politics of a dictatorship, like that of an absolute monarchy, normally consist of mere court intrigue. If this is increasingly less true of the Second Empire, that is because it was rather a weak and half-hearted dictatorship. The simple preservation of parliamentary forms is not particularly significant; nor can we learn much from the elections, at least in the earlier years. Dictatorships, since they cannot tolerate opposition, normally suppress it by force, as the Second Empire did in the beginning. But Napoleon III also liked to pretend that it did not exist. This belief was made the easier by the fact that the majority of the nation undoubtedly supported him to the end. However, nothing less than a hundred per cent support is really satisfactory to a dictator. To secure the appearance of almost unanimous support the Second Empire relied on electoral management.

After 1852, the next elections were held in 1857. Opposition was still weak and the government was supported by just over 84 per cent of those voting (62 per cent of the electorate) as against 83 per cent in 1852. The prefects and their subordinates secured the election of the official candidates in all except thirteen constituencies; and of those who succeeded without the blessing of the Minister of the Interior eight were independents whose opposition to the regime was very mild. The remaining five were republicans, four, including Jules Favre, Émile Ollivier, and Ernest Picard from Paris, and one from Lyons. The Party of Five, as it was known, counted for rather more than its minute size might suggest, because the eloquence of Ollivier and Favre, and the wit of Picard, made a striking contrast to the dull pomposities of most of the yes-men of the prefects. But the fact that these republicans had accepted a seat in the Legislative Body was already a long step in the direction of reconciliation with the regime. The Italian war, with which they sympathized, carried them still farther. By 1859 the emperor felt his position so thoroughly consolidated that he offered an amnesty to all political exiles, with the solitary exception—and this is significant—not of any of the socialists but of the leader of the red republicans, Ledru-Rollin.

In 1860 the first step away from dictatorship and in the direction of a real parliamentary system was taken. Since the Empire was at the height of its success and under no necessity to make concessions, and the change was introduced against the advice of the ministers except Morny, it must be attributed to Napoleon III himself. His motives, as always, remain inscrutable. One possibility is that he may have found himself too much at the mercy of his ministers, having neither the expert knowledge nor the assiduity to examine and control all they said or did in his name. He now allowed the Legislative Body and the Senate to hold annual debates on the speech from the throne, in the presence of ministers who were to reply to them on behalf of the government. An official report of debates was also to be published.

In 1861 a further step was taken. The vote of the budget by sections, instead of *en bloc*, was conceded. Political life was reviving, and in 1863 for the first time the government went into the election faced by a real, if hopelessly divided, opposition. This only won 32 seats, 15 to the Catholic opposition and 17 to the left. The Empire still had rather over five million votes out of over seven millions, but the opposition obtained a vote of two millions, compared with under half that figure in 1852 and 1857. An ominous fact was that out of the twenty-two largest towns in France, eighteen had given a majority to the opposition candidates. Paris elected Thiers and eight republicans.

These elections had been managed by the devoted Persigny, who had followed the star of Louis Bonaparte from Strasbourg to the Tuileries. Minister of the Interior after the *coup d'état*, and subsequently ambassador in London, he had returned to the Ministry of the Interior in 1860. It was characteristically inconsequent that Louis Napoleon should have put back into the key position this enthusiastic, authoritarian Bonapartist, just at the time when an attempt was being made to moderate authoritarianism. Persigny's ruthless application of the system of official candidatures in the election of 1863 could only have been justified by conspicuous and increased success. The absence of this was equivalent to failure, and the resentment that his methods aroused suggested that they were becoming anachronistic. So Persigny had to go, with a dukedom as a consolation prize.

The leading influence over the domestic policy of the emperor for the next two years was to be that of Morny, the most brilliant, unscrupulous, and from a political point of view perhaps the ablest and wisest of the emperor's collaborators. The duc de Morny had a special qualification for his role, since he was the emperor's half-brother. He was the son of Hortense Beauharnais, Louis Napoleon's mother, by General de Flahaut, her lover, himself an illegitimate son of Talleyrand. This double illegitimacy was to add up to a great dignitary of the Second Empire, but already under Louis-Philippe, Morny had won a fortune by speculation and a seat in the Orleanist Chamber of Deputies. He, more than anyone else, perhaps even more than Louis Napoleon himself, was the architect of the *coup d'état*. He quarrelled with the emperor over the confiscation of Orleanist property, which may perhaps be set off against some of his own rather dubious financial transactions. In 1854 he became President of the Legislative Body, and he believed all through that France must return to a qualified parliamentary regime, in which the position of Napoleon III would perhaps not be so very different from that of Louis-Philippe. Morny's charm, his capacity for managing men, his combination of bonhomie with the air of a *grand seigneur*, his dashing ways with women and with wealth, his shrewdness and essential sense of the possible, made him one of the chief assets of the Second Empire and an ideal agent for the transformation of the regime into what was to be called the Liberal Empire. Morny envisaged an imperial government freed from the incubus of the rigid authoritarians, the unimaginative conservatives; a parliamentary Empire, which should be led and managed by himself and in which the oratorical talent which he lacked should be supplied by some brilliant orator of the left, such as Émile Ollivier. Among a crowd of technicians, *fonctionnaires*, political managers, and general second-raters, he stands out as something like a statesman. If he had lived, his ability might increasingly have supplemented the failing powers of Napoleon III. His death, at the age of fifty-four, in 1865, was perhaps the single most disastrous event for the Second Empire in a period that was increasingly filled with disasters. It postponed the coming of the Liberal Empire for five years, and meant that when it did come, it should be under much less favourable auspices.

The series of disasters in foreign and colonial policy bears witness to the strength rather than the weakness of the Second Empire. In all of them, it is true, public opinion was the accomplice of the emperor, as it had been in December 1851; but a regime with less support could not have passed through them with such immunity, nor have been so little shaken by the growing opposition in France.

This opposition was now coming as much from the right as from the left. The relations of the Empire with the Catholics had changed markedly since 1852. At the time of the *coup d'état* a few bishops, like Sibour of Paris, saw ultimate dangers for the Church in too close an identification with the new regime. Lacordaire despaired, but most Catholics welcomed it. Montalembert only hesitated for a few days; Veuillot was enthusiastic. Napoleon III paid part of the price for the support of the Church by increasing the financial contribution of the state to the Church, thus enabling clerical salaries and pensions to be raised. Legal recognition was accorded to congregations of women and a large loophole was left for congregations of men. Between 1852 and 1862, 982 new religious congregations were authorized. The Panthéon was restored to religious use.

Under state patronage the Church in France grew in size and vigour. Membership of religious orders increased from some 37,000 at the beginning of the Second Empire to nearly 190,000 by the end, mostly of course women but three times what it had been in 1789. This was not a mere numerical growth; religious zeal mounted as well as numbers. The episcopate was distinguished by scholars, administrators, politicians, theologians. The lower clergy, disciplined by their training in the seminaries and their total subjection to the bishops, showed none of the dangerous independence of the eighteenth century. The laity was kept in a state of religious zeal by a well-organized propaganda. Perpetual Adoration became general and the cult of the Virgin occupied an increasingly dominant position in religious worship. In 1854 the doctrine of the Immaculate Conception of the Virgin Mary, supported by the Jesuits and opposed by the Dominicans, was promulgated. Visions were seen and miracles happened. In 1858 the events occurred at Lourdes that were to make it the greatest holy place of modern Catholicism. In these circumstances where all the anti-clericals of the Third Republic were to come from seems a mystery.

Perhaps they might have been fewer if the liberal Catholics of the Second Empire had been more; but these were only a tiny minority. The organ of liberal Catholicism was *Le Correspondant* of Montalembert; and with such collaborators as Albert de Broglie, Dupanloup, Falloux, and Lacordaire, its intellectual distinction was guaranteed. On the other side were those for whom the *loi Falloux*, by which clerical control of education had been greatly extended, was not enough. The law was attacked bitterly by the Intransigents, the leader of whom was the powerful Catholic journalist, Louis Veuillot. Born of peasant stock, trained as a lawyer's clerk, as editor of *L'Univers* he was the voice of the Church militant and spared neither opponents nor allies. Any concession was a crime; persecution was a sacred duty. Veuillot was one of the athletes of faith: to call any happening a miracle was for him to render it *ipso facto* worthy of faith. The liberal Catholics were worse than infidels or heretics.

At the opposite pole to Veuillot was Dupanloup, Bishop of Orleans, a politician, a frequenter of salons and academies, and as restless and fervid a controversialist as Veuillot himself. Dupanloup had most of the intellectuals of the Church behind him. Veuillot had—what was more important—Rome; and through him French Ultramontanism was identified with the religious views that prevailed at the Vatican under Pius IX. The publication of the *Syllabus of Errors* in 1864, if it might easily have been foreseen as the inevitable recognition of the need to condemn and ban all liberal ideas, came as a shock to the French liberal Catholics. It aroused the latent Gallicanism of the French Church. The opposition to Rome was led by the Archbishop of Paris, Mgr Darboy, appointed in 1863 and destined to die before a Communard firing squad in 1871. The conflict between liberal Catholics and Ultramontanes reached its peak in 1869–70 with the Council summoned at Rome to proclaim the dogma of papal infallibility. Dupanloup agitated in press and pamphlet; Darboy tried to bring in Napoleon III against the papalists; but it was no time for the tottering emperor to assert himself. Veuillot sent back from Rome brilliant reports for *L'Univers*, demolishing the enemies of the Pope. It was doubtless significant of something that the most powerful voice among the French Catholics was now that of a successful journalist. The victory of the Ultramontanes was complete.

It was during the Second Empire that the cleavage between the majority of French intellectuals and the Church, which had begun under Louis XIV, was renewed. Even the political alliance of the Church with the state began to wear thin before the end of the Second Empire. The Italian war alienated the sympathies of many Catholics, who manifested their dissatisfaction in the elections of 1863. The emperor, in turn displeased, not only removed the pro-clerical Walewski from Foreign Affairs but appointed Victor Duruy as Minister of Education, to defend the interests of the lay University against the clericals and struggle for the emancipation of education from religion. Duruy cautiously modified the educational system, increasing the number of state schools and reducing the fees, as first steps towards free and compulsory education. He also introduced changes into the traditional syllabus, including a more secular education for girls. In these years, also, anti-clericalism was spreading and becoming more aggressive. Among the middle classes freemasonry, now more or less purged of the misty illuminism of the eighteenth century, was one of the chief means by which it was expressed. And because of the alliance—however strained it had become—between the Church and the Second Empire, anti-clericalism was associated with republicanism.

The growing opposition, of both right and left, is much more interesting than the time-serving politicians and bureaucrats of the Empire. This should not lead us to exaggerate the size or strength of the oppositions. To the end there was no possibility that either could have obtained a majority in the country, still less have overthrown the regime. Their chief effect was in weakening its self-confidence, and in leading the emperor, who was acutely conscious of changes in public opinion, to feel the need for concessions. Another factor in the situation was his own declining health, which both weakened his grasp and made him more conscious of the problem of the succession. As has been said, the death in 1865 of Morny, who might have been able to guide the regime into more liberal paths with the alliance of Émile Ollivier, delayed the changes which Napoleon probably already had in mind; but in a letter of January 1867 he announced coming constitutional reforms. They may not seem to amount to very much—the chief were that the right of interpellating ministers in the Legislative Body was to be substituted for the debate on the address, that ministers were to speak in support of their legislative proposals, and that the control of the press was to be somewhat relaxed—but conservative resistance held up the new press law for a year.

Until 1868 the press had been kept by direct or indirect methods under effective governmental control. A paper could only be published with government permission and on depositing substantial caution money to meet the fines it might incur. For any article that the authorities disliked it could be warned, and after two warnings was liable to suspension. As well as banning the publication of hostile articles, the government also circulated favourable ones, which were reproduced throughout the country by journals which wished for official support. Most of them did, for it brought advantages in the form of access to information from government sources, such as in England *The Times* had, and also more direct forms of favour—the publication of official notices amounted to a disguised form of subsidy and outright payments were not unknown.

The press law of 1868 ended this administrative control of the press and allowed new journals to be established without preliminary authorization. It was much more dangerous for the regime than any of the constitutional reforms. Immediately there was a proliferation of new sheets, among them the notorious *La Lanterne* of Henri Rochefort, which reached a sale of half a million by June 1868. After three months of calculated and brilliant, if irresponsible, insults against the whole Bonapartist establishment, it was suppressed by legal action. Another episode resulting from the relaxation of the press laws occurred in 1868, when the stalwart *quarante-huitard* Delescluze and another journalist started a fund in their papers to erect a monument to the deputy Baudin, who had been killed in the *coup d'état* of 1851. The government made the mistake of prosecuting them. The trial provided the opportunity for a young defence lawyer, just beginning his political career, to deliver a resounding denunciation of the crime of December and all who had been accomplices in it. Gambetta had made his appearance on the political scene.

Everything seemed to be conspiring against Napoleon III in the last, unhappy years of his rule. Economic progress, which had been the great idea, and up to a point the great achievement, of the regime, slackened. There was a severe crisis in the cotton industry in the 'sixties, attributable mainly to the effects of the American Civil War and to increased competition within France as a result of the development of rail transport. The silk industry suffered from a disease of the silk worm. In the vineyards the appearance of phylloxera in 1863, to become widespread after 1875, began to produce depression. The later 'sixties indeed belied some of the golden hopes which the economic development of the 'fifties had raised, though they did not undo the progress that had already been achieved.

The financial crisis was more dangerous for the regime. The Second Empire had been founded on credit, it flourished while the credit lasted, and began to break down when the springs of credit dried up. The steadily increasing threat of war undermined confidence increasingly in the eighteen sixties. Monied men ceased to invest and left their money idle in the bank: this was known as the *grève du milliard*—the thousand million francs that went on strike. Those with capital to invest feared the adventurous disposition of the emperor now that he had ceased to want adventures. With more reason they were alarmed by the deterioration in the international situation.

The great financial house which was most closely identified with the Second Empire was naturally the one which suffered most in this crisis. The Crédit Mobilier found in 1866 that its commitments had outrun its mobilizable resources. Its titles to property were still extensive, and given time and the co-operation of other financial houses it could have weathered the storm. But the adventurous methods introduced by the Péreire brothers had alienated the world of orthodox finance, which cheerfully allowed them to sink. In the course of 1867 their shares fell from 1,982 francs to 140, and their credit to the point at which the legitimist lawyer Berryer, in a lawsuit arising out of the crisis, could describe the Crédit Mobilier as 'the greatest gaming house in the world'. The Rothschilds and the more traditional bankers now took their revenge for the earlier triumphs of the Péreires; and the emperor—for all their services to his regime—could only make a weak and unsuccessful attempt to come to their rescue. As soon as they had safely gone under for the third time, the Crédit Mobilier was refloated by rival houses. But in ruining the Péreires and launching a campaign against 'Saint-Simonian finance' the orthodox bankers had delivered a deadly blow to the already tottering credit of the Second Empire. Perhaps this was not altogether unintentional. They had been suspicious of Louis Napoleon from the beginning, and now they were beginning to believe that a parliamentary government might be more conservative and a better guarantee of property and wealth than an emperor. As so often, we see the prefigured shape of a coming regime appearing behind the increasingly blurred outlines of the existing one.

The government that had to cope with this critical situation was one from which the paladins of the Second Empire had disappeared, but the party hacks, the official spokesmen, and—at best—the administrators remained. The Empire had not been able to renew its cadres or its leaders. Fould, uncommitted rival of the Péreires from the beginning, was at the Ministry of Finances. Haussmann ruled Paris. In 1863 Baroche added Cultes to Justice, and Rouher became joint Minister of State with Billault, who had been the voice of the Empire in the Legislative Body. Before the session opened Billault had died, and the chief burden was to fall on the broad shoulders of Rouher.

The question which contemporaries and historians have asked themselves is whether henceforth Rouher or the emperor determined the policy of the declining Empire. Ollivier called the minister the vice-emperor; the wits declared that France had not a government but a 'Rouhernement'; high officials and foreign diplomats looked to him for the best indication of the policy of the emperor. He had been a notable servant of the Second Empire from the beginning. With a capacity for hard work and intrigue, a determination pushed to the point of obstinacy in pursuing a fixed line of action, and the rather crude cunning of an Auvergnat, Rouher rapidly made himself almost indispensable to an emperor whose own powers were noticeably weakening. With the close collaboration of Fould and Baroche, he built up a subservient clientele in the Legislative Body. Yet he could never feel quite sure of his position: there were many rivals round the emperor, and he could not afford to make a mistake or a concession. His position was essentially that of a political manager and an advocate rather than a statesman. He envisaged his task as one of defending a regime and implementing its policy, not of supplying the policy himself. Garde des Sceaux on the eve of the *coup d'état* of December 2nd, Rouher had probably had a larger share in drawing up the Constitution of 1852 than anyone. He was thus committed to the Bonapartist idea from the outset, that is to a dictatorship which rested on universal suffrage—in other words to the official candidature and electoral management. By character, training, and conviction he was opposed to any liberal concessions. He could only hold his position and continue to function so long as the political system which needed him, and which he had done so much to create, lasted. The death of Morny left him free to pursue his own authoritarian tendencies, one sign of which was the appointment to the Ministry of the Interior of La Valette, who combined a heavy hand with a light head.

Yet the government of Rouher was essentially weak, as was shown when it was faced by the one really vital issue, that of rearmament. The series of military defeats inflicted on the Austrian Empire, begun—by Napoleon III's own act—at Magenta, and culminating at Sadowa, had changed the balance of power in Europe. In face of the rise of Prussia and the isolation of France, only a rapid French rearmament could redress the situation. A commission, appointed after Sadowa in 1866, revealed the weakness of the army—the exemption, in practice, of the sons of the better-off classes from military service; the reliance mainly on professional soldiers and only such as were attracted by the meagre pay and not worried by the dullness of life in barracks; the slowness to adopt the new weapon, the *chassepot*, which only began to be introduced in 1866. But, when, early in 1867, the commission produced proposals which would have made military service less easy to avoid and created an effective reserve, there was an almost universal outcry. Government supporters in the Legislative Body feared for their seats; opponents saw a stick with which to beat the government.

Finance was the other major obstacle to rearmament. The earlier wars, colonial expeditions, the Mexican adventure, had still to be paid for. A programme of public works was needed to check the growth of unemployment. The government could not face, at the same time, extensive borrowing to modernize the army. Eventually a few relics of the proposed reforms were passed in the Army Law of January 1868, amid demonstrations of protest from the republicans in the cities, and even these reforms were not put into practice effectively. Throughout the years of increasing international tension the republicans and monarchists opposed rearmament. Napoleon III, who saw the dangers of the international situation, had not the strength either to avoid, or prepare for, the coming clash; and Rouher seems to have been pinning his hopes on a policy of peace at almost any price.

Although Rouher was the main target for the attacks of the opposition and a sufficiently large if pachydermous one, almost as fierce a fire was concentrated on another apparently permanent feature of the Second Empire. This was the prefect of the Seine, Baron Haussmann. Like the Péreire brothers and Rouher, what particularly singled him out for attack was his close association with Napoleon III; and again the attack was launched with the aid of the Rothschilds, as well as with ammunition furnished by Fould from the Ministry of Finances. For Haussmann, to rebuild Paris, had relied on unorthodox methods of raising credit. As building costs increased, and with the slackening of economic activity, speculators who were willing to invest in the property values his new roads created became less easy to find, he was driven to more and more daring expedients to finance his operations. When all these were exhausted, in 1868 he had to come to the Legislative Body to ask for retrospective sanction for a loan amounting to about a quarter of the whole French budget. Fundamentally, the financial position of the rebuilding of Paris was probably sound, but it had been achieved by daring methods which even a parliament still largely composed of official candidates could hardly accept. Rouher, who, like Fould, had no love for Haussmann, practically disavowed him. A future minister of the Third Republic, Jules Ferry, made his mark on the political scene with a pamphlet entitled *Les Comptes fantastiques d'Haussmann*. The emperor did not yet abandon the prefect who had served him so well, but the fate of Haussmann, and of more than Haussmann, was to turn on the elections of May 1869.

In this situation the wisest policy for Napoleon III might have been to attempt to raise his regime above the electoral battle. There was, after all, no serious possibility of a movement to overthrow the Empire. Legitimists, Orleanists, conservative republicans, men of property, and peasants, the Empire was still what divided them least. Napoleon III could have afforded to leave the election in 1869 comparatively free; but Rouher could not. He flung everything he had into the struggle, though his own unpopularity was such that his support was the greatest handicap he could inflict on his own candidates. Paris, Lyons, and all the big cities produced crushing majorities against the government. The opposition won some 3,300,000 votes (a million and a half more than in 1863) to 4,400,000 for the official candidates, and it yet remained to be seen how far the latter would be loyal to Rouher.

The emperor, ill and exhausted, was in no state to enter on a stern struggle in defence of his minister. Persigny was warning him of the unpopularity of Rouher and Baroche; his always inconvenient relative, Prince Napoleon, was intriguing; the Legislative Body was evidently on the point of escaping from Rouher's control.

Unwilling to resign in time, the 'vice-emperor' found himself, when Napoleon at last decided to yield to the demands of the opposition, faced with the bitter task of announcing the abandonment of his own policy and the concession of the parliamentary liberties which he had consistently and uncompromisingly refused. This was the end of the Bonapartist constitution that had been set up in 1852;

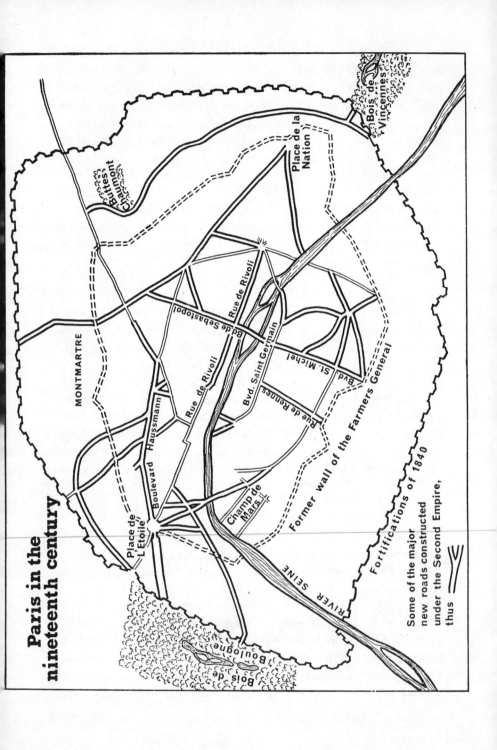

Paris in the nineteenth century

Bois de Vincennes

Buttes Chaumont

Place de la Nation

MONTMARTRE

Rue de Rivoli

Bd de Sébastopol

Rue de Rivoli

Bvd. Saint Germain

St. Michel

Rue de Rennes

Boulevard Haussmann

Place de L'Etoile

Champ de Mars

Former wall of the Farmers General

Fortifications of 1840

RIVER SEINE

Bois de Boulogne

Some of the major
new roads constructed
under the Second Empire,
thus

and the building having tumbled down in ruins, it was inevitable that its chief architect should go. The same evening Rouher tendered his resignation: Haussmann was to follow him in January 1870. It is hardly necessary to enumerate the constitutional changes that followed, they were to endure so short a while.

The year 1870 opened with the choice of Émile Ollivier, whom Morny had picked out for the role five years earlier, as head of the first and last parliamentary government of the Second Empire. Ollivier had been chosen, partly doubtless in the belief that his eloquence would help to sustain the new regime, but partly because he was an *isolé*, not committed to any party and therefore supported by none. He was a dazzling orator, full of good intentions, enthusiastic for the Liberal Empire, and convinced of his own ability to play the role for which he had been cast. Whether this belief was right or wrong, whether the Liberal Empire could have endured, or how it might have evolved, was never to be known.

The new constitution was put into formal shape in April 1870: it established government by a cabinet responsible to parliament. Evidence of the new spirit that it was intended to introduce into the political life of France was a circular of the Minister of the Interior to the prefects: 'You will take care not to subordinate the administration to politics, and you will treat with equal impartiality worthy men [*les honnêtes gens*] of all parties.' The liberal reforms were submitted to a plebiscite on May 8th and approved by 7,358,000 votes against 1,572,000 with 1,894,000 abstentions. It was a triumph for the Empire: republicans and monarchists both recognized it as such. Napoleon III had obtained practically the same number of affirmative votes as in 1852, despite a long series of misfortunes. Although the towns were the centres of opposition, it is claimed that the attachment of the workers to Napoleon III remained lively to the end of the Empire. At any rate, when they did revolt it was only after the Empire had fallen. In the early summer of 1870, though the Empire was in process of evolution, there seemed not the slightest danger of revolution.

❦

CHAPTER SIX

THE PRICE OF DICTATORSHIP

NEMESIS was to come in the shape of war, not unjustly, on an Empire that had denied its own promise that it was peace. The complicated international manœuvres that led up to the Franco-Prussian War have been narrated many times and given various interpretations. The offer of the throne of Spain to a Hohenzollern prince, and its acceptance—after much hesitation—in June 1870, precipitated the crisis that had been threatening ever since Sadowa. French opinion was outraged, and the Foreign Minister, the duc de Gramont, a light-weight to have to deal with such a serious situation and an opponent such as Bismarck, declared that a Hohenzollern king in Madrid would be a *casus belli*. In spite of attempts, after the war, to suggest that Napoleon III had dragged an unwilling country into war, the evidence is strong that public opinion throughout France felt that the time had come to make a stand against Prussian aggression. France had been out-manœuvred by Prussia too many times in the recent past to be in a mood to accept one more humiliation. The empress and the court at Saint-Cloud expressed the general sentiments of the nation when they called for a firm stand, and if necessary war. The popular demonstrations in Paris were described by republican politicians after 1870 as 'organized by the police'. There seems to be no justification for this view. Nor should they be dismissed as the mere outburst of a frivolous populace. They were the natural reaction to the history of the previous ten years. Émile Ollivier himself is alleged to have declared, 'Enough humiliation: it is no longer Rouher who controls the government of France.'

However, Ollivier was no fire-eater, and when the acceptance oɪ the Spanish throne was withdrawn by the Hohenzollern prince, he rejoiced that peace had been saved. Napoleon III, who knew the real weakness of the French army, and had been striving by personal approaches to the other European courts to secure a Hohenzollern withdrawal, without which, he realized, he could not avoid war, also believed that peace was saved. He counted without the French need, after years of humiliation, for a victory, if only on paper; and one seemed at last within grasp. Let France demand something more secure than a mere withdrawal, something in the nature of guarantees: the Legislative Body would probably have overthrown Ollivier if he had not done this, and it reflected a widespread opinion, at least among the politically vocal classes. What the peasants thought, or if they thought, cannot be known. Equally, what Ollivier would have done in the face of this movement of opinion cannot be known, for the liberal Empire was too new to permit the normal processes of a parliamentary and cabinet government to operate.

The crucial decision was taken not in parliament or by the head of the government, but at the court of Saint-Cloud, and by a little, and in every sense irresponsible, group headed by the empress, with the acquiescence of the emperor. The only minister present was Gramont, who telegraphed immediately after the meeting at Saint-Cloud to Benedetti, French ambassador at Berlin, instructing him to demand a personal guarantee of the withdrawal of the Hohenzollern candidature from the Prussian King, which, it was added, he could hardly refuse 's'il n'est véritablement animé d'aucune arrière-pensée'. However much this may look like a deliberate attempt to snatch war from the jaws of peace, such an interpretation would be mistaken. The empress and her entourage were still haunted by the insecurity of a dictatorial regime, which they felt to be more insecure than ever now that it had been launched on the experiment of liberalization. Only a striking diplomatic victory, they believed, could restore the tottering prestige of the Bonapartist cause. And the man over whom they expected to gain this victory was Bismarck.

The king of Prussia seems to have behaved with complete propriety, but of course refused Benedetti's demand for a declaration which would have been almost an admission of his own dishonesty. Bismarck, to whom the episode was reported, saw his opportunity and gave the press a short statement which read like a brusque rebuff from William I to Benedetti: there is no doubt that he knew what he was doing. This was the so-called Ems telegram. When it was

published in France a wave of emotion swept through the country —
the empress, Gramont, Ollivier reflected the feeling that practically
all the newspapers were proclaiming, and that was manifested on the
boulevards of Paris and in the streets and squares of every town in
France.

On the day after the interview at Ems, the Imperial Council met
repeatedly, with the empress present, and decided on mobilization.
The emperor was too incapacitated by illness to oppose the irresistible current of opinion, even if he wanted to; but when Ollivier
reported to the Legislative Body, it was seen that the current was not
quite as irresistible as it had seemed. Certainly it was resisted. The
centre and the left envisaged the approaching war as an attempt to
undo the concessions of the liberal Empire, which in part it was, and
they had a spokesman in Thiers, who in private had already been
one of the few in France to foresee defeat, and in public denounced
a policy which involved shedding torrents of blood to avenge a few
insulting words. Ollivier, whatever his earlier doubts, was now carried away by his own eloquence, and — in one of those phrases with
which a man can damn his own reputation for ever — declared that
he accepted the responsibility of war 'with a light heart'. On July
19th war was declared on Prussia.

The blunders of Napoleon III's foreign policy ensured that France
should enter the war with no allies, but on the side of the government
hardly anyone, except perhaps the emperor himself, supposed that
there was any need for them. 'À Berlin' was the war-cry on the
boulevards and the password of the army. There was a run on maps
of Germany in the shops; it would have been unpatriotic, defeatist,
and absurd to suggest that maps of France might be more useful.
As recently as 1859 France had been patently the leading military
power of Europe, and the revelation of defects in the French army
had not affected public confidence. Yet from the beginning the
French army was out-numbered, out-gunned, and out-manœuvred.
The mobilization was so muddled that the Prussians, unexpectedly
even to themselves, were able to take the offensive at once. The
French, nominally under the supreme command of the emperor, who
was suffering cruelly from his illness and could only sit his horse in
agony, experienced a series of defeats — at Wissembourg, Frösch-

willer and Forbach—in the first week of August. Alsace was lost and Lorraine invaded. The Prussian generals made their share of mistakes, but they showed more capacity for coping with the new conditions of warfare created by the railway and intensive use of artillery than did the French, conditioned by thirty years of North African warfare to the cultivation of elan and the neglect of logistics.

The conduct of the campaign on the French side was rendered even more ineffective by the emperor's continual hesitations, and the absence of any coherent plan of campaign. After the initial defeats he was coolly pushed out of his nominal supreme command by the generals, who were as responsible for them as he was. In his place Bazaine became commander-in-chief. He had risen from the ranks, was known for his personal courage, and had lost the favour of the court after dubious conduct in the Mexican campaign. This was sufficient to make him the favoured candidate of the left, and public opinion practically forced him on Napoleon. But the emperor, while he was in the field, could not avoid the ultimate responsibility for military decisions; and Bazaine was not the man to take any positive action on his own. He withdrew with a large army on Metz, where the Prussians cut him off by a victory at Gravelotte. Meanwhile, the emperor, with Marshal MacMahon, was gathering a new army on the Marne at Châlons.

When the news of the defeats reached Paris, the empress, left behind as regent, summoned the Legislative Body, which called for the dismissal of the ministers and generals whom it held responsible for the defeat, and the appointment of a new government chosen by the Assembly. Eugénie at least had the courage of her lack of judgment and did not yield to this. She appointed a Bonapartist ministry under General Cousin de Montauban, comte de Palikao, who took his title from a victory in China, in place of the defunct government of Ollivier. It was patent to everyone that only a military victory could save the Empire. Palikao's order to MacMahon to march to the relief of Bazaine, unjustifiable from a military point of view, was dictated by political considerations; failing this, he said, revolution would break out in Paris. In a forlorn hope, MacMahon and the emperor led their army in the direction of Metz, where Bazaine remained in a state of inaction that was later to bring the charge of treachery on him. His motives were at least peculiar—but then he had always been what he looked, rather a peculiar individual. In their turn, MacMahon and Napoleon found themselves penned in at Sedan. Under the bombardment of the Prussian artillery a continuation of the struggle meant only futile slaughter of the encircled troops. On September 1st, beaten and broken, the emperor surrendered with 84,000 men, 2,700 officers, and 39 generals.

At Paris, recently so gay with optimism, opinion was reeling under the report of defeat after defeat. The news from Sedan brought revolutionary crowds out into the streets. Eugénie and the Prince Imperial fled to England. The Second Empire disappeared: it had become such a phantom that the mob was not even concerned to take revenge on its adherents. Napoleon III was perhaps never less hated or more pitied than in his fall. The Legislative Body, to anticipate a revolutionary movement from the extreme left, proclaimed a provisional Government of National Defence. It was headed by General Trochu, already military governor of Paris, and it included the leaders of the parliamentary opposition, but not Thiers. Far too shrewd to allow himself to be put in a position of responsibility for what he foresaw as inevitably a humiliating defeat, Thiers undertook instead a futile mission to the courts of Europe to plead for intervention.

The usual kind of vulgar libels were produced by the Parisian journalists against Eugénie, as formerly against Marie-Antoinette. Now it was 'la femme Bonaparte, ses amants, ses orgies'. But there was surprisingly little anti-Bonapartist demonstration. Patriotic enthusiasm and a belief that, as in 1792, the republic would spell victory, excluded other emotions. Of course, the political machine of the Second Empire collapsed. The new Minister of the Interior, Gambetta, replaced all the prefects of the fallen regime. He began preparing for a national war. The size of the National Guard in Paris was doubled, and at the end of the month it contained 360,000 men. By this time Paris had been surrounded by German forces, which had pushed on beyond the city and occupied all France north and east of Orleans except for Paris. The Government of National Defence was now deprived of contact with the rest of the country and with its own delegation at Tours, whither Crémieux, a venerable survivor of '48, had been sent, on the ground that he was the oldest.

When it became evident that a more energetic leadership was needed, it was decided to dispatch Gambetta, on October 7th, across the German lines by balloon to Tours, where he assumed the functions of Minister of War along with those of the Interior. The son of an Italian immigrant and a Frenchwoman from Gascony, and born at Cahors, Gambetta was a southerner by birth and upbringing. His comparatively humble origins left their mark in his uncouth appearance and manners, which did not conceal his charm and ability or diminish his oratorical powers. In all these respects he reminded his contemporaries—and perhaps was not sorry that they should be reminded—of another great Frenchman in another time of troubles, Danton. An early career in the law led on to politics, and in 1869, at the age of thirty-one, Gambetta was elected to the Legislative Body as a member for Belleville, on the strength of the radical programme of political reform known as the Belleville programme. In the autumn of 1870, as heir of the *quarante-huitards* and of the Jacobins of '92, he believed that even in this crisis the republic could save France and hurl back the invader.

To second him at the improvised Ministry of War Gambetta chose the engineer Charles de Freycinet, as cool as Gambetta was excitable, but equally determined. In spite of the reluctance of the rural masses, who were now longing only for peace, the two civilians summoned from the soil of France huge new armies in a way that the generals could never have done; but to provide them with efficient officers was not possible, and to train and arm them time was needed. They had hardly begun to take the field before another military disaster occurred. Bazaine, passive in Metz, intriguing with Bismarck for the restoration of the Empire, perhaps hoping to march his troops back to suppress the republic in Paris, playing, as formerly in Mexico, an equivocal role, capitulated with 173,000 men. The only military objective left now—and it was a forlorn hope—was the relief of Paris. The army that Gambetta had formed on the Loire, under the command of a Bonapartist general with a reputation for ruthlessness, d'Aurelle de Paladines, won an initial victory at Coulmiers and on November 7th reoccupied Orleans.

A full-scale sortie from Paris, attempting to join forces with the army of the Loire, was driven back, but already d'Aurelle de Paladines had decided that he could go no farther and had been dismissed by Gambetta. His army was now split by a German counter-attack into two forces, one led inadequately by Bourbaki, another general of the old school, pessimistic, passive, lacking like Bazaine in all the qualities of leadership; and the other with skill by Chanzy, one of the few French generals in the war who, if he was defeated, at least did not go into battle expecting it in advance. In the north-east Faidherbe was struggling ably to contain the German advance, with temporary success.

The sudden, unexpected, heroic resistance of republican France, after the imperial armies and generals had crumpled up so ignominiously, had taken the Prussian command by surprise; but when they recovered from the shock and deployed the forces freed by the capitulations at Sedan and Metz, the result was a foregone conclusion. By January 1871, Chanzy had been driven back fighting from Le Mans to Mayenne. Faidherbe was in retreat. Bourbaki, sent to the east to threaten German communications, led his army into internment in Switzerland. The delegation at Tours, no longer safe there, withdrew to Bordeaux.

Resistance was concentrated now in Paris, where, in numbers at least, there was a formidable force, well armed and gathered behind powerful fortifications. In numbers, indeed, the besieged were superior to the besiegers. Trained troops of course were lacking, though a Mobile Guard of reservists had some military value and a small volunteer body of *francs-tireurs* combined courage with lack of discipline. Practically the whole male able-bodied population of Paris was enrolled in the National Guard, to the number of some 350,000 men, whose duty it was to man the defences of the city. There they became simply a semi-armed rabble, demoralized by lack of military training or occupation of any kind, for the Prussians had no intention of taking Paris by storm when it could so much more easily be starved into surrender. The circle round Paris had been completed on September 25th and the beleaguered population, much larger than was estimated at first, in a fever of patriotism and hope awaited relief from without by the new armies of Gambetta, joining with a victorious sortie from within. It had little information of what was happening in the rest of France, for while balloons could carry letters out of Paris, they could not, because of the prevailing westerly winds, return.

Shortage of food rapidly made itself felt. The poorer suffered greatly, and the lower middle class, whose small shops and trades were ruined, perhaps most of all. On the other hand, luxury restaurants remained open with full menus, apart from vegetables and sea fish, throughout the siege, even if exotic dishes such as kangaroo or elephant, and humble ones like cat, had to appear on the list. As winter came on, cold was as great an enemy as hunger. The trees in the Champs-Élysées were cut down and a swarm descended on them to seize firewood, like the ragged army that daily prowled in the no man's land beyond the fortifications to bring back roots and greenstuff. The Seine began to ice over and soldiers were frozen at their posts. From cold and hunger the death rate mounted. The quest for food became a universal occupation. Edmond de Goncourt, walking in the dusk, hears a girl murmur — 'Monsieur, voulez-vous monter chez moi ... pour un morceau de pain.'

Bismarck, impatient and seeing political dangers in delay, was pressing for a bombardment of Paris, believing that this would terrorize the inhabitants into surrender. The German generals resisted his pressure for some time, partly because the experiment had already been tried of bombarding Strasbourg, with marked lack of success. However, on January 5th, the weapon of terror was added by the bombardment of Paris. It lasted several hours each night for twenty-three nights. About 12,000 shells fell on the city, killing or wounding some 400 persons, helping to found the modern German tradition of war, but having little effect on the spirit of resistance in Paris.

The extremists of the left, who had emerged from hiding or prison with the fall of the Empire, were now the leaders of republican patriotism. 'The Frenchmen of 1870 are the sons of those Gauls for whom battles were holidays,' declared Delescluze. Blanqui entitled the journal he founded *La Patrie en danger* and proclaimed the determination of the people to fight to the death and to save Paris at all costs. Believing as they did in the necessary victory of republican forces, defeat naturally was equated with treachery. When the Parisian offensive of October 27th was beaten back three days later, and at the same time arrived the news of the capitulation of Metz, the left-wing leaders called out the mob, invaded the Hôtel de Ville, and began to organize a revolutionary government. Loyal battalions were fetched up and brought the situation under control. There was a similar reaction to a final *sortie en masse* on January 19th, which failed with heavy loss. It has been regarded as an attempt by Trochu to demonstrate to the Parisians the hopelessness of the situation and so prepare the way for capitulation, but as he put himself at the head of the troops this may not be altogether fair to him. The defeat led to another march on the Hôtel de Ville, which was dispersed by the Mobile Guard. The transformation of the patriotic struggle against the invaders into a social struggle inside France was beginning. Elsewhere—in Lyons, Marseilles, Toulouse—revolutionary communes had already been set up, but had been brought under control by Gambetta's prefects.

The propertied classes, who had most to lose from the continuance of the war, had long been ready to abandon the struggle. Thiers had all along believed in negotiating with the enemy, under the impression that the price of peace would be cheaper the sooner it was concluded. After the failure of the left-wing rising of January 22nd the government in Paris felt safe in accepting the inevitable armistice. By its terms Paris was to capitulate and there was to be a three weeks' suspension of hostilities to allow for the election of an assembly which could negotiate a peace.

The war was over. It was the defeat of an army in which were reflected all the defects of the state and society created by the Revolution and Napoleon. The army, like successive French regimes, was possessed by the blind belief in itself of an all-powerful bureaucracy, and by a corresponding inability to make adjustments to cope with the unexpected. The result was total collapse in the face of a crisis. The army also reflected the inherent social conflicts in France. The older aristocratic families had given up their traditional military role rather than serve a state which had abandoned the legitimate monarchy. The bourgeoisie saw no attractions in such an underpaid and despised profession as the army; it was able to avoid the selective service, if its sons drew an unlucky number, by the system of paying for a substitute. The officers of the army were largely drawn from the ranks and their position was the reward of bravery and brawn rather than brains. The higher command went by court favour. What the officer corps lacked in tradition and social background was not made good by the system of military education, for this was as conservative and inappropriate to a post-seventeenth-century world as all other education. When the Minister of War, Lebœuf, said that the army was ready, he spoke truth by its own standards. In fact, sunk in an inspissated conservatism, the French army, a true mirror in this respect of French society, was quite unprepared to meet the challenge of a new age. It was still, for all effective purposes, an *ancien régime* army, with all its defects and lacking only some of its virtues. 'French troops', writes Mr Michael Howard, 'straggled, looted and drank as European armies had for four hundred years past.' It had to meet a German army which in comparison was an organized and disciplined military machine. The successes of the German gunners showed, Mr Howard says, that a new age of applied technology in war had begun; the disasters that befell the French cavalry that an old age had ended. 'The German victories, as was universally recognized, had been won by superior organization, superior military education, and, in the initial stages of the war at least, superior man-power.'

The new armies of France, called out of the earth by the genius of Gambetta and organized by Freycinet, represented an even newer response to the problem of modern war, but in 1870 a brilliant improvisation that could not succeed. Gambetta, his policy of national defence having failed, resigned. Although he was elected by nine departments, the result of the elections was overwhelmingly against him. He recognized defeat and withdrew from France.

The electoral decree was issued on January 24th and the election held on February 8th. To bring to an end the electoral management of the Second Empire, *scrutin de liste* was introduced in place of single-member constituencies. The new prefects had not the influence to make the election, and in any case had been instructed not to do so. The vote was largely a plebiscite for peace and against the dictatorship of Gambetta. Many electors were prisoners or in the new armies; over 40 departments were occupied by the enemy. The population, which could only look for guidance to its local notables and clergy, returned conservative lists everywhere save in Paris and some other large towns, in parts of the east, and in a few southern departments. There were 400 monarchists, 214 of them Orleanist, 182 legitimists mostly from the west and south-west; 78 moderates who were to become conservative republicans; 150 republicans, about 40 of a radical tinge; Bonapartism was reduced to a mere 20, only 4, and these in Corsica, daring to proclaim themselves as such. Some third of the new Assembly was *noblesse*; only 175 had ever sat in an Assembly before; their average age was fifty-three.

It was an exceptional body, elected under exceptional conditions, for a single purpose—to make peace. The shadow of things to come might have been seen in the election as President of the Assembly of Jules Grévy, the republican who had warned in 1848 against the constitutional arrangements which opened the door to Louis Napoleon. Thiers, for whom the election had practically been a plebiscite, with 2,000,000 votes accumulated in multiple candidatures and election in 26 departments, was the almost inevitable choice as head of the Executive. France invariably looks to those it has known for many years when a national crisis emerges. Nevertheless, an overwhelmingly monarchist assembly had begun by placing in the key positions two republicans; and Thiers' three leading ministers, Favre, Picard, and Simon, were also republicans.

But there was more than one kind of republican in the minority of the Assembly. Paris had sent a group of deputies, including Louis Blanc, Victor Hugo, Delescluze, Ledru-Rollin, Rochefort, Quinet, whose names were like a roll-call of '48. To the monarchist majority they were intolerable and in fact were so little tolerated that some eight of them resigned. The National Assembly, under the leadership of Thiers, was determined to eliminate the danger from the left, and now this meant almost exclusively Paris. A court martial sentenced Blanqui and Flourens, as leaders of the October 31st rising, to death in their absence. The former Bonapartist, d'Aurelle de Paladines, dismissed by Gambetta, was put in command of the Paris National Guard. The Assembly was brought back from Bordeaux to Versailles instead of to Paris. Finally, Thiers gave orders for the 400 guns in the hands of the National Guard of Paris to be removed on March 18th. It has been described as a deliberate provocation, which Thiers never expected to succeed in any other respect; but he did not expect his troops from Versailles to fraternize with the Parisians, and he expected the National Guard from the middle-class quarters of Paris to give his policy support. This was to underestimate the effect of two fatal measures passed by the Assembly. The first had ended the moratorium on the promissory notes through which much of the business of Paris was conducted; the second was to make rents which had remained unpaid during the war immediately payable. These decisions seemed very reasonable to the landed gentry of the Assembly, to the financiers who had speculated in paper and rents, and to Thiers. They spelt ruin to the lower middle classes of Paris.

Thiers' attempted seizure of the guns was the spark which set off revolution in Paris. After a riot and a few murders, he ordered the abandonment of Paris by all the legal authorities. The only organized body left in the city was the moderate Central Committee of the National Guard, which found itself obliged to take over the essential services, abandoned by Thiers' orders. Naturally those who came to the front in this emergency were the stronger and extremer leaders, bred in the red clubs which had flourished during the siege of Paris. The eternal conspirator, Blanqui, temporarily not the eternal prisoner, had been the inspiring genius of the most famous of the clubs, meeting in the Halles. His *club rouge* has been described as 'a chapel consecrated to an orthodox classical cult of conspiracy, in which the doors were wide open to everyone, but to which one only returned if one was a convert'. Blanqui himself presided over the cult, with 'his delicate, superior, calm countenance, his narrow, piercing eyes shot across now and again with a dangerous, sinister light'—an unusually favourable picture of the conspirator described by Victor Hugo as 'a sort of baleful apparition in whom seemed to be incarnated all the hatred born of every misery'.

The Blanquists were only a tiny fraction, the rest of the Parisian rebels felt the need to legitimize their position by holding elections. A municipal government, to be known by the historic but alarming name of Commune, was elected on March 26th. The name of the

Commune was a memory of the year 11, of the Jacobins of Robespierre and the sans-culottes of Hébert. It was a symbol beneath which
the most opposed schools of revolutionary thought could rally.
Four separate groups can be distinguished among its members — the
pure revolutionaries, divided between Blanquists and Jacobins, the
federalists following Proudhon, and the adherents of the First
International. The conservatives or moderates returned in the first
election of the Commune resigned, and after complementary elections there was a revolutionary majority of some 57 Blanquists and
Jacobins, and a socialist and Proudhonist minority of about 22.

It is a mistake to regard the Commune as Marxist in inspiration;
only one of its members can be described as a Marxist. Equally it was
not a government of the working-class. Though there were 25
ouvriers, there were more than twice as many lesser bourgeois or
professional men. The 'Declaration to the French People' issued by
the Commune on April 19th represents the federalist tendencies of
the minority. As soon as the active struggle began, the Blanquists,
weakened by the absence of their prophet, who had been arrested
and returned to jail as soon as danger began to threaten in Paris, and
the Jacobins, headed by Delescluze, took control in a temporary
alliance, to be followed, as in 1793, by bitter quarrels. On May 1st
they set up a Committee of Public Safety by 45 votes to 23.

The second siege of Paris began on Palm Sunday, April 2nd, by a
Versailles army in a wretched state of disorganization and lack of
material and morale. Its first military achievement was to shoot five
prisoners. The forces of the Commune retaliated with a wild sortie
in the direction of Versailles, which was easily dispersed with the
loss of some 1,000 prisoners captured by the Versaillais, who picked
out those they thought were the leaders and shot them. Given a small
measure of capacity and unity, at the outset the Commune should
have been able to take the offensive with success. It had many more
men and guns than Versailles, and a base in the fortified camp of
Paris which could be provisioned through the neutral Prussian
lines. These advantages were gradually lost. While the leaders of the
Commune talked and small bodies of men defended the forts, the
life of Paris, theatres, concerts, the busy traffic of the streets, went
on much as usual and far more normally than during the Prussian

siege. Such changes as were deliberately debated and brought about by the Commune were hardly of major importance. The old revolutionary calendar was revived and May 1871 became *floréal* year LXXIX. The Vendôme column was pulled down in a great public ceremony.

Meanwhile the military strength of Versailles was growing. On May 8th a general bombardment of the fortifications began. The forts round the south of Paris, gallantly defended by isolated groups of men, fell one by one. On May 21st a section of the walls near the porte de Saint-Cloud was discovered to be undefended, and by nightfall the Versaillais had a large body of men within Paris. On the same day the Commune held its last official meeting, devoted typically to a trial of its own military commander. Both he and his successor had failed to secure a reasonable measure of military behaviour from the forces of the Commune. Now that Paris was at bay, the old Jacobin Delescluze proclaimed a war of the people, not conducted by staff officers and military discipline, but by the people, the *bras-nus*. And now that all was really lost the Communards at last began to fight in earnest, in the traditional way, the only way that the people of Paris knew. It was a street battle of barricades, which was to rage for seven days across the breadth of Paris from west to east.

The Versaillais, strong in the knowledge that they were defending order and public morality, throughout the fighting showed more barbarity than the Communards. Apart from the initial episode and the actual fighting, there were practically no shootings of opponents or suspected opponents in Paris until the last stages were reached, though hostages were seized. The Versaillais systematically shot their prisoners. This was one motive of the subsequent murders of hostages that accompanied the final battle in the streets of Paris; but also, it is true, there was a group of ruthless men among the leaders of the Commune, who had not distinguished themselves in the fighting but had had their eye on the hostages all the time. Now they had their chance and particularly chose priests, including the Archbishop of Paris, for their victims. To the horror of the street fighting and massacres on both sides was added fire. Incendiary shells from the Versaillais, the burning of buildings by the Communards to clear lines of fire or form a barrier, destroyed much. The Tuileries and

o

other public buildings were fired in a last act of defiance by desperate men, though the story of the *pétroleuses* is a mere piece of propaganda.

In its final phase the defence of the Commune degenerated into unco-ordinated episodes of heroism or cruelty. Delescluze, in the dress of a deputy of '48, top hat, frock coat, and red sash, cane in hand, all being now lost, mounted a barricade to be shot. The last combat of any size was among the graves of the Cemetery of Père-Lachaise; and there, on the next day, against the wall that was to become a place of pilgrimage, 147 Communards were shot. Military justice continued to take its toll. The Versaillais lost about 1,000 dead in the fighting; the death roll of the Communards was probably not less than 20,000. Thiers had won a notable victory in the class war; the illusions of 1789 and 1792 had drawn the people of Paris into the bloodiest and most merciless of all its defeats; the Second Empire had ended in disgraceful surrender, revolution and repression, blood and tears; but it was an assembly of monarchists, under a conservative republican head of state, that first provoked and then put to fire and sword the people of Paris.

⚜

CHAPTER SEVEN

PLUS ÇA CHANGE

THE collapse of the Second Empire ends the monarchical and Bonapartist phase in French history. Yet, just as the ghost of the legitimate monarchy haunted the century after its fall, so a disembodied Bonapartism without a Bonaparte was to be a sort of Pepper's ghost, periodically appearing and disappearing on the political stage during the hundred years after the collapse of the Second Empire. Politically, it was far from clear in 1871 whether France was going on to something new or merely back to stale revivals of the past. In art and literature, also, 1871 was not a dividing line. The rebel movements of the third quarter of the century had already inaugurated what was to be one of the great ages of French painting and letters. Above all, in its basic pattern French society seemed to be, and indeed was, unaffected by the passing of an Empire.

If, having said all this, and admitting the artificiality of such divisions in history, we nevertheless have to end one volume and begin another in 1871, this is because there is, after all, something significant in the political calendar. The major changes in political institutions that resulted from the fall of the Second Empire were a determining factor in a fundamental though gradual transformation of French society, and without its opening years the history of the Third Republic would be robbed of the political developments that are essential for its understanding. There is another reason why we must make the break here. The disaster that befell the army, the unresisted collapse of the political system, the social *stasis* that burst out in the bloody class war of the Commune, all inflicted a psychological shock that, if the first result was to numb the national spirit, in the end stimulated it to new endeavour. Although, therefore, the disappearance of Napoleon III from the scene was not like that of a Louis XIV or a Napoleon I—it did not mark an epoch and hardly left a void—there are reasons for accepting the division of French history at this point and pausing to reflect on the significance of the generations that had elapsed between eighteenth brumaire and Sedan.

It is revealing to look back even earlier to 1770, when Louis XV had been making a new political experiment, as Louis Napoleon was in 1870, and consider the passage of an eventful hundred years, in the course of which France had experienced three major revolutions and moved backwards and forwards between monarchy, republic, and empire. How much during this century had French society really changed? If we imagine a Rip van Winkle who fell asleep in France, and alternatively in England, in 1770, and woke again in 1870, and ask him in which country there had been a series of revolutions, there can be little doubt what his answer would be. He would remember eighteenth-century England as a small, rural community of country-towns, villages and hamlets, with sea-ports, but with no great centre of population outside London, its communications by coach on the new turnpike roads where they existed or by pack-horse along tracks, its industry mainly carried on, in town or country, in the homes of domestic workers. Much of this could also apply to the France of 1770, except that in England an agrarian revolution was already under way, while in France the ports were finer and urbanization had produced a crop of elegant provincial towns; also that France was a country with a population of over twenty millions, about three times that of Great Britain. Politically and socially there were more significant differences, but in both countries the powers of monarchy were in practice strictly limited by the influence of the aristocracy, which in turn had to respect the interests of a rising middle class.

Waking in 1870, the sleeper for a hundred years would find changes in England such as he would hardly credit. An industrial revolution that had transformed the appearance of large tracts of country, a population multiplied by five, an urgent political life, with two great parties which had brought political consciousness and activity to large sections of the community, an empire spreading to the four corners of the world: this was the England of Queen Victoria and Mr Gladstone. What was the France of Napoleon III and Ollivier?

It was a country which seemed in many ways never to have left the eighteenth century. There was an emperor who was the effective head of the government, instead of a king who was only its nominal head; a court at Saint-Cloud instead of Versailles, with fewer old names and more *ennoblis*; a parliament, it is true, but one which lacked the independence, for good or ill, of the juridical parlements of the *ancien régime*; there were still great financiers, and they still exercised some political, and even more social, power; the Church was again in alliance with the state, and again used its influence to frustrate national policies and obstruct reforms; Paris was swollen and rebuilt, its poorer population expelled to the periphery, and the city itself even more than formerly the centre of administration and government, art and letters, finance and banking. Provincial France, apart from isolated patches of industrialization, and the railways that had been driven across it under the Second Empire, remained very much as it had been a century earlier, administered in *départements* by prefects instead of in *généralités* by intendants. For the ordinary man the pattern of daily life, the food he ate and the way in which he ate it, his social relations, his interests, his upbringing and his formal education, had changed little; for the peasantry life had changed hardly at all.

If we ask the reason for the intense conservatism of such a politically revolutionary country as France, we must first look at its economy, its ways of earning and spending. The Second Empire, under the inspiration of the Saint-Simonians, had inaugurated a minor industrial revolution, and in particular endowed France with a railway system. This was a sign of new things stirring, like the rebuilding of Paris by Haussmann, and of Lyons by Vaïsse. But it was attributable to the inspiration of Louis Napoleon himself, with a small group of advisers, and forced through against the opposition of the established powers of French society, just as had been the lesser efforts at economic progress of the Orleanist regime; the main financial and business interests of France seemed to have a vested interest in social conservatism and economic backwardness. The powerful Bank of France, whose two hundred regents formed the central citadel of wealth, had been given the task, from its Napoleonic beginnings, of guarding against social or economic change.

A stable currency, unaffected by wars or revolutions, was one proof of its success. Industry was similarly guarded against experiment or change. In the nineteenth century it was impossible to keep technical improvements out entirely, or to prevent the appearance of some large-scale enterprises. But these were exceptional, and until Napoleon III forced through, against bitter opposition, his new commercial policy, a rigid protectionism shielded French industry from competition and the compulsion of progress.

However, industrialists and financiers and commercial men were not a dominant factor in French society. Men of property and rentiers were the main constituents in the structure of the French upper classes. Their ideas were supplied to them by professional men and writers who were equally conservative in their intellectual formation. They were men of property on the Forsyte model, interested in the accumulation of land and houses, or the collection of government bonds, in which they had a pathetic faith, playing for safety as they thought, and content with modest gains so long as no risks were taken. Ordinary business they rather despised. England in these days was still damned, in Napoleonic phrase, as a nation of shopkeepers. 'La France', Michelet truly said and he meant it as praise, 'n'a pas d'âme marchande.' The French elite in the nineteenth century was an elite of bourgeois, but their aim was to be, as in the eighteenth century, 'bourgeois vivant noblement'.

The ideal of a stable, unchanging society seemed one that was capable of achievement at the time. The pressure which, in the eighteenth century and the earlier part of the nineteenth, produced social unrest and forced speculation about ways to remedy it, the pressure of population on a country already over-populated in relation to its productivity, had slackened. Above all, France remained rural, the masses of the nation scattered in small country towns, villages or hamlets, where a class of peasant proprietors, however lacking in worldly goods or the amenities of life they may have been themselves, were acutely conscious of their interests as property owners, intensely suspicious of anything which seemed to offer the threat of change in the pattern of French agrarian society.

Thus a revolution had laid the foundations of an intensely conservative society, nor is this difficult to understand. The classes which

consolidated their victory in the Revolution were the peasant proprietors in the country and the men of property in the towns,
neither with any vision beyond the preservation of their own
economic interests, conceived in the narrowest and most restrictive
sense. A Church devoted — apart from an occasional easily crushed
rebel — to the interests of the wealthy propertied classes provided
the moral justification for their wealth, and spiritual sanctions against
those who would attack it. The small Huguenot minority was, if
possible, even more devoted to the protection of the interests of
property than the great Catholic majority. A powerful, centralized
administrative structure and judicial system, recruited almost exclusively from the upper sectors of society, strengthened the defences of
the existing order. If this was bourgeois society, it was an economically
reactionary and backward bourgeoisie that it represented, having
nothing in common with the inventors and entrepreneurs, the ruthless financiers, the cut-throat competition of the builders and makers
of industrial capitalism. The society which emerged in France from
the revolutionary decade and was stabilized by Napoleon, under
whom the pattern was fixed which it was to keep with little change
for the next three-quarters of a century, was a far more static society
than the one which had entered the Revolution with such high hopes.

It was also a society torn by periodic gusts of violent and bloody
political disturbance. The paradox is not in the political instability,
but in the fact that this also is evidence of the conservatism of a
society stuck with an unfinished revolution on its hands, one which
it seemed under the compulsion to try to re-enact periodically, not
because of any social necessity, but because it was now part of the
national tradition, a set pattern of behaviour that had to be repeated
whenever the coincidence of political and economic crises provided
the appropriate stimulus. Then, while some took up the traditional
revolutionary stances, others dreamed of reviving the counter-
revolution. But since the balance of society remained essentially
unchanged, when the smoke had cleared away and the turmoil died
down, it was seen that nothing fundamental had changed. Different
actors might now be in the front of the stage, but they were still
performing the same play.

For this reason the revolutions of 1830, 1848, 1870, though not the frustrated revolution of 1871, each in turn give the impression of being the result of a chapter of accidents. This is in fact what they were, but it does not mean that they were of no importance and had no effect on national history. What they did was successively to remove most of the political, and in some cases even the administrative personnel of the previous regime, sometimes only temporarily, but sometimes permanently. In addition, they destroyed the reputations and prospects of many of the leaders of revolution themselves. Seldom has a great nation been so wasteful of its elites. Regularly, generation after generation, those who had acquired political or administrative experience were thrown on the scrap-heap of a usually remunerative retirement.

What kept France going, apart from the stability of its social structure, was the rigid framework of a centralized administration, staffed in all its higher levels by the sons of the same propertied class that controlled the nation's economy. So long as their property and their jobs were safe, they were prepared to serve any regime. France has often been taken as the awful example of a country whose politics have been blighted by the curse of ideology. The strong, but unfortunately not silent, men in our universities who advocate a highly principled lack of political principle, and have tried to deny the legitimacy of rational thought about ends and means in politics, have looked to France to illustrate the danger of having ideas in politics, whereas Great Britain shows the virtue of a happy empiricism, not sicklied over by the pale cast of thought. Historically, this is the most arrant nonsense. The interplay between rational political thinking and empirical politics, which was a dominant feature of British political life for four centuries, was lacking in France. The influence of Rousseau on the French Revolution is a legend. The theocrats may have been too lunatic, and the doctrinaires too rational, but the failure of the Restoration was nothing to do with either, any more than the July Monarchy or the Second Republic were influenced by the Utopian Socialists. Benjamin Constant and de Tocqueville were both distinguished political thinkers, but if they were recognized as such, and had any practical influence, it was in England not in France.

In nineteenth-century France political life was the expression of the most blatant materialism. France between 1799 and 1871 was a working model of the instability of a political system without moral and ideological bases. The Napoleonic Empire naturally had none; it was a war dictatorship, with no more principle behind it than the Golden Horde, probably a good deal less. The Restoration came to a nation which had already made many compromises with the revolutionary and Napoleonic state, and could not return to the *ancien régime*, which anyhow had already lost its intellectual justification before it met its violent end. The revolution of 1830 merely demonstrated that France could not recover an age that was lost, and that 1789 was irreversible. The raison d'être of the July Monarchy was to protect the interests of property, and when Louis-Philippe was no longer able to do so, after a brief interval Louis Napoleon took up the task. With Saint-Simonian inspiration, the Second Empire came a little closer to grips with the problems of French society. If it had not been for the disaster of the Franco-Prussian War, the Liberal Empire might have survived and merged into a parliamentary regime not so very different from that of the Third Republic. But it could only have done this by giving some real content to the principle of the sovereignty of the people to which it paid lip service, and this meant in effect the Republic.

If the Revolution had any ideological basis it was the sovereignty of the people; and if this idea had any honest meaning (which is doubtful) it was universal suffrage. Again it will be enlightening to draw a comparison with England. Once the theoretical democrats of the revolutionary period — never very influential in practice — had been defeated, the extension of the franchise in Great Britain had been argued mainly on practical, utilitarian grounds, as a means of winning improved conditions of life for successive layers of the population. In France politics and economics were curiously separated. The case for universal suffrage was argued as a political right of the individual, a sort of magical gesture. Sovereignty of the people became an incantation, a secular religion. It had its prophets, chiefly concerned with their own spiritual sanctity, its dervishes, prepared to suffer or inflict any pain in the service of the cult, and a political priesthood, anxious above all that no doctrines should be taken so seriously as to endanger vested interests.

Electoral management for a time succeeded in controlling the popular vote, but even in a restricted franchise the electorate sometimes refused to be managed, as the history of the Restoration and the July Monarchy showed. The only alternative, since the one-party state had not yet been invented, was the Bonapartist plebiscitary dictatorship. Beyond this we need not ask what Bonapartism was: it was the party of the men with property and jobs, as Orleanism had been before it, and as Legitimism had tried with less success to be during the Restoration. There was no Bonapartist, just as there was no Orleanist ideology. French politics between 1815 and 1870 was a Namierite paradise, with no Burke to distort the play of self-interested political intrigue, a model machine for the demonstration of politics as a self-sufficient activity.

The trouble is that real life will keep breaking in, disturbing the happy meaninglessness of the Namierite or Oakeshottian political game, in which every ladder has its corresponding snake and the game is never-ending, for it has no goal just as it had no beginning. Unfortunately, as we discover in the last resort, and sometimes even earlier, it cannot always be kept on the level of a game. So the history of nineteenth-century France showed. There were vital issues, which politicians and *fonctionnaires* might try to ignore, but which periodically took charge of the players; and then the ladders soared to the skies and the snakes devoured their victims.

The instability of French politics did not just arise out of the throw of the dice. There were real issues at stake. One of these was religion. To what extent religion in the West has ever been a cement of society is a matter of doubt. In France it certainly was not so in the century of the religious wars, or in that of the persecution and destruction of the Huguenots, or when the Jansenist controversy was bedevilling Church and state. The Revolution created a new religious schism which was dangerous because the anti-clerical minority was large and influential. The constant attempts of the Church to use the machinery of the state to recover its influence over society, to interfere in secular matters and especially to control education, built up an anti-clerical opposition, which was not conciliated by the rise of a proselytizing spirit and a militant ultramontanism which aroused national and Gallican hostility as well.

Although many unbelievers in the propertied classes were prepared to accept the power of the Church as a means of keeping the lower orders in the station to which God had called them, they could not enthusiastically support clerical influence over government. They were glad enough to have their daughters brought up in purdah and general ignorance by nuns, but they wanted a better education for their sons. As for the lower orders, whom religion was supposed to be keeping in a state of proper respect, they were steadily being alienated by a Church which seemed to be devoted exclusively to the protection of the interests of the rich. After 1794, however, anti-clericalism never offered a serious threat to the Church in this period, while clericalism was never strong enough to put the clock back to the seventeenth century as it might have liked. This conflict, therefore, produced tension in society, but no dangerous cleavage as yet.

The class conflict, which was not unconnected with this one, was more immediately alarming. Its nature must not be misunderstood. It was not the class conflict of a modern industrial society, with organized labour waging war for improved conditions and higher wages. Only in Lyons was there, on a small scale, something like this pattern. In the country—and France remained overwhelmingly rural—the peasant proprietors, with no vision beyond their commune, were more concerned to guard their own petty privileges against the rural proletariat than to envisage anything better for themselves. As men of property they could always be called on to rally to the defence of property against the 'anarchists' of Paris. Only in the capital was there a sufficiently large proletariat to offer a real threat to the established order and here it was in the form of an unorganized horde, living in depression and degradation, capable—as in 1789—of being called out by political leaders in the interests of a change of regime, but not capable of conceiving or fighting for a programme of economic reform to better its own conditions. The Parisian populace was a threat, in fact, not to the social system, which seemed irrefrangible, but to political stability.

It is true that in this intensely conservative society ideologies proliferated. Their numbers and their wildness bore witness to their remoteness from practicality. An ineffective left-wing now acquired the tradition of irresponsibility which comes from the divorce from political power, and which the right had inherited from the frondeur aristocracy of the *ancien régime*; while the various parties of the centre, sunk in a squalid defence of their vested interests, squabbled, and sometimes fought, for power and places and the rewards that went with them.

The picture is a depressing one, of a society which had forgotten most of the ideals inherited from the age of the Enlightenment and the earlier days of the Revolution and from which all who held to these, or to newer ideals, felt themselves alienated. Despairing of political and economic life, finding little solace in religion, they turned to art and literature and inaugurated the tradition of a divorce between these and society, the mutual contempt of the artist and the bourgeois. Instead of a mirror in which were reflected the highest values of contemporary civilization, the arts in France became a protest against a society which rejected them and which they rejected. Victor Hugo with the victims of justice and property in *Les Misérables*, Daumier in his drawings of the Orleanist bourgeoisie— lawyers and men of affairs, with greed, envy, malice and all uncharitableness written in their countenances, Flaubert and the empty life of the Paris rentier or the provincial lady of fashion, Courbet painting the cold, pinched faces of poverty or the leer of success in Church and state—in these there was conscious social comment; in Gautier and others a turning away from contemporary society to art for art's sake, a rejection of bourgeois values, of the moral and religious phrases that provided the alibi for unfeeling hearts, and of the repetition of stereotypes that was a substitute for thought in obtuse heads. To those who could not accept gross and philistine standards the life of the rich was a spiritual void and that of the poor a material hell. In a sordid cult of dirt, drugs, and debauchery, the artist sought an artificial paradise, which yet in a Baudelaire could reach to the heights of poetry.

The *vie de Bohème* was a conscious protest against bourgeois values, but it was a pathetically unavailing protest. The aristocracy and bourgeoisie of the eighteenth century had kissed the rods that chastised them: Montesquieu, Voltaire, Rousseau, the Encyclopedists were their idols. Orleanists and Bonapartists just ignored their critics. The age enclosed by the two Napoleons, looked at from the point of view of the high hopes of the Enlightenment and 1789, is bound to seem disappointing and disillusioning. The achievements of the Frenchmen of that age were unimpressive even to themselves, and they remain unimpressive in retrospect. The exciting new developments of the nineteenth century passed France by. In an age of change the French nation appeared to have chosen stagnation without stability. The more the kaleidoscope of its politics changed, the more France remained the same.

Yet, looking forward, it will be seen that this could not have been the whole story. The First Republic succeeded to a great age of reform, and sadly misused its heritage. The Third Republic was to come into a much less promising inheritance and great things were to be made of it. But if this can be said, then there must be a different way from that which I have adopted of summing up the France of the monarchies and the empires. Under the frozen surface of sterile egoism we should detect the early shoots of the creative achievements of the Third Republic. These beginnings have been passed over slightly or not mentioned in this volume. They can be brought in more appropriately later, when they were coming to fruition. For the moment, in 1871, there was little enough evidence of a more hopeful future. It was the end of an unattractive chapter in the history of France. It was not the end of the whole story.

CHRONOLOGICAL TABLE

❦

1799	November. *Coup d'état* of 18 brumaire
	December. Constitution of year VIII. Bonaparte First Consul
1800	February. Foundation of Bank of France
	Law of 28 pluviôse year VIII establishes prefectoral system
	Pacification of the West
	June. Marengo
	December. Hohenlinden
	Royalist bomb plot
1801	Armed Neutrality
	February. Treaty of Lunéville
	April. Copenhagen
	August. French army in Egypt capitulates
1802	Chateaubriand's *Le Génie du Christianisme*
	March. Peace of Amiens
	April. Concordat promulgated
	May. Bonaparte Consul for life
1803	April. British ultimatum
	May. Renewal of war with Great Britain
	Sale of Louisiana to United States
1804	March. Civil Code promulgated
	Cadoudal plot
	Execution of duc d'Enghien
	May. Proclamation of Empire
	Camp at Boulogne
	December 2nd. Coronation of Napoleon
1805	August. Third Coalition
	October 15th. Ulm
	October 21st. Trafalgar
	December 2nd. Austerlitz
1806	January. Peace of Pressburg
	June. Confederation of the Rhine formed
	July. Maida
	October. Jena
	Auerstädt
	November. Berlin Decrees
1807	February. Eylau

1807	June. Friedland
	July. Treaty of Tilsit
	October. Invasion of Portugal
	November, December. Milan Decrees
1808	Establishment of the University
	May. Joseph Bonaparte King of Spain
	July. Capitulation of Baylen
	August. Vimiero
	Convention of Cintra
	December. Napoleon invades Spain
1809	January. Corunna
	March. Invasion of Portugal
	April. Austrian offensive
	Disgrace of Talleyrand
	May. Annexation of Papal States
	Imprisonment of Pius VII
	July. Wagram
	October. Peace of Schönbrunn
1810	Divorce of Josephine
	April. Marriage of Napoleon to Marie-Louise
	Disgrace of Fouché
	Mme de Staël's *De l'Allemagne*
	September. Lines of Torres Vedras
1811	Economic crisis
1812	June 24th. Grand Army crosses the Niemen
	September. Borodino
	September 14th–October 14th. Occupation of Moscow
	October. Malet plot in Paris
	November 27th. Crossing of Beresina
	December 14th. Ney recrosses Niemen
1813	May. Lützen
	Bautzen
	June. Vittoria
	August. Dresden
	October. Leipzig
	Wellington crosses the Pyrenees
1814	January. Allied invasion of France
	February, March. Negotiations at Châtillon
	March 31st. Capitulation of Paris
	April 6th. Abdication of Napoleon

1814   April 10th. Toulouse. Defeat of Soult by Wellington
April 11th. Treaty of Fontainebleau
May 1st. First Treaty of Paris
May 2nd. Declaration of Saint-Ouen
June 4th. Constitutional Charter of Louis XVIII
September. Congress of Vienna meets

1815   March 1st. Napoleon lands at Fréjus
March 20th. Napoleon enters Paris
June 16th. Ligny and Quatre-Bras
June 18th. Waterloo
June 22nd. Second abdication of Napoleon
July 8th. Second Restoration
Government of Talleyrand and Fouché
White Terror in Midi
August. Election of Chambre introuvable
September. Talleyrand and Fouché resign
Richelieu ministry
November. Second Treaty of Paris
December. Execution of Marshal Ney

1816   September. Dissolution of Chambre introuvable
Election of new Chamber

1818   November. Occupation of France ended
December. Richelieu replaced by Decazes

1819   de Maistre's *Du Pape*
Géricault's 'The Raft of the Medusa'

1820   February. Assassination of duc de Berry
Recall of Richelieu
September. Birth of comte de Chambord

1821   Death of Napoleon
Revolutionary movement of the Carbonari
December. Fall of second Richelieu ministry. Ultras take over
    government

1822   March. Plot of four sergeants of La Rochelle
September. Villèle President of the Council

1823   April. Expedition into Spain

1824   March. Elections return an Ultra Chamber
June. Dismissal of Chateaubriand
Delacroix's 'The Massacres of Scio'
September. Death of Louis XVIII
Succession of Charles X

1825	Law against sacrilege
	Indemnity to émigrés voted
	May. Coronation of Charles X at Reims
1827	Victor Hugo's *Cromwell*
	October. Battle of Navarino
	November. Elections
	December. Fall of Villèle
1828	January. Government of Martignac
1829	August. Polignac government
1830	Victor Hugo's *Hernani*
	Berlioz's *Symphonie Fantastique*
	June. Elections
	July. Capture of Algiers
	July 25th. Four Ordinances
	July 28th–30th. Revolution in Paris
	July 31st. Duke of Orleans accepts lieutenant-generalcy of France
	August 2nd. Abdication of Charles X
1831	Victor Hugo's *Notre-Dame de Paris*
	Stendhal's *Le Rouge et le Noir*
	February. Anti-clerical riots
	March. Casimir-Périer ministry
	August. French expel Dutch from Belgium
	October–November. Revolt in Lyons
1831–2	Cholera epidemic
1832	Death of duc de Reichstadt
	May. Attempt of duchesse de Berry to rouse Vendée
	Death of Casimir-Périer
1833	Guizot's education law
1834	Revolt in Lyons
	Massacre in rue Transnonain
	Lamennais' *Paroles d'un croyant*
	Balzac's *Le Père Goriot*
	Louis Blanc's *L'Organisation du travail*
1835	July. Fieschi bomb plot
	Gautier's *Mademoiselle de Maupin*
	Vigny's *Chatterton*
1836	Attempt of Louis Bonaparte at Strasbourg
	September. Government of Molé
1838	Rachel plays in Racine

P

1839	Revolt of Abd-el-Kader
	March. Fall of Molé
	Louis Bonaparte's *Les Idées napoléoniennes*
1840	Re-burial of Napoleon in the Invalides
	Attempt of Louis Bonaparte at Boulogne
	March. Government of Thiers
	Mehemet Ali crisis
	October. Fall of Thiers
	Ministry of Guizot
	Proudhon's *Qu'est-ce que la propriété?*
1841	Entente cordiale of Aberdeen and Guizot
1842	Comte's *Cours de philosophie positive* completed
	Sue's *Les Mystères de Paris*
	Death of duc d'Orléans
	Guizot's railway law
1842–6	Railway mania
1844	Pritchard affair in Tahiti
	Dumas' *Le Comte de Monte-Cristo*
1846	Escape of Louis Napoleon Bonaparte from Ham
	October. Spanish marriages
1847	Economic crisis
	Capture of Abd-el-Kader
	May. Teste trial
	August. Murder by duc de Praslin
	July–December. Campaign of banquets
1848	February 23rd. Revolution in Paris. Resignation of Guizot
	February 24th. Abdication of Louis-Philippe
	Provisional Government set up
	Proclamation of universal suffrage
	Abolition of slavery
	March 16th. Demonstration of *bonnets à poil*
	March 17th. Left-wing demonstration
	April 23rd. Election of Constituent Assembly
	May 15th. Demonstration of the clubs
	June 22nd–26th. June Days
	Government of Cavaignac
	November 4th. Constitution of Second Republic
	December 10th. Election of Louis Napoleon Bonaparte as president
	Government of Odilon Barrot

1849	April. Expeditionary corps sent to Rome
	May. Election of Legislative Assembly
	June 13th. Attempted rising in Paris
	July. Fall of Roman Republic
	October. Dismissal of Barrot ministry
1850	March. *Loi Falloux* on education
	Left-wing victories in by-elections
	May. Law restricting franchise
1851	July. Legislative Assembly fails to accept constitutional reform
	December 2nd. *Coup d'état*
	December 14th. Plebiscite
1852	January. Constitution
	November 20th–21st. Plebiscite on Empire
	December 1st. Proclamation of Empire
	Foundation of Crédit Foncier and Crédit Mobilier
1853	January. Marriage of Napoleon III and Eugénie
1854	March. War with Russia
	September. Siege of Sebastopol
1854–65	Faidherbe in Senegal
1855	Paris Exhibition
	September. Fall of Sebastopol
1856	Peace Congress in Paris
1857	Prosecution of *Madame Bovary* and *Les Fleurs du Mal*
	Port of Dakar founded
1858	January. Orsini bomb plot
	July. Conference of Napoleon III and Cavour at Plombières
	Vision at Lourdes
1859	Construction of Suez Canal begun
	Amnesty
	April. War of Italian Unification
	June. Magenta
	Solferino
	July. Armistice of Villafranca
1860	Annexation of Savoy and Nice
	Free-trade treaty with Great Britain
	Anglo-French occupation of Peking
	Expedition to Syria
	First Constitutional changes
1861	October. Expedition to Mexico

1862   Annexation of Cochin-China
        French troops remain in Mexico
1863   Revolt of Poland
        Renan's *Vie de Jésus*
        Salon des refusés
        Manet's 'Le Déjeuner sur l'herbe'
        May. Legislative elections
        Fall of Persigny
        Rouher Minister of State
1864   Schleswig-Holstein War
        Maximilian proclaimed Emperor in Mexico
        Papal *Syllabus of Errors*
1865   Death of Morny
        Educational reforms of Duruy
1866   Austro-Prussian War
        French troops evacuate Mexico
1867   January. Letter of Napoleon III announcing constitutional
            changes
        February. Proposals for rearmament
        Crisis of Crédit Mobilier
        June. Execution of Maximilian
        November. Garibaldi repelled at Mentana
1868   May. Press laws relaxed
1869   Flaubert's *L'Éducation sentimentale*
        Suez Canal opened
        May. Elections
        Election of Gambetta on Belleville programme
        Government of Ollivier
1870   May. Plebiscite on constitutional changes
        June. Hohenzollern acceptance of throne of Spain, sub-
            sequently withdrawn
        July 14th. Ems telegram
        July 19th. French declaration of war on Prussia
        August. French defeats
        Fall of Ollivier
        September 1st. Surrender of Napoleon III and MacMahon at
            Sedan
        September 4th. Government of National Defence set up
        September 19th. Paris besieged
        October 10th. Gambetta arrives at Tours

1870	October 27th. Capitulation of Bazaine at Metz
	November. Victory at Coulmiers
	Reoccupation of Orleans by French
1871	January 19th. Failure of *sortie en masse* from Paris
	January 28th. Armistice
	February 8th. Election of Assembly
	Government of Thiers
	March 1st. Terms of peace ratified by National Assembly
	March 18th. Troops fail to remove guns from Montmartre
	March 28th. Election of Commune
	May 10th. Treaty of Frankfort
	May 21st. Versaillais enter Paris
	May 28th. End of the Commune

FURTHER READING

THE fullest general history of France in the nineteenth century is still Lavisse, *Histoire de France contemporaine* (1920–22); reference to specific volumes will be made later. There are useful bibliographies in these, in the volumes of the *Peuples et civilisations* series, and in *Clio*: L. Villat: *La Révolution et l'Empire, ii. Napoléon* (1936); *L'Époque contemporaine*, i. Droz, Genet et Vidalenc: *Restaurations et révolutions 1815–1871* (1939), ii. Renouvin, Préclin et Hardy: *La paix armée et la Grande Guerre 1871–1919* (1939. 2nd ed., 1947). Excellent general histories, in less detail than Lavisse, are J. P. T. Bury: *France 1814–1940* (2nd ed., 1951); *Histoire de la France pour tous les Français*, G. Lefebvre: *de 1774 à 1815*, C. H. Pouthas: *de 1815 à 1878*, M. Baumont: *de 1878 à nos jours* (1950); and M. Reinhard's finely illustrated *Histoire de France, ii. de 1715 à 1946*; J. Vidalenc: *Le Premier Empire, la Restauration*; L. Girard: *Le Règne de Louis-Philippe, La Révolution de 1848, Le Second Empire*; M. Sorre: *La Troisième République*; L. Genet: *La France au XXe siècle* (1954). A selection of works on special aspects of French history since 1799 follows.

The best short account of French constitutional developments is given in the Introduction to the earlier editions of Duguit, Monnier et Bonnard: *Les Constitutions et les principales lois politiques de la France depuis 1789*. M. Deslandres: *Histoire constitutionelle de la France depuis 1789 jusqu'à 1870, ii* (1932) is long and rather arid but it contains useful material that cannot easily be obtained elsewhere. An interesting sketch of right-wing movements, perhaps unduly schematized, is R. Rémond, *La Droite en France de 1815 à nos jours* (1954). An essential book for understanding the operation of parliamentary institutions in France is D. W. S. Lidderdale's *The Parliament of France* (1951).

French historians are only now beginning to work on the economic history of nineteenth-century France. J. H. Clapham's *Economic Development of France and Germany 1815–1914* (4th ed., 1936) is an able survey on the basis of the material available when it was written. The trade policies of France are traced by S. B. Clough in *France, a History of National Economics, 1789–1939* (1939), a useful book though written to a theme which does not necessarily command acceptance. An account of religious developments is given by C. S. Philips in *The Church in France, 1789–1907* (2 vols., 1929, 1936), and more recently in the series edited by Fliche and Martin, especially *La Crise révolutionnaire 1789–1846* (1949)

by J. Leflon. The study of the interaction of Church and state in France
by P. H. Spencer in *The Politics of Belief in Nineteenth-Century France*
(1954) is thoughtful and illuminating. Concise and impartial summaries
of foreign problems and policies, with bibliographies, are given in the
Histoire des relations internationales, edited and in these volumes written
by P. Renouvin—*Le XIXe siècle: i. 1815–71, l'Europe des nationalités et
l'éveil de nouveaux mondes, ii. 1811–71, L'Apopée de L'Europe* (1954–5);
Les Crises du XXe siècle (2 vols., 1957–8). On French colonies a competent survey with sufficient detail for the non-specialist is the *Histoire de
la colonisation française* (1946) by H. Blet, while the ideas behind French
colonization are described in H. Deschamps' *Méthodes et doctrines
coloniales de la France du XVI siècle à nos jours* (2 vols., 1953). R. Girardet's
La Société militaire dans la France contemporaine 1815–1939 (1953) has
interesting *aperçus* on the history of the army but is rather slight. A more
scholarly work, containing much new material, is P. Chalmin, *L'Officier
français de 1815 à 1870* (1957). In place of various rather dull histories of
education may be mentioned G. Duveau's *Les Instituteurs* (1957), slight
and opinionated but also lively and realistic. A well-documented study of
the press laws is *The Government and the Newspaper Press in France
1814–1881* (1959) by Irene Collins. It is difficult to pick out a single book
on French art for mention, but a stimulating general history of architecture is P. Lavedan's *French Architecture* (1944, trans., 1956). The *Oxford
Companion to French Literature* (1959) is a useful work of reference.
R. Soltau's *French Political Ideas in the Nineteenth Century* (1931) is a
helpful if uninspired survey. Selections from a number of leading French
social and political thinkers, with introductory notes on their authors, are
edited by A. Bayet and F. Albert under the title, *Les Écrivains politiques
du XIXe siècle* (1907).

Turning to special periods, we find the nineteenth century very unevenly served by secondary works. The literature on Napoleon I is
immense. The best life in English is J. M. Thompson's *Napoleon Bonaparte: his Rise and Fall* (1952), though the arrangement is a little con-
fusing. F. M. H. Markham's *Napoleon and the Awakening of Europe* (1954)
is a well-written and judicious short account. In French may be mentioned G. Lefebvre's *Napoléon* (1935) in the *Peuples et Civilisations* series,
and the brief survey by F. Ponteil, *Napoléon Ier et l'organisation autoritaire
de la France* (1956). The changing views on Napoleon during the subsequent century are summarized by P. Geyl in *Napoleon For and Against*
(trans., 1949). A well-presented collection of contemporary verdicts which
takes some of the gilt off the Napoleonic gingerbread is J. Savant's

Napoleon in his Time (1954, trans., 1958). Works on special aspects of the meteoric career of the emperor from one little island to another, and on all those who impinged on it from his marshals to his mistresses, are so many and so detailed that the effort to pick out particular volumes for mention here has had to be abandoned. The histories already referred to will provide an introduction to the voluminous Napoleonic bibliography.

The counter-revolution and the opposition to Napoleon has been served much less well, but its importance for the future intellectual development of France is indicated in F. Baldensperger's *Le Mouvement des idées dans l'émigration française, 1789–1815* (1924). There is now an excellent history of the evanescent but unduly depreciated regime that followed the catastrophe of Napoleon, in G. de Bertier de Sauvigny's *La Restauration* (1955). Sympathetic to the Catholic and royalist ideals of the Restoration, it is therefore perhaps a little hard on parliamentarians like Decazes and Villèle.

The July Monarchy lacks any good recent general history and even specialized studies are comparatively rare. Competent accounts of the reign of Louis-Philippe are the volume in Lavisse by S. Charléty, *La Monarchie de juillet* (1921) and P. de la Gorce, *Louis-Philippe 1830–1848* (1931). A useful light on the politics of the reign is thrown by S. Kent in *Electoral Procedure under Louis-Philippe* (1937). The economic and social problems of a still mainly pre-industrial society have not been adequately studied, but indications are to be found in C. H. Pouthas, *La Population française pendant la première moitié du XIXe siècle* (1956), L. Chevalier's authoritative *La Formation de la population parisienne au XIXe siècle* (1950), the same author's stimulating *Classes laborieuses et classes dangereuses à Paris pendant la première moitié du XIXe siècle* (1958), and J. B. Duroselle's *Les Débuts du catholicisme social en France 1822–70* (1951).

With the Second Republic and the Second Empire we come to a period in which our problem is not to find titles to include, but rather to know what to omit. The best history of the Second Republic is the volume in Lavisse by C. Seignobos, *La Révolution de 1848 et l'Empire* (1921), which reflects a great deal of archival research, unfortunately—for lack of references—all to be done again. One traditional misinterpretation was eliminated by D. C. MacKay in *The National Workshops, a study in the French Revolution of 1848* (1933); and something to rescue the reputation of Ledru-Rollin from excessive contempt was achieved by A. R. Calman's *Ledru-Rollin and the Second French Republic* (1922). Karl Marx's *Class Struggle in France 1848–50* was a brilliant analysis for its time but is naturally inadequate by the standards of modern economic history. F. A. Simpson's *Louis Napoleon and the Recovery of France 1848–56* (1930. 3rd edition 1956) is well written but lacks the research that might have given it more lasting value. The same author's *Rise of Louis Napoleon* (1909) is brilliantly written and amusing but very slight, and H. A. L. Fisher's *Bonapartism* (1914) is somewhat misleading. Louis Napoleon's own *Des idées napoléoniennes* (1939) is essential for the understanding of the Second Empire. Karl Marx's *The Eighteenth Brumaire of Louis Bonaparte* is a brilliant piece of contemporary history.

Among general histories of the Second Empire the volumes by Seignobos in Lavisse are probably still the best. A. L. Guérard's *Napoleon III* (1943) is a bright account and J. M. Thompson's *Louis Napoleon and the Second Empire* (1954) is of value as a study of the personality of Napoleon III. A thoughtful introduction to the economic policy of the Second Empire is H. N. Boon's *Rêve et réalité dans l'œuvre économique et sociale de Napoléon III* (1936). There is a thorough and well-documented study of the Chevalier-Cobden commercial negotiations in *The Anglo-French Treaty of 1860* (1930) by A. L. Dunham. D. H. Pinkney's *Napoleon III and the Rebuilding of Paris* (1958) is a well-balanced account based on original sources. A competent life of the rebuilder of Paris, derived from printed materials, is *The Life and Times of Baron Haussmann* (1957) by J. M. and Brian Chapman. L. Girard's *La Politique des travaux publics du second empire* (1952) is authoritative. On the other side of the medal is the detailed but impressionistic *La Vie ouvrière en France sous le second empire* (1946) by G. Duveau. The membership of the legislative assemblies is sketched by T. Zeldin in *The Political System of Napoleon III* (1958), which combines the brilliance and the narrowness of the Namier approach. A revealing picture of political life under the Second Empire can be obtained from biographies, such as R. Schnerb's thorough and penetrating *Rouher et le Second Empire* (1949). There are many studies of the foreign policy of Napoleon III. One of the most illuminating, which uses the reports of the procureurs, is L. M. Case, *French Opinion on War and Diplomacy during the Second Empire* (1954). The Franco-Prussian War belongs as much to European as to French history and has an extensive literature of which *The Franco-Prussian War* (1961) by Michael Howard is now authoritative. A detailed though rather anti-French account of *The Siege of Paris 1870–1871* (1950) is by M. Kranzberg. The attempt of France to fight back after the collapse of the Empire is well described by J. P. T. Bury in *Gambetta and the National Defence* (1936). F. Jellinek's *The Paris Commune of 1871* (1937) is lively but to be used with caution.

A scholarly account of the ideological conflicts among the Communards is given by C. Rihs in *La Commune de Paris* (1955).

Contemporary writings are, of course, very enlightening to the historian, perhaps particularly so in France where literature has so often been 'engagé'. The list that follows represents merely a sample of the riches that French literature holds for the historian. Chateaubriand's *Mémoires d'outre-tombe* is better for conveying atmosphere than facts. In *Choses vues* Victor Hugo gives a series of political and social vignettes, largely of the period of the July Monarchy. De Tocqueville's *Souvenirs* contain a penetrating study of the social and political errors, in which the author shared, of the Second Republic. The comte de Falloux's *Mémoires d'un royaliste* reveal the limitations of the clerical and conservative mind. In *L'Éducation sentimentale* Flaubert sets the gradual disillusionment of a young bourgeois, haunting the Paris boulevards with no end in life, against the tragic events of revolution and class war. Zola wrote, under the Third Republic, the *Rougon-Macquart* cycle of twenty novels, portraying in lurid detail a Second Empire society made up almost wholly of an amalgam of luxury, crime, misery, and vice. The *Journal* of the Goncourts describes literary and artistic society in the second half of the nineteenth century. Nor should the kind of literature with no apparent political reference be forgotten. Balzac's novels were deliberately conceived as a many-faceted reflection of the *Comédie humaine* in the first thirty years of the nineteenth century.

BOOK III

✤

France of the Republics

CONTENTS

INTRODUCTION   9

PART ONE: THE RISE OF THE THIRD REPUBLIC

1. The Making of the Republic   13
2. The Triumph of the Republic   24
3. The Conservative Republic   37
4. The Dreyfus Affair   49
5. Prologue to Reform   58
6. An Age of Greatness   72

PART TWO: THE DECLINE OF THE REPUBLIC

1. Rumours of War   85
2. The First World War   106
3. Bloc National   118
4. Cartel des Gauches   124
5. The hey-day of the Leagues   133
6. Popular Front   142

PART THREE: THE FALL OF THE REPUBLIC

1. The Quest for Peace   155
2. The Drift to War   165
3. Vichy France   176
4. Collaboration and Resistance   184
5. Constitution-making   193
6. The Fourth Republic   203
7. Doubts and questionings   218
8. The Regime of May Thirteenth   225

CHRONOLOGICAL TABLE   241
FURTHER READING   251

MAPS

1   The French Empire in Asia: Indo-China and India   32

2   The Western Front 1914–1918   107

3   France in the Second World War   171

4   French Empire in Africa   233

INTRODUCTION

THE need to write a third volume in this history of modern France has provided a stimulus to reflection on the slow struggle of republican France to escape from its history. For a thousand years France was a monarchy; it has been a republic for less than a hundred. Monarchical traditions necessarily went deep in French society, and the establishment and consolidation of the republic was bound to be a long-drawn-out and uncertain struggle against them. When the trials of two world wars are added, it may well seem surprising that the republic, even in a series of numerical metamorphoses, should have survived. The work of those who founded and consolidated it, between 1871 and the beginning of the age of wars in 1914, must have been sounder than their critics, or perhaps even they themselves, knew. Monarchy and empire have attracted more attention and far more admiration from historians than the republic. But if the former had their moments of glory, the latter now begins to be seen as more truly an age of greatness. But it was marred by a social pattern of economic conservatism and class rigidity inherited from *ancien régime*, revolution and empire, which produced intense political conflicts and governmental instability.

There was a time when the history of republican France seemed a tiresome story of repetitious failure, the history of a regime too weak and governments too ephemeral to master circumstances, and of would-be rebels too futile and merely negative to take their place. If this were all, there would be little justification for the production of yet another account of how one Radical Socialist replaced another Radical Socialist on the banks of the Seine and the Rhône. But in history the past gains significance from the future, and the Fourth and Fifth Republics have given a posthumous justification to the Third by the achievement of social and international aims which had seemed doomed to perpetual frustration. A merely political history of the French republics is bound to seem trivial and superficial; but envisaged in terms of the evolution of a society, the history of modern France acquires a deeper dimension. As such it has a significance which as an account of the vagaries of day-to-day, or even year-to-year politics it was bound to lack. Social history has also to be seen on a longer time-scale than political. The history of each age throws light on those that preceded and those that followed it. In writing a third volume on France of the Republics I have constantly found myself referred back by echoes of earlier regimes, and sometimes sent forward by anticipations of the latest one. The Fifth Republic seems to draw the threads of modern French history together. It has already concluded much hitherto unfinished business. But if it provides a suitable terminus for this history, it is not so much because it represents an end, as because it also represents a beginning.

✣

PART ONE

THE RISE OF THE THIRD REPUBLIC

✤

CHAPTER ONE

THE MAKING OF THE REPUBLIC

T HE defeat that wrote finis to the rule of Napoleon III was an external event not an internal development. The Second Empire was not ended by the will of the people. The last plebiscite gave the Emperor almost as large a majority as the first. It was not destroyed by revolution: there was no revolutionary party with the power to overthrow it. The Empire had simply, in the person of a defeated, aged and ailing Emperor, been overthrown in war, and capitulated to the invader. Its disappearance, before no predestined successor, left only a void. France was thrust into a new age, not deliberately by her own action, or in the fullness of time by the presence of new social forces, but accidentally and prematurely by the fact of military defeat. The intense conservatism of French society in 1871 was revealed by the savage reaction to the Commune of Paris, as it had been in 1848 by the repression of the revolt of the June days. The aim of the ruling classes in 1871 remained what it had been when the Empire was set up, to preserve the fabric of society unchanged, not to make a new France but to save the old one. This was the task which the National Assembly at Bordeaux, elected to get France out of the German war as quickly as possible, took upon itself.

It was an assembly of notables in more than one sense: intellectuals from all shades of the political spectrum – Louis Blanc, Edgar Quinet, Victor Hugo, Littré, Albert de Broglie, Dupanloup; old republicans like Ledru-Rollin and Delescluze, and Orleanists like Dufaure and Thiers; the as yet untried leaders of the future Republic, including moderates like Waddington, Méline, Léon Say, and those who were then accounted of the left – Jules Simon, Jules Favre, Grévy, Ferry – and so far out that he resigned when the Assembly made war on the Commune, the Mayor of Montmartre, Clemenceau. More noticeable at the moment, since no one knew that they already belonged to a *temps perdu* and had a future only in the volumes of Proust, were the Noailles, the Harcourt, Haussonville, la Rochefoucauld – the old *noblesse de cour* come back to Versailles to haunt the galleries and corridors of its former greatness for the last time. They might, if they had possessed sufficient perception, have perceived an omen in the fact that despite its predominantly monarchical complexion, the Assembly chose the republican Jules Grévy – admittedly known as the enemy both of the Empire and of Gambetta – as its first President. More significant was the fact that Thiers had been elected in twenty-six departments and thus practically chosen by a national vote to form the new government. He appointed three republicans, Favre, Picard and Simon, to the key posts of Foreign Affairs, Interior and Education respectively.

The first task was to make peace. Thiers settled with the Germans even before he settled with Paris. The southern part of Lorraine, all Alsace except Belfort, the payment of what seemed at the time a huge indemnity of two milliard francs, German occupation of the eastern departments of France until the indemnity had been paid, and of Paris until the treaty was ratified – such was the cost of defeat in war. The Assembly, desiring peace and a return to normal conditions before everything else, accepted the terms as soon as they were presented, and so reduced the German military occupation of Paris to a parade of a single day. By the peace France lost a population of nearly a million and a half, though there was a considerable migration to France from the surrendered territories. She lost the mines and industries of Lorraine, the textile mills of Alsace, and the great provincial capital of Strasbourg, a French city since the time, two hundred years earlier, when Louis XIV had marched his armies to the Rhine. The sums necessary to pay off the indemnity were raised, by means of loans, far more rapidly than had been expected. The first half-milliard was paid in July 1871 and brought the evacuation of five out of twenty-one occupied departments. In March 1873 Thiers was able to pay another half-milliard, and the remainder was paid in four monthly instalments from June to September. The last German soldier left France in

September 1873. In spite of the burden of the indemnity, the French budget, with the aid of favourable world economic conditions, was balanced by 1875.

Elected to liquidate the war, Thiers and the National Assembly had succeeded in their task by the simple process of paying the price demanded by the victors. The Assembly found the other task, for which it had not been elected but which it took upon itself, that of framing a new constitution for France, a more difficult one. The only solution which at first seemed definitely excluded was the Bonapartist one. In 1871 the political and administrative personnel of the Second Empire had followed its predecessors into the increasingly overcrowded Valhalla of defunct regimes, whose memory filled the history books and whose ghosts haunted the French political scene. It was not quite the end of Bonapartism. A nostalgia for the high days of the Empire survived among army commanders, high ecclesiastics, dispossessed officials and Corsicans; and the death of Napoleon III in 1873 was to leave the young Prince Imperial as a more appealing representative of the dynasty. Subsequently the selfish policies of monarchists and conservative republicans revived Bonapartist sentiments among those suffering from economic distress; and yet later it was to be seen that plebiscitary dictatorship had not exhausted its attraction for the people. But for the time being, at least, Bonapartism was excluded from the political agenda.

If the elections of February 1871 had adequately represented the political wishes of France, a restoration of the monarchy should have been a foregone conclusion. Even if they did not, the predominance of monarchists in the Assembly would have brought the same result if the fatal division of monarchist forces had not stood in the way. The legitimist claimant was the comte de Chambord, *l'enfant du miracle*, posthumous son of the duc de Berry, who had passed his life with a little court of exiles in a castle in Austria. Devout to the point of mysticism, trained as he said himself to expect everything from God and nothing from man, free from worldly ambition or knowledge, lame, isolated, living in and for the past, perhaps the noblest of his line, he was beyond doubt now the last for he had no children. In this fact seemed to lie the possibility of a deal with the rival house of Orleans, by which the comte de Chambord might occupy the throne while he lived, and on his death be followed on the throne in due line of succession by his Orleanist heir.

This seemed a very reasonable plan to the Orleanist comte de Paris, a very different kind of person, who knew the world and might seem almost to have modelled himself on the career of Louis Napoleon in preparing his own candidature to the throne. He had studied trade unionism in England, travelled widely and written books to describe his travels, fought in the American Civil War and written a history of it. Unfortunately for the hopes of the Orleanists it was quite out of the comte de Chambord's character to do a deal with anybody, or offer any concession to obtain his legitimate rights. He made this plain in a manifesto issued as early as July 1871, when he declared that he would never abandon the white flag and fleur-de-lis of his ancestors: 'I will not let the standard of Henry IV, of Francis I, of Jeanne d'Arc be torn from my hands.' Decentralization, provincial liberties – the old demands of the aristocratic revolt of 1787 – universal suffrage 'honestly applied' (whatever that meant), parliamentary government: these he could and did promise. He was willing to give up the substance so long as he kept the shadow, the symbols of legitimate monarchy, which had a mystical value in his eyes. This was his first and his last word and it was fatal to the prospect of a restoration, for these were the symbols that France had twice rejected.

For some years the French monarchists continued to hope for a compromise and to pursue their vain negotiations with Chambord. Indeed, in the autumn of 1873 their envoy returned with the glad news that he had accepted the national flag. Preparations were at once set on foot for the *joyeuse entrée* of the last of the Bourbons into his capital, which shows how crucial was the question of the flag. Alas, it was all a misunderstanding. Chambord issued a repudiation of the report. Notwithstanding this, with ineffable faith and that contempt for the facts which was the hallmark of the French royalists, he still continued to believe, apparently, that all he had to do was to appear in France for his right divine to be recognized. When he did come, in 1874, it was to arrive in secret and return in silence.

The one thing that Chambord and his supporters could do was to block the path to a restoration of the hated house of Orleans. That under neither dynasty would it have been an easy or peaceful restoration was shown by the first elections to be held under normal conditions. These were the supplementary elections of July 1871, in which 99 republicans, as against 9 Orleanists, 3 legitimists and 3 Bonapartists, were elected. Subsequent by-elections continued the same trend: between 1871 and 1874, 126 republicans were elected and only 23 monarchists and 10 Bonapartists. There was thus a great change in the composition of the Assembly, which explains in part how an initially monarchist assembly came to agree to a republican constitution. At the same time, the significance of the election results must not be exaggerated.

In 1873, however, the monarchist majority still surviving in the Assembly was becoming increasingly restive under the yoke of the republican ministers it had felt obliged to accept in 1871. If the monarchists could not set up their own regime, at least, they felt, they did not have to endure the rule of their enemies. Grévy was forced out of the presidency of the Assembly in favour of an intransigent clerical. Thiers, who had made up his mind that the Republic was going to win and had cautiously been throwing his influence on that side, had not been quite cautious enough for the taste of the monarchists of the majority. When it became evident that he was no longer a safe bulwark against the advance of the left they repudiated him. This was after a Paris by-election in which the conservative candidate, Thiers's own Foreign Minister, was well beaten by the republican candidate Barodet, a former mayor of Lyons who had been dismissed by the government for his advanced views. After this the Assembly decided to rid itself of Thiers. By a vote of May 24th, 1873, the monarchists repudiated the old man, who now seemed to them only an embarrassment, and he resigned.

In his place as head of the state they chose Marshal MacMahon, whose reputation had somehow survived defeat. Perhaps defeat itself was not so loathsome if it bore the precious jewel of a restoration in its head. MacMahon, although a former Bonapartist marshal, was reckoned sympathetic to the cause of monarchs. He was rather stupid and did not understand politics. The headship of the government was now separated from that of the state and was taken over by the Orleanist duc de Broglie. The abnormal situation in which practically supreme authority had been concentrated in the hands of a single man was thus brought to an end and replaced by a parliamentary government. Ironically, the monarchists in 1873, as after 1815, were temporarily and for their own ends the restorers of parliamentary government. It was restored under very aristocratic auspices. Along with Broglie the government included Decazes and d'Audiffret-Pasquier, only three it is true, but enough to let historians dub the new regime the republic of the dukes. The witticism may have some point if it is true that the aim was as much to preserve the rule of a now rather adulterated *noblesse* as to restore that of an over-pure monarch.

Until legitimists and Orleanists had reached an agreement, and the legitimist claimant had given way on the question of the flag, the restoration of the monarchy was not practical politics. MacMahon himself, when Chambord made his secret journey into France in the autumn of 1874, had sufficient common sense to see what patent folly an attempt at restoration would be and Chambord returned to his castle as he had come, incognito. Broglie, seeing that the monarchy could not be restored in the person of Chambord, and unwilling to accept the Republic, fell back on the device of prolonging the provisional. Chambord and his flag, an Orleanist may have thought, would not stand in the way of a restoration for ever. The solution was the *septennat* of November 1873, by which MacMahon was to be head of the state for seven years. This settled nothing but it enabled Broglie to remain in office pursuing a resolutely conservative policy.

The failure of the restoration should not lead us to underestimate the strength of monarchist feeling in the country, just as the strength of the republicans had been underestimated a few years earlier. In the Assembly, and the country, right and left were – as they were to be throughout the history of the Third Republic – fairly evenly balanced. The future government of France was to depend on which could win the support of the body of opinion in the centre which held the balance.

The weakness of the monarchists lay, where their strength also lay, in their religious affiliations. The religious revival that had begun early in the century was still strong. Religious sentiments played their part in the masochistic tendencies manifested by the French right after 1871, as they had been after 1815 and were to be again in 1940. The nation was called to repentance by the Church for the sins that had brought disaster on it. There was also a general fear of social revolution, and religion was, perhaps more than ever before, seen as a social sanction. The identification of the Church with the protection of the interests of birth, wealth and social status became almost total with the Third Republic. The *noblesse* were now practising Catholics almost to a man – and even more woman – and the bourgeoisie, at least since 1848, had come to feel that religion was necessary both to protect the virtue of their daughters and to keep the socially dangerous classes at bay.

The strength of the religious bulwark of society had greatly increased under the Second Empire. The numbers in the male religious orders had multiplied by ten to some thirty thousand, and in women's orders by four to about a hundred and twenty thousand. Much of boys' and practically all of girls' education was under their control, as was assistance to the poor, aged, and infirm. Influence over the voters was, however, more easily won by an appeal to their sentiments than to their intellect or even their interests. The propaganda motive, as well as the dominance in the Church of a wealthy class with peculiarly little aesthetic sense, may have been responsible for the remarkable vulgarity of most of the religious art of the period. The attempt to win back the people to religion was above all the work of the new order of the Assumptionists, founded in 1845, who promoted a raging, tearing propaganda, one feature of which was the development on a vast scale of the cult of the Sacred Heart. The foundation stone of a great new church, dedicated to the Sacré-Cœur, was laid in 1873 on the heights of Montmartre, where Loyola and his first group of followers had met and the Counter-reformation had in a sense begun. Its building was conceived as an act of national penitence. Individual penitence took the form of great mass pilgrimages to Lourdes and other shrines, organized with the aid of special railway excursions. The methods of the popular press were brought into play in the cause of religion by the Assumptionist paper *La Croix*, which attained a circulation of half a million.

Religious agitation was, as usual, not unconnected with political aims. Linked with the cult of the Sacred Heart and the sorrows of France were those of a Church whose head was now the prisoner of the Vatican. In July 1871 the French bishops petitioned the Assembly to take action to restore the temporal power of the Pope. In the churches Roman Catholics prayed 'Sauvez Rome et la France au nom du Sacré-Cœur.' The restoration of the monarchy to France and of the Pope to his temporal domains became the joint aims of French Catholicism, but such militancy was to the taste of only a minority. To those who were less ardent the prospect of war with Italy for the sake of the temporal possessions of the Papacy, and a parallel agitation against the religious policy of Bismarck which threatened further hostilities with Germany, were alarming. The result of the close link between legitimacy and the Church was to saddle the monarchists with the joint encumbrance of clericalism and war-mongering. Meanwhile they were falling out among themselves. To serve permanently under an Orleanist was more than some legitimists could manage, and the two legitimists in Broglie's government retired in November 1873. In May 1874 the extremer legitimists, who were known from the name of the street where they had their headquarters as the *chevau-légers*, voted to the number of fifty with the republican opposition to overthrow Broglie. He had to resign and MacMahon set up a caretaker government in his place.

At the same time the republicans, including Gambetta who had returned to active politics in 1872, had been behaving with conspicuous moderation which was gradually conciliating centre opinion. Both republicans and moderate monarchists were now becoming alarmed at signs of a recrudescence of Bonapartism. In the National Assembly there were some twenty-five to thirty admitted Bonapartists, led by the Second Empire survivor Rouher. This was not many, but enough, given the narrow margin of votes separating republicans and monarchists, for them to inaugurate the wrecking policy which was to be the hallmark of Bonapartism without a Bonaparte, as it was later to be of monarchism without a monarch, under the Third Republic. The Bonapartists played their part in bringing down Thiers in 1873 and Broglie in 1874, and so long as France remained without a constitution, even of the most provisional kind, the door seemed open to a Bonapartist revival.

In January 1875 a motion defining the government of the Republic was defeated by only 359 votes to 336. It was followed, on February 25th, by the famous *amendement Wallon*, which laid down the method of electing the successors to MacMahon at the head of the state. The effect of this was to turn the presidency of the Republic from a temporary expedient into a permanent institution. 'My conclusion,' Wallon ended his speech, 'is that it is necessary to leave the provisional. If the monarchy is possible, show that it will be accepted, propose it. If on the contrary it is not possible, I do not say to you: decide for the republic, but I say: recognize the government now established, which is the government of the republic. I do not ask you to proclaim it as definitive – what is definitive? But all the same do not call it provisional.' The amendment was passed by 353 votes to 352, so that it could be said that the Republic was established by a majority of one vote.

The Third Republic never had a constitution. In its place there was passed a series of constitutional laws, determined more by practical than theoretical considerations. The monarchists, knowing that they would lose heavily in a general election, were prepared to compromise to avoid a dissolution of the Assembly. So it came about that a republic was set up by an Assembly which still had a monarchist majority. Naturally the constitutional laws included as many potentially conservative elements as the Assembly could manage to introduce into them. The President, chosen for seven years and re-eligible, with extensive and broadly defined political powers, including, with the agreement of the Senate, the dissolution of the Chamber of Deputies, to which he was not personally responsible, was the next best thing to a king; and the door for an easy transition from republic to monarchy was kept open by establishing a simple procedure for constitutional revision. While republican institutions lasted, the conservative interests in society were to be entrenched in an upper chamber, or Senate, with powers in theory practically equal to those of the Chamber of Deputies. One-third of the members of the Senate were to be chosen for life by the existing monarchical Assembly, while the remainder were to be elected indirectly by electoral colleges drawn from local government bodies, with a strong weightage in favour of the small, rural communes. The elected Senators, moreover, were to hold office for nine years, one-third retiring every three years.

What happened was, of course, very different from what had been expected. Only in the later years of the Third Republic did the Senate come to assume the conservative role planned for it, while the strong executive intended for the presidency was never to materialize. However, the natural play of social forces ensured that the Chamber of Deputies should itself be for long immunized against social experiment.

Having given birth if not to a constitution at least to a small litter of constitutional laws, the National Assembly had no longer any reason for existence. It was dissolved in December 1875. The elections of 1876 produced a Chamber with over 340 republicans against under 200 on the right including, most significantly, a Bonapartist group of about 75. When the new Chamber chose the life members of the Senate, the legitimists of the committee of the rue des Chevau-légers vented their hatred on the Orleanists by joining with the republicans in an electoral manoeuvre which produced 57 republican life Senators out of 75.

After the elections MacMahon found himself in the position of a President elected by a defunct Assembly which had been repudiated by the country, and faced with a republican Chamber which could claim to represent the voice of the people. If the monarchists accepted this situation they abandoned any hope of achieving their aim in the foreseeable future. Rather than do this they played the only card in their hand: MacMahon dissolved the Chamber on May 16th, 1877. This became known as the *coup d'état* of *seize mai*, though in fact he was acting strictly within his constitutional rights. He called Broglie to lead a government which was to make – literally it was hoped – the new elections. The ground was prepared by a wholesale administrative purge. Over 70 prefects and 226 sub-prefects and secretaries general were replaced, 1,743 municipal councils dissolved and their mayors dismissed. To conduct the new elections Broglie had to call in the only men with experience in the job of electoral management, those who had run the former Bonapartist political machine. All the traditional methods of influence were revived. Pressure was brought to bear on government officials or employees; opposition journals were prosecuted, opposition cafés were closed and licences to sell pamphlets were revoked. MacMahon was sent to tour the provinces, making speeches in the larger towns, and with the whole-hearted backing of the Church and the *bien-pensant* gentry whose authority customarily dominated the small towns and villages of France, he and Broglie might reasonably have felt confident of success.

The left replied with a policy of republican concentration under Gambetta and Thiers. When, in the middle of the campaign, Thiers died, Paris forgot that he had made war on it and turned his funeral into a great republican demonstration. His place at the head of the republican coalition was taken by Jules Grévy, a provincial lawyer from Franche-Comté with a reputation for moderate republicanism, a safe man on all matters affecting property and particularly interested, the *chansonniers* alleged, in its acquisition, which was to involve him in difficulties later.

The election of 1877 can be regarded as the real foundation of the Third Republic. It was not only a political turning-point, it was a more decisive social revolution than anything that had occurred in 1830, 1848 or 1871. It was the point at which rural France repudiated the authority of the notables, those men of landed estate, composed of an amalgam of *noblesse* from a series of regimes with *haute bourgeoisie*, conservative and clerical, whose influence had kept the great rural masses of France steadily on the side of social conservatism whatever political changes might come about. The attempt to make the elections was a total failure: the republicans won 326 seats and the right 207. After this there was nothing for MacMahon to do but resign. Broglie naturally disappeared and was followed into the wilderness by his prefects. Also, to bear witness that this was a major defeat for the executive, the Vice-President of the Conseil d'État and nine Conseillers were dismissed, the first and last such purge until 1945. Grévy moved into the vacant presidential chair.

CHAPTER TWO

THE TRIUMPH OF THE
REPUBLIC

THE crisis of 1877 had done more than register the failure of the monarchists. In his first message the new President declared, 'Subject to the great law of the parliamentary regime, I will never enter into opposition against the national will expressed by its constitutional organs.' The balance of the constitution had been decisively shifted in favour of the Chamber and against the Senate and the President. The Senate was for long after this to be a mere 'theatre of the Left Bank', not a stage on which the greater dramas of national life were enacted. Its influence gradually increased, but it was only in the last years of the Third Republic that it became practically the headquarters of the general staff of republican politics. The presidency, on the other hand, never recovered from the failure of MacMahon's attempt to make himself an effective head of state. It became practically a constitutional convention of the Third Republic that no strong statesman should be elected President; Poincaré in 1913 was an exception attributable to the threatening international situation. The President's duties were henceforth mainly honorific: he has been described as an elderly gentleman whose function it was to wear evening dress in day-time. Yet he alone was in a position to provide continuity in policy – very necessary in a regime of rapidly changing governments, and his right to nominate the new head of the ministry made him the key figure when a government fell. His skill in manoeuvring could often determine whether a political crisis should be of short duration, or long and severe. But at best the President could do no more than grease the wheels of politics. After 1877 power resided in the parliament and chiefly in the Chamber of Deputies.

The years 1877 to 1881 witnessed the establishment of the republican regime. It was fortunate in that it came to birth at a time when economic affairs were prospering and the budget was balanced. It was also fortunate, considering the strongly conservative nature of French society, in coming to power with a conservative policy and bias. The attempted *coup* of the *seize mai* had saddled the right with a tradition of unconstitutional action which alarmed moderate opinion. The republicans had previously been committed to radical demands based on Gambetta's Belleville programme of 1869, including separation of Church and state, liberty of press and meeting, free and compulsory public education, removal of the laws against trade unions. The *seize mai* was a not altogether unwelcome diversion, which enabled them to escape from these advanced proposals, and when they came to power it was with more modest commitments. The abandonment of the 1876 programme was also responsible for the description of Opportunists, given them by the satirical journalist Rochefort.

The ruling personnel, as well as the policy of the new Republic, was to be conservative. Grévy was determined that a popular tribune with dangerous reforming ideas, such as Gambetta, should be kept out of power. When it was necessary to choose, in December 1879, he therefore called to office not Gambetta but his former aide in the Prussian war, Freycinet – small, dapper, aloof, subtle, insinuating, who was for a whole generation to run up and down the corridors of the Third Republic like a little white mouse, which was what the political world called him, not a great figure but a useful, worthy, likable one, eminently a serviceable man.

The defeat of the right in the legislative elections of 1877 was followed by a corresponding republican victory in the local elections of 1878, which was bound in due course to influence the composition of the Senate. After further elections in 1881, the republicans had control of some twenty thousand communes out of thirty-six thousand, and a majority in sixty-six departmental councils out of eighty-seven. This has been called the *révolution des mairies*. The notables, having been defeated in their struggle for the central government, had also lost control of the provinces.

A series of political changes marked the increasing republicanism of the regime. *La Marseillaise* became the national anthem and July 14th a national holiday. In 1879 the Chamber of Deputies and

the Senate returned to Paris from Versailles. This was a less dangerous move than it might have been a generation earlier, for Paris
was ceasing to be the left-wing and proletarian city of the past
hundred years.

The major political problem for the left was presented by the
exiled Communards of 1871. The agitation on their behalf was led
by small groups of socialists, for whom it provided a focus of unity
which in other respects they lacked. The tiny group of French
Marxists, which was just beginning to appear, seized on the Commune as a ready-made historical legend for themselves and began
the propaganda which was to root the cult of the Commune deeply
in French working-class consciousness. A partial amnesty, granted
in spring 1879, reduced the number of Communard prisoners or
exiles to about one thousand. Those who were released were the best
plea for an amnesty to the remainder. Ill, wasted, and in rags, they
staggered off the ships that had brought them back across half the
world, and the appeal of humanity was stronger than the fears of
property and respectability. With new elections due in 1881, the
republicans were anxious to remove from the political agenda a
question which divided them, though the socialists were now less
keen for an amnesty which would rob them of one of their strongest
grounds for agitation against the regime. Freycinet introduced the
proposal for a full amnesty in June 1880, but it was the authority of
Gambetta which carried the measure. Among other progressive
measures of the same year were a law freeing public meetings from
the requirement of official authorization; and a press law abolishing
'crimes of opinion', leaving only direct provocation to crime or to
disturbance of the peace, insults against the President, defamation
and the like as press offences. The latitude allowed to the press to
slander and incite to violence with almost total impunity was not
yet seen as the danger to democratic institutions that it was to
become later.

The legislative elections of 1881 continued the swing to the left,
giving the republicans a large majority in the Chamber. The Republican Union of Gambetta emerged as the strongest group with
over two hundred members; but perhaps the most significant
feature was the continued growth of the Bonapartists, who included

half the strength of the conservative forces in the Chamber. Clearly the right was changing, and with hindsight we might say that it was ominously evident in what direction.

With the constitutional crisis settled, the chief area of strategic conflict between left and right now shifted to the field of education, in which political and social divisions were exacerbated by their identification with religious ones. In 1879 a determined opponent of clerical control, Jules Ferry, had become Minister of Education. He belonged to a distinguished family of the Vosges and had been a strong critic of the Second Empire and a member of the Government of National Defence. Though able and determined, he was too rigid and uncompromising to win popularity. Conservative in social matters, he was a convinced republican and fiercely secularist in educational policy. There was a general feeling, in republican circles, that French education did not meet the requirements of the time. The disaster of 1870 was regarded as a victory for the German teacher. Whereas German schools provided instruction in the sciences and modern languages, French education, it was alleged, was still following the methods and aims of the seventeenth century. An attempt at modernization in 1872, by Jules Simon, had been frustrated by the influence of the Church, particularly of the great cleric, Dupanloup, and it seemed unlikely that reform would be possible so long as education remained in clerical hands. As the clergy were in the main monarchist in their political sympathies this was another reason for fearing their influence on the educational system.

Ferry launched his attack with characteristic single-mindedness and vigour. He began by secularizing the Conseil Supérieur de l'Instruction Publique, expelling the bishops and other high ecclesiastics from it. He confined the granting of degrees and other educational qualifications to the state. Education in the public primary schools was made free and by a subsequent law compulsory. For the training of women teachers, écoles normales for girls, which hardly existed as yet, were to be founded in every department. Religious instruction was excluded from the state schools: it was the coming of the 'école sans Dieu', declared Broglie.

The bitterest opposition to Ferry's educational laws was provoked by the notorious article 7: 'No one is allowed to take part in state or independent education, or to control an educational establishment of any kind if he belongs to an unauthorized congregation.' Among the unauthorized congregations were Jesuits, Marists, Dominicans, and indeed all but five of the orders for men. The Senate rejected the article but the government retaliated by taking advantage of the distinction drawn by Napoleonic legislation between religious bodies that were legally authorized and those that were merely tolerated. It decreed the dissolution of the Society of Jesus and ordered that the other orders should apply for official recognition. Ferry himself was prepared to let the parish priests give religious education in secular schools, but the extremists on both sides rejected this compromise and Catholics and anti-clericals united to vote it down. The premier, Freycinet, a Protestant, was willing to agree to a compromise in respect of all orders except the Jesuits, and the Pope, Leo XIII, was prepared to accept an agreement by which the government would abandon its demand for official authorization and in return the orders would renounce their political opposition to the Republic, though without affording it formal recognition. This was too much, on one side for the superiors of the orders and the French hierarchy, monarchist almost to a man, and on the other for the extreme anti-clericals. As soon as information about the proposed compromise leaked out, Freycinet, attacked from both right and left, was driven out of office.

The clerical party did not gain by this, for Ferry took his place and began a piecemeal expulsion of the unauthorized orders. The decrees presented a real *crise de conscience* to many good men. Two hundred magistrates, who had scruples about applying them, resigned their positions. Members of the orders often barricaded their houses, though they generally did not wait in them to be arrested when the police, or sometimes the army, occupied the empty premises. This was only a preliminary skirmish, not the major battle. After the passions aroused by the struggle had died down, the orders filtered back, with even less love for the Republic than before, while the decrees were allowed to fall quietly into disuse. It was the beginning of a conflict which was to embitter the politics of the Third Republic almost to the end.

In spite of the success of the republicans, their real leader, Gambetta, had remained excluded from office. Grévy reflected conservative hostility against the man whom Thiers had damned as the 'fou furieux'. It was the first of many occasions during the Third Republic when the reasonable, sensible, moderate, intriguing, little men, of whom Grévy was no unworthy representative, joined to exclude a man whose greater stature made him seem dangerous. Not until 1881 did Gambetta form a ministry and then it proved a sad anti-climax. Whether as a result of Grévy's continual hostility against him, or of the suspicions of other politicians, or of Gambetta's own dictatorial temperament, his great ministry proved to be a cabinet of lesser lights, including none of the brighter luminaries of the republican galaxy. Perhaps, also, Gambetta was too much a man of panaceas. He attributed the weakness that was already affecting republican politics to the influence of the electoral system of single-member constituencies – *mares stagnantes* as they were later to be called – and began his legislative programme by introducing a law to replace *scrutin d'arrondissement* (single-member constituencies) by *scrutin de liste* (voting on a departmental basis). When the Chamber rejected the proposal he resigned, in January 1882, less than three months after taking office. The same year he died prematurely, at the age of forty-four, taking many hopes and fears for the new Republic with him.

After a short hiatus Ferry, the biggest figure among the republicans after Gambetta, came again to office. The membership of Ferry's two ministries of 1880 and 1883 reads like a roll-call of future premiers and presidents. In his second ministry, beginning in February 1883, Ferry continued the task of republican consolidation with the notable law on municipalities of 1884, which established the free election of *maires* by the local councils everywhere except in Paris. The full importance of this step can only be appreciated if we realize the extent of the powers of the *maire* – the agent of the state for proclaiming and carrying out the laws and regulations of the central government; registrar of births, marriages and deaths; a judicial officer entitled to denounce breaches of the law, and in default of the police commissioner prosecute them in the courts; the executive agent of the commune, the president of the meetings of the local council, who prepares its agenda and draws up its budget. In the light of all this it is not difficult to see why the Republic has been described as the regime of the elected *maire*.

Other laws passed at this time included a prohibition of any revision of the republican form of government, and of the election of any member of a family which formerly reigned in France to the presidency; the abolition of life Senators as and when the existing ones died; the recognition of trade unions; and the introduction of a law of divorce. These were the work of Ferry and those moderate republicans whom their critics condemned as Opportunists. Ferry's achievement has seemed greater to historians than it did to his contemporaries, dominated by a personal hatred of the man. Hardly any other politician of the time aroused such bitter hostility; but it was not his domestic policy but his contribution to building a new colonial empire that brought about his downfall.

It is ironic that the Third Republic should have been the regime which built up France's great colonial empire, for at least in the earlier stages this was against the will of most of its political groups. The left was opposed to colonial conquests on principle, as well as to anything that might increase the influence of the army, while the right regarded overseas acquisitions as a diversion from the task of revenge on Germany. The creation of the colonial empire under the Third Republic has been explained in terms of the personal policy of Ferry, but this is to attribute too much to the influence of one man, as well as to read back into Ferry's actions at the time a colonial policy that may never have been in his mind, or have been thought of only later, when he had undeservedly suffered for what was supposed to be his policy. Coming from an industrialized area of the Vosges and from a family of manufacturers and financiers, it is easy to suppose that he might have envisaged colonies as providing markets for surplus manufactures and a source of supply of raw materials. But this is to read an economic motivation into the colonial policies of the Third Republic for which there was at the time little evidence. A more important factor than the economic may well have been the religious one, for France was the great missionary power of the Roman Catholic world in the nineteenth century. By the time of the Third Republic among some four thousand five hundred missionary priests outside Europe three-quarters were French. If trade followed the flag, the flag sometimes followed the cassock. More influential than either economics or religion was perhaps mere prestige. When France occupied Tunis, in 1881, Gambetta wrote to Ferry that she was resuming her rank as a great Power.

In spite of such motives, the reluctance of politicians to launch France on extensive colonial enterprises was clearly exhibited when a debt-collecting Anglo-French fleet sailed to Alexandria to overthrow Colonel Arabi in 1882. The Chamber of Deputies reacted against the possibility of being entangled in a war in Egypt and left the liquidation of the affair to the British. A little earlier, in 1881, a decision had been taken by Ferry to establish a protectorate over Tunisia, but this was for strategic reasons and under pressure from the army and the Foreign Office. The whole of the decaying Turkish empire of North Africa had fallen into a state of chaos in which the only stable point was the French military hold on Algeria. It was evident that either France or Italy would move into the vacuum in Tunis, and Bismarck's diplomacy encouraged the French to do so, both to divert French interests from Europe and to alienate Italy from France. It was not even necessary to organize a *casus belli*: in those days retaliation by the stronger against aggression by the weaker was not invariably regarded as a form of international immorality. Forays into Algeria by Tunisian tribes provided the army with an excuse to take action, and after minor military operations the Treaty of Bardo, in 1881, established a French protectorate over Tunisia in the name of a puppet Bey.

Ferry's next major colonial commitment was also hardly the result of deliberate choice. The Second Empire had established a foothold in Indo-China. Trouble with pirates and the loss of a small French force there turned a minor expedition for police purposes into a substantial war with China for the possession of Tonkin. The credits required for the expedition were resented and there was a heavy loss of life from disease. As the colonial war dragged on it became more and more unpopular in a country that was not interested in colonial expeditions and had unhappy memories of the Mexican adventure, which had followed rather a similar pattern.

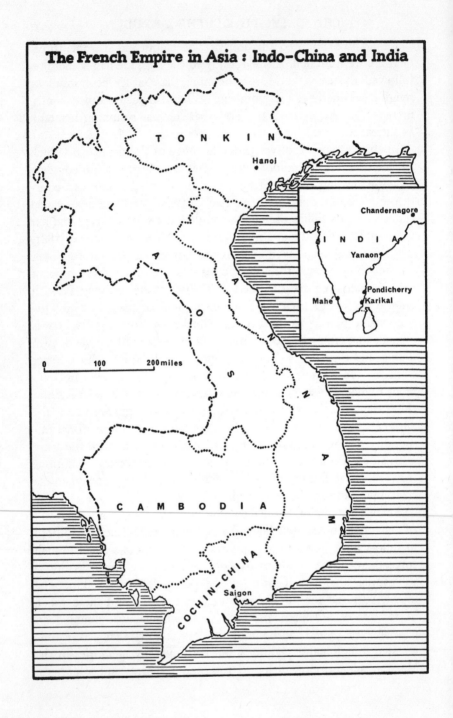

The French Empire in Asia : Indo-China and India

T O N K I N

Hanoi

L

A

O

S

Chandernagore

I N D I A

Yanaon

Mahé   Pondicherry
        Karikal

0   100   200 miles

A

N

N

A

M

C A M B O D I A

COCHIN–CHINA

Saigon

When, in 1885, the report arrived of a French reverse, the enemies of Ferry saw their opportunity. Led by Clemenceau from the extreme left, they shouted him down with cries of 'Tonkin-Ferry' and hurled him from office. The Tonkin affair was soon afterwards concluded successfully, but Ferry's name had been linked with colonial aggression and disaster and his reputation never recovered from the attack.

He fell at a time when political and economic developments were leading up to the first great crisis of the Third Republic. Economic conditions, which had given the Republic a good start in the 'seventies, became much less favourable in the 'eighties. The world slump, which had begun in 1875, was now affecting France, always slower than most other countries to experience the effect of external economic regression. In addition, competition from America was bringing down agricultural prices and land values were falling with them. The disease of phylloxera, which had begun to affect the vineyards in 1865, continued to spread until 1885, when the vines were reconstituted by grafting on immune American stock. Finally, a financial crisis developed in 1882, when one of the leading banks, the Union Générale, established under Catholic influence to challenge the financial dominance of Protestants and Jews, suspended payment. Speculation in central Europe had brought the bank into a conflict with the more powerful Rothschilds from which it emerged the loser. The failure of this Catholic financial venture, a panic on the Bourse, and a number of bankruptcies, were perhaps not unconnected with a growing agitation against Jewish financiers. Also, for the first time under the Third Republic, there was a deficit on the budget in 1882, which continued until 1887. A general industrial slump, in which prices and wages fell and unemployment rose, followed the financial crisis. The conclusion was drawn that economic depression was the result of the weak and unstable policies of republican governments, whereas in fact it would have been more reasonable to suppose that it was their cause.

The republican parties therefore entered the elections of 1885 in unfavourable conditions. They were disunited because of the growth of a left wing, now beginning to be called Intransigents or Radicals, who were hostile to the social conservatism as well as to

B

the colonial policy of the dominant Opportunists. The right, on the other hand, as a result of the deaths of the Prince Imperial in 1879 and of the comte de Chambord in 1883, were left with only one candidate for the throne, the Orleanist comte de Paris. It is true that the more rigid legitimists never reconciled themselves to his claim, and that the Bonapartist tradition was to develop in a different direction, but for the moment the monarchists were less divided than usual. Throughout the history of the Third Republic the strength of the right in the country was greater than their generally inferior position in the Chamber of Deputies would lead one to suppose, but this permanent parliamentary inferiority was partly responsible for their tendency to flirt with revolution. In the elections of 1885, which were conducted under the system of *scrutin de liste*, they had 3,500,000 votes against the republican 4,100,000. The obvious danger forced an electoral coalition on the republican parties in the second ballot, which gave them 383 seats against 201 to their opponents.

In the new Chamber the Opportunists secured the re-election of Grévy as President, but they were able to form a government only with the aid of the more radical republicans, and to this extent were at their mercy. The left wing – and particularly its leading figure, Clemenceau – was now responsible for a miscalculation which endangered the Republic. The later development of his political career had already been foreshadowed in the transfer of Clemenceau from his working-class constituency of Paris to the representation of the old Jacobin stronghold of Draguignan in the Var. A new left was appearing which he could not but repudiate. He would not follow it, he declared, into the barracks and convents of socialism. He was more attracted, as indeed were many on the left, by a reforming general, whose martial air and panache had aroused the enthusiasm of the crowd. Boulanger was appointed Minister of War, largely by the influence of Clemenceau, in January 1886. When, by a law passed soon after, the heads of families which had formerly ruled in France were excluded from the territory of the nation, Boulanger manifested his republicanism by going a step farther. Despite earlier indebtedness to Aumale, he rather meanly stripped the Orleanist princes of their military rank. This doubtless won him some support from the left. The attention that Boulanger in his new office paid to the welfare of the troops also increased his popularity, which was not diminished by German attacks on him for verbal fireworks directed against Germany. The Opportunists becoming alarmed, in May 1887 he was dropped from the ministry; but he was now a national figure, round whom opposition, from left and right, began to rally. Popular discontent, arising from economic difficulties as much as anything, found a cause to concentrate on in November 1887, when it was revealed that the President's son-in-law, Daniel Wilson, had been turning the Élysée Palace into a market for the sale of decorations and other favours in the presidential gift. Grévy, though discredited by these revelations, clung to office until he was forced out. The obvious successor was Ferry, but the popular hatred that had been built up against him was such that his nomination might well have provoked a revolution. Instead, therefore, Sadi Carnot, a worthy moderate republican and the bearer of a great republican name, was elected.

The situation was still dangerous, for the right had now taken up Boulanger. They saw in his popularity a lever with which they might overturn the Republic. The episode that followed is a watershed in the history of French politics. It marks the end of the old-fashioned monarchist tradition, whether of legitimists or Orleanists, and the beginning of a new nationalist, plebiscitary, anti-parliamentary one, based on an appeal to left and right against the centre and relying on the cult of a man rather than on a policy. Summed up, it was Bonapartism without a Bonaparte. The government gave Boulanger and his supporters their opportunity by forcing him into retirement from the army in March 1888. He had now lost the backing of most of the radical leaders but not necessarily of their voters. On the extreme left Blanquists were attracted to a potential dictator. Many socialists, in their enmity to the conservative republic, favoured Boulanger, and unemployment brought the workers on to his side. Rochefort, once editor of *La Lanterne*, who had returned to France with the amnesty of 1880 and as editor of *L'Intransigeant* conducted a guerilla war against the Republic, contributed to his clientèle. Boulanger was backed by a committee of monarchists and Bonapartists, his campaign was financed by the legitimist duchesse d'Uzès, and he had much support in the army and the Church. In a series of by-elections he won overwhelming majorities culminating in a victory by 244,149 to 162,410 in the Paris election of January 1889.

When the Paris result was announced huge excited mobs surrounded Boulanger crying 'À l'Élysée'. The Ligue des Patriotes, founded in 1882 by Paul Déroulède with the intention of reviving French national spirit by a mass appeal, was ready to give the lead, which many would have followed, for a *coup d'état*. It is difficult to see what but his own faint-heartedness – unless the persuasion of his ailing mistress – stopped Boulanger from attempting to seize power. He has been charged with losing his head in this crisis and with an unmilitary preference for parliamentary methods, but this is to forget that, apart from Louis Napoleon who had the First Empire and the Napoleonic tradition behind him, there was as yet no modern precedent, outside Latin America, for this kind of dictatorial seizure of power. Possibly Boulanger may have realized – what was certainly true – that his supporters were so diverse that they could never have agreed on a coherent policy. If they had obtained power they would not have known what to do with it. It is more difficult to explain why he gave up the game altogether. When a comparatively weak government began legal proceedings against Boulanger and he believed himself in danger of arrest he fled the country, to commit suicide on the grave of his mistress a few years later. With his flight the whole movement collapsed. In the elections of September 1889 conservatives and Boulangists could win no more than 210 seats; the republicans gained 366. Among them the Opportunists with some 216 were the dominant element, for the Radicals suffered because of their flirtation with Boulanger.

CHAPTER THREE

✠

THE CONSERVATIVE
REPUBLIC

T HE next ten years was a period of confused and changing
policies. Superficially it could be described in terms of personal
rivalries and the political intrigues of parties and factions, but
to do so would be to miss the real significance of the decade. A
summary of political developments is perhaps necessary in the first
place.

The new Chamber of September 1889 continued to support the
cabinet of republican concentration which had weathered the
Boulangist storms. It was 'replastered', to use the French term,
twice, under different leaders, but achieved nothing in particular
until November 1892, when under a nondescript republican premier,
Loubet, it had to face a new crisis, caused by the collapse of the
Panama Canal Company. After his triumph with the Suez Canal,
Ferdinand de Lesseps had launched a plan to drive a canal through
the isthmus of Panama. This proved a much more difficult under-
taking than had been expected and called for far more capital than
had originally been envisaged. To raise the new money the Panama
Company issued shares repayable at an enhanced price and by lot,
which required parliamentary authorization. In spite of the new
money, the difficulties of the canal project proved too much for the
resources of de Lesseps and the company went bankrupt to the
tune of some £60 million, all sunk without hope in the hills and
mosquito-ridden swamps of Panama.

Two survivors of the Boulangist movement, the author Maurice
Barrès, who had been elected by Nancy to the Chamber in 1889,
and Édouard Drumont, editor of the anti-semitic *La Libre Parole*,
saw in the affairs of the Panama Company an opportunity to discredit the parliamentary regime. Drumont opened the attack with
Les Dessous de Panama, an exposure of the bribery of politicians

that had accompanied the promotion of the company and the raising of funds for it. He based himself on information supplied by a baron Jacques de Reinach. This was curious, since Reinach had himself been the agent responsible for the bribery. Possibly he was trying to confuse the issue and so conceal his own activities; but when he died, suddenly and possibly by suicide in November 1892, it appeared that he himself had not been a free agent. For years he had been blackmailed by an international adventurer named Cornelius Herz, who, as was the way of international adventurers, was well placed in the social world of Paris and had influential political connections. With Reinach's death the scandal burst out into the open. The names of deputies and journalists charged with receiving bribes were published. Violent scenes occurred in the Chamber. Ministers resigned, the government fell. A judicial inquiry was instituted. Among those implicated in the affair were the Minister of Finance, Rouvier, the President of the Chamber, Floquet, and the *franc-tireur* of the left, Clemenceau.

It was on the head of Clemenceau, whose ruthless attacks had earned him so many enemies, that the most violent storm fell. Though he came from Catholic and royalist Vendée, Clemenceau's ancestors, small proprietors and doctors, were anti-clerical and Jacobin. La Reveillière-Lépeaux, regicide and Director, had been a cousin. Clemenceau's father narrowly escaped deportation under the Second Empire. He himself was *maire* of Montmartre during the siege of Paris, and one of the *maires* who attempted to mediate between the Commune and Versailles. In the Chamber of Deputies he became the most feared of the guerillas of the left, notorious for his violent speeches, vitriolic articles, and duels. Now he was to fall a victim to the kind of onslaught he himself knew so well how to launch. Suspicion that he had been the power behind Cornelius Herz was crystallized in a speech by Paul Déroulède. Everyone knew who was the guilty man, Déroulède proclaimed, but they dared not say it for they feared three things – his tongue, his pistol, and his pen. 'I defy all three and name him: it is M. Clemenceau.' A duel naturally followed, which was bloodless, but the fatal blow had been struck. Clemenceau was hounded out of public life with cries of 'Aoh yes!', for to the charge of Panama corruption was added, to sink him beyond hope of rescue, that of being an English agent.

The republicans, having shed their more compromised members, got over the Panama affair as well as they could. The elections of August 1893, in which there were many abstentions, returned a majority of about 310 moderate republicans, some 150 radical republicans, and a small group of independents or socialists on the extreme left – these last the electoral witness of rising social unrest. The republican cabinets of the next few years had to govern amid a wave of violence which culminated, in June 1894, in the assassination of Sadi Carnot. Casimir-Périer, who replaced him as President, held office for only six months, after which, frustrated at the powerlessness of the presidency, he resigned. In his place was chosen the amiable man-of-the-world, Félix Faure. The new government of June 1894 was more notable for its members than for its head. With Delcassé, aged forty-three, Hanotaux forty-two, Poincaré thirty-three, and Barthou thirty-one, it was evident that a new generation and a notable one, was entering republican politics. In November 1895, under Léon Bourgeois, for the first time a radical cabinet took office. It was undermined by its attempt to introduce financial reforms, including an income tax, and in April 1896 was replaced by a cabinet of moderates under Méline, who had no such dangerous ideas. General elections in May 1898 once again proved that despite all the faults of the republican parties the country remained republican. But now a new crisis had unexpectedly arisen. In January 1898 Zola published in the journal which Clemenceau used as his political forum after his parliamentary debacle, an open letter, 'J'accuse', and the Dreyfus affair broke.

Before this, however, and behind the petty political manoeuvring of the 'nineties, major developments had taken place, which fundamentally changed the meaning of right and left. First, the old right, the monarchists, whether legitimist or Orleanist, ceased to be an effective political force. The Boulangist movement showed the pattern of the future right, in which neither Church nor king, nor the inherited traditions of the old monarchist parties, were to have much real part to play.

There had been, after the failure of Boulangism, an attempt to refashion the right on different lines, which must first be mentioned. This was the Ralliement. So long as Pius IX remained on the papal throne there had been no possibility of any relation between the Church and the Republic other than a state of open or barely concealed war. The accession of Leo XIII in 1878 brought the opportunity of a *détente*, especially after the death of the comte de Chambord in 1883 had made an Orleanist prince the claimant to the throne. In 1884 a papal encyclical enjoined the French bishops not to exhibit hostility to the established authorities of the state. Papal awareness of the strength of anti-republican sentiments among French Catholics was shown by the long interval that elapsed before a further step was taken towards a *rapprochement* with the Republic.

This came in 1890 and its chosen agent was the tall, bearded, authoritarian, irascible primate of Africa, Cardinal Lavigerie. A Bonapartist prelate, though converted after 1870 to legitimacy, and the embodiment of French missionary zeal, he was an odd choice for the role. The occasion of the announcement of the new policy was equally unexpected. It was a banquet at Algiers to the officers of the Mediterranean fleet, monarchist and reactionary to a man. Though Lavigerie had acted under instructions, that he had accurately represented papal policy was not made clear before 1892, when Leo XIII issued the encyclical *Au milieu des sollicitudes*, which advised French Catholics to rally to the Republic and defend the interests of the Church by taking part in political life.

The policy of *ralliement* was not the only evidence of a new wind blowing from the Vatican. Leo XIII also saw that the increasing alienation of the Church from the poorer sections of society, which resulted from the identification of its interests with those of the wealthier classes, had already gone a long way towards duplicating the social cleavage in urban society with a religious one. The encyclical *Rerum Novarum*, of 1891, called on Catholics to adopt a positive attitude towards the problem of wages and hours and the social welfare of the workers. The French hierarchy, confined to the society of the *haute bourgeoisie* and *noblesse*, took but a languid interest in the new ideas enunciated by Rome; but lower down appeared a sprinkling of what came to be called – not necessarily in praise – democratic priests, who engaged in missionary activity among the poor and even went so far as to suggest that they might have rights as well as duties. The hierarchy and the *bien-pensant* upper classes could hardly be expected to tolerate this. Like the followers of Lamennais and the Catholic democrats of 1848 earlier, or the worker-priests much later, the democratic priests of the 'nineties went further than respectable society was willing to accept or than Rome was ready to follow them. The implicit repudiation, in 1901, by the Vatican of these steps towards social *rapprochement* was a severe blow to the Ralliement, because it drew its main strength from the areas that were both Catholic and industrial, especially the departments of the Nord and the Pas-de-Calais.

Heirs of the Social Catholics of half a century earlier, the *ralliés* drew their leaders largely from old legitimist families. Albert de Mun, an orator of the extreme right but also a social reformer, was their most notable figure, but perhaps the most influential convert in the long run was a young cavalry officer named Lyautey. Under the influence of the new school of Catholic thought, he put forward, in an article in the *Revue des Deux Mondes* in 1891, a new role for the army, now composed mostly of conscripts spending their time in peaceable manoeuvres or kicking their heels in barracks. The army, said Lyautey, should be a school of citizenship and the officer an educator. All that an attempt to put his ideas into practice with his own squadron gained for the young officer was a severe reprimand and the advice to transfer himself and his unsuitable ideas to the colonies. Curiously, the first steps towards putting his ideas into practice in France were taken after 1901 by the anti-clerical War Minister, André.

Between the radical anti-clericals and the dervishes of the Catholic revival, there was never much room for a party of liberal Catholicism. Even Dupanloup, whose liberalism was very diluted, had never been made a cardinal. As an effort to reconcile the Catholic Church and the Republic, the Ralliement proved almost a complete failure. Faced with the choice between the advice of a Pope (which another Pope might reverse) and their deeply ingrained hatred of republican ideas, most of the monarchists and Catholics remained irreconcilable. Even the bishops closed their ears to the appeal from Rome. There is this to be said for them, that it was not a mere matter of accepting republican institutions, but also republican symbols and dogmas, which were profoundly secularist and anti-clerical. On the republican side, while the moderates were prepared to accept the support of Catholics, the radicals feared them even when they brought gifts.

The failure of the Ralliement meant that the conservative and monarchist right ceased to be a real force, or to have more than a nuisance value, in French politics. Even though the monarchy was still a flag that was waved, a different party now fought under the same banner and directed its efforts towards a different objective. The logic of the situation made it a revolutionary party, and being this it had to adopt a revolutionary pattern of behaviour. It still found its allies naturally in the two great professional bodies which had not been reconciled to the republic – the army and the Church. Hence militarism and clericalism became the hallmarks of the new right. From Bonapartism it inherited a contempt for parliamentary government and from Panama had learnt the cry of 'À bas les voleurs'. It took over from the Opportunists a belief in the colonial mission of France, which it added to the hope of revenge on Germany and the recovery of Alsace-Lorraine. Therefore it stood for war, as well as, and perhaps partly as a means towards, the overthrow of the regime. It drew its support largely from the urban middle classes. Never more than a revolutionary minority, with only a small representation in parliament, it could provoke a permanent feeling of insecurity by continual agitation. Henceforth the Republic had always to live on the brink of a threatened *coup d'état* and the conservative elements that should have provided ballast for the state were weakened by the existence of a revolutionary party on their right, which might capsize the ship by a sudden lurch at any moment.

The conservatives, properly so-called, were to be found among the right-wing republicans, and the minority Catholics of the Ralliement naturally gravitated towards them. This alliance was, however, not without its harmful effect on the original social ideals of the Ralliement; for the conservative republicans, who were now changing the title of Opportunists for that of Progressivists, had taken over from the Orleanist and Second Empire notables the defence of property. The bitter class struggles of 1848 and 1871 were now a historical memory, labour was beginning to organize itself, and socialist parties were effecting a breach in republican politics. But the wealthy propertied classes were still prepared to resist all concessions and to do no more to improve the conditions of the lower classes than they were compelled to. As has already been mentioned, when, in 1896, Léon Bourgeois proposed a reform of the inequitable system of taxation by the introduction of a modest income tax, the Chamber of Deputies reacted violently and turned to Méline to save them from what they saw as a monstrous attack on the rights of property, involving an inquisition into the jealously guarded secrets of individual wealth.

Financial reform had little chance in a nation in which social influence and administrative position were still largely in the hands of the wealthy, and political power rested with the votes of peasant proprietors and independent shopkeepers and artisans. The influence of organized labour was too weak to do much to redress the balance. This situation accounts for the backwardness of social legislation in France. Even the reforms that were passed into law often remained ineffective for lack of the machinery to put them into practice. One can hardly count the abolition of the worker's *livret* in 1890 as such; in fact it had fallen into disuse much earlier, for it involved obligations on employers as well as on their workers. A law of 1892 establishing labour conciliation remained unapplied. Such modest reforms as passed, usually did so only after a prolonged struggle and much delay.

Freedom of individual enterprise, however, did not involve any dogmatic adherence to ideas of free trade. Gradually an alliance of agriculturalists and manufacturers, aided by the slump of the late 'seventies, secured the abandonment of the liberal commercial policy of the Second Empire. In 1881 a tariff law imposed duties of between 10 per cent and 30 per cent on imported manufactures. Agriculture, which had been suffering from bad harvests and the competition of overseas products, demanded protection in its turn. Its cause was championed by the Minister of Agriculture, Méline. A senator from the Vosges, he particularly represented agricultural interests, and was the spokesman of the economic Bourbons of the

Third Republic, for whom economic progress equalled social danger. He combined a policy of energetic state aid and protection for agriculture with strenuous opposition to any interference with the free play of economic forces in industry. Méline's campaign reached a successful conclusion in 1892 with the introduction of a tariff covering practically the whole of agricultural and industrial production. The system of high protection provided a platform on which small and big men, peasant proprietors and large farmers, craftsmen and capitalists, could stand together, the rich uniting to defend the poor against cheap food and cheap manufactures. France was one of the greatest wheat-producers of the world, but the price of wheat inside France remained far above the world level.

The interests of the propertied classes were even more closely touched by the question of taxation. In 1895 and 1896, as we have seen, proposals were tabled for a progressive income tax, with a compulsory declaration of income to be officially checked. Some such way of making French tax methods more modern, more elastic, and more equitable was badly needed, and it had been part of the programme of the radical wing of the republicans. The moderates and the right reacted almost unanimously against the proposal. Here, again, the small businessman and the peasant provided the rank and file of the army that fought in defence of the social irresponsibility of wealth. Méline, who had already been the agent of class interests in his protectionist campaign, became premier with the task of defending the interests of property against the new tax proposals. This was practically the only policy of his cabinet, but it was enough to guarantee it a solid majority for over two years, from 1896 to the elections of 1898.

France evidently remained under the Republic what it had been under the Monarchy and the Empire, socially an intensely conservative country. Political and social changes had indeed increased the strength of conservative forces. The peasantry had been a revolutionary element in 1789; 1848 demonstrated that they were on the side of law and the established order; and the fact that this was now a republican order did not materially change its social implications. Paris also had ceased to be a stronghold of the left, as Boulangism showed. This was the point at which the political kaleidoscope was given the decisive twist which settled French politics in their new pattern. Although the Boulangist movement was followed by Radical victories in the capital, changes in the social composition of Paris proper, consequent on Haussmann's rebuilding, finally found political expression in the municipal elections of 1900 and 1902, when the right gained control of the municipal council. It was the end of the *bras-nus* and the barricades. Only a few Blanquists and their successors among Marxist or Leninist historians continued to hanker after the legend of the revolutionary *journées*. The excitement of the descent *dans la rue*, of swirling mobs surging through the streets, beleaguering the Hôtel de Ville, breaking into the Assembly, now passed from left to right. The threat of revolution was henceforth to come from the other end of the political spectrum.

In the industrial regions there was a growing, but in relation to the whole population still small, wage-earning proletariat of factory and mine, disciplined by its conditions of life, lacking the initiative or the political instincts of the master craftsmen and the middle class, more capable of the dumb, passive resistance of the strike than the active effort to overthrow governments and seize power by *journée* or *coup d'état*, lacking also the middle-class leadership that can usually be traced in the revolutionary mobs of the past. What the industrial proletariat was capable of, what indeed it was conditioned to accept, was organization in trade union or political party. The 'nineties saw the real development of the trade unions, or *syndicats*, and of the Socialist party or rather parties, though the previous decade had been one of preparation for them.

After the Commune, left-wing leadership had temporarily been eliminated from France; the older socialist ideologies were moribund, and the new influence of Marx had as yet hardly penetrated to France. The first positive step towards the organization of a socialist political party was taken by a Congress at Marseilles in 1879, which formed a Fédération des Travailleurs Socialistes, with a very moderate programme of nationalization. The return of the exiled Communards after the amnesty of 1880 gave an impetus to the left-wing movement but also introduced strong elements of dissension. The Blanquists formed a Central Revolutionary

Committee under Vaillant. Their opponents joined the Federation, but it split in 1883, when Jules Guesde, the earliest of the Marxist leaders in France, repudiated the policy of social reform and founded a new Parti Ouvrier, drawing its chief support from the areas of mining and heavy industry in the north-east and the centre.

The passing of the law of 1884 authorizing the formation of trade unions, or *syndicats*, was evidence that the Opportunists recognized the existence of a new force in French society, though the unions were bitterly opposed by employers, and state employees, including railway workers, were prohibited from joining them. The new unions were profoundly suspicious of politics and politicians; they believed in direct action to improve the workers' conditions, and distrusted the Socialist leaders as mere bourgeois ideologists. In fact, all except one of these, Allemane, were middle-class. However, under the Marxist influence of Guesde a Fédération Nationale des Syndicats was formed for political action in 1886. In opposition to this, Bourses de Travail, founded in 1887 as popularly controlled centres of mutual aid, workers' education, and employment exchanges, formed a national federation in 1892. The period from 1889 to 1892 was one of economic progress, when the membership of the *syndicats*, 140,000 in 1890, multiplied by three; then, in a period of economic recession, it rose very slowly and was still only 580,000 in 1899 – this in a country with a total population of some 39 millions. Even this modest progress of the *syndicats* was marked by strikes, violence on both sides, and repression. In 1890, May 1st was recognized as the annual Labour Day. Its first celebration, in 1891, served to demonstrate the reality of class fears and hatred in French industrial society. A demonstration in the Nord for an eight-hour day got out of hand. Troops were called in and opened fire on the crowds, killing nine demonstrators, including four young girls, and wounding over one hundred.

The situation darkened when 1893 brought an industrial slump, and about this time also the infection of anarchism, hitherto not much more than a literary freak, broke out in France. The anarchists upheld a doctrine of propaganda by action, in which bombs were the chief form of conversion, though a knife was used to kill President Carnot in June 1894. The disease worked itself out after

a year or two, but provided a justification for the cabinet of Casimir–
Périer to pass what the left called the '*lois scélérates*', imposing severe
penalties on press offences and on the instigation or organization
of attacks on persons or property.

However, the left was now in a better position to defend itself
politically. Socialist and syndicalist agitation had created an effective
workers' vote, which in some constituencies could materially
influence or even decide the elections. The result was the arrival in
the Chamber of Radical Socialists (strictly 'socialist radicals') and
even Socialists. The four Socialist parties, with the aid of the votes
of former Boulangists and of radicals upset by the Panama scandal,
won eighteen seats. In addition there were some thirty independent
Socialists, including Alexandre Millerand and Jean Jaurès, who had
moved over from the Radicals or Opportunists. They were too
few in number to provide more than a small weight in the political
balance, but they offered a reminder that though politically the
Republic had survived longer than any other regime France had
known since 1789, the social problem still remained. A hard struggle
was evidently ahead between the intensely conservative propertied
classes and the growing class of employees. The agricultural
population, which had been suffering from a prolonged depression,
had not yet awoken to the use of its potential political power to
secure better conditions, but even this was to come. These issues,
however, could be fought out by ballot box and in the debating
chamber: they did not threaten the stability of the regime. Though
the ideology of the Socialists was revolutionary, they were already
beginning to show their capacity for being absorbed by the parliamentary system. The real danger arose from the fact that there were
other elements, which were unreconciled to the Republic and
fundamentally opposed to its ideology.

The Ralliement, by its very failure, had underlined the hostility
of the Catholics to a political regime which was on principle secular
and seemed to be the deadly enemy of religion. Though the political
personnel was now overwhelmingly republican, the higher ranks of
the administration continued to be recruited from families of the
haute bourgeoisie which, whatever their origins, now had, or were
rapidly acquiring, Catholic connections. Literature in France has

always tended to lean towards the opposition, and the opposition was now on the right. Most important of all, a new political trend was appearing which may loosely be called nationalism and which appealed to a new generation of angry young men in revolt against the boredom of a regime that had lasted for a quarter of a century. In their enmity to the parliamentary regime the nationalists were the heirs of Bonapartism, with which Boulangism was the link, while their anti-intellectualism harked back to the theocrats. The most characteristic, and indeed the common feature of all sections of nationalism was a peculiarly vicious strain of anti-semitism. The new right drew, geographically, on the traditional centres of right-wing support. Despite the changes in name, and even in ideology, the electoral geography of France remained remarkably stable, except that, as well as Paris, Lorraine moved, after 1871 when many Alsatians settled there, to the right. In 1898 the nationalists elected fifteen deputies, to whom might be added four anti-semites from Algeria. In 1902 their strength had risen to fifty-nine. Their support in the nation was limited. The danger they presented to the Republic lay not so much in their political power as in their ideological hold over Church and army. Though the nationalists of the early years of the twentieth century often used bellicose language and were xenophobic, their aggression was directed more against their compatriots than against foreigners.

⚜

CHAPTER FOUR

THE DREYFUS AFFAIR

ONE of the most important developments in the Third Republic was the change in the composition of the officer class in the army. The older legitimist families had abandoned the army, as well as all other forms of government service, after 1830; while the sons of the wealthy bourgeoisie avoided a career that brought neither gain nor social prestige. However, this situation did not last. Gradually, during the Second Empire, the status of the army officer rose and recruitment from aristocratic families revived. This tendency was intensified, rather unexpectedly, in the early years of the Third Republic, perhaps because the agricultural depression made a profession more necessary for the sons of the old landed class. The result was that by the end of the century, when in other fields the republicanization of the state was becoming effective, the higher ranks of the army were an almost solidly conservative, monarchist, and Catholic monopoly. There were the ingredients here of a dangerously explosive situation, though no one could have guessed in advance what was to be the spark that would set it off.

This came in 1894, though the train that led to a nation-wide conflagration was a long and slow-burning one. In September 1894 a list of French military documents, apparently handed to the Germans, was rescued by a minor French agent, in the normal process of collecting information, from a waste-paper basket in the German Embassy. This was the famous *bordereau* or memorandum. It was examined by the counter-espionage branch of the French army, which operated under the title of the Statistical Section and was practically a law to itself, being answerable only to the Chief of Staff. It followed its own ways – rather eccentric and devious ones, be it said – in blithe freedom from all outside control. The dominant influence in the little office – its staff numbered only some seven altogether – was a career officer who had risen by his own ability from the ranks, one Major Henry, a heavy and powerful peasant type, brave, ruthless and, as it turned out, with peasant cunning and an extraordinary gift of invention that accorded ill with his blunt, bull-like appearance. It was evident from the *bordereau* that there was a spy at work in the French officer corps, and looking for a culprit, the Statistical Section hit on the name of Captain Alfred Dreyfus. Member of a wealthy, textile-manufacturing family of Alsatian Jews which had chosen French nationality in 1871, Dreyfus entered the army as an artillery officer, and had recently been seconded to the War Office in Paris. The evidence against him was not merely negligible, it was entirely non-existent. Even the writing on the *bordereau*, the one material fact, did not resemble Dreyfus's hand. In the whole story, while we meet, naturally, with some ingenious rogues, what strikes one most is the monumental stupidity that was exhibited, not least in the Intelligence branch, by the army.

What settled the fate of Dreyfus was the fact that he was a Jew and as such a rare – possibly unique – phenomenon on the General Staff. Anti-semitism, formerly, in so far as it existed in France, a prejudice of the left and the people, under the Third Republic had moved over to the right and become a mark of those who were, and therefore of those who wished to be regarded as, socially superior. Before about 1890 there had been some eighty thousand Jews in France, mostly well assimilated except in Alsace. By the end of the century immigration from eastern Europe had more than doubled their numbers and this great influx of a new and obviously alien element into French society provided an opportunity and stimulus for the spread of anti-semitism on a much wider scale than before. Its chief propagandist was the journalist Édouard Drumont, who founded in 1892 a paper called *La Libre Parole* to inculcate his ideas. One of the earliest features was a series called 'Les Juifs dans l'armée'. In 1886 he had given the anti-semites a textbook in *La France Juive*, and in 1889 he founded the Anti-semitic League.

The one part of France in which anti-semitism was indigenous – it had appeared in 1789 and again in the revolution of 1848 – was Alsace. Now, not only was Dreyfus an Alsatian Jew, but the head

of the Statistical Section was also Alsatian: this may have helped
him to settle on Dreyfus as the guilty man. He reported his discovery to the War Office. The Minister, General Mercier, who was
to play a sinister role from beginning to end of the affair, ordered
a court martial. It might have been thought that the absence of
evidence would prove a difficulty at this stage. By now, however,
the press was on the scent. With its usual determination that justice
shall be done, or at least seem to be done, and a victim be found,
it proclaimed that a rich Jewish traitor was about to buy himself
immunity for his crimes. The War Office being anxious not to
provide any opening for such a suspicion, the conviction of Dreyfus
became a political necessity. Major Henry, who was a practised
hand at producing forged papers to be planted on foreign agents,
supplied the necessary evidence. Though the result was rather
crude, it was good enough for a secret court martial which had, to
use French legal terminology, an intimate conviction of the guilt
of the accused. Dreyfus was unanimously found guilty and
sentenced to be cashiered and deported for life. There was a good
deal of public indignation that he was to escape being shot. Clemenceau, admitting that in the past he had supported the abolition of
the death penalty, urged that here if anywhere was a case for its
infliction. The Socialist leader, Jaurès, expressed his alarm at the
evidence of sinister forces at work: a rich Jew, who was a proved
spy and traitor, was going to escape his rightful punishment.

The War Ministry did not really deserve this criticism. Enraged
that Dreyfus had refused to commit suicide as a gentleman should
when found out, or even to confesss, although promised better
treatment if he would do so, General Mercier ordered him to be sent
to the severest possible solitary confinement on Devil's Island.
The order was faithfully carried out for the next four years.

The case was now closed, but there was still a desire to get to
the bottom of the crime. What was the motive of Dreyfus? What
was he after? It could hardly be money for he was a wealthy man.
Efforts were made to discover a woman. A secret love nest was in
fact ferreted out, but it proved to be only a mare's nest, belonging
to quite a different Dreyfus. Moreover staff papers continued to
disappear and the invaluable waste-paper basket of the German

Embassy produced another document, this time an express letter – a *petit-bleu* – addressed by name to a French officer named Esterhazy. There was now a new head at the Statistical Section, Major Picquart, yet another Alsatian, who had represented the War Office in the trial of Dreyfus. Put on the track of Esterhazy by the *petit-bleu*, Picquart obtained specimens of his writing and discovered to his astonishment its similarity to the writing on the *bordereau*. One might have thought that this would be the end of the case: it was only the beginning. Major Henry rapidly appreciated the danger of the situation and proceeded to manufacture some better evidence against Dreyfus for Mercier to use. The War Office also became alarmed, and before he could cause trouble by any more inconvenient discoveries Picquart was removed from his position, sent to Tunisia, and subsequently ordered to the fighting area where there was at least a chance that his inconsiderate activities might be brought to an end.

Major Henry's mind was still not at ease, and his alarm was shared by two highly placed members of the War Office, General Gonse and the Marquis du Paty de Clam, who had taken part in the original investigation of Dreyfus. Gonse was a good office man, and as it turned out prepared to lie through thick and thin to cover up for the office. Du Paty de Clam had been a dashing young officer and still fancied himself as something out of a romantic novel. Henry, who was obviously the brains of the triumvirate, now had the fantastic idea of using Esterhazy to consolidate the case against Dreyfus, with a promise of protection, though he was a notorious debauchee, permanently in debt, and known to the foreign attachés, if not to the Intelligence branch, as prepared to do anything for money. But he was also the son of a French general, had himself formerly been a member of the Statistical Section, and had an imposing aristocratic air. Because of the discovery of the *petit-bleu* it was not possible to avoid a court martial, which took only three minutes to acquit him. Esterhazy's sardonic imagination was now added to the cruder cunning of Henry, and more and more officers were entangled in a web of forgery and false evidence so complicated that even its inventors began to lose the threads.

The family of Dreyfus had all this while been struggling unavailingly to reopen the case. They had obtained only a little outside support and that chiefly from other Jews; but Picquart, who had already sacrificed his career to his sense of justice, was trying from a distance to prevent his suspicions from dying with him. He therefore sent a statement to a friend in Paris, who, armed with this, approached the eminent Alsatian senator, Scheurer-Kestner, who was convinced by it of the need for a retrial. Scheurer-Kestner interpellated the government in December 1897 but received no satisfaction. Indeed, Méline prematurely announced, 'Il n'y a pas d'affaire Dreyfus'. This made it an affair on the political level. Public interest was aroused: evidently something mysterious was going on. It burst on the general public in January 1898, when the novelist Zola, who had already written one or two articles expressing his concern, published in Clemenceau's *L'Aurore* an open letter to the President of the Republic – the famous 'J'accuse' – indicting the War Office of a judicial crime. The Office and the government fought back – they could do nothing else – even though it meant bringing out some of the secret evidence against Dreyfus. Zola was tried, found guilty, and eventually took refuge in flight to England. Picquart was charged with indiscipline and dismissed the service. Surely the case was now closed.

The case may have been closed, the Affair had just begun. Press and public opinion were aroused and a campaign for revision of the sentence on Dreyfus was started. For some, justice and the fate of an innocent man were at stake; for others it was a heaven-sent opportunity for a campaign against the enemies of the Republic. A petition calling for revision of the judgment on Dreyfus was signed by leading writers and artists – Lanson, Seignobos, Brunot, Viollet, Blum, Langevin, Anatole France, Proust, Halévy, Briand, Herr, Péguy, and many others. The League for the Defence of the Rights of Man was founded. Naturally, the majority of those who took an active part in the campaign for revision were anti-clericals, freemasons, Protestants, and Jews. The army, monarchists, Catholics, nationalists, found themselves attacked by all those they hated most. The veil that had been cast over old grievances was rudely torn aside and recent attempts at reconciliation went for nothing. The *anti-dreyfusards* had most of the press behind them and the campaign against the revisionists was waged without mercy. The small party of Catholic reformers was committed by Albert de Mun to the defence of the army, and though there were Catholic *dreyfusards* neither side was willing to draw attention to their existence. One who could not be ignored was Péguy, for whom the stake in the Affair was not the physical safety of France, which the army and the politicians imagined themselves to be defending, but its spiritual salvation.

The Archbishop of Paris had a different idea of what was needed spiritually; he became the patron of the Laborum League of anti-semitic army officers. In its journal *La Croix* the Assumptionist Order carried the Church into the struggle with a raging, tearing campaign which did much to stir up anti-clerical feeling on the other side. The question, wrote one commentator, is not whether a wretched individual is guilty or innocent, it is whether the Jews and the Protestants are, or are not, the masters of this country. The factions of the right had the incitement to fight back against enemies whose political control of France had seemed unshakable, and in anti-semitism they had a symbol, a flag, a common cause to bind them together. Anti-Jewish riots broke out in many towns; in Algiers there was widespread looting of Jewish property.

The line between *dreyfusards* and *anti-dreyfusards* did not invariably coincide with other divisions; old associations were broken and families split. The political parties of the left at first tried to keep themselves uncommitted. The Radicals were anti-revisionist, the Socialist groups unwilling to be outbid in patriotism by the Radicals and themselves not uninfluenced by anti-semitic feeling. The Foreign Minister, Hanotaux, believed that a retrial would weaken the French image abroad. A manifesto drawn up by Guesde and Jaurès called on the proletariat not to enlist in either of the clans of a bourgeois civil war. Jaurès, however, found his sense of justice stronger than his socialist ideology and became one of the leading advocates of revision. Politically, the fate of Dreyfus had come to be bound up with the survival of the Third Republic. The attempt to pretend that this was not the issue collapsed with the resignation of Méline in June 1898. The War Office had so far played its cards with complete success – this was not so difficult since Major Henry was always there to provide it with extra aces whenever they were needed. General Mercier, in particular, fought each move in the direction of revision with every weapon he had. The fanatical obstinacy of the War Office has led some historians to the supposition that there was somebody much more powerful than Esterhazy involved in espionage, who was determined to use the supposed guilt of Dreyfus to cover himself. Indeed it does seem possible that a second spy had been at work, though beyond this we cannot go. Whatever the reason, in its anxiety to beat down all criticism the War Office committed the tactical blunder of prosecuting Picquart, perhaps forgetting that since it had already expelled him from the army this involved an examination of the case against him in a civil court. It was now discovered that one of the documents presented to the court was a blatant forgery. Major Henry, whose capacity for covering up one forgery with another had at last come to an end, was put under fortress arrest. He was a brave man who had done his best for the Office without thought of personal reward. Realizing he could do no more, he cut his throat that night. Esterhazy, realizing that *his* game was up, fled to England.

In fact the game was not yet up. To admit the innocence of Dreyfus would be to incriminate the War Office, the aristocracy, and the Church. A Ligue de la Patrie Française rallied intellectuals, artists, poets – Charles Maurras, Émile Faguet, Mistral, François Coppée, Heredia, Lemaître, Rambaud, Jules Verne, Léon Daudet, Forain, and many others – in their defence. The most powerful writer among the *anti-dreyfusards*, Maurice Barrès, converted what had become a defensive struggle against the revisionists into a mystical offensive on behalf of the nation. The country seemed on the verge of civil war.

What saved it was perhaps that spirit of *fonctionnarisme* with which the army, like the other great organizations which emerged from the Consulate and Empire, was imbued. Its officers in the last resort were servants of the state, bound by an oath to whoever held the legal authority of the government. Hence, of all the revolutions or *coups d'état* between 1815 and 1958, none was made and none was prevented by the army. The revolutionary move had to come from civilians. The poet-politician Paul Déroulède, who had

founded his Ligue des Patriotes for such a purpose, saw an opportunity to exploit the feverish state of public opinion early in 1899,
when the President, Félix Faure, collapsed in the Élysée and the
arms of a terrified lady friend. His funeral was used by the Ligue
des Patriotes to stage an attempt at a *coup*; it was a farcical failure.

The tide was now running fast the other way. There is no need
to recount the delaying tactics by which one barrier to revision after
another was set up. In September 1898 the case of Dreyfus was
referred to the appeal court; in June 1899 it decided for a new trial,
and Dreyfus, in total ignorance of everything that had happened
since his trial, was brought back from Devil's Island, white-haired
and broken. He was to be tried again, before a new court martial,
at Rennes. It was no better conducted than the former trial: the
generals and colonels lied like troopers in defence of the honour of
the army. By five to two the court reached the ridiculous verdict that
Dreyfus was guilty of treachery with extenuating circumstances
and sentenced him to ten years' detention. It was clear that no
military court would admit to an error of justice. A presidential
pardon was therefore issued. A retrial before the appeal court in
1906 quashed the Rennes verdict, but the case was really over
in 1899.

In the summer of 1899 it had seemed that the republican regime
was breaking down. A trivial incident in June proved the turning-
point. In the course of a visit to the races at Auteuil by the new
President, Loubet, a royalist baron knocked his hat off with a stick.
This was going too far. It was only a straw but it came at the end
of a history that had aroused intense passion. At last the republicans,
moderates as well as the extremer factions, had had enough. The
compromising, appeasing cabinets that had held office so far during
the Affair came to an end. In June 1899 a cabinet of republican
defence was formed under Waldeck-Rousseau, a conservative
republican and a former colleague of Gambetta and Ferry. The
new premier was a distinguished lawyer with a clear mind, a cool
temperament and a cold manner. He was a moderate in his political
views, but added a sense of justice to his sense of order, and he was
capable of giving the country what it needed most, a government
that would govern. Perhaps only Ferry, among the politicians of

the Third Republic, had an equal sense of authority, and Ferry aroused too many enmities. Waldeck-Rousseau drew his ministers from the whole gamut of republican politics. Their names are worth remembering for it was a cabinet of strong men, not afraid of taking decisions, chosen for what they were rather than for the number of parliamentary votes they could bring with them. General de Gallifet at the Ministry of War, hated by the left as the 'executioner' of 1871, was balanced against the Socialist Millerand, even if the latter's acceptance of a ministerial post aroused resentment among other Socialists; Delcassé was at the Quai d'Orsay, Caillaux at the Ministry of Finances; Lépine, strongest and most popular of Prefects of Police, brought Paris back to order.

The Waldeck-Rousseau cabinet obtained a majority of only twenty-five, but the new premier was not deterred from taking energetic measures. The appointment of the new Minister of War, though it aroused bitter opposition from the left, was in one respect a stroke of genius. Gallifet was a professional in the best sense of the word, not a political general like Mercier, and free from any inclination to play at politics. His reputation with the army put him beyond attack on that side and enabled him to quell all symptoms of unrest in it. To subject the Church to republican discipline was to be a longer and most costly process. But the critical decade had passed. The Affair, though at a heavy price both at the time and in drafts on the future, had ended in the triumph of the Republic. It was to survive for another forty years, and then to be overthrown only by a foreign enemy.

✦

CHAPTER FIVE

PROLOGUE TO REFORM

THE struggle for justice in the Dreyfus affair had united, as perhaps nothing else could have done, the republican forces in France. Under a premier like Waldeck-Rousseau this meant justice not only for Dreyfus but also – of a retributive kind – for the enemies of the Republic. One of the first steps of the new government was to order the arrest and trial of those who had attempted to exploit the affair in the interests of revolution. Something also had to be done about the Assumptionist Fathers, who in their papers had been conducting a Holy War against the Republic and the Jews. They had been rather unwise in thus putting themselves in the forefront of the political battle, for as an unauthorized congregation they were in a weak position if the government chose to take action against them. Not without provocation – one of the last efforts of the Order had been to subsidize opposition candidates in the election – it did take action and the Order was dissolved.

Waldeck-Rousseau was not anxious to extend the attack to those religious bodies which had not flung themselves into the political struggle. He put forward, in November 1899, a scheme compelling religious congregations to apply for legal recognition. It also included certain steps for assimilating clerical and lay schools, so that, as he said, there should no longer be *deux jeunesses* in France. It is doubtful if the Church would have accepted such proposals in any case, but the plan was diverted from its original intention. One of the basic weaknesses of the parliamentary system of the Third Republic was that no government had control of its own legislation. Its proposals were seldom voted on in the form in which they were presented; they automatically went into the machine of the Commissions of the Chambers, from which they might emerge in an almost unrecognizable shape. Thus Waldeck-Rousseau's proposals, when they became law on July 1st, 1901, had been vastly changed.

By the new law each congregation had to apply for legal authorization or be dissolved, and no member of an unauthorized congregation was to be allowed to teach. However, the law was applied with moderation and did not seem likely to provoke serious opposition.

The country registered its approval, after a close electoral struggle, in May 1902. The government won some 370 seats against 220 held by the opposition, though once again the division was a much more even one than these figures might suggest, for in actual votes there was only some two hundred thousand difference between the two blocs. But they were now divided by the whole gulf of the Dreyfus affair. The bitterness of the feelings that had been aroused by the series of attempts to overthrow the Republic, and the moral revulsion against appeals to violence and anti-semitism, were now added to the traditional anti-clericalism; and a strong element of class hostility reinforced the attack on a Church which was identified with the ruling class. The aristocracy was pretty solidly Catholic, the wealthier middle classes and higher officials had largely abandoned their former scepticism or indifference to religion and now supported the Church. On the other hand the lower middle classes and lesser officials retained all their fervid anti-clericalism, and the breach between many of the workers and Roman Catholicism was becoming total. The attitude of the peasantry varied greatly. In the south there was widespread anti-clericalism; elsewhere – for instance in Brittany, the Vendée, Normandy, and Lorraine – the Church was still deeply rooted.

The particular form which anti-clericalism took among the middle and lower middle classes was freemasonry, which was also closely linked with radicalism in politics. In 1896 there were 364 lodges and about 24,000 freemasons. By 1926 the numbers had risen to 583 and 52,000, though possibly at the price of some dilution of quality. Indeed, by this time the masonic movement could be described, not altogether unfairly, as very largely an employment agency for lower civil servants. Being a secret society, its actual activities and membership can only be guessed at, but it undoubtedly exercised considerable political influence.

The extremer anti-clericals regarded the elections of 1902 as their particular victory. Waldeck-Rousseau was left behind by the violence of the passions that had been aroused in the course of the electoral struggle. Unwilling to give the new majority what it wanted, he resigned in June 1902 and in 1903 strongly attacked the policy of his successor, though without any effect. He died a year later. His place was taken by a second-rate, elderly senator named Combes, indicated for such high office only by the fact that as an ardent anti-clerical himself he might be expected to hold an anti-clerical majority together. No one has a good word to say for this product of a seminary education, who would have made a typical narrow-minded and vindictive bishop in a backward diocese, for Combes was originally intended for the priesthood. He added to the *odium theologicum* the petty malignancies of small-town politics and carried both into national life. The corrupting influence of clerical-ism and anti-clericalism on French public life can be seen fully dis-played, the first in the Dreyfus affair and the second in the ministry of Combes.

With Combes in office everything was subordinated to the anti-clerical campaign. To reassure the interests of property, the Ministry of Finances was given to Rouvier, who – as had been shown in the Panama affair – had close, if in the past a little shady, connections with the financial world. To keep his parliamentary majority in line Combes set up a Délégation des Gauches as a sort of occult govern-ment in the Chamber. It arranged parliamentary strategy, disciplined individuals who were tempted to act on their own, and checked any tendency on the part of moderate elements in the left to compromise with the right. The Socialists were divided in their attitude to the new government. For Guesde and the more orthodox Marxists the radical onslaught on the Church was a distraction from the class struggle; on the other hand, Jaurès played a leading part in the work of the Délégation des Gauches. Along with the majority of the parliamentary Socialists he believed that the weakening of clerical influence was a necessary preliminary to the introduction of Social-ism. Like the philosopher of the liberal republic, Renouvier, he saw the French Church as a fortress for the defence of the privileges of the wealthy bourgeoisie.

In the country Combes brought the whole administrative machinery into play in support of his anti-clerical campaign. A circular of June 1902 instructed the prefects to reserve 'the favours which the Republic disposes of' for supporters of the government. In communes where the *maire* belonged to the opposition an 'administrative delegate' was appointed instead, to advise the government on the distribution of these favours. The law against congregations was applied ruthlessly. Those that asked for legal recognition under the new law found, with few exceptions, their requests rejected: 81 congregations of women were dissolved and 54 of men, the latter containing some 20,000 members in 1,500 houses. By October 1903 more than 10,000 schools conducted by unauthorized orders had been closed, though some 6,000 were to be reopened later, still under religious control. A law of July 1904 prohibited members of religious orders from teaching. Priests were excluded from the state examination for the *agrégation*; responsibility for burials was attributed to the secular authorities and crucifixes were removed from law-courts. The property of the banned orders was put up for sale and conscientious anti-clericals felt it their duty to support the government by purchasing it, often at prices well below its real value.

It is surprising that such measures, though they produced demonstrations of protest, did not lead to more violent resistance, especially in the large areas of France where Catholicism was dominant. These formed a kind of ring, beginning in the mountains of Savoy and Franche-Comté, and passing through Lorraine, Flanders and Artois, Normandy, Brittany and the Vendée, down through the Bordelais to the Basque country and Béarn in the extreme south-west; in the Massif Central also there were strong Catholic enclaves. Yet only in Brittany did disturbances worthy of the name occur.

Combes found an enemy of his own metal in Rome. There Leo XIII had died in 1903. The representative of the Emperor of Austria in the Sacred College vetoed the election of a francophile candidate who seemed to be leading the field, and the choice fell on Pius X, a simple priest with little knowledge of the world but a great sense of the authority of his office, who appointed as his Secretary of State the young and uncompromising Spanish cardinal, Merry del Val. The conflict with Rome which the policy of the French government had prepared was precipitated by an official visit of President Loubet to the King of Italy. A papal protest against the visit leaked out and the French government recalled its ambassador to the Vatican. The action of the Papacy was widely resented in France, and the French cabinet's retaliation was endorsed by a vote of 427 to 95 in the Chamber. The conflict was exacerbated by differences between Rome and Paris over the appointment and dismissal of bishops. Finally, in November 1904, Combes, not very reluctantly, tabled a law for the separation of Church and state.

Though his majority was weakening, it still held together, and it was in fact not his anti-clerical legislation that brought down the government of the 'petit père' Combes but the indiscretions of his Minister of War, General André. One of Gallifet's reforms had been the reorganization of the Army Council and the attribution to the Minister of War of all promotions and appointments in the army. This was obviously a desirable measure, on condition that it was put into effect with discretion, which was the quality André lacked. He had been chosen as the only general with strong republican sympathies, and had suffered throughout his career for his views. It was therefore with enthusiasm that he set about breaking down the Catholic and monarchist monopoly of the higher command. Its fantastic behaviour in the course of the Dreyfus affair did indeed suggest that drastic changes were needed, and Gallifet had taken the first steps towards them. André turned the tables with a vengeance. Promotion now went only to those who could demonstrate their sound republican and anti-clerical sentiments. This was not altogether unreasonable in a republic, though it was not guaranteed to improve the morale or quality of the army command. To obtain the necessary information, André organized, with the aid of informers, especially freemasons and often from the lower commissioned or non-commissioned ranks, a great collection of *fiches* on the religious affiliations of the members of the officer corps. In October 1904 his system was revealed by an employee of the Masonic Grand Orient, and public indignation was such that the Minister had to resign. Combes followed him in January 1905.

The problem of separatism had still to be tackled. In a new ministry it was taken over by a young lawyer and journalist from Nantes, Aristide Briand, who had begun his political career as a Socialist but was too little a doctrinaire and too much a politician to stay in any of the Socialist groups. Supple, conciliating and infinitely persuasive, Briand was to move in and out of the highest posts of government with equal nonchalance for the space of nearly thirty years. His gift for political manoeuvre secured the passage, in December 1905, of a law of separation which, he hoped, would offend the religious susceptibilities of the Catholics as little as possible. In principle it went back beyond the Napoleonic Concordat to the year III, recognizing absolute liberty of religion but denying that any Church had special claims to the patronage of the state. Religious bodies were to be allowed to keep their property, including religious edifices, on condition of forming recognized associations to manage it. Thus the state would not have to contaminate itself by having any dealings with the Catholic Church as such, which would satisfy the anti-clericals, while the Churches would continue to function legally and preserve their corporate identity under a different name.

The French bishops, mostly appointed during the comparatively liberal regime of Leo XIII, were prepared to make the best of the situation by accepting Briand's conciliatory proposals and working the proposed religious associations, but for Rome separation meant the creation of a godless state and Piux X was in no mood for compromise. Besides, whatever the original intention of the Napoleonic Concordat, in practice it had proved too favourable to the interests of the Church for the Vatican to be willing to abandon it without a struggle. The papal encyclical *Vehementer* therefore barred the road to compromise and prevented the French Church from forming the religious associations provided for by the new law.

In practice, of course, there had to be some kind of compromise. An unofficial modus vivendi, worked out by the Conseil d'État, allowed the use of Church premises for religious ceremonies and permitted religious processions. The opposition of Rome merely underlined the fact that the anti-clericals had won a great victory. 'We have torn human consciences from the clutches of credulity,' proclaimed Viviani; 'we have demonstrated that behind the clouds there are nothing but chimeras. With a magnificent gesture we have put out the lights of heaven and they will never be lighted again.'

One unanticipated result of the law of separation was greatly to increase papal control over the Church in France. The Papacy could now appoint bishops without, as it normally had done in the past, taking into account the preferences of the French government. Moreover the poverty which fell upon the lower clergy, which made their recruitment more difficult, at the same time helped to ensure that only those with a real religious vocation entered the priesthood. The *curés* and *vicaires*, who in the nineteenth century had represented a privileged class in the villages, perhaps gained more respect now that economically they were no better off than their parishioners; whereas the *instituteur*, the teacher, who had been one of themselves to the village people when he was a downtrodden usher eking out a meagre living by acting as bell-ringer, clerk, and general drudge to the *curé*, now that he was a better-paid official of the state seemed to represent a superior and alien element. Paradoxically, the Concordat, framed, at least in the mind of the Vatican, to protect the interests of the Roman Church in France, had in the long run done it much harm; the separation, which was so bitterly resisted, was to prepare the way for the recovery of some of its lost spiritual authority.

On the whole separation, while it temporarily exacerbated relations, in the end tended to reduce the tension between Church and state. The majority of the Catholics were not yet reconciled to the Republic, but with the decline of clerical interference in politics the violence of anti-clerical sentiment inevitably declined. The discredit resulting from the methods and narrowness of Combes was to some extent wiped out by the moderation of Briand. On the other hand, the policy of the Vatican remained rigid and uncompromising. Its victims were inside as well as outside the Church. Those who were suspected of having been infected by the abbé Loisy with the taint of modernism came under severe disciplinary measures.

Another French movement which incurred papal censure was Le Sillon. This was the creation of Marc Sangnier, who in 1898 gave up an army career to devote himself to proselytizing the laity. He was a spellbinder, capable of winning total devotion, though even at its height Le Sillon never had more than some twenty-five thousand adherents and never formulated any clearly defined programme of action. This did not matter, for Marc Sangnier envisaged its task as the formation of an elite, and its essential coherence in loyalty to his own person. He drew his followers largely from students and the lower middle classes. To protect his meetings he organized a 'young guard', which was treated as a sort of modern order of knighthood with ritual observances and a uniform. Opposition to the authority of the leader was not tolerated. All this might sound as though Le Sillon was a sort of religious Fascism; though its bias was towards the left rather than the right. Politically the aim of Le Sillon was to reconcile the Church with the Republic. Socially it upheld the idea of co-operation. Because he acted in independence of the hierarchy, Sangnier was viewed with suspicion by the Church. His movement was particularly opposed by the *Action Française*, which directed its propaganda at a similar clientèle and also hoped to spread its views by the indoctrination of an elite. To the influence of the *Action Française* has been attributed the papal condemnation, in 1910, of Le Sillon as a movement 'placing authority in the hands of the people and tending towards the levelling of classes', which was perhaps to give it too much credit.

Thrust back upon themselves by their defeat in the struggle with the state, the leaders of the Church identified the spirit of conciliation with weakness or covert disloyalty. The attempt to come to terms with the Republic, which had begun when Cardinal Lavigerie made his speech at Algiers in 1890, had failed, and on the whole it may be said that the Republic had emerged strengthened from the prolonged crisis. The hold of the republicans on the state, even though still based on a narrow electoral margin, was unshaken. It was reaffirmed by the elections of May 1906. And now it seemed possible that the social and political reforms, held up while the dog-fight between the Church and state had been going on, might at last have a chance of enactment. In October 1906 Clemenceau, *bête noire* of the right, for the first time formed a government, towards what might have seemed the end of such a long and chequered career. After his disastrous involvement in the Panama affair of 1893 even the staunch Jacobins of the Var had rejected him and he had turned back to journalism. His daily article in *La Justice* kept him still a force in the country. Back in parliament, he resumed the role of hunter-out of scandals – he liked to call himself 'le premier flic de France' – and

c

destroyer of governments, that suited a republican with no faith in the people. At last in office, he chose a cabinet inclining to the left and announced an impressive programme of reforms, few of which were to be carried into effect even though his government was to last for the astonishingly long period of three years.

One of the first steps of the new parliament was to increase the pay of its members from nine to fifteen thousand francs a month – a gift not only to themselves but to the agitators of the right, who now had a new anti-parliamentarian cry in denunciation of the *quinze mille*. The Clemenceau ministry also passed a law nationalizing the Chemin de fer de l'Ouest, which had for long been surviving only with the aid of a subsidy from the state. After this its reforming ardour lapsed. The trouble was that the social reforms that were urgently needed could not be carried through without injury to the interests of the great mass of property-owners which constituted its electoral clientèle. A pensions law was passed by the Chamber of Deputies, but as usual opposition in the Senate could be relied on to safeguard the Chamber from the effects of its own generosity and the law was held up until 1914.

The issue which aroused the strongest feeling was the proposal for an income tax. First discussed by the Chamber in 1888, this took a whole generation to be passed into law and come into effect. The government of Léon Bourgeois had brought it forward again in 1896, only to be defeated by the Senate. Caillaux introduced an income tax bill in 1907, and after two years succeeded in getting it through the Chamber. Naturally, the Senate vetoed the bill. Only on the eve of war, in 1914, did the Senate relax its opposition as part of a political deal over military service, and a very modest income-tax law came into effect, finally, in 1917.

The party which should have represented the cause of social reform, the Socialist, was weakened, as throughout its history, by internal divisions. It achieved little in the pre-war years, despite the leadership of the man who must count as one of the greatest of French politicians of the time. Jean Jaurès was an orator who could sway the masses, an inspiring personality who won the loyalty of individuals, a distinguished historian whose work on the French Revolution is still a major historical contribution, a powerful journalist, editor of the Socialist daily paper *L'Humanité*, a Socialist who had learnt Marxism at the *école normale*, and at the same time a liberal idealist. His genius bestrode the French political stage but could not overcome the opposition of the great body of small property-owners, whose votes kept the Radicals in power and the Socialists out. Even among the Socialists the power of Jaurès was limited by the rivalry of the sterner Marxist, Guesde, the pope of French Socialism and certainly papal in his anathemas and excommunications.

On the surface the two main tendencies into which the French Socialists were split had been brought together by the mediation of the Second International in 1905. The Socialists were united as the Section Française de l'International Ouvrière – S.F.I.O. The development of a specifically Socialist, as distinct from a republican, French revolutionary mystique, was symbolized by the abandonment of *La Carmagnole* and the substitution for it of *L'Internationalale* as the party song. Born at Lille in 1888, sung at the Congress of Troyes in 1895, it had become the official anthem by 1899.

In the policy of the new party the more doctrinaire views of Guesde prevailed over the belief of Jaurès in the possibility of collaboration with bourgeois parties and progress by constitutional methods. Both sides could appeal to the experience of Millerand's entry into the Waldeck-Rousseau cabinet. Millerand was not merely a traitor, he had introduced an element of reformism into a non-Socialist government. He created a labour section inside his Ministry of Commerce to deal with the problem of social insurance, established arbitration tribunals and inspectors of labour, brought representatives of the workers into the Conseil supérieur de travail, prescribed minimum wages and maximum hours of labour for all work undertaken by public authorities, and established an eight-hour day for postal workers. The maximum working day of eleven hours instituted in 1900 was reduced to ten hours in 1904. These were not negligible achievements but they did not win Millerand any favour from his former Socialist colleagues, who believed that half a loaf was much worse than no bread.

The Socialist movement was further split by the cleavage between its political and industrial sides. The trade union organization, the

Confédération Générale du Travail, under the influence of former Blanquists and anarchists, and more recently of Georges Sorel's *Réflexions sur la violence* (1906), was profoundly suspicious of the political movement. It advocated revolutionary syndicalism and believed in the myth of the General Strike, which had been accepted as the basis of trade-union action at a congress in 1892 by a large majority, under the influence of an eloquent speech by a young Socialist named Briand. In 1906 a congress at Amiens laid down the programme known as the Amiens Charter and reaffirmed the General Strike as the means of achieving it.

At this time the membership of the C.G.T. was rising, from some 715,000 in 1904 to nearly a million in 1909, and militancy was increasing. Strikes were often accompanied by violence, which was not confined to industrial workers. In 1907 the vineyard owners of the south reacted to over-production and a fall in the price of wine by a series of outbursts, in one of which the prefecture at Perpignan was looted and burnt. The government retaliated against strikers by sending in troops and arresting and imprisoning the leaders. Clemenceau, though relying on a majority of the left, repressed such movements ruthlessly, but it remained for his successor, Briand, to invent and put into use the decisive weapon. In 1910 a strike on the Chemin de fer du Nord, for an increase in wages and a weekly day off work, developed into a general railway strike. Briand smashed it by the simple process of mobilizing the strikers and sending them back to work as soldiers.

While industrial action by the trade unions was becoming more vigorous, politically the years from 1906 to 1914 were a period of evolution towards the right. The Radicals, losing votes on the left to the Socialists, who in the election of 1910 garnered over a million votes and by 1914 had one hundred deputies in the Chamber, turned for support to the right in a sort of anticipation of the later Bloc National tactic. The history of the Third Republic bore out the saying that France was politically to the left and socially to the right. Governments of the left could achieve and keep power only on condition of not using it to introduce social reforms.

Whatever the political trend, the social structure of France was a guarantee of conservatism. Nearly half the labour of France was still engaged in agriculture. Of some 40 million population, 17 to 18 million, or nearly half, lived in communes of under 2,000. Nearly 40 per cent of the 5,700,000 farms in France were less than 2½ acres in size; and only 33,000 over 250 acres. The electoral system still overweighted the rural vote. The small peasants, who were politically dominant in the Third Republic, were not disposed to favour social reforms in the interest of the workers of the towns. Apart from occasional depressions, such as that which produced the outbreak of 1907 in the south, they had reason for satisfaction with the Third Republic, under which they were at last beginning to escape from the depressed conditions of life that had been their lot from time immemorial. In their farm-houses floor-boards were replacing beaten earth and tiles the more picturesque thatch; oil lamps and coal stoves were coming in; the blue blouse and sabot were disappearing. The Méline tariff kept the price of agricultural produce high; and because of the railways its transport to the towns was now easier. The opening years of the twentieth century were a period of agricultural prosperity. Although agricultural methods were still very backward, France was second only to the United States and Russia in the production of grain, and produced more wine than any country except Italy.

Industry was also mainly on a small scale. Out of 1,100,000 workshops, 1,000,000 had fewer than 5 employees, and only 600 employed over 500. At the same time, the process of industrialization begun under the Second Empire was continuing under the Third Republic, particularly between 1890 and 1914. The use of steam power in industry (excluding transport) multiplied ten times between 1870 and 1914. Between 1880 and 1914 the production of coal doubled, from 20 to 40 million tons, that of cast iron went up nearly four times and that of steel was multiplied by twelve.

What French production still lacked in quantity it made up in quality. France was what Louis XIV and Colbert had made it, the world's chief producer of luxury goods – fine fabrics, *haute couture*, perfumes and cosmetics, *objets d'art* in general. The race of craftsmen still survived and there is no irrelevance in adding that Paris under the Third Republic was more than ever the artistic capital of the world. The picture of French social conservatism and economic backwardness in this period must therefore not be exaggerated. There were, of course, reasons why the economic development of France was lagging behind that of other Western countries. The structure of a society dominated at the top by the official and professional classes and *rentiers*, and at a lower level by peasants and small employers, was not favourable to economic progress. The family was dominant not only in social life but also in business, and the preservation of the family business took precedence over expansion or even efficiency. This helped to preserve a host of small family firms from the pressures of competition, while the larger ones were protected by cartelization. Firmly prevented from interference in the interests of the workers by the electoral influence of the mass of small employers and proprietors, the state was biased by the same influences in their own favour, particularly through the protective system of tariffs. While private enterprise would not take the risk of starting new undertakings, it could prevent the state from supplementing its deficiency; as was shown in 1879, when Freycinet, a real technocrat, put forward plans for the development of roads, canals, and feeder railways, only to be defeated by the opposition of the great banks.

One must not forget, of course, that France was not well endowed in the natural resources of the industrial revolution. French production of coal in 1913 was one-seventh of British or German production. In iron and steel she produced less than a third as much as Germany. The slow growth of population was also a handicap. France, so long predominant in Europe, had been overtaken. In 1871 the population of France, at 36 millions, had been above that of Great Britain and only slightly lower than that of all Germany. By 1914 France had grown only to 39½ millions, Great Britain had 45 millions, and the German Empire 67 millions. Various explanations have been given for the stagnation of the French population, such as the influence of the rule of the division of inheritance among all children, generalized by the Napoleonic Code, or the persistence of a high rate of infant mortality, itself not unconnected with the absence of social reforms.

While French economy suffered from lack of capital, the savings of the French flowed out to fertilize the rest of the world, nearly one-quarter of the foreign investments being – for reasons not un-connected with high politics – placed in Russia. By 1914 French investments abroad, at about 50 milliard francs, represented one sixth of the national wealth, but only 4 milliards of this was in-vested in France's own colonies. The large commissions which went to the credit houses which handled the loans were, of course, not a negligible factor in determining their direction and ensuring their success.

When all this has been said, it must be added that in the first decade of the twentieth century France was clearly beginning to move out of the phase of social rigidity which had marked its history in the nineteenth century. The political conflicts on which attention had been concentrated were beginning to give place to social prob-lems in the public mind, and the balance was beginning to be weighted on the side of reform.

CHAPTER SIX

AN AGE OF GREATNESS

I F survival was a test of political success, the Third Republic had passed it. By 1914 it had long outlasted all previous regimes since 1789. Its economic progress had been slow, but only in comparison with that of the more advanced industrial countries. The status and economic conditions of the peasantry, who constituted the largest section of the French nation, had risen to the point at which it would not have been very exaggerated to describe France as a peasants' republic. What, more than anything else, made this one of the great ages of French history was its achievement in arts, letters and sciences. Its periodization in this respect reflects unusually closely the political calendar. As in the political history of the Third Republic, 1914 is something like an end, though 1871 is in no sense a beginning. The fall of the Second Empire was not a date in artistic, literary or scientific history. French art and literature had already revolted against the philistinism of the Second Empire before 1870. It is significant of an age of individualism that the public arts of architecture and town-planning, which had reached a high degree of excellence under the *ancien régime*, continued to decline. The only advantage that the official architecture of the Third Republic has over that of the Second Empire is that there is possibly less of it, though ecclesiastical building, unfortunately, flourished. Sculpture did not develop beyond the romantic tradition, but it reached a level of mastery that won immediate appreciation with the popular and powerful work of Rodin (1840–1917). A less dramatic but persisting appeal is to be seen in the lovely nudes of Maillol (1861–1944). Not all was of this quality. The sculpture of the Third Republic, like its architecture, was largely dependent on the commissions of nineteenth-century officials and bourgeois, who, unlike their predecessors of the previous century, were notably lacking in taste.

Painting would equally have suffered from the philistinism of society if it had not been a comparatively cheap art, which the artist could pursue for his own pleasure and that of a few friends. France, of course, had an Academy art, like Great Britain, of painters whose works, having gratified a generation of town councillors, civil servants and politicians, now clutter up provincial museums and whose names are forgotten. The mid-century had not been a period of great distinction in painting. A pastoral spirit, like that of the Berrichon romances of George Sand, illumined the poetic landscapes of Corot (1796–1874) and the Barbizon school. The growth of a social conscience had appeared in the paintings and cartoons of Daumier (1808–79), in the harsh realism of the Socialist and Communard Gustave Courbet (1819–77), and the unsentimentalized and affecting peasants of Millet (1814–75). A combination of realism with a purer interest in pictorial values appears in such paintings as the 'Déjeuner sur l'herbe' (1863) of Manet, whose naked girl at the picnic seemed so much more shocking than all the romantic odalisques who had preceded her, or in his 'Bar aux Folies Bergères' (1882).

Manet forms the link with the great school of the Third Republic, the Impressionists, who inaugurated an artistic renaissance which casts a glow over the society which in their own day rejected them. Paris of the Third Republic, damned by the Hôtel de Ville and Sacré-Cœur, is saved by the painters it despised or ignored. A roll of honour of artists decorates its days – Monet, Pissarro, Sisley, Degas, Gauguin, Seurat, Toulouse-Lautrec, the douanier Rousseau, and the great names of Cézanne, Renoir, Matisse; nor should it be forgotten that Picasso and Braque, both born in 1881, belong to the Third Republic. To see in this galaxy of artists an element of greatness is obviously justifiable. To go beyond this is perhaps not justifiable, but it is tempting to see also the reflection of an intensely vital society, full of colour and character, in which the individual vision mattered most, a fundamentally stable society in which experiments were possible because they were firmly rooted in tradition, and which through them rose to the achievement of a great classical art.

The Third Republic came to its greater musicians more slowly. Offenbach had delighted Second Empire society, but after him the world of music was bestridden by Wagner. *Carmen* was first performed in 1875 and *Manon* in 1884, but Bizet, César Franck, Massenet, Saint-Saens could hardly challenge Wagner's genius. A new note was heard in 1902 with the production of *Pelléas et Mélisande* by Debussy. Soon after, Ravel joined him, and with composers such as Gabriel Fauré, Paul Dukas, Erik Satie, the Third Republic had a school of music of its own, not unworthy to be mentioned along with its great painters.

In letters the great names of the first half of the century had been succeeded by somewhat of a hiatus during the Second Empire. Romantic'sm, when the gloss had been worn off, was felt to be meretricious and false. A period of 'realism' in literature followed; its greatest figure, Flaubert, produced an exposure of romantic love in *Madame Bovary* (1857) which was also a detailed anatomy of life in a provincial town; and a picture of Paris from the Orleanist monarchy to the Second Empire in *L'Education sentimentale* (1869). None of the other realists of this time has left work that counts besides Flaubert's masterpieces. Notable writers appeared later in the century under the label of 'naturalism', which was merely realism pushed to a more brutal extreme and given a scientific theory by Taine. Vice and virtue, he proclaimed, are but products like vitriol or sugar; the three factors of race, environment, and conjuncture (which he called *moment*) determine absolutely the character of men and nations. The novelist therefore is really a kind of social scientist registering and recording the facts of social life which added together explain the men and women of his day. The Goncourt brothers applied this theory to writing the social and artistic history of the eighteenth century; they recorded the literary history of their own time; and they produced under the Second Empire a series of novels describing on the basis of a careful documentation the more sordid aspects of French life. They were followed on a monumental scale by Zola, whose *Les Rougon-Macquart* is the natural and social history of a family under the Second Empire. It appeared in twenty novels between 1871 and 1893 and its characters – all drawn from the same family circle and revealing in combination after combination the same hereditary traits – range from scheming senators or financiers and the dissolute high society of the Empire to the degraded and wretched victims of social injustice and their own vices and follies at the bottom of the social scale. Sheer power carries Zola's sordid concerns and pseudo-scientific theories into the rank of literary art. The other naturalists are lighter in weight. Guy de Maupassant, a disciple of Flaubert and Zola, still remains the greatest master of the *conte*. Another important contributor to *Les Soirées de Médan* (1880), a naturalistic symposium in which Maupassant published *Boule de suif*, was J.-K. Huysmans, but he was to move on to the higher realms of decadence and religious mysticism.

Naturalism in literature may be regarded as in some sense the reflection of the positivist movement in philosophy. This was itself the secular reflection of the religious revival of the nineteenth century, it was *la foi des sans foi*, envisaged by its prophet, Comte, as a sort of religion of science based on the laws of social progress. Freemasonry also, in some aspects, was a kind of secular faith. This semi-religious element in French freemasonry explains why it met with such bitter opposition from rival faiths like Roman Catholicism and later Communism.

That the fundamental influence of positivist social thought was conservative was shown by the historical writings of Taine. His hatred of democracy and fear of the people antedates the shock of the Commune of Paris, to which it is sometimes attributed, and is inherent in his positivist social philosophy. It is arguable that Taine played a larger part than any other writer in the development of an anti-democratic trend of thought among the intellectuals of the Third Republic. A whole generation of French students learned from him to condemn the Revolution which had founded French republicanism, and to see Jacobinism as the source of all social evil. The '*petits faits bien choisis*' of his history, presented in a coruscating style, were convincing, and if Taine's gems are now seen to be paste, they still have the power to dazzle. Even the greatest of the republican historians who came after Taine, Georges Lefebvre, could not but pay a somewhat reluctant tribute to his power of social analysis, which should remind us that in spite of all other differences they both shared the tradition of positivism. Another great influence among the positivists was Émile Littré (1801–81), who began life as a student of medicine, became a disciple of Comte, and won his fame as the compiler of the masterly *Dictionnaire de la langue française* (1863–73). He combined a rigidly materialist determinism with an idealistic conception of human progress.

From the positivists also grew a school of sociology, in which the greatest name was that of Émile Durkheim. Theories of group or mass psychology were developed, which exposed the irrational content of democratic action and taught the enemies of democracy how to exploit its weaknesses against it.

Positivism exercised a surprising influence over the academic world during the Third Republic, but both its austerities and its dogmatism stood in the way of a wider influence. A more inspiring form of scientific idealism was derived from the writings of Ernest Renan (1823–92). A Breton, educated in a seminary, he became a distinguished Hebrew scholar. When he published the first volume of his *Vie de Jésus* in 1863, its literary charm could not make up for its unduly rational and historical attitude to the founder of Christianity and Renan was expelled from his chair as Professor of Hebrew at the Collège de France. In many later works he developed the views on religion as an historical phenomenon which he had sketched out in *L'Avenir de la science*, written as early as 1848 though not published till 1890. Religious dogmatism was in much more danger from such moderate, historical criticism than from its more violent enemies. Even a religious historian and archaeologist like Duchesne (1843–1922), Professor of Ecclesiastical History at the Catholic Institute in Paris and achieving the rank of Monseigneur, contributed to the undermining of nineteenth-century orthodoxy by applying the methods of historical criticism to many a cherished legend of the Church.

Reference has already been made to the modernist controversy in the Roman Catholic Church, stirred up by the writings of the abbé Loisy (1857–1940). A professor at the Catholic Institute, he also applied historical criticism to the Scriptures, showing how religious ideas had changed and developed in the course of their long history. In this Loisy, however, went much farther than Duchesne, and farther than the Church could follow him. He was removed from the Institute and sent to be chaplain at a girls' boarding school in a fashionable suburb of Paris, where it was presumably hoped that his dangerous historical inquiries would do no harm. Unfortunately he continued to write and to acquire followers by his writings. He was excommunicated but this did not prevent him from being appointed Professor of the History of Religion at the Collège de France.

Not only a heretic like Loisy, but many other French ecclesiastics and laity, whose orthodoxy was hardly suspect, were to suffer in the early years of the twentieth century from a witch-hunt run from Rome, under the patronage of Pius X, by those who called themselves 'integral Catholics'. The lead in this anti-modernist campaign was taken by the journal *Correspondance de Rome* and a secret international federation of Catholic groups associated with a neo-Thomist revival. The bitterness of the attacks, and the strength of the modernist defence, were at least evidence of the vitality of religious interests.

On the other side, philosophy was moving back towards a neo-Kantian idealism with Charles Renouvier (1815–1903), whose optimistic belief was in progress towards rationality, marking the moral advance of the human race – for reason was still, at the end of the nineteenth century, in the ascendant and along with it science and history. The need to cultivate science seemed to be one of the lessons taught by defeat in the Franco-Prussian War. The Third Republic continued the great tradition of French science with names such as those of Henri Poincaré, the mathematician, the Curies, famous for their work on radium, the chemist Berthelot, and Pasteur, genius of the famous Institute founded in 1888 and named after him. On a lower level, yet not without significance for the future, was the technological development shown when, in 1894, the Lumière brothers made the first short films in France and in 1896 Méliès built the first film studio.

The same empirical spirit produced a school of critical historians, centred on the Sorbonne and the École des Chartes, with Fustel de Coulanges, Lavisse, Seignobos, Halphen, Lot, among many others. Even the Académie Française included an Albert Sorel among its members – though the historians in its ranks were mostly on a much lower level. There was a deep gulf between the historical scholarship of the University and the smart-society historical journalism of the Academy. Of course, the scientific and historical achievements of

French genius were confined to a small elite. It is remarkable that they were possible at all, for tradition was still so strong in French education that the predominantly literary culture of the schools was as yet hardly affected by the newer disciplines.

Even in literature, however, new trends were appearing towards the end of the century. In poetry, as in the other arts, there had been a sort of pause after the ebb of the flood-tide of romanticism. It was occupied by the Parnassians, whose aim was to write a more classical verse, free from the passionate individual and social concerns of romanticism. They had learnt the doctrine of 'art for art's sake' from Théophile Gautier. Among them were Leconte de Lisle, Sully-Prudhomme and José-Maria de Heredia, whose sonnets, *Les Trophées*, published in 1893, are still the most read poems of the school.

A profounder and more permanent influence than that of Gautier flowed from Baudelaire, whose *Les Fleurs du Mal* had appeared, only to be burnt as indecent, as early as 1857, and who died in 1867. His poems, and even more his literary criticisms, were only appreciated at their real value by a subsequent generation. Baudelaire is the real founder of symbolism, which began to put forth its fruits when Verlaine met the boy Arthur Rimbaud and the latter wrote *Le Bateau ivre* in 1871. Verlaine's own *Romances sans paroles* followed in 1874 and Mallarmé's *L'Après-midi d'un faune* in 1876. The influence of symbolism was to be continued into the heart of the twentieth century in the rare poems of Paul Valéry.

The last decade of the nineteenth century saw the passing of a great generation in literature. Rimbaud, Verlaine, Mallarmé ceased to write then. Renan died in 1892, Taine in 1893, Edmond de Goncourt, author with his brother (who died much earlier) of the *Journal* which is the literary history of their time, in 1896. Maupassant died in 1893 and his master Zola in 1902; among the Parnassians Leconte de Lisle in 1894.

The new age in literature opened on a lower level, with the decadence and mysticism of *fin de siècle*. The critic and novelist Rémy de Gourmont continued the symbolist movement, but his novels, combining mysticism with physiological naturalism, illustrate its weaknesses rather than its strength. The half-Dutch Joris-Karl Huysmans moved from a naturalism in which he tried to outdo Zola to a literary cult of Satanism, with the usual appurtenances of black magic, orgies, sacrilege, and religiosity. Like the hero of his own novel, *Là-bas* (1891), he then moved over to religion, becoming for a time an oblate in a Benedictine abbey. By way of decadence and mysticism the road back to religion in literature was opening up. Barbey d'Aurevilly (1808–89), flamboyant critic and novelist, anticipates the militant royalist and Catholic writers of the next generation, such as Léon Bloy (1846–1917), whose apocalyptic writings preached death and destruction on existing society.

With religious and secular inspiration, from both left and right a politically committed literature was appearing. The growing pressure of politics can be traced in the life and writings of Anatole France (1844–1924), for whom, as for many, the Dreyfus affair was the catalyst which brought literature and political life together in a more active, and in some cases even an explosive reaction. Anatole France's erudition, his scepticism, irony, moderation, the patina of the past with which he misted over nearly everything he wrote, the sense of being too consciously a literary man, have robbed him of much of the adulation that he received in his lifetime. His fine novel of the French Revolution, *Les Dieux ont soif* (1912) could be disliked equally by those who favoured the Revolution and the Counter-revolution. *L'Île des pingouins* (1906), a satiric history of the Third Republic, and the four volumes of *L'Histoire contemporaine* (1896–1901), were too understanding to political enemies, too lukewarm to friends, and altogether too humane, to appeal to the generation that followed him. It is a curious comment on changing ideas that France, who to his predecessors seemed to have sacrificed literature to his commitment to social and political causes, was seen by the next generation as a mere man of letters, too lacking in serious interests to be taken seriously.

Another writer, primarily a music critic, also brought into political consciousness by the Dreyfus case, was Romain Rolland (1868–1944), in whom the commitment was above all to the problem of international relations and peace. His ten-volume *roman fleuve*, *Jean-Christophe*, published between 1906 and 1912, reflects the shift in the main concentration of French interests from domestic to foreign problems. Its hero, a German musician who makes his home in France, is the embodiment of Rolland's belief in the need for Franco-German friendship. This was also to be expressed in 1915, during the First World War, by his pamphlet *Au-dessus de la mêlée*, an appeal for international understanding which was not to be listened to until another generation had been sacrificed in another World War.

In Anatole France and Romain Rolland reason was still in the ascendant. The influence of the second-rate mysticism of the 'nineties had so far done little to weaken it. But times were changing. Perhaps the strongest single influence over French thought in the opening years of the twentieth century was the philosophy of Henri-Louis Bergson (1859–1941). *L'Évolution créatrice*, published in 1906, which elevated Bergson to the rank of one of the society stars of the Collège de France, postulated the existence of an *élan vital* inspiring all life. Reality, he proclaimed, is discovered not by the intelligence but by intuition. The problems that he propounded were perhaps more important than his solutions, and both Bergson and his brilliant literary style have long been out of favour. But philosophy has its fashions and these are as much a reflection of the spirit of an age as is its fiction. The philosophy of *élan vital* belongs to a period when rationalism was passing under a cloud.

The anti-intellectualism which had risen to the surface in the last years of the old century and which marks the decline of a great age in French literature, was becoming dominant in the years before the First World War. A straw, which showed the way the wind was blowing, was thrown up in 1909 by the Italian poet Marinetti. His *Manifesto of Futurism*, an appeal to and glorification of war, chaos and destruction, was more prophetic of the future than its adherents guessed or could have hoped. It anticipated both the dadaism of the war years by its apotheosis of meaninglessness, and the surrealism of post-war years by its suggestions of sinister hidden meanings.

The inculcation of violence as a legitimate method in domestic politics was a more immediately significant development, and one in which literature and politics came closest together. One of the peculiarities of the Third Republic was that revolution, hitherto a force of the left, was now transferred to the right. It was essentially an inheritance from Bonapartism, and the transition from Bonapartism to the new right came in the Boulangist movement. Among the supporters of Boulanger was a young writer from Lorraine, Maurice Barrès. The German annexation of what he felt to be part of the French nation and French soil was the first conditioning factor in his life. A second was the dislike of a provincial for the centralizing influence of Paris. In *Les Déracinés* (1897) Barrès portrays the disillusionment of a group of young Lorrainers robbed of their traditions by the indoctrination of a Kantian schoolmaster, and of their roots in their native soil by transplantation to Paris. Barrès was the chief literary exponent of nationalism in France, but his literary interests, though dominated by a nationalist ideology, were never completely subjected by it. The same cannot be said of his friend Charles Maurras, with whom we leave the category of literature and enter that of political journalism.

Literature and politics met and influenced one another in the cafés of the Left Bank, but the spirit of the greater literature, as of the painting and music of the Third Republic, transcended its passing political interests. By its writers and painters and musicians, even if the society of their time failed to recognize their full stature, the Third Republic becomes one of the great ages of French history. They represent the flowering of a free and vital society. Time has only magnified their achievement. In the poetry of the symbolists, the painting of Impressionism, and the music of Debussy, Fauré or Ravel, can be detected a common artistic vision, which transcends physical reality but never abandons the world of the senses, which intensifies the significance of sensations by seizing them in the immediacy of the single moment with a piercing clarity. What they lacked, and it was perhaps an artistic loss, was self-confidence. There is in them all a last, fading glow of romantic melancholy, a feeling of impermanence, of the transient as the all, as though something were coming to an end, which becomes the dominant note in the last and greatest of the writers of the age before the World Wars.

Marcel Proust, born with the Third Republic in 1871, produced the first volume of *À la recherche du temps perdu* in 1913. When he completed the work and his genius was recognized, shortly after the First World War, it was becoming clear that something had indeed come to an end. Yet the fundamental optimism, the belief in their world that is radiant in the Impressionists, persists in spite of everything in the Combray of Proust, and by it he belongs to a Republic in which, after so many uncertain and changing regimes, France seemed at last to have found the security of firm achievement and faith in the future.

PART TWO

THE DECLINE OF THE REPUBLIC

CHAPTER ONE

RUMOURS OF WAR

B Y 1910 it might have seemed that the major political problems of the Third Republic had all been solved or were well on their way to solution. Political divisions could still arouse intense feeling but there was no real danger of the Republic collapsing by its own weakness or being overthrown by the strength of its enemies. Social problems still remained to be tackled, but however powerful the forces of opposition, social reform was at least on the agenda.

There were signs in the general election of 1910, however, that France might be taking a new turn and one that was less encouraging. In that year over two hundred new deputies were elected, and the new Chamber represented a marked swing to the right. On the other hand, the left-wing elections of 1914 were to show that this was not necessarily a permanent trend. More significant were new developments appearing in the realm of ideas. A mystical Catholicism and conservatism was manifest in the works of Paul Claudel, who, although he was born in 1868, only became recognized with his poetic drama *L'Annonce faite à Marie* in 1912; but his real influence belongs to the post-war years. A rather different figure is Charles Péguy, Catholic and *dreyfusard*, Socialist and patriot, killed on the Marne in 1914, who left behind him a legend to which some of the finer elements of both left and right could look back. Even Péguy, however, represented a reaction against republican politics in the name of some undefined superior authority. His saying 'Tout commence en mystique et tout finit en politique' became classic, but in fact it was the other way round. The real trouble lay in the tendency to introduce religious mystique into politics. This was the work above all of the movement known as the Action Française.

Its founder, Charles Maurras, has some claim to be considered the evil genius of the Third Republic. Born and bred in the little provincial town of Aix-en-Provence, son of a minor official who died when Maurras was six, thin, dark, solitary, from the age of fourteen deaf, he came to Paris when he was seventeen to make his way in the literary world. Though he became, and was to remain, a permanent feature of the Paris literary scene for the rest of his long life, he soon took up and never shed the perhaps more genuine pose of that other provincial, Barrès, against the cosmopolitan capital that was his adopted home, and was so different from what he believed to be the real France. It was the kind of romantic nostalgia for the scenes of boyhood and youth that Rousseau had once felt for *Les Charmettes* and Annecy, and that Proust was to express in his memories of Combray, given a less peaceful and a more feverish form in the politics of the anti-republican, right-wing, Paris journalism, and the Left Bank cafés.

Maurras's first aim was literary success. He endeavoured to chisel his early works like a classical statue, with a cold rejection of emotion; but in the course of the Dreyfus affair he adopted a passionate political commitment, the keystone of which was anti-semitism. The argument ran – Dreyfus was a Jew, therefore he was a traitor. Since he was a traitor, any method of bringing him to justice was rightful: hence Henry's forgery was justified, or rather, since its purpose was to establish the truth it could not be a forgery at all. From beginning to end anti-semitism was the essence of the teaching of Maurras. It provided the motive for the foundation in 1898, by a little group of young writers, of the Comité de l'Action Française, which struggled on in obscurity, but only began to make an impression on the public in 1908, when its journal, the *Action Française*, with the aid of unexpected financial support, became a daily paper. Its editor, Léon Daudet, was one of the most brilliant and unscrupulous political journalists of the day. A fanatical nationalist and lion of cosmopolitan society, a practising Catholic and the author of pornographic novels, with the physical appearance of a *bonhomme* and the qualities of a *faux bonhomme*, a dangerous man by his gifts and his lack of scruple, Daudet was a master of invective who could give literary shape and expression to a mass of disorganized hatreds and resentments. Another frequent contributor to the *Action Française*, Jacques Bainville, made a successful career out of writing popular histories with a royalist bias.

We have now moved away from literature and into the field of politics. If the *Action Française* was to be a successful organ of propaganda it had not only to be distributed to members of the league of the Action Française but to be sold to the general public on the streets. For this purpose a volunteer corps of *Camelots du roi* was recruited. This turned out to be a brilliant innovation: the *Camelots* were the first of the organized, later shirted and booted, street-fighters and agitators of the political leagues. Their title is a reminder that the Action Française was a royalist organization. This was curious, for the movement and its leaders were descended in no way from the old royalist parties, which indeed had largely sunk into apathy and faded out of political life. The business and financial interests which had formerly provided the royalists with their funds had now largely transferred their support to the conservative republicans. The Action Française as a monarchist organization was the creation of Maurras. He claimed to be a monarchist because the monarchy stood for order and the classic discipline in literature, because it was the antithesis of a hated parliamentarism, because as the living embodiment of French history a king stood for the permanent interests of the nation against the transitory selfishness of the individual. Yet, on a closer inspection, one cannot help asking whether the royalism of the Action Française was ever more than a stalking-horse for different and more sinister designs. It is remarkable what a little part the monarchy seems to play in the actual political proposals of Maurras, so far as he had any. They were never given coherent and systematic expression, but certain leading themes can be picked out. Thus he takes up the agitation of the nineteenth-century regionalists for a revival of the old provincial divisions of France. He would limit the duties of the central government to the control of foreign policy, military and naval affairs, national finance, and justice. All other functions should be left in the hands of local or corporate bodies. In order to provide a new ruling class great landed estates and industrial corporations should be created, or re-created and to prevent them from being split up, the rule of equal inheritance abolished. This is essentially an aristocratic creed, calculated for the promotion of an independent, governing elite, in no way in the tradition of Bourbon absolutism. It looks back not to the monarchy but to the ultra-royalists of the Restoration and beyond to the Counter-revolution and the *révolte nobiliaire* of the seventeen eighties which set its mark on all subsequent right-wing movements in France.

So long as the men of wealth and position remained in effective control of France, as they did up to 1870, there was little scope for such a creed. With the Third Republic it found a real target. Maurras supplied all those who resented the arrival of even a limited measure of political democracy and social egalitarianism with an outlet for their resentment and a rationale for views based primarily on self-interest. For a generation after 1871 the right had been on the defensive, continually out-manoeuvred and defeated and driven back from the positions it took up. Politically it continued to be beaten, but at least it was now on the offensive. This is why Maurras and the Action Française won the sympathy of many who were not willing to go all the way with them. Maurras provided the conservative classes with a stimulus for their morale which they so badly needed, but they did not reflect on the illogicality of basing a conservative creed on the advocacy of revolution. The supposed classic rationality of Maurras is an illusion, only possible because he put forward his ideas fragmentarily, through the medium of daily journalism. The king was the least essential element in his political scheme. If it ever came to the point he would have been as expendable as Louis XVI and Marie Antoinette had been for the Counter-revolutionaries. The deafness which afflicted Maurras may have assisted him to isolate himself from political reality and create an illusion of doctrinaire consistency, which he inculcated with remorseless fanaticism for the space of over half a century.

The Action Française recruited its support because it offered a specific for social as well as for political discontents. Its local leadership was often in the hands of members of noble families disgruntled at their elimination from political life, though rarely of the higher aristocracy. Some half of its adherents were professional men, often lawyers, and there was a fair proportion from the lower middle class – shopkeepers, commercial travellers and so on, either attracted by its snob value or finding an outlet for their natural resentment against a society which did not give them the rewards they felt their due.

The student element in the Action Française, at least before the First World War, seems to have been less numerous than the vociferous rowdiness of those who did belong suggested. It was numerous enough, however, to stage impressive student riots in Paris, such as those of the academic year 1908–9, when one M. Thalamas proposed to deliver a course of lectures on what might have been thought the not very provocative subject of pedagogical method. However, several years earlier the same M. Thalamas had distinguished himself by making rude remarks about Jeanne d'Arc, who had been adopted as a sort of nationalist patron saint by the Action Française, and this made him a suitable object for a rather artificial outburst. The Vatican seemed to give its blessing to the proceedings by announcing, in April 1909, the beatification of Jeanne d'Arc.

In spite of the atheism of Maurras and the libertine novels of Daudet, the Action Française won the sympathy of many French Catholics and was treated as an ally by Pius X. The French hierarchy was less certain of the value of its support and a number of French bishops laid an information in Rome against the writings of Maurras. The congregation of the Index could hardly avoid prohibiting them in 1914, but the Pope ordered that the decree should be kept secret and the Action Française continued to retain the allegiance of good Catholics. Moreover the complexion of the hierarchy was gradually being changed under Pius X by the appointment of bishops who were favourable to the movement. On the other hand, the methods by which the Action Française was endeavouring to promote the causes of the monarchy were a little too crude for old-fashioned royalists and in 1910 the Pretender disavowed it. Conservative society was not yet accustomed to the use of irresponsible youth to create rowdy demonstrations, chanting slogans and smashing up private and public property.

In the columns of the *Action Française* an unremitting war was conducted, with all the weapons of slander, denunciation, and incitement to violence, against the Third Republic. The French Marianne, converted by the Bonapartist journalist, Paul de Cassagnac, with the anti-patriotism characteristic of the French right, into *la gueuse* – the slut – was the daily target of venomous darts in

Maurras's journal. The corruption of politicians was a consistent theme, usually in combination with an appeal to the anti-semitism of nationalists and Catholics. Yet in spite of the brilliance of its propaganda the Action Française never became a real political party or more than a merely destructive force. After the First World War, when there were evident signs of the onset of social disintegration, the vultures might gather with better hope, but it would be a mistake to regard the Action Française in the years before 1914 as other than a noisy nuisance and a symbol of dangers to come.

Nationalism in France before the First World War, whether in the form of the Action Française or any other form, was directed primarily against domestic enemies. It became more significant when in place of imaginary foes at home it found real ones abroad, but this situation was slow to develop. The one major external threat to the peaceful progress of the Third Republic was the prospect of war with Germany, and for some time this, despite the nationalist cult of *la revanche*, seemed to be receding. After 1871 France had recovered her position among the Great Powers with remarkable speed. A system of alliances had been built up which enabled her to enter the conference room on equal terms with Germany; and despite the agitation on the right, and a genuine if fading regret for the lost provinces, there was no serious thought of aggressive war to recover them. The international situation, of course, was far too complex to be summed up briefly. All we can do here is to attempt to trace in outline the evolution of French foreign policy under the Third Republic.

In the first years after 1871 clerical agitation kept both Germany and Italy concerned with the possibility of a French attempt at intervention in either country in support of the Roman Catholic Church against the state. Despite the agitation of the bishops this was never a very serious danger, and the republican victory in the elections of 1877 eliminated it as a source of international tension. The condition of almost total isolation that the Republic had inherited from the Second Empire came to an end when French representatives took their seats at the Congress of Berlin.

It was understood, in the course of conversations at the Congress, that the other Powers in Europe would not regard colonial expansion by France as a threat to their security. Indeed, it was felt that the diversion of French interests outside Europe might take the French mind off Alsace-Lorraine and help to stabilize the international situation. Whether or not it actually had this result, the colonial activity of France during the Third Republic was remarkable both for its scope and its success. Yet if the French colonial empire was not acquired in a fit of absence of mind, it can hardly be described as a conscious creation of French government. There was not the machinery for a deliberate and coherent colonial policy. Colonial affairs had been the direct responsibility of the Ministry of the Marine until 1881 when Ferry put them under a sub-department. Only in 1894 did they have a separate ministry of their own, and even then Tunis and Madagascar, as protectorates, as well as the Indo-Chinese colonies, were under the Foreign Office.

A beginning had been made on the re-creation of a colonial empire earlier in the nineteenth century, but only in Algeria had the process been an extensive and continuous one, though punctuated by savagely fought Algerian revolts. After 1871 the European population was increased by the immigration of a considerable number of Alsatians, followed later by Italians, Spaniards, and others. By the end of the century there were some 665,000 Europeans in Algeria, though less than half of these were French in origin. They came to Algeria with different languages and different traditions and if there were to be a policy of assimilation in the colony it needed to be applied to the European immigrants in the first place. At the same time assimilation seemed possible, since there were only some two and a half million native Algerians.

The policy of assimilation was therefore not an unreasonable one. Algeria was divided into three departments and given representation in the parliament at Paris. A major step was taken in 1881, when most of the Algerian public services were put directly under the ministries at Paris. In 1896, however, there was a move in the opposite direction, towards decentralization, which greatly increased the powers of the Governor General at Algiers. The fatal weakness in the policy of assimilation was one that might not have been anticipated in the colonial policy of a state that was secular on principle and often anti-clerical in practice. The essential condition laid down for the extension of political rights to native Algerians was acceptance of the Napoleonic Code. One cannot help wondering how far this was a conscious device for excluding the native population from political rights. It certainly did this, for no follower of Islam could fulfil the prescribed condition. On the other hand the Jews of Algeria, numbering some thirty thousand, had been enfranchised by a decree of October 1870 by Crémieux, which helped to precipitate an Algerian revolt at the time. The new republican government re-pressed it ruthlessly, but the privileged position of the Jews of Algeria was one of the causes of the anti-semitism which was par-ticularly marked there. Possession of the franchise was not a mere symbol of status. It brought with it more specific advantages in law, and with the aid of these, when the French land laws were intro-duced, a large part of the more fertile area was taken over by European settlers. With the coming of phylloxera to France, Alger-ian vineyards developed on a large scale. The benefit was almost wholly to the Europeans. The native Algerian population remained a rural proletariat working the great European *latifundia*.

The establishment of a protectorate in Tunis in the early 'eighties has already been mentioned. The fall of Ferry did not mean the abandonment of colonial ambitions in Indo-China. Cochin-China, Annam, Cambodia, and Tonkin were united under French rule in 1887, Laos being added in 1899. In 1885 a loose protectorate was established in Madagascar, and in 1895 once again a badly pre-pared and unsuccessful military expedition – in which some six thousand out of fifteen thousand young French soldiers died, mostly from fever – proved the prologue to annexation. Farther north, in East Africa, France found a foothold in Djibouti, though trade or discovery did not draw her beyond the coastline there.

In the West it was a very different story. From trading centres in Guinea, the Ivory Coast, Dahomey, and above all from Faidherbe's colony of Senegal, French traders, explorers, missionaries, expedi-tionary forces – not necessarily in that order – extended French rule deep into the interior. After the usual set-back to a premature and inadequate force in 1893, Timbuktu was successfully occupied by a column under a young officer named Joffre.

Although North Africa was a natural area for French expansion, there were other powers in the same field. In 1890 a Franco-British convention fixed a line of demarcation between the respective spheres of interest of the two countries in Africa from the Niger to Lake Chad, in spite of which a point of collision was reached in 1898. A French plan to stake out a claim to the southern Sudan by expeditions from the east and west coasts was only belatedly and inadequately implemented. The leader of the latter expedition landed in July 1896 and struck out from the basin of the Congo in April 1897. Colonel Marchand's foray across the heart of desert Africa, with a handful of French and about a hundred and fifty Senegalese, was a brilliant exploit. By July 1898 his small expedition had reached Fashoda, a strong point of the Sudan, only to be met in September by Kitchener with a British force ten times as large coming down from the north, where he had destroyed a Sudanese army at Omdurman. To send reinforcements to Marchand was practically impossible, and the French Foreign Minister, Delcassé, was not prepared to go to war for the sake of a large area of what Lord Salisbury called light agricultural territory. He was already looking to Great Britain as a potential ally against Germany. Therefore, in spite of popular fury in France, Marchand was given the order to withdraw and French and British zones of influence in the Sudan were delimited.

By now the room for expansion in the extra-European world was much more restricted. In Africa only Morocco remained. French intervention here was to produce a series of international crises. But before this the attention of French governments had been drawn back to Europe. The inherent contradictions in the Bismarckian system made it increasingly difficult for Germany to keep in step with Russia and Austria at the same time. The discontent of Russia with the results of the German alliance provided an opportunity for French diplomacy, as the monetary needs of the Tsarist government did for French finance. In 1888 the Russian government borrowed five hundred million francs on the French market. Other loans followed, promoted with the aid of an extensive Russian-subsidized campaign in the French press. Franco-Russian friendship was further stimulated when, in 1891, the French fleet paid a formal visit to the Russian naval base at Cronstadt, returned by the Russian fleet in the following year. Finally, in January 1894, a Franco-Russian defensive alliance was announced. The *rapprochement* with Russia was immensely popular in France which no longer felt itself isolated. Though it was a natural and inevitable reply to the Bismarckian system of anti-French alliances, it is not quite so obvious now as it seemed at the time that the Russian alliance was ultimately in the interests of France. Even then some feared that – like Austria in the eighteenth century – Russia might turn the alliance to her own exclusive interests without any consideration for her ally; and that if she made a serious mistake she might drag France into an un-necessary war with her. Such doubts hardly existed in 1896 and 1897, when the Tsar and the French President exchanged highly successful visits.

After this, France was swallowed up in the Dreyfus affair and its sequel, and too preoccupied with the domestic problem to pay much attention to foreign affairs. They remained for seven years, under five successive premiers, in charge of the same Foreign Minister. This was Delcassé, small, dark, short, a provincial from the remote Pyrenees, apparently insignificant, bureaucratic, but immensely hard-working, pertinacious and secretive, and above all, a passionate enemy of Germany, determined to build up a counter to the now decaying Bismarckian system. His aim was, without damaging the Russian connection, to bring Great Britain into the French alliance, to restore friendship with Italy, and to consolidate the French position in the Mediterranean by securing control of Morocco. Only Delcassé's unreasonable optimism could have conceived the possibility of achieving such incompatible ends. If he did achieve them it was partly owing to the maladroitness of German diplomacy, and partly owing to the skill with which his chief agents executed his policy in the capitals of Europe.

The Third Republic had a brilliant corps of diplomats, notably the two Cambon brothers – Paul at London from 1898 to 1920, Jules at Berlin from 1907 until his ambassadorial career there was brought to an abrupt end in 1914. Launched into the Foreign Service by Ferry, they bore a name that evoked memories of the Convention, the First French Republic and the struggle of the year I.

Another great ambassador, who had been given his start by Gambetta, was Camille Barère, at Rome from 1897 to 1922. A further element in Delcassé's success was that he had the work of his predecessor at the Quai d'Orsay, Gabriel Hanotaux, to build on. Hanotaux's achievements have hardly received adequate recognition, but it was Hanotaux who took the essential steps towards the alliance with Russia and the first step to the *rapprochement* with Italy. In 1898, when Delcassé became Foreign Minister, France had already taken the first moves towards what was to be a major diplomatic revolution.

The success with Russia was followed up, in 1900, by a secret understanding with Italy. France agreed that Italy should have a free hand in Tripoli, in return for Italian recognition of French interests in Morocco. In 1902, when Italy renewed the Triple Alliance with the Central Powers, a further secret declaration promised that she would not join in any aggressive action against France. Thus by 1902 Russia was an ally, and Italy was in effect neutralized in any future Franco-German conflict.

Relations with Great Britain presented a more difficult problem. The key to the situation was Morocco, artificially preserved in its native state of anarchy by British concern that no other great Power should hold the southern shore of the Straits of Gibraltar. French intervention there could only take place by agreement with Great Britain, but the British government, uneasily conscious of its isolation at the time of the Boer War, was looking towards Germany, while French opinion was violently Anglophobe. Fashoda was not quickly forgotten. The right-wing press alternated anti-British and anti-semitic cartoons, repulsive enough to have satisfied the most exacting demands of the Nazis, who did indeed make use of them in their propaganda forty years later. Delcassé's approaches to the British government had therefore to be made cautiously and under cover, by way of the French ambassador in London, Paul Cambon. An exchange of visits by Edward VII and the French President Loubet in 1903 did something to replace the mutual hostility of their two countries by a more cordial atmosphere. In 1904, behind the innocuous terms of a diplomatic expression of friendship, the Entente Cordiale, were negotiated secret clauses by which France and

Great Britain recognized each other's freedom of action respectively in Egypt and Morocco. Even more significant for the future were the accompanying military and naval conversations, though it is doubtful if the British government realized at the time, or even much later, how far they committed it.

The change in the international atmosphere, and the restoration of France to an effective weight in the diplomatic balance, was revealed in the successive crises, provoked mainly by Germany, over the Moroccan situation. To the German government it seemed that the time had come to put a limit to the rapid improvement in France's international position. The defeat of France's ally Russia in the Far East, and the unrest produced in the French army by the policy of the Combes government, apparently provided a favourable moment for intervention. The Emperor Wilhelm II was therefore sent to Tangier, where he insisted, in a speech that was calculated to resound through Europe, on the independence of the Sultan and the maintenance of German interests in Morocco. This was in effect a demand that France should repudiate the policy of Delcassé, who was prepared to accept the challenge by a formal rejection of the German *démarche*. The Chamber was less bellicose and did not support his demand for an uncompromising reply. Moreover his influence in parliament, which he had almost totally abandoned for work in his bureaux, had greatly diminished. The German government therefore had the satisfaction of having forced his resignation. It was a Pyrrhic victory, for an international conference, held at Algeciras in 1906, recognized as well as the general international interest in Morocco the primary role of France there.

This was a rebuff to Germany, which had gained nothing by her bellicose gesture, and the progressive military occupation of Morocco by French troops continued. In 1908 an affair of German deserters from the French Foreign Legion produced another international incident, without any serious consequences this time. In 1911, a further French military advance brought the sending of the German gunboat, the *Panther*, to Agadir, to reinforce a German demand for territorial compensation in the French Congo. The international situation, which up to this point had never been more than a minor sub-plot in the history of the Third Republic, now takes the centre of the stage. Three times, in 1905, 1908, and 1911, Germany had rattled the sabre – not, it is true, without some cause on each occasion, but the effect was cumulative. In 1911 the French and German Foreign Offices were prepared to work up a nice little war between them, but the French Premier Caillaux and the German Foreign Minister Kiderlen-Wächter chose to compromise: Germany recognized a French protectorate in Morocco, and France ceded part of the Cameroons to Germany, to the fury of the nationalists on both sides.

Nationalist agitation in France was now directed against external as well as internal enemies. The international crisis of 1911 marks a real turning-point in French politics. Already in February 1911, with the defeat of Briand's ministry, the dominance of the great republican bloc, which Waldeck-Rousseau had gathered behind him when he formed his cabinet in 1899, had come to an end. The influence of the Union Républicaine Démocratique, founded in 1903 and led by Louis Marin, was increasing. Representing Catholic and conservative France, and backed by much of the landed and industrial wealth of the country, it provided a responsible rallying-point for the more sober elements of the right. But even these were undergoing the influence of Action Française propaganda, which had an effect well beyond the circles that accepted the political creed of Maurras and Daudet. Through its influence in the world of letters it was changing the spirit of *tout Paris*, as Roger Martin du Gard shows in his novel *Jean Barois*.

The vociferous nationalist minority which seemed to dominate Paris society and journalism was, of course, far from representative of France. On the left there was a strong vein of pacifism and internationalism, which had been one of the reasons why the Socialists abandoned the left-wing alliance in 1905. French intervention in Morocco did not go unopposed in France; the Russo-Japanese war suggested that the Russian ally might be a liability; the suppression of the revolution of 1905 alienated the Socialists, and the money the Tsarist government was known to spend on the French press did not conciliate them. The leading spokesman of Socialist pacifism, Gustave Hervé, was a former teacher, who had set out on a demagogic career which was to bring him in the end to near-Fascist

D

journalism and the authorship of *C'est Pétain qu'il nous faut.* This was a long way ahead. Before the First World War, he was editor of *La Guerre Sociale.* 'Notre patrie', he wrote, 'c'est notre classe', and called for revolution if mobilization were proclaimed. This was only an exaggerated statement of a common illusion of the left. Jaurès, who did not go so far, himself believed that the international action of Socialism could prevent the outbreak of war.

The moderate and the right-wing parties are hardly to be blamed if they did not share these optimistic illusions. It did not require any very great foresight to be alarmed about the international situation by 1912. A left-wing cabinet under Caillaux found a compromise solution to the international crisis of 1911, but Caillaux was not the man to cope adequately with any major crisis, domestic or foreign. Son of a cabinet minister, recruited into the bureaucratic elite of the Inspectors of Finances, at an early age Minister of Finances in the great Waldeck-Rousseau government, in Caillaux technical ability and a powerful intelligence were combined with fatal conceit, ambition, intolerance and a weakness – surprising in one who was by birth a member of the republican elite – for hob-nobbing with shady characters in journalism and politics. He had no love for his fellow politicians and they had little for him. For his loss of office in January 1912, however, he was hardly to blame: the reasonable compromise he had found for the international crisis drove the nationalists to fury.

Foreign policy was now increasingly pushing domestic issues into the background, and the Chamber turned to a very different type of politician to lead a government of national union. Raymond Poincaré, lawyer cousin of the mathematician Henri, belonged to a University and Polytechnic family. Deputy in 1887 and senator in 1903, he was profoundly conservative but counted as a man of the left since he was also an anti-clerical. He had the nationalist sentiments of a Lorrainer. Aloof, cold and unsympathetic – Curzon, worsted in a diplomatic encounter after the First World War, was to call him 'that horrid little man' – Poincaré was one of the great technocrats of the Republic. He had intellectual powers at least equal to those of Caillaux, and combined them with a rarer personal integrity and an inexorable pursuit of the policy he thought right for his country. His reputation, and his combination of nationalism with anti-clericalism, and republicanism with conservative social views, made him the essential man for the situation. His premiership in January 1912 was only a step to the presidency, to which he was elected with the support of the right by a majority of 483 to 296 in January 1913.

The international sky continued to darken. Before the threat of growing German military power it seemed necessary to increase the period of conscription in France to three years. This had been reduced to two years in 1905, though – since the previous term of three years had been riddled with exceptions for those who possessed educational qualifications, which in effect had meant those from the better-off sections of society – this had not involved as great a reduction in man-power as might have been supposed. The bitter conservative resentment at the reduction to two years, along with a removal of the exemptions, was therefore not entirely on patriotic grounds. In spite of the energetic opposition by Jaurès and Caillaux, a law was passed in August 1913 prescribing three years' service, with seven years in the territorial army and a further seven years in the reserve.

The question that now arose was how the necessary rearmament was to be paid for. This produced an even bitterer controversy. The French bourgeoisie remained, like its predecessors of the *noblesse*, willing to sacrifice everything rather than accept a more equitable system of taxation. Caillaux's attempt to revive the income tax proposals of 1909 added to the intense hatred which he gained from the right by opposing the three-years law. A fanfare of wrath, probably orchestrated by Poincaré from the Élysée, blew round his head. His own capacity for equivocation and making enemies did not help him. Ruin came when Mme Caillaux assassinated the editor of *Le Figaro*, who had played a leading part in a very dirty campaign against her husband including the publication of early love-letters.

Judging by the press and Paris, France was on the point of being carried away on a wave of nationalist and bellicose ardour. The legislative elections that came in 1914 revealed the true sentiments of the country. Joint opposition to the three-years law on the part of

Radicals and Socialists brought them together again in a revived left-wing bloc. The noisy nationalists of *tout Paris* kept the support of the traditional conservative and Catholic crescent stretching round from the Vendée, through Brittany and Normandy, with a gap in the industrial regions of the north-east, but strengthening again in the border departments of the east. For once there was a clear-cut issue between left and right, and the line of cleavage was not confused, as was more usual, by an active clerical and anti-clerical issue. The right set up Caillaux as a bogey-man, with his *grand fonctionnaire* personality and association with high finance, which went so ill with his presidency of the Radical Socialist party. Opposition to the three-years law was denounced as unpatriotic. On the other hand the left was at least excusable in believing the seriousness of the international situation to be exaggerated when it found the right unwilling to pay an extra sou for the defence of the country. The election proved that even in the existing state of international tension French opinion was profoundly pacific and non-aggressive. Memories of 1870 were fading, colonial conquests only really interested a minority, the political consolidation of the Republic seemed completed and the task of social reform ready to begin. To the left, the threat of war was obviously a fifth ace smuggled into the hand of the right and smacked triumphantly on the table to take the electoral trick; the idealistic Radicals and Socialists refused to believe it could be true. The country was so little warlike that it agreed with them. The result of the elections was a victory for the left, with 104 United Socialists, 24 Republican Socialists, and 172 Radicals and Radical Socialists. On the right were 37 members of the Republican Federation, 23 Liberal Action, 15 Right, and 44 Independents, 119 in all. The centre and the centre left included 66 Radical Left, 23 Republican Radical Socialist Union, 7 'Dissidents', 53 Republicans of the Left, and 32 Democratic Left, making a floating vote of 181. This catalogue well illustrates the leading features of the French political system: the dominance of the group system; the bias to the left, so strong that the real left only began where parties ceased to label themselves as such; the inability of the members of the extreme right to present a coherent programme and their disposition to disguise themselves as independents; and the disproportionate influence that could be exercised by small groups in the – perhaps literally – dead centre of French politics, which were in a position, by throwing their votes on one side or the other, to bargain for office and set up and destroy governments at will.

The intense political struggle going on inside France was dramatically demonstrated now by the appearance and disappearance, in a single day, of the shortest of all the short-lived governments of the Third Republic. When the conservative Ribot presented his cabinet to the Chamber, on June 12th, 1914, it was immediately shouted out of office by the parties of the left.

An unusual element in the political situation at this time was the presence of a President who was not content with the normal restricted role of his office. Despite the verdict of the electorate Poincaré was determined to maintain the three-years law. After failing to obtain a premier from the right, he accepted Viviani, now a member of a small group mid-way between the Radicals and the Socialists, who agreed not to press for the immediate reversal of the law on condition of the Senate's lifting its *non possumus* on the income tax. The tax was in fact voted in principle, though the details were not to be worked out until 1917, by which time France had accumulated a colossal burden of war debt. With the three-years law respited, President and Premier, on July 16th, took ship for a state visit to the Tsar arranged earlier in the year.

Nobody knew that the event that was to lead to the First World War had already occurred. On June 28th, 1914, a Jugoslav criminal, or nationalist, brutally murdered the Austrian Archduke Francis Ferdinand and his wife at Serajevo. The situation evolved at first slowly, while the peaceful populations of Europe went about their work and their pleasures in the warm summer weather. It seemed that this crisis would be got over, as had so many others in the recent past, peacefully; but there were those, in Vienna and Berlin, who thought otherwise. When Poincaré and Viviani left Russia, on July 23rd, their visit concluded, they did not yet know of the Austrian ultimatum, on the same day, to Servia.

It is not necessary to summarize here the fatal events of July 1914, through most of which France could only stand by and watch passively the moves on the international board that were pushing her helplessly and inexorably into war. That the most pacific Chamber the country had ever known should have led France into a World War was ironic. One might be tempted to transfer the blame back earlier on to that policy of the Russian alliance which tied France to the support of her Russian ally; but in fact the struggle of the great military despotisms of Germany and Austria-Hungary against Russia was written on the tablets of fate – or avoidable only on the supposition of quite different governments in the three countries. In such a struggle Russia was bound to be defeated, and to assume that after this victory the Reich would abandon the path of conquest, and that the German eagle would settle peacefully on its perch, side by side with the rather clamorous but essentially domesticated Gallic cock, would have been to expect the impossible. Whether France would stick to her alliance with Russia, and equally what the entente with England would amount to in practice, did not really concern the directors of German strategic policy. They viewed British military potential with contempt, and the French, even if they got as far as honouring their commitments to Russia, as a decadent race of immoral artists and corrupt politicians incapable of standing up to the *furor Teutonicus*. It was to be a short war. The great German General Staff had its Schlieffen plan, according to which the German army, by disregarding an old and therefore obsolete treaty of neutrality and marching through Belgium – obviously a justifiable measure because Belgium could offer little serious opposition – would be able to turn the flank of the French army and crush resistance within a few weeks.

On July 28th Austria-Hungary declared war on Servia. The next day Poincaré and Viviani landed at Dunkirk. On July 31st Germany, having issued an ultimatum to Russia, called on France to declare what she would do in the event of war between Germany and Russia. This seemed a clever move: if France replied with a declaration that she would stand in shining armour beside Russia (as Wilhelm II had in relation to Austria-Hungary a few years earlier) this could be presented as a threat of aggression; if, on the other hand, the French offered to remain neutral, then Germany intended to demand the occupation of Toul and Verdun as a guarantee. Viviani escaped the trap by replying evasively that France would consult her interests. Public opinion was now becoming excited in all countries. In France, mounting nationalist fervour, fed by years of irresponsible agitation, led to the assassination of Jaurès by a fanatic, but there was no widespread agitation for war. Small chauvinist demonstrations were easily suppressed by the police. *La revanche*, or the thought of recovering Alsace-Lorraine, hardly entered into the mind of the French people, whose only hope was for the preservation of peace. The government had one other concern: what would be the attitude of Great Britain if Germany attacked? The entente, even the military and naval conversations, were far from binding her to intervene. A personal letter from the French President to King George V asked for an assurance that Great Britain would not remain neutral if the Central Powers attacked France, but the British government refused to commit itself. The probability is that the German and Austro-Hungarian General Staffs were already so far determined on war, and that such civilian opposition as there was in high places in Germany had been so effectively stifled, that no action by the British could have prevented war; but it was a reasonable conclusion for the French to draw after the catastrophe that a clear statement of the British position (which unfortunately was far from clear) might have averted it. This was to have much influence on French policy after 1918.

The French government could only wait on the course of events and take such precautions as were possible to safeguard itself from any possible charge of French aggression. When the French cabinet acceded to the demand of the General Staff that covering troops be sent to the frontier, on July 30th, it was on condition that they be kept ten kilometres behind it, to prevent the development of any incidents. The Commander-in-Chief, Joffre, agreed to this, though he protested strongly against the failure to call up reservists and the order that only those troops who could do so by moving on foot should take up their war-time stations. Meanwhile military preparations for war were rapidly and inexorably proceeding in Central and Eastern Europe. On August 1st the French government issued the order for general mobilization. On August 2nd Germany occupied Luxembourg and German patrols crossed the French frontier.

Joffre was now given freedom of action, but while ordering the repulsion of incursions into French territory, he instructed his commanders not to pursue enemy troops into Germany. He believed that the Germans would attack France without a declaration of war, as indeed they did, but not from the direction anticipated. In 1914 there was still a general expectation that treaties would be kept until they were formally denounced. It is difficult to think back now to a time when the German disregard of Belgian neutrality was regarded as a shattering blow to normal conventions of international behaviour, something that no other great Power – or so it was believed and perhaps rightly then – could have done, or hardly so blatantly. On August 2nd the German government demanded the right of passage for its troops through Belgium, on the ground of its knowledge of French plans to invade Germany from the same quarter. This was a patent lie. The next day Germany declared war on France, alleging with equal mendacity French attacks on Germany. German policy had achieved what a little earlier would have seemed the impossible – a stubborn if hopeless Belgian resistance to the German army, a declaration of war by Great Britain on August 4th, and the entry of France into the war with total national unity from extreme right to extreme left. The Third Republic in 1914 had no Fifth Column.

In the armed camp that Europe had become in 1914, with the atmosphere of tension created by the irresponsible nationalists of all countries, and given the interlocking and opposed systems of alliances, it is all too easy, and correct in a sense, to present the outbreak of the First World War as the result of an international anarchy to which all countries contributed, and the responsibility for which was so divided that if there were any guilt all were equally guilty. To the French in 1914 this would have seemed nonsense. They understood, for they had been through a struggle over the same issue themselves, that Germany was a country where the General Staff could override the civil authorities, and the executive was largely independent of the legislature; its government had repeatedly used the threat of war as a diplomatic instrument. Other countries had their wild men. France was particularly afflicted by the 'integral nationalist', anti-semitic, war-mongering elements in the conservative and Catholic sectors of opinion; but the pacifist and defensive sentiments which prevailed in French policy on the eve of the First World War reflected a general national temper, which had gradually risen to dominance with the triumph and consolidation of the democratic Republic. It was difficult for civilized, humane men of the stamp of Jaurès to believe that the rulers of a great European Power could be so wicked or irresponsible, and their subjects so passively obedient, as to plan and put into operation, or accept without question, a major war. More pessimistically, a Delcassé or a Poincaré had believed in the inherent aggressiveness of the German state; but their contribution to the increase in French defensive capacity, in arms and allies, was in no way intended as a preliminary to starting a war on Germany. This is not to deny that the increasing strength of France and her allies was an important factor in provoking war, for 1914 seemed to the Central Powers perhaps the last moment at which it might be launched with a maximum prospect of rapid success. It is difficult to see what France could have done that would have averted the war, short of repudiating her treaty bonds with Russia and recognizing German military and political hegemony over Europe. This was not contemplated in 1914. No one could have been expected to know that the coming struggle, and even ultimate victory, would be almost as fatal to the ideals and achievements of the Third Republic as defeat could have been.

Though developments in the years before 1914 foreshadowed the change that was coming, it was the First World War that marked the turning-point in the history of the Third Republic, and in a sense the end of its greatness. Henceforth it was to live in the shadow of war and rumours of wars. Social cohesion and political stability were to vanish in the civil discord and social hatreds bred by a climate of international war and revolution. As Marcel Proust had felt, something was indeed coming to an end. Looking back, we can see in retrospect that what was ending was a great age in the history of France.

CHAPTER TWO

THE FIRST WORLD WAR

ON the outbreak of war Poincaré's call for a *union sacrée* met
with practically universal acceptance. All divisions in the
nation disappeared. Monarchists and republicans, employers,
workers and peasants, rich and poor, united in defence of the
patrie. The peace-time battle of clerical and anti-clerical was forgotten. Priests joined up and fought side by side with laity. Most
remarkable of all, defeat was not followed by the cry of 'Nous
sommes trahis'. There was no Fifth Column: that was an improvement of a later age. The notorious *carnet B*, containing the names
of all the supposed dangerous revolutionaries in France, whom it
was proposed to arrest and intern in the event of war, was wisely
left undisturbed in the files of the Ministry of the Interior. The
Socialists sang the 'Marseillaise'; Gustave Hervé praised patriotism;
the tradition of Jacobin patriotism was invoked by Édouard
Vaillant, Communard and Blanquist of 1871.

The man of the moment was the Commander-in-Chief, Joffre,
appointed in 1911 as a moderate republican general, rock-like in
appearance, stolid and unemotional in manner. The son of a cooper,
he was evidence of the possibility of *la carrière ouverte aux talents*
even in the army. Not lacking in the intellectual qualities needed
to gain a place in the École Polytechnique, he was endowed with a
peasant shrewdness that was to enable him to meet and often beat
the politicians at their own game. Above all he was a man who gave
the impression of being reliable. He shared, of course, the views on
the nature of the coming war and the correct policy for the French
army that prevailed in the General Staff. Something more than the
normal decline of a peace-time army is needed to explain the thrice-
repeated – in 1870, 1914 and 1940 – failure of the French General
Staff to judge correctly the nature of the war which each time it
believed to be coming and for which it was preparing. In 1914 it

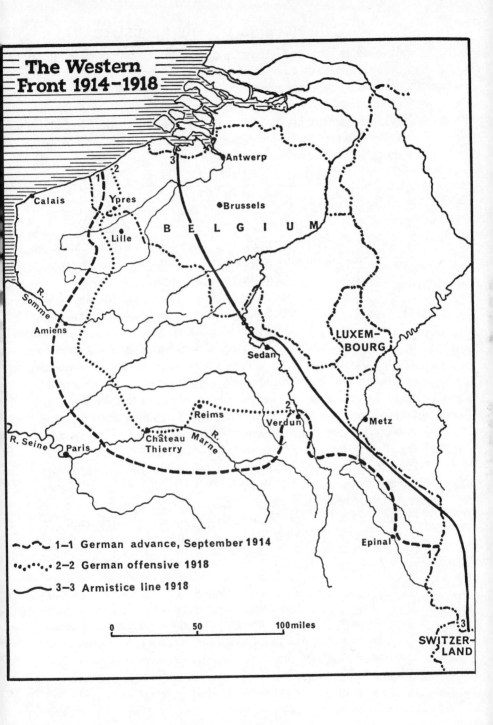

The Western
Front 1914–1918

Antwerp

Calais

Ypres

Brussels

Lille

B E L G I U M

R.
Somme

Amiens

LUXEM-
BOURG

Sedan

Reims

Verdun

Metz

R. Seine

Paris

Château
Thierry

Marne

R.

Epinal

~~~ 1–1 German advance, September 1914

•••••• 2–2 German offensive 1918

—— 3–3 Armistice line 1918

0   50   100 miles

SWITZER-
LAND

calculated, as also the Germans did, on a short war, which could be won by a sharp, decisive offensive.

The most influential theorist of the General Staff, Colonel de Grandmaison, had inculcated the doctrine of the *offensive à outrance*. In accordance with his strategic teaching, the French army began the war by advancing into German-occupied Lorraine and Alsace, across a hilly and wooded terrain that gave all the advantages to the defensive. For a brief moment Mulhouse was taken, only to be rapidly lost again. The German artillery once more exhibited a crushing superiority. Meanwhile the Germans, recognizing that their direct route into France was blocked by the great French fortresses, took the easier route through Belgium, which in the circumstances they regarded as morally forced on them, and after a brief delay they swept under Von Kluck into northern France.

Before the mounting military threat Viviani strengthened his cabinet and made it truly a government of national union, by calling Delcassé to the Ministry of Foreign Affairs, Millerand to the Ministry of War, Briand to Justice, and bringing in Guesde and another Socialist. The government needed all the strength it could get. Kluck was approaching so close to Paris that, to avoid a repetition of 1870, on September 1st the government left for Bordeaux, where it was to stay for some three months. There was no suggestion of yielding. If any defeatists existed in France they were silent and there were no pro-Germans, so different was the situation from what it was to be in 1940. Again unlike the later campaign, the armies maintained their cohesion, and the general kept his head and never lost control of the situation. On September 5th Galliéni, in command of the troops defending Paris, saw the opportunity to counter-attack. Joffre let him loose on the right flank of the advancing Germans and the battle of the Marne saved Paris. There followed the 'race to the sea', the consolidation of the front from the Alps to the beaches, and the beginning of what no one yet knew was to be four years of exhausting trench warfare. France, in the first four months, had lost in dead, missing, wounded, or prisoners some 850,000 men, and had yielded up some of her most important industrial and agricultural areas to enemy possession.

Despite the experience of 1914 the French General Staff

continued to be dominated by the mystique of the offensive. In 1915 the 'young Turks' of Joffre's headquarters adopted the policy of what was called a 'war of attrition' by launching continual petty attacks on the enemy. Since the offensive was invariably more costly than the defensive, it is fairly clear which army was being worn down by this policy. Governmental nerves also were becoming frayed, and in October 1915 internal differences of opinion, and criticisms from outside, brought about the fall of the Viviani cabinet. Briand took over the premiership, still at the head of a broad coalition preserving the *union sacrée*.

But politics was now beginning to re-emerge and affect the conduct of the war. In 1915 Joffre, finding that one of his generals, Sarrail, after an early success, was involved in serious reverses, and moreover was intriguing against his commander-in-chief, removed him from his command. Sarrail was later to be compensated by a command on the Balkan front, where his ill luck followed him; but unfortunately he was the model of a republican, anti-clerical general, and his dismissal brought the Radicals and Socialists on to the battle-field, politically speaking, in defence of their hero.

The next year, 1916, was the year of Verdun. In February a massive German attack on the Verdun salient was launched. It was a cleverly worked out strategic move. The great fortress was in an exposed situation and would be expensive to defend; but the Germans had studied history and knew that Verdun had a particular meaning for France. By making it their main objective they could practically force the French army to defend it, because of the moral value of its retention and the pessimism that would be engendered by its loss. In spite of this the French High Command had not taken the steps that seemed called for if Verdun were to be treated as a vital position. Joffre, with his usual common sense, was probably prepared to abandon it and shorten the French line when the Germans had paid a sufficient price. Briand, however, knew that the fall of Verdun would not only seriously affect French morale, it would also be fatal to his government. He gave the order to defend Verdun at all costs, and the defence was conducted with a skill, stubbornness, and heroism that made the reputation of General Philippe Pétain. However, the German High Command had achieved its object of enticing the French to sacrifice their man-power for the purpose of holding a fortress of mainly symbolic value. It was the war of attrition in reverse, applied with Teutonic thoroughness. France was to be 'bled white' at Verdun. German losses were also heavy but, starting the war with a population of sixty-six millions against the French thirty-nine millions, the German Command doubtless thought it could better afford exten-sive blood-letting. By the time the German attack had worn itself out each army had lost about a quarter of a million men in the fighting. In July, to relieve the pressure, Joffre began a counter-offensive on the Somme, which gained a little territory; the Allied and German armies lost another half-million men between them in this sector.

The continuous and calamitous loss of life, to no apparent gain, inevitably had its effect on the national spirit. By the end of 1916 disillusionment was widespread. A change of leadership was psychologically necessary and a veiled press campaign was launched against Joffre, who for all his cunning was no match for Briand. The responsibility for the carnage of Verdun was gently but firmly placed on the General's shoulders. When his prestige was sufficiently undermined he was promoted chief military adviser to the govern-ment, in which post he was ignored and from which he soon resigned. The new Commander-in-Chief of the French armies on the Western Front was to be General Nivelle, who had achieved a number of tactical successes and was affable and popular with the politicians. He was believed, and probably believed himself, to have the secret which had evaded Joffre of breaking the enemy line.

Briand's victory over Joffre did not enable his government to hold out much longer. He fell in March 1917 and was replaced by an elderly, conservative nonentity, Ribot. The first measure of the new government was to approve a great offensive projected by Nivelle. The previous War Minister, Lyautey, the great colonial admini-strator, whose political maladroitness had in fact brought Briand's ministry down, had not concealed his belief that Nivelle's plans were mad. Lyautey's successor in the War Ministry, the mathe-matician Painlevé, was himself profoundly sceptical; but Nivelle, asked to modify or postpone his offensive, threatened to resign.

Ribot, who saw that this would involve the fall of his government, and Poincaré, who believed in generals, supported him. Although every sane calculation was against it and Nivelle's plan was, in the words of Lyautey, only suitable for the army of the Grand Duchess of Gerolstein, he was allowed to go ahead with it and walk into the trap laid by the Germans, who by now, after all the discussions between politicians and generals, knew the details of the coming offensive almost as well as the French themselves.

The German commander Ludendorff laid his plans for the antici- pated French offensive by preparing a defensive line to withdraw to. On April 16th, having been delayed for a week by torrential rain, which reduced the fields to a quagmire and should by itself have caused the offensive to be called off, the misconceived, mis- conducted French advance began. Their peasant armies moved forward across devastated territory, with its houses blown up or booby-trapped, wells poisoned, and even fruit trees sawn off, sights which were not calculated to weaken the increasing bitterness with which the war was being fought, until they came up against the impassable obstacle of the so-called Hindenburg line, against which Nivelle flung his troops in senseless and apparently endless slaughter.

Painlevé, who was struggling to remove the amiable, incom- petent, obstinate general from his command and bring the offensive to an end, found himself opposed on all sides. The anti-clerical Minister of the Interior, Malvy, supported Nivelle because he was a Protestant and likely to be succeeded by a Catholic, the British General Haig because the offensive helped to concentrate the fighting on the Western Front where Haig was in command and avoid 'side-shows', Poincaré because he had committed himself, in the face of warnings, to the Nivelle plan. But in the end the evidence of continued and useless loss of life was irresistible. On May 15th Painlevé succeeded in removing Nivelle. He was replaced by Pétain, who was known to prefer the defensive, with Foch as Chief of Staff. The team had been found that, after waiting while waiting was necessary until France's allies had filled the gaps left by a death roll of well over a million men since 1914, was in due course to win the war.

Despite military mistakes, the Third Republic had stood the test of the most appalling of wars with remarkable cohesion and constancy. Even Verdun and the Somme had not produced more than a demand for a change in leadership. After the pointless massacres of Nivelle's offensive the crack came. In May 1917 scattered mutinies broke out. Pétain dealt with a critical situation with intelligence, tact, firmness, and humanity. He established personal contact with as many units as he could, improved the troops' conditions so far as was possible, limited the military operations that had to be undertaken, minimized losses, and restored discipline at the cost of no more than twenty-three executions of mutineers.

Equally dangerous unrest, developing in civilian quarters, was exposed to the public gaze in a series of political scandals. A campaign against the alliance with Great Britain, against the President, and surreptitiously against the war, was appearing in the press. A minor left-wing journal called *Le Bonnet rouge*, edited by a journalistic adventurer named Vigo-Almereyda, took a prominent part in this campaign. The *Action Française*, with information supplied by police headquarters, in its turn attacked *Le Bonnet rouge*, aided by a League against subversive forces which operated from its offices, to preside over which General Mercier, of Dreyfus-affair notoriety, was brought out of his well-deserved obscurity. Behind *Le Bonnet rouge* the real objectives of the attack were the Radical ministers, Malvy and Caillaux, who were suspected of being prepared for a negotiated peace. In fact Malvy's ministry had bribed *Le Bonnet rouge*, like some other papers, early in the war, to keep it quiet. He stopped his subsidies when it began anti-war propaganda but German money probably took its place. In July 1917 Clemenceau used this connection to launch an attack on Malvy in the Senate. Almereyda was arrested, and in the curious way that more than once happened with arrested persons who know too much for the good of the state apparently strangled himself, with a boot-lace or a piece of string, in his cell. Malvy, however, had to resign.

Trouble did not end there. A deputy was discovered with a large packet of Swiss francs, for the possession of which he could give no explanation. There followed the cases of an absurd adventurer named Bolo, supplied with German money to spread defeatist propaganda, and the dramatized woman spy Mata Hari. In November the Painlevé cabinet, tarred with all these scandals and in its turn charged with weakness, was overthrown.

Something more serious was at issue than the machinations of petty German agents and spies. The belief had begun to spread, especially among the parties of the left, that a negotiated peace was the only alternative to endless, meaningless slaughter. The idea of a common humanity and unity among the workers of the world, roughly shaken when the German Socialists wheeled into line behind their government's aggression in 1914, was reviving. The Russian Revolution aroused an idealistic echo in the West; but when an international Socialist congress was called at Stockholm to attempt mediation between the warring nations, the French Socialists were refused passports to attend. They now left the Sacred Union and gave up participation in the government. Industrial strikes, which had hitherto been conspicuously absent, began to develop. Caillaux, re-emerging into political life, with characteristic lack of tact prematurely spoke in public of the possibility of a compromise peace. Even Briand was not unsympathetic to the idea of eventual negotiations with Germany. Reason and humanity suggested that at least the possibility should be explored, though passion and politics prohibited it. The age of slogans had come upon the warring world – the war to end wars could not be abandoned half-won; the propaganda-mongers were caught in their own toils. It must also be recognized that German policy now brought its nemesis: what trust could be put in a regime that had launched a World War by flagrant aggression and justified it by blatant mendacity? Moreover, the recovery of Alsace-Lorraine had now become a war aim for France and only total defeat would bring a German government to envisage this. It might be said that, in spite of all this, nothing would have been lost by allowing the enemy to expose his intransigence, but any willingness to contemplate a compromise peace was interpreted as weakness. Pétain, asked by the President if he could keep his troops under control should there be discussions with the Germans at Stockholm – a loaded question – replied firmly, No. The *Action Française* began to resume its characteristic activity with a charge by Léon Daudet that the ex-Minister of the Interior, Malvy, had betrayed French battle-plans to the Germans.

The lead among those who were determined that there should be no negotiated peace was taken by the old 'tiger' of French politics, Clemenceau, now aged seventy-six. He was an isolated figure, cut off from all parties by temperament and the bitter struggles of the past, and belonging to a different generation. His incessant attacks on the conduct of the war, in the parliament and in the pages of his paper *L'Homme libre*, renamed under war censorship *L'Homme enchaîné*, marked him out in the public mind as the man who could put things right. Poincaré, with his usual clear-sightedness, saw that a choice had to be made, either Caillaux or Clemenceau, and though he hated Clemenceau, he hated Caillaux and the idea of peace without victory even more. He called Clemenceau to office. The prospect of a compromise peace was at an end, though it is impossible to believe that the German General Staff, now on the eve of its greatest victory in the East, would have contemplated such a peace in the West.

The new premier turned on the would-be negotiators – defeatists, to use the language of the time – savagely. Briand received a fright which sent him into retirement until the war was over; Malvy was put on trial; Caillaux, arrested and charged with intelligence with the enemy, was to stay in prison for two years. Many lesser actual or alleged 'pro-Germans' experienced attacks in which personal enmities were given ample scope, and accusations of treachery were flung about wildly. The right wing welcomed these steps, which brought the needed temporary unity, but also introduced a cleavage into French politics more permanent and deeper than had been known since the struggle over Dreyfus.

So far as winning the war, or not losing it, was concerned, Clemenceau had not come to power too soon. He was his own War Minister and collected round him a cabinet of nonentities: he described them as the geese who by their cackling saved Rome. The situation when he assumed office seemed desperate. In December 1917 an armistice was signed on the Eastern Front and the German Command was free to concentrate its forces on the West, where American reinforcements were only slowly arriving. In March

1918 the Ludendorff offensive drove deep into the Allied lines. An attempt, earlier in the year, to take the first step towards a badly needed unity of command over the Allied armies, by putting the most widely respected French general, Foch, in charge of a Reserve Force for the whole front, had been frustrated by an unholy alliance between Haig and Pétain, concerned with their own prestige. When the German break-through came, Pétain's deep temperamental pessimism seemed likely to prohibit a vigorous reaction; but the situation was now so obviously critical that the political leaders were able to impose Foch as supreme commander over both the jealous generals. From March to July Ludendorff desperately let loose offensive after offensive, penetrating as deep into the Allied lines as Château-Thierry and the Marne. Foch bided his time, stoically supported by Clemenceau. At last, on July 18th, he began the counter-offensive, which was not to stop until the German army had been driven back to its own frontier and on November 11th accepted an armistice.

It was, or it seemed to be, the most glorious hour in the history of the Third Republic. France had borne the brunt of the struggle against the military power of the German Reich and had survived with her national life, her ideals, and her institutions intact. The Republic had emerged triumphant from the severest of all tests, though at a cost that in the moment of triumph was hardly realized. Part of the price of victory had already been paid in some million and a quarter military, and half a million civilian dead or soon to die, and three-quarters of a million permanently injured; in the invaded departments looted and devastated; and in a national debt of huge proportions. The price was to continue to be paid for another generation in the loss of the high hopes which might reasonably have been held in the opening decade of the twentieth century.

In 1918, on the morrow of victory, such pessimism would have seemed absurd. Looking back one can see that a good peace was inconceivable. That the peace was as bad as it proved to be may be attributed partly to the degradation of the public spirit in all the belligerent countries that resulted from the punitive death roll of the war, and the vicious and mendacious propaganda that had been used as a major weapon on all sides; partly to the fact that the common purpose which had united the Western Allies inevitably failed to survive victory.

The Peace Conference at Paris revealed their divergent aims and ideals. France, in the person of Clemenceau, knew what she wanted – first the return of Alsace-Lorraine, and on this there was no dispute; secondly, security; and thirdly, reparations. Even with Alsace-Lorraine, France would remain weaker in population and resources than Germany. The main aim of Clemenceau was to redress this balance. He secured the reduction of the German army to a maximum of a hundred thousand men, without air force or heavy artillery, though, contrary to French wishes, it was, on mistaken British ideas, to be a long-service force, and therefore capable of rapidly providing the trained cadres for a conscript army. To counterbalance the loss of resources in the French devastated areas, the great mining basin of the Saar was put under international control; but this was only for fifteen years, after which it was to decide its future by plebiscite.

Over the terms of the peace a bitter conflict broke out between the two chief French architects of victory, Foch and Clemenceau. Foch, disbelieving in the efficacy or permanence of treaties of disarmament, insisted that the only solution to the French problem of security was the Rhine frontier. Clemenceau, as a politician, knew that it would be impossible ever to extract from Great Britain and from America, committed to the principle of national self-determination, agreement to such a proposal. He settled for the best terms he could get his allies to agree to – the occupation of three bridge-heads on the right bank of the Rhine for five, ten, and fifteen years respectively, an Anglo-American guarantee against future German aggression, and a demilitarized zone in the Rhineland.

Foch and the nationalists condemned Clemenceau for his failure to secure the left bank of the Rhine for France. The internationalists, such as Léon Bourgeois, put their faith in an international army. Great Britain and the United States were unwilling to contemplate either road to security. They frustrated one French plan after another, and although Clemenceau obtained a joint Anglo-American guarantee of assistance to France if Germany should make an unprovoked attack it was to be repudiated by the United States and the repudiation used by Great Britain as an excuse for cancelling her obligation. Clemenceau was certainly no Talleyrand and he tried to make obstinacy do the work of finesse, but given the American misjudgment of the European situation, and the shiftiness of British policy, it is difficult to see what more he could have rescued from the wreck of the alliance. He did at least provide, by clauses which could have been brought into effect at the critical moment in 1936 if there had then been the will to do so, for a French reoccupation of the Rhineland in the event of a German attempt to remilitarize it.

The other great aim of the French negotiators was one which she shared with all her allies – to make somebody else pay for the war; the only difference was that whereas Great Britain and the European allies were determined to make Germany pay, the Americans were determined to make their allies pay. Every war cost that could be thought of was added to the bill for reparations in a frantic competition to draw up an astronomical total. In this way it was hoped to avoid the painful necessity of raising money by taxation. The result was that further borrowing was added to the already huge French war debt and the budget was balanced on the promise of German reparations. The inflation that was the inevitable result was to be a powerful factor in undermining the stability of French society.

By the end of the peace negotiations tempers were frayed and the victorious alliance was dead, but somehow a document was produced which was called the Treaty of Versailles and signed in the Hall of Mirrors on June 28th, 1919.

✤

CHAPTER THREE

BLOC NATIONAL

WITH the restoration of peace the normal processes of politics were resumed in France. The Chamber of Deputies, which had been elected in 1914, was dissolved and elections for a new Chamber were held in November 1919. Clemenceau in France, like Lloyd George in England, was determined to let no scruples of any kind stand in the way of dealing the knock-out blow to his political enemies on the home front that he had already dealt to the Germans on the military front. The degradation of national standards, in the victorious as well as the vanquished nations, that resulted from the First World War, was first clearly shown in the general elections in Great Britain and France. The director of Clemenceau's personal 'cabinet', Georges Mandel – destined to end his political career with more honour than he began – managed the French elections in the interests of the parties of the right, allied in a Bloc National and led by the ex-Socialist Millerand. In the feverish dawn of victory after a night of misery and bloodshed, the right wing, which had stood for the fight to a finish and total victory, was bound to win. The name of Clemenceau – 'père la Victoire' as the newspapers with a typical touch named him – was itself almost a guarantee of success.

The first signs now appeared, also, of a new trend which was to exert a sinister influence on French politics during the inter-war years. Henri Massis, who, as one of two journalists writing under the name of 'Agathon' before the war, had purported to show by various pseudo-scientific inquiries that the youth of France was moving towards Catholicism and patriotism, and so had played a part in stimulating such a movement, continued his pre-war propaganda with the issue, in July 1919, of the manifesto of the 'parti de l'Intelligence', and followed this up in the next year by founding a review with a Fascist bias. This was premature. The only political group which as yet went as far as this in its sympathies, was the Action Française, which had very slight electoral success though Léon Daudet was elected for Paris.

Behind such literary guerillas the big battalions of the right were moving into action. The heavy industries of France had long been organized in close cartels, the most famous of which was the Comité des Forges, established in 1864. Closely linked with the big banking interests, and together largely controlling national finances through the Regents of the Banque de France, they were able to bring a powerful influence to bear on the elections. Their principal aims were, first, to maintain the military power of France and her armaments, in which patriotism, a wise scepticism about the stability of the European situation, and a not unnatural concern for profits, were happily combined; and secondly, to make sure that they did not have to pay in the shape of higher taxation on wealth for the achievement of their first aim. A third object, which was also the main propaganda theme, was the defence of civilization against Communism, symbolized by a brilliant placard of a bandit with a ferocious countenance gritting a knife between his teeth.

In the cause of electoral victory, the conservative parties dropped the old struggle of clerical and anti-clerical, with the aid of a piece of meaningless verbiage: this said that, 'Secularization must be compatible with the liberties and rights of all citizens whatever their religion.' The left, on the other hand, was more than usually divided. The Radicals were alarmed at the rise of Communism and suspicious of the Communist sympathies of part of the Socialist Party, which was itself split into those who clung to Socialist orthodoxy and those who followed the lure of Leninism. Finally, for this election a system of multi-membered constituencies was adopted. Supposed to give a fairer proportional representation, in fact it exaggerated the swing which would have occurred in any case away from the left-wing and pacifist chamber of 1914. Grouped in the Bloc National, the parties of the right won 433 seats, against a mere 86 Radicals and 104 Socialists. It was a new *Chambre introuvable*, called the *Chambre horizon bleu*.

One of the earliest actions of the new Chamber was to turn on its creator. When Clemenceau posed his candidature for the presidency on the end of Poincaré's term in February 1920, Briand got his revenge for 1917 by organizing the election, against Clemenceau, of Paul Deschanel, an amiable nonentity who was President of the Chamber of Deputies. The nationalists voted against Clemenceau because they were discontented with Versailles, and the Catholics out of alarm at the thought that if he died in office, as was not impossible considering his age, the presidential funeral would be a secular one. This was an important factor, for in 1919, for the first time under the Third Republic, France had a Chamber in which there was a majority of practising Catholics. It made possible the negotiation of an exchange of envoys between Paris and the Vatican. The pre-war alliance of nationalism and Catholicism was cemented with the canonization by Benedict XV of Jeanne d'Arc, in the presence of a large contingent of French parliamentarians. The sky-blue Chamber played its part by making her fête day into a national holiday. None of this would have been possible under Clemenceau, but after his rebuff in the presidential election he had withdrawn from office, to be succeeded by Millerand. However, in September 1920, only some six months after the election, his successful rival for the presidency, Deschanel, had to retire to a mental home. This unfortunate episode perhaps led the politicians to make the unusual experiment of choosing a strong President, in the person of Millerand himself.

Public attention, immediately after the war, was still largely concentrated on foreign affairs. Into the vacuum left by the collapse of the Central Empires, the forces of Russian Communism seemed to be advancing. The government of Millerand took what might well be considered a decision of major historical importance when, in the summer of 1920, it sent Foch's right-hand man, Weygand, to fight the battle of Warsaw. This turned the tide in eastern Europe, but though the Communist armies were thrust back, the attempt to intervene in the Russian civil war proved a disastrous failure. The best that could be produced was a *cordon sanitaire* across eastern Europe, a sort of Iron Curtain, destined to be revived in reverse some thirty years later, when it was the East that feared the contagion of Western ideas rather than vice versa.

Suspicious, and rightly so, of the reliability of American or

British guarantees, France looked elsewhere for possible support against an eventual revival of German military power. Since the Russian Empire lay in ruins and an alliance with a Communist state would anyhow not have been contemplated, treaties of mutual support were concluded with the successor states to the Austro-Hungarian Empire – Czechoslovakia, Jugoslavia and Rumania, united by their common interest in preserving the new territorial arrangements in what was called the Little Entente. A Franco-Polish treaty was subsequently added to the French system of alliances, which looked formidable on paper. What was not realized was that no combination of however many small states could equal one great state. The strength of the French system was the strength of France, no more and no less. It would survive so long as France had the strength and the will to defend her allies and herself. That she would have this hardly anyone questioned in 1920. Indeed, already in Britain and America voices were being raised against the bellicose militarism of a country that had committed the unforgivable crime of winning, at the price of unprecedented sacrifices, a war that had been forced upon it.

While the government was devoting much of its attention to the problem of security, the French people set about the hard task of rebuilding their shattered land and economy. Within seven years the ten depopulated and devastated departments of the north-east had been restored to normal activity. Unfortunately reconstruction, like arms and military interventions, cost money, and the bankers and industrialists of the Bloc National, as well as their lesser clientèle in the propertied classes, were determined not to foot the bill. The current expenses of the war had been met by borrowing at home and abroad and by printing notes. It was easiest to continue the same system, putting all that could not be paid for out of revenue into a separate budget, and hoping to meet it by the receipt of reparations from the Germans. These were not finally settled, and the French share of the fairy gold not determined, until April 1921.

Meanwhile there was a weary and fruitless round of international conferences, at which Britain and France, particularly in the persons of Briand and Lloyd George, manoeuvred for financial and diplomatic advantage in the name of justice and international peace.

Franco-British relations were also complicated by a little struggle they were waging in the Near East. Having agreed, by the secret Sykes-Picot agreement in 1916, on the partition of the Turkish Empire and implemented the agreement by the Treaty of Sèvres of May 1920, the two Western Allies were split by the resurgence of Turkish power under Kemal Pasha, when Kemalist armies drove the Greeks, who had invaded Asia Minor with British aid and encouragement, into the sea at Smyrna. When the Turks advanced on the Allied lines guarding the Straits at Chanak, the French concluded an armistice and withdrew their troops. Although a settlement was eventually reached in the Treaty of Lausanne in 1923, it was only after Franco-British relations had been strained almost to breaking point.

In January 1922 the strong man of the conservative parties, Poincaré, took office with the task of collecting reparations. When, after a year, he had failed to do so, in January 1923 he sent a French army into the great industrial complex of the Ruhr to collect them on the spot. French attempts to encourage Rhineland separatism, German passive resistance and sabotage, the final collapse of the German mark, all having produced nothing save an as yet un-noticed crop of dragon's teeth, France had to recognize that the Poincaré experiment had failed. The problem was thrown back again on an international conference in November 1923. This pro-duced the Dawes plan, by which credits were to be extended to Germany for the restoration of her economy in the present, on the strength of which the Germans promised to begin reparation pay-ments at some date in the future. France liquidated the Ruhr adventure and in the spring of 1924 Poincaré accepted the Dawes plan in principle. The belief that reparations would balance the French budget was now patently an illusion and the national finances were on the point of collapse.

Reflected in these muddied waters the colour of the 'sky-blue' Chamber of 1919 looked a good deal less attractive, and it was due to face the electorate in the course of the coming year. The elections of 1924 were to be conducted in a very different atmosphere from those of 1919, one of disillusionment with the policy of glory and the iron fist. The name of Poincaré was not the vote-catching bait that the name of Clemenceau had been. Of course, we must be careful not to give an exaggerated impression of the change in public opinion. As in all the elections of the Third Republic, an extensive shift in the balance of parties in the Chamber came about without any equally extensive change in the electorate. The transfer of votes from right to left was comparatively slight. The most important development was that the right was now split. The failure of its domestic and foreign policy had, naturally, brought disarray to the ranks of the Bloc National; and there was a revival of the antagonism of Catholics and anti-clericals, the cabinets of the sky-blue Chamber having gone rather too far for the latter in their concessions to Catholic opinion. On the other hand, Radicals and Socialists managed to form for electoral purposes a Cartel des Gauches, which the Communists were not yet strong enough to weaken seriously. Given the electoral system of 1919 a small change-over in votes could bring about a much greater change in the membership of the Chamber. The Cartel des Gauches won 270 seats against 210 to the Bloc National, with about 50 of the Gauche Radicale in the middle, and a flanking group of some 30 Communists. It was not a safe majority but sufficient to enable the Cartel des Gauches to take over the government.

CHAPTER FOUR

CARTEL DES GAUCHES

THE first objective of the victorious Cartel was to drive Millerand, identified with the Bloc National first as its leader and then as President, out of the Elysée. The new Chamber voted, almost as soon as it met, that his continuance as President was a threat to the Republic. To enforce this view the majority went on strike and refused to form a ministry while Millerand remained President. Within a fortnight he had been forced out, though the Cartel failed to replace him with its own candidate, Paul Painlevé, and had to see the moderate President of the Senate, Doumergue, elected. The Radical victims of the purge of 1917, Caillaux and Malvy, were rehabilitated, and as a gesture to the Socialists the ashes of Jaurès were transported to the Panthéon.

The leader of the Radicals, Édouard Herriot, formed the first Cartel government. Solid and serious in mind and body, as befitted a man who was to be elected and re-elected *maire* of Lyons for a whole generation, Herriot had unshakable patriotism and a genuine desire for the well-being of ordinary provincial Frenchmen, of whom he was so obviously one. Modest in his origins, lacking panache, but having a pipe, a friendly smile, and intellectual and artistic tastes, a sentimental turn of mind and real political shrewdness, what he lacked was a cutting edge to his mind and an appreciation of the fact that France had to come to terms with the twentieth century. But even if Herriot had been less of a politician and more of a statesman the political balance of forces in France would have denied success to the Cartel des Gauches. The left was now to show, what was repeatedly to be demonstrated, that it could hold together only during an election, and that the problem of agreeing on a policy in office was more than it could manage.

Politically allied to the Socialists, in basic social ideas the

Radicals were far removed from them. Both the strength and weakness of the Radicals can be seen in the writings of the teacher of philosophy who wrote under the name of Alain. Our only programme, he declared in his *Éléments d'une doctrine radicale* in 1925, 'is to have no other ideal than government in conformity with the will of the majority.' 'The elite is worthless ... Because it is destined to exercise power, the elite is destined to be corrupted by power.' 'What I call liberty is the close dependence of the elected on the elector.' 'In a democracy, not only does no party have power, but even better, there is no power properly speaking.' Basically, Radicalism believed in reducing government to a minimum, which was a recipe for failure at a time when political and social problems were urgently demanding positive action; but it suited the peasant proprietors, small employers, and shopkeepers who voted Radical and who represented a great vested interest in economic backwardness.

The partners of the Radicals in the Cartel, the Socialists, naturally had a much more positive attitude towards the economic functions of government, though they shared the faith of the Radicals in political democracy. But they were in a weak position because, since the Russian Revolution of 1917, they had to face the growing threat of a Communist party, always ready to outbid them and taking full advantage of the traditional republican *mystique de gauche*, the principle of 'no enemies on the left'.

For the hopes of the left in France, and therefore for the prospect of social reform, the Russian Revolution was a disaster. In the beginning, of course, it aroused strong Socialist sympathies. The French Socialist Party, which had been agitating against French intervention in Russia, sent two representatives to the Bolshevik Congress of 1920 in Moscow. There they were presented with Lenin's twenty-one conditions for membership of the Third International. These conditions were bound to exclude a large proportion of the Western Socialists. This was their object, for Lenin, in adherence to the Blanquist technique he had adopted, was concerned to secure the adhesion of a ruthless revolutionary elite rather than the sheep-like masses and their idealistic leaders. When the emissaries returned and presented the terms laid down by

Moscow to the Congress of the Socialist Party at Tours in December 1920, they were rejected by the established leadership. The Socialism of Jaurès, declared Jean Longuet, cannot go to Moscow with a cord round its neck and ashes on its head. A leading role in the debate was taken by the brilliant Jewish technician and intellectual, Léon Blum. He saw that the Moscow theses represented a reversal of existing Socialist theory and involved the creation of an occult party directory controlled from Moscow. When he went on to declare that Socialists should defend their country against aggression, this provoked an outburst of pacifist sentiment and cries of 'À bas la guerre'. The pro-Communist faction under the returned emissaries, Cachin and Frossard, carried the day by a three-to-one majority.

The victorious majority set up the French Communist Party, which retained control of the Socialist Party organization and funds and its daily paper, *L'Humanité*. On the other hand, as an attempt to capture the political elite of the Socialist Party the Leninist manoeuvre, though it had been brilliantly executed, missed its mark. Most of the Socialists on local bodies and at the head of the local parties remained faithful to the traditional leadership and policy, and only 13 out of 68 of the Socialists in parliament joined the Communists. In spite of a concentrated attack, the Communists failed to consolidate their victory. As early as 1924 the situation of majority and minority had been reversed, and by 1932 the Socialists could poll nearly 2,000,000 votes against a Communist 800,000. There was a similar reversal of fortunes in the trade union movement. The Communist Confédération Générale du Travail Unitaire (C.G.T.U.) began with the support of some 500,000 trade unionists, against 370,000 who followed the Confédération Générale du Travail. By the early 'thirties, however, the C.G.T.U. had only some 300,000 against the C.G.T.'s 900,000. The real significance of the schism was that it created two left-wing parties in bitter rivalry with one another. Henceforth the presence of the Communists on their left prevented the Socialists from co-operating whole-heartedly with the Radicals, for fear of losing their own clientèle to the former. The Communists could always employ the emotional appeal to the tradition of revolution, and there was an ample supply of social grievances and injustices in French society to provide motivation for a revolutionary party. In pursuance of well-considered Russian policy they concentrated their fire on the Socialists.

The division between Socialists and Radicals, along with the guerilla attacks of the Communists on their left, provide the fundamental reason for the failure of the Cartel des Gauches. In addition it had inherited major problems in the colonies, and was to create problems in France for itself which precipitated its collapse.

Since, after they had disposed of Millerand, almost the only other policy that the parties of the left had in common was anti-clericalism, an attempt was made to maintain their cohesion by that rather dried-up cement. The time and the place for applying it were both ill-chosen. The Vatican had just, after several years' negotiation, approved of the setting up of religious associations to operate under the laws of separation, despite the opposition and delaying tactics of the extremist bishops appointed in France by Pius X. Instead of welcoming this as a step towards recognition of the Republic and its laws, the government of Herriot, under the influence of a rather old-fashioned, dogmatic anti-clericalism, attempted to withdraw the French representation at the Vatican and to extend the laws of separation to the regained territory of Alsace-Lorraine.

The restoration of the lost province of Alsace to the Gallic bosom from which it had been so roughly torn some fifty years earlier, had not proved as easy as had been anticipated in the first flush of patriotic emotion. In particular, language presented an administrative and educational problem, for the language of the province was the Alsatian dialect, supplemented usually by German, but with very little knowledge of French. Again, in the German Empire Alsace had possessed a decentralized local administration. After its return to France, a High Commissioner was appointed to supervise a cautious reintegration with the French state. The process had been too slow for the parties of the left. They were anxious to introduce the laws of separation, to substitute lay for Church schools, and to impose French as the medium of instruction. Local Alsatian opposition to these measures took the form of an Autonomist movement, which seemed for a short period to be assuming dangerous proportions. Fortunately, as difficulties accumulated the government's enthusiasm for forceful assimilation declined and it reverted to more gradual methods.

It is not possible to assess the connection between the revival of anti-clericalism and the increased militancy, which appeared at the same time, of the Catholics. A National Catholic Federation was founded in 1924 under the presidency of the monarchist General de Castelnau, with the right-wing *Echo de Paris* as its organ. Just as anti-clericalism was identified with the left, so Catholicism was with the right. Among the spokesmen of the Church militant were such future Nazi collaborators as Philippe Henriot and Xavier Vallat. The conflict of Catholicism and anti-clericalism, which had always had strong political overtones, was now largely a cover for social and political enmities.

A major part in the association between French Catholics and right-wing politics was played by the influence of the Action Française, which in the 'twenties acquired an astonishing domination, that nothing in its intellectual content seemed to justify, over Catholic writers and intellectuals. Its journal was alleged to be widely read in Catholic seminaries, where the anti-semitic racialism in which it specialized was appreciated. At the same time it kept nationalist sentiment at fever pitch, played on xenophobic emotions and did all it could to prevent a Franco-German *rapprochement*. For this, among other reasons, Pius XI, who had aspirations towards international reconciliation, determined to discipline the movement by bringing out of its pigeon-hole the condemnation of 1914. It turned out that this had been mislaid in the Vatican archives, perhaps not entirely by accident; but despite strong opposition within the Church the Pope remained firm in his resolve to deal with the movement. Following the method employed in starting the Ralliement, he used a French cardinal, the Archbishop of Bordeaux, to initiate the attack. Many French Catholics, including the neo-Thomist journalist, Jacques Maritain, sprang to the defence. Polemics between the Action Française and the Vatican became increasingly bitter, until, late in 1926, the condemnation of 1914, now rediscovered, was published. It was reinforced by a ban on the journal, and a declaration from the French Church condemning the leaders of the Action Française as 'men who, by their writings, have put themselves in opposition to Catholic faith and morality'.

Maurras's gladiators now turned their almost unmatched powers of vituperation against Rome, which retaliated with punitive measures against priests suspected of sympathizing with the movement. In 1928 episcopal regulations prohibited adherents of the Action Française from receiving religious rites, such as those for marriage or burial. All this was less effective than might have been supposed, for many priests, as well as laity, sympathized with Maurras and his ideas and gave only a half-hearted adherence to the orders of Rome. However, the circulation of the *Action Française*, which was the life-blood of the movement, shrank to about half of what it had been before the ban was imposed.

Communists and Action Française as yet had only a nuisance value in the history of the Republic. They were not strong enough to bring down the Cartel des Gauches. That was achieved by its own mistakes. The treatment of Alsace was one of these. A second difficulty, and one which it had inherited rather than created, was presented by the colonies. In Morocco the rebel chief, Abd-el-Krim, had been in arms since 1921; he was not to surrender till 1926. For the disastrous events in Syria, the one French mandate which had emerged from the Franco-British Near Eastern imbroglio, the government of Herriot was largely responsible. Unlucky on the Western Front, unlucky in the Balkans, Sarrail still remained *par excellence* the republican general. As such he was sent to replace the Catholic Weygand in Syria. His bad luck had not deserted him, for a revolt broke out in Syria in 1925 and Sarrail found himself in the position of bombarding his own capital, Damascus. The situation was never more than temporarily redressed and the revolt dragged on until 1936, when France promised the Syrians independence, though not at once.

The crucial difficulty for Herriot's government, however, appeared at home. The illusion that the huge gap in the French budget would be filled by reparations died hard. It provided an excuse for the wealthier classes, represented by the parties of the right, to resist any increase in direct taxation, and the parties of the left to oppose increases in indirect taxation. The only alternative was inflation.

E

As the national debt rose the value of the franc sank. By 1926 the pound sterling, which itself had not preserved its 1914 value, stood at 243 francs. The parties of the right and the big financial interests, which had no desire to see the Cartel overcome its difficulties, waged a violent campaign to discredit its financial policy. The millions of small property-owners and investors saw their savings vanishing, and employees their real wages shrinking. The Herriot cabinet, incapable of agreeing on any policy to meet the crisis, broke up. Caillaux, brought back from political ostracism as the former financial genius of the left, found himself out of touch with postwar politics; Briand employed his skill at building bridges in vain; and the franc continued to fall in value. The public was increasingly restive. There were demonstrations before the Chamber of Deputies. The Cartel, it began to be felt, had shown itself incapable of governing.

The centre groups which had so far supported the Cartel, though not very enthusiastically, now withdrew their support. The Chamber turned again to the one strong man and elder statesman it possessed, Poincaré, who formed a government of national union including a galaxy of leading politicians – Herriot himself, Briand, Barthou, Painlevé, Tardieu, Louis Marin. Poincaré was given power to deal with the financial crisis by decree-laws – the first admission that the French parliament might be unworkable in a crisis. It enabled him to restore confidence by the fairly simple method, which could never have been put into effect by the ordinary legislative process, of increasing taxes and reducing expenditure. The large part played by speculation in the collapse of the franc was shown by its rapid recovery from 250 to 125 to the pound sterling. With the return of confidence in the government, the real wealth of the country was shown by the ease with which the loans issued in 1926 were absorbed. The small property-owners, whose suspicion – not unjustified – of the financial policy of the Cartel had caused the crisis, were reassured by the name of Poincaré. It was a guarantee of social conservatism, financial orthodoxy and republican order. To the Socialists and Radicals, constitutionally suspicious of hard economic facts, the financial catastrophe which had brought them down seemed the result of a deep-laid plot. They saw themselves as the victims of the *mur d'argent*, erected as a barrier against social progress. And so in a sense they were; but it was a plot in which the great mass of small property-owners of France were fellow conspirators. With the restoration of confidence in the government, financial improvement during the next two years, from 1926 to 1928, was amazing. The 3 per cent *rentes* rose from 48·25 to 67·60 francs, the balance of the Treasury in the Bank of France was multiplied by sixty, and the franc was stabilized at 25·52 francs to the American dollar.

Meanwhile the Cartel des Gauches lay shattered in fragments, and only the approach of new elections could put it together again. It reunited temporarily in 1927 to pass a new electoral law, restoring single-member constituencies with a double ballot, which was expected to be more favourable to the left; but the elections of 1928, held under the influence of the financial success of the Poincarist experiment, proved a disappointment. The Communist party was not yet in a position to secure many seats for itself, but it was strong enough successfully to pursue a wrecking policy. That doctrinaire intolerance which, for example, forbade its members to be freemasons, was called into operation. Under instructions from Moscow, there were to be no electoral pacts. The Party consequently maintained its candidates at the second ballot, securing only 14 seats with over a million votes, but handing over some 60 or 70 seats to the parties of the right, which won 330 seats out of 610.

There was now open war between the Socialists and Communists. The Socialist leader, Léon Blum, was the son of a wealthy manufacturer from Alsace. He had passed into the highest ranks of the French bureaucracy, and at the same time made a distinguished literary reputation with dramatic criticism, a work on Stendhal, and another on marriage which shocked the bourgeois. He entered parliament in 1919 and almost at once came to the front. Not a great orator, with a shrill and unimpressive voice, Blum held his leading position by his elevation of character and power of intellect. He had played a leading role in meeting the challenge of the Communists at the Tours Conference of 1920, and never ceased to regard them as the confirmed enemies of social and democratic ideals. He believed that the unity of the workers had as its necessary condition the destruction of the Communist cadres. In fact neither Communists nor Socialists were likely to make much headway in the late 'twenties, when economic prosperity and progress were at last returning to France.

International tensions also were beginning to relax under the careful diplomacy of Briand, who, becoming Foreign Minister in April 1925, was to continue in the same post, apart from a gap of two days, until 1932. The climate of Versailles had now passed away. Belief in total victory no longer survived. French military predominance would evidently not last for ever and the need for another basis of French security was beginning to be felt. Briand looked to the League of Nations for the machinery of a peaceful consolidation of the status quo. After the Ruhr episode France did not wish to find herself again, in peace or in war, tête-à-tête with Germany. It was therefore necessary to bring back Great Britain into the European balance. The first attempt to do this, the Geneva Protocol of 1924 and the consequent disarmament plan, was wrecked by the British government of Baldwin; but the Locarno agreements of 1925 led up to the admission of Germany to the League of Nations in 1926. Briand devoted his last years to the noblest work of his life – the attempt at a genuine reconciliation with Germany and the creation of a peaceful international order. The greatest difficulty, the fog of reparations which had spread like a miasma over the international scene, seemed at last to be dissipated when the plan named after the American banker, Young, was accepted by both France and Germany in 1930. It was followed by the French evacuation of the Rhineland, five years before the appointed time.

❧

CHAPTER FIVE

THE HEY-DAY OF THE LEAGUES

B UT already at this high noon of inter-war hopes ominous clouds were gathering. In October 1929 occurred the Wall Street crash, from which all the disasters of the following decades date. This destroyed the recent reparations settlement even before it had been put into practice. Under pressure from the American President Hoover, a moratorium was imposed on the payment of reparations by Germany, while at the same time Hoover insisted on the payment of the war debts that France owed to the United States. Another cloud also darkened the prospects of Franco-German reconciliation. In 1930, hard on the heels of the last French soldier leaving the Rhineland, 107 Nazi followers of Hitler took their seats in the Reichstag. The failure of Briand's efforts was already written in the realities of the international scene and nothing he or France could have done would have prevented it. In 1931, with Doumergue's term as President ended, Briand had hoped to crown his long service to the state with the highest of its offices. Once again the most distinguished was rejected. Paul Doumer, who was chosen, was to be assassinated by a mad Russian in May 1932, but Briand, disappointed, worn out and ill, was already dead. He was replaced at the Quai d'Orsay by Pierre Laval, not yet seen as quite the significant figure he was later to appear.

By 1932 also, when a new Chamber was elected, the world slump had not yet seriously affected France, nor had the deterioration of the international situation become a major factor in domestic politics. The reversal of electoral fortunes was therefore to be attributed to different considerations. Four years in opposition had brought the Radicals and Socialists together again, while the Communists, obedient to the policy of isolation and *poing brandi contre le parti socialiste*, continued to lose support. Right and left were still, in votes, extraordinarily evenly balanced, but given the system of a second ballot a small change could alter the complexion of the Chamber drastically. Radicals and Socialists, along with their smaller partners, now held 334 seats, while the right won 257 and the Communists, benefiting from no electoral alliances, a mere 12. The Radicals and Socialists had again won an election. Their misfortune, during the inter-war years, was that each time they achieved an electoral victory – in 1924, 1932 and 1936 – the swing against the right occurred, naturally enough, when its policies or world conditions had brought France to the eve of a grave economic or financial crisis. The left was thus repeatedly presented with the need for taking decisions which either it could not take, or which, if taken, almost inevitably destroyed its naturally weak cohesion.

The majority of 1932 came to power in a France which had resisted the effects of the world economic crisis better than most countries. The apparent immunity of France from world economic diseases was however an illusion. By 1933 there were 1,300,000 unemployed and both agriculture and industry were in difficulties. Herriot, called to office by the new President, Lebrun, a worthy political hack who had replaced the assassinated Doumer, had once again to face economic problems of the kind with which his majority was least fitted to deal. This time, with his former unhappy experience to warn him, he made, as is customary, the opposite mistake. Determined not to be swamped by the flood of inflation as in 1926, he chose a rigidly orthodox Minister of Finances, who drew up a budget on the homoeopathic principle of orthodox finance, by which the remedy for the evils of deflation was yet more deflation. Expenditure was to be reduced by cutting the salaries of civil servants, reducing ex-service pensions, and closing down public works, and revenue increased by taxing consumer goods. The whole policy amounted to a direct attack on the interests of the electoral clientèle which had voted the government into office. This was more than the parliamentary majority could stand: it therefore rejected at the outset of the new parliament the financial proposals of its own government. The right, on the other hand, thoroughly approved of the policy of deflation but had no intention of helping Herriot to apply it; far better to allow the left to sink in a morass of its own making, and the national finances along with it, so creating a situation to which the Radicals and Socialists would almost inevitably react with opposed policies. After the left was hopelessly split, the right might regain its influence in the Assembly, and finally return to power on a wave of public disillusionment with the left. This programme was almost too successful. Despite his failure to secure the passage of his government's budget, which at least represented a policy even if a mistaken one, Herriot continued in office, though since he now had no policy for what purpose was not very clear.

It was a financial question, though of a different nature, which brought down his government before the year was out. Reparations, which had been troubling the international scene and causing periodic disturbances on the national stage since the end of the First World War, now made their final appearance. The Young plan, which came into operation in May 1930, had scaled down reparations to what was believed to be a practicable level. The world economic crisis made it an impracticable one. In June 1931 Germany had declared her inability to pay the forthcoming instalment of reparations. President Hoover announced in the following month a moratorium for one year on international debt payments. France, which had just paid a half-yearly instalment on her war debt to the United States, was not quite convinced that the timing of Hoover's proposal was all that might have been desired on the highest principles of international justice, but under American pressure acceded to it. Many Frenchmen suspected that this was a way of ending reparations, and it turned out that they were not wrong. Inter-Allied debts still remained, and with the conclusion of the moratorium in 1932 France was called on to pay another instalment on her debt to the United States. Herriot invited the Chamber to authorize the payment. This was to fly so obviously in the face of a bitterly anti-American public opinion, as well as of the views of the majority in parliament, as to lead one to speculate whether he was simply seeking an excuse to get out of office without exposing the fundamental divisions in the left which had in fact made his position untenable. Inevitably he was defeated and resigned.

His successors were no luckier, for French politics had now reached an impasse. The cabinet of the independent Socialist, Paul

Boncourt, lasted barely a month. Another Radical, Daladier, survived from January to October 1933 by abandoning the attempt to get any financial proposals through the Chamber. When, in the autumn, he at last had to present them, and tried to insist on plans which included a 6 per cent reduction in official salaries, the Socialists overthrew his government. The government of another Radical, Albert Sarraut, was brought down a few weeks later for the same reason and in the same way. Yet another Radical, Camille Chautemps, succeeded Sarraut, and under him Daladier's not very drastic proposals were at last agreed to, the Socialists walking out of the Chamber before the vote to avoid the responsibility for either supporting the proposals or else overthrowing yet another government.

The repeated slaughter of cabinets had already provided an opportunity for Communists and Fascists to concentrate their fire from left and right on the incompetence and corruption of republican politics. The calendar seemed to be turning back to Boulanger and Panama. Indeed, at the psychological moment, in the autumn of 1933, a new affair did in fact break on the political world. A shady financier named Stavisky, who for years had kept one step ahead of the law, not without the aid of influential acquaintances in the world of high society and politics, at last overreached himself. He floated a loan of millions of francs' worth of bonds, allegedly to finance the little municipal pawnshop of Bayonne. This was too ambitious a trick for one who was not really in the first class of financial wizards, and as the bonds began to appear, Stavisky had only one recourse left, to disappear. Tracked to the other side of France, he shot himself in January 1934. Continuing the traditional pattern the Radical premier, Chautemps, tried to hush the matter up. The parties of the right, equally traditionally, alleged that Stavisky had been murdered to prevent him from betraying the names of his influential protectors. Compared with château-bottled affairs like Panama or the Union Générale, the Stavisky affair was small beer, or at least *vin ordinaire*, but circumstances allowed it to develop, or be built up, into a major political crisis. Under the lead of demagogues of the right such as Philippe Henriot, deputy for Bordeaux, the forces of anti-semitism and the old Catholic suspicions of Radical freemasonry were evoked. Ministers who had been connected with Stavisky were driven from office, and Chautemps, himself not the purest of the pure, had to resign.

His place was taken by Daladier, another Radical. Son of a small-town baker in Provence, Daladier, who before entering politics had been a history teacher, had the appearance and manner of a real Jacobin of the Midi. Throughout his career he appealed to, and had the support of, the socially conservative but politically advanced peasantry of the south. Short and solidly built, with a Napoleonic frame and cast of countenance, he seemed a strong man; and a strong man was needed, for the situation was rapidly getting out of hand. The police had been as uncertain and divided in their handling of the Stavisky affair as the politicians. Indeed there were grounds for suspicion that the Sûreté itself had been partly responsible for Stavisky's long immunity from prosecution. When, however, the police official charged with the investigation was found dead on a railway line, tied up and poisoned, the papers of the right attributed his death to murder at the hands of politicians whose complicity with Stavisky he had uncovered. A more probable hypothesis is suicide, arranged for personal reasons to look like murder.

However, the Paris Préfecture de Police, the great rival of the Sûreté, was safely on the other side of the fence. Its head, the Corsican Chiappe, was notorious for his right-wing sympathies. He was suspected, not without reason, of having tolerated, or even encouraged demonstrations against the government. One of Daladier's first acts, therefore, was to dismiss him, though the effect of this gesture of strength was somewhat weakened by offering him as a consolation prize the Governor Generalship of Morocco. To reduce matters to the level of a farce, Daladier then dismissed the director of the Comédie Française, who had just produced *Coriolanus* with its patent incitement to anti-democratic demonstrations, and replaced him by the police chief of the Sûreté Générale. Whether at Chiappe's instigation or not, this proved the signal for an attempt at a right-wing *coup* on February 6th.

Of the leagues that joined in this Blanquist-type *putsch* from the right, the Action Française – still dragging its ever-frustrated fol-lowers like a long, attenuated snake through the Paris literary and political jungle, its leaders, Maurras and Daudet, still spitting poison from the head – deserves to be mentioned first, at least on grounds of seniority. Though ideologically the Action Française looked to the past rather than to the future, in its methods it set the pattern for the Fascist leagues that were proliferating in the 'thirties. Its supporters included many of the old gentry, or of those who aspired to be regarded as such, and it still kept the support of clerics whose political commitment exceeded their loyalty to Rome; but it also drew recruits from the professional classes, especially lawyers, doctors, and chemists, and from small businessmen, shop-keepers and artisans, whose social and economic status was declining under new social pressures and who saw themselves as an elite under attack from the forces of egalitarian democracy and unegalitarian finance. Jewish pre-eminence in the world of finance, joined to traditional religious prejudices, made anti-semitism the chief bond uniting these diverse groups. Cultural *snobbisme* drew literary aspirants to the *Action Française*, which provided a training-ground for the more vicious Paris journalists, many of whom, having served their apprenticeship with Maurras and Daudet, moved on later to the pro-Nazi papers. It still had some appeal to the University student population, which in France was traditionally polarized between extreme left and extreme right. But though it still attracted new generations of adherents, the Action Française belonged to the past rather than the future. It had shown throughout a remarkable inability to produce new leaders, and now Maurras at sixty-six, Daudet at sixty-seven, were rather old to start a revolution. Indeed, the secular canonization of Maurras, and the recognition that he was not, after all, a literary genius, may be said to have been effected a few years later, in 1937, when he was elected to the Académie Française. The purely destructive nature of his propaganda had been demonstrated once again by the ineffectiveness of the Action Française in the elections of 1932. Moreover, it now no longer stood alone as the representative of the revolutionary right.

After the First World War rival movements had begun to appear, though they did not crystallize until the victory of the Cartel des Gauches in 1924 offered a specific political challenge. Then Pierre Taittinger founded the Jeunesses Patriotes, wearing blue raincoats and berets, and drawing from the University some of the students who in an earlier generation would have been *Camelots du roi*. The new model was provided by the Fascist movement of Mussolini. Coty, the perfume and cosmetics millionaire who used his wealth to promote French Fascism, financed an anti-democratic journal to which this would-be Marat of the right gave the name *L'ami du peuple*, and founded the Solidarité Française. A smaller league was the anti-semitic Francistes. Much the biggest was the Croix de Feu, an ex-servicemen's organization headed by a retired lieutenant-colonel, de la Roque, who with a gift for mob oratory and wealthy if occult backers, turned it between 1931 and 1933 into a mass movement against Socialism and internationalism.

Besides the agitation of the leagues, right-wing opinion was whipped up by the Paris press. In addition to the usual popular journals of the right, such as *Le Matin* and *Le Journal*, there sprang up a crop of venomous weeklies like *Candide*, xenophobic and anti-republican, which dated from the early 'twenties, *Je suis partout*, founded in 1930, and edited at first by the historical writer Gaxotte, and somewhat later *Gringoire*. These specialized in slandering politicians of the centre or left and outdid even *l'Action Française* in indecency and invective. The part played by the journalists of the right, many of whom ended as collaborators of the Nazis in the Second World War, in sapping the moral fibre and powers of resistance of the Third Republic can hardly be exaggerated.

The strength of the anti-republican movement lay in the concentration of so much of its strength in Paris, its weakness in its divisions and lack of any real constructive programme. The feverish excitement which the leagues and their journalists could whip up was itself fatal to the possibility of a cool calculation of tactics and chances, such as was needed for political success. Why they chose to act on February 6th must always remain a little mysterious. Certainly the projected revolution went off at half-cock. Perhaps the leagues themselves believed in the legend of Daladier as the strong man and felt a need to prevent his government from consolidating itself when it met the Chamber on that day; perhaps they thought they could capitalize on the dismissal of Chiappe and use him as a martyr; perhaps they were just carried away by the wave of emotion they themselves had stirred up. An organized attack on the Chamber must have been planned, for the forces of the various organizations were summoned to meet on the evening of February 6th at varying rallying-points and at times which would enable them to converge simultaneously on the Chamber of Deputies. What was especially sinister was the presence, among the assault groups, of the Communist-controlled Association Républicaine des Anciens Combattants, summoned to the fray by an appeal in *L'Humanité*.

There was nothing secret about the preparations either for attack or defence. Police had been massed across the bridge leading from the place de la Concorde and on all the other routes of access to the Chamber of Deputies. As the forces of the leagues gathered, pressure on the forces of law and order built up. The confused history of some six hours of street-fighting between thousands of demonstrators, who lost fourteen killed and over two hundred sufficiently seriously injured to be taken to hospital, and about eight hundred police, whose corresponding losses were one dead and just under a hundred injured, need not be traced here. By midnight yet another Parisian *journée* had failed.

It is not possible to say whether the threat might or might not have been renewed. What we can say is that it could not have been as serious as it seemed at the time, for no more was needed than the resignation of Daladier and the formation of a centre government, including the leading parliamentarians, under the former President, Doumergue, for the agitation to collapse. The Communists organized a bloody street affray of their own on February 9th at the other end of Paris, but the object of this could not be ascertained, except in so far as it was intended to efface the memory of February 6th when they had fought side by side with royalists and Fascists in an attempt to overthrow the Republic.

The new government restored confidence but it restored nothing else. The economic crisis continued. Doumergue, aged, vain and mediocre, rapidly demonstrated that he was not another Poincaré. He began a series of wireless addresses to the nation which discontented his colleagues, whose disillusionment was completed by his attempts to promote constitutional changes which would increase the powers of the premier. In principle this was badly needed, but Doumergue was not the man to exercise such powers; nor were the political parties ready to concede the measures that might have strengthened the executive. His cabinet of national union collapsed under the strain, and the usual shift to the right that occurred in the latter years of the life of a Chamber continued with the accession of Laval to the premiership.

CHAPTER SIX

✤

POPULAR FRONT

THE most important consequence of February 6th was the traumatic effect it had on the French left. At any time after the sky-blue elections of 1919 France ought, if the balance of social forces and political opinion had been adequately represented, to have had a government of the moderate left. The conflicting social ideals of Radicals and Socialists, as well as the differing sectional interests they represented, along with the wrecking policy of the Communists, stood in the way of this. It is tempting to say that the shock delivered by the attempted *coup* of 1934 brought the parties of the left to their senses and forced a broad collaboration on them, but this did not happen at once. The French Communist Party continued its bitter attacks on the 'criminal policy' of the Socialists, and rebuffed attempts at a *rapprochement* from the Socialist left. The change when it came was the result not of internal but of foreign developments. The triumph of the Nazis in Germany belatedly aroused the Russians to a realization of the international consequences of the line they had laid down for foreign Communist parties. It is, of course, rarely possible to say of a switch in the policy of any Communist party how far it was the result of a directive from Moscow, or how far the local party may have taken the initiative. In practice this was not a matter of much significance. Wherever the change in the party line originated, the fact is that the Communist policy of treating the Socialist Party as the first enemy was tacitly suspended. In June 1934 the French Communist leaders proposed joint action against Fascism. Despite Socialist suspicions an agreement was reached in July for common political action.

From February 1934 to April 1936 French politics seems to bifurcate into two distinct and separate streams. On the one hand the parties of the left were struggling to rebuild on a broader basis, taking in the Communists, the twice-shattered Cartel des Gauches;

on the other, a series of governments leaning to the right had practically given up the attempt to cope with the internal social and economic problems of France, but were still attempting, though with almost total lack of success, to stem the rapidly advancing tide of international disaster.

The process of uniting the left was slow and painful, but the Communists were now as persistent in wooing the other parties of the left as they had formerly been, and were later to be again, in vilifying them. The hand of friendship was extended to include the Radicals. In July 1935 Daladier, Blum and Thorez addressed a combined meeting of their three parties. The great Bastille day procession of July 14th, 1935, saw three or four hundred thousand Socialists, Communists and Radicals marching together through the streets of Paris. With that concentration of attention on the problem of political power that Lenin had taught them, the Communists were pressing for a working political alliance as the first step. Blum and the Socialists, on the other hand, insisted that the formulation of a common policy must precede such an alliance. By January 1936 it was possible to publish the programme of the Popular Front. This called for a return to the system of collective security and the consolidation of the recently concluded Franco-Soviet pact, for the dissolution of the Fascist leagues, along with other internal political changes; and for an extensive programme of economic and social reform. Its slogan was 'bread, peace and liberty'; and its enemy was identified as the 'two hundred families' – the reference being to the Regents of the Bank of France, taken to symbolize, or indeed to embody in fact, the power of organized wealth.

The long weary years of economic depression had prepared the country for drastic political change. Governments of the centre and right were obviously unable to cope with the economic difficulties of France. Laval, after the failure of Doumergue to repeat the success of Poincaré, had been given authority to restore the economic situation by decree-laws. He sent Parliament on holiday and engaged on a thorough-going policy of deflation, which naturally increased unemployment, decreased the wages of those who remained in employment, and disillusioned even many of the small property-owners who were the natural electoral clientèle of the right. It is only fair to record that the Popular Front, fearful of antagonizing the small proprietors, also pledged itself against devaluation of the franc. Among leading politicians, Paul Reynaud was practically alone in being prepared to draw the logical conclusion to a generation of inflation by accepting the idea of devaluation, which merely won him vituperation from both right and left as the tool of international finance.

The continued appeal of the right to violence, which since February 1934 had been alarming moderate opinion, was responsible for an incident that occurred shortly before the elections of 1936. Léon Blum, on his way back from the Chamber, had the misfortune to encounter the funeral cortège of the Action Française historian, Jacques Bainville. Recognized by the mourners, he was seized on, and saved from probable lynching, though not from injury, only by the intervention of near-by building workers. Even the French courts could not ignore this, and Maurras, who had quite recently reminded his readers of what was their duty in such circumstances, was tried for incitement to murder and given a short prison sentence, which made him more of a hero to his supporters than ever.

While the right was continuing to demonstrate its irresponsibility and trying to create a revolutionary situation, Thorez was cooing like the dove of peace, stretching out his hand – over the national broadcasting system – even to the Catholics, as brothers oppressed with the same burdens. The Communist appeal was above all national and patriotic – 'Pour une France libre, forte et heureuse'. Only the leaders can have known how odd the appeal to liberty was from the followers of Stalin and presumably they did not care.

The new political alliance of the left had been well cemented by the time when the Chamber was dissolved. The elections of April 1936 were marked by a remarkable coherence among the electors of the Popular Front, and a corresponding disarray among the supporters of the right. The result was a shift from right to left, which gave the Popular Front about 380 deputies against 237 on the right. Within the Popular Front the Communists were the principal gainers, with an increase of some 62 seats; the Socialists gained 39 and the independent Socialists 12. On the other hand the Radicals lost 43 seats, which was not calculated to ensure their continued loyalty to the Popular Front.

In spite of this big swing in representation, once again it must not be supposed that there was an equally marked change in the balance of political forces in the nation. In actual votes the parties of the right and the centre had lost only some two hundred thousand votes. The uneasy balance of strength which condemned the nation to permanent political instability therefore still survived. Indeed the omens for political stability were worse than ever. The right, baulked at the polls, began to turn even more to the thought of extra-constitutional action. The Action Française, in the person of a former *Camelot du roi*, Eugène Deloncle, was to give birth to the Comité Secret d'Action Révolutionnaire (C.S.A.R.), whose members became known later as the 'Cagoulards' or Hooded Men from their cult of secrecy. In this respect they achieved more notoriety than success for it seems likely that the police had planted informers in their ranks from the beginning.

The largest of the leagues, the Croix de Feu, underwent a series of curious changes. It had already, in October 1935, become a para-constitutional organization under the name of Mouvement Social Français. When, in June 1936, the new government of the left decreed the dissolution of the leagues, it formed itself into the Parti Social Français, aiming to gain power by electoral methods. This was equal to an acknowledgment of the failure of the revolutionary agitation of the leagues, made by the biggest and most powerful of them. The P.S.F. swelled in numbers – by 1938 it claimed three million members; but as it grew in size it diminished in significance. The failure of the leagues to achieve more than an – admittedly very considerable – nuisance value must however not be taken as evidence of the strength of the Third Republic in its last years; the weakness of French politics and society was a conservative clinging to the past, not an irresponsible adventuring into new ways.

The same lesson can be drawn from the failure of an attempt to organize the farmers for revolutionary action. Badly hit by the fall in agricultural prices, peasant discontent had been given leadership by Henri Dorgères, who founded in 1935 the Front Paysan, with a spear-head of Greenshirts as its fighting force. For a moment the

Front Paysan seemed to present a serious danger to the regime, but it was only a transient one. A modest rise in prices in the autumn, a reaction against the outbreak of violence, and the traditional conservatism of the peasantry came into play again and Dorgères and his movement faded out.

What was more serious was the general discrediting of parliamentary institutions. Tardieu was writing a series of books against them. The cult of Péguy from one point of view represented the search for a *mystique* in place of *politique*. The left was not immune from these tendencies. Indeed in the long run the dissident and crypto-revolutionary movements of the left were to prove more dangerous than those of the right. A group of disillusioned Socialists, led by Marcel Déat and the Mayor of Bordeaux, Adrien Marquet, proclaimed the bankruptcy of Marxism before the problems of the twentieth century and formed a schismatic party of neo-Socialists. Their appeal to nationalism, call for the restoration of authority, and hostility to parliamentary methods, would indicate, even if we did not know of their later record as collaborationists with the Nazis, their kinship with Fascism and National Socialism.

The blue-eyed boy of the Communists, Jacques Doriot, Mayor of St Denis and leader in the Chamber of Deputies, impressed by the rise of Hitler, was also looking for a new path. In 1934, after a premature demand for an alliance of the parties of the left, which was then still anathema to the Communists, he split with the party. Instead of accepting the official policy he began a campaign to change it. Summoned, with his chief opponent, Thorez, to the arbitrement of Moscow, he refused to go. Thorez returned with authority to deal with Doriot, who was expelled. In the elections of 1936 he managed to hold his fief of St Denis against his former party, in rivalry with which he founded the Parti Populaire Français. The new Chamber was to contain ten dissident Communists under Doriot, and twenty-six neo-Socialists.

As leader of the largest party and also of the middle party in the coalition, the premiership in the new government naturally fell to Léon Blum. He came into a troubled social situation as well as a depressed economic one. The victory of the Popular Front aroused hopes that the agitation for social reform, frustrated for over a generation, was at last to reap its fruits. In a sense the workers of France might be said to have staked out their claim to a share in the rewards of society, as well as its labours, over a century earlier, in 1792. After nearly a century and a half of frustration, they were determined, to adopt the words of Carlyle, not to have their pockets picked, once again, of a millennium – though indeed their demands were more modest and more practical than that. Some impatience was natural and no political agitation need be hypothesized to account for it.

The elections of April–May 1936 were immediately followed by an outburst of strikes in the aircraft factories of the Paris region. They were a spontaneous reaction to the electoral victory of the left and took the Communists themselves by surprise. Though the Communist Party had declined to share in the responsibility of the government it had played so large a part in making, it was not prepared to smash it at the outset. The tradition of the French industrial workers, not Communist propaganda, was responsible for the Utopian belief of at least the more militant among them that the factories were to be handed over to them to run. Until this happy consummation they proposed to occupy them passively. As sit-down strikes spread from industry to industry, the economic life of the country was brought almost to a standstill. The first task of the new government was therefore by the restoration of industrial peace to start the wheels of production turning again.

A conference of representatives of employers and trade unions was held at the hotel Matignon, the premier's official residence, where alarm at what seemed a revolutionary situation extracted revolutionary concessions from the employers. The larger industrial enterprises, of course, were those that were mainly represented and these were more prepared to recognize economic and political realities than the smaller propertied classes. On June 9th the Matignon agreement was signed. By this there was to be a rise on an average of 12 per cent in wages, which was to be accompanied by an increase in the pay of civil servants; armaments works were to be nationalized and government control extended over the Bank of France. Perhaps the most valuable and permanent gain, and one which in the long run was to have far-reaching social consequences, was the achievement of the *congés payés* – holidays with pay. The most risky was the introduction of the forty-hour week. The employers recognized the right of the trade unions to represent the workers and in return the unions withdrew their claim to direct action, which was tacitly to repudiate the occupation of the factories. Both sides agreed to start discussions for collective agreements. The Matignon settlement was a triumph for Blum; the workers rightly believed that they had made great gains, though spasmodic strikes continued into 1937, and the propertied classes were relieved to have escaped from a threatening situation.

The new reforms were rapidly put into effect. The only problem that remained was how to pay for them. The answer was by the expansion of government borrowing, the full extent of this being concealed by the old expedient of putting part of the deficit into an 'extraordinary budget'. The parties of the left had so often in the past attributed the inflationary result of government policies to the machinations of the men of wealth who knew how to escape from its consequences or turn them to their own advantage, that they had come to believe that this was the only cause of inflation. Blum had tied his hands in advance against effective remedial measures by committing himself to maintaining the gold value of the franc. Consequently the increasing disproportion between internal and external prices, combined with the continuance of industrial unrest though on a less massive scale, and fear of Communist influence on the government, began another flight from the franc. On October 1st, 1936, the government swallowed its pledges and reconciled itself to what had been inevitable from the beginning, and would have been much more efficacious if done then: it devalued the franc in terms of gold. This did not have the stimulating effect on French economy that was expected. Production – partly because of the introduction of the forty-hour week – was much lower than it had been in 1929 and unemployment remained high. The financial crisis continued to be acute.

By March 1937 Léon Blum had come to feel that the only way to restore confidence was to proclaim a 'pause' in the reforms of the Popular Front. This merely encouraged the attacks of its enemies,

who were determined to drive it out of power at whatever cost
and so to have their revenge for the fright they had been given and
the concessions that had been forced from them. The bitterness of
the opposition to Blum's government was shown in the vicious
attacks on the Minister of the Interior, Roger Salengro, Mayor of
Lille and deputy for the Nord. An old Communist slander against
him, of desertion in the First World War, was taken up by one of
the most venemous of the journals of the right, *Gringoire*, and
the subsequent press campaign drove him to suicide. At the same
time, the international situation, which must be dealt with in the
next section, continued to exacerbate the domestic situation.

Blum had trouble from his nominal supporters as well as from his
opponents. The 'pause' gave the Communists, and even more the
militants of the Socialist left, an excuse for attacking his government. In the usual way the extreme left and right played into each
other's hands. A party of some two hundred Croix de Feu, with
their women and children, attended a demonstration at a cinema,
held rather unnecessarily in the working-class suburb of Clichy.
They were attacked by a Popular Front counter-demonstration.
Police opened fire and the resulting casualties gave the now reunited and Communist-controlled C.G.T. a reason for calling a
twenty-four-hour general strike. Apart from this, industrial peace
was still very unsettled. Sporadic strikes continued to break out,
like a' smouldering heath-fire, in town and country. The middle
classes, already bitterly resentful at what seemed to them the
arrogance of their inferiors in a country where consciousness of
class distinctions was acute, found their usual seaside and country
resorts swamped by hordes of workers in the summer of 1937,
leaving for the first time on *congés payés*. It seemed like a new
barbarian invasion.

To complete the troubles of the government, despite the devaluation of the previous year there were renewed signs of a flight from
the franc. The leaders of industry and finance were recovering their
confidence. Influential papers like *Le Temps* and *Le Journal des
Débats* were largely under their control, and the state of public
opinion made a counter-attack on the weakening and divided
Popular Front possible. The rumour began to spread, 'better Hitler

than Blum'. Even apart from this agitation, it seemed to Blum that some assertion of governmental strength was needed to redress the economic situation. The index of industrial production, 140 in 1929, was still only 101 in 1937; and unemployment remained at the level it had reached in 1934. Since he knew that his majority would never vote the measures he thought necessary, in June 1937 Blum resorted to the old expedient of decree-laws with the intention of establishing control of the exchanges. The Radicals in the Chamber of Deputies accepted the proposals, knowing that they could rely on the Senate to emasculate them. In the upper chamber, the old president of the Financial Commission, Joseph Caillaux, launched a bitter attack in the name of financial orthodoxy, thus performing the last public act in a career marked throughout by an extraordinary capacity for political misjudgment. The Senate, by excluding exchange control from the scope of the decree-laws, delivered the *coup de grâce* to the government of Blum, as it had to that of Herriot in 1925, so far had the upper house risen from its insignificance in the early days of the Third Republic. Blum resigned. For the third time an electoral victory of the left had been reversed within two years of the election.

With the forces of organized wealth thus conciliated, and the left once again shattered by its own internal stresses, weak Radical governments were able to take over, while the financial sky brightened and the propertied classes basked in a final and imbecile euphoria. Unfortunately finance was no longer what mattered most. The economy of France remained in a state of chronic weakness and needed drastic treatment. Even if they had been prepared to give it or the country to support them, the last governments of the Third Republic had little time left in which to attempt a reform and little attention to spare from the international situation.

It is tempting to trace the economic malaise of France between the wars to the effects of the First World War. Approximately 1,300,000 Frenchmen had been killed, apart from the injured, and France seemed a nation of old men, widows, and *mutilés de guerre*. This was partly the reason why, by 1938, it had 140 persons in 1,000 over sixty, compared with, say, Holland's 94; and why the death-rate was 150 in 10,000 as against 107 in the United States and

117 in the United Kingdom. By 1939 the population of France was practically what it had been in 1913, and even this figure had only been reached with the aid of massive immigration. By 1936 the foreign immigrants numbered 3,000,000, bringing needed, though usually unskilled, labour with them but also creating serious social stresses. The decline in population was most obvious in the country-side, especially in the agriculturally poorer areas of the Massif Central, south-east and south. The balance of population, which at the beginning of the century had been roughly 42·5 per cent urban to 57·5 per cent rural (i.e. living in communes of under 2,000 inhabitants), had changed by 1936 to 52 per cent urban and 47 per cent rural. Although the social consequences were bitterly deplored, the decline in the numbers of small uneconomic farms was little loss, but the productivity in proportion to the number of agri-cultural workers was still only half what it was in Great Britain. The number fed for each agricultural worker was 5·1 in France as against 14·8 in the United States. French farming was preserved in its state of inefficiency and prices were kept far above the world level, by a long-standing policy of protection. In the summer of 1939 the price of wheat in France was three times its price in London. The electoral pressure that could be exercised by the rural constituencies prevented any attempt to allow French prices to come closer to the world level. One of the most powerful pressure groups was that of the sugar-beet growers, whose surplus produc-tion the state had to purchase at an uneconomic price for conversion into fuel alcohol.

In industry, as well as in agriculture, the small scale of production was a cause of economic backwardness. For each active worker British industry commanded nearly three times as much horse-power and American nearly five times as much as French industry. There were, of course, signs of modernization appearing here and there. Hydro-electric power was being developed, though it was not as yet put to much industrial use. André Citroën had introduced American methods of mass production into the manufacture of motor-cars, but this was practically an isolated example. The powers of finance and industry, gathered in great associations such as the Comité des Forges or the Bank of France with its fifteen

Regents and Council of two hundred, formed great monopolistic groups, which operated behind the cover of the mass of small employers whose inefficiency helped to keep prices up and wages down and whose numbers provided a political clientèle for use against left-wing governments. Even when reforming legislation, such as the social insurance laws of 1928 and 1930, was passed, the employers' associations were able by working up a press campaign against them largely to nullify their application.

In elections the left might win its victories, but the real power in the state remained in the hands of its enemies, not only industry and finance but also in the professions and administration. Higher education, in lycées or universities or institutes, was expensive and scholarships were few. The Faculties of Law and the École des Sciences Politiques, the almost essential gateway to a career in the higher ranks of the administration, were conservative, Catholic, Action Française or even Fascist in their sympathies. Economic backwardness and acute class conflict produced the political instability which repeatedly threatened the Third Republic between the wars with total collapse. Yet the danger must not be exaggerated. Neither economic nor political weakness brought the Third Republic down. This was the result of defeat in war and foreign occupation. All through the 'thirties a ground swell of international trouble had been rising and diverting attention from domestic problems, until it finally overwhelmed them and drowned the nation in the tide of war.

PART THREE

THE FALL OF THE REPUBLIC

❧

CHAPTER ONE

THE QUEST FOR PEACE

BY 1937 French foreign policy lay in ruins about a nation that was divided in everything except the desire to avoid a second World War. Whatever the blame that may be attached to individuals and parties or even whole classes for the failures of French domestic policy, an air of fatality can be seen, in retrospect, to surround the development of international relations from the high hopes of 1918 to the total despair of 1939.

The peace of 1919, it was said at the time, was one that passed human understanding. It started badly, with American repudiation and British evasion of the guarantees promised to France at the Conference of Paris. In exchange the French fell back on their treaties with the Little Entente and Poland. For some years reparations dominated French policy. Conference followed conference round the more desirable resorts of Western Europe. The Ruhr adventure brought no gain. With the defeat of the Bloc National in 1924 more rational international policies emerged; but by this date the possibility – a real one in the years immediately after the war – of integrating a peaceful Germany into the structure of Western society had largely been dissipated, though it was another six years before this was to be inescapably evident. The Dawes plan of October 1924 represented the first attempt to reduce reparations to serious economic proportions, and between 1924 and 1930 Germany paid nearly £400 million.

Reparations might have been more easily dealt with if the problem had not been tied up, practically if not logically, with the basic French search for international security. The ostracism of Bolshevik Russia, the isolationism of the American Republican Party, and the weakness and folly of British Conservative governments, prohibited any solution. In September 1923 a draft treaty of Mutual Assistance was rejected by Great Britain. In 1924 the Labour government negotiated the Geneva Protocol. Generally welcomed by European statesmen, it collapsed with the defeat of the Labour government and the return of the Conservatives to power. The British rejection of the Protocol, for which the French press and statesmen had been passionately pleading, left France determined to maintain the practical safeguards she still had in the form of occupied territory and the Allied mission of control over German armament.

Meanwhile German foreign policy came under the control of Stresemann and French under that of Briand. Perhaps for different reasons, they both desired a *détente* in Franco-German relations, and as the British Foreign Minister, Austen Chamberlain, was also prepared for a European solution to the international impasse so long as the commitment was not too high, the three Powers signed a pact at Locarno in October 1925. This was followed by the evacuation of the occupied zone of Cologne and the admission of Germany to the League of Nations with a permanent seat on the Council.

Even after the elections of 1928 had strengthened the French right, Briand remained at the Quai d'Orsay, attempting to build international peace on a Franco-German *rapprochement*, set – to guard against the undue predominance of Germany – in a broad European cadre. It might be argued that Briand carried the country with him for so long only by means of a calculated ambiguity, allowing the right to see in his policy a strengthening of the French system of alliances, and the left an extension of the Locarno treaties. That Briand was sincerely working for the preservation of international peace cannot be doubted; and he can hardly be criticized if his policy was also in the interests of French security. In September 1929 he proposed a European Federal Union. In the same year a final attempt was made to put reparations on a practical basis. This was the Young Plan. In return for German agreement to the plan, France offered to evacuate her occupied zones of the Rhineland. In May 1930 ratifications of the Young plan were completed. In June the last French troops left the occupied territory. Three months later the German elections were marked by sensational Nazi gains which carried the representation of the National Socialists in the German parliament from 12 to 107.

The French government, while not abandoning its pacific intentions, now began to turn back to more positive ways of strengthening its position. Military service had been reduced in 1928 from eighteen months to one year, but to make up for the consequent decline in man-power the Maginot line had been begun, as a continuous defensive line from the Belgian to the Swiss frontier. These works were now pushed on more energetically. There was a move towards greater friendship with Soviet Russia, which, however, had the effect of weakening the Polish alliance; attempts were made to conciliate Italy; and the states of the Little Entente huddled closer together for protection. In 1931 France was still strong enough to veto a proposed Austro-German customs union. It was almost a last demonstration of strength.

The international Disarmament Conference, opening in February 1932, could not have begun under more unfavourable auspices. Briand's noble and far-seeing struggle to bring France and Germany together in friendship had obviously failed with the rise of the Nazis. He still struggled for an international solution, but this was just what his enemies on the right did not want. At the beginning of 1932 they drove him from office and robbed him of the reward of the presidency. Worn out and disillusioned, the cynical old roué who had given his last years to the noblest of illusions died. Neither he, nor anyone else, could have guessed that he had laid foundations which, after another generation of bloodshed and ruin, were to prove the only ones on which a tolerable future could be built.

He was replaced at the Quai d'Orsay by Pierre Laval – only briefly, for Laval's day had not yet come – but it was a symbol of the passage of France from an age of coherent policies and ideals to one of temporary devices and opportunism. If circumstances in the coming years were too great for the men who had to deal with them, the men were also too small.

By a curious but quite natural reversal of positions, it was henceforth to be on the left that the policy of resistance to Germany was to find support, and the right that was increasingly to favour concessions. On neither side was there any confidence in the future, though much of the kind of facile optimism that was ready to seize on any straw. When, in January 1933, Hitler became Chancellor of the German Reich and did not immediately declare war, fears momentarily faded. The Nazi leader, with his genius for telling the right lies at the right time and his understanding of human psychology, knew that if people wanted to believe, the bigger the lie that gave them what they wanted the better. He hastened to announce his devotion to peace and readiness to sign any international agreements that would guarantee it. Many on the French right, thus reassured, began to feel that the Nazi accession to power might even be a good thing. After all, they shared many of the same ideas. They had been anti-semitic and opposed to democratic government long before Hitler. They had the same enemies – Jews, Communists, Socialists, democrats, internationalists. They were equally prepared to use violence in domestic politics to eliminate an 'ignoble parliamentarism'.

The French government was therefore prepared to accept the Four-Power Pact, which Mussolini, playing on the British Prime Minister's vanity, had sold to Ramsay MacDonald. By it, France, Germany, Italy and Great Britain were to form a sort of condominium of Great Powers to settle the affairs of Europe. This was a way of by-passing the League of Nations. It was also equivalent to delivering notice to the smaller states of Europe that their fate was likely to be settled over their heads. It is extraordinary that the French right should have been so ready to come to terms with the Fascists and Nazis, and so anxious to deliver a blow to the hated League of Nations, that they failed to appreciate that they had also gone a long way towards undermining their own cherished system of alliances. The Four-Power Pact was signed in July 1933. In October Germany walked out of the disarmament conference. Still the French right, which had never wanted disarmament, refused to see the writing on the wall; while the left pathetically continued to believe that Nazi Germany was only a transient phenomenon which could not really survive in the twentieth century.

A strong and coherent foreign policy could hardly have been expected from the series of weak Radical cabinets which followed one another in 1933. The following year, opening with the crisis of February 6th, promised no better; but in the government of national union under Doumergue a new Foreign Minister began a revival of French diplomacy. Louis Barthou was a politician of the right, but he was also a statesman of the old school, author – twenty years earlier – of the three-years law of 1913. In a diplomatic tour of Eastern Europe Barthou reinvigorated the Little Entente and took the first steps towards a revival of the old Russian alliance. The new threat from Germany obviously demanded some such reply, even though it involved a danger of alienating Poland, which was already playing with the suicidal idea of saving herself by a separate arrangement with Germany. On the other hand Mussolini, alarmed at Nazi-instigated movements for a German *Anschluss* with Austria, showed signs of moving into the anti-German camp. The ground plan of a grand alliance was being sketched out, by which a reborn aggressive Germany might yet be contained. Whether it could ever have been more than a sketch must remain in doubt, for in October 1934, when, as part of Barthou's plan, King Alexander of Jugoslavia paid a state visit to France, he and the French Foreign Minister were both assassinated by a Macedonian terrorist at Marseilles. The hope of a revived French foreign policy was ended.

The successor to Barthou at the Quai d'Orsay was Laval, hardly the man to have become a dominant figure in the greater days of the Third Republic, but in his element when the fabric was rotting and crumbling on all sides. Son of a small-town butcher in poverty-stricken Auvergne, he came to the Faculty of Law in Paris, itself a great achievement for a poor boy. In Paris, before the First World War, Laval was a left-wing Socialist, his humanitarian ideals finding expression in voluntary service as a 'poor man's lawyer'. In 1914 he was elected as deputy for the Paris working-class suburb of Aubervilliers; and during the First World War one of the permanent motives which ran through his life appeared. This was the desire for peace at any price. As a young Socialist deputy he opposed the military service law. In 1917 he was a member of what was labelled the defeatist group in the Chamber, and in the nationalist elections of 1919 he lost his seat. Now began a gradual move to the right, which characteristically, aided by his natural camaraderie, he effected without losing his personal links with the left.

Laval's first move away from the left brought him into association with Caillaux and the Radicals. He supported Briand's attempts at a Franco-German *rapprochement*. He claimed, and probably genuinely believed, that ideologies or forms of government were irrelevant to foreign policy – 'Les régimes se succèdent, les révolutions s'accomplissent, mais la géographie subsiste toujours.' When he became Foreign Minister, however, although he continued the negotiations, begun by Barthou, for a Franco-Soviet pact, he delayed ratification as long as he could. In fact, although the negotiations were concluded in May 1935, the treaty was not ratified by France, after the fall of Laval, until April 1936. The other side of Laval's indifference to ideologies and ideals was his respect for strength, or what he took to be such, and it is probable that he already saw European peace as dependent on agreement with Nazi Germany.

Meanwhile Hitler was progressing from strength to strength. In January 1935 the Saar, under French rule for the past fifteen years, held the plebiscite prescribed by the Peace Treaty to determine its future and voted overwhelmingly for return to the Reich. In March compulsory military service was re-established in Germany. France was now facing the 'lean years' of 1935 to 1939, when the annual number of recruits, as a result of the First World War, would be halved. The period of compulsory military service was therefore extended to two years, in spite of the opposition of the Socialists led by Blum, who denounced the militarism and aggressive spirit of what was probably the weakest and most defensively-minded General Staff that France has ever had. If the Germans attacked, Blum declared, the workers would rise as one man to defend their class and country in a far stronger force than any conscript army – so completely was a most intelligent man humbugged by his own wishful thinking and an historical legend. A young officer named de Gaulle, who was at this time trying to persuade both soldiers and civilians that tanks might be a better defence than either bare arms or big battalions, merely earned denunciation as a Fascist for having such dangerous ideas.

The imputation would not have been an insult to Laval, who was already negotiating with that other ex-Socialist, Mussolini. In April 1935 the conference at Stresa united France, Great Britain and Italy in a declaration of resistance to any unilateral repudiation of the treaty agreements on which the European status quo was based. This might have been a little more than a pious gesture if two months later the British government, living up to its reputation of *perfide Albion*, had not signed a naval agreement with Germany without consulting its allies. The line where stupidity merged into treachery in British policy was naturally a difficult one for the French to draw.

Meanwhile, however, the Italian dictator, looking for a little cheap glory, had decided on Abyssinia as a foe he could measure his troops against without undue risk, having prepared his rear in advance by the Stresa agreement. The Italian army invaded Abyssinia in the autumn of 1935. In spite of the reluctance of the Great Powers, the League of Nations could hardly avoid decreeing sanctions against such a flagrant international aggression. Opinion in France was hopelessly divided. The left saw in Mussolini's action yet one more example of the international menace of Fascism. Yet its pacifism was so deeply rooted that when British battleships were sent to the Mediterranean, Blum wrote an article under the heading 'England's Error', in which he made it plain that he was not prepared to go beyond economic sanctions. Even these were too much for the parties of the right, which, partly by natural affinity, and partly as a result of Italian propaganda and bribes, had adopted Mussolini's cause as their own. In September 1935 the *Action Française* published a list of a hundred and forty deputies who favoured economic sanctions against Italy, with the warning that if war resulted their blood would be the first to flow. The extent to which Fascist ideas had permeated the French intelligentsia was shown by a manifesto of solidarity with Italy signed in October by over eight hundred and fifty intellectuals. Laval, one of nature's go-betweens, persuaded the British Foreign Minister, Sir Samual Hoare, to do a deal with Italy. Revealed to the British public, which looked upon right and wrong in the international scene with a less impartial and sophisticated eye than its government, the Hoare-Laval agreement produced an outburst of indignation. To save his government, the Prime Minister sacrified Hoare in December 1935, and in January Laval himself fell, bitterly resenting what he regarded as yet another British betrayal.

A caretaker government took office to see out the last few months of the Chamber, and it was this government which was faced with

F

what was perhaps the most critical decision in the whole of the inter-war period. In March 1936 Hitler denounced the Locarno treaties, proclaimed the remilitarization of the Rhineland, and sent in a token force of German troops. Even at the time there were many who realized that this was a moment of destiny. The French premier, Albert Sarraut, a typical professional politician of the Radical Party, rather surprisingly favoured a military reaction by France. The Foreign Minister, Flandin, was intelligent enough to see the real importance of the crisis and also at first thought of positive action, in spite of the fact that the right was certain to shriek to the skies if there were any attempt to resist the Nazi move, to such a pitch of pacifist defeatism had their perverted nationalism reached. This reaction might have been discounted. More serious was the fact that the General Staff was not only imbued with right-wing ideas and ideologically more in sympathy with the Fascists and Nazis than with its own Radical government, but its military thinking and preparations, under the influence of Marshal Pétain, had become purely defensive. The lessons of the First World War, and the temperament of Pétain, both dictated a policy of defence, which had been given concrete form by the construction of the great Maginot line. Yet, though the French army in 1936 could have taken the offensive only by a drastic readjustment of its plans and redeployment of its forces, there is little doubt that the small army Hitler had committed to the Rhineland could have been thrown back, and that France still had a sufficient military superiority over Germany to defeat any possible German resistance.

The Sarraut government might have disregarded the opposition of the right and the unpreparedness of the military but for another and decisive obstacle. This was the attitude of the British government. Anthony Eden, who had taken Sir Samuel Hoare's place at the Foreign Office, might have been willing to support French military intervention. The Cabinet as a whole was unprepared for action; it seems probable that the decisive influence at this crisis, when the inevitability or avoidance of a second World War hung in the balance, was that of Lord Halifax. Ambiguities in the Locarno treaties provided the British government with a way of evading, with legality if not with honour, the action which even at the time some saw as the only hope of checking the rush to the Second World War. Though Sarraut and Flandin have had to bear the blame for their tame acquiescence in the remilitarization of the Rhineland, the greater responsibility lies with Pétain and the French General Staff for decisions taken years before, and with the British cabinet for the decisions it evaded at the time.

Hitler had succeeded in his greatest gamble. The result of the remilitarization of the Rhineland was the crumbling of the whole French system of alliances. The Eastern Allies drew the logical conclusion that henceforth France neither could nor would do anything to defend them if Germany attacked. Consequently they tried to come to terms with the Nazis. Belgium attempted to shelter from the coming storm by a declaration of neutrality, apparently having forgotten what was the value of its neutrality in 1914. The Versailles settlement lay in ruins. The French strategic position had been turned. During the next three years a steady retreat was to degenerate into rout and end in final collapse.

The Popular Front came into power when it was probably already too late to redress the situation. It is doubtful if it had the will to do so in any case. The Socialist Party, which was the dominant partner in the new government, had inherited deep-rooted pacifist instincts from Jean Jaurès, to whose memory Léon Blum constantly appealed. He was faced with a less decisive but more long-drawn-out crisis in the second half of 1936, in the shape of the civil war that had broken out in Spain. The left pressed for intervention to aid the Spanish republicans, the right passionately supported General Franco. Blum later declared that his reason for not helping the Spanish government in 1936 was that it would have brought about a civil war in France. This was perhaps to avoid the admission that the pacifism of the left was as strong a factor behind the policy of neutralism as the pro-Fascist sentiments of the right. British influence was also brought to bear on the same side. The result was that France watched passively while with German and Italian aid a new Fascist dictator established himself on her Spanish frontier. Mussolini, who had flirted with Laval while it seemed to his advantage, now saw on which side lay the strength and concluded the Berlin–Rome axis.

Frustrated in its domestic policy and paralysed in foreign policy, the government of the Popular Front collapsed in June 1937. The natural history of left-wing majorities in the Chamber prescribed a gradual move to the right. The place of Blum was taken by Camille Chautemps, well fitted to follow a policy of hesitating compromises, while the international situation boiled up to its next crisis. In March 1938 Hitler achieved the *Anschluss* with Austria, when momentarily Blum was back in office. In the desperate state of affairs he envisaged a government of national union, but this was a weapon of the right, repeatedly used to block social change, not one that they were prepared to hand over to the leader of the left. All the long-nourished enmities of the right against Blum burst out and he was driven from office. His place was taken by the Radical Daladier, with a government now including Paul Reynaud and three other moderates. Once again Daladier could appear as the strong man of French politics; heading a government of national defence in a mounting domestic and foreign crisis. The Popular Front was a thing of the past.

❦

CHAPTER TWO

THE DRIFT TO WAR

THE German *Anschluss* with Austria was followed by a Nazi agitation for the annexation of the German minority areas of Czechoslovakia. The weakness of France, and the inability of the government of Daladier to take any firm line of its own, were shown by the passivity with which it followed the British lead throughout 1938 and 1939. It is true that the Chamberlain government was providing France with an excuse for a policy to which it was condemned anyhow by the state of French politics. The level to which Western diplomacy had now been reduced was demonstrated by the fact that it was being mainly conducted personally by Neville Chamberlain. On September 15th, at Berchtesgaden, Chamberlain, under the pathetic illusion that he was purchasing peace, agreed to the cession of the Sudetan areas of Czechoslovakia to Germany. At Godesberg, soon after, he discovered that the amount of the Danegeld he was prepared to pay – at the expense of another country, it is true – had suddenly been doubled. The patent treachery of Hitler produced a psychological shock and for the first time there were signs that Britain and France might, however unwillingly, be driven into resistance.

But now the mixture of pacifism and pro-Nazi sentiments in France emerged as a major influence over French policy. The Socialist Party was hopelessly split over the issue of resistance to the Nazis. Its secretary general, Paul Faure, who led the pacifist wing, wrote articles against resistance in *Le Populaire*, while René Belin carried the C.G.T. and the trade-union journal, *Syndicats*, on to the same side. *Le Canard Enchaîné*, spoilt child of left-wing journalism, echoed British politicians in asking, 'What do we care if three million Germans want to be German?' On the right the nationalists, fearing above all the menace of social reform and conscious of their ideological links with Fascists and Nazis, had completely abandoned the

foreign policy of the 'twenties. The Action Française found itself
in the happy situation of being able to combine 'À bas la guerre'
with 'Down with the Jews'. Flandin had a manifesto against war
posted up in Paris. In the French cabinet a strong pacifist group included the Foreign Minister, Georges Bonnet.

In this situation the initiative was again left to the British government, which had no better idea than to propose another four-power
conference. Chamberlain, Daladier, Mussolini and Hitler therefore
met at Munich on September 29th. The Western Powers once more
yielded to threats and accepted the partition of Czechoslovakia. The
Versailles settlement and the French system of alliances lay in ruins;
but when Daladier, who unlike Chamberlain knew what he was doing, stepped off the plane that brought him back to Paris, half expecting to be greeted with hisses and brickbats, he was cheered by
crowds who believed the menace of war had been lifted from them.
Léon Blum wrote in *Le Populaire* that every man and woman in
France would pay their just tribute of gratitude to Chamberlain and
Daladier. In the Chamber the whole Socialist Party, with one
exception, voted for the government. The Communist Party, which
denounced the 'treason of Munich' – Russia having been excluded
from the negotiations – thereby only saddled itself with the onus of
being the war party. In December the German Foreign Minister,
Ribbentrop, came to Paris to sign a Declaration of Friendship. All
was well.

Meanwhile, though foreign affairs occupied the centre of the
stage, there were still economic difficulties for the French government. In October Daladier had obtained plenary powers to deal
with them. He appointed the dapper and self-confident little Paul
Reynaud, a politician of the centre and opposed to the Popular
Front, but also one of the anti-Munich section of the government, as
Finance Minister. Reynaud produced plans for new taxation, a
reduction in the number of government employees, and an increase
in the length of the working week, with the object of restoring international confidence in the French franc. The C.G.T. proclaimed
a one-day general strike on November 30th in protest against these
measures, and the Communist Party seized on it as an opportunity
for a great demonstration of protest. But the life had gone out of

the left wing, which was now also torn by bitter differences over Munich. Public opinion was against the strike. The railways and public services were requisitioned by the government to keep them working. When workers at the great Renault car works attempted a stay-in strike, *gardes mobiles* were sent in and cleared the factory by midnight. The strike was a total failure for the Communist Party, which had led it. The wealthy classes and international finance being thus reassured, the financial situation showed a marked improvement. Economic recovery still lagged in France, but of the social gains of the Popular Front not all had been lost. France thus entered 1939 with the appearance of restored social stability and under what seemed a strong government. In April 1939 Daladier secured the re-election of the mediocre but safe Albert Lebrun as President.

True, this optimism could only be preserved by scrupulously shutting one's eyes to everything that was happening outside France. Hitler and the Nazis were momentarily quiescent: experience should have suggested (yet to many it did not, to such a pitch had the habit of cultivating illusory hopes reached in the Western democracies) that this would not be for long. Mussolini was looking for more cheap colonial conquests, now at the expense of France. The Spanish Civil War was in its last throes, with France as hopelessly divided in its sympathies as ever. The left was still ignorant of the deeds of the Communist commissars against their political rivals in the republican ranks; and if a few Catholic writers, such as Mauriac, and Bernanos in his *Les Grands Cimetières sous la Lune*, had raised their voices in protest against the deeds of Franco and his men, the French right as a whole rejoiced when Barcelona fell in January 1939 and the war was over. The rule by which French Chambers beginning on the left ended on the right was demonstrated when the same Chamber that had set up the government of the Popular Front voted by 363 to 261 for the recognition of Franco. France's most famous soldier, Marshal Pétain, was sent as ambassador to conciliate the new Spanish regime.

This Indian summer of the Third Republic was all too brief. The euphoria engendered by Munich lasted a bare five months. In March 1939 German troops occupied the rump of Czechoslovakia in disregard of the undertakings at Munich, while Great Britain and

France watched helplessly. Daladier, true to his conception of himself, and the popular image of him, as a strong man, whereas in fact he was merely a well-intentioned one, had himself voted plenary powers. The British government of Chamberlain, at last beginning to understand dimly something of the situation into which it had led its country, tried to stem the rush to war by guaranteeing to support Poland against aggression. It was a sign of the state to which the French government had been reduced that Chamberlain had to speak for France as well as for Great Britain, though France was, of course, committed by her treaty of 1921 to go to the help of Poland. Marcel Déat in *L'Œuvre*, the former Radical paper which was now subsidized secretly by the Italian government, asked if Frenchmen were to die for Danzig. Daladier cancelled this by issuing a statement supporting the Polish position in Danzig and French pressure forced Chamberlain to adopt a similar position. Meanwhile, Daladier's Foreign Minister, Bonnet, was negotiating behind the scenes with Italy.

Belatedly and reluctantly Great Britain and France came to realize that the only possibility of preserving peace lay in redressing the European balance by bringing in Russia. They sent a military mission to Moscow in August, but it was already too late. On August 21st the conclusion of a German-Soviet Non-aggression Pact was announced, but not the secret agreement for the partition of Poland. Bonnet was now feverishly trying to prevent war in the only way that remained, by persuading Poland not to resist. Daladier, on the other hand, was prepared in the last resort to accept the inevitability of war. On September 1st the Germans invaded Poland, and on September 3rd Great Britain and France declared war on Germany.

The minister under whom France entered the Second World War was conscientious and intelligent, but, like his country, for the last five years Daladier had been following events without the power to control them. His vice-premier, Chautemps, a typical political middleman, had not emerged unscathed from the Stavisky scandal. The Foreign Minister, Georges Bonnet, had clung to appeasement as long as he could; he was moved to another ministry but remained in the cabinet. From the beginning it can hardly be said that the government was united on the conduct of the war, and the optimistic propaganda with which it concealed its own doubts did little to prepare the country for the trials to come. The pro-Nazi opposition was comparatively subdued at the beginning, though biding its time. The Communist Party also, discredited by the Hitler-Stalin pact, was not able to take strong action against the war at first; indeed, there were signs that patriotic sentiments were struggling with party solidarity. *L'Humanité*, in a confiscated issue of August 26th, carried the leader 'Union of the French nation against the Hitlerian aggressor'. However, the temptation of patriotism was largely removed from the party by the actions of the government itself On September 2nd the Communist deputies voted for the military credits; but on September 26th the party was dissolved by law and all its publications banned. In January 1940 all the Communist deputies, many of whom had already fled or gone into hiding, were declared to have forfeited their seats. The indignation of the politicians and journalists of the right, many of whom were only too anxious to do a deal with Hitler, that Stalin, with world Communism behind him, should have done the same, rescued the party from the impossible task of trying to justify Russian policy to the country. It was able to go underground and prepare for the day when the last imperialist war would have ushered in the awaited revolution.

The war, launched by a German *Blitzkrieg* on Poland, began very differently in the West. In the Franco-Polish military conventions of May 1939 Gamelin had promised that, if Poland were invaded, France would attack Germany with the main body of her forces within fifteen days of mobilization. Even if the promise had been kept it would have been of little avail to Poland. The German armies were at the gates of Warsaw at the end of the first week, Russia invaded Poland in the middle of the month, and by the end of September Warsaw had surrendered. Meanwhile France had garrisoned the Maginot line and manned the Belgian frontier; and the British, moving more slowly than in 1914, had landed a small force of eighty thousand men at the ports of western France, and were gradually organizing long lines of communication to the north-eastern frontier. France, which called up its conscripts rapidly, was even more backward than Great Britain in its material preparations for the war. Daladier had refused to set up a Ministry of Munitions in peace time, perhaps because it would have involved keeping industrial workers out of the army and so once more allotting to the peasants their traditional role as the major source of cannon-fodder. When such a ministry was set up, after the war had begun, it had to recall between 100,000 and 150,000 men from the armies. The 'business as usual' mentality also prevented preparations for rationing which Reynaud as Minister of Finances urged, while the Minister of Agriculture, Queuille, in the interests of the peasants, opposed it.

Even those who were not defeatists believed that somehow or other the war would be a bloodless one for France. Safe within the Maginot line, the French troops would let the enemy army bleed itself white in fruitless assaults, while the Anglo-French blockade excluded the vital raw materials and slowly strangled the economy of Germany. The French and British armies, which had done practically nothing to assist the Poles, passively sat on the defensive waiting to be attacked. It was a *drôle de guerre* all that winter. After the Russian attack on Finland, on November 30th, there was more enthusiasm for aiding the Finns against the Russians than for fighting the Germans; and when the Finns, after a stubborn resistance, capitulated in March 1940, the outcry against Daladier brought his ministry down. He was replaced by Paul Reynaud, dapper, dynamic, optimistic. Daladier, with the Radical Socialist party behind him, clung to the Ministry of Defence and saved the Commander-in-Chief, Gamelin, in whom he had implicit confidence, but Bonnet was at last eliminated from the cabinet. On the other hand, Paul Baudouin, who had been used by Bonnet in negotiations with Italy before the outbreak of war, was brought in as under-secretary to the Prime Minister. With the support of 268 votes, as against 156 opponents and 111 abstentions, Reynaud had a bare majority. To improve his position he obtained from Great Britain an agreement that neither state would initiate separate peace negotiations.

On May 10th, 1940, the German army invaded the Low Countries. The French and British, abandoning their prepared positions, moved into Belgium to meet them. Reynaud took the opportunity

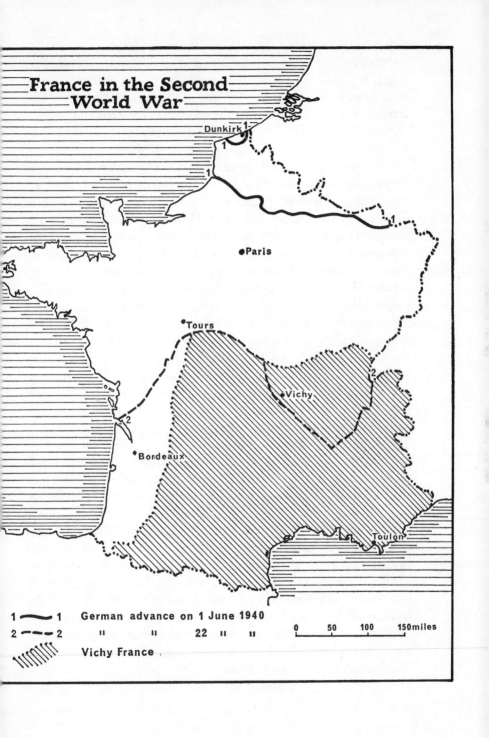

France in the Second World War

Dunkirk

●Paris

●Tours

●Vichy

●Bordeaux

Toulon

1 ———— 1 German advance on 1 June 1940

2 – – – 2   "   "   22   "   "

////// Vichy France

0   50   100   150 miles

to broaden his government by taking in more representatives of the right. It was the beginning of a trend that was to go much further than he expected. In spite of the strategic writings before the war of a minor French officer, de Gaulle, which had been passed over, like their author, by the French General Staff but carefully studied by the Germans, and the subsequent lessons of the Polish campaign, the *blitz* campaign that now descended on the Allied armies took them by surprise. Holland and Belgium were rapidly overrun. The German offensive against France developed on the Meuse, south of Sedan, where the nature of the ground was supposed to prohibit it. By May 15th the debris of the French army of the Meuse was everywhere in retreat, the defences of France had been breached and the Panzer columns were ranging the French countryside.

The disaster gave Reynaud the chance at last to eliminate his enemy Daladier from the Ministry of Defence, though, conducting a stubborn retreat, the Radical leader only moved to the Ministry of Foreign Affairs. Reynaud, who took over the Ministry of Defence, at once removed Gamelin, who in the depth of his bureaux had progressed from slow motion to almost total inaction. Weygand was called back from Syria to assume command of the lost battle, and Pétain from Spain to become vice-premier and chief military adviser to Reynaud.

In calling back these distinguished if aged figures from the past, Reynaud was aiming to restore the morale of the country, and in this he had a momentary success; but more than morale was needed to hold back the German onrush. The military situation was already out of the control of any general. Practically all trust between the French and British commands had disappeared. Politically, disillusionment was degenerating into recrimination and despair. The Western alliance was breaking up. The Belgian armistice let loose a flood of bitter invective against the Belgian king. In the Dunkirk evacuation the French troops found themselves left to the last on the beaches while the British were evacuated first; it was taken as a sign of British desertion. On June 9th the Council of Ministers moved from Paris to scattered châteaux in the Tours area and on June 14th the German army entered the capital.

Weygand and Pétain were without hope from the beginning; they had come in, as liquidators of a bankrupt regime, to bring hostilities to an end. For them the architects of ruin were the politicians of the Third Republic; but however devoutly they believed this, the defeat of France, it must be emphasized, was a military defeat. The French army had been launched into a war it was quite unprepared to fight, against a weight of armour and an air force that outclassed it, and tactics it did not know how to cope with. The military disaster gave their chance to the defeatist and pro-Nazi elements – Georges Bonnet and the 'Munichois', Faure and the Socialist pacifists, the Fascist and Germanophile groups strong in Paris and among the journalists, and the Communists demanding the end of an imperialist war. The new Minister of the Interior, Mandel, who had worked with Clemenceau and inherited some of his spirit, for the first time took strong action against the Germanophiles. But it was clear that the military defeat of France was total. The only question before the cabinet was how and by whom the fighting in France should be brought to an end.

Weygand was determined that France should leave the war and that the government and not the army should have the onus of concluding an armistice. Reynaud, and those who supported him in the cabinet, wanted the military command to take the responsibility for the armistice, and were prepared to remove the government to North Africa and continue the struggle from there. On the other hand Weygand, like Bazaine in 1870, was concerned to preserve an army in France to maintain law and order and repress the anticipated Communist rising. Both he and Pétain were also determined that the government should not leave the soil of France, and this was undoubtedly the view of the majority in both official and political circles. It would probably have been shared by the great masses of the people if, bewildered, harassed, overwhelmed, pouring in endless streams along the roads of France, or despairingly awaiting the next blow and not knowing from which direction it would come, they had been capable of having an opinion. Their one hope was in the man who had been summoned in the extremity to save France. Pétain, with the aloofness from immediate concerns and the impassive reaction to misfortune of extreme old age, was already thinking of the future, and the task, to which he believed himself called, of regeneration of a France weakened and corrupted by the ideologies of the left. Defeat was almost to be welcomed if it could bring this about.

On June 14th the government moved to Bordeaux, where the last scene in the tragedy was to be enacted. Relations with Great Britain, in a state of mutual misunderstanding and general confusion, were steadily deteriorating as the pressure for a separate peace increased. A group of ministers behind Chautemps now joined in the demand for an armistice. Outside the cabinet, Laval and his clique, including many who had belonged to the pro-German propagandist organization France-Allemagne, were intriguing. Reynaud yielded to the pressure and resigned on June 16th. Pétain was the obvious successor, and the next day the old Marshal broadcast to the nation a message in which he said that it was necessary to end hostilities and seek an honourable peace with Germany as between soldiers. This completed the demoralization of the army.

It had still not been settled whether the government should transfer itself to North Africa and continue the struggle from there. Twenty-four deputies, including Daladier and Mandel, sailed in the *Massilia* with the intention of doing so, only to be prevented from landing in North Africa, sent back ignominiously and condemned as *fuyards* by official propaganda. De Gaulle, promoted general after a successful armoured engagement, and called back from the fighting to join the government as Under-secretary for War on June 5th, made a dramatic escape to England and appealed for continued resistance, but only a handful joined him. On June 22nd the armistice was signed with Germany in the same railway carriage, at Compiègne, in which Foch had presented his terms to a German delegation in 1918. And on June 24th Italy, which had entered the war on June 10th, when it was quite clear that France was safely beaten, and had conquered the outskirts of Menton, also concluded hostilities.

By the terms of the armistice France was divided into Occupied and Unoccupied Zones. The former covered the whole of the Atlantic and Channel coasts and included all the richer areas of western, northern and eastern France. The French army was to be disarmed and demobilized; and the navy to be demobilized under

German supervision. The latter condition aroused intense British suspicion that it would be handed over to, or seized by, the Germans. This suspicion, though natural, was unjust, for its Admiral, Darlan, was determined to keep the last card in his hand and sink the navy rather than give it up; but it was to lead to a British attack on the fleet of their so-recent allies at Mers-el-Kébir.

The two clauses in the armistice which gave Germany a stranglehold over France were the agreement for the payment by France of unlimited costs of an undefined army of occupation and the retention in German hands of the great army of French prisoners of war until the conclusion of peace. No one – not even the Germans – saw the significance of these clauses, for no one believed that the war could last more than a few weeks, or at most a month or two, now that Great Britain was left alone to face the irresistible German military machine.

CHAPTER THREE

VICHY FRANCE

WHILE metropolitan France lay plunged in a state of numbed confusion, the first reaction to the armistice of generals and governors in the French overseas possessions was one of refusal to accept defeat. Perhaps this represented an inability to face facts rather than determination to continue the struggle, for as soon as the news of the formation of a government under Pétain reached the colonies, with very few exceptions their authorities, both military and civilian, came into line. The most notable resister, General Catroux in Indo-China, was immediately dismissed. The tradition of hierarchical subordination to Paris, and the spirit of defeatism with which the French upper classes were permeated, prohibited any different reaction. This was also shown by the absence of response to General de Gaulle's broadcast appeal from England. His military career before the war had been injured by the publication of a prophetic book, *Vers l'armée de métier*, in which he had shown the conditions in which a future war would be fought. He seemed destined to be the advocate of lost causes. 'La France a perdu une bataille,' he cried, 'mais la France n'a pas perdu la guerre!' It fell on deaf ears. Pétain's authority was accepted inside France and throughout practically the whole of the vast French Empire. By a tacit but nation-wide plebiscite he was entrusted with the task of taking France out of the war.

The government of the armistice, seeking for a suitable capital in the Unoccupied Zone but fearful of exposure to popular pressure in a large town, moved to the health resort of Vichy, there to await the moment, which it believed could not be long delayed, when, the Germans having defeated Great Britain, the war would be over and Pétain and his ministers could transfer their authority back to Paris. They did not guess that Vichy was to be their home for far longer than they conceived possible, to become the symbol of many hopes and fears, and the visible centre and name of the ailments of a nation.

It would be a mistake to suppose that the Vichy regime began in the spirit of benumbed despair which was that of the average Frenchman after the military collapse of France. On the contrary, while some of its supporters, particularly among the right-wing journalists, even rejoiced in defeat because it had brought the end of the Republic, many more found at least a consolation in this consequence. Even the parliamentarians themselves were prepared fatalistically to accept what seemed to be the verdict of history. Convoked at Vichy in extraordinary session, the Senate voted with a single dissentient (the aged marquis de Chambrun, descendant – perhaps he remembered – of La Fayette), and the Chamber of Deputies by 395 out of 398 present, for the revision of the constitutional laws. And now Laval came into his own. His feverish activity secured the almost unopposed suspension of the constitutional laws of the Third Republic and the establishment of the new regime. 'Laval,' Pétain said, of this period, 'a été inouï.'

The first act of Pétain was to declare himself *Chef de l'État français*, thus avoiding the use of the term 'republic', a dirty word to his more ardent supporters. With the headship of the state he combined the headship of the government. In two days France passed from a parliamentary to a personal regime, reminiscent rather of Bonapartism than of royalism, despite the enthusiastic support from the Action Française which the Vichy government received. The essential and only cement of the new regime was loyalty to its head. We need waste no space over its constitutional arrangements: they were of no significance. The titular head was the Marshal, and the real government, from beginning to end of the Vichy episode, was the bureaucracy. The heads of the ministries were for the most part, since Pétain was suspicious of politicians, high officials. The problems they had to face were enormous – not least those created by the division of France into two zones. Their technical ability kept the machinery of state in operation, even in appalling conditions, though on a lower level of administration a deplorable collection of rogues and adventurers flocked into the ranks of Vichy, while at the centre there was only, in the words of the American ambassador, 'a feeble, frightened old man, surrounded by self-seeking conspirators'.

Many of the hangers-on of politics and fashionable society, who gathered at Vichy in the first winter, soon returned to Paris where the money was, as well as the Germans, leaving Vichy to pursue its dream of a National Revolution. This was conceived in terms of the campaign so long conducted against the Third Republic by the Action Française and more recently by the Fascist leagues. For many of the upper bourgeoisie, the officers of the army and navy, and high officials, defeat was the price paid for the sins of the Republic and at least it provided an opportunity for the creation of a new and better social and political order. A memorandum by Weygand called for an end to be put to the masonic, cosmopolitan, capitalistic state, to class war, demagogy and the cult of pleasure, and a return to the principles of religion, the *patrie* and the family. In place of an egoistic individualism, the National Revolution put forward the corporative ideal. This involved the dissolution of the trade unions and an attempt to replace them by professional corporations, in which the interests of employers, workers and the state would all be represented and reconciled. Though, in practice, this never amounted to more than the bureaucratic control of industry, it would be unfair to deny the existence of a genuine desire for social reform. It found expression in laws, only very partially applied, introducing old-age pensions and physical training of the young, and penalizing alcoholism. Decrees making divorce more difficult and favouring large families reflect the increased influence of the Roman Catholic Church, which provided strong support for Pétain's government. An attempt to restore religious control of education ran into serious opposition, and a labour charter was also of very limited practical effect.

Vichy was more successful in destroying than in rebuilding. The ending of the parliamentary regime was followed by the abolition of elected local councils in all communes of over two thousand inhabitants. The leading politicians of the defunct Republic, including Daladier, Blum, Vincent Auriol, Jules Moch, Reynaud and Mandel, were interned; but when a small group, including Daladier and Blum, was, after many postponements, tried at Riom in the spring of 1942, the defendants were able to turn the hearings into a debate over the causes of the defeat of France. So much discredit was cast on Pétain and the General Staff by the evidence, that the trial was stopped and the case never reached a conclusion.

The anti-semitic tendencies of the French right found expression, as early as October 1940, in a law excluding Jews from all positions in government service, teaching, and state-subsidized industries, from managerial positions in the press, radio and cinema, and fixing a quota for their entry into the liberal professions. The Action Française had been relieved of the papal condemnation on the eve of the war. Pius XII, almost as soon as he ascended the papal throne, in February 1939, began negotiations and the ban was lifted in July. This made little difference to its influence and none to its policy. The defeat of France and the fall of the Republic should have seemed to Maurras as though, at the end of his life, the gates of the Kingdom were being opened; but the old man had lived too long with his hates to forget them now. Published in Unoccupied France, the *Action Française* intensified its campaign for the exclusion of Jews, freemasons, and 'metics' of non-French parentage from the state services. Anti-semitic legislation gradually became severer, though it lagged far behind the standard set by the Nazis.

All this hardly amounted to a policy. Indeed, Vichy was too preoccupied with urgent economic and administrative problems to have much scope for applying one. Hordes of refugees and demobilized soldiers had to be returned to their homes, in spite of which nearly two million prisoners of war remained in German hands. Raw materials, machinery and supplies of all kinds were requisitioned by the Germans and payment left to the French authorities. An artificial rate of exchange enabled the occupying troops to go through the French shops like an army of locusts. The cost of the occupation was assessed at the colossal figure of four hundred million francs a day, while the division of France left the richer half, with 60 per cent of the cultivated land and 65 per cent of the industrial works, in the hands of the Germans. A British blockade closed the Atlantic and Channel ports. A bad harvest, made worse by the chaos of the summer of 1940 and the absence of labour, reduced the country, in the winter of 1940–1, to the verge of starvation. Faced with these conditions, Vichy had to introduce economic controls of a severity that France had not known since the government of the

Committee of Public Safety, including rationing and strict control of wages and prices.

The greatest, indeed the only real asset of the regime was the name of Pétain, and the cult of the Marshal was promoted by all the usual devices of totalitarian propaganda. His photograph, in all sizes, was omnipresent. The Marseillaise of the National Revolution – '*Maréchal, nous voilà*' – was chanted all over the country by bands of youths and girls. Pétain made personal tours through the Unoccupied Zone in the autumn and winter of 1940–1. But though his cult was stimulated it was not created by propaganda. The country had greeted him, wrote *Le Temps* in December 1940, as a saviour. It believed he had saved the nation from revolution and social chaos. The Church surrounded him with an almost religious aura of respect. He is the incarnation of suffering France, declared the Archbishop of Lyons, one might have thought a little blasphemously.

The personal qualities of Pétain in no way explain this almost mystical adulation. His name was linked with the defence of Verdun in the First World War and he had earned a reputation for humanity by his treatment of the mutinies in the French army. His disastrous influence on the General Staff during the inter-war years and his responsibility for the weakness of the French army was not known. The right-wing parties had had some success in building him up as a potential leader in the 'thirties, when the Fascist leagues also tried to make use of him. He was honest, unpretentious in his way of life, calm and dignified, with an almost royal capacity for impassivity. Above all, he supplied the need that the average Frenchman felt in the hour of total defeat for someone to believe in, a saviour of society. His own mediocrity helped to fit him for the role, for he had neither positive qualities to stand in the way, nor the self-critical faculty which might have inhibited his adoption of it. 'I offer France the gift of my person to assuage her ills,' he declared in his first broadcast, revealing the vanity which was a marked feature of his personality. Apart from the normal prejudices of an army officer and a man of the right, Pétain had no political ideas; nor had he the mental capacity to control his cabinet or frame its policy. His actions were those of the group or individual which influenced him at the moment, though there were to be limits beyond which he could not be pushed in the direction of collaboration with the Germans.

The first illusion of Vichy was the belief that France, by accepting the armistice, had succeeded in withdrawing herself from a world at war and creating a little oasis of peace. The conclusions drawn from this varied. There was a conflict between those, like Laval, who wanted France to enter the German camp at once and earn the reward for her prompt recognition of the new order in Europe, and those, like most of the supporters of the Action Française, who believed a policy of independence was still possible. While Laval's star was in the ascendant, Vichy propaganda was violently anti-British. The British attack on the French fleet at Mers-el-Kébir on July 3rd, 1940, under the belief that it might be handed over to the Germans, intensified the wave of Anglophobia. Laval gave the impression of having been deterred from declaring war on Great Britain only by a total lack of the resources necessary for waging it. It is difficult, in fact, to believe that he was unaware of this, or that it was other than a manoeuvre to impress the Germans. His more serious plan for a reversal of alliances culminated in the famous interview which he arranged in a railway carriage at Montoire, on October 24th, between Pétain and Hitler. The apparent triumph of Laval's policy was marked by his appointment, a few days later, as Foreign Minister, while Pétain, in a broadcast speech, proclaimed a policy of sincere collaboration with the Germans. Attempts have been made to present this Montoire policy as a subtle Machiavellian scheme for bringing about the defeat of Germany. This is nonsense: even after the failure of the German air attack on England, doubts about German victory hardly existed at Vichy. Collaboration was no deep-laid scheme for bringing France back into the war on the British side: it was what it called itself, collaboration.

The first blow to the hope of Franco-German reconciliation was dealt by the Germans themselves in their treatment of Alsace and Lorraine. Ruthless Germanization of the two provinces was accompanied by the expulsion of up to two hundred thousand of their inhabitants, who were regarded as unassimilable. In spite of this Laval did not turn back. Under cover of the negotiations with the Germans, he was extending his influence over the government. To complete the process of capturing it, a plot was concocted in which the essential element was the return of the remains of Napoleon I's son, for burial at the Invalides. It was proposed that Pétain should go to Paris for the ceremony; and once there, it was not intended that he should be allowed to return to Vichy. Laval and the Germanophiles would instead set up in his name a French government at Versailles under German control. The Marshal might have fallen into the trap, but the rest of the government, who had no desire to hand over total control to Laval, organized a cabinet plot against him and secured his dismissal. The first attempt at total collaboration had failed.

A struggle now began between the neutralists at Vichy, conservative and Catholic in bias, and the ardent collaborationist politicians and journalists of Paris, drawn largely from the extremist left- and right-wing politicians of the pre-war Fascist leagues. Among these the most prominent were the former Communist Doriot and the former Socialist, Marcel Déat. In January 1941 they founded the Rassemblement National Populaire to advocate full co-operation with the Nazis in the creation of the new European order.

At Vichy a period of governmental confusion after the fall of Laval was succeeded by the rise to the chief position, under Pétain, of Admiral Darlan, Commander-in-Chief of the French navy from the beginning of the war. He had managed to keep control of the navy. Undefeated, with its prestige increased by exploits against the Germans before the armistice and against the British after, the French navy was in good shape and morale. It supplied governors for many of the colonies and administrators for Vichy France, who provided an effective backing for Laval. In politics Darlan was a complete opportunist. Like Laval, he had decided that since the Germans had won the war, an understanding with them was the best policy, possibly for France and certainly for his own personal ambitions.

The most important decisions with which Darlan was to be faced in the course of 1941 were those affecting the future of the French Empire. The French West Indies and Djibouti had remained under the control of governors who supported Vichy. Indo-China, nominally governed by Vichy, became perforce practically a Japanese base. In Syria a High Commissioner of doubtful loyalty to Vichy was dismissed in 1940 and the former police chief Chiappe, who had played such an equivocal role in the attempted *coup* of February 6th, was sent out to replace him. Chiappe was killed when his plane was shot down and his place was taken by General Dentz, who had to deal with the consequences of the temporary success, in April 1941, of a pro-Nazi *coup* in Iraq. This made it necessary, if aid was to be sent to Iraq, for Germany to obtain the use of Syrian airfields. It was also desirable, in the interests of the Axis campaign in North Africa, for the Germans to be able to use French North Africa for supplies and transport. Darlan saw in this situation the possibility of a deal with Germany. In May 1941 he was received by Hitler at Berchtesgaden and out of the discussion emerged the May Protocols, giving the Germans military facilities in Syria and North Africa. What France got in return was so insignificant that the agreement can only be explained as an attempt by Darlan to buy German support for himself by showing that he could produce better results for them than Laval had been able to. The consequence was a British and Free French attack on Syria, which expelled Dentz and his troops. The other members of the Vichy government, alarmed at Darlan's apparent willingness to sell out completely to the Germans, called Weygand back from his governorship in North Africa to oppose him; and after Weygand's influence had been thrown into the balance the Protocols became a dead letter. The Germans had their revenge in November 1941, when they secured the dismissal of Weygand. They did not deal more firmly with the growing spirit of *attentisme* at Vichy, which was encouraged by continued British resistance, Axis defeats in the Mediterranean area, and the opening of a second front in Russia, because they were unwilling to pay the price of more effective French collaboration, and as yet unready to impose it by further exercise of force.

✣

COLLABORATION AND
RESISTANCE

FOR a year the situation in France remained essentially static
despite frequent changes in the personnel of Pétain's cabinet, in
which Vichy seemed to be perpetuating the governmental instability of the Third Republic. What altered the situation was the
German invasion of Russia in June 1941. Vichy was divided in its
reaction. Pétain, in a broadcast, described the Nazis as the defenders
of civilization against Communism. The Paris collaborationists
were vociferous and organized an Anti-Bolshevik Legion, which
received little active support. For the first time, however, a large
body of opinion, even among the adherents of Vichy, now became
doubtful of ultimate German victory.

The most important consequence within France of the German
invasion of Russia was the development of the Resistance movement, which had hitherto operated on a very limited scale, though
small Resistance networks had been formed, mainly in the Unoccupied Zone. From the time of the Hitler–Stalin pact the French
Communist Party had been the tacit ally of the Nazis. After the
armistice it called for fraternization with the occupying troops,
denounced economic sabotage in the factories and advocated collaboration on the basis of the German–Soviet alliance. The Nazis had
not received these advances in the friendly spirit with which they
were put forward and the Communist Party had to remain underground, but it continued to attack de Gaulle and the British im-
perialists. The outbreak of war between Germany and Russia
changed the situation overnight. Former enemies now became allies.
The Communist Party launched its militants into the Resistance
with the advantage of possessing a widespread underground
organization. They began with attacks on individual members of
the occupying forces, to which the Germans replied by taking

hostages, especially Jews, and shooting them in batches of fifty at a time.

Meanwhile, the stalemate between the Nazis, trying to get something for nothing, and Vichy, only willing to sell its aid at a price, continued. Both sides were becoming increasingly discontented with Darlan. Pétain himself was jealous of the Admiral's prominence and the pomp with which he surrounded himself. Laval, who had been negotiating with the Germans for his own return to power, at last convinced them that he would serve their purposes better than the Admiral. On April 18th, 1942, therefore, Darlan was moved down to the post of Commander-in-Chief, and Laval became the head of a government which represented a more pro-Nazi orientation though it did not go as far in this direction as the Paris collaborationists desired.

Laval was still convinced of the inevitability of German victory. He had the intellectual limitations and the inability to escape from fixed ideas that often go with a capacity for successful intrigue. Before the armistice he had made up his mind that the fate of France was bound up indissolubly with that of Germany, and that collaboration was necessary to the salvation of France and the restoration of peace. The one thread, apart from devotion to his own career, that runs through his life is a sincere and almost unqualified pacifism. This was what made him an ideal instrument for the Nazis. Moreover, convinced of the invincibility of the German military machine, he was determined that a Laval should not be found on the losing side. Back in office again, and more convinced of his own astuteness than ever, he picked up the threads of his policy where he had dropped them in December 1940. In a broadcast of June 1942, he burnt his bridges behind him with the notorious words, 'Je souhaite la victoire de l'Allemagne.' That this was not a mere uncalculated gesture, was shown by the phrase with which he concluded the sentence – 'car sans elle, le communisme s'installera partout en Europe.' He saw the future of the world as determined either by Nazism–Fascism or by Communism and had thrown in his lot with the former.

The next turning-point in the history of war-time France came not in France itself but in North Africa. There, Weygand had been succeeded by General Juin, who continued the same policy of loyalty to Pétain. The Americans, meanwhile, had been preparing for a landing. Their representatives in North Africa had persuaded themselves, and the American government, of the existence of effective support for intervention. When the American expedition arrived off North Africa on November 8th, 1942, it therefore expected to be welcomed by a strong body of supporters. These hopes proved false, and what at first sight seemed worse was that Darlan himself happened by chance to be in Algiers. In fact, his Machiavellian traits proved the salvation of the American expedition. Telegrams passed between Algiers and Vichy. Their real import has never been established but it seems probable that Pétain gave Darlan full powers to deal with the emergency, though not necessarily expecting him to do what he did. Impressed by the size of the American armada, he switched sides and, followed a little belatedly by General Juin, proclaimed a cease-fire. Opposition at Casablanca led to a short but sharp bout of fighting, after which Morocco followed Algiers. Tunis, on the other hand, was seized by the Germans. Darlan himself was not to profit long by his change of sides. Some six weeks later he was shot. The assassination seems to have been connected with a royalist intrigue, but its motivation remains obscure.

The Germans reacted to the invasion of North Africa by putting into operation a long-prepared plan for the occupation of the whole of France. What they wanted above all was the French fleet, riding at anchor in the great naval harbour of Toulon. On November 27th, after a promise that so long as the French pledged themselves to defend the port and the navy against Allied aggression, it would be immune from seizure, the German army pounced. Laval and the admirals at Vichy played the German game loyally by sending orders to Toulon to avoid resistance. But now at last Darlan was to be justified. For two years the orders he had signed in 1940 for the sabotage of the French fleet to prevent it from falling into German hands had rested in inviolable secrecy. Now at last they were put into effect, and even faster than the German mechanized units could speed through Toulon, explosion after explosion sounded the death-knell of the last great French navy.

November 1942 was the real end of Vichy and the 'National Revolution'. It was already little more than an agency for the Nazi exploitation of France. This took many forms. Occupation costs were raised, after the invasion of North Africa, from three hundred million to five hundred million francs a day. The vast amount of credit which the German authorities accumulated in this way was used for the acquisition of raw materials and food-stuffs, French securities and works of art, for payments to the dependants of French workers recruited for labour in Germany, and to finance all the civil and military services of the occupying Power. To prevent the French from following the precedent set by the Germans at the time of the occupation of the Ruhr and using inflation as a weapon of economic defence, the Germans insisted on a policy of controlled wages and prices. This resulted in the growth of a vast and nation-wide black market, which the occupying authorities themselves tolerated and used with an appropriate rake-off.

Behind the financial exploitation of France, which was largely a matter of book-keeping, there was the reality of systematically stripping France of raw materials, food-stuffs and manufactured products. In addition, the German war machine required an ever-increasing supply of foreign workers. Up to the summer of 1942 the exportation of French labour was kept down to the fairly low figure of about 70,000. After Laval returned to office stronger pressure, combined with his need to retain Nazi support, brought greatly increased numbers. Laval, characteristically, tried to win German favour and popularity in France at the same time by nego-tiating an agreement for the release of French prisoners of war in return for an increase in the supply of French workers for Ger-many. By the autumn of 1943 it was estimated that French workers constituted one-fourth of all foreign male workers in Germany and amounted to 605,000 men as well as some 44,000 women. The con-scription of this great mass of labour was not effected, of course, without much evasion and opposition; and in the last stages of the occupation the flight of workers to avoid compulsory transfer to Germany was one of the chief sources of the Resistance.

After November 1942 it is difficult to regard Pétain and Laval and their little group of ministers, operating in increasing isolation at Vichy, as a government. Laval remained in office, perhaps because the Nazis could find no one more serviceable to put in his place.

Moreover, up to an extraordinarily late date he appears to have clung to his long-standing belief in the invincibility of the German war machine. He had the stupidity in big things that can go with excessive cleverness in little ones. Much of his energy had to be devoted to defending his position from the Paris collaborationists, still trying to outbid him for Nazi favour. In September 1943, led by Déat and Darnand, they produced a plan for a French *parti unique* on the Nazi model, to bring France into full alliance with Germany. This alarmed the more moderate advisers of Pétain, who was induced to prepare a constitutional amendment transferring power, after his death, back to the National Assembly. Laval, who did not intend to be by-passed in this way, informed the German authorities who blocked Pétain's proposal. After some delay they moved against those who had counselled him. Laval was instructed to re-form the government 'in a sense which would guarantee collaboration'. This meant that he had to accept as his colleagues the whole gang of extreme collaborationists from Paris, with the exception of his bitterest personal enemies and rivals, Déat and Doriot. Even Déat was able to force his way in soon after, in March 1944.

Long before this, France was in a state of virtual civil war, as the resistance movement, from inside and outside France, grew in size. French North Africa had passed out of the German sphere of control with the Allied landings and the subsequent defeat of the armies of Rommel. It was not at first clear into whose hands it had passed. Darlan's hour there, as we have seen, was a brief one. If the royalists were implicated in his murder, they gained nothing from it. The claimant to the throne, the comte de Paris, spent the war hanging about behind the scenes, occasionally making a tentative approach to one of the leading players, but never succeeding in getting on the stage himself. If, even in this crisis, he was to be pushed on one side and ignored, it was clear that for all the sound and fury of the monarchists their cause was dead.

Darlan was succeeded as civil and military head of the North African government by General Giraud, who, after a picturesque escape from Nazi captivity had been chosen by the Americans as their candidate for authority over the regained colonial territories. There was, however, another candidate, who, it might almost be said, had chosen himself. This was General de Gaulle. His initial appeal from Great Britain had rallied only the governors of French Equatorial Africa and the French Cameroons to his cause. A small Gaullist naval expedition to Dakar in September 1940 had been repulsed rather humiliatingly. The Free French Movement, as the small body of supporters who had gathered round de Gaulle called themselves, made a very poor start.

Although the British government welcomed de Gaulle and provided him with moral support and material facilities, it was not sure of the wisdom of committing itself to the Free French Movement, and relations were often difficult, while the Americans were profoundly suspicious of de Gaulle and his ambitions. However, by means of wireless propaganda from his Free French Movement in London, his was becoming the one name that was associated in France with continued resistance to the Germans. In January 1942 the Free French sent the former prefect, Jean Moulin, into France to co-ordinate the small resistance movements that were growing up. He became the first head of a National Council of Resistance, which met in Paris in May 1943; but Moulin himself was arrested, tortured and killed a month later. His successor was Georges Bidault.

The Allied conquest of North Africa had meanwhile provided an opportunity for de Gaulle to measure his strength and assert himself as the single leader of resistance outside metropolitan France. To begin with Giraud held apparently all the winning cards in North Africa. His total lack of political capacity, combined with the skill with which de Gaulle played his own weaker hand, determined the outcome. Giraud was gradually eliminated and de Gaulle remained in sole control as the acknowledged leader of the Free French (now called 'La France Combattante') Movement outside, and the Resistance movement within France.

In France Nazi repression kept pace with resistance. The first high-ranking German officer was assassinated in October 1941. Fifty hostages were killed in retaliation. When, a few days later, a German major was shot, fifty more were destroyed. Vichy and the Nazis agreed that the acts of assassination or sabotage must be the work of Jews or of Communists. One result of this was to restore to the Communists the patriotic reputation they had lost at the time of the Nazi–Soviet alliance.

The campaign of the occupying forces against the Resistance was partly misdirected because of the lunatic Nazi preoccupation with the Jews, who were singled out for seizure as hostages, and for execution, whether they were implicated in the Resistance or not. The French anti-semites also were now given their chance, and after the Germans had moved into the Unoccupied Zone this ceased to provide a partial refuge for Jews. In the last stages of the occupation the extremist factions and the French Militia under Darnand joined enthusiastically in the hunt. The most effective French aid in repression did in fact come from this Militia, founded in January 1943 by Joseph Darnand, which was in the end to be more feared and hated than the S.S. troops themselves.

The first triumph of the Resistance was the liberation of Corsica in September 1943 by a force from North Africa. From the Corsican resistance groups, operating in wild country, came the name of *maquis*. In France the numbers of coherent groups in the *maquis* and the membership of the Resistance greatly increased in 1943 and 1944, though on the eve of the Allied landings in France the Allied Supreme Command had little faith in their military value. Equally, the Allies refused to believe that de Gaulle had become a name to conjure with in France. His influence was, in fact, at this moment to be of decisive importance for the future history of France. The Communist influence in the Resistance had become increasingly strong, and the Communist leadership never forgot its ultimate aim of converting liberation into a Communist take-over. The effective, if subtle, preparations for countering the Communist plan were taken by de Gaulle. He set up, parallel with the Council of the Resistance inside France, a Délégation Générale, which was to represent the interests of the state and be above the parties. A committee headed by the future Fifth Republic premier, Michel Debré, drew up a list of *préfets* and *commissaires* to take over the administration of France as it was freed from the German occupation. The effectiveness of these preparations is shown by the fact that out of eighty future *préfets* on the list as many as forty-five in due course assumed that office. On the military side, in April 1944 General Koenig, hero of the defence of Bir-Hakeim in the North African campaign, was appointed Commander-in-Chief of the French Forces of the Interior. The captain of engineers who took the *nom de guerre* of Colonel Passy, and a former professor of anthropology named Jacques Soustelle, headed the organization of secret agents which provided intelligence from France both for the Free French and the Allies.

It cannot be pretended that the Free French preparations were taken seriously by their Allies. Throughout the war American policy towards France was strongly influenced by the reports of Admiral Leahy, the ambassador to Vichy, and Robert Murphy, special envoy in Algiers, who both felt some affinity with the Pétainist regime. New York and Washington also had their quota of French exiles, politicians of the defunct regime like Camille Chautemps, who presented de Gaulle to the Americans as a would-be military dictator. Alternatively, or at the same time, he was treated as a mere British puppet, which could hardly have been further from the truth. He was certainly a difficult ally and was not taken into serious consideration in Allied plans for the organization of France after liberation. Instead, it was proposed that an Allied Military Government should assume responsibility for the liberated territories.

The reckless gossip, as a result of which the ill-fated Dakar expedition had practically become public knowledge before it even set out, made the Allied higher command reluctant to communicate its plans to its French allies. Moreover, the British and Americans were sceptical of de Gaulle's authority over the internal Resistance. So it was that he was not informed of the imminence of D-day until the eve of the invasion. In spite of this the Allies called the forces of the Resistance into action by broadcast messages, summoning them to start general guerilla activity and sabotage. This led, inevitably, in parts of France, to premature risings, with serious loss of life and much subsequent recrimination. The need for a general call, if the specific areas of invasion were not to be revealed to the Germans, was accepted by Koenig and the French command, though it involved such a tragedy as the revolt of Vercors, where some 700 *maquisards* out of 3,500 were lost in pitched battle with 20,000 Germans. In the whole of France it has been reckoned that 140,000 *maquisards* were armed by the Allies in parachute droppings, in addition to those who captured arms from the Germans; 24,000 were officially reported as killed in battle. The *maquis* of Brittany, about 30,000 strong, distinguished itself by the military effectiveness of its operations in a strategic zone on the flank of the invasions. Everywhere the cutting of railways and destruction of bridges hampered German movements.

The Anglo-American command intended to set up a military government of French territory as it was liberated. There was no intention of allowing General de Gaulle to interfere with this plan. However, it was difficult to prevent him from visiting the bridgeheads in France. On June 14th he appeared in Bayeux and the neighbouring towns in Allied possession, and when he departed left behind him his representatives, who proceeded to take over the sub-prefectures peacefully from the Vichy incumbents. The Allied command, presented with a *fait accompli*, had no alternative but to accept it. North of the Loire and east of the Rhône, where, as soon as the Germans were driven out by Allied armies, Gaullist administrators appeared on the heels of the invading forces or revealed themselves in the midst of the population, the transition was orderly and free from excesses. Elsewhere things were very different. Particularly in the south-west, when the German troops withdrew, a Communist and Resistance terror followed the Nazi and collaborationist one.

Vichy, of course, was not even a name now. On August 17th, when his German masters ordered Laval to transfer the French government to Belfort, for the first time he refused to obey. Pétain also refused to leave Vichy but the Nazis were determined that those who had served them so well in the past should not escape them now. The Marshal, Laval and as many of the ministers as they could lay hands on were carried off, first to Belfort and then to Germany. The ultra-collaborationists needed no compulsion. In a general *sauve-qui-peut* the less conspicuous ones tried to sink into obscurity or insinuate themselves into the ranks of the Resistance. The more prominent collaborationists fled with the retreating German armies to Germany. At Sigmaringen they set up, still in the name of Pétain, the last French government of the war, achieving, on German soil and under the defeated and disintegrating regime of the former all-powerful Nazi conqueror, the object for which they had intrigued and agitated during five years of occupation and war.

⚜

CHAPTER FIVE

CONSTITUTION-MAKING

In the Second World War republican France passed from the humiliation of total collapse to the moral ambiguity of divided allegiance. Sabotage and rebellion were the deeds of patriots, loyalty and obedience the virtues of defeatists and collaborators, murder and torture part of the normal machinery of government, and assassination the method of opposition. On more than one side honour was rooted in dishonour and faith unfaithful kept men falsely true. It seemed impossible that anything but civil war and chaos could appear when the Vichy administration collapsed and the German armies retreated. The immediate setting up of an independent and coherent government, and the restoration, within a reasonable time, of law and order all over France, was due to the existence of de Gaulle. His name had become identified with the idea of French national independence for millions who knew no more than his name. But if he was a symbol he was also a symbol who knew very well what he was doing, and he was determined that a liberated France should be free and united and independent.

Of course, there was inevitably some settling of accounts by private action. In areas like the south-west, where local resistance bodies, particularly the Communists, were able to take control temporarily after the German withdrawal, there was a good deal of this, both private and public. How many of the more prominent collaborators were summarily executed, and how many other persons were disposed of in the pursuance of local feuds, cannot be estimated. The official figure of some three or four thousand is a gross understatement which must be multiplied at least by ten. Where the new Gaullist authorities were set up at once, the summary executions of collaborators, stripping and shaving of female associates of the Nazis, dispossessions and expulsions, were held in check. Everywhere, sooner or later, courts created to deal with

collaborators formally handed out penalties ranging from depriva-
tion of civic rights through fines and imprisonment to death. A
High Court was established to try the more notable collaborators.
The reports of a series of *causes célèbres* provide valuable source
material for the historian, though they do not shine as bright models
of the judicial process at work. The trial of Laval, in particular, was
conducted with such miserable pettiness by the prosecuting lawyers,
and senile incompetence by the presiding judge, that it merely
provided the greatest of the collaborators with a platform for
turning the accusers into the accused. With scant regard for the
forms of law he was silenced and sentenced, allowed to poison
himself in the night and ignominiously resuscitated for the sake of
being hauled out at dawn and shot. Pétain, in the remoteness of
great age, did not, or perhaps could not, deign to pay more than
momentary attention to his own trial. He was sentenced to detention
in a fortress for the rest of his life.

In place of the defunct authorities of Vichy, the government in
exile, set up by General de Gaulle in Algiers, came to Paris. A Con-
sultative Assembly, formed of the advisory body constituted at
Algiers together with representatives of the resistance movements
within France, was joined to it. For all effective purposes the
government of France for fourteen months after his entry into Paris
on August 26th, 1944, was in the hands of General de Gaulle. There
is a tendency to regard this as the lost year, when vital opportunities
were missed. The speed with which France returned to normal,
peaceful conditions, is really the more remarkable phenomenon.
To blame de Gaulle, in his capacity as head of the provisional
government, for lost opportunities, is to exaggerate the extent of
his personal authority. It is not possible to praise him for his
abstention from setting up a dictatorial regime and at the same time
blame him for not imposing solutions of the many problems pressing
on the country. It should also not be forgotten that a war was still
being waged on the soil of France. Even when most of the territory
had been liberated, fighting continued round the Atlantic pockets of
German resistance and in the eastern frontier region.

Looking back, it is easier now than it was at the time to see that
de Gaulle had one prime object – to contain the Communists,

which he pursued with characteristic subtlety and indirection. Because the Communist Party did not aim – it was not in their tradition nor was it possible in the circumstances – to seize power by a military *coup*, it must not be supposed that they had no hope of capturing the citadels of authority by the methods of infiltration that – aided by the benevolent proximity of Soviet armies – were to prove so efficacious in central and eastern Europe. They came out of the war with many advantages. The memory of the Hitler–Stalin pact had been washed out in the blood of Communist resistance fighters. The Communists were the one party that had retained its identity and its cadres intact throughout the underground struggle. Its leader, Maurice Thorez, former miner and trade-union organizer, one of the few genuine sons of the people to rise to the top in French politics, implacable in devotion to the strategy of the party line laid down by Moscow, yet conciliating and flexible in the day-to-day tactics of political life, returned from Russia, where he had fled by some unknown route in 1939, to lead the party. Their victory seemed to the Communists a foregone conclusion. Many of their opponents in France would have agreed with them, all the more because General de Gaulle seemed to be playing their game for them. Looking backward, or possibly further forward than was justifiable at the time or perhaps for long to come, he made a bid for a renewal of the old Franco-Russian alliance. He went to Moscow to sign a treaty with the Soviet government. This bid for support for his new and shaky regime from Stalinite Russia rather than America seemed to many misguided in foreign policy. It made better sense in domestic affairs, if it was conceived as the first step towards drawing the teeth of the French Communist Party. De Gaulle's ultimate objective was never easy to judge from his immediate actions. He knew that the prospect of a Gaullist military dictatorship was being used by the Communists to gather the support of the left behind them, and by his conspicuous moderation gradually dissipated this fear. The failure of the Communist take-over bid was all the more remarkable in the atmosphere of French politics during the first years after the war, which were marked by the strength of the left, the political annihilation of the right, and the discredit of the centre.

The first positive decision that had to be taken concerned the future regime in France. Given the general desire for a new beginning, the result of the referendum of October 1945 was a foregone conclusion. By an overwhelming vote of 96 per cent the French people rejected the idea of continuing, or reviving, the Third Republic. The Assembly that was elected in the same month was therefore a Constituent Assembly, with the task of making a new Constitution. It was naturally one in which the left was overwhelmingly represented: many collaborationists were disenfranchised and the memory of Vichy was too recent to allow its known adherents to influence the voting. There was, however, one new and major factor on the other side. The franchise had now been extended to women, and this, as the left-wing parties which had opposed it had always believed, meant a great accession of strength to the Catholic interest. The result of the election was what might have been expected from the combination of these factors. The vote for the right wing fell from its customary strength of something just under 50 per cent to a mere 16 per cent. The once great Radical centre, socially conservative and anti-clerical, suffered on both counts and was now a mere 10 per cent. The parties of the old left, Communists with 25 per cent and Socialists with 23 per cent, came near to winning an absolute majority. Their success was natural and expected. What was not anticipated and what was a new phenomenon, was the rise of a large and progressive Catholic party, born out of the small pre-war group of Popular Democrats. It had the prestige of possessing, in the person of the pre-war history teacher, Georges Bidault, the president of the Resistance Council at the end of the war. Catholic organizations had survived better than any others, except the underground Communist party, during the occupation. The new party, the Mouvement Républicain Populaire, was that which was closest to General de Gaulle in its political outlook, and could therefore draw on the prestige of his name, even though he himself kept rigorously out of party politics. It was headed by a group of able Catholic intellectuals, little dreaming of the success they were about to achieve. Many from the right, whose support for its ideals was less than lukewarm, undoubtedly voted for the M.R.P. as the least of three evils. Support snowballed and the M.R.P. emerged from the election with some 24 per cent of the popular vote.

With the meeting of the Constituent Assembly, de Gaulle became the head of a parliamentary government, a role for which he was suited neither by his nature and training nor his political beliefs. However, he used his position to take the next trick from the Communists by excluding them, in the tripartite ministry which he formed, from the three key ministries of Foreign Affairs, Interior, and Defence, to one of which, at least, they seemed entitled as the largest party in the Assembly. This was only the beginning of a series of conflicts between the head of the government and his Communist and Socialist ministers. Even with the M.R.P. Foreign Minister, Bidault, de Gaulle's relations were strained, and the seeds were sown of a resentment which was to produce bitter fruits later.

The basic issue was whether there was to be a unified policy determined by the head of the executive, or whether policy was to emerge, as in the past, from party compromises in the legislature. In January 1946 de Gaulle recognized that he could not govern on the lines in which he believed with parliament; he was unwilling to attempt to govern against it, and so resigned. Tripartism continued, the Socialists, as the middle party, providing the premier, while the Assembly set about the task of constitution making.

The most important constitutional issue had already been tacitly settled before the Fourth Republic began. General de Gaulle had stood for a presidential as against a parliamentary executive. When his views were rejected he resigned. There was a strong tradition of personal government in France, which had only been broken by the defunct Third Republic. The strength of the tradition was the measure of the hostility to it, which made it certain that a left-wing Assembly would react against it. De Gaulle said ironically that the Assembly was determined to make the President a mere figurehead for fear that Charles de Gaulle might one day become president. The first president of the Fourth Republic, the Socialist Vincent Auriol, was in fact, because of his personal prestige and political skill, able to play an important role behind the scenes, but it was still, like that of presidents of the Third Republic, mainly one combining the functions of prompter and scene-shifter. His successor, René Coty, was even closer to the presidential tradition of the Third Republic.

The left-wing majority in the Constituent Assembly, if it was agreed that the government should be a parliamentary and not a presidential one, was far from agreed on anything else. The Communists, anticipating a new Popular Front majority through which they might turn tripartism gradually into one-party rule, and the Socialists, clinging to their old Jacobin traditions, stood out for a single, omnicompetent legislative chamber. This was included in the terms of the first constitutional draft, which Communists and Socialists carried in the Assembly by 309 votes to 249. It was submitted to the country for ratification in May 1946. The triumphant Communist Party swept the country in a great political campaign with the cry, 'Thorez au pouvoir!' and the country replied with a vote of nine and a half million for the Constitution but ten and a half million against it, nearly six million not voting. Even at a time when the right was discredited, its leaders in prison or disenfranchised and its supporters in total disarray, the French people, or at least a majority of them, set their sails against the dominant winds of the left and veered back to the centre.

A second Constituent Assembly was elected in June 1946. The Socialists lost votes because of their association with the Communists. The M.R.P., which had led the campaign against the first Constitution, now became the largest party, with a popular vote of 28 per cent. Only time could show whether its predominance was to be a permanent feature of the political landscape, but for the present it had the gravitational force which drew the unwilling Socialists, as in the previous Assembly they had been drawn by the Communist Party, towards it. The new constitutional draft established a second chamber, to be called the Council of the Republic, while the lower house retained the name of National Assembly by which the whole parliament had traditionally been known. The second chamber was, to begin with, more a symbol than an effective political force. It was described as a chamber of reflection and in its first years did indeed do little but reflect the views of the other house.

The new Constitution, though closer to that of the Third Republic than the first draft had been, would, it was hoped, avoid the major weaknesses of the old regime. Specific provisions were introduced to deal with governmental instability. To prevent the use of *interpellations* to upset governments at a moment's notice, it was laid down that a government could be overthrown only by a formal vote of no confidence, for which twenty-four hours' notice had to be given. To rob deputies of their power of destroying governments one after another without running the risk of a dissolution of parliament, some rather complicated arrangements, intended to provide for compulsory dissolution after the fall of a government on a vote of no confidence, were included. Thirdly, by weighting the constitutional arrangements in favour of large parties it was hoped to escape from the group system with its built-in bias towards instability. For a time, indeed, the three great parties practically monopolized power: they behaved, it was complained, more like orchestras under a conductor than the cacophony of political virtuosos which France seemed to have preferred in its public life. The three parties naturally were not averse from proposals calculated to perpetuate their own monopoly of power. Indeed they subsequently organized the electoral system with the specific object of preserving it.

All this was well and effectively contrived on paper, but it was to prove easier to change a nation's laws than its political habits. The demise of the Third Republic may have been voted: its successor was to follow so closely in its steps that the observer might well feel that it had merely changed to remain the same thing. In one way or another governments fell without having received the fatal vote of no confidence and the first legislative assembly of the Fourth Republic was to last nearly its full term, from December 1946 to June 1951. Its eight ministries averaged just under seven months each; and, as in the past, while governments changed, their personnel remained much the same. Those who were regarded as *ministrables* appeared and reappeared in successive ministries, often in the same office. Thus year after year the Quai d'Orsay witnessed a *pas de deux* in which the two M.R.P. ministers, Bidault and Schuman, replaced one another in turn. The group system gradually re-emerged. Of the three great parties, only the

Communists succeeded in retaining their monolithic character, while in the centre and to the right smaller groups began to reappear.

None of the three major parties felt very enthusiastic about the new Constitution they had made; but if a poor thing it was the best they could manage. With muted voices and little enthusiasm they recommended it to the country, to the accompaniment of a blast of denunciation from de Gaulle and opposition from an extra-political Gaullist Union set up in his name. The Constitution won the acceptance of the country in the referendum of October 1946 by the narrow margin of nine million votes to eight million; but one wonders if the real voice of France were not better expressed by the eight million who abstained. It cannot be said that the Fourth Republic had got off to a flying start. General public opinion was perhaps illustrated by the advertisement which was familiar on Métro walls in those days: it represented four painters inscribing the figures I to IV respectively on one another's back, and bore the inscription, 'Republics pass but so-and-so's paint stays'.

While the politicians had been debating the terms of the Constitution, the French had somehow or other been putting their shattered country together. The essential first step was the restoration of the railways. In proportion as this was accomplished so economic life gradually revived. As after the First World War, though the problem was now a nation-wide one, reconstruction proceeded at a remarkable pace. The political dominance of the parties of the left provided an opportunity for it to be accompanied this time by a programme of social reform. Laws of social insurance voted in April 1946 were added to the *Code de la Famille* of 1939. One result was a dramatic rise in the birth-rate.

In the Resistance movement, as well as the ideal of social reform the whole economic ideology of the Popular Front had been reborn. The powers of finance and capitalist industry had been discredited by collaboration, and the left-wing coalition which came to power in October 1945 was determined to carry through an extensive programme of nationalization and workers' control. The latter amounted to no more than an increase in the powers and responsibilities of the trade unions; and while de Gaulle was in office the policy of nationalization was pursued with calculated slowness.

However, the state took over the great Renault motor works, the north-eastern coal field and Air France. The first Constituent Assembly carried the policy a good deal farther by adding the Bank of France and the larger private banks, insurance, gas, electricity and the whole coal-mining industry.

Except in so far as they helped to weaken the hold of big business on national life, the nationalizations were really less significant than either those who supported or those who opposed them expected. The development of a system of social security affected national life more widely and deeply. But perhaps the most important of the economic decisions in the period immediately after liberation was taken in the field of finance. During the war German policy had simultaneously swollen the supply of paper money by the demand for occupation costs, and prevented the inflated note circulation from having its natural effect by enforcing, with the co-operation of Vichy, a rigid policy of wage and price controls, to which the accompaniment had been a nation-wide black market, especially in food-stuffs. With the disappearance of the Vichy authorities the system of control, such as it was, collapsed; and at the same time new and heavy obligations – for the support of an army in the field, the reconstruction of transport and industry, the import of raw materials and other supplies of which France had been starved – pressed on the French economy. The Minister for National Economy, the Radical Mendès-France, proposed a policy of *blocage* of the notes, combined with a tax on capital gains, control of wages and prices, and strict rationing. This policy was supported by the Socialists. It was challenged by the Minister of Finance, Pleven, who, with a background in business, believed in the free play of economic forces to cure economic ills. De Gaulle, with little technical economic knowledge, accepted the arguments of Pleven, and Mendès-France resigned. Both men were justified in the event, Pleven by the remarkable speed of reconstruction, and his opponent by the even more remarkable speed of the inflation which accompanied it.

Whether political pressures would have allowed even the simple step of blocking the circulation of occupation notes is doubtful. The rivalry of the three main parties stood in the way of the adoption of a policy which was bound to be unpopular with important sections of the electorate. The peasants, who had accumulated such quantities of notes during the war that they were said to keep them not in the traditional stockings but in *lessiveuses* – washing coppers – would have resented their formal devaluation by the government bitterly, and the result might have been a reduction in the much-needed agricultural production. The Communists, who were alleged to have accumulated great quantities of hot money during liberation, were also opposed to a policy of monetary control. Perhaps, also, they were not unaware that inflation can be a great revolutionary force. The circulation of notes, which had been about a hundred milliard francs in 1939, had risen to six hundred milliard by 1944. By the end of 1947 it was nine hundred milliard. In the two years from December 1945 to December 1947 the value of money was divided by three, and the process was to continue. In so far as inflation was a running sore of the Fourth Republic, as it had been of the Third, and one which was a basic cause of its political weakness, it could be said that the death-warrant of the Fourth Republic had been written before its birth. However, for the time inflation did not hamper, and may even have assisted, material reconstruction. The necessary foreign imports, which the weakness of French currency might have prevented, were made possible by massive American aid.

CHAPTER SIX

THE FOURTH REPUBLIC

ENERAL DE GAULLE was neither by training nor disposition a politician. Therefore he did not play the game according to the established rules. Instead of flinging himself into opposition to a constitution which he believed to be unworkable, a course of action which would have compromised him irretrievably and made impossible for the future the role of national leader that he had reserved for himself, he withdrew from active political life. When his admirers in the spring of 1946 formed a Gaullist Union, he took no part in it. Only a year later, in a speech at Strasbourg on April 7th, 1947, did he issue a call for the formation of a Rally of the French People – Rassemblement du Peuple Français, or R.P.F. This was, paradoxically, to be a party against parties. It rapidly gathered support. Gallup polls assessing the proportion of the electorate that was prepared to vote '*de Gaulle au pouvoir*' produced results rising from 31 per cent in spring 1946 to 36 per cent in January 1947, with the aid of the faults of the existing parties, the skilfulness of Gaullist propaganda and avoidance of positive proposals.

The Gaullist policy was an attractive one. It demanded that the taxes should be paid, but without specifying who should pay them. It proposed 'associations' in industry and a paternalist organization which for its critics was reminiscent of the ideals of Vichy. It appealed in non-committal terms to the army, the peasants, the bourgeois, the workers, the industrialists, for a great national union. De Gaulle's campaign was reminiscent in many ways of that conducted between 1848 and 1851 by Louis Napoleon Bonaparte, particularly in its concentration on the provinces, where the General made a series of major speeches. It is true that Paris is only one-fifteenth of France, and that since 1871 the provinces, and not Paris, have decided the government of the country. Like Louis Bonaparte, also, de Gaulle had a profound belief in his destiny. His career provided a Gaullist *mystique* to take the place of the Bonapartist legend. At St Étienne, in 1947, a miner's lamp, presented to the General, bore the inscription, 'To General de Gaulle, who lightened us in our darkness'. Unfortunately, the success of the R.P.F. was fatal to his ambitions. The combination of progressive and conservative forces within the Rassemblement undermined its unity. When it won a considerable body of seats in the Assembly, it became difficult for it not to behave as yet one more political party. Realizing that his time had not yet come, de Gaulle disassociated himself from the movement, leaving its members divided and leaderless and its future uncertain.

However, he had established his claim as a potential residuary legatee of the Fourth Republic if it had the misfortune to die. Meanwhile, the Communist Party had not abandoned its own hope of taking over the state. The general election of June 1946 revealed two new factors in the political situation – first, that the Socialist Party was beginning to suffer the usual fate of middle parties by attrition from both sides, losing its supporters to Communists on the one side and M.R.P. on the other; and secondly that the pendulum had already begun to swing back to the right, which (if the M.R.P. is included) now obtained 53 per cent of the votes, against 47 per cent for the Communists and Socialists.

For the first months of the Fourth Republic, in 1947, an uneasy truce was maintained and the three big parties shared the government. Inflation, however, produced an agitation for wage increases, and in May 1947 strikes, which the Communist Party, at first somewhat reluctantly, supported, although they were directed against the government to which it belonged. The Socialist premier, Ramadier, instead of resigning, took the bold and novel step of dismissing the Communist ministers. It was the end of tripartism and the beginning of the open war of Communists against Socialists and M.R.P. Communist-led strikes in November–December 1947 provided a critical test of the party's power. Their failure showed not merely that France could be governed without the Communists, but that it could even be governed against them, despite their hold on the trade union movement – they had recaptured the C.G.T. in 1946 – on the majority of the industrial workers and on about one-quarter of the whole electorate. The result of their use of the strike weapon for political ends, which went against the French syndicalist tradition, was to blunt it in their hands.

Perhaps the turning-point in France, and indeed in the history of the whole world after the Second World War, came with General Marshall's speech of June 1947 on economic aid. The Communist Party rapidly moved into the attack with a denunciation, in December, of French acceptance of American aid. It was 'the subjection of France to the aggressive designs of American imperialism', they said, and the preparation for a new world war in which France would be the battle-field. In the course of the autumn strikes, the Communist Secretary General of the C.G.T. announced the plan of his party: the denunciation of all military agreements, dissolution of the Gaullist Rassemblement, rejection of Marshall aid and the development of economic relations with the U.S.S.R. Unfortunately, France badly needed economic aid, which only America could give. The general public must vaguely have felt this, or perhaps it felt that Communist warnings were not entirely disinterested. In any case the strikes failed and their only effect was to assist a swing to the right.

Since the Gaullist Rassemblement had won some of its national support as an insurance against the danger of a Communist take-over, the apparent weakening of the Communists brought about a corresponding weakening of the Gaullists. Between them there was room for a Third Force, which was formed, in January 1948, by an alliance of Socialists, Radicals and M.R.P. Shortly before, a break-away from the Communist-controlled C.G.T. had formed a Force Ouvrière among the trade unions.

The basic problem of the Third Force, as of previous governments, remained inflation, and the Third Force was as powerless to deal with this as the Cartel des Gauches before the war. The laissez-faire traditions of the Radicals prohibited them from accepting measures of state intervention in economic matters which the Socialists put forward; and the M.R.P. was increasingly divided between its more reactionary and more progressive supporters. Disunity in the Third Force was increased by the conflict between Radical and Socialist anti-clericalism and the attempt of the M.R.P.

to protect the interests of Catholic education, and by the reluctance of the Socialists to vote for the army estimates. In such divisions it was becoming ever more apparent that the traditions of the Third Republic lived on in the Fourth.

As the centre of gravity of French politics moved towards the right, so M.R.P. and Radical replaced Socialist premiers. The pre-war Radical Minister of Agriculture, Queuille, formed a ministry in September 1948 which was to survive till 1949, with the aid of his Socialist Minister of the Interior, Jules Moch, who defeated new Communist strikes in October–November 1948; also with the aid of a good harvest and some measures of price control. The cost of living remained stable throughout 1949. By the autumn of 1949, however, there were signs that this economic miracle was only a temporary one, while the old conflicts between the partners in the Third Force were becoming acute once again. The Queuille ministry fell in October 1949. The Third Force reverted to the worst habits of the past and the last eighteen months of the first Assembly of the Fourth Republic witnessed a sorry procession of weak and short-lived ministries.

The one point on which the three government parties managed to agree in the last days of the parliament was in passing an electoral law intended to keep both Communists and Gaullists out of power. By a complicated arrangement combining proportional representation where it suited them with a majority vote where that was likely to be favourable, the parties of the centre hoped to achieve this result. Their calculations were not mistaken. When the elections were held, in June 1951, the parties of the Third Force obtained 62·5 per cent of the seats, with 51 per cent of the votes; while the Gaullists had 19·6 per cent with 21·7 per cent, and the Communists, with 900,000 votes more than the R.P.F., had only 17·8 per cent of the seats to represent an electoral vote of 25·9 per cent.

In spite of this electoral victory it was apparent that the Fourth Republic could rely on the support of barely half the nation, and that those who did support it were too hopelessly divided among themselves ever to be able to form a strong or stable government. The Third Force was still split over the question of state aid to Catholic schools and a proposal to allow their pupils to be eligible for scholarships. The shift to the right continued. In March 1952 the new Assembly produced, in the person of Pinay, the first premier from the right since the war. In May Pinay fell and there was a gap of five weeks before a new government could be formed. Reynaud could describe France as 'the sick man of Europe'.

Yet there were elements of stability, behind the political instability, which should not be ignored. For the first ten years after liberation, up to the summer of 1954, the Quai d'Orsay was practically monopolized by two ministers, Georges Bidault and Robert Schuman, both belonging to the same party, the M.R.P. The reshaping of the French economy was largely free from the vagaries of party politics. It was entrusted to a Commission inspired and headed by the brilliant technocrat, Jean Monnet. If the political and financial weakness of the Fourth Republic is stressed, it is only fair also to give due weight to its positive achievements. These were particularly in the fields of foreign and economic policy.

During the Second World War France had practically been eliminated from the community of nations. The Free French outside, and the Resistance movement inside, began the process of recovery while France was still under enemy occupation. In foreign policy the problem of the Fourth Republic was not essentially different from that which had faced the Third. During the centuries when military strength depended primarily on man-power, France, with by far the largest population in Europe, was its greatest military power. The balance of power shifted in the nineteenth century with the change in comparative populations. The military decline of France was accentuated by comparative backwardness in industrial development. To keep in the ranks of the Great Powers France had to find allies to redress the balance. Before the First World War Russia, and after it for a time the small states of Central and Eastern Europe, filled the gap. The parties of the right clung to a belief in the military efficacy of the Little Entente up to and beyond the point at which it had patently become an illusion. But long before this, after the victory of the Cartel des Gauches in 1924, Herriot opened a new chapter by appealing for a United States of Europe. The theme was taken up by Briand in 1929. In the 'thirties the European idea, transmuted into the strange dream of a Fascist international, found support from the right. After the German victory of 1940 a substantial body of opinion saw France's future as the favourite *Gau* of the German Führer. At the other extreme, the Communists had, of course, for long dreamed of, and worked for, a Moscow-orientated grouping of what were not yet thought of as satellite states. Thus by the Second World War many sections of opinion in France had come to envisage the future in terms of internationalism, though the nature of the international association envisaged varied through all shades of the political spectrum.

After the war a strong current of neutralism found expression in the influential columns of *Le Monde*; but the experience of the inter-war and the war years did not suggest that France could cut herself off from international affairs and find security in isolation. The creation of the Third Force in French domestic politics naturally led to the speculation whether there might not be a Third Force also in international politics, between the Communist and capitalist colossi of East and West.

In April 1948 the Gaullist Conference called for European federal institutions. 'Economic union,' it declared, 'is clearly the indispensable basis of political union. It is Zollvereins which make federations.' The governments of the Third Force put these ideas into practice. As early as March 1948, the Brussels Pact, a Treaty of Mutual Assistance between France, Great Britain, Belgium, the Netherlands and Luxembourg, was the first step. At the first session of a new Council of Europe, in 1949, Bidault spoke of a possible German accession to the Council. At the same time France had strengthened her ties with the West by the Dunkirk Treaty of Alliance with Great Britain in March 1947 and the North Atlantic Treaty of April 1949; but the memory of their policies between 1918 and 1939 stood in the way of any unqualified reliance on British and American guarantees. A *rapprochement* with a defeated Germany and a real identification of economic and political interests, seemed to offer a better prospect for French security.

The prospects of economic co-operation also seemed brighter with European neighbours. Significantly it was the moderate Catholic M.R.P. leader from Alsace, Robert Schuman, who put forward, in May 1950, the plan for a pooling of the coal and steel industries of Western Europe. In April 1951 a coal and steel agreement was signed by the governments of France, Germany, Italy, Belgium, Holland and Luxembourg.

Political and economic links had now been established in Western Europe. A military treaty proved more difficult to negotiate. In October 1950, Pleven proposed the formation of a European army under the authority of a European Minister of Defence and the Strasbourg Assembly. Robert Schuman did not shirk the implications of the Pleven plan. 'States,' he said, 'must reconcile themselves to the abandonment of part of their autonomy to a collective authority in which they will participate.' However, this proposal had a more difficult passage than its predecessors. The Communists rightly regarded it as intended primarily to form a European bulwark against Soviet advance. It also went too far for the Gaullists, who accepted the idea of Federal Europe only so long as in making the omelette of federation the eggs of national sovereignty were left intact. Socialists and Radicals approved in principle but were suspicious in practice, not least because the M.R.P., and the Catholic parties in Germany and Italy had taken the lead in promoting the plan for a European Defence Community. It was denounced as a Catholic plot, a plan for *la petite Europe vaticane*. It could even be regarded as a continuation of the ideas of Albert de Mun and the Christian Socialists at the end of the nineteenth century, with behind them a long clericalist ancestry of legitimism, the Austrian alliance of the eighteenth century, the *parti dévot* against Richelieu and the Spanish satellite *Ligue* which fought against Henry IV. This was going rather far back in the search for a discreditable ancestry, but French politics have often been fought, like an Homeric combat, over the dead bodies of former heroes.

On a more practical level, the fear of being dragged into a conflict with Russia, the prospect, with French troops heavily committed overseas, of being left in an embarrassing tête-à-tête with a more powerful Germany, and resentment at the idea of putting the French army under international control, also produced opposition. British entry into E.D.C. might have resolved these doubts but it was not forthcoming. Because the discussions had been largely conducted by experts behind the scenes, the plan was denounced as the dream of irresponsible technocrats. For nearly three years the controversy bedevilled French politics. No government dared submit the draft treaty to the Assembly in the face of almost certain rejection. Finally, in 1954, Pierre Mendès-France, who himself had little enthusiasm for the Defence Community, submitted the plan to the Assembly, which by 319 to 264 voted for a postponement *sine die*. This was equivalent to burying it.

The collapse of the hopes based on E.D.C. was, however, not the end. There were supporters of the European idea in every political group, with the exception of the Communists. Relations with Germany continued to become closer; the return of the Saar to German sovereignty in 1956 removed the only outstanding territorial dispute between the two countries; and the European idea gradually strengthened.

In the economic life of the nation, also, fundamental change was coming to France under the Fourth Republic. It was to an extraordinary extent the work of one man, Jean Monnet. The coalition of three parties of the left in the Provisional Government, to the exclusion of the right compromised by collaboration and Vichy, provided what in a sense was the fortuitous circumstance which enabled a start to be made on the reform, as well as the reconstruction, of the economy of France. In January 1946 General de Gaulle signed the decree setting up a *Commissariat du Plan*, under Jean Monnet, with this task. The First Plan dealt mainly with the nationalized industries of railways, mines and electricity, though it also intended to promote other basic industries, in particular steel, cement and farm machinery. From 1947 to 1951 the equivalent of some £2,300 million was invested in railways, electrical power plants, coal, shipping, petroleum refineries and various lesser industries. Hydro-electric plants, which in 1929 had produced only 15, in 1951 produced 40 milliard kilowatts. Coal and steel recovered the level of productivity of 1929. The number of tractors on the land was multiplied by 5 over the pre-war figure. In 1939 60 per cent of French imports had been paid for by exports: the comparable figure for 1951 was 80 per cent. By 1954 the productivity of fifteen of the twenty main industries had passed that of the boom year of 1929.

Marshall aid – and the flow of credit from America continued in one form or another up to 1955 – played an essential part in French recovery, but much of the capital required for the restoration and modernization of French industry came from domestic sources, not least by way of monetary inflation. One result was an increase, compared with the position before the war, in the proportion of the national income that went to profits and a corresponding decline in the share of salaries and wages. The resulting combination of distressing poverty with ostentatious wealth seemed to be made to assist the Communists and their failure to exploit the situation successfully is all the more remarkable. To some extent the new forms of social assistance introduced by the Provisional Government helped to redress the balance, and in 1952 wages were tied to prices by a sliding scale.

An exception to the general progress of the French economy was agriculture. The peasants had done well during the food shortages of the Second World War, but inflation wiped out much of the value of their accumulations of paper money. There was a good deal of depression among the poorer peasants, following antiquated methods on uneconomically small farms with scattered holdings, especially in the centre and south-west. They were protected from world competition by high tariffs, maintained because of the electoral pressures they were able to exert; but although the average yield of the crops was low, there were regular surpluses which the market could not absorb. Even the great increase in the number of tractors, from under 16,000 in 1938 to nearly 630,000 in 1959, did not represent the increase in efficiency that might have been supposed. Often bought on credit as a status symbol rather than for their actual use on many of the tiny farms, their most effective use may have been for blocking roads in the peasant demonstrations periodically organized against the falling prices resulting from overproduction, or to dump surpluses of such commodities as beets and artichokes in the towns as a visible protest.

A steady decline in the numbers of the rural population was evidence of economic progress, but naturally not a welcome progress to the peasants who were being eliminated. It is estimated that between 1949 and 1954 over one-quarter of the working population in rural occupations left the land. Though France still had a much higher proportion of its population on the land than other large Western countries, urbanization was proceeding rapidly. The Paris region doubled its population in the twentieth century, and urban standards of living were higher than rural, though even the agricultural population was not uninfluenced by changing standards. The expectations of the peasants were no longer essentially different from those of the urban population. France was ceasing to be two nations.

While the population of the rural areas was declining, the general tendency for the birth-rate to fall had been halted and indeed drastically reversed. The process had begun even before the Second World War, with the passing of legislation to favour larger families. The net reproduction rate, which had been only 87 in 1911, and the same in 1935, was 132 in 1953 and 128 in 1959. Improved social services also reduced the high death-rate among infants. In the first ten years after the Second World War the population of France rose by three million.

Despite inflation the Fourth Republic was making remarkable economic and social progress. Whatever the electoral strength of Communists and Gaullists, the Third Force might well feel that it deserved well of the country and was presiding over a period of remarkable recovery and increasing prosperity. True, all progress is bought at the expense of those who cannot go along with it. The France of small employers, small shopkeepers, small peasants, slowly but remorselessly being squeezed out, did not like the process. Electoral pressure could check the passage of legislation unfavourable to them, but could not stop the operation of economic forces. The small shopkeepers found a leader in the person of Pierre Poujade, from the backward Massif Central, who organized a local revolt against taxes, which naturally attracted a good deal of support. He moved into national politics and in the general election of 1956 the Poujadists were to win fifty seats and collect a total vote of three millions; but their leader exhibited a total lack of political capacity. His only programme was the evasion of taxes, and his followers already did that to the best of their ability. When Poujade attempted to revive his movement by contesting a by-election in Paris, he was crushed. Those of his followers who had any serious political ambitions transferred their allegiance to other right-wing parties and the movement disappeared.

The fatality for the Third Force, and ultimately for the Fourth Republic, lay not in its domestic or even its foreign policy, but in the problem of the colonies. During the war the policy of the Vichy government, and its powerlessness, had laid the whole of the French Empire open to either enemy or Allied occupation. France's allies had promised to respect the territorial integrity of her Empire, but at the end of the war this promise had not been interpreted as requiring active steps for the restoration of French rule in the colonies. The independence of Syria and the Lebanon, promised before the Second World War, was turned into a *fait accompli* by the Allied forces of occupation: it was not forgotten in France that the decisive step had been the expulsion of the Vichy General Dentz's troops by the British. In Indo-China a temporary occupation by British forces gave the nationalist Viet Minh a chance to establish itself.

Concern about the future of the Empire was perhaps not widespread in France. For the average Frenchman, on the morrow of liberation, the problems of France itself were quite enough. However, some of the opponents of Vichy, and particularly de Gaulle, returned from their overseas bases with new ideas on the colonies, inspired partly by their wartime experiences and partly perhaps by the British example. De Gaulle had the idea of converting the Empire into a Federal Union, for the headship of which his own constitutional proposals would have been more appropriate than a parliamentary executive. The parties of the left envisaged a slower development in the direction of federation, although this went counter to their inherited tradition of Jacobin centralization. The M.R.P., on the other hand, perhaps not without thought for the interests of the Roman Catholic Church in the colonies, wanted the maintenance of French influence.

The Constitution of the Fourth Republic proclaimed that the French Union was 'based upon equality of rights and duties without distinction of race or religion', but its constitutional provisions were so soon to be rendered anachronistic by the winds of change that we need not delay over them. The two essential articles were that whereas in France the National Assembly alone had the right of legislation, in the overseas territory the President could decree special provisions; and that organic laws were to determine the conditions of representation in the colonies. The effect was to leave all real power in the hands of the French government. As regards local representation, the crucial case was Algeria, where there were to be two electoral colleges – one including some nine hundred thousand mainly of European descent, the other seven to eight million native Algerians, each college being represented equally.

It would be unfair to give a picture which did not mention the introduction of social and economic reforms in the Empire – the legalization of trade unions, a labour code, progress in education, plans for capital investment. But the dominant fact was the rise of nationalist movements and the consequent antagonism between European and non-European populations. This was all the more acute because of economic competition for jobs, provoked especially by the French habit of using Frenchmen for even the minor official posts in the colonies.

Changes in the French colonial Empire were formal rather than actual. Paris, not unnaturally, had been unable to grasp the extent to which the whole condition of empire had changed in the course of the Second World War. The states of Indo-China – Laos, Cambodia and Vietnam – were elevated to the rank of Associated States in 1948 and 1949, but already in 1945 Ho Chi Minh, the nationalist leader in Vietnam, had proclaimed its independence. In 1947 a revolt broke out in Madagascar; North Africa was in ferment; but it was Indo-China that produced the first great crisis. There, a state of open war was proving a heavy drain on French military and financial resources. Though the rank and file of the French army in Indo-China included many African troops and many other non-French of the Foreign Legion, the loss of French commissioned and non-commissioned officers was heavy and continuous. Above all there was the psychological strain of an apparently unending war in a country of which the average Frenchman had little knowledge and in which he had little interest. There was also the steady pressure of American anti-colonialism against the French presence in the Far East. Without the brilliance of the French general de Lattre de Tassigny the crisis might have come earlier. When, in 1954, the French strong point of Dien Bien Phu, the defence of which had become symbolic, fell, the balance was tilted decisively against a continuation of the war.

Pierre Mendès-France, most energetic and incisive of the Radical leaders, who had consistently and correctly prophesied the failure of most of the policies of the Fourth Republic, was elected premier largely because it was believed that he would get France out of the Indo-Chinese impasse. There was no choice but total withdrawal. The relief in France was reflected in the vote of the French Assembly approving the Indo-China settlement by 471 votes to 14. While most Frenchmen accepted the loss of French possessions in the Far East as inevitable, the leaders of M.R.P. opposed what was not only an abandonment of political but also of religious influence; the elements in the upper classes that had interests in colonial investment and government resented their loss; while for the army officers, who had fought on so long, with such inadequate resources, it was the final stab in the back by the mandarins of Paris.

Elsewhere, too, the government of Mendès-France recognized that the colonial age was coming to an end. Autonomy was offered to Tunis, where nationalist agitation was making the traditional method of government through a puppet sultan impossible; and in June 1955 agreement on self-government was reached with Bourguiba, the leader of the nationalist party, the Néo-Destour. Negotiations for a settlement with Morocco were also begun. Algeria remained round the neck of the Fourth Republic, a heavier burden and one, because of its large French, or European, minority, much more difficult to cut away.

The ambitions of Mendès-France went much further than finding a solution to the problem of the colonies. He had taken control of the Radical Party out of the hands of older, traditional leaders for the purpose of giving it a new ethos and using it to steer an unwilling France into the twentieth century; but the party was no suitable instrument for such a policy. It soon broke in his hands, a large section following Edgar Faure into opposition. However, it was a coalition of the right and the M.R.P. with the Communists which finally overthrew his government. Its fall showed that the parties of the Third Force could only hold together, and even only maintain themselves as parties, by refusing to face the national problems that demanded a solution. M.R.P. could not accept the colonial policy of Mendès-France; the Radicals could not face the prospect of economic and social reforms that would be contrary to the interests of a large part of their electoral clientèle; and the Socialists seemed to belong, more clearly than any other party, to a France that was dying. In their old industrial strongholds of the North and Centre they were in retreat. The industrial proletariat had long since passed over to the Communists. The active membership of the party fell from 353,000 in 1946 to 117,000 in 1956. Its cadres were getting old. It had become a petit-bourgeois, small-town, provincial party, looking for support to backward areas like the south-west or Franche-Comté. Its greatest support came from the lower ranks of officialdom, in both the public and private sectors. Behind the revolutionary verbiage of tradition it had become profoundly conservative and opposed to change.

The disarray of French politics was reflected in the instability of governments. From January 1947, when the Fourth Republic began, to the election of Mendès-France in June 1954, there were fifteen cabinets, keeping up the average rate of change of the Third Republic. The presidential election of December 1953, after the conclusion of Vincent Auriol's term of office, demonstrated strikingly the acuteness of political conflicts. There was an unprecedented delay in the election and only after thirteen ballots did a majority rally round the name of René Coty, a worthy but undistinguished Norman conservative politician. His succession to a Socialist President showed how far the centre of politics had shifted to the right in seven years. The success of the Poujadists, in the general election of 1956, which has already been mentioned, also seemed to confirm this swing, though in the same elections there were also Socialist and Communist gains. The centrifugal tendencies of French politics were evidently reasserting themselves.

Immediately after the general election a cabinet headed by the

Socialist, Guy Mollet, took office, supported by a 'Front républicain' which even included the Communists. This was merely a gesture to the memory of the Popular Front. It had no political future; the fact was already becoming evident that no coherent majority existed in the Assembly or even in the country at large.

DOUBTS AND QUESTIONINGS

THERE was a paradox about the situation of France ten years after liberation. Economically and in the international sphere remarkable progress had been made: politically the Fourth Republic was in what seemed a hopeless impasse, which reflected only too well the general frame of mind of her people. The hoped-for recovery and rebirth of the state which was to follow liberation had not come about. Objectively there had been progress; subjectively, to the French people, France in the 'fifties seemed to be much what she had been in the 'thirties. Indeed, we can go further back. Two World Wars had apparently had little effect on the mind of France. This, at least, is the impression that one obtains from the literature of the twentieth century. The notes that were to be dominant later had all been struck in the years before the First World War. Even the strong pacifist theme, which might reasonably have seemed a consequence of that holocaust, in fact predates 1914. It was continued in anti-war novels, such as Henri Barbusse's *Le Feu* of 1916, or *Les Croix de Bois* by Roland Dorgelès in 1919. And, alongside protests against war, the normal, peace-time habits of the French middle classes were narrated, after the war as before and in much the same terms, by novelists such as Jules Romains, Georges Duhamel or Roger Martin du Gard. Bridging the gap, the Saint-Simon of the Third Republic, his colours shining with the glory of its great days, and turning in anticipation to the angry hues of the setting sun after the storm of war, Marcel Proust, in 1918 with only a few years yet to live, was able, from his sanctuary in the place Vendôme, to see something of the glow that *À la recherche du temps perdu* was to cast over the declining Republic. The war had brought no break in French literary history. Péguy and the author of *Le Grand Meaulnes* died in it; but the better-known literary figures of the inter-war years –

Claudel, Mauriac, Bernanos, Gide, Colette, Giraudoux, Maritain, Valéry – were all established writers before the First World War.

One who looked far back as well as forward, Paul Valéry, provided a link with the symbolism of the nineteenth century and the rationalism of the world before 1914. *La Jeune Parque* of 1917, and *Le Cimetière marin* of 1922, mysterious and beautiful poems, evoke a world not of the time or place any of his contemporaries knew. On a lower level, the revival of Catholic thought, that had begun before the war, continued. Neo-Thomism, strongly supported in the Dominican Order, found its most influential advocate when Jacques Maritain passed over from Bergsonism. His *Trois Réformateurs* of 1925 was a powerful denunciation of the three men who embodied what he saw as the three great heresies of the postmedieval world – the Protestantism of Luther, the rationalism of Descartes and the romanticism of Rousseau. In a different way the cause of religion was proclaimed in the prose-poetry of the former symbolist poet and diplomat, Paul Claudel, from the medieval *L'Annonce faite à Marie* of 1912 to the sixteenth-century Spanish *Le Soulier de satin* in 1943.

In painting, also, the themes dropped in 1914 were resumed in 1918. Cubism, created about 1907 in succession to an Impressionism that was losing its inspiration, reached its height in the few years after 1918. The greatest of French painters of the time – Picasso, Spanish by origin, Juan Gris, Fernand Léger, Braque – passed through it, and through Cubism Braque attained to a classical serenity which was in striking contrast to the restlessness of the age.

Paris was the Mecca of artists and writers from the whole world in the nineteen twenties. At the tables of the Dôme and the Coupole and Le Select, along the short length of the boulevard Montparnasse, levelled by the Ateliers Nationaux for what purpose they knew not, seventy years earlier, gathered the great and the less great, the classic and the romantic and the merely queer. Among the fevered and poverty-stricken exiles of a war-time Paris, but also repeating the experience of pre-war futurism, developed dadaism – a philosophy of meaninglessness, a literature of incoherence, an art of destruction. Its adepts would have counted it the supreme irony if they had known that their nonsense was to make all too much sense in the years that were to come. Dadaism, like any other outburst of lunacy, however consciously willed, could not survive, but out of it grew surrealism, a more methodical madness, and a more sinister, because rationalized, kind of irrationalism. Its manifesto was written by the poet André Breton in 1924 and rewritten by him several times after. The future Communist poets Paul Éluard and Louis Aragon began as surrealists, and in painting its best advertised exponent was Salvador Dali. The aim of surrealism was to create shock and revulsion by the association of incompatible and unpleasantly combined images. The surrealists wanted not to imitate reality but to present the clear-cut representational image in such a way that it had the hallucinatory, frightening reality of a nightmare. Attempting to dredge up its images and associations from the unconscious mind, surrealism had affiliations with the new Freudian psychology and the methods of psycho-analysis.

The new psychology was, however, less influential in France than elsewhere; perhaps an education in Cartesian rationalism was not favourable to it. But, with or without the aid of psycho-analysis, it was an age of self-questioning moral uncertainty and introspection. The Marcel of Proust's great novel, in his agonizing doubts and hesitations, illustrated the times, though in his final achievement of the ultimate certainties he rose above them. André Gide, born two years before Proust and to live nearly thirty years after him, whose productive career stretches for sixty years from 1891 to 1951, is a better representative of the inter-war years. Protestant by descent and education, beset with religious and moral anxiety, tormented by egocentric introspection, paradoxically finding morality only through the experience of immorality in the *acte gratuit*, the motiveless crime, craving love but unable to concede it, in books like *L'Immoraliste* of 1902, *Les Faux-Monnayeurs* of 1925, and perhaps most of all in his *Journal*, published in 1939, Gide exposed the quivering flesh of a generation that seemed to have lost its protective covering and to have its nerve ends bare to the assaults of a hostile world. Similar introspective anxieties can be found in the Catholic writers of the 'thirties. For Georges Bernanos man was the victim of original sin; there was no other way, for him, of coping with the agony of the Spanish Civil War, which presented moral problems to both right and left. François Mauriac saw life as a battle-ground between good and evil, and painted the passions seething beneath bourgeois respectability. To writers without the consolation of religion, like Céline, whose *Voyage au bout de la nuit*, if we did not know that it was written in 1932, might have been thought to reflect the moral chaos of the years of occupation, the world was a cess-pit, portrayed with the disgust but without the humanity of a Voltaire.

Of course this is not the whole picture. There were other writers, perhaps historically less significant, more detached, less imbued with the pessimism of the age: Jean Cocteau, who moved from dadaism to neo-classicism, was a brilliant amateur of all the arts; Colette was the prose painter of the sensual world, translating the immediacy of sensations into words as the Impressionists seized and put in paint the transience of the seen world.

The other arts often carried the same message as literature. In Picasso, who led the fashion in painting for nearly sixty years, there was a tragic sense of life. Matisse, Braque and Léger preserved a less committed art. Music set out on a new course with the Swiss-born Arthur Honegger and Darius Milhaud. In the cinema the brilliant, light-hearted, tender comedies of René Clair offered a moment of sunshine in a clouding sky. Politics and violence swept over the scene in the 'thirties. Henry de Montherlant eulogized war, the bull-fight, physical endeavour. André Malraux sought a solution in political action; and found his way through Communism in China, the Spanish Civil War and the Resistance, to de Gaulle and office in the Fifth Republic.

Over all, increasingly, hung the cloud of impending war. In 1935 Jean Giraudoux's *La Guerre de Troie n'aura pas lieu* shows Hector, victorious in battle but hating war, struggling for a peaceful solution to the quarrel begun by the abduction of Helen. Success, up to the last moment, is wrecked when a sudden drunken killing makes war inevitable, and the great gates of Troy, opened only in time of war, slowly begin to part. The last comment, on the stupidity of war as well as its inevitability, is the sight of Helen, revealed within the gates in the arms of yet another lover. Here, as elsewhere, we see the intense pacifism, combined with pessimism, of France in the inter-war years.

The Second World War and the occupation seem to have contributed little, at least for the time, to French literature or art. In the clandestine writings of the Resistance, Vecors's *Le Silence de la mer* stood out for its presentation of the dilemmas of conscience created by the enemy occupation. Anouilh's *Antigone* (1942) reflected the conflict between loyalty and obedience to established authority and loyalty to the higher law of the conscience. In his other plays, Anouilh continued the pre-war concern with moral issues, with the same inability to resolve them. *La Peste* (1947), by Albert Camus, could be seen either as an allegory of France under German occupation or of the whole predicament of humanity in the face of unavoidable evil.

The conflict of good and evil, already in Gide becoming so confused that each could assume the character of the other, was intensified by the moral problems of occupation and liberation. Increased scepticsm seemed the main result. The religious revival continued but without any notable intellectual or artistic substance. It was marked by an increased tolerance – the fire of integral Catholicism and the Action Française seemed to have died out – and a corresponding decline in anti-clericalism. The readmission of the Action Française to the fold by Pius XII in July 1939, the religious adulation with which Pétain was surrounded, and the attempt under Vichy to revive clerical control of education; the collaborationist activities of some clerics, notably of Cardinal Baudrillart, the aged director of the Catholic Institute of Paris – all this was counter-balanced by the anti-Nazi policy of *Action Catholique* and the Dominican Fathers, and the underground resistance of the Christian Democrats. After the war 'worker-priests' went into the factories, to revive the Church in proletarian quarters. There was some doubt how far they were converting the proletariat they lived and worked with, and how far the proletariat was converting the priests, perhaps to socially dangerous views, and the Vatican brought the experiment to an end.

After the war Communism, like Catholicism, increased the number of its adherents, and yet somehow seemed to have lost its intellectual vigour, despite all the efforts of such a brilliant leader as

Thorez to preserve its militancy. Aragon wrote pleasing lyrics, Picasso continued to bestride the artistic world and designed the dove of peace for Stalin. The memory of the Hitler-Stalin pact had been partly obliterated by the deeds of the Communist resistance; but later revelations about the Stalinist terror, and the suppression of the Hungarian rising, were daggers in the hearts of many of the Communist-oriented intellectuals. The party militants were better conditioned to accept whatever came from Moscow, as thoroughly as Pavlov's wretched dogs salivating at the sound of the master's bell.

The one intellectual movement which, though it had its origins before the Second World War, seemed for a time to offer something new after it, and to give an answer to a generation that only knew how to ask questions, was existentialism. Its origins were to be found in the religious mysticism of the mid-nineteenth-century Danish writer, Kierkegaard. It penetrated to France by way of the contemporary German philosophers, Heidegger and Jaspers. The earlier existentialist writings of its chief French exponent, Jean-Paul Sartre, precede the Second World War. They reflect the subjectivism and pessimism of those years. After the war, his titles – *Les Mouches* (1943), *Les mains sales* (1948) – are a programme in themselves. *Huis clos*, in 1944, is little to do with war, resistance or liberation. It is a denial of the possibility of liberation from the self-made chains of evil binding man. To be, to endure, is to sin and suffer, each man in his own self-created and self-perpetuating hell. Merely to be is to deny life; to exist is to act, to choose freely; yet freedom of choice is what man cannot have – all he can do is to choose to engage himself in the world, as Sartre himself did in left-wing politics.

The mental confusion of the intelligentsia, struggling with the problems of politics and literature in the left-bank cafés of Paris after the war, is portrayed in less abstruse form in Simone de Beauvoir's *Les Mandarins*. Here, also, and in her *Le Deuxième Sexe*, appears another feature of the post-war scene – the changing position of women in French society, emerging now as individuals capable of playing a part in public life, yet still with all the hesitation of the first steps adding to the uncertainties of the general atmosphere.

Existentialism itself denied the possibility of rational choice and preserved the dignity of man only by falling back on irrational choice, such as the choice of rules to break for no purpose other than breaking them. But this was nothing new: it was a return to the *acte gratuit* of the inter-war years. At the end of his search for the consistently anti-social, Sartre found a writer from the underworld, only again to be disappointed, for Jean Genet achieved literary success, which is a very social kind of thing. And twenty years after liberation, existentialism had lost its philosophical respectability. If the works of Anouilh, Camus, Sartre, de Beauvoir, Genet, continued to have social relevance, it was to a France that might soon belong to history.

⚜

THE REGIME OF MAY
THIRTEENTH

THE political and psychological malaise of France after the First World War was a chronic rather than an acute condition. It took a second war and an overwhelming military defeat to shatter the Third Republic. The fabric of the Fourth Republic was more fragile, but even so only war, though this time a smaller and a colonial war, cracked it. Before this the coherence of the Republic had obviously been weakening. In November 1955, for the second time during the life of the Assembly, a cabinet was defeated on a vote of confidence and the conditions for a dissolution existed. The Assembly was dissolved, and as it had been unable to agree on a new electoral law the system of 1951 still applied. This time it operated chiefly against the parties of the right which lost forty seats. The Social Republicans (the name adopted by the former Gaullists) lost forty-six, while the Communists and their allies gained fifty-two. Any possibility that the Communists might consolidate their position and become again a real force in the Fourth Republic was frustrated, first by the Russian revelation of some part of the Stalinite atrocities – the image of the Communist leader Thorez was closely linked with that of Stalin; and secondly by the crisis of conscience which affected many of the Communist intellectuals after the repression of the Hungarian revolution.

The election did nothing to alter the state of paralysis which had stricken the Fourth Republic. The parties retained just enough life to inhibit action by their opponents, but not enough to take any themselves. The nation was the less concerned about this situation because it was losing interest in politics. Even the disastrous and humiliating failure of an Anglo-French adventure in the Near East, provoked by Egyptian nationalization of the Suez Canal, made no profound impact on the national consciousness.

In many ways the Fourth Republic had not served the nation badly. France was adapting herself to the new situation in Europe. In December 1956 the French government agreed, in return for economic concessions, to the return of the Saar to Germany. This ended territorial disputes between the two countries, and began the real possibility of finding in new European institutions an end to the millennial struggle of West and East Franks, and therefore an answer to the problem of security. In January 1957, rather more than a year before its collapse, the Fourth Republic began negotiations for a Common Market with Germany, Italy and the Benelux countries. In March, the Rome Treaties setting up the Common Market were ratified by the Assembly. Within France, economic prosperity, even if unevenly distributed, was spreading, and social reforms had removed some of the worst social evils.

An important step was taken towards a solution of the colonial problem when, in March 1956, the independence of Morocco and Tunisia was recognized. In June a law extending local self-government in the other African possessions prepared them for a future grant of independence. This left still unresolved the most intractable of the colonial struggles that bedevilled France after the Second World War, the Algerian revolt. It entered the acute stage in November 1954, when the nationalists initiated a campaign of terrorism. By 1955 France had 170,000 troops stationed in Algeria in an attempt to contain the revolt, while another 100,000 were still in Morocco. The General Secretary of the Socialist Party, Guy Mollet, who became premier after the election of 1956, began with an attempt to apply the Socialist policy of negotiation with the rebels. A visit to Algiers and the hostile demonstrations of a mob of Europeans revealed to him the violence of feelings of the *colons*. This experience seems to have shocked him into a remarkable reversal of policy, from one of concessions to one of resistance. More French reinforcements, many only just back from the Far East, were poured into Algeria until some 350,000 men were there, to contain the activities of some 15,000 active rebels. Despite the size of the French forces, the remoter, mountainous parts of the country remained largely under rebel control, and in the more settled areas continuous terrorist outrages made normal life difficult.

Government increasingly passed into the hands of the military. They recruited native forces, settled villages under armed guard and engaged in a campaign of education and indoctrination. The Algerian nationalists intensified their campaign of largely indiscriminate murder, while the army organized underground counter-terrorist services. Terrorism was met by counter-terrorism and torture by torture. It was becoming increasingly a private war, waged with the utmost barbarism, between the army and the *colons* on one side and the Algerian rebels on the other. The French people as a whole, heartily sick of colonial wars, which had never been other than unpopular in France from the time of the first conquest of Algiers in 1830, felt itself committed to the Algerian war only through the army of young French conscripts, sent out to wage the kind of struggle imposed on them by the Algerians, by methods of which the nation, in spite of the censorship, was becoming uneasily aware, and at a price in human life that it increasingly resented. The injury done by the Algerian war to French interests went on mounting. France could not exercise her European influence while the bulk of the army was tied down on the other side of the Mediterranean; the expense of the war was prohibitive of sound national finances; Algerian terrorist outrages were spreading to France itself; and while the struggle continued there seemed no hope of stability in domestic politics.

In autumn 1957 France was without a government for five weeks because of the inability to get any majority together to support one. As governments fell, one after another, the stock of possible premiers was rapidly being exhausted. When a government fell in April 1958 it was again a month before a new one could be put together. The desire somehow to end the struggle and get out of Algeria was reaching a pitch at which it was an obvious threat to the aims of the army and the interests of the *colons*, a few rich but hundreds of thousands of poor whites, who saw no future for themselves in what was the only homeland they had if the native Algerians took control. It only needed the choice of a premier who was reputed to favour negotiation to fire the explosive atmosphere in the European quarters of the Algerian towns.

On May 13th, 1958, when Pierre Pflimlin was to present his

cabinet to the Assembly, the extremists struck. The army was determined that it should not be stabbed in the back yet again, as it believed it had repeatedly been, by the civilians in Paris. The Europeans of Algeria, driven to hysteria by being for years the target of bloody and indiscriminate terrorist attacks, marched and screamed and harangued to the tune of innumerable pots and pans and motor-horns blaring out the beat of 'Algérie française'. A mass demonstration in Algiers invaded the government offices and a self-elected revolutionary committee seized control. Paris was powerless to check the revolt so long as the army was on the side of the *colons*. The question was rather whether the extremists in Algiers, and their sympathizers in the French parties of the right, could extend the movement to metropolitan France. The rebels succeeded, some ten days later, in getting control of Corsica.

For the first time since 1799 it seemed as though a military *coup* might overthrow a legitimate government of France. In fact the position of the army and the *colons* was much weaker than either the leaders of the *coup*, or the Republican politicians now stricken with terror, supposed. The army could not invade France without losing such hold as it had on Algeria. Moreover it began to be suspected that the rank and file of the troops, if called into action to overthrow the government in Paris, might refuse to march. The officer class, right-wing in its political sympathies, often following a family profession, career men whose loyalties were to their colonels and generals rather than to the politicians of Paris, was ripe for revolt. The Foreign Legion and the parachute regiments might have followed them. The weakness, of which they were probably not aware till it was put to the test, was that the rank and file of the army were young temporary soldiers, conscripts who, back in France, would be no proper metal for rebellion, and even in Algeria manifested their unwillingness to be used to overthrow the Republic. The leaders of the revolt, therefore, saw no way of following up their success, though the political authorities in Paris were in daily expectation of disaster. For a fortnight there was a stalemate.

The one person who saw what might be done with a situation which he had been anticipating for years was General de Gaulle. He had long been convinced that the Fourth Republic could not

survive and that when the crisis came he would be called on to save
the state. He had done nothing to bring about the crisis, and even
now that it had come his only act was to announce, on May 15th,
that he held himself in readiness if he were called upon. At the
same time he made it clear that he would contemplate no move that
was not strictly legal. Among those who saw the return to power
of de Gaulle as the only solution there were three main groups.
The Gaullists proper were personally devoted to the General.
They believed that only by accepting his principle of presidential
government could France escape from the political impasse which
seemed to be the inevitable result of government by Assembly.
Secondly, there were many – conservatives, Radicals, even Socialists – who were reluctant to accept either de Gaulle's personal
authority or his political principles, but who saw the Fourth Republic lurching inevitably towards a condition in which government would become impossible and law and order completely
break down: they were prepared to accept the authority of the
General as a temporary solution to the crisis, a *faute de mieux*.
Finally, there were those of the right, especially the 'colonels' leading the revolt who – with typical political naivety – could not
believe that a general could do other than share their views, and, in
spite of his whole record and everything he had said, looked to de
Gaulle as the man who would establish a more or less Fascist
dictatorship based on the army and use it to save an Algérie
française.

De Gaulle let them, and any other potential supporters, believe
what they pleased. He remained in a masterly silence. The situation
grew more and more tense and everyone else's nerves gave signs of
breaking. The President, René Coty, occupied the strategic position. It was customary for Presidents to negotiate the transfer of
government from one premier to another, less usual for them to
arrange for the fall of one Republic and the transfer of power to
another; but this is what Coty did. Everything followed the correct
formal channels. Pflimlin resigned. De Gaulle was appointed
premier. On June 1st the Assembly accepted him by a majority of
about a hundred. The Communists voted solidly against him, the
right generally in his favour, and the Radicals and Socialists were

hopelessly divided. The new premier laid it down as a condition of accepting office that he should have decree powers for six months, and at the end of that time should submit a new Constitution to the vote of the whole nation.

From the time of liberation de Gaulle had consistently argued that France could only recover political stability and national strength by means of a government based on a presidential rather than a parliamentary executive. He used the six months of personal rule to put into law a host of badly-needed reforms which it had hitherto proved impossible to get through the Assembly, and for the preparation, particularly by his former war-time colleague and future premier, Michel Debré, of a new constitution. It was submitted to a referendum in September 1958 and accepted by a majority of about 80 per cent of the voters. It changed the whole balance of French politics by transferring effective legislative powers from the Assembly to the premier, making ministerial office incompatible with membership of the Assembly, and attributing the nomination of the prime minister to the President. Despite the deep-rooted prejudice, dating back to the election of Louis Napoleon Bonaparte in 1848, against a popular election of the President, he was made the representative of the sovereignty of the nation by becoming the nominee of a large electoral college of members of local government bodies, with a considerable bias in favour of the rural communes. The general effect of the changes was to weight the constitution heavily in favour of the executive and against the legislature.

The development of a conflict between the President and the Assembly, such as might have been anticipated, was eliminated, so far as the opening stages of the Fifth Republic went, by a surprisingly complete victory in the election of Gaullist candidates. The electoral system of single-member constituencies, with second ballot, produced some remarkable results. The overwhelming majority that supported the new Constitution were in effect voting in a plebiscite for General de Gaulle. Immediately after, the nation gave a third of its votes to his main opponents – 19 per cent to the Communists and 15·5 per cent to the Socialists. But after the second ballot the Communists, in electoral isolation, were left with a pitiable 10 seats; the Socialists, with fewer votes, were better off with 44, but even so many of their most prominent men disappeared from parliament. In the second ballot there was a nation-wide swing over to candidates who put themselves forward as supporting de Gaulle, with the result that the new Gaullist party, the Union pour la Nouvelle République (U.N.R.), obtained some 200 seats. The Radicals, with 13 seats, were practically eliminated; M.R.P. survived with about 56; the Independent-Peasant bloc of the right did well with 118. The significant fact was the overwhelming national support for de Gaulle, which unexpectedly gave him not only a large party in the Assembly, but also the means of controlling his own majority if it were to become recalcitrant. A referendum in January 1961 confirmed his hold on the country with 75 per cent for and 24 per cent, mostly Communist, against him. In April 1962 it was to be 90·7 per cent against 9·3 per cent.

However unrepresentative the membership of the Assembly may have been, the electoral massacre of the old parties, and the appointment of ministers from outside their ranks by de Gaulle, produced a second great political change – a revolution in political personnel. The Fourth Republic had been run by men whose political habits had been formed under the Third Republic, just as the Second Empire had depended on the political management of many former Orleanists. The Fifth Republic, like the Third, began with something more important than a change in laws, and that is a change in men. The *ministrables* lost their monopoly of office, though not to their old enemies of the extreme right and left. Their fault had been their failure to provide France with a government. Both the old left and the old right had been condemned to frustration by their own inherent contradictions. The right, with the support of the conservative, wealthy, Catholic classes, had stood for the overthrow of the Republic, if necessary by force. Too many of the wealthier, more religious, conservative elements in society, who should have served as the ballast of the ship, had spent their time talking, and sometimes even acting, revolution. They had succeeded to the fatal inheritance bequeathed from the *ancien régime* of an irresponsible *frondeur noblesse*. The parties of the left, on the other hand, Radicals, Socialists and Communists,

depending on the electoral support of *les petits*, were tied to out-
dated interests and followed intensely conservative social policies,
while at the same time they had inherited the historical tradition of
Jacobinism and continued to make appropriate revolutionary
gestures. As for the extreme right and extreme left, neither was as
influential as the size of its electoral support, or the volume of the
noise it made, suggested. To interpret French politics in terms of a
polarization between extremes is profoundly mistaken. Ever since
1871 the ruling element has been the centre. Continual instability
must be seen in terms of comparatively small movements to right
or left about an always dominant centre. Within the loose coalitions
formed for electoral purposes by left and right, the divergences were
always greater than those between the moderates on either side of
the dividing line; and in the last resort these would always join to
save the state from the extremists. This was what happened in 1958.
The Fourth Republic had already dealt successfully with the threat
of Communist extremism from the left; it fell, and the nation
accepted de Gaulle, because it was unable to deal equally successfully
with the army and the Algerian extremists from the right.

In the light of these considerations it is easier to understand why
the break in continuity that was effected as a result of the Algerian
coup of May 13th, which seemed so great at the time, especially to
the politicians who had ruled France and now found themselves
cast into the political wilderness, may appear much less dramatic
when it is looked at in historical perspective. To exaggerate the
change is to underestimate the achievements of the Fourth Republic. Even in respect of the problem of the overseas territories the
Fourth Republic had advanced to the edge of a solution. The
abandonment of Indo-China had been a forced one; but the independence of Morocco and Tunisia was negotiated; and the legislation of 1956, endowing the overseas territories with local assemblies
elected by universal suffrage, was an important preparation for
later developments. When, in the Constitution of the Fifth Republic,
the last and the boldest step was taken, it only carried to its conclusion the policy that governments had pursued, inevitably if
erratically, since liberation. Under the new constitutional laws ten
West and Equatorial African territories, and Madagascar, chose to

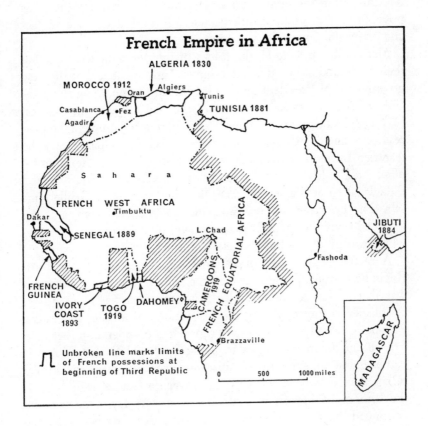

French Empire in Africa

ALGERIA 1830

MOROCCO 1912

Algiers

Oran

Tunis

Casablanca

Fez

TUNISIA 1881

Agadir

S a h a r a

FRENCH WEST AFRICA

Timbuktu

Dakar

JIBUTI 1884

SENEGAL 1889

L. Chad

FRENCH EQUATORIAL AFRICA

Fashoda

FRENCH GUINEA

IVORY COAST 1893

TOGO 1919

DAHOMEY

CAMEROONS 1919

Brazzaville

Unbroken line marks limits of French possessions at beginning of Third Republic

0   500   1000 miles

MADAGASCAR

H

be self-governing member states of the French Community of States, while five smaller and remoter colonies remained as overseas territories. General de Gaulle had added one other possibility, which no previous government could have put forward without being overthrown in the midst of a violent outcry from the right. This possibility, that of total independence from France, was in fact chosen by only one colony, Guinea.

Meanwhile, in Algeria, the forces of the old right were making their last stand, when it became increasingly evident that the new government of President de Gaulle, instead of upholding the principle of Algérie française, as those who had initiated the *coup* on May 13th had expected of him, was preparing to complete the process of recognizing Algerian independence. In January 1960 the Algerian Europeans, the *pieds noirs*, supported by a group of army officers and a few old and once faithful Gaullists like Soustelle and Bidault, attempted a second *coup*, this time against de Gaulle himself. The government, this time, did not yield an inch, and the intended revolution rapidly degenerated into a terrorist conspiracy, which was gradually but ruthlessly crushed.

A second major field of national activity in which the Fifth Republic continued and extended the achievements of the Fourth was that of foreign policy. The European idea was already well established before 1958. As the institutions of a federal Western Europe gradually took shape, economic co-operation between France and Germany began to replace political rivalry. While it had been in opposition the Gaullist movement had stressed national rather than European interests: in power de Gaulle made himself the symbol of French national traditions. At the same time he continued the work of reconciliation with Germany begun by the Fourth Republic, in particular by establishing a close personal relationship with the German Chancellor, Adenauer. The economic institutions of a Western European community therefore continued to develop. The stress was now on a Europe of *patries* rather than a federal Europe, but this might be considered a necessary recognition of facts rather than a repudiation of the European idea.

In one field, however, in which the Fifth Republic inherited a problem, it can hardly be said to have inherited the line of action on which a solution could be found. This was the problem of national finances. Forty years of inflation had reduced the franc of 1914 to near-worthlessness, and in a period of increasing government expenditure such as the twentieth century, finance was something which a French parliament was ideally suited not to cope with. The Fifth Republic adopted the method of decree-laws, which the Third Republic had fallen back on in successive financial crises, to increase taxes and reduce expenditure. There was a partial devaluation, though French prices still remained high by world standards. To establish the psychological conditions for a fresh start a metallic coinage was restored for the lower values, and a new franc was created worth one hundred old francs. Although large sums continued to be poured out in aid to the former colonies in the French Community, the cessation of expenditure on colonial wars, along with a continued increase in economic activity, and more settled government, kept prices fairly stable for a time, though the spectre of inflation still haunted the Fifth Republic, and remained potentially the greatest threat still unexorcized to French political stability and economic progress.

Inflation, as we have seen, had not prevented economic progress, and France emerged from the Fourth Republic in very different shape from that in which she entered it. French economy, so stagnant during the inter-war years, had become dynamic. The genius of a great technician, Jean Monnet, turned French economy into new paths when he inaugurated the first of a series of national plans, drawn up and supervised by a permanent *Commissariat du Plan*.

The First Plan was remarkably successful in laying the foundations of economic revival, but the secondary sectors did not keep pace with the basic reconstruction and the economic atmosphere of the early 'fifties was still one of modified pessimism. After some hesitation a Second Plan, with a broader scope, was drawn up, to cover the years 1954 to 1957. Paradoxically this period, marked by the instability and decay of the political institutions of the Republic, economically was the time of the real break-through. Technically and managerially French industry set out on a process of radical change. Even more important, the habits of the French consumer – for the expansion was still dependent mainly on the exploitation of the home market – underwent a fundamental transformation. There was a marked shift in the direction of mass consumption. The result was an annual rate of growth of the economy, between 1954 and 1959, of $5\frac{1}{2}$ per cent. The total output in 1957 was 30 per cent above that of 1954, and this conceals an even greater rate of industrial progress of 46 per cent, obscured by a much smaller agricultural growth of 19 per cent. Most remarkable of all, prices and the balance of payments remained passably stable.

A Third Plan, from 1958 to 1961, brought in more sectors and attempted a comprehensive cover of the whole national economy. Production now began to take more account of the export market. Aided by the devaluation of the franc in December 1958, the balance of exports to imports between 1958 to 1961 was in the neighbourhood of 100 per cent. The preliminary steps in France towards the development of a European Common Market were thus facilitated.

Economic progress was, of course, patchy. The division was largely one of geography. In the west of France the average income was half what it was in the east, where 80 per cent of the industry was concentrated. Ironically, it was the generally more conservative France of the east that was progressive, and the politically advanced France of the centre and south-west that remained economically conservative. The famous *mystique de gauche*, which kept France politically to the left, also operated to keep her economically backward. It was an inheritance from the time when, in a nation still predominantly made up of peasants and craftsmen, the rights of the individual needed to be asserted against the pressures of authority, the interests of the weaker against the demands of the stronger, and the ideals of the little man against the egoism of the great. Admirable, perhaps, in its day, still carrying into the twentieth century the nostalgic memory of a Rousseauist ideal, imbued with all the sentimentality that the idea of *les petits* can evoke in the French mind, the *mystique de gauche* had become a protective covering for economic inefficiencies and social evils that were tolerated because they worked to the immediate advantage of the mass of petty peasants and small businessmen. They were also a professional interest of left-wing politicians, whose political careers depended on the survival of abuses they devoted their time to denouncing, and they were the basis of the recurrent alliance of left and right against the centre. The interests of *les petits* were not only a stalking-horse for political career-hunters, they were a camouflage for what the Fourth Republic learnt to call *les richesses inciviques*. The *mystique de gauche* was also an indirect means of perpetuating the rule of an *haute bourgeoisie* which still kept its hold on the strategic centres of power.

The very economic success of the first three plans made the survival of poverty, of social evils, and class inequalities more patent and shocking, and emphasized the contrast between the prosperous north and north-east and the remainder of the country. The political weakness of the left, which, apart from anything else, the division between Communists and the rest was guaranteed to perpetuate, prohibited any effective political pressure for a change in the distribution of wealth or income. But poverty is inefficient, and under the Fifth Republic the Fourth Plan, which was to cover the years 1962 to 1965, began a war of attrition against it by adding social to economic ends. Private investment was now deliberately restrained in order to promote development in the public sector. Housing, schools, hospitals – none too soon – appeared more prominently on the lists of priorities. Universities were added, not soon enough to forestall violent student demonstrations, though this problem, it is true, was made worse by a tendency to believe that the Sorbonne was the only university in France and Paris the only place where a real education could be obtained.

The problem of the backward regions was tackled by the encouragement of industrial development, for example in Brittany and the Massif Central. The Rhône Valley down to Marseilles, and the Côte d'Or, were already experiencing economic development even without government stimulus. Areas untouched by economic progress still remained, but they were slowly being penetrated by the new economic forces. The lowest-paid workers also remained a wretched, unimproved stratum of misery at the bottom of the social structure, but in proportion there were now fewer even of these.

The effect of the series of Plans on France was revolutionary.

Within fifteen years France had, in large sectors of her economy, caught up with the twentieth century. It had been done by a means which largely bypassed the normal processes of politics. This indeed was a necessary condition of economic and social progress. Not merely the party politicians, many of whom undoubtedly knew what the country needed but saw no advantage in trying to secure it at the price of political suicide and so failing to secure it anyhow, but the social forces represented by the parties, were irreconcilable with such progress. In fact, the political parties showed themselves extraordinarily disinterested in the Plans, when they were not actively opposed to them. The Communist-controlled Confédération Générale du Travail did its best, unsuccessfully, to sabotage them, and it represented a large majority of the workers. The mass of small businessmen, shopkeepers and farmers were opposed to any kind of planning, which directly conflicted with their interests and threatened their very survival. Though the Plans began and were well advanced under the Fourth Republic, the latest and more advanced stages of planning, carried out under the auspices of the Fifth Republic, could hardly have survived the political pressures inherent in the previous parliamentary regime, for French society, as has been said, had a built-in resistance to economic progress and social amelioration. The fatality for the Fourth Republic was that its political habits did not keep pace with the demands for social and economic progress.

Scientists, technicians, industrialists, civil servants, experts from *écoles polytechniques*, gathered to provide the extra-political pressure which was needed to force through the reshaping of France's economy. In them might be seen the reappearance of what France had known in the days of Turgot, or of Colbert, of Sully and Villeroy – a great reforming bureaucracy. The task of government was taken over, as in the past, by servants of the state, tracing their ancestry back through Conseillers d'état and prefects, intendants, Secretaries, *officiers*, to the royal lawyers of the medieval monarchy. Time and again they had held the country together and provided it with government in a political vacuum. Such were the men who began under the Fourth Republic, and continued under General de Gaulle, what was essentially a technical revolution. Their expertise was remarkable as was their capacity for dealing, in a pragmatic way, with the problems of national economy. The specialized training in practical economics given to some of the French higher civil servants now proved its value. The ease with which they could move between executive posts in the administration and in private business, while obviously open to abuse, meant in fact that the directors and managers of private enterprise and their opposite numbers in the *Commissariat du Plan* had the same intellectual background and outlook, spoke the same language, and largely envisaged the same ends.

On the other hand, the political parties, with their commitment to the issues of the past and seeming indifference to the needs of the present, gave the impression of being prepared to leave the task of reform to the bureaucracy. It should perhaps not have been entirely unexpected when the country in its turn rejected the politicians and looked once again for the head of its government to a super-bureaucrat.

The Fifth Republic is already putting the Fourth into proportion. Its politics are sinking into insignificance, a preparation for the revolution of May 13th, which itself now seems of significance mainly as ensuring the continuance of the economic and technical changes that embody the real revolution of contemporary France. The traditional enmity of *les gros* and *les petits* still survives, perhaps more acutely than ever a class war of rich against poor, as does the unholy alliance of parties of the left and right with a vested interest in its perpetuation. It is still an open question whether economic progress, in the absence of a spirit of humanitarian reform, will so transform the social fabric that the older pattern of social strife will cease to have relevance. The least we can say is that under both the Fourth and Fifth Republics the ancient strongholds of anarchy, on left and right, were falling before the pressure of an advancing economy. The Fifth Republic stands as an end, but also as a beginning. Not, indeed, that any historian could venture to anticipate the fate of its political system, or even guess whether an incomes policy will be evolved and the menace of inflation, with its probable political consequences, avoided. The Fifth Republic provides a suitable point at which to end, for a time, a history of modern France. It initiates a new phase in the history of France not because of a dubious and possibly undurable constitution, but because under it the social and economic revolution has been carried to a point of no return. One of the greatest traditionalists of France has presided over a revolution which is none the less fundamental for being peaceful. The conditions of French development in the future will not be what they were in the past. This is the end of one book. Fortunately it is not my task to prophesy what will have to be written in the next.

CHRONOLOGICAL TABLE

❧

1871	January 28th: Armistice
	February 8th: Election of Assembly
	Government of Thiers
	March 1st: Terms of peace ratified by National Assembly
	March 18th: Troops fail to remove guns from Montmartre
	March 28th: Election of Commune
	May 10th: Treaty of Frankfort
	May 21st: Versaillais enter Paris
	May 28th: End of the Commune
	July 5th: Manifesto of comte de Chambord
	July: Evacuation of five departments by Prussians
	Supplementary elections
	Bishops' petition for restoration of temporal power of Pope
	Rimbaud's *Le Bateau ivre*
1873	Death of Napoleon III
	May: Resignation of Thiers. Appointment of MacMahon
	September: End of German occupation
	October: Letter of comte de Chambord
	Foundation stone of Sacré-Cœur laid
	November: Law of the *septennat*
1874	May: Defeat of Broglie's government
1875	February: *Amendement Wallon*
	Constitutional laws passed
	December: Dissolution of National Assembly
1876	Mallarmé's *L'Après-midi d'un faune*
	Election of new Chamber
1877	May 16th: Dissolution of Chamber by MacMahon
	De Broglie government
	September: Death of Thiers
	October: Legislative elections: republican victory
1879	Republican majority in Senate
	Resignation of MacMahon
	Grévy elected President
	Death of Prince Imperial
	Parliament returns to Paris
	Partial amnesty to Communards

1879–82   Educational reforms of Ferry
1880   Full amnesty to the exiles of the Commune
          Les Soirées de Médan
          September: First ministry of Ferry
1881   May: Protectorate over Tunisia
                Legislative elections
                Tariff law
          November: Fall of Ferry
                Ministry of Gambetta
1882   January: Union Générale crash
          February: Fall of Gambetta
                Anglo-French demonstration at Alexandria
                Foundation of Ligue des Patriotes
          December: Death of Gambetta
1883   February: Second ministry of Ferry
                Death of comte de Chambord
1884   Trade unions legalized
          Law of municipalities
1885   Tonkin reverse
          Fall of Ferry
          Legislative elections: revival of right
          December: Grévy re-elected President
                Protectorate over Madagascar
1886   January: Boulanger Minister of War
                Foundation of Fédération Nationale des Syndi-
                cats
1887   Formation of Indo-Chinese union
          May: Boulanger loses office
                Foundation of Bourses de Travail
          November: Wilson scandal
          December: Resignation of Grévy
                Sadi Carnot elected President
1887–9   Building of Eiffel Tower
1888   Boulangist campaign
          Foundation of Pasteur Institute
1889   January: Election of Boulanger at Paris
          April: Flight of Boulanger
                Paris exhibition
          September: Elections: republican victory
1890   November: Cardinal Lavigerie starts the Ralliement

1891   May: Encyclical: *Rerum Novarum*
          Labour Day shootings
          French fleet visits Cronstadt

1892   Méline tariff
          Encyclical: *Au milieu des sollicitudes*
          November: Panama scandal

1893   August: Elections: moderate majority
               Heredia's *Les Trophées*

1894   Franco-Russian defensive alliance
          Lumière brothers make first film
          June: Assassination of Sadi Carnot
               Casimir-Périer President for six months
          December: Condemnation of Dreyfus

1895   January: Félix Faure elected President
               Establishment of Confédération Générale du Travail
               Repression of Madagascar rising
          November: Radical cabinet of Léon Bourgeois

1896   April: Cabinet of Méline
               Annexation of Madagascar

1897   Barrès's *Les Déracinés*

1898   January: Zola's 'J'accuse'
          June: Resignation of Méline
          June 1898–June 1905: Delcassé Foreign Minister
          September: Marchand at Fashoda
                    Formation of Comité de l'Action Française

1899   Death of Faure
          Election of Loubet as President
          June: Government of republican defence under Waldeck-
            Rousseau
          September: Court martial finds Dreyfus guilty of high treason
            with extenuating circumstances

1900   Franco-Italian secret agreement

1901   July: Law on congregations

1902   Debussy's *Pelléas et Mélisande*
          May: Legislative elections: victory of Bloc Républicain
          June: Resignation of Waldeck-Rousseau
               Government of Combes

1903   Edward VII and President Loubet exchange visits

1904   April: Anglo-French Entente
               Grand Orient scandal. Resignation of General André

1904   April: Ten-hour day law
        November: Law for separation of Church and state introduced
1905   January: Resignation of Combes
                Foundation of S.F.I.O.
        March: Wilhelm II at Tangier
        June: Resignation of Delcassé
        December: Law of separation of Church and state passed
1906   Conference at Algeciras
        Amiens Labour Charter
        May: Legislative elections
                Presidency of Armand Fallières
        October: Government of Clemenceau
                Sorel's *Réflexions sur la violence*
                Bergson's *L'Évolution créatrice*
1908   Anatole France's *L'Île des pingouins*
        L'Action Française becomes a daily paper
        Thalamas student riots
        Affair of German deserters in Morocco
1909   Wave of strikes
        Income tax law passed by Chamber, vetoed by Senate
        Marinetti's *Manifesto of Futurism*
        Beatification of Jeanne d'Arc
1910   November: Railway strike broken by Briand
                Papal condemnation of Le Sillon
                Legislative elections
1911   July: Government of Caillaux
                The *Panther* sent to Agadir
1912   January: Fall of Caillaux
                Government of Poincaré
                Claudel's *L'Annonce faite à Marie*
                French protectorate over Morocco set up
1913   Proust's *Du côté de chez Swann*
        January: Poincaré elected president
        August: Law of three years' military service
1914   Secret papal condemnation of Action Française
        April–May: Legislative elections: victory of left
                Government of Viviani
        June 28th: Assassination of Archduke at Serajevo
        July 16th–23rd: Visit of Poincaré and Viviani to Russia
        July 23rd: Austrian ultimatum to Servia

1914   July 28th: Austrian declaration of war on Servia
July 30th: Russian mobilization
July 31st: German ultimatum to Russia
       Assassination of Jaurès
August 1st: German declaration of war on Russia
       French mobilization
August 3rd: German declaration of war on France
August 4th: British declaration of war on Germany
August 22nd: French defeated in the Ardennes
August 23rd: Viviani government re-formed
September 1st: French government leaves for Bordeaux
September 5th–12th: Battle of the Marne
December: French government returns to Paris

1915   October: Fall of Viviani
       Briand ministry

1916   February 21st: Battle of Verdun begins
July 1st–September: Battle of the Somme
       Sykes-Picot agreement for partition of
       Turkish Empire
December: Nivelle appointed Commander-in-Chief

1917   March: Fall of Briand government
       Ribot ministry
April 16th: Nivelle offensive
May 15th: Dismissal of Nivelle
May: Mutinies in French army
     Appointment of Foch and Pétain
     Trouble among workers
     Bonnet rouge affair
     Fall of Ribot government
September 13th: Ministry of Painlevé
       Bolo affair
November 13th: Fall of Painlevé
       Clemenceau government

1918   March–July: Ludendorff offensive
July 18th: Counter-offensive of Foch
November 11th: Armistice

1919   June 28th: Signature of Treaty of Versailles
November: Election of Assembly: victory of Bloc National

1920   January: Paul Deschanel elected President against Clemenceau
       Resignation of Clemenceau

1920   May: Treaty of Sèvres
         Government of Millerand
         Weygand mission to Poland: Battle of Warsaw
     September: Resignation of Deschanel
            Millerand elected President
     December: Socialist Congress at Tours

1921   Trade union split

1922   January: Government of Poincaré
         Le Cimetière marin of Paul Valéry

1923   January: Occupation of Ruhr
         Treaty of Lausanne

1924   May: Election: victory of Cartel des Gauches
     June: Resignation of Millerand
         Doumergue elected President
         André Breton's Manifesto of Surrealism
         Government of Herriot
     September: Geneva Protocol
     October: Dawes plan

1925   April: Fall of Herriot
         1925–32: Briand Foreign Minister
     July: Evacuation of Ruhr begins
         Revolt in Syria
     October: Locarno agreements

1926   July: Government of Poincaré – decree-laws
         Papal condemnation of Action Française published

1928   Military service reduced to one year
     Decision to build Maginot line

1929   July: Retirement of Poincaré
     September: Briand proposes European Federal Union
     October: Wall Street crash

1930   May: Young plan comes into operation
     June: French evacuation of Rhineland
     September: Election of 107 Nazis to Reichstag

1931   May: Paul Doumer elected President

1932   May: Assassination of Doumer
         Lebrun elected President
         Election of Chamber: success of Cartel des Gauches
         Government of Herriot

1933   January: Hitler becomes Reich Chancellor
     January–October: Government of Daladier

1933	July: Four-Power Pact
	Stavisky affair
1934	February 6th: Attempted *coup d'état* of the Leagues
	February 9th: Government of Doumergue. Communist demonstration
	October 9th: Assassination of Barthou and King Alexander
	Doriot breaks away from Communist Party
	Laval becomes Foreign Minister
	November: Fall of Doumergue
1935	January: Saar votes for reunion with Germany
	April: Stresa pact
	May: Franco-Soviet pact negotiated
	September: Italian attack on Abyssinia
	Giraudoux's *La Guerre de Troie n'aura pas lieu*
	December: Hoare-Laval agreement
1936	January: Fall of Laval
	January: Manifesto of Popular Front
	March: Remilitarization of Rhineland
	April: Ratification of Franco-Soviet pact
	April, May: Election of Chamber: victory of Popular Front
	Government of Blum
	Occupation of factories
	Matignon agreement
	October: Devaluation of franc
	Spanish Civil War
1937	March: Léon Blum announces 'pause'
	June: Fall of Blum government
1938	April: Government of Daladier
	September: Munich
	October: Reynaud becomes Finance Minister
	December: Ribbentrop visits Paris: Declaration of Friendship
1939	February. French recognition of government of Franco
	March: Germany occupies Czechoslovakia
	Daladier voted plenary powers
	March: Anglo-French guarantee to Poland
	April: Re-election of Lebrun as President
	August 12th: Anglo-French mission at Moscow
	August 21st: Russo-German agreement announced
	August 22nd: French Communist Party supports Nazi-Communist pact

1939 September 1st: German invasion of Poland
September 3rd: Great Britain and France declare war on Germany
September 17th: Russian invasion of Poland
September 26th: Daladier dissolves Communist Party

1940 March 20th: Reynaud succeeds Daladier
May 10th: German invasion of Low Countries
May 13th–14th: French front broken on Meuse
May 18th: Reynaud becomes Minister of National Defence in place of Daladier
May 19th: Gamelin replaced by Weygand
Pétain enters government
May 29th–June 4th: Dunkirk evacuation
June 10th: French government in Touraine
Italy enters war
June 14th: Germans enter Paris
Government moves to Bordeaux
June 16th: Resignation of Reynaud. Succeeded by Pétain
June 18th: General de Gaulle calls from London for continued resistance
June 22nd: Armistice with Germany
June 24th: Armistice with Italy
July 1st: French government moves to Vichy
July 3rd: Mers-el-Kébir. British attack on French fleet
July 10th: National Assembly votes full powers to Pétain
July 11th: Vote of constitutional laws
Ministry of Laval
September: Free French expedition to Dakar fails
Japanese forces enter Indo-China
October 24th: Hitler-Pétain interview at Montoire
December 13th: Dismissal of Laval

1941 January: Foundation of Rassemblement National Populaire
February: Darlan in control of government
May: May Protocols
June: Syrian campaign
German invasion of Russia
Communists begin resistance
November: Dismissal of Weygand

1942 April: Trial at Riom of Blum, Daladier, etc., abandoned
April: Laval returns to power

1942   November 8th: Invasion of North Africa
        November 11th: Germans move into unoccupied France
        November 27th: French fleet sunk at Toulon
        December 24th: Assassination of Darlan
1943   June: Committee of National Liberation formed at Algiers
                under de Gaulle and Giraud
        September: Liberation of Corsica
1944   January: Paris collaborationists enter government
                Sartre's *Huis clos*
        June 6th: Allied landing in Normandy
        August 20th: Pétain transferred to Belfort
        August 26th: De Gaulle enters Paris
                Ho Chi Minh proclaims independence of Viet-
                nam
1945   October 21st: Referendum ends Third Republic
                Election of Constituent Assembly
1946   January: Resignation of de Gaulle
        May: France votes against first Constitution
        June: Election of Second Constituent Assembly
        October: Second Constitution accepted by referendum
1947   January: Election of Vincent Auriol as President
        March: Anglo-French Treaty of Dunkirk
        April: Formation of Gaullist Rassemblement
                Revolt in Madagascar
        May: Ramadier dismisses Communist ministers
        June: Marshall speech on aid
        November–December: Communist-led strikes
                Albert Camus's *La Peste*
1948   January: Formation of Third Force
        March: Treaty of Mutual Assistance
        October–November: Strikes
1949   April: Signature of North Atlantic Treaty
1950   May: Schuman proposes coal and steel plan
        October: Pleven plan for European army
1951   April: Coal and steel agreement between France, Germany,
                Italy and Benelux
        May: Electoral reform bill
        June: General election
1952   March: Government of Pinay
1953   Formation of Poujadist league

1953   December: Election of René Coty as President
1954   May: Fall of Dien Bien Phu
        June: Government of Mendès-France
        July: French Assembly approves Indo-China settlement
            French Assembly rejects European Defence Community
        November: Algerian revolt
1955   June: Agreement with Néo-Destour in Tunisia
1956   January: General election
                Front républicain government under Guy Mollet
        March: Independence of Morocco and Tunisia recognized
        June: Law extending self-government in colonies
        November: Suez affair
        December: Return of Saar to German sovereignty
1957   March: Rome Treaties for Common Market ratified by Assembly
        May: Resignation of Mollet government
        August: Partial devaluation of franc
1958   April 16th: Fall of Gaillard government
        May 13th: Revolt of Europeans and army in Algeria
        May 14th: Government of M. Pflimlin
        June 1st: Government of General de Gaulle accepted by Assembly
        June 3rd: French parliament adjourns till October
        September 28th: Constitution of Fifth Republic accepted by referendum
        December 21st: General de Gaulle elected President
        December 27th: Devaluation of franc
1959   January 8th: General de Gaulle proclaimed President of Fifth Republic; Michel Debré, premier
1960   January: Introduction of 'new' franc
        February: First French nuclear bomb exploded
1961   January: Referendum on future of Algeria
        April: Army revolt in Algeria collapses
1962   March: Franco-Algerian agreement
        April: Resignation of M. Debré
        July: Independence of Algeria proclaimed
        October: Referendum approves future presidential election by universal suffrage

FURTHER READING

⚜

Some of the works mentioned in the reading list to Volume 2 must be repeated here, among them the general histories – Lavisse: *Histoire de France contemporaine* (1920–2), vol. 8; Ch. Seignobos: *L'Évolution de la Troisième République* (1875–1914); Renouvin, Préclin et Hardy: *La paix armée et la Grande Guerre, 1871–1939, (Clio*, 2nd ed., 1947); J. P. T. Bury: *France, 1814–1940* (2nd ed., 1951); Lefebvre, Pouthas et Baumont: *Histoire de la France pour tous les Français* (1950); M. Reinhard (ed.): *Histoire de France*, ii, *de 1715 à 1946* (1954). To these may be added, Gordon Wright: *France in modern times, 1760 to the present* (1962), a thoughtful and informed survey, with very full bibliographical discussions which should be consulted; D. W. Brogan's *The Development of Modern France* (1940), encyclopaedic in its scope; and David Thomson's *Democracy in France* (3rd ed., 1958), the best single analysis of French politics since 1871. The texts of successive French constitutions are given in Duguit, Monnier et Bonnard: *Les Constitutions et les principales lois politiques de la France depuis 1789* (various editions: the earlier ones contain an introduction which is the best short survey of French constitutional history since 1789).

General interpretations of the course of French politics are R. Rémond: *La Droite en France de 1815 à nos jours* (1954) and F. Goguel: *La Politique des partis sous la IIIe république* (1946), both interesting and suggestive, but both also tending to reduce French political history to an unduly artificial pattern. D. W. S. Lidderdale's *The Parliament of France* (1951) is essential for understanding the weakness of parliamentary institutions in France.

An interesting contemporary English interpretation of the first quarter-century of the Third Republic is J. E. C. Bodley's *France* (revised ed., 1902). The opening years of the Third Republic are those that have been best served by historians. The constitutional debates are described in detail by M. Deslandres: *Histoire constitutionnelle de la France*, iii, *L'Avènement de la IIIe République, la constitution de 1875* (1937). *The Beginning of the Third Republic in France* (1940), by F. H. Brabant is a witty account with sympathetic sketches of the legitimist, Orleanist, and republican personalities of the time. Daniel Halévy provides an individual interpretation in *La Fin des notables* (1930) and *La République des ducs* (1937). The contribution that can be made to historical interpretation by a scholarly piece of electoral analysis is shown by J. Goualt's *Comment la*

France est devenue républicaine (1954). The classic work in the field of political analysis is A. Siegfried's *Tableau politique de la France de l'Ouest sous la IIIe République* (1913). Among many books on the Dreyfus affair, perhaps the most thorough and impartial is G. Chapman on *The Dreyfus Case* (1955). A clear and concise analysis of the political institutions of the Third Republic is J. Barthélemy's *Le gouvernement de la France* (edition of 1934). W. L. Middleton's *The French Political System* (1932) is a lively description, and A. Siegfried gives a pungent verdict on French parties in *Tableau des Partis en France* (1930). Right-wing critiques of the republican parties are R. de Jouvenel's *La République des Camarades* (1934) and A. Thibaudet's *La République des Professeurs* (1927).

It is not easy to find party or social histories in France which are not over-committed. A thorough and detailed, but excessively orthodox history of the Socialist party is *Histoire du Socialisme en France (1871–1961)* (1962), by D. Ligou. E. Dolléans's *Histoire du Mouvement Ouvrier, 1830 à nos jours* (1947–53) is useful but also rather uncritical. A rather ambivalent history is G. Walker's *Histoire du parti communiste français* (1948). A good, reasonably short account of *The Action Française* (1962) is by E. R. Tannenbaum. *Republican Ideas and the Liberal Tradition in France 1870–1914* (1951) by J. A. Scott is interesting but tries to link the politics of the Third Republic rather too closely to political traditions inherited from the French Revolution. The political ideas of the French parties are best studied in the writings of the time, for example, *Éléments d'une Doctrine Radicale* (1925) by Alain; Léon Blum's *L'histoire jugera* (1945), a selection of articles and speeches; and *Une politique de grandeur française* (1945) by Maurice Thorez. To the last of these it would be wise to add some of the material that the Party would prefer to suppress, such as *Les cahiers du bolchevisme pendant la campagne 1939–1940* (1951) collected by A. Rossi. A lively and penetrating survey of the period when French party divisions reached almost to the point of civil war was made by the English left-wing journalist, A. Werth, in *The Twilight of France, 1933–40* (1942). There are hardly any outstanding biographies for this period, though the English reader will find J. Hampden Jackson's *Clemenceau and the Third Republic* (1946) an interesting sketch of the most striking individual in its political history.

The economic history of France has been neglected. Val Lorwin has written on *The French Labor Movement* (1954). The *Bilan de l'économie française, 1919–1946* (1947) by C. Bettelheim is a useful survey of the period, with a fair amount of statistical information. On religion the best account is A. Dansette's *Histoire religieuse de la France contemporaine* (1948–51); and on the colonies, up to the dates of their publication, H. Blet's *Histoire de la colonisation française* (1946) and H. Deschamps's *Méthodes et doctrines coloniales de la France du XVIe siècle à nos jours* (1953). On foreign policy general histories of international relations are apt to give a more balanced picture than histories of the policy of a single country. In addition to the appropriate volumes of P. Renouvin's *Histoire des relations internationales*: *Le XIXe siècle*, ii, *de 1871 à 1914* (1955); *Les crises du XXe siècle*, i, *de 1914 à 1929*, ii, *de 1929 à 1945* (1958) give clear short summaries of international affairs from a French point of view; and there is also J.-B. Duroselle's *Histoire diplomatique de 1919 à nos jours* (1957). Two difficult phases in French foreign policy are studied by J. C. King in *Foch versus Clemenceau* (1960) and Adrienne Hytier in *Two Years of French Foreign Policy: Vichy 1940–1942* (1958). The crucial problem of relations between Great Britain and France during the inter-war years is considered by A. Wolfers in *Britain and France between the Two Wars* (1940) and W. M. Jordan in *Great Britain, France and the German Problem, 1918–39* (1943).

The last phase of the Third Republic was described by a great historian, Marc Bloch, in *L'Étrange défaite* (1949), translated as *Strange Defeat*. The most revealing of many memoirs on the Vichy regime is by Pétain's first secretary, Henri du Moulin de Labarthète: *Le Temps des illusions: souvenirs juillet 1940–avril 1942* (1946). An account of Vichy France based on contemporary sources is given in my contribution to *Hitler's Europe* (1954), pp. 338–434, edited by A. and V. M. Toynbee. There is a short sketch of the Resistance in H. Michel's *Histoire de la résistance* (1950), though much more material on this struggle is gradually being brought out. General de Gaulle's *Mémoires de guerre* (1954–9) is a classic. R. Aron, who has written a history of Vichy, has also collected much first-hand material in *Histoire de la Libération de la France* (1959), translated as *De Gaulle before Paris* (1962), and *De Gaulle triumphant* (1964). Gordon Wright describes the complicated political manoeuvres before the setting up of the Fourth Republic in *The Reshaping of French Democracy* (1948); and the Fourth Republic itself is ably analysed by Dorothy Pickles in *French Politics: the First Year of the Fourth Republic* (1953) and Philip Williams in *Politics in Post-war France* (2nd ed., 1958). Mrs Pickles has continued her conscientious and perceptive study of French politics in *The Fifth French Republic* (1960). The most thorough account, so far, of the important series of Plans is *Economic Planning in France* (1963) by J. and A-M. Hackett.

To pick out a limited number of works of fiction which throw light on the history of recent times is even more difficult than to make a selection for earlier periods. The development of nationalist feeling is illustrated by the novels of Maurice Barrès, such as *Les Déracinés*. Anatole France's *L'Île des pingouins* is a satiric history of the earlier years of the Third Republic, and Georges Duhamel's *Chronique des Pasquier* (1933–45) a sober account of the fortunes of a bourgeois family. Marcel Proust in the many volumes of *À la recherche du temps perdu* not only looks back to the apparently stable society of the years before the First World War but also prophetically forward to an age of decay and disaster. Direct responses to the tragedy of war, such as Henri Barbusse's *Le Feu* show the intensity of feeling it aroused, but now seem to go less deep than Proust's more indirect approach to an age of national decay. Disillusionment and despair are reflected in Céline's *Voyage au bout de la nuit* (1932) and Camus's *La Peste* (1947). The plays of Sartre, written mostly after the Second World War, continue to reflect the state of depression of the inter-war years; Simone de Beauvoir's semi-autobiographical *Les Mandarins*, on a lower artistic level, gives an impression of the self-questioning futility of politicians and intellectuals after the Second World War. The new France is so far little reflected in literature; one would hardly expect, or perhaps even desire, to find a technological revolution in the poetry or fiction of a nation.

INDEX

✤

BOOK I

ABOUKIR BAY, BATTLE OF, 251
Académie des Inscriptions, 87
Académie des Sciences, 16
Académie Français, 128
Adélaide, Mme Princess of France, 102
Africa, 27, 42
Agriculture, 50-1, 106, 111, 139-40, 142, 167,
    191, 252, see also Famine
Aguesseau, Henri François d', 36
Aiguillon, Armand duc d', 159
Aiguillon, Emmanuel duc d', 96, 98-9, 101
Aix-la-Chapelle, Treaty of, 74
Alberoni, Guilio cardinal, 30
Alembert, Jean le Rond d', 104
Alexandre, 194
Alsace, 157, 174
Amelot de Chaillou, 36, 72
American Independence, War of, 111, 117
    122-4, 127, 135, 164, 190, 193, 202
Ami du Peuple, 193
Ancien régime, 16, 39, 40, 69, 100, 110, 113,
    125, 138, 155, 164-5, 169, 171, 204, 211,
    231, 245, 255
Angervilliers, d', 36
Angivillier, d', 116
Anglophobia, 208-9
Antilles, 42, 75, 174
Architecture, 43-5
Argens, marquis d', 104
Argenson, comte d', 55, 63, 72-4
Argenson, marquis d', 81, 87
Aristocratic plots, fear of, 157-8, 192
Army, 94, 108, 110, 176, 225, 231
Arnouville, comte Machault d', 63-4, 81, 90,
    99, 130
Arouet, François Marie, see Voltaire
Artois, comte d', see Charles X
Assemblies, provincial (estates), 132
Assembly, National (also constituent and
    legislative), 134, 145-6, 159, 160, 162-7,
    170, 172-7, 179-186, 188, 190-1, 194-5,
    197-9, 206, 216, 218-19, 258-9
Assembly of Notables, 127-9, 133
Assignats, 172, 191, 211, 223, 226, 247
Aubusson tapestries, 57
Augereau, Pierre, marshal, duc de Castig-
    lione, 231, 249, 250
August days, 196-9

Augustus II, Elector of Saxony, 37
Augustus III, Elector of Saxony, King of
    Poland, 37
Austrian succession, war of, 63, 71-4
Avignon, 173, 187

BABEUF, FRANÇOIS EMILE, 248
Bailly, Jean Sylvain, 144, 148, 154, 182, 195
Balzac, Honoré de, 218
Barbaroux, Charles Jean Marie, 208, 213
Barère de Vieuzac, Bertrand, 214, 218-19,
    232, 235, 240-2
Barnave, Antoine Pierre Joseph Marie, 154,
    168, 182-3
Barras, vicomte Paul de, 236, 238, 246, 249,
    251
Barry, Mme du, 78, 96, 102, 115, 222
Barthélemy, marquis de, 248-9
Bastille, 112, 148-9, 153-4, 158, 167-8, 197,
    228, 257
Bavaria, Charles Albert Elector of, 71, 110
Bayle, Pierre, 85-7
Beauharnais, Joséphine de, 247
Beaumarchais, Pierre Augustin Caron de,
    117
Beaumont, Christophe de (Archbishop of
    Paris), 66
Beauvais tapestries, 57
Beauvillier, duc de, 24
Becker, Carl, 90
Belle Isle, comte de, 53, 70-2, 74, 77, 80
Bentham, Jeremy, 87
Bernard, Samuel, 40
Bernis, cardinal de, 54, 77, 80
Bertier de Sauvigny, Louis Jean, 153-4
Berwick, marshal duke of, 38
Billaud-Varenne, Jean Nicolas, 92, 215, 217,
    225, 227, 235, 238, 240-1
Blois, 169
Bodin, Jean, 14, 32
Boissy d'anglas, comte de, 242, 244-6
Bolingbroke, Viscount, 87
Bonaparte, Lucien, 253
Bonaparte, Napoleon, 13-14, 29, 47, 99, 100,
    122, 205, 225, 231, 242, 244-6, 249-50,
    253-4, 260
Bordeaux, 43, 45, 50, 60, 132, 221
Boscawen, Admiral Sir Edward, 75

Bossuet, Jacques, Bénigne Bishop of Meaux, 18
Boucher, François, 57
Bouillé, marquis de, 176, 181
Boulainvillier, comte de, 87
Bourbon, duc de, 28, 31-2
Bourbon kings: see Charles X, Henri IV, Louis XIV, Louis XV, Louis XVI, Louis XVII, Louis XVIII
Bourgeoisie, triumph of, 259, see also Third Estate
Braddock, General, 75
Bread shortages, see Famines
Breteuil, baron de, 112, 119-20, 128-9, 147-8, 150, 187
Breton club, see Jacobin
Brienne, Loménie de Archbishop of Toulouse, 128-33
Brissot, Jacques Pierre, 184-5, 188-9, 191-7, 200-1, 206-7, 209-13, 219-20, 222, 224
Brittany, 47, 95, 132, 136, 160, 173, 181, 221, 252
Broglie, comte de, 71-2, 77, 99, 100
Broglie, marshal de, 146, 148
Brune, marshal, 231
Brunswick, Duke of, 80, 191, 194, 198-9, 201-3
Brussels, 191, 204, 210
Buffon, comte de, 88
Burgoyne, General John, 121
Burgundy, Duke of, 24
Burke, Edmund, 179, 186
Byng, Admiral John, 79

Cabarrus, Thérèse, see Tallien, Thérèse
Cagliostro, comte de, 120
Cahiers, 141-2, 155, 157, 175
Ça ira, 194, 223
Calas, Jean, 64, 89
Calendar, republican, 222
Calonne, Charles Alexandre de, 112, 127-9, 132, 186
Cambon, Joseph, 238
Camisard revolt, see Huguenots
Campan, Mme de, 115
Camperdown, battle of, 250
Campo-Formio, Treaty of, 250
Canada, 27, 42, 74-6, 80-1, 93
Cardinals, reign of, see Mazarin and Richelieu
Carlyle, Thomas, 236, 254
Carnot, Lazare, 215, 217-18, 232, 234, 238, 243, 248-9
Caron, Pierre Augustin, see Beaumarchais
Carrier, Jean Baptiste, 221, 234, 240-1
Castries, marquis de, 129, 232
Catherine II, Empress of Russia, 99, 121, 187
Catholic church, see Roman Catholic
Cellamare, prince de, 30
Censorship, 87, 89

Châlons, 181
Champ de Mars, 182, 184, 216
Champs Élysées, 44
Chancellor, office of, 34
Chardin, Jean Baptiste, 116
Charette de la Contrie, François, 245
Charles VI, Holy Roman Emperor, 70
Charles X, King (comte d'Artois), 127-8, 145, 148, 150, 186-7, 244
Charles Edward Stuart, Prince (the Young Pretender), 72
Châteauroux, duchesse de, 53, 55, 70, 72-3
Châteauvieux, regiment of, 176
Chatham, Earl of (William Pitt the Elder), 79
Chaumette, 224
Chauvelin, Bernard Louis marquis de, 36-8, 53-4, 70, 77
Chauvelin, François Bernard marquis de, 190, 208-9
Chenier, André, 236-7
Cherbourg, 119, 127
Chevreuse, duc de, 24
Chimay, princesse de, see Tallien, Thérèse
China, Company of, 27
Choiseul, duc de, 77, 81, 90, 93-9, 108, 110-11, 115, 119
Choiseul-Praslin, duc de, 81, 93, 97
Cisalpine Republic, 250
Civic fêtes, see Fêtes
Civil Constitution, see Constitution and Roman Catholic
Classicism, 178-9
Clavière, Etienne, 190, 214, 222
Clermont, 45
Clive, Robert, 80
Clootz, Anacharsis, 177
Clubs, revolutionary, see Revolutionary clubs
Coal mining, 47
Coburg, General, 211, 225, 232
Colbert, Jean Baptiste, 16, 18, 36, 45-6, 48, 60
Collot d'Herbois, Jean Marie, 215, 217, 223, 227, 233, 235, 238, 240-1
Commerce, see Trade and industry
Commerce, bureau de, 42
Committee of General Security, 210, 225, 233, 240
Committee of Public Safety, 177, 212, 215-19, 223-6, 230-5, 238-41, 243-4, 246, 258
Committee of Public Safety, call for new, 252
Common land, 155
Commune, 195-6, 200-1, 203, 213, 220, 223, 235-6, 239, 244
Companies, trading, see China and Indes
Companies of the Sun, see Sun
Company of Jesus, see Jesus, Company of
Condé, prince de, 30, 150
Condillac, Etienne Bonnot de, 88, 104
Condorcet, marquis de, 104, 135, 222
Conscription, 225

Constituent Assembly, *see* Assembly
Constitution, 160, 166-7, 183-4, 195, 198, 215, 228, 241-2, 244-6, 251
Consulate, 252
Conti, prince de, 28, 77
Controller-General, office of, 34
Convention, National, 159, 197, 201, 206-7, 208-16, 220-3, 228, 230, 234-6, 239-44, 246, 248
Corday, Charlotte, 221
Cordeliers, club des, 177, 184, 203, 211, 221, 238, 239
Cornwallis, General Lord, 122
Corsica, 95, 186
Corvée, 49
Council of the Five Hundred, 252-3
Councils, royal, 25-7, 33-4, 54-5, 60, 99, 125
Counter-revolution from abroad, plans for, 104, 163, 187, 192
Couperin, François, 57
Court at Versailles, *see* Versailles
Courts, sovereign, *see* Parlements
Couthon, Georges, 214, 218, 233, 234, 236
Crébillon, Prosper Jolyot de, 56, 58
Cröy, duc de, 54
Crozat, marquis du Châtel, 40
Cuchod, Suzanne, *see* Necker, Suzanne
Cumberland, Duke of, 79
Currency, *see* Finance
Custine, comte de, 190, 204, 211
Customs and tolls, 48, 62

Dakin, Dr Douglas, 106
Damiens, Robert François, 81
Danton, Georges Jacques, 168, 177, 195, 197, 203-4, 207-8, 214, 226-7, 231, 235, 239
Darien, 28
Dauphiné, 132-3
David, Jacques Louis, 178-9, 219, 228-9, 222
Davout, marshal Louis duc d'Auerstaedt, 231
Declaration of Rights, 164-5, 168, 174
Deffand, Mme du, 128-9
Departments, division of France into, 169
Descartes, Rene, 85-6, 88, 103
Desmoulins, Camille, 177-8, 218, 222, 227
Diamond necklace scandal, 100, 119-21
Diderot, Denis, 88, 116
Dijon, 132
Directory of Five, 246-52
Divine right, theory of rule of king by, 165
Divorce, 174
Dubois, Guillaume cardinal, 30, 35
Dumont, Pierre, 180
Dumouriez, Charles François, 189-90, 202-4, 208-11, 212
Dunkirk, 43
Dupleix, Joseph, 75-6
Dupont de Nemours, Pierre, 112
Duport, Adrien, 135
Dyon, 50

East India Company, 75
East Indies, 27, 75, 94, 122
Economic situation, *see* Finance
Education, 91-2, 106, 230
Edward, the Black Prince, 157
Égalité, Phillipe, *see* Orléans, duc d'
Egypt, expedition to, 250-2
Élisabeth, Mme Princess of France, 181, 222
Elizabeth, Farnese, Queen of Spain, 29
Emigration under *ançien régime*, 50
Émigrées, 150, 185-7, 212, 244-5, 248
Encyclopedia of Arts and Crafts, 16
Encyclopedists, 86, 88
Enragés, les, 211, 223-4, 239, 247
Entresol, club de l', 87
Éon, chevalier d', 99-100
Epidemics, *see* Plague
Estrées, duc d', 79
Étoiles, Charles Guillaume le Normant d', 56
Étoiles, Jeanne le Normant d', *see* Pompadour, marquise de
Evelyn, John, 13

Fabre d'Eglantine, 177
Falkland Islands, 97
Family Compact, 81, 93, 97, 186
Famines and other food shortages, 18, 50, 52, 100, 139-41, 155, 161-2, 191, 211, 232, 242, 247
Farmers-General, 27, 41, 48, 62, 99, 100, 126, 247, 258, *see also* names
Fashions, 46, 115, 247
Fédérés, les, 194, 196
Fenélon, François de Salignac de la Mothe, Archbishop of Cambrai, 24, 32, 87
Ferrières, marquis de, 183
Ferson, count Axel von, 118-20, 181
Fêtes, civic, 168, 222, 228, 234, 236
Feuillants club, 182, 184
Figaro, as spirit of revolution, 117
Finance, 16, 18, 26, 29, 40-2, 44-6, 49, 50, 52-3, 58, 60-4, 69, 106-7, 112, 124-8, 133, 139-40, 169-70, 176, 191, 211, 220, 223-4, 233, 242, 247, 252, *see also* Assignats, Law, John and Taxation
First Estate, *see* Roman Catholic
Fishing, 42-3
Flanders, 47
Flanders regiment, 160, 162, 168
Fleurus, 232, 234
Fleury, André Hercule cardinal de, Bishop of Fréjus, 32, 35-40, 53-4, 62, 69-72, 87, 93, 128, 255
Fontenelle, Bernard le bovier de, 56, 103
Foreign policy, 29, 40, 69-81, 101, 125
Fouché, Joseph duc d'Otranto, 92, 217, 234, 255
Foullon, Joseph François, 153-4
Fouquet, Nicolas, 14, 70
Fouquier-Tinville, Antoine, 221, 241

Fournier, Claude, 193
Fragonard, Jean Honoré, 116, 178-9
Franche-Comté, 157
Francis, I, Holy Roman Emperor, 114
Francis of Lorraine, 38
François I, King, 256
Franklin, Benjamin, 121, 168
Frederick II, King of Prussia, 71, 73, 76, 78-80, 203
Fréjus, 252
Fréjus, Bishop of, see Fleury, cardinal
Fréron, Louis, 234-5, 238-9, 241
Fronde, 14-5, 65, 147, 154, 157, 256
Fructidor, 249, 252

GABELLE, 62
Gebrielle, A.-J., 43-4
Gardes Françaises, 148-9
Germinal riots, 241-2
George I, King of England, 30
Gibbon, Edward, 124
Gilds, 45-7, 109
Girondins, 185, 189, 206, 214
Givet, 191
Gluck, Christophe, 117
Gobelin tapestries, 18, 46, 57
Gournay, seigneur de, 106
Granville, 225
Grasse, admiral de, 122
Gray, Thomas, 58
Great Fear, The, 57-8, 199
Grenoble, 50, 60, 132-3
Greuze, Jean Baptiste, 116
Gribeauval, general J.-B. Vaquette de, 94, 110, 202
Guiana, 241, 249
Guibert, comte de, 250
Guillotine, 175, 192, 221, 227, 233-6, 249
Gunpowder, 108

HANRIOT, FRANÇOIS, 214, 235-6
Hébert, Jacques Réné, 193, 219, 224, 226, 239
Henri II, King, 120
Henri IV, King, 79
Hérault de Séchelles, Marie Jean, 215-17
Hobbes, Thomas, 13
Hoche, general Lazare, 225, 231, 245
Holker, John, 46-7
Holy Roman Empire, 38, 70, 114
Hood, Admiral Lord, 122
Howe, Admiral Lord, 232
Huguenots, 18, 19, 64, 86, 89, 108, 111, 174

Incroyables, 247
Indes, Compagnie des, 27, 42-3, 75-6, 94, 126
India, 42, 71, 75, 80
Industry, see Trade
Inflation, see Finance

Intendants, names, 16, 69, see also
Invasion of England projects, 121-2
Isnard, Maximum, 188, 212
Italian campaign of Bonaparte, 249-50

JACOBIN CLUBS, 158-9, 176-9, 182, 184-5, 192, 195-6, 201, 206, 209, 211, 214, 221, 228-30, 239-43, 246, 248, 251-2
Jacquard, 47
Jacqueries, 154
Jansenists, 13, 22, 39, 65-6, 69, 89, 90
Jeanbon Saint-André, 214, 218, 232
Jemappes, battle of, 205, 210
Jesus, Company of, 240
Jesus, Society of (Jesuits), 22, 63, 65-6, 90-1, 93, 103
Jeunesse dorée, 239, 247
Jews, 111, 174
Jourdan, Coupe-Tête, 192, 225, 231-2
Jurieu, Pierre, 86
Justice, Chamber of, 26

KAUNITZ, COUNT, 76-7
Keeper of the Seals, office of, 34
Kellermann, François Christophe, duc de Valmy, 202, 226
Kersaint, comte de, 209
King as whole Government, idea of, 32-3
Kloster-Zeven, Convention of, 79-80

LA BARRE, CHEVALIER DE, 89-90
La Bouexière, 41
Labour control, 47-8, see also Gilds
La Bruyère, Jean de, 24
La Chalotais, 96
La Fayette, marquis de, 121-2, 135, 154, 161-2, 180, 182, 190-1, 195, 199, 202, 211
Laincourt, de, 135
La Luzerne, 129
Lamballe, princesse de, 118, 201
La Mettrie, 88
La Motte de Valois, comtesse de, 120
La Motte de Vayer, 86
Lanjuinais, 213
La Revellière-Lépeaux, 249
La Rochefoucauld, duc de, 135
La Rochelle, 43
Launay, de, 148-9
Lavalette, abbé, 91
Lavater, 120
Lavoisier, Antoine Laurent, 51, 104, 108, 202, 222
La Vrillière, marquis de, 108
Law, John, 26-30, 40-1, 43, 70, 172
Lazowski, 193
Lebrun, consul, 99, 209, 213
Leczinska, Marie, see Marie Leczinska
Leczinski, Stanilaus, see Stanilaus Leczinski
Lefebre, 231
Legal reform proposals, 131, 174-5

Legendre, 193, 213
Legislative Assembly, see Assembly
Le Havre, 43
Leibniz, Gottfried, 86
Le Laboureur, abbé, 24
Leopold Holy Roman Emperor, 187
Le Sage, Alain Réné, 23
Lettres de cachet, 33, 98, 112
Levant, 42-3, 252
Levassor, Michel, 24
Lévis, duc de, 118
Liège, 191
Lille, 191, 248
Limousin, 105-6
Lindet, Robert, 214, 218, 234, 238
Liverpool, 43
Local government, 169-70, 225
Locke, John, 85-6, 88, 130
Longwy, 198-9
Lorient, 28-9, 43
Lorraine, 37-8, 95, 142, 174
Lorraine, Francis of, see Francis
Louis IX, King (Saint Louis), 114
Louis XIV, King, 13-16, 18-27, 29, 32-3,
    35-6, 38-40, 42, 44, 48, 50, 52, 54, 58, 60,
    64-5, 68, 70, 85-7, 101, 114, 126, 162, 208,
    254-6
Louis XV, King, 22, 25, 30-4, 41, 44, 53-6,
    63, 70, 72-4, 76-81, 87, 91, 95-8, 100-2, 107,
    107, 114-16, 118, 141, 188, 255-6 (for
    regency during minority; see Orleans,
    duc d' and Regency)
Louis XVI, King, 26, 96, 100, 102, 105, 107,
    109, 111, 114, 117, 119, 121, 123, 125-6,
    128, 131-3, 135-6, 138-9, 143-6, 148, 161-3,
    165-6, 169, 180-3, 185-6, 188, 194-5,
    197-8, 208-10, 244, 255-6
Louis XVII, King (never reigned), 210,
    244-5
Louis XVIII, King (comte de Provence),
    118, 244-5
Louis Philippe, King of the French (duc
    d'Orléans), 242
Louisiana, 27-8, 40, 42, 74-5, 81
Low countries, 37
Lyons, 45, 47-9, 50, 60, 221, 225, 240

MABLY, BONNET DE, 168
Mack, General, 211
Mâconnais, 157
Maestricht, 210
Mailly, comtesse de, 53
Maine, duc de, 21
Maintenon, marquise de, 22-3
Mainz, 204
Malesherbes, Lamoignon de, 108, 110,
    129-31, 133
Mallet du Pin, 245
Marat, Jean Paul, 167, 193, 197, 201, 206-7,
    221, 224, 238-9, 241

Maria Teresa, Empress of Austria, 70-2, 74,
    76, 96, 100, 114-15, 118-19
Marie Antoinette, Queen, 96, 100, 112,
    114-16, 118-21, 124, 126, 128, 145-6, 161-3,
    172, 180-3, 184, 187, 192, 221-2, 244
Marie Leczinska, Queen, 31, 71, 73
Marigny, marquis de, 57
Marivaux, Pierre de, 58
Marriage, 111, 174
Marseilles, 43, 50, 196, 221
Marx, Karl, 197
Masonic plot, alleged, 135
Masséna, André, marshal duke of Rivoli, 231
Maupeou, Réné Charles de, 97-9, 101-3, 106,
    109, 117, 131, 141
Maupertuis, Pierre Louis Moreau de, 103
Maurepas, comte de, 36, 72, 79, 102, 105-6,
    109-10, 124-5
Mazarin, Jules cardinal, 14, 16, 22, 24, 35-6,
    79, 93
Meaux, 182
Meaux, Bishop of, see Bossuet
Meissen china, 57
Meissonier, Louis, 57
Mercy, count, 118
Merveilleuses, 247
Meslier, abbé, 88
Mesmer, Friedrich Anton, 120
Metz, 149, 181, 191, 198, 228
Mirabeau, marquis de, 106, 133, 135, 174,
    179-81, 184, 190, 203, 235
Miromesnil, 108
Mississipi, 29
Montaigne, Michel de, 85-6
Montcalm de St Véran, marquis de, 80
Montespan, marquise de, 21
Montesquieu, baron de, 29, 32, 56, 87-8,
    129, 166, 229
Montmorin, 128-9
Moreau, 231
Mountain, the, 206-7, 212-14, 217, 219-20,
    222-3, 226, 229, 234, 236, 239-40, 244, 246
Muscadins, 239

NANCY, 44, 176, 181
Nantes, 43, 221, 240
Napoleon Bonaparte, see Bonaparte, Napo-
    leon
Narbonne, comte de, 188-9
National Assembly, see Assembly
National Debt, see Finance
National Guards, 154, 158, 162, 168, 180-2,
    192-4, 196, 199, 205, 208, 213, 221-2, 241-4
Nattier, Jean Marc, 57, 116
Navy, 25, 94, 111, 176, 232
Necker, Jacques, 111-12, 124-9, 132-3, 135-6,
    142-3, 145-8, 180
Necker, Mme Suzanne, 124
Neerwinden, 210
Nelson, Horatio Viscount, 251

Nesle sisters, de, *see* Chateauroux, duchesse de, Mailly, comtesse de, and Vintimille, marquise de
New Orleans, 28-9
Newton, Isaac, 85, 88, 103-4
Nice, 204, 250
Nîmes, 44
Noailles, duc de, 26, 54, 87
Noailles, Mme de, 118
Noailles, marshal de, 53
Noailles, Mgr, Archbishop of Paris, 65
Noailles, vicomte de, 159
Noblesse de l'épée et de la robe, 15-16, 24-5, 28, 43, 103, 110, 132, 134, 136, 138, 142, 144, 155-7, 159, 180, 233, 256, 258
Nootka Sound, 186
Normandy, 47, 157, 180, 227
Notre Dame de Paris, 222
Notre Dame de Thermidor, *see* Tallien, Thérèse
Notables, Assembly of, 127-9, 133

October Days, 160, 162-3, 167, 197
Orange, Prince of, 123
Oratorians, 91-2
Orléans, 60
Orléans, Louis Philippe duc d', *see* Louis Philippe
Orléans, Philippe II duc d', 21-2, 24-6, 30-1, 36, 77
Orléans, Philippe III duc d', 132, 147, 162, 184, 222
Orry, Jean Henri, 36, 47, 49, 62-3, 72
Ottoman Empire, 38, 42

Pantheon, 178, 241
Paoli, General, 95
Paris, 43-4, 49, 50, 60, 147, 149, 153-4, 158, 161-2, 167, 191, 195-6, 220, 236, 242
Paris, Archbishops of, *see* Beaumont, Mgr and Noailles, Mgr
Paris, Treaty of, 81
Pâris-Duverney, 36, 41, 55, 62, 71, 79, 126
Parlements, 22, 32, 39, 63-5, 68-9, 89-91, 95-6, 98-9, 102, 109, 129-34, 136, 138, 145, 156, 164, 256
Pascal, Blaise, 65, 85
Patriote française, 184
Pau, 132, 141
Pere Duchesne, 193, 224, 226
Perrault, Charles, 23
Pétion, 196, 222
Petit Trianon, 115, 118
Philip V, King of Spain, 19, 21, 29-30, 54
Philippe Égalité, *see* Orléans, duc d'
Philosophes, les, 103-5, 124, 128, 164, 173, 260
Physiocrats, 105-6
Picardy, 47
Pichegru, 231
Pilnitz, Manifesto of, 187

Pitt, William the Elder, *see* Chatham, Earl of
Pitt, William the Younger, 112, 186
Place de la Concorde (Place de la Révolution, Place Louis XV), 44-5, 208
Plague and other epidemics, 50
Plain, the, 206, 234
Pluché, abbé, 103
Poisson, François, 55
Poisson, Jeanne Antoinette, *see* Pompadour, marquise de
Poisson de Vandieres, Abel, *see* Marigny, marquis de
Poitiers, 45
Poland, 37-8, 76-7, 99
Poland, ex-King of, *see* Stanilaus Leczinski
Polignac, cardinal de, 66
Polignac, comtesse de, 118, 127, 150
Polysynodie, 23, 30
Pompadour, marquise de, 55-8, 63, 72, 78-81, 95-6, 115, 118
Population, 50-1, 140, 155
Port-Royal, *see* Jansenists
Postal services, 108
Pragmatic Sanction, 38
Prairial, law of, 233-5, 244
Press, 126, 174-5, 227, 234, *see also* names of journals
Prévost, abbé, 23, 28
Prices, 140, 220, 223
Prie, Mme de, 31-2
Prieur, of Côte d'Or, 214, 217, 234, 238
Prieur, of Marne, 214, 217
Prime Minister, office equivalent to, 35, 53, 95
Prisons, 111, *see also* Bastille and Vincennes
Protestant minority, *see* Huguenots
Provence, comte de, *see* Louis XVIII
Provincial assemblies (estates), 132

Quesnay, François, 105
Quesnel, 65

Rabelais, François, 85
Racine, Jean, 23
Rameau, Jean Philippe, 57
Ramsay, chevalier, 24, 87
Rastadt, Treaty of, 20
Rayneval, 123, 169
Reaumur, Réné Antoine de, 104
Récamier, Mme de, 247
Regency during minority of Louis XV, 21, 23-5, *see also* Orléans, duc d'
Reims, 47
Remonstrances, 130, 164
Rennes, 41, 44, 50, 95-6, 132
Republic, 182, 206, 209
Restoration of the monarchy, 242
Reubell, 249, 251
Réveillon, 147

Revolts, 52, 95, 108, 132, 139-40, 162, 191, 241, *see also* names of places and Jacqueries and Revolution
Revolution of 1789, 137, 146-7, 149, 150, 153, 158-9, 168
'Revolutionary army', 227
Revolutionary clubs, 176-7, *see also* names
Revolutionary committees, 244
Revolutionary ideas, 85-92, 103, 113, 117, 121-3, 137-8, 153, 163, 166, 169, 186, 188
Revolutionary Tribunal, 212, 221, 233-4, 240
Revolutionary wars, 185, 187-92, 199, 202, 205, 209-10, 219, 223, 231, 249
Richelieu, Armand cardinal duc de, 14, 22, 24, 35-6, 64, 79, 93
Richelieu, Louis duc de, 53, 80
Richer, Edmond, 66, 143
Rigaud, Hyacinthe, 32
Roads, 49, 112
Robert, Hubert, 178
Robespierre, Augustin, 236
Robespierre, Maximilian, 137, 167-8, 177, 182-3, 189, 195-7, 201, 206-7, 209, 212, 214, 218-19, 223, 226-31, 233-6, 238-9, 241, 251
Rochambeau, comte de, 122
Rohan, cardinal de, 66, 100, 119-20
Roland de la Platière, Jean, 191, 192-4, 197, 203, 206, 222, 224
Roland de la Platière, Mme, 190, 193, 195, 207, 213
Roman Catholic Church, 51, 53, 62-6, 85, 87, 90-1, 111, 128, 132, 143-4, 155, 170, 172, 186, 222-3, 256, *see also* Huguenots, Jansenists, Jesus, Society of and Oratorians
Rossignol, 193
Rotundo, 193
Rouen, 46, 60, 130, 180
Rouillé, comte de, 77
Rousseau, Jean Jacques, 23, 57, 114, 116, 164-5, 168, 223, 241
Roux, Jacques, 211, 223
Roveray, du, 208

St Domingo, 191
Saint-Germain, comte de, 108, 110-11
Saint-Germain, faubourg de, 43
Saint-Germain-des-Prés, 222
Saint-Honoré, faubourg de, 43
Saint-Huruge, marquis de, 193
Saint-Just, Armand, 214, 218, 229, 234-6
Saint Malo, 42-3
Saint-Pierre, abbé de, 87, 104
Saint-Simon, duc de, 14, 18-19, 22, 24-5, 36
St Vincent, battle of, 250
Sainte Geneviève, church of, 178
Sainte-Menehould, 182
Sans-culottes, 224, 227, 243
Santerre, 193, 196, 205

Sardinia, 250
Sartine, 111
Savoy, 205, 226, 256
Saxe, marshal de, 72-4, 77, 110
Scheldt, 208-9
Schweitzer, Albert, 113
Science, 49, 103-4
Second Estate, *see* Noblesse
Secretaries of State, 23, 34-5, 53-4, 71, 93
Sedan, 198
Ségur, comte de, 104, 128-9
Seine, river, 49
Senegal, 27
September massacres, 158, 199-201
Sérurier, 231
Seven Years War, 42, 75-6, 81, 93-4, 97, 208
Sèvres china, 46, 56
Sieyes, abbé, 135, 144, 165-7, 248, 251-3
Silk, 45-8
Six Edicts, 109
Slavery, 42-3, 174
Soissons, 196
Sorel, 19
Soubise, prince de, 80, 100
Soulavie, 115
South Sea Bubble, 28
Sovereign courts, *see* Parlements
Spain, 19-20, 29-30, 71
Spires, 205
Staël, Mme de, 188, 247
Stainville, comte de, *see* Choiseul, duc de
Stanhope, 30
Stanislaus Leczinski, 31, 37-8, 44, 95, 238
Stanislaus Poniatowski, 99
States-General, 26, 130-1, 133, 138-9, 141-6, 165, 184, 186
Stuart, Charles Edward, *see* Charles Edward
Suffren, *bailli* de, 122
Sun, Companies of the, 240
Superstitions, 120
Swiss Guard, 162, 196-7, 200

Taille, 60
Taine, Hippolyte Adolphe, 51
Tallien, 234-5, 238, 243
Tallien, Thérèse, 238, 247
Talleyrand-Périgord, Charles Maurice de Bishop of Autun, Prince de Benevento, 135, 171, 190, 208, 253
Taxation, 26-7, 60, 62-4, 99, 126-8, 131, 133, 141, 170
Teissier, 41
Tencin, cardinal de, 53-4
Tencin, Mme de, 53
Tennis court oath, 145, 168
Terray, abbé, 97-9, 101, 106-7, 125-6
Terror, the, 178, 202, 212, 216, 226, 230, 232-4, 239-41, 243, 247, 249, 258
Theatres, 174
Thermidor, 235-6, 238-41, 243-6, 251, 258

Third Eastate, 134-5, 137, 139, 141-7, 150,
   153-4, 157-8, 163, 165, 167, 170, 180, 184,
   233, 257-8
Thirty, Society of, 135
Toiles peintes, 46-7
Torcy, 20
Torture, 111-2, 174
Toulon, 221, 225, 232, 250
Toulouse, 128-30, 132, 228
Toulouse, Archbishop of, *see* Brienne,
   Loménie de
Toulouse, comte de, 21
Tournai, 191
Townshend, Viscount, 37
Trade and industry, 16, 42, 47-8, 50-1, 94,
   175
Travel, 49
Triple Alliance, 30
Troyes, 131
Tuileries, 25, 44, 162, 194, 196-7, 199, 207
Turgot, Anne Robert Jacques, 105-8, 111-
   12, 125

UNEMPLOYMENT, 140
Utrecht, Treaty of, 20, 42

VADIER, 235, 238
Valenciennes, 221
Valois, club de, 177
Valois, comtesse de la Motte de, *see* la Motte
   de Valois
Valois kings, *see* François I, Henri II and
   Louis IX
Valmy, battle of, 202-3
Van Loo, Carlo, 57
Varennes, 181, 184
Varlet, 211, 223
Vauban, marshal de, 27

Vaucanson, 47
Venaissin, 174, 186
Vendée, 160, 181, 211, 225, 232, 245
Vendémiare, 246, 248-50
Venice, 250
Verdun, 198-9
Vergennes, 108, 112, 121, 123, 128, 176
Vergniaud, 194, 207, 222
Versailles, 15, 24-5, 41, 53, 60, 63, 106,
   114-16, 142, 146, 161-2, 256-7
Versailles, Treaty of, 78, 122
Veto, royal power to, 166, 193
Vienna, Treaty of, 37
Vieux Cordelier, 227
Vigée le Brun, 116, 178
Villars, marshal duc de, 20, 38
Vincennes, 25
Vintimille, marquise de, 53
Voltaire (François Marie Arouet), 13, 15,
   56-7, 86, 88-90, 99, 103-5, 173, 238
Vosges, 225

WALPOLE, SIR ROBERT, 36-7, 71
Watteau, Antoine, 23
Wattignies, 225
West, Company of the, 27
West Indies, 27, 42, 75-6, 80-1, 94, 122
Westminster, Convention of, 76, 78
Westphalia, Treaty of, 79
White Terror, 240
Wickham, William, 248
Windham, 186-7
Wolfe, General James, 80
Wordsworth, William, 170
Worms, 206

YOUNG, ARTHUR, 43, 49, 60, 155, 186
Young Pretender, the, *see* Charles Edward

INDEX

BOOK II

ABADIE, 116
Abd-el-Kader, 109–10
Aberdeen, Lord, 112
Académie Française, 117
Academy of Moral and Political Sciences, 39
Acte additionel, 68
Affre, mgr, 124
Aide-toi, le ciel t'aidera, 89
Albert, Alexandre Martin, 136–7
Alexander I, 46, 61, 65–6
Alexander II, 178
Algeria, Algiers, 43, 90, 109–10, 144, 157, 173–4
Alsace-Lorraine, 199
Amiens, Treaty of, 19–20, 23, 33, 41, 44–5, 50
Ampère, 39, 84
Angoulême, cathedral of, 116
Angoulême, duc d', 65
anti-clericalism, 84, 87–8, 99–100, 124, 133, 153, 187
Arago, François, 39, 122, 136
architecture, French, 38–9, 115–16
Armed Neutrality, 19
army, French, 47–9, 67, 145, 191–2, 204–5
Army Law of 1868, 192
Artois, comte d', 66, 69, 75, 78, 82, *see also* Charles X
Aumale, duc d', 106, 110, 129
Aurelle de Paladines, Louis d', 201–2, 206
Austerlitz, battle of, 46, 59, 110, 155
Austro-Prussian War, 178–9

BALZAC, HONORÉ DE, 98, 117, 120
Bank of France, 31, 213
banquets, reform, 126–7
Barante, baron de, 79, 85, 151
Barbès, Armand, 141
Barère de Vieuzac, 49
Baroche, Pierre-Jules, 190–1, 193
Barrot, Odilon, 125, 136, 149, 151, 153
Batavian republic, 19, 46
Baudin, Dr, 155, 189
Bautzen, battle of, 63
Bayeux tapestry, 45
Baylen, Capitulation of, 59, 67
Bazaine, marshal, 181, 199–200, 201
Beauharnais, Eugène, 47, 55, 165
Beauharnais, Hortense, 157, 184
Beauregard, comtesse de, *see* Howard, Miss
Belgian revolution of 1830, 96, 107
Belleville programme, 201
Benedetti, 197
Béranger, 120, 150

Beresina, crossing of, 62
Berlin Decrees, 51
Berlioz, 85
Bernadotte, marshal, Charles XIV of Sweden, 61, 63
Berry, duc de, 29, 81, 85, 100, 168
Berry, duchesse de, 101
Berryer, Antoine, 190
Berthier, marshal, 24
Berthollet, Claude-Louis, 50
Billault, Adolphe-Augustin, 190
Bismarck, 177–9, 196–7
Blanc, Louis, 119, 136–7, 206
Blanqui, Auguste, 141, 203, 206–7
Blanquists, 207–8
Blücher, marshal, 69
Bonald, Louis de, 79, 83
Bonaparte, Caroline, 47
Bonaparte, Jerome, 46
Bonaparte, Joseph, 47, 55, 59, 85
Bonaparte, Louis, 46, 54–5, 159
Bonaparte, Louis Napoleon, *see* Napoleon III
Bonaparte, Lucien, 24, 27
Bonaparte, Napoleon, *see* Napoleon I
bonapartism, 106–7, 112–13, 120, 147–51, 205, 211, 218
Bordeaux, 54, 65, 202, 206
Borodino, battle of, 23, 62
Bossuet, 92
Boulogne, attempt of Louis Bonaparte, 107, 113, 118
Boulogne camp, 45
Bourbaki, general, 202
Bourbon, île, 89
Bourmont, marshal, 89–90
Broglie, Jacques-Victor-Albert, duc de, 186
Broglie, Victor, duc de, 79, 95, 97, 104–5
brumaire, *coup d'état* of, 16
Buchez, Pierre-Joseph-Benjamin, 119
Buffon, 84
Bugeaud, marshal, 110, 128

CABANIS, GEORGES, 39
Cabet, Étienne, 19
Cadoudal, Georges, 20
Cambacérès, 55
Cambodia, 174
Campan, Mme, 55
canals, 122
Carbonari, 89, 159, 181
Carnot, Hippolyte, 118, 140, 152
Carnot, Lazare, 18, 68
Carnot, Sadi, 85
Casimir-Périer, 95, 101–2, 104–5

Cavaignac, general, 110, 143, 146–7, 151
Cavour, 171–3, 177
Cayenne, 157
Cayla, comtesse de, 81–2
censorship of press, 31, 37, 81, 99, 104
Chambord, comte de, 101
Chambre introuvable, 77
Changarnier, general, 110, 136, 154
Chanzy, general, 202
Chaptal, 27, 58
Charles X, 80, 83–4, 86–92, 94–6, 102, *see also* Artois, comte d'
Charter of Louis XVIII, 68, 73–6
Charter of 1830, 96–7
Chateaubriand, 34, 37, 73, 78, 85–7, 114, 150
Châtillon, negotiations, 64
Chevalier, Michel, 118, 162, 175–6
Chevaliers de la Foi, 65, 78, 81
cholera epidemic, 102
Cintra, Convention of, 59
Cisalpine republic, 19, 43
Cluny, abbey of, 115
Cobden Treaty, 175–6
Cochin-China, 174
Code Napoléon, 30–1
Colbert, 30
colonies, French, 41–3, 89–90, 109–10, 173–5
Comédie française, 37
Commune of Paris, 207–10
Comptoir d'Escompte, 163
Comte, Auguste, 118, 120, 161
Concordat, 33–5, 57–8, 83–4
Condorcet, 161
Confederation of the Rhine, 46
Congregation, Jesuit, 83, 87
Conseil d'état, 25–6, 158
Constant, Benjamin, 68, 78, 216
Consulate, 16–40
Continental System, 46, 49–54, 60–1
Copenhagen, bombardment of, 19
Corunna, battle of, 59
Coulmiers, battle of, 201
Courbet, Gustave, 168, 220
Courvoisier, Jean-Joseph-Antoine, 89
Crédit Agricole, 163
Crédit Foncier, 163
Crédit Lyonnais, 163
Crédit Mobilier, 163, 189–90
Crémieux, Isaac, 136, 200
Crimean War, 170, 172
Cuvier, Georges, 39, 84

D'AGUESSEAU, 30
Dakar, 174
Darboy, mgr, 186–7
Daumier, Honoré, 103–4, 115, 117, 168
David, Jacques-Louis, 37–8
Decazes, duc, 78–80

Delacroix, Eugène, 85, 115
Delescluze, Louis-Charles, 151, 189, 203, 206, 208–10
Desai, general, 18
Destutt de Tracy, 39
doctrinaires, 79, 104
Dresden, battle of, 63
Drouyn de Lhuys, 179
Dumas, Alexandre, 120
Dupanloup, mgr, 186–7
Dupont de l'Eure, 94, 152
Dupont, general, 67
Duruy, Victor, 187

ÉCOLE DES CHARTES, 85
education, 35–7, 84, 88, 123–4, 153, 187
Egypt, 19, 41–2
Elba, 66–7
émigrés, 67, 75, 87, 93
empire, French overseas, *see* colonies
Ems telegram, 197
Enfantin, père, 119, 161
Enghien, duc d', murder of, 20
entente, Anglo-French, of Louis-Philippe, 110–11
Eugénie, Empress, 160–1, 197–200
Exhibition of 1855, 169
Eylau, battle of, 46

FAIDHERBE, GENERAL, 174, 202
Falloux, comte de, 136, 142–3, 150, 153, 186
Farmers General, Wall of, 13, 167
Favre, Jules, 182, 206
February days, 127–9, 136
Ferdinand of Spain, 58
Ferry, Jules, 193
Fesch, cardinal, 60
Fieschi plot, 104
finances, French, 31, 67, 78, 87, 138, 165, 189–90
Flahaut, Charles de, general, 184
Flaubert, Gustave, 136, 144–5, 220
Flocon, 136
Flourens, Gustave, 206
Fontanes, Louis de, 37
Forbach, battle of, 199
Fouché, 24, 33, 57, 60, 69–70, 73, 77
Fould, Achille, 150, 163, 176, 190–3
Fourcroy, Antoine-François, 36, 50
Fourier, 119
Four Ordinances, 90
Fragonard, 37
Francis Joseph, emperor, 173
Franco-Prussian War, 196, 198–205
Frayssinous, mgr, 84
Free French movement, 308–9
freemasons, freemasonry, 187
free trade treaties, 175–7
Fresnel, Augustin, 84–5

Freycinet, Charles de, 205
Friedland, battle of, 46
Fröschwiller, battle of, 198–9

GALLICANISM, 33, 83, 186
Gambetta, 189, 200–2, 204–5
Garibaldi, 180
Garnier, Charles, 167
Garnier-Pagès, Louis Antoine, 136, 152
Gaudin, duc de Gaète, 24, 31
Gautier, Théophile, 114, 120, 220
Genlis, mme de, 106
Gérard, marshal, 94
Géricault, 38, 85, 115
Girardin, Émile de, 151
Giselle, 114
Godoy, 58
Goncourt, Edmond de, 203
Gorée, 89
Goya, 38
Gramont, duc de, 196–8
Grandville, 104
Gravelotte, battle of, 199
Grégoire, bishop, 81
grève du milliard, 189
Grévy, Jules, 147, 206
Gros, baron, 38
Guadeloupe, 42, 89
Guiana, French, 89
Guibert, cardinal, 140
Guibert, general, 49
Guizot, François, 79, 85, 95, 97, 102, 104–5,
  108–12, 122–8, 135

HAM, CASTLE OF, 148
Haussmann, baron, 165–7, 190, 192–5, 213
Helvetic republic, 19, 46
Hohenlinden, battle of, 18, 20
Hohenzollern candidature, 196–8
Howard, Miss, 150, 161
Hugo, Victor, 85–6, 110, 114–17, 120, 128,
  145–6, 150, 155, 166, 168, 206–7, 220
Hundred Days, 67–70, 74–6

INDUSTRY IN FRANCE, 50–4, 117, 121–2,
  164, 176, 189
Ingres, Jean-Auguste-Dominique, 38
Intransigents, clerical, 186
Ionian islands, 46, 64
Isabella, queen, of Spain, 112
Italian War, 172–3, 183, 187

JACOBINS, 20, 27, 208
Jemappes, battle of, 96
Jena, battle of, 46, 179
Jessaint, prefect, 29
Jesuits, 83, 87, 124, 186
Jeune France, 89
Joinville, prince de, 106–7
Josephine, empress, 21, 38, 42, 57, 60, 159

Juarez, president, 180
June Days, 142–5, 153, 170

LABICHE, EUGÈNE, 168
La Bourdonnaye, 77, 89
Lacordaire, père, 99, 168, 185–6
La Fayette, 81, 94–5
Lafitte, Jacques, 89, 91, 95, 101–2
Lafon, l'abbé, 62
Lagrange, Joseph-Louis, 39
Lamarck, Jean-Baptiste de, 39, 84
Lamarque, general, funeral of, 101
Lamartine, 85, 113, 114, 136, 141, 147, 151–2
Lamennais, 79, 83, 99, 118, 168
Lamoricière, general, 110
Lampedusa, 44
La Lanterne, 188
Laplace, Pierre-Simon de, 39
La Presse, 151
La Réforme, 125, 127, 150
La Rochelle, four sergeants of, 81, 144
La Valette, 191
L'Avenir, 99
Lavoisier, 39, 50
Laws, Napoleonic Code of, 30–1
Le Bas, Philippe, 159
Lebœuf, 205
Lebrun, consul, 55
Le Charivari, 117
Leclerc, general, 43
Le Correspondant, 186
Le Creusot, 164
Ledru-Rollin, 125, 136, 138–41, 146–8,
  151–2, 157, 183, 206
Legion of Honour, 55
legitimism, legitimists, 99–101, 106, 124
Leipzig, battle of, 63
Le Journal des débats, 87
Lemaître, Frédéric, 117
Le National, 89–90, 125, 127, 151–2
Lenoir, Richard, 50
Leroux, Pierre, 119
Lesseps, Ferdinand de, 175
L'Événement, 151
Liberal Empire, 195
Ligsy, battle of, 69
Ligurian republic, 19, 43
livret, 51
Loi Falloux, 153, 186
Louis XVIII, 66, 68, 70, 73–8, 81–2, 83,
  85–6
Louis, baron, 67, 95
Louis Napoleon Bonaparte, see Napoleon III
Louis-Philippe, 96–7, 101–2, 104–13, 116–17,
  127–9, 133, 157–9, 178
Louisiana, 43, 180
Lourdes, 186
Lunéville, treaty of, 19, 33
L'Univers, 124, 186–7
Lützen, battle of, 63

lycées, 32–7
Lyons, 54, 66, 165, 219; revolt in, 98–9, 103

MACAIRE, ROBERT, 117
Mack, general, 46
MacMahon, marshal, 199–200
Madagascar, 90
Magenta, battle of, 172, 193
Maida, battle of, 47
Maistre, Joseph de, 37, 79, 83
Malet conspiracy, 62
Malta, 44, 54
Marengo, battle of, 18–19
Marie-Amélie, queen, 106
Marie-Antoinette, queen, 55
Marie-Louise, empress, 60, 65
Marie, Alexandre-Thomas, 136–7, 152
Marmont, marshal, 65, 90–1
Marrast, Armand, 125, 136, 152
Martignac, vicomte de, 88
Martinique, 89
Marx, Karl, 135
Massiac, club, 41
Maupas, Charlemagne Émile de, 155
Maximilian, emperor, 180–1
Mehemet Ali, 107–8, 110
Mentana, battle of, 180
Mérimée, Prosper, 85, 115, 120
Metternich, 60, 69
Metz, 199, 201–2, 204
Mexican expedition, 175, 180–1
Michelet, Jules, 124, 214
Mignet, François-Auguste, 85, 89, 91, 96
Milan Decrees, 51
Millet, Jean-François, 168
Miquelon, 89
Mirari vos, 99
Molé, count, 105, 107, 128
Monge, Gaspard, 39
Montalembert, Charles Forbes, comte de, 99, 115, 124, 140, 150, 185–6
Montmorency, Mathieu, duc de, 78, 86
Montpensier, duc de, 106, 112
Moore, general, 59
Moreau, general, 18, 20, 62–3
Morny, duc de, 155, 166, 180, 183–5, 188, 191, 193
Mortier, marshal, 59
Moscow, 62
Mulhouse, 54
municipal laws, 98
Murat, Joachim, marshal, 47, 55, 57, 63
Musset, Alfred de, 114

NAPOLEON I, 16–70, 147, 164; his personality, 17, 20–3
Napoleon III, 107, 112, 118, 147–200
Napoleon, Prince, 193
National Guard, 88, 94–5, 99, 100–1, 103, 127, 136, 138, 142–4

National Workshops, 137, 142–3
Navarino, battle of, 88
Nemours, duc de, 96, 106
Nerval, Gérard de, 115, 120
Ney, marshal, 59, 62, 68–9, 77
Nice, 173

OFFENBACH, 168
Oldenburg, annexation of, 61
Ollivier, Émile, 171, 183, 185, 188, 190, 195, 197–9
Opera, Paris, 167–8
Organic Articles, 33–4
Orléans, duc d', 91, see also Louis-Philippe
Orléans, Ferdinand-Philippe, duc d', 106, 117, 129
Orléans, Hélène, duchesse d', 117, 136
Orleanism, 94, 163
Orsini plot, 168, 171
Ossian, 37
Otranto, duc d', see Fouché
Oudinot, marshal, 152
Ouvrard, Gabriel-Julien, 86

PAINTING, FRENCH, 37–8, 85, 115
Palikao, comte de, 199
Palmerston, Lord, 112
Panthéon, 84, 185
Papal States, annexation of, 47, 58
Paris, 13–14, 39, 117, 134–5, 165–8; Commune of, 207–10; comte de, 129; Congress of, 171, 175; siege of, 202–4
Paul I, assassination of, 19
Peking, occupation of, 174
Peninsular War, 58–9
Péreire brothers, 118, 150, 163, 190, 192
Persigny, Victor Fialin, duc de, 155, 183–4
phylloxera, 189
Picard, Ernest, 182, 206
Pichegru, general, 20
Pitt, William, 19, 50
Pius VII, 21, 33
Pius IX, 152, 186
plebiscite of 1799, 17; of 1804, 20–1; of 1852, 159
Plombières, meeting at, 171
Poland, 141, 178
Polignac, Jules, prince de, 78, 88–90, 94
population, 15, 93, 117, 135, 164
Positivism, 120–1
Praslin, duc de, 126
prefects, 27–9, 55, 80, 102, 109, 139, 158
Pressburg, treaty of, 46
press laws, 37, 78, 81, 104, 157–8, 188
Prince Imperial, 161, 200
Pritchard incident, 112
Protestants, French, 35
Proudhon, Pierre-Joseph, 119–20, 208
Prud'hon, Pierre, 38

QUATRE-BRAS, BATTLE OF, 69
Quinet, Edgar, 124, 206

RACHEL, 120
railways, 122, 163–4
Raspail, François-Vincent, 147, 151
Réal, Pierre-François, comte, 22
Reichstadt, duc de, 60, 65, 107, 159
religion, 32–5, 75–6, 83–4, 99–100, 114, 118, 124, 185–7
Rémusat, Charles de, 79
Renan, Ernest, 121
Restoration, First, 65–8; Second, 73
Revocation of Edict of Nantes, 92
Richelieu, duc de, 77–81
Robespierre, 16, 19
Rochefort, Henri, 188, 206
Roederer, Pierre-Louis, 25, 36
Roman republic, 152
romanticism, 114–16, 120
Rome, French garrison in, 180; king of, see Reichstadt, duc de
Rossini, 85
Rothschilds, 190, 192
Rouher, Eugène, 157, 179, 190–5, 196
Rousseau, Jean-Jacques, 18, 30, 82, 113, 118
Royer-Collard, Pierre-Paul, 76
rue de Poitiers, committee of, 151
Ruhr, 51
Russo-Turkish War, 170

SAAR, 70
sacrilege, law of, 84
Sadowa, battle of, 191, 196
Saint-Antoine, faubourg of, 14–19
Saint-Arnaud, general, 155
St Domingo, 41–3
Saint-Germain, faubourg of, 97
Saint-Germain d'Auxerrois, riot of, 100
Saint-Omer, declaration of, 66
Saint-Pierre, Bernardin, de, 114
Saint-Pierre, île de, 90
Saint-Simon, comte de, 116, 118–19, 120, 161–2, 165
Saint-Simonianism, Saint-Simonians, 118, 150, 161–2, 190, 217
Salon des Refusés, 168
Sand, George, 114, 118, 120
Savoy, 173
Schleswig-Holstein, 178
Schneider brothers, 164
Sébastiani, marshal, 43–4, 94
Sebastopol, 170
Sedan, 200, 202
Ségur, Philippe de, 67
Sénégal, 89–90, 174
Sibour, archbishop, 185
Sieyes, 16–17
Simon, Jules, 206
slavery, slave trade, 42, 137

Société des Amis des Noirs, 41
Society of the Rights of Man, 102, 104
Solferino, battle of, 172–3
Solidarité Républicaine, 151
Soult, marshal, 59, 65, 104
Spain, French invasion of 1823, 86–7; Napoleonic War in, 58–9
Spanish marriages, 112
Staël, mme de, 37, 85, 115
Stendhal, 85, 120
Strasbourg, attempt of Louis Bonaparte, 107, 112, 148
Stuart, general, 47
Sue, Eugène, 116, 120, 154
Suez canal, 175
Surcouf, 51
Syllabus of Errors, 186
Syria, expedition of 1860, 175

TAHITI, 112
Taine, Hippolyte, 35, 121
Talleyrand, 24, 57, 60, 65, 67, 69, 73, 77, 80, 89, 96, 184
Ternaux, Guillaume-Louis, baron, 50
Teste affair, 126
theocrats, 79
Thierry, Augustin, 85, 118
Thiers, Adolphe, 85, 89–91, 95–6, 102, 104–5, 107–8, 110, 122, 125–6, 128, 149, 153–4, 179, 183, 198, 200, 204, 206–7, 210
Third Coalition, 40
Thomas, Albert, 137
Tilsit, Congress of, 46, 49, 57, 61
Tocqueville, Alexis de, 26, 125, 135, 142–4, 147, 149, 216
Toulouse, battle of, 66
Toussaint-Louverture, 42–3
Trafalgar, battle of, 45, 49
Transnonain, massacre of the rue, 103
tricolore, 67, 96
Trochu, general, 200, 204
Tunis, 43
Tussaud, madame, 38

ULM, BATTLE OF, 46
Ultramontanes, 83, 186–7
ultra-royalists, 78–80, 84
universal suffrage, 113, 126, 136, 139, 154, 217
University, 36, 84, 153

VAÏSSE, 165, 213
Vendée, pacification of, 32; revolts in, 69, 93, 101
Vendôme column, 39, 107, 209
Vera Cruz, 180
Vernet, Horace, 114
Veuillot, Louis, 124, 185–7
Victor, marshal, 59
Victoria, queen, 110, 159

Vigny, Alfred de, 85, 114–16
Villafranca, armistice of, 173
Villèle, comte de, 78, 80, 82, 86–8
Villeneuve, admiral, 45
Vimiero, battle of, 59
Viollet-le-Duc, 115, 166
Voltaire, 14, 84

WAGRAM, BATTLE OF, 59
Walcheren expedition, 59
Walewski, comte, 173, 176, 187
Warsaw, Grand Duchy of, 46, 61

Waterloo, battle of, 69, 89
Weber, 85
Wellington, Duke of, 23, 59, 63, 65–6, 69, 73, 77
West Indies, French, 41–3
Westphalia, kingdom of, 46
White Terror, 77, 89
Winterhalter, 161
Wissembourg, battle of, 198

YOUNG, ARTHUR, 14

INDEX

⚜

BOOK III

ABD-EL-KRIM, 129
Abyssinia, Italian invasion of, 161
Académie Française, 77, 138
Action Catholique, 222
Action Française, 86–90, 97, 113, 128–9, 137–8, 144–5, 152, 166, 177–9, 181, 222; *l'Action Française*, 65, 86–90, 112, 129, 138–9, 179
Adenauer, Chancellor, 234
Africa, French Equitorial, 189
Africa, North, May Protocols, 183; American invasion of, 186
Agadir, 96
'Agathon', 118
Agriculture, French, 47, 69, 151, 211–12, 236
'Alain' (E.-A. Chartier), 125
À la recherche du temps perdu, 81, 218
Alexander, King, 159
Alexandria, bombardment of, 31
Algeciras, Conference of, 96
Algiers, Algeria, 31, 40, 48, 91–2, 186, 191, 214–15, 226–9, 232–4
Allemane, Jean, 46
Alsace, 14, 50, 127
Alsace-Lorraine, 42, 91, 103, 108, 116, 127, 181
Alsatians, 48, 51
amendement Wallon, 21
Amiens Charter, 68
anarchism, anarchists, 46, 68
André, General, 41, 62
Anglo-American guarantee of 1919, 116, 155
Anglo-French entente, 95, 102–3
Anglophobia, 95
Annam, 92
Anouilh, Jean, 222, 224
Anschluss, 159, 164–5
Anti-Bolshevik Legion, 184
anti-clericalism, anti-clericals, 28, 53–4, 59–64, 98, 127–8, 205, 222
Antigone, 222
anti-intellectualism, 80, 220

anti-semitism, anti-semites, 48, 50, 54, 86, 90, 92, 128, 136, 158, 166, 179, 190
Anti-semitic League, 50
Arabi, Colonel, 31
Aragon, Louis, 220, 223
architecture, 72
armistice of 1918, 115; of 1940, 174–5
army, French, 41, 49, 55, 57, 62, 99, 228
Association Républicaine des Anciens Combattants, 140
Assumptionists, 19–20, 54, 58
Audiffret-Pasquier, duc d', 18
Aumale, duc d', 34
Au milieu des sollicitudes, 40
Aurevilly, Barbey d', 79
Auriol, Vincent, President, 178, 197, 216
Austrian ultimatum to Servia, 101
Austro-German customs union, 157

BAINVILLE, JACQUES, 86, 144
Baldwin, Stanley, 132
Banque de France, 119, 143, 151, 201
Barbizon school, 73
Barbusse, Henri, 218
Bardo, Treaty of, 31
Barère, Camille, 95
Barodet, Désiré, 17
Barrès, Maurice, 37, 55, 81, 86
Barthou, Louis, 39, 130, 159–60
Baudelaire, Charles, 78
Baudouin, Paul, 170
Baudrillart, Cardinal, 222
Bayeux, 192
Bazaine, Marshal, 173
Beauvoir, Simone de, 222–3
Belfort, 14, 192
Belgium, 163; invasion of in 1914, 104, 108; and war of 1940, 170, 172
Bélin, René, 165
Belleville programme, 25
Benedict XV, 120
Berchtesgaden, 165
Bergson, Henri, 80

Berlin–Rome Axis, 163
Bernanos, Georges, 167, 219–20
Berry, duc de, 15
Berthelot, Marcellin, 77
Bidault, Georges, 189, 196–7, 199, 207, 234
Bir-Hakeim, defence of, 190
Bismarck, 20, 31; Bismarckian diplomacy, 93–4
Bizet, 75
Blanc, Louis, 13
Blanquists, 35, 45, 68
Bloc National, 118–19, 121, 123
Bloy, Léon, 79
Blum, Léon, 160–1, 163–4, 166, 178
Bolo, 112
Bonapartism, 15, 17, 20–3, 48, 80, 177, 203–4
Boncourt, Paul, 135–6
Bonnet, Georges, 166, 168, 170, 173
Bordeaux, 13, 108, 174
Bordeaux, Archbishop of, 128
Boulanger, General, Boulangism, 34–7, 39, 44–5, 47–8, 81
Boule-de-suif, 75
Bourgeois, Léon, 39, 43, 66, 116
Bourguiba, 215
Bourses de Travail, 46
Braque, Georges, 73, 221
Breton, André, 220
Briand, Aristide, 53, 62–4, 68, 97, 108–10, 113–14, 120–1, 130, 132–3, 156–7, 207
Broglie, Albert de, 13, 18, 20–3, 27
Brunot, Ferdinand, 53
Brussels Pact, 208
Budget, French, *see* finances

Cachin, Marcel, 126
Cagoulards, 145
Caillaux, Joseph, 57, 66, 97–100, 112–14, 124, 130, 150, 159
Caillaux, Mme, 99
Cambodia, 65
Cambon, Jules, 94
Cambon, Paul, 94–5
Camelots du roi, 87, 139
Cameroons, French, 97, 189
Camus, Albert, 222, 224
Candide, 139
Carmen, 74
Carnet B, 106
Carnot, Sadi, President, 35, 39, 46
Cartel des Gauches, 123–5, 127, 129–31

Casablanca, 186
Casimir-Périer, President, 39, 47
Cassagnac, Paul de, 89
Castelnau, General de, 128
Catholics, Integral, 77
Catholics, Social, 41
Catroux, General, 176
Céline, Louis-Ferdinand, 221
Cézanne, Paul, 73
Chamberlain, Austen, 156
Chamberlain, Neville, 165–6, 168
Chamber of Deputies, of Third Republic, 21–2, 24–5; of 1914, 100; of 1919, 119
Chambord, comte de, 15–18, 34, 40
Chambrun, marquis de, 177
Chanak, 122
Château-Thierry, 115
Chautemps, Camille, 136–7, 164, 168, 191
Chevau-légers, 20, 22
Chiappe, Jean, 137, 139, 183
Church in France, Roman Catholic, 19–20, 27, 40–2, 63–5, 178, 222
Cinema, French, 77, 221
Citroën, André, 151
Clair, René, 221
Claudel, Paul, 85, 219
Clemenceau, Georges, 14, 33–4, 38–9, 51, 53, 65–6, 114–20, 173
clericalism, 19–20, 27–8, 42
Clichy, 149
Coal and steel agreement of 1951, 209
Cochin-China, 92
Cocteau, Jean, 221
Colette, 219, 221
Collaboration, collaborationists, collaborators, 139, 182–3, 188, 192
Colonial convention, Franco-British, 93
colonies, colonial policy, 30–3, 91–3, 129, 183, 213–15, 226–8, 232–4; colonies, in 1940, 176; after 1944, 65, 69, 71
Combes, Émile, 60–2, 64, 96
Comité des Forges, 119, 151
Comité Secret d'Action Révolutionnaire (C.S.A.R.), 145
Common Market, 226, 236
Communards, amnesty of, 26, 45
Commune of Paris, 13, 26, 38, 75
Communist Party, Communism, Communists, 119, 123, 125–7, 129, 131–3, 136, 140, 142–4, 146–9, 167, 169, 173, 184–5, 189–90, 193, 195–8, 200, 202, 204–6, 208, 212, 214–17, 222–3, 225, 229, 231–2, 237
Compiègne, 174

Comte, Auguste, 75
Concordat, Napoleonic, 63–4
Confédération Générale du Travail (C.G.T.), 68, 126, 149, 165–6, 204–5, 238
Confédération Générale du Travail Unitaire (C.G.T.U.), 126
congregations, see religious orders
Congress of Berlin, 90
conscription, three years law, 99, 101
Constituent Assembly of 1945, 196–8
Constitutional Laws of Third Republic, 21–2
Constitution of Fifth Republic, 230
Constitution of Fourth Republic, 198–200
Coppée, François, 55
cordon sanitaire, 120
Corot, 73
Correspondance de Rome, 77
Corsica, liberation of, 190; Corsica, in 1958, 228
Coty, François, 139
Coty, René, President, 198, 216, 229
Council of the Republic, 198
Courbet, Gustave, 73
Crémieux, Isaac, 92
Croix de Feu, 139, 145
Cubism, 219
Curie, Marie and Pierre, 77
Czechoslovakia, 165–8

Dadaism, 80, 219, 220, 221
Dakar, 189, 191
Daladier, Édouard, 136–7, 139–40, 143, 164–8, 170, 172, 174, 178
Dali, Salvador, 220
Damascus, bombardment of, 129
Danzig, 168
Darlan, Admiral, 175, 182–3, 185–6, 188
Darnand, Joseph, 188, 190
Daudet, Léon, 55, 86, 97, 113, 119, 137–8
Daumier, Honoré, 73
Dawes Plan, 122, 155
Déat, Marcel, 146, 182, 188
Debré, Michel, 190, 230
Debussy, Claude-Achille, 74, 81
Decazes, duc de, 18
decree-laws of 1926, 130; of 1934, 143; of 1937, 150
Degas, Edgar, 73
Delcassé, Théophile, 39, 57, 94–6, 105, 108
Délégation des Gauches, 60
Delescluze, Louis-Charles, 13
Deloncle, Eugène, 145

Dentz, General, 183, 213
Déroulède, Paul, 36, 38, 55–6
Deschanel, Paul, 120
Dien Bien Phu, 215
diplomacy of Third Republic, 90, 93–105
Disarmament Conference, 157–8
divorce, law of, 30
Djibouti, 92, 182
Dorgelès, Roland, 218
Dorgères, Henri, 145–6
Doriot, Jacques, 146, 182, 188
Doumer, Paul, President, 133–4
Doumergue, President, 124, 133, 140–1, 143, 158
Draguignan, 34
Dreyfus affair, 39, 49–57, 79, 86, 94
drôle de guerre, 170
Drumont, Édouard, 37, 50
Duchesne, Monseigneur, 76
Dufaure, Jules, 13
Duhamel, Georges, 218
Dukas, Paul, 74
Dunkirk evacuation, 172
Dupanloup, Monseigneur, 13, 27, 41
Durkheim, Émile, 76

École des Chartes, 77
École des Sciences Politiques, 152
Eden, Anthony, 162
education, clerical, 19, 27–8, 58–9, 61, 222
education, higher, 152, 237
education laws, 27–8, 58–9, 61
Edward VII, king, 95
Egypt, 31, 96
Egypt, Anglo-French attack on, 225
election of 1871, 13–15; of 1876, 22–3; of 1877, 23, 90; of 1881, 26–7; of 1885, 33–4; of 1889, 36; of 1893, 39; of 1898, 44; of 1902, 59; of 1906, 65; of 1910, 85; of 1914, 99–100; of 1919, 118–19; of 1924, 122–3; of 1928, 131; of 1932, 133–4; of 1945, 196–7; of 1946, 198; of 1956, 212, 216, 225; of 1958, 230–1
electoral law of 1951, 225
Éléments d'une doctrine radicale, 125
Éluard, Paul, 220
Entente cordiale, 95, 102–3
Esterhazy, Commandant, 52, 55
European army, plan for, 209
European Defence Community (E.D.C.), 209–10
European federation, 209, 234
Existentialism, 223

FAGUET, ÉMILE, 55
Faidherbe, General, 92
Fascism, Fascists, Fascist Leagues, 136, 139, 145, 165, 173
Fashoda, 93, 95
Faure, Edgar, 216
Faure, Félix, President, 39, 56
Fauré, Gabriel, 74, 81
Faure, Paul, 165, 173
Favre, Jules, 13–14
Federal Union of Europe, 156
Fédération Nationale des Syndicats, 46
Fédération des Travailleurs Socialistes, 45
Ferry, Jules, 13, 27–33, 56, 91–2
finances, French, 15, 43, 99, 101, 117, 119, 121, 129–31, 134–6, 148, 149–51, 201–2, 235
Finland, Russian invasion of, 170
Flandin, Pierre-Étienne, 162–3, 166
Flaubert, Gustave, 74–5
Floquet, Charles, 38
Foch, Marshal, 111, 115–16, 174
Forain, Jean-Louis, 55
Force Ouvrière, 205
Foreign Legion, affair of German deserters, 96
Four-Power Pact, 158
Fourth Republic, 203–17
France, Anatole, 53, 79–80
France-Allemagne, 174
franchise, female, 196
Francis Ferdinand, Archduke, murder of, 101
Francistes, 139
Franck, Cézar, 74
Franco, General, 167
Franco-Polish treaty, 121
Franco-Russian alliance, 93–4, 96, 102
Franco-Soviet pact, 143, 160
Free French Movement, 189–92
freemasonry, freemasons, 53, 59, 62, 75, 136
Freycinet, Charles de, 25–6, 28, 70
Front Paysan, 145–6
Frossard, 126
Fustel de Coulanges, 77
Futurism, 80

GALLIÉNI, GENERAL, 108
Gallifet, General de, 57, 62
Gambetta, Léon, 14, 23, 25–6, 29, 31, 56, 95
Gamelin, General, 169–70, 172
Gaulle, General de, 160, 172, 174, 176, 189–97, 200–1, 203–5, 213, 228–34

Gaullist Union, 203–5
Gauguin, Paul, 73
Gautier, Théophile, 78
Gaxotte, Pierre, 139
General Staff, French, 103, 106, 108–9, 160, 162–3, 172, 179
General Strike, myth of, 68
Genet, Jean, 224
Geneva Protocol, 156
German–Soviet Non-aggression Pact, 168
Germany, diplomatic relations, 20, 31, 35, 96–7, 102, 155–63, 165–9
Germany, strategic plans of, in 1914, 102–4
Gide, André, 219–20, 222
Giraud, General, 188–9
Giraudoux, Jean, 219, 221
Godesberg, 165
Goncourt, Jules and Edmond, 74, 78
Gonse, General, 52
Gourmont, Rémy de, 78
Grandmaison, Colonel de, 108
Great Britain, relations with, 93–6, 103, 155–6, 208
Grévy, Jules, President, 13–14, 17, 23, 25, 29, 34–5
Gringoire, 139, 149
Gris, Juan, 219
Guesde, Jules, 46, 54, 60, 67, 108
Guinea, French, 71, 234

HAIG, GENERAL, 111, 115
Halévy, Élie, 53
Halifax, Lord, 162
Halphen, Louis, 77
Hanotaux, Gabriel, 39, 54, 95
Harcourt, duc d', 14
Haussonville, duc d', 14
Heidegger, 223
Henriot, Philippe, 128, 136
Henry, Major, 50–2, 55, 86
Heredia, José-Maria de, 55, 78
Herr, Lucien, 53
Herriot, Édouard, 124, 127, 129–30, 134–5, 207
Hervé, Gustave, 97, 106
Herz, Cornelius, 38
Hitler, Adolf, 133, 149, 157–8, 162–3, 165–6, 169, 181
Hoare, Sir Samuel, 161–2
Ho Chi Minh, 214
Honneger, Arthur, 221
Hoover, President, 133, 135
Hugo, Victor, 13

Huis clos, 223
Huysmans, Joris-Karl, 75, 78

IMPRESSIONISM, IMPRESSIONISTS, 73, 81–2, 219, 221
income tax, 39, 43–4, 66, 99, 101
Indo-China, 31, 91–2, 176, 182, 213–15, 232
industry, French, 70, 134, 210–11
inflation, 129–30, 144, 148, 201–2, 205, 211
interpellations, 199
Intransigents, 33
investment abroad, French, 70–1
Italy, 20, 31; relations with France, 95; armistice with France, 174
Ivory Coast, 92

J'accuse, 39, 53
Jaspers, Karl, 223
Jaurès, Jean, 47, 51, 54, 60, 66–7, 99, 103, 105, 124, 126, 163
Jean Barois, 97
Jean-Christophe, 79
Jeanne d'Arc, beatification of, 89; canonization of, 120
Je suis partout, 139
Jesuits, 28
Jeunesses Patriotes, 138
Joffre, General, 92, 103–4, 106, 108–10
Juin, General, 185–6
June Days, 13

KEMAL PASHA, MUSTAPHA, 122
Kiderlen-Wächter, 97
Kierkegaard, 223
Kitchener, General, 93
Kluck, General von, 108
Koenig, General, 190–1

LÀ-BAS, 79
Laborum League, 54
Labour Day, 1891, shootings, 46
labour laws, 67
La Croix, 20, 54
Lamennais, 41
l'Ami du peuple, 139
La France Juive, 50
La Guerre de Troie n'aura pas lieu, 221
La Guerre Sociale, 98
La Jeune Parque, 219
la Justice, 65
la Lanterne, 35
la Libre Parole, 37, 50

Langevin, Paul, 53
L'Annonce faite à Marie, 85, 219
Lanson, Gustave, 53
Laos, 92, 214
La Peste, 222
L'Après-midi d'un faune, 78
La Revellière-Lépeaux, 38
La Rochefoucauld, duc de, 14
Lattre de Tassigny, General de, 215
l'Aurore, 53
Lausanne, Treaty of, 122
Laval, Pierre, 133, 141, 143, 157, 159–61, 163, 177, 181–2, 185–8, 192, 194
L'Avenir de la Science, 76
Lavigerie, Cardinal, 40, 65
Lavisse, Ernest, 77
League for the Defence of the Rights of Man, 53
League of Nations, 132, 156, 158, 161
Leahy, Admiral, 191
Lebanon, 213
Le Bonnet rouge, 112
Lebrun, Albert, President, 134, 167
Le Canard Enchaîné, 165
l'Echo de Paris, 128
Le Cimetière marin, 219
Le Deuxième Sexe, 223
Ledru-Rollin, 13
L'Éducation sentimentale, 74
Lefebvre, Georges, 75
Le Feu, 218
le Figaro, murder of editor, 99
Léger, Fernand, 219, 221
Legitimists, 15, 17–18, 20, 22, 34, 35
Le Grand Meaulnes, 218
le Journal, 139
le Journal des Débats, 149
Lemaître, Jules, 55
le Marseillaise, 25, 106
le Matin, 139
le Monde, 208
Lenin, 125, 143
Leo XIII, 28, 40, 61, 63
Lépine, prefect of police, 57
le Populaire, 165–6
Les Croix de Bois, 218
Les Déracinés, 81
Les Dessous de Panama, 37
Les Dieux ont soif, 79
Les Faux-Monnayeurs, 220
Les Fleurs du Mal, 78
Les Grands Cimetières sous la Lune, 167
Le Silence de la mer, 222

Le Sillon, 64–5
Les Mains sales, 223
Les Mandarins, 223
Les Mouches, 223
Le Soulier de Satin, 219
Les Rougon-Macquart, 74
Lesseps, Ferdinand de, 37
Les Soirées de Médan, 75
Les Trophées, 78
le Temps, 149
L'Évolution créatrice, 80
L'Histoire contemporaine, 79
l'Homme enchaîné, 114
l'Homme libre, 114
l'Humanité, 67, 126, 140, 169
Ligue de la Patrie française, 55
Ligue des Patriotes, 36, 56
L'Île des pingouins, 79
L'Immoraliste, 220
L'Internationale, 67
l'Intransigeant, 35
Lisle, Leconte de, 78
Little Entente, 121, 155, 157, 159, 207
Littré, Émile, 13, 75
livret, 43
Lloyd George, David, 118, 121
local elections of 1878, 25
Locarno agreements, 132, 156, 162
l'Oeuvre, 168
lois scélérates, 47
Loisy, abbé, 64, 76–7
Longuet, Jean, 126
Lorraine, 14, 48, 81
Lot, Ferdinand, 77
Loubet, President, 37, 56, 61, 95
Louis XIV, 14
Lourdes, 19
Ludendorff, General, 111, 115
Lumière brothers, 77
Lyautey, Marshal, 41, 110
Lyons, 17

MacMahon, Marshal, 17–18, 21–4
Madagascar, 91–2, 214, 232
Madame Bovary, 74
Maginot line, 157, 162, 169–70
Maillol, Aristide, 72
maires, 29–30
Mallarmé, Stéphane, 78
Malraux, André, 221
Malvy, Louis-Jean, 111–12, 114, 124
Mandel, Georges, 118, 173–4, 178
Manet, Édouard, 73

Manon, 74
maquis, 191–2
Marchand, Colonel, 93
Marin, Louis, 97, 130
Marinetti, 80
Maritain, Jacques, 128, 219
Marne, battle of the, 108
Marquet, Adrien, 146
Marshall aid, 205, 211
Martin du Gard, Roger, 97, 218
Marx, Karl, 45
Massenet, 74
Massilia, 174
Massis, Henri, 118
Mata Hari, 113
Matignon agreements, 147
Matisse, Henri, 73, 221
Maupassant, Guy de, 75, 78
Mauriac, François, 167, 219, 221
Maurras, Charles, 55, 81, 85–90, 129, 137–8,
    144, 179
May Protocols, 183
Méliès, 77
Méline, Jules, 13, 39, 43–4, 53
Mendès-France, Pierre, 201, 210, 215–16
Menton, 174
Mercier, General, 51–2, 55, 57, 112
Merry del Val, Cardinal, 61
Mers-el-Kébir, 175, 181
Meuse, battle of the, 172
Milhaud, Darius, 221
Militia, Darnand, 190
Millerand, Alexandre, 47, 57, 67, 108, 118,
    120, 124
Millet, Jean-François, 73
missionaries, French, 30–1
Mistral, 55
Moch, Jules, 178, 206
Mollet, Guy, 217, 226
monarchists, royalists, 15–22, 24, 34–6, 87–8,
    186, 188
Monet, Claude, 73
Monnet, Jean, 207, 210, 235
Monnet Plan, 210, 235–9
Montherlant, Henry de, 221
Montmartre, 13–14
Montoire interview, 181
Montparnasse, boulevard, 219
Morocco, 94–7, 129, 137, 215, 226, 232
Moulin, Jean, 189
Mouvement Républicain Populaire, 196–9,
    204–7, 209, 213, 215–16, 231
Mouvement Social Français, 145

Mulhouse, 108
Mun, Albert de, 41, 54, 209
Munich Conference, 166–7
municipalities, law of, 29
Murphy, Robert, 191
music, French, 73–4, 221
Mussolini, 158–61, 163, 166–7
Mutual Assistance, Treaty of, 155
mystique de gauche, 236

NAPOLEON III, 13, 15, 203
National Assembly, 13–15, 17–18, 20–2
National Assembly of Fourth Republic, 198–9
National Catholic Federation, 128
nationalism, nationalists, 48, 90, 97–100, 104, 120, 128, 146, 165
nationalizations, 200–1
'National Revolution', 178–9, 186
naturalism, 74–5
navy, French, 174–5, 181, 186
Nazis, 95, 133, 142, 158–60, 162–3, 165, 185–90, 192
Néo-Destour, 215
neo-Kantism, 77
neo-socialists, 146
neo-Thomism, 77, 219
Nivelle, General, 110–12
Noailles, duc de, 14
noblesse, 14, 18
North Atlantic Treaty of 1949, 208

OCCUPATION OF FRANCE, NAZI, 179, 187
Offenbach, 73
Omdurman, 93
Opportunists, 25, 34–6, 42
Orleanists, 16–18, 20, 22, 39, 42

PACIFISM, 100, 165–6, 218, 221–2
Painlevé, Paul, 111, 113, 130
Panama affair, 37–9
Panthéon, 124
Panther, 96
Papacy, papal policy, 20, 28, 40–1, 61–4, 127–9
Paris, 14, 17, 44–5, 73, 81, 86, 203, 219
Paris, comte de, 16, 34, 188
Paris, Peace Conference of, 116–17
Parnassians, 78
parties in 1914, 100
Parti Ouvrier, 46
Parti Populaire Français, 146

Parti Social Français, 145
Passy, Colonel, 191
Pasteur, Louis, 77
Paty de Clam, marquis du, 52
peasants, 44, 69, 72, 145–6, 202, 211–12, 236
Péguy, Charles, 53–4, 81, 146, 218
Pelléas et Mélisande, 74
pensions, law of, 66
Perpignan, attack on prefecture, 68
Pétain, Marshal Philippe, 111–13, 115, 162–3, 172–4, 176–82, 185–8, 192, 222
Pflimlin, Pierre, 227, 229
phylloxera, 33, 92
Picard, Ernest, 14
Picasso, Pablo, 73, 219, 221
Picquart, Major, 52–3, 55
Pinay, Antoine, 207
Pissarro, Camille, 73
Pius IX, 40
Pius X, 61, 63, 77, 127
Pius XI, 128
Pius XII, 179, 222
Pleven, René, 201, 209
Poincaré, Henri, 77, 98
Poincaré, Raymond, 24, 39, 98–9, 101–3, 111, 114, 120, 122, 130
Poland, 120–1, 168–9; alliance with, 121, 158, 159, 168; Nazi invasion of, 169
Popular Front, 144–9, 164
population, 70, 151, 212
positivism, 75
Poujade, Pierre, Poujardists, 212–13, 216
President, of Third Republic, 21, 24; of Fourth Republic, 197; of Fifth Republic, 230
press laws, 25, 47
priests, democratic, 40–1; worker, 222
Prince Imperial, 15, 34
Progressivists, 42
Proust, Marcel, 14, 53, 81–2, 105, 218, 220
psychology, Freudian, 220

QUEUILLE, HENRI, 170, 206
Quinet, Edgar, 13

RADICAL PARTY, 33, 36, 47
Radical Socialists, 47, 68, 99, 119, 124–5, 130, 134, 196, 205, 215–16, 231
railway, nationalization of, 66
railway strike of 1910, 68
Ralliement, 40–2, 47
Ramadier, Paul, 204
Rambaud, Alfred, 55

Rassemblement du Peuple Français (R.P.F.), 203–6
Ravel, Maurice, 74, 81
realism, 74
referendum of 1945, 196; of 1958, 230; of 1961, 231
Réflexions sur la violence, 68
Reinach, Jacques de, 38
religious orders, and legislation on, 19–20, 28, 61, 64
Renan, Ernest, 76
Renault works, 201
Renoir, Pierre-Auguste, 73
Renouvier, Charles, 60, 77
reparations, of 1871, 14; of 1919, 117, 121–2, 129, 135, 155–6
Republican Union, 26
Rerum novarum, 40
Resistance, 184, 187–92
Resistance, National Council of, 189
Revue des Deux Mondes, 41
Reynaud, Paul, 144, 166, 170–4, 178
Rhineland, evacuation of, 133, 156
Rhineland, occupation of, 116–17
Rhineland, remilitarization of, 162–3
Ribbentrop, 166
Ribot, Alexandre, 101, 110–11
Rimbaud, Arthur, 78
Riom trials, 178
Rochefort, Henri de, 25, 35
Rocque, Colonel de la, 139
Rodin, Auguste, 72
Rolland, Romain, 79–80
Romains, Jules, 218
romanticism, 74, 78
Rommel, General, 188
Rouher, Eugène, 20
Rousseau, le douanier, 73
Rouvier, Maurice, 38, 60
Ruhr, occupation of, 122, 132
Russia, alliance with, 93–7, 102, 105
Russia, French loans to, 71, 93
Russia, Nazi invasion of, 184
Russia, Soviet, relations with, 143, 157, 159, 195
Russia, state visit of 1914 to, 101–2
Russian Revolution, 113, 125
Russo-Japanese War, 96

SAAR, 116, 160, 210, 226
Sacré Coeur, 19, 73
Saint-Saens, 74
Salengro, Roger, 149

Salisbury, Lord, 93
Sand, George, 73
Sangnier, Marc, 64–5
Sarrail, General, 109, 129
Sarraut, Albert, 136, 162–3
Sartre, Jean-Paul, 223–4
Satie, Erik, 74
Say, Léon, 13
Scheurer-Kestner, 53
Schuman, Robert, 199, 206–7
science, 77
Scrutin d'arrondissement, 29
Scrutin de liste, 29, 34
sculpture, French, 72
Second Empire, 13, 15, 36, 69
Second International, 67
Section Française de l'International Ouvrière (S.F.I.O.), 67
Seignobos, Charles, 53, 77
seize mai, coup d'état of, 22–3
Senate, of Third Republic, 21–2, 30, 66, 150, 177
Senators, life, 22, 30
Senegal, 93
Separation of Church and State, law of, 62–4, 127
septennat, 18
Seurat, Georges, 73
Sèvres, Treaty of, 122
Sigmaringen, 192
Simon, Jules, 13–14, 27
Sisley, Alfred, 73
Smyrna, 122
social legislation, 46, 147–8, 200
Socialist Congress at Marseilles, 45
Socialists, Socialist Party, 26, 45–7, 60, 66–8, 97, 113, 119, 124–7, 130–6, 143–4, 146, 148, 160, 163, 165–6, 197–8, 204–6, 209, 216, 229–31
Solidarité Française, 139
Somme, battle of the, 110
Sorel, Albert, 77
Sorel, Georges, 68
Soustelle, Jacques, 191, 234
Spanish Civil War, 167, 225
Stavisky affair, 136–7
Stockholm, Socialist Congress at, 113
Strasbourg, 14
Stresa, Conference of, 161
Stresemann, Gustav, 156
Sudan, 93
Sully-Prudhomme, 78
Sûreté Générale, 137

surrealism, 220
Sykes–Picot agreement, 122
symbolism, 78, 81, 219
Syndicats, 165
Syria, 129, 183, 213

TAINE, HIPPOLYTE, 74–5, 78
Taittinger, Pierre, 138
Tangier, 96
Tardieu, André, 130, 146
tariffs, 43, 69
Thalamas riots, 89
Thiers, Adolphe, 13–15, 17, 21, 23, 29
Third Force, 205–6, 208, 212–13
Thorez, Maurice, 143, 146, 195, 198, 223, 225
Timbuktu, 92
Tonkin, 31, 33, 92
Toul, 102
Toulon, 186
Toulouse-Lautrec, 73
Tours, 172
Tours, Socialist Congress of, 126, 131
trade unions, 30, 45–6, 68
tricolour, 16
Tripoli, 95
Trois Réformateurs, 219
Troyes, Congress of, 67
Tunis, Tunisia, 31, 91–2, 186, 215, 226, 232

UNION GÉNÉRALE CRASH, 33
Union pour la Nouvelle République (U.N.R.), 231
Union Républicaine Democratique, 97
union sacrée, 106, 109, 113
Uzès, duchesse d', 36

VAILLANT, ÉDOUARD, 46, 106
Valéry, Paul, 78, 219
Vallat, Xavier, 128
Vatican, *see* papacy

Vehementer, 63
Vercors, battle of, 191
Vercors (Jean Bruller), 222
Verdun, 102, 109–10
Verlaine, Paul, 78
Verne, Jules, 55
Versailles, 14, 26
Versailles, Treaty of, 116–17
Vers l'armée de métier, 176
Vichy, government of, 176–92
Vie de Jésus, 76
Viet Minh, 213
Vietnam, 214
Vigo-Almereyda, 112
Viollet, 53
Viviani, René, 63, 101–2, 108–9
Voyage au bout de la nuit, 221

WADDINGTON, WILLIAM, 13
Wagner, Richard, 74
Waldeck-Rousseau, Waldeck-Rousseau government, 56–9, 97
Wallon, Henri, 21
Wall Street crash, 133
war debts, 133
War Office, 50–2, 55
Warsaw, 120, 169
West Indies, French, 182
Weygand, General, 120, 129, 172–3, 183
Wilhelm II, 96, 102
Wilson, Daniel, 35
women, position in French society, 196, 223
worker-priests, 222

YOUNG PLAN, 132, 135, 156

ZOLA, ÉMILE, 39, 53, 74–5
Zones of France, Occupied and Unoccupied, 174–5